BEHAVIOR MODIFICATION

BEHAVIOR MODIFICATION

PRINCIPLES, ISSUES, AND APPLICATIONS

Second Edition

W. Edward Craighead

The Pennsylvania State University

Alan E. Kazdin

Western Psychiatric Institute and Clinic
University of Pittsburgh School of Medicine

Michael J. Mahoney

The Pennsylvania State University

HOUGHTON MIFFLIN COMPANY   BOSTON
Dallas   Geneva, Illinois   Hopewell, New Jersey
Palo Alto   London

For
Glynn and Christine Craighead
Leon N. Kazdin
Daniel and Zita Mahoney

Printed in the U.S.A.

Library of Congress Catalog Card Number: 80-83115

ISBN: 0-395-29721-4

CONTENTS

PREFACE

As its title implies, this text is intended to familiarize the reader with three different aspects of behavior modification—its basic principles, some of its major assumptions and issues, and the applications to which it has been put in recent years. In Part One, we begin with a discussion of the conceptual and methodological bases of behavior modification. This section also provides an overview of the behavioral model and a discussion of the basic principles that have been derived from other experimental areas of psychology and have been utilized in behavior modification. Our initial discussion of basic issues and principles is supplemented, in Part Two, by fourteen original contributions demonstrating how behavior modification has been employed across a wide range of settings, populations, and behaviors. Because it is difficult to define many of the terms out of the context in which they are used in behavior modification, we have not included a glossary. Rather, the locations of the definitions of the important terms are provided in the subject index.

This text is primarily intended for use by undergraduates in courses on behavior modification and behavior therapy in departments of psychology, education, human development, nursing, counseling, and law enforcement. With lecture or written supplements, it can also be of use in other courses, such as psychopathology or abnormal psychology, learning, adjustment, and counseling. It may also be helpful to professionals working in applied settings where the use of behavior modification is appropriate.

We have attempted to reach a balance between breadth and depth, giving both an overview and an expansion of each aspect. A lengthy list of references is also provided for those who would like to delve more deeply into specific areas. More than anything else, however, our goal has been to stress the personal relevance of behavior modification for the reader: personal relevance both in improving the quality of one's life through better self-management skills and in providing the knowledge and skills to help others. In the chapters that follow, a wide variety of techniques and illustrations have been employed in achieving that goal. We have written not only for the psychology student, but also for the nurse, the social worker, the teacher, the counselor, the parent, the law enforcement professional, and, in many respects, for every concerned person. We hope that our overview and our frequent use of illustrations and case histories will encourage an appreciation of the difficulty and the promise of employing scientific methods to reduce human suffering.

In some ways, writing a book can be compared to going through adolescence. It is usually impossible to tell exactly when or where either process began and, in retrospect, the whole experience may seem like a confusing series of insights and frustrations. But perhaps the closest parallel is the realization that change is not just a single aspect of the adventure; it is the critical essence. For both adolescents and authors, a large part of the motivation to continue coping and growing is the somewhat naive assumption that there is an end to the whole process. Adolescents strive for an "adulthood" when life will be free of the continual flux of emotions and problems. In like manner, authors work toward that day when a book will be "finished," thinking that their task will then be complete. The fact of the matter in both situations is that there is no end to life's challenges and there is no completely satisfactory signal that a book has reached the pinnacle of an author's expression or adequacy.

We have grown a lot in the current undertaking. As the following chapters will attest, we abide by the primary assumption that human behavior can be studied and therapeutically enriched by a sensitive scientific approach. However, the reader will find very few pat answers in what follows. Although behavior modification research has significantly contributed to our understanding of the thoughts, feelings, and activities that characterize both adaptive and maladaptive behavior patterns, we are still a long way from any complacency about the extent of our knowledge or the power of our techniques consistently to alleviate suffering and enrich human functioning. Our approach in this text is thus one of cautious optimism: we seem to be on the right road, but our journey is far from complete. We see this tentative hopefulness and commitment to continued pursuit as an asset rather than a liability. Two of the most important aspects of maturity are the ability to endure uncertainty and the acceptance of change as inevitable. Both life and science are processes rather than outcomes and, as this text will emphasize, it may be more accurate to approach each as a journey rather than a destination. We welcome you to begin that journey in one recent and promising scientific development: behavior modification.

Many individuals have lent their professional and personal skills to the production of this book, and it would be impossible to do justice to all of them without adding an entire chapter of acknowledgments. We would like to thank collectively our students and colleagues for their contributions to the completion of this project. Fortunately, those who have been integral in the production of this text are already aware of our gratitude and indebtedness. We wish to express our appreciation to the following reviewers, who provided us with useful comments and suggestions: Steven Paul Schinke, University of Washington; and Herbert H. Severson, University of Oregon. We are especially grateful to the Houghton Mifflin staff for their assistance. We would like to express our appreciation to our secretaries, Ellie Adams, Sandy Ranio, and Esther Strause, for their roles in the production of the manuscript of this book. Last, we would like to thank all of the authors who contributed the chapters in Part Two.

W. Edward Craighead
Alan E. Kazdin
Michael J. Mahoney

LIST OF CONTRIBUTORS

Gene G. Abel, College of Physicians and Surgeons, Columbia University

Beverly M. Atkeson, Department of Psychology, University of Georgia, Athens, Georgia

David H. Barlow, Department of Psychology, SUNY at Albany, Albany, New York

Alan S. Bellack, Department of Psychology, University of Pittsburgh, Pittsburgh, Pennsylvania

Douglas A. Bernstein, Department of Psychology, University of Illinois at Urbana-Champaign, Urbana, Illinois

Kelly D. Brownell, Department of Psychiatry, University of Pennsylvania, Philadelphia, Pennsylvania

Linda Wilcoxon Craighead, Division of Counseling and Educational Psychology, The Pennsylvania State University, University Park, Pennsylvania

James P. Curran, Veterans Administration Medical Center, Brown University Medical School, Providence, Rhode Island

Mercedes Dallas, Department of Psychology, University of Iowa, Iowa City, Iowa

Dennis M. Donovan, Department of Psychology, University of Washington, Seattle, Washington

Ronald S. Drabman, University of Mississippi Medical Center, Jackson, Mississippi

Rex Forehand, Department of Psychology, University of Georgia, Athens, Georgia

Michel Hersen, Western Psychiatric Institute and Clinic, University of Pittsburgh School of Medicine, Pittsburgh, Pennsylvania

John J. Horan, Division of Counseling and Educational Psychology, The Pennsylvania State University, University Park, Pennsylvania

Neil S. Jacobson, Department of Psychology, University of Washington, Seattle, Washington

Philip C. Kendall, Department of Psychology, University of Minnesota, Minneapolis, Minnesota

Benjamin B. Lahey, Department of Psychology, University of Georgia, Athens, Georgia

Joseph LoPiccolo, Department of Psychiatry and Behavioral Science, SUNY at Stony Brook, Long Island, New York

G. Alan Marlatt, Department of Psychology, University of Washington, Seattle, Washington

Peter D. McLean, Department of Psychiatry, University of British Columbia, Vancouver, B.C., Canada

Andrew W. Meyers, Department of Psychology, Memphis State University, Memphis, Tennessee

Bruce Richards Reed, Department of Psychiatry and Behavioral Science, SUNY at Stony Brook, Long Island, New York

Robert Schleser, Department of Psychology, Memphis State University, Memphis, Tennessee

Jerome S. Stumphauzer, University of Southern California School of Medicine, Child Adolescent Clinic, Los Angeles, California

Carolyn L. Williams, Department of Psychology, University of Minnesota, Minneapolis, Minnesota

BEHAVIOR MODIFICATION

PRINCIPLES AND ISSUES OF BEHAVIOR MODIFICATION

PART ONE

Imagine for a moment that you have come home for the holidays. It has been one of those long, grueling terms, full of surprise quizzes and boring instructors. You are really looking forward to unwinding a bit, and you may even be so homesick that seeing your parents actually sounds good. On your first night home you stay up until three in the morning talking with your parents and brother about the "thrill of victory and agony of defeat" in college life. Your parents finally go to bed, and the conversation with your little brother continues. The excitement of the first few hours has toned down a bit now—you have already exchanged new jokes and shared the highlights of the last few months. Suddenly, your brother turns more serious and starts asking how many psychology courses you have taken. After beating around the bush for a few minutes, he confides that a friend of his is having dating problems and would like to know how and where to get help. This friend, it seems, has trouble getting dates, and when he does get one, he falls all over himself trying to be "cool." He is also anxious about sexual adequacy, not to mention a weight problem and acne. As you sit there listening patiently, it gradually becomes clear that the "friend" is actually your younger brother and that, for the first time in years, he is earnestly asking for your help. You may be a psychology major, and this isn't the first time family or friends have asked your advice on personal problems. But this time it is your own little brother, and you feel a mixture of sensations. It is gratifying to know that he respects your opinion and feels close enough to turn to you for help. On the other hand, you are well aware of the limitations in your technical knowledge.

We hope that after having read this book, you will be able to deal with situations like the one we have described with more confidence in your ability to help. Although this book is not intended primarily as an introduction to clinical methods, it is designed to expand your technical knowledge in ways that should be relevant to your everyday life. It will familiarize you with some of the issues and evidence that bear on human dysfunction. You will not become a clinician by reading this book, but you will obtain some technical information, which could be valuable for troubled friends and relatives; information on the success rates of various techniques of behavior modification, sources of counseling, and basic processes of behavior change. Moreover, we have written this book in such a way that it may also help you personally.

The applied science of therapeutic behavior change is much like other sciences in the sense that it has its foundations in an extensive body of basic research. These fundamental principles are essential prerequisites for the choice and evaluation of clinical techniques. We therefore begin our presentation in this part of the text with some of the more basic aspects of behavioral science—its principles, methodology, and issues. You will then be in a position to look at its products—the therapeutic applications.

CHAPTER 1

BEHAVIOR MODIFICATION:
AN OVERVIEW

Perhaps more than any other subsection of modern psychology, behavior modification has gained prominence among both professionals and the general public as one of the most exciting and promising developments in contemporary behavioral science. This broad interest is reflected in the proliferation of behavior modification articles both in professional journals and in the popular media. Although the foundations of behavior modification were developed years ago in the experimental laboratories, its impact on personal and social problems has been very recent. Its success rate has elicited an enormous expansion of applications and a growing list of adherents. Recent developments include the adoption of behavior modification by individual therapists, school systems, correctional facilities, industry, psychiatric hospitals, and even middle-class parents. All in all, its versatility, recency, increasing popularity, and impressive success rate have made behavior modification an exciting, productive area for research and application.

This surge of popularity, however, has generated a number of problems. Perhaps the greatest one surrounds the definition of behavior modification. Since in a very literal sense any procedure that results in a behavior change may be labeled behavior modification, it is apparent why this is a difficult issue. For example, removal of part of the brain undoubtedly changes behavior. Is psychosurgery therefore a form of behavior modification? The injection of huge quantities of certain tranquilizing drugs into an organism undoubtedly changes that organism's behavior. Is psychopharmacotherapy therefore a form of behavior modification? Although the public media and popular publications have occasionally labeled such procedures as behavior modification, behavior therapists would reject these two clinical procedures as being unrelated to the field of behavior modification. Clearly, there exists a great deal of confusion regarding the definition of behavior modification. While we do not expect to provide a complete resolution of this issue, we do hope that as a result of reading this book, you will have a clearer notion of what behavior modification is and, just as importantly, what it is not.

DEFINITION OF BEHAVIOR MODIFICATION

One reason for the difficulty in determining whether a clinical intervention procedure should be labeled behavior modification is that no unequivocal definition of behavior modification exists. In fact, the richness of creativity demonstrated by the generation of definitions causes one to be amazed that behavior modifiers should ever be criticized for their lack of creativity. The lack of a single, accepted definition not only has elicited considerable theoretical discussion, but also has had a significant impact at the practical level. For example, with no definition of behavior modification, insurance companies have had a difficult time deciding what clinical procedures constitute behavior modification and thus should be reimbursable. There has been great controversy recently over whether certification should be required for the practice of behavior modification. Even if such certification is deemed desirable, who would be a bona fide behavior modifier? This controversy has resulted in renewed discussion of "What is behavior modification?"

A common question associated with the defining of behavior modification centers on the relationship between behavior modification and behavior therapy. There are now several books and professional journals whose titles include the terms *behavior modification* or *behavior therapy* or even both. However, there is no consistent relationship between these titles and the particular content of the books or journals; one cannot judge the book by its title. Similarly, the distinction between behavior modification and behavior therapy breaks down in clinical practice. What one clinician calls behavior modification, the next calls behavior therapy, and vice versa. Both conceptually and practically, the terms have been interchangeable, and we will employ them synonymously in this book.

Definitions of behavior modification have ranged from the application of the principles of operant conditioning (for example, Skinner, 1953, 1971) or classical conditioning (Wolpe, 1958), to something called, more generally, principles of learning (Ullmann & Krasner, 1975), to the more broadly based clinical approaches of Bandura (1977b) and Lazarus (1971). Most of these definitions are characterized by an appeal to the content of the underlying principles of behavior change. An alternative approach is to define behavior modification by its concern with methodology and functional behavior relationships. Many previous definitions have assumed the existence of a singular theoretical model or technology of behavior modification. Such a state of affairs would solve many conceptual and practical issues, but it does not exist.

In this book we will use the following criteria, adopted from Mahoney, Kazdin, and Lesswing (1974), in defining behavior modification:

(1) use of a broadly defined set of clinical procedures whose description and rationale often rely on the experimental findings of psychological research (Goldstein, Heller, and Sechrest, 1966); and (2) an experimental and functionally analytic approach to clinical data, relying on objective and measurable outcome (Goldfried and Pomeranz, 1968) (p. 14).

This view of behavior modification allows for the study of an extremely wide range of factors that may affect behavior and that may be employed in the modification of behavior; principles from many areas of study may be utilized. For example, principles of modeling and operant conditioning may be combined to teach new social-interaction skills; findings from developmental psychology may be important in clinical work with children, such as teaching clients to talk or to engage in more constructive self-talk; and, basic nutrition may be directly relevant to the treatment of obesity. The functionally analytic aspect of the definition means that the behavior modifier undertakes an experimental analysis of the problem behavior. Behavior modification is best defined by a rationale and a methodology and not by a specified theory or set of principles. For a procedure to be called behavioral, it must be empirically evaluated. Although it is not always possible, behavior therapists ideally evaluate a clinical procedure each time it is employed; as a minimum, they attempt to utilize clinical procedures that have been empirically demonstrated to be effective.

This approach to the study of behavior is called *methodological behaviorism* and was introduced by John B. Watson in 1913. Behavior modification does not refer to a *specified* set of clinical procedures derived from a unified learning theory nor to a *completed* collection of facts or experimental outcomes. Instead, behavior modification draws from an ever changing body of experimental findings and represents a scientific approach to the study of behavior and its modification.

Yet many people, both friend and foe, identify behavior modification as an "arrived-at," specified set of procedures based on the application of an "arrived-at" set of principles. Undoubtedly, glimpses of that view will appear in this book. But we believe that the greatest progress in understanding and modifying behavior will be made when behavior modification is seen as the application of the scientific approach of methodological behaviorism. We now turn to a brief history of the development of this approach to the study of behavior.

THE HISTORY OF BEHAVIOR MODIFICATION

To the extent that the behavioral model presented in this book represents the real world, the history of behavior modification is as old as the history of human beings. Although individuals have always modified their own, their spouses', their children's, and even their animals' behaviors, they usually have not specified that they modeled, prompted, shaped, and chained responses. Nevertheless, they have used these principles of behavior change.

The study of the systematic application of behavior modification is a comparatively new endeavor. As previously noted, the person who is usually given credit for introducing behavior modification is John B. Watson (1878–1958). He did most of his work at the University of Chicago and Johns Hopkins University during the first quarter of this century. It was he who advocated the use of methodological behaviorism in the scientific study of human behavior. Although he is best remembered for what is popularly labeled *radical behaviorism,* which maintains that psychologists should only study overt behaviors or responses, it was his emphasis on methodology and his scientific approach to the study of behavior that make him truly the founder of behavior modification. Although Watson laid the groundwork and reported the well-known case study of Little Albert (Watson & Rayner, 1920), behavior modification was not widely adopted for clinical application. In fact, except for a few sporadic case reports, the study of human behavior based on this approach occurred primarily in the laboratory until about twenty to twenty-five years ago.

The current widespread interest in behavior modification began in the 1950s.[1] The last twenty years have witnessed an enormous growth in both laboratory studies and applied evaluations. Although considerable discussion has occurred regarding who should be credited with beginning the current era of behavior modification, there is little doubt that the most

1. This brief history is not intended to be exhaustive; therefore, the work and writings of a number of significant contributors are not included. For a more exhaustive review, see Kazdin (1978c).

John B. Watson

Photo courtesy of The Ferdinand Hamburger Jr. Archives, Johns Hopkins University.

widely known and most controversial behavior modifier is B. F. Skinner. It was he and his colleagues who, in 1953, systematically studied the use of the principles of operant conditioning with psychotic patients at the Laboratory for Behavior Research at Metropolitan State Hospital in Waltham, Massachusetts. His landmark book, *Science and Human Behavior,* was published in 1953.

At about the same time, Joseph Wolpe, later joined by Arnold Lazarus, began work in what was presented as the application of certain physiological findings and the principles of conditioning based on Hull's (1943) learning theory. Their early work, most noted for the clinical procedure of

B. F. Skinner
Photo courtesy of B. F. Skinner.

systematic desensitization, was a major force in determining the direction of behavior modification. Hans J. Eysenck is usually included among the group of clinicians who claimed an alliance with the clinical applications of classical conditioning. As we shall see later, much of the early classical-conditioning research was conducted by Pavlov and others in Russia. Eysenck argued strongly against the psychoanalytic model and the general effectiveness of psychotherapy, and his behavior therapy oriented books of 1960, 1964, and 1966 set the tone for many behavior modifiers in their rejection of the quasi-medical (Freudian or psychoanalytic) model of abnormal behavior and their call for an empirical evaluation of therapy procedures.

Thus, the stage was set—the psychoanalytic model was rejected and the principles of behavior modification were then synonymous with the clinical application of the principles of operant and classical conditioning. This resulted in the conceptualization of behavior modification as follows: (1) normal and abnormal behavior develop according to the same principles, and (2) all behavior is modified or changed according to principles of

Ivan Pavlov
Photo courtesy of Brown Brothers.

learning (meaning principles of operant and classical conditioning).[2] To the extent that the psychoanalytic model failed to be verified empirically and the application of the principles of learning could be empirically validated, this view of behavior modification was scientifically acceptable. But to maintain that behavior modification had "arrived," that the methods of change could be derived from the principles of operant and classical conditioning, and that the conceptual model was completed was not scientifically acceptable. As indicated, however, there very quickly developed

2. This view was evident in the first (and seminal) summary of the work done in behavior modification, the introduction to Ullmann and Krasner's *Case Studies in Behavior Modification* (1965).

Joseph Wolpe
Photo courtesy of Joseph Wolpe.

an alignment of learning theory and behavior modification, and the latter became synonymous with the application of principles of learning. Empirically oriented clinicians looked for their foundations in the learning laboratories. Additionally, some psychologists in the field of learning began to study the effects of clinical applications.

However, this equation of learning theory and behavior modification was premature, and behavioral-change agents, who favored an empirical approach to understanding behavior and helping their clients, began to look to other areas of research for empirical data that might enhance their understanding, prediction, and modification of behavior. These experimental findings were incorporated into a growing set of empirically validated principles of behavior change. This is clearly demonstrated in two 1969 books which, perhaps more than any others, have served as a positive force in the popularization of behavior modification. L. P. Ullmann and L. Krasner's *A Psychological Approach to Abnormal Behavior* incorporated extensive findings from sociology into a psychosocial model of abnormal behavior. Albert Bandura's *Principles of Behavior Modification* went

Hans J. Eysenck
Photo by A. L. Greeman. Courtesy the American Psychological Association.

well beyond the principles of operant and classical conditioning in incorporating data regarding symbolic, cognitive processes into a behavioral model. It set the tone for methodological behaviorism or the experimental/clinical approach to the study of human problems in living (see Davison & Neale, 1974, 1978).

Two recent developments have spawned the view of behavior modification offered in this book. The first was the development of cognitive

Albert Bandura
Photo courtesy of Albert Bandura.

(Beck, 1976) and rational-emotive therapies (Ellis, 1962). The systematic evaluation of these therapies and their integration with the more traditional behavior-therapy procedures has led to the use of the term *cognitive behavior therapy* to define these therapies (Mahoney, 1974a; Meichenbaum, 1977). This approach to therapeutic change maintains the behavioral emphasis on empirical evaluation, but the primary focus is on the modification of irrational thought patterns by changing what people say to themselves and what they visualize. The self-statements and mental images are called cognitions, and it is these cognitions that are modified in cognitive behavior therapy. Traditional learning-oriented behavior therapy focused on overt observable behaviors and physiological responses, whereas cognitive behavior therapy has focused almost exclusively on cognitive or covert behaviors, which are observable only by the individual engaging in those behaviors. These cognitive variables will be discussed at length in Chapter 8.

The definition of behavior modification (therapy) which we have set forth in this book maintains that somatic-motor, cognitive, and physiological variables are all components of an adequate model of behavior change. The following chapters will discuss how these variables may be measured as well as their roles in the explanation, prediction, and changing of human response. This broader model incorporating the study of cognitive as well as overt behaviors and physiological variables has recently been labeled *social learning theory* (Bandura, 1977a). Consequently, we view the terms *behavior modification* and *behavior therapy* as synonymous, and consider them to be the application of social learning theory. We prefer the use of the terms *behavior modification* and *behavior therapy* to the development of a new term like *social learning therapy*.

A major factor in the development of behavior therapy has been the formation and growth of the Association for Advancement of Behavior Therapy (AABT). This organization was formed in 1966 for the purpose of advancing knowledge regarding behavior change and has grown from a membership of 671 in 1970 to approximately 3,000 in 1980. This group has facilitated the advancement of behavior therapy through its annual conferences, educational programs, and its journals, *Behavior Therapy,* which began in 1970, and *Behavioral Assessment,* which began in 1979.

The increased interest in and broadened emphasis on behavior modification has been further reflected in the appearance of several behavioral journals in addition to increased publication of behavioral articles in the American Psychological Association (APA) journals. The first behavioral journal, *Behaviour Research and Therapy,* was begun in 1963 and was edited by Eysenck. The second, *Journal of Applied Behavior Analysis,* emphasized the application of operant procedures and began in 1968. In addition to these journals and those of the AABT, there are numerous recent journals that emphasize behavior-therapy research. These include: *Journal of Behavior Therapy and Experimental Psychiatry* (1970), *Behavior Modification* (1977), *Cognitive Therapy and Research* (1977), *Journal of Behavior Assessment* (1980), and *Behavioral Counseling Quarterly* (1980).

BEHAVIOR MODIFICATION AND
MENTAL HEALTH PROFESSIONS

Much of the application of behavior modification developed within the framework of the mental health professions. Although behavior modification's foundations were laid in experimental laboratories, it has been successful clinical applications that have led to its increased utilization and present status. While many additional areas could be included today, the traditional mental health professions are social work, clinical and counseling psychology, and clinical psychiatry.

In the period 1830 to 1850 mental health problems were viewed simply as problems in living and were treated in a rather common sense, straightforward manner that was later labeled *moral treatment* (Bockoven, 1963). However, this was gradually replaced by the assumption that people with problems in living suffer from a disease; most methods of treatment in this country have been based on this medical model.

For our purposes it is adequate to note that the medical model refers to the view that abnormal behavior has a physiological or biochemical cause. Behavioral problems develop from an underlying physical ailment. Although the data supporting such a model are minimal, it was essentially *the* model for mental health professionals during the last half of the nineteenth century and the first quarter of this century, and it remains the most broadly accepted model in the field. Within this model the social worker did social histories, the psychologist gave tests and made diagnoses, and the psychiatrists did therapy.

Between World War I and World War II, the medical model was partially replaced by the quasi-medical model.[3] This model has also been labeled the Freudian or psychoanalytic model. It is called quasi-medical because the medical model is accepted, but the underlying cause of abnormal behavior is viewed as psychological rather than physical in nature. Thus, the development of the term *mental illness*. The roles of the mental health professionals remained essentially unchanged within this model, although a few social workers sneaked in some casework and clinical psychologists did a little therapy.

A third model, represented by the nondirective therapy of Carl Rogers, developed in the late 1940s and early 1950s within the fields of educational counseling and clinical psychology. According to this model, people developed problems because they could not admit their visceral experiences

---

3. This distinction between medical and quasi-medical models is presented in Bandura (1969), but there is no such distinction in Ullmann & Krasner (1969). The models will be discussed in more detail in Chapter 6.

into awareness; the real self and the ideal self were not congruent. It was believed that each person had within himself or herself a self-actualizing tendency and that nondirective therapy would enable one's "selves" to become more congruent. It was the school psychologists, counselors, and clinical psychologists who provided therapy within this model. It should also be noted that the shortage of therapists during World War II had resulted in increased clinical activities by social workers and clinical psychologists.

During the 1950s and early 1960s a new model, the behavioral one, was introduced into social work, clinical and counseling psychology, and clinical psychiatry. This model, like the others, has been characterized to some extent by its reference to a particular theory and/or a specified set of clinical procedures. The behavioral model, perhaps because of its partial derivation from and association with the experimental laboratory, has placed greater emphasis on a scientific approach to the study of human behavior. It is this characteristic that is used to define the behavioral model in this book. The next section will demonstrate this, and the model will be presented in detail in Chapter 6.

A fifth model might best be labeled the existential or phenomenological model and is exemplified by the work and conceptualizations of Frederick Perls and, more recently, Carl Rogers. The emphasis is on immediate subjective experience and its meaning for the client. Although some authors favor an empirical evaluation of this model, typically the scientific approach is not considered appropriate. Sometimes this model is equated with humanistic psychology, but as we will see later, humanistic psychology is a much broader and more encompassing concept. It should be identified with any of the previously discussed models only to the extent that a particular model is indeed humanistic. This notion will be discussed further in Chapter 10.

While there are more conceptual models that find clinical expression, most of the clinical work done by mental health professionals can be derived from one of these five models. There are some similarities and some obvious differences among them. One advantage of the behavioral model as defined here is that it presents no a priori basis for rejecting clinical procedures derived from any other model, but it does demand a scientific evaluation of those procedures. The clinician may engage in activities that have not been empirically validated and the experimental clinician may develop a clinical procedure from some other area of research, but those activities and procedures should still undergo empirical validation if they are to be called behavioral. This requirement should not thwart such clinical activities, but rather provide criteria for determining which procedures should become a part of the endeavor of behavior change. Even though such procedures may come from clinical innovation or deduction from other areas of research, they should find broad application only after they have been demonstrated to be effective. Those principles and procedures that are empirically validated are incorporated into behavior modification; by the same token, principles and procedures are part of behavior modification only to the extent that they are scientifically verified.

BEHAVIOR MODIFICATION AT WORK

Perhaps the best way to provide an overview of behavior modification and its scientific emphasis is by means of a case history. The following case history is drawn from a study by Haughton and Ayllon (1965, pp. 94–98). The subject was a fifty-four-year-old mental patient who had been hospitalized for twenty-three years and diagnosed as schizophrenic. One behavior that drew the attention of the researchers was broom holding. Over the course of several days, the patient began carrying a broom with her wherever she went and even slept with it nearby. This rather bizarre behavior will constitute our point of departure for a discussion of the scientific emphasis in behavior modification, One obvious problem in this case history is the cause of the broom-holding behavior. Why did the patient begin carrying a broom around with her? We are assuming that her behavior was in some way determined or *caused,* and a clarification of this term will be required. First, however, our interest lies not only in the cause of her behavior but also in the means that would be necessary to modify that behavior. Excessive broom holding is not a socially acceptable behavior (except perhaps around Halloween, and not even then if engaged in by former mental patients) and therefore must be modified if the patient is to return to the community. We might also want to determine whether the patient's broom-holding behavior is one that we may observe at some future date. Perhaps some characteristic of this patient or of her history would allow us to predict future outbreaks of excessive broom-holding behavior. Notice that we have already set ourselves three goals regarding the patient's behavior: we would like to *explain* it, *control* it, and *predict* its future occurrence. Explanation, prediction, and control are the essential goals of science as a whole. Our inclusion of these goals in this example is not in any way artificial; they provide challenging and desirable objectives. These goals characterize behavior modification, and it is not a coincidence that they are also the goals of science in general. Indeed, *the most singular characteristic of behavior modification is its scientific emphasis.* This has been viewed as both a merit and a flaw in the behavior modifier's framework. However, since it is such an integral part of that framework, we will devote all of Chapter 2 to an examination of the scientific emphasis in behavior modification. There we will discuss the relevance of rigorous empirical investigation, the emphasis on scientific rationale and method, and the advantages and disadvantages of the scientific approach. There are alternatives to science; for example, in the preceding case history, one might simply speculate about the possible causes of the bizarre behavior. Although such speculation might take place in the early stages of a scientific analysis, it would not, by itself, constitute a scientific approach to the problem. Such speculations often replace scientific approaches in everyday life. We may wonder why the girl next door always takes a gym bag with her when she goes on a date. Our speculations might run rampant, but unless we put them to the test (either by asking to look in the gym bag or by asking the girl for a date, or both), they remain prescientific. In the case of the broom-holding woman, simple speculation about the significance and/or cause of her bizarre behavior is no more than a guess. It may turn out that the guess is correct, but the only means of determining that is a test. Enter science, stage right.

Behavior as Subject Matter

Speculations about the causes of the broom-holding behavior might range from conservative hypotheses to abstract and complex theories. Haughton and Ayllon (1965) asked two psychiatrists to observe and evaluate their patient. The first psychiatrist expressed the following view:

The broom represents to this patient some essential perceptual element in her field of consciousness . . . it is certainly a stereotyped form of behavior such as is commonly seen in rather regressed schizophrenics and is rather analogous to the way small children or infants refuse to be parted from some favorite toy, piece of rag, etc. (p. 97)

The second psychiatrist evaluated the patient's behavior as follows:

Her constant and compulsive pacing holding a broom in the manner she does could be seen as a ritualistic procedure, a magical action. When regression conquers the associative process, primitive and archaic forms of thinking control the behavior. Symbolism is a predominant mode of expression of deep seated unfulfilled desires and instinctual impulses. By magic, she controls others, cosmic powers are at her disposal and inanimate objects become living creatures.
  Her broom could be then:
  1. a child that gives her love and she gives him in return her devotion;
  2. a phallic symbol;
  3. the sceptre of an omnipotent queen. (pp. 97–98)

Both evaluations attribute a symbolic significance to the excessive broom holding; the second psychiatrist's interpretation is much more abstract. Note that neither evaluation ignores the patient's behavior. However, both go beyond that behavior and relegate it to a secondary role. The broom holding is assumed to be an expression of more deep-seated problems, such as unfulfilled desires and instincts. Either hypothesis or both may be correct. However, unless their accuracy can be tested, we have nothing more than two professional-sounding hypotheses about a problem behavior. One problem with such intriguing speculations about behavior is that they often take the place of an attempt to modify the behavior. To label a behavior as symbolic, schizophrenic, or primitive does not explain the behavior, let alone predict or control it. Because speculations tend to get in the way of scientific investigation, behavior modifiers have chosen to restrict their dialogues and treatment strategies to definable and measurable behaviors and to limit their speculations to scientifically testable ones. For example, talk of repressed sexual needs makes for good conversation at a party, but raises all kinds of research problems. How does one verify that such repressed needs exist? By verbal responses or performance on an ambiguous psychological test? One cannot observe a repressed sexual need. One can only measure a behavior (be it on paper or in bed) that is assumed to be representative of the speculated need. The convention in behavior modification is to stick with the definable and measurable. This is not to say that behavior modifiers deny the existence of repressed sexual needs. However, since the ultimate interchange must deal with definable and measurable behaviors, behavior modifiers elect to remain parsimonious with their interpretations and explanations of behavior.

The *principle of parsimony* (also known as Occam's Razor) states that one should never employ a more complex explanation of an event when a less complex one will suffice. The principle, which is a convention not a truth, is often misinterpreted as encouraging simple-mindedness. The gist of this principle is that allegations, assertions, interpretations, and predictions should be as conservative as possible. It may, of course, turn out that a highly complicated, abstract, and unparsimonious rendition is the most accurate. However, in our blissful ignorance, we adopt the convention that keeps us closest to our evidence. Moreover, practical experience with parsimonious and unparsimonious undertakings has often found the former to be more useful.

This decision to remain parsimonious is often a difficult one, since there are many instances when one is tempted to go beyond the facts and speculate about unobserved phenomena. However, in the strictly scientific sphere, one must speak in a language that enables virtually all of one's professional colleagues to agree on what has been observed. In the case mentioned, the two psychiatrists saw the patient performing what they considered to be a symbolic act—the behavior of broom holding. However, their evaluation of the patient diverged considerably. Behavior modifiers hope to eliminate such divergence by restricting their analyses to definable and measurable behaviors.[4]

Thus we see that *behavior is the ultimate datum in behavior modification.* In order for internal or external events to be studied, they must be defined as behaviors and be amenable to observation and measurement. Inference, or going from some observed behavior to some unobserved phenomenon, is discouraged because of the many problems that can arise when one gets too far from one's data. Such issues as the problems with mental states, the emphasis on behavior, and the role of inference will be discussed at greater length in Chapter 3.

Choice of Methodology

Let us return to the broom-holding mental patient. We have decided that the goal is to explain, control, and predict her behavior. We have entertained some speculations about the causes of her behavior but have decided to concentrate on her observable behaviors rather than on hypothesized internal states. It is now time to choose a methodology for investigating the cause of the problem behavior. Two general classes of methodology are open to the researcher in behavior modification: (1) begin testing preconceptions and hypotheses about the behavior in question, or (2) explore and manipulate various aspects of the patient's environment to test their effect on behavior. Both methodologies contain subvarieties that allow for considerable diversity in research techniques. At times the distinction between them is far from obvious. However, these two general classes of methodology constitute an issue in current behavior-modification research. Many workers prefer one type over the other. The hypothesis-testing approach is often called *hypotheticodeductive* or *theoretical,* because the researcher begins with a theory or hypothesis about behavior and deduces from it an experimental test. The second approach is often termed *free research* or *atheoretical,* since it is allegedly free of a theoretical framework. In our case history, we would have to choose between testing some of our speculations about the cause of the patient's behavior and simply exploring the patient's environment for potential causes. For example, if we wanted to

---

4. Recent research trends have allowed for pioneering efforts in the application of behavior-modification techniques to client-reported behaviors that are not measurable by anyone other than clients themselves (for example, the client may record the frequency of saying, "I am worthless"). Such definition and measurement of variables *previously* labeled internal or mental, and therefore not available for study by the behaviorist, have increased in frequency.

test the second psychiatrist's interpretation of her behavior, we might provide the patient with a doll, an artificial penis, or a queen's scepter.[5] If the patient discontinued her broom holding after being given any of these objects, this might lend credence to the second psychiatrist's interpretation. An alternative approach would be to observe the conditions antecedent and consequent to broom holding. Perhaps the patient exhibits that behavior only when in the presence of a particular nurse or another patient. We could manipulate the presence of that other person to test its effect on the broom-holding behavior. Likewise, we might observe that the patient receives quite a bit of attention from staff members whenever she carries the broom. We might then wish to test a hunch by withholding staff attention during broom-holding episodes. Note that hypotheses do enter into the free-research approach, even though their arrival is somewhat later and less formalized than in the hypotheticodeductive method.

Let us choose the free-research approach in the present situation. Next we must choose between a single-subject design or a group design. In the single-subject design (also known as *intrasubject*), only one subject is studied. Thus, we would restrict our observations and eventual conclusions to a single broom-holding woman. In the group design (also known as *intersubject*), many subjects are studied simultaneously. In our example, we could look for other broom-holding patients and submit them as a group to an experimental test. There are many relative advantages and disadvantages in both of these designs, just as there are advantages and disadvantages in hypothesis-testing and free-research methodologies. We will discuss these at length in Chapters 4 and 5. For the time being, let us assume that a single-subject design is appropriate for the problem in question.

Drawing Conclusions

We have now resolved three questions: (1) we have chosen scientific goals (the explanation, prediction, and control of a behavior); (2) we have restricted our immediate attention to an observable behavior (broom holding); and (3) we have decided on a research methodology involving an atheoretical, single-subject design. Our immediate task is the collection and interpretation of data. The collection of data cannot be easily separated from the scientific emphasis in behavior modification. Indeed, as will be

5. Actually, it is unlikely that the second psychiatrist would accept this as a test of the hypothesis. A major contention of more speculative and traditional psychotherapists is that symbolic expressions of inner needs are effective only because they are subtle and ambiguous. This is one reason why hypotheses regarding psychic symbolism are hard to test.

seen in Chapter 4, data reign supreme in behavioral quarters. As might be anticipated, there are several means by which data may be collected, and there are different types of data. Although there is some dispute over how data should be collected and what types of data are important, there is little disagreement regarding the necessity for data collection in behavior modification. If an individual can cite reliable data to support some contention, the behavior modifier will usually sit up and listen. Dataless speculations are rather rudely received.

The interpretation of data, however, often creates controversy. Several researchers may agree on the reliability of a particular set of data but may strongly disagree on the import or message in the data. The issue is one of how to weigh or evaluate the evidence. There are two popular means of data evaluation in behavior modification. The simpler method is herein called *nonstatistical data analysis:* data, in either numerical or graph form, are examined, and it is decided whether some difference is apparent. The more complicated method is *statistical data analysis* and involves mathematical evaluation of data. Both methods have as their goal the interpretation of evidence. The relative advantages and disadvantages of statistical and nonstatistical data analysis will be discussed in Chapter 5.

Haughton and Ayllon used the nonstatistical approach in the case of the broom-holding woman. First, they obtained data on the original frequency of the problem behavior; then they tested the effect of removing an experimental variable from the broom-holding situation. This resulted in a decline in the frequency of the problem behavior. Continued absence of the experimental variable eventually resulted in a total cessation of broom holding. The nature of that variable and of the research itself will be discussed next. For the moment, let us review the research strategy employed by Haughton and Ayllon. They sought to explain, control, and predict the problem behavior. After choosing the broom-holding behavior as their subject matter, they proceeded to test the effect of an experimental variable in a single-subject design. They collected data and then evaluated them in a nonstatistical fashion. Their conclusions about the "cause" of the problem behavior were colored by their research strategy.

A brief digression may re-emphasize the need for parsimony in behavior-modification research. Haughton and Ayllon (1965) were able experimentally to induce and later eliminate a typically bizarre psychotic behavior. Their data indicated that control over the problem behavior was obtained and that its "cause" related to a cigarette contingency. What conclusions can parsimoniously be drawn from this case study? Can we conclude that all psychotic symptoms are generated by similar learning conditions? Are all psychiatric evaluations as unhelpful as those cited in getting at the root of the behavioral problem? Can we conclude that when a learning principle is employed in the modification of a behavior, then a

learning principle was necessarily involved in the development of that behavior? A parsimonious response to all of these questions would be a tentative no. These issues and some additional questions raised by this particular case study are discussed by Davison (1969, pp. 270–275).

Unfortunately, many sweeping conclusions have been drawn from the
broom-holding case study. Again, parsimony and conservatism would
seem to be overlooked antidotes. Behavior modifiers take pride in their
scientific bent. However, cool scientific conservatism is often overtaken
by the enthusiasm generated by the progress and promise of the behavioral
approach. It is just such enthusiasm that needs to be tempered if the area of
behavior modification is to retain its empirical aura. It is difficult to contain one's excitement when a vegetative mental patient makes a first vocal
response in seventeen years as a result of the implementation of some
behavior-modification technique. However, such excitement should be
channeled toward continuing and expanding behavioral research rather
than making unwarranted predictions and premature theorizations. It is
the intent of this book to provide a few reminders of the empirical rigor
and scientific conservatism that should be the byword of researchers in behavior modification.

Ethical Issues

The case history of the broom-holding woman was chosen because it is
frequently cited by behavior modifiers (see Ayllon, Haughton, & Hughes,
1965; Ullmann & Krasner, 1965, 1969; Wenrich, 1970). It is actually an
illustration of an experimentally induced "symptom." By employing the
behavior-modification techniques of shaping and intermittent reinforcement, Haughton and Ayllon (1965) were able to create a symptom in a
fifty-four-year-old patient. That this behavior was similar to many of
those exhibited by mental patients is demonstrated by the two psychiatrists' evaluations. The development of the deviant behavior was programmed by rewarding the patient with cigarettes whenever she engaged
in broom-holding behavior. After the behavior had stabilized at a fairly
high frequency of occurrence, two unsuspecting psychiatrists were asked
to observe and evaluate the patient. Their speculative interpretations were
later used as examples of the futility of nonbehavioral analyses. The
broom-holding behavior was eliminated by withholding cigarettes, the experimental variable considered responsible for the maintenance of the behavior. The case history illustrates much more than the speculative pen-
chant of many psychiatrists. It also touches upon the ethical issues that
underlie any attempt at behavioral control. Is it ethically justifiable to ex-

perimentally induce symptoms? Does the fact that the researchers were aware of the conditions that generated the broom-holding behavior make their request for a psychiatric diagnosis unethical? If Haughton and Ayllon had come upon an example of excessive broom holding that they had not programmed, would there be any ethical impediments to their modification of that behavior? These and many other issues regarding the ethics of behavior control will be discussed in Chapter 10. Suffice it to say for the moment that the control of behavior and, indeed, even the scientific investigation of behavior principles have been challenged by many contemporary psychologists on the grounds that they are unethical. We will explore some of their arguments in Chapter 10.

Another topic that will be discussed in Chapter 10 is the quasi-schism between behavioral approaches and what have come to be called humanistic approaches. For some time now there has been a mistaken assumption that some inherent incompatibility exists between humanistic concerns and scientific analyses of behavior. To be sure, some behavioral researchers have allowed their scientific coolness to generalize to their everyday interactions, so that a cold, austere prototype has been intermittently reinforced. However, most behavior modifiers are a very humane lot. They do not eye their sexual companions with a cold, objective stare, and only a handful of them carry a cumulative recorder to bed. The main contention of the final chapter is that the ultimate humanism is based on behavioral science. Knowing how to program the most rewarding of all worlds— where individuals function in harmony with their talents, interests, values, and the needs of their community—is one goal on which both humanists and behavior modifiers alike can agree.

THE RELEVANCE OF BEHAVIOR MODIFICATION

Why should you read this book or undertake a course of study in behavior modification? We would like to suggest a number of reasons in response to that question. The first is a point that was noted earlier; namely, to the extent that the behavioral model unravels the puzzle of behavior and behavior change, it will provide information regarding how we change our behavior, how we modify the behavior of others, and perhaps most importantly, how other people modify our behavior. The basic point is that the findings of behavior modification not only tell us how better to deal with clinical and social problems, but they also provide useful information relevant to all aspects of our lives. Such findings can help us improve interpersonal relationships, work habits, child-rearing practices, and methods of self-control.

Beyond the personal-management sphere, there are a number of reasons why the study of behavior modification is relevant to your life. If you expect to work in the area of mental health, the applicability of the behavioral approach and its emphasis on evaluation should be apparent by now. The relationship of behavior modification to the rest of psychology and related disciplines warrants its study by the serious student in psychology. This is especially true of the methodological behaviorism espoused in this book, because the emphasis is on the integration of clinical work with that of other areas of psychological research and theory. The rapidly expanding application of behavior modification to the prevention and alleviation of social problems at the community level is further reason to study behavior modification. These applications at the community level, such as increasing bus ridership and decreasing racial prejudice, are exciting but they raise a number of questions, especially ethical ones. You can adequately resolve these issues only by understanding what behavior modification is and is not.

Our final suggestion, which is one that will appear throughout the book, is that the more you know about yourself, your social learning history, and the empirically validated principles of behavior change, the more choices you will have, the more self-control you will exhibit, and the more freedom and dignity you will possess.

SUMMARY

Behavior modification, or behavior therapy, is one of the fastest growing and most promising fields of psychology. Behavior modification is tentatively defined as (1) the use of a broadly defined set of clinical procedures whose description and rationale often rely on the experimental findings of psychological research, and (2) an experimental and functionally analytic approach to clinical data, relying on an objective and measurable outcome. This definition is consistent with Watson's scientific method of investigation labeled methodological behaviorism on which behavior modification is based. The principles and procedures of behavior modification change as new research findings become available; there is no "arrived-at" set of principles or procedures.

Mental health professionals from such fields as clinical and counseling psychology, clinical psychiatry, and social work engage in behavior therapy. This, however, is a recent phenomenon and is related to the historical development of the various models for behavior change. The most singular characteristic of behavior modification is its scientific emphasis or its reliance on methodological behaviorism. Behavior modification has as its goals the explanation, prediction, and control of behavior. The example of the broom-holding mental hospital resident demonstrates the chief characteristics of behavior modification, as well as some difficulties encountered in its application.

Since behavior modification has widespread applications and is relevant to so much of one's life, it is an important area of study. With this overview of behavior therapy we are ready to launch into a discussion of the scientific method on which it is based.

SUGGESTED READINGS

Bandura, A. *Social learning theory*. Englewood Cliffs, N.J.: Prentice-Hall, 1977.

Davison, G. C. & Neale, J. M. *Abnormal psychology: An experimental clinical approach*. New York: Wiley, 1977. Chapters 1 and 2.

Mahoney, M. J. *Cognition and behavior modification*. Cambridge, Mass.: Ballinger, 1974. Chapters 1 and 2.

Ullmann, L. P., & Krasner, L. *A psychological approach to abnormal behavior*. Englewood Cliffs, N.J.: Prentice-Hall, 1975. Chapters 7, 8, and 11.

CHAPTER 2

THE SCIENTIFIC EMPHASIS
IN BEHAVIOR MODIFICATION

A main characteristic of behavior modification is its emphasis on a scientific approach. This emphasis is expressed in such ways as rigorous definition of concepts, a heavy reliance on data, and so on. The scientific approach is not easily defined. There are several subvarieties of scientific approaches, and there are many issues that may differentiate one behavior modifier's concept of science from another's. Science is not a circumscribed body of knowledge or a collection of how-to-do-it techniques. There is considerable flexibility within the scientific framework which allows for the expression of individual research biases and philosophical bents. It is the purpose of this chapter to acquaint the reader with some of the major goals and issues that characterize the nebulous entity called the scientific approach. Familiarity with the rationale and limitations of that approach is an ever present necessity for the behavioral researcher.

THE GOALS OF A SCIENTIFIC APPROACH

In simplest terms, science might be described as a search for order. It seeks to discover, describe, and utilize lawful relationships among events. The events may range from the activity of a single brain cell to the actions of a large social group. It is often useful to classify events into one of two categories: *independent variables* and *dependent variables*. They are called variables because they may vary in terms of such things as quantity, quality, and type. Science seeks orderly relationships between values of these variables. In the simplest instance, the value of a variable may be its presence or absence. In more complex cases, the value may take the form of a number, such as age, or a category, such as male. Regardless of how one assigns different values to them, the independent and dependent variables constitute the subject matter of scientific investigation. The range of possible variables is, of course, infinite, and the scope of science is therefore virtually limitless.

The distinction between independent and dependent variables is a very important one. Basically, the *independent variable* (IV) is the variable that one manipulates in order to produce changes in the *dependent variable* (DV). The IV is independent in that it is the isolated focus of a given experiment, and the DV is dependent in that its value may or may not be affected by changes in the IV. One may roughly conceptualize their relationship as one of cause and effect[1] wherein changes in the independent variable cause some change in the dependent variable. A popular toothpaste advertisement offers one illustration. In evaluating the effects of two brands of toothpaste on dental cavities, the brands (A and B) are IVs and number of cavities is the DV. If fewer cavities are encountered after use of brand A than after use of brand B, then the researcher concludes that brand A is a better product. He or she must be careful, however, to make sure that other IVs were not responsible for the observed difference in cavities. Suppose, for example, that more candy was eaten during the evaluation of brand B. The difference might then be due to a third unwanted or extraneous IV, namely, the difference in candy consumption. The careful isolation of IVs is an important characteristic of scientific methods.

Although the decision as to which variable is which may sometimes be arbitrary, most variable pairs can be classified easily. The search for order is pursued in hopes that if a lawful relationship exists between the two variables, it will be discovered and described. For example, if some value of the independent variable is always associated with some consistent change in the dependent variable, then a lawful relationship has been discovered. The relationship is lawful in that it conforms to a regular pattern.

The goals of science, then, are the discovery and description of lawful relationships among variables. Once such relationships have been observed, they may be utilized in prediction and control. To observe that some value of variable A consistently results in some change in variable B allows one to predict and control variable B. The prediction, of course, simply involves an "if-then" restatement of the observed lawful relationship. Control means that the predicted change in variable B can be

---

1. See pp. 35–37 for discussion of some problems in cause-effect conceptualizations.

produced or avoided simply by appropriately manipulating variable A. Closely tied with the scientific goals of prediction and control is the concept of *replication*. In order to be maximally useful, a lawful relationship between two variables must be applicable to future, similar occurrences. In other words, the observed relationships must be repeatable, or replicable. Ideally, future occurrences would be identical occurrences; however, exact replication never occurs. Thus we must speak of future, similar occurrences. Replication then refers to the process of extending an observed relationship from one instance to future, similar ones. For example, if a popular reducing diet is the IV and weight change is the DV, one might wish to determine whether any observed regularity could be applied to the same person at a later time or to other people. If the relationship did hold in both situations, then it would be tentatively classified as replicable. A failure to replicate would, of course, necessitate appropriate qualifications in the description of the relationship. Note that unreplicable results are not unscientific; they are simply more circumscribed in their relevance. However, they are often looked upon unfavorably. This is because a failure to replicate may indicate that some previous finding was spurious because of poor experimental design, chance factors, or a failure to control extraneous IVs. The replicability criterion stems from an emphasis on public observability in the scientific approach.

To summarize, science might be defined as a search for order. It entails the discovery and description of lawful relationships among variables (events). Such discovery and description make possible the prediction and control of future, similar occurrences. Control, of course, is a utilization of the observed regularity. Replicability ensures that the observed relationship was neither unique nor accidental and that it may be usefully applied to future, similar situations.

TRUTH, CERTAINTY, AND PROBABLE INFERENCE

It is a common assumption, especially among laypersons, that science is "the royal road to truth." Perhaps because of modern emphases on scientific progress, many people look up to science as the ultimate means of obtaining certainty and indisputable facts. However, a brief look at the philosophy on which science is based will illustrate the error in this conception. Some basic generalizations about the nature of scientific knowledge–gathering may be worth noting.

1. Truth is an unattainable ideal. Science will never allow us to know the truth; it can only allow us to increase our relative confidence in the accuracy of our assumptions and theories about the world.

2. Science denies finality. Its search for order is a never ending one.

3. Certainty and proof apply only to abstract logical systems like mathematics and not to concrete, real-life events. Science can deal only with probabilities; it cannot claim certainty. This distinction is slightly technical but worthy of elaboration. Recall that science strives to discover and describe orderly relationships in nature. There are two broad categories of such relationships in science: (a) *analytic,* or those dealing with symbols, such as words and numbers; and (b) *synthetic,* or those involving real-life experience. The truth value or validity of a statement depends on which kind of relationship it predicts. Generally, the terms *truth* and *proof* are used in reference to symbolic statements and *probability* and *evidence* are applied to experiential statements. One can be certain that "all bachelors are unmarried" because this statement is true by definition. Its validity is guaranteed by the respective meanings of the symbols (terms) *bachelor* and *unmarried.* On the other hand, one cannot be certain that it will snow next winter in Toronto. Although it is very probable that this event will occur (based on previous evidence), there is a very remote possibility that it won't. A good rule of thumb for distinguishing between analytic and synthetic assertions is the *principle of conceivable negation.* For any given statement, if you can conceive of its being false, then it is synthetic, or experimental (regardless of how probable it may be). If the statement cannot conceivably be negated, it is analytic, or symbolic. For example, consider the proposal, "A triangle has three sides." Can you conceive of its being false? Can you conceive of a two-sided triangle? Of course not. The statement is true by definition. How about the statement, "Vitamin C helps prevent colds"? Can you conceive of the possibility that it does not? The answer is yes, and the proposition can therefore only claim evidence, not proof, and a probability of validity, not certainty.

4. Science is a self-appraising discipline. The scientist continually reexamines both the facts and the methods of inquiry used to collect information. Evidence is accepted regardless of its appeal or implication for popular conceptions of reality. A scientist is dependent upon the data for an evaluation of current conceptions of lawful relationships among events. If the data do not fit the popular conception, then the conception must be altered to fit the data.

5. All scientific facts are relative and tentative. Nothing about science is unchangeable. It used to be a "fact" that the earth is flat. This seeming bit of truth changed, however, as contradictory evidence appeared. Contemporary "facts" are no less susceptible to change. When we use the terms *scientific fact* or *fact* later in the book, we refer to evidence that is relative and tentative and not to the popular concept of *fact* as a proven bit of truth.

6. Science assumes some degree of determinism or order in nature. If event B consistently follows event A, then their relationship is considered

an orderly and determined one. Rhetorically, one might say that in future situations when event A occurs, the scientist assumes that nature is obliged to follow through with event B.

7.   Science is a thoroughly human undertaking. Being human, the behavior of scientists is not unlike that of other individuals and the scientist is therefore quite susceptible to theoretical prejudices, emotionality, and the like. As a fallible human endeavor, science is never totally objective.

CRITERIA IN SCIENCE
Testability

The scientist's confidence in the probable validity of a statement depends on the relevant evidence. This brings up still another characteristic of scientific inquiry, namely, its reliance on empirical tests in the evaluation of statements. A prediction or hypothesis is supposed to be judged by the data encountered in its experimental assessment. Not all statements, however, are testable, and philosophers of science have long debated the status of such hypotheses. Some have argued that untestable propositions are scientifically meaningless; others have imposed different criteria on hypotheses (see Weimer, 1979). In everyday research, however, the contemporary scientist seldom entertains hypotheses that do not specify potential tests of their validity. A testable statement, of course, is one for which potentially supportive or disconfirming evidence is conceivable.

Without pursuing the logical arguments and philosophical issues pertaining to the testability criterion, we might consider some of its more prominent aspects and give a few examples. Originally, the testability criterion required that an empirical statement be verifiable. Thus, a scientific evaluation of the statement, "There is a God," would have required specification of the conditions that would give support to the statement or contribute to its verification. For reasons that the interested reader may wish to pursue (see Mahoney, 1976; Weimer, 1979), the verifiability criterion was supplemented by a falsifiability criterion, so that empirical statements had to be *verifiable or falsifiable in principle*. The qualification "in principle" stressed the fact that the statement in question need not be immediately testable; there need only be some conceivable means for testing it. For example, the statement, "There is life in other galaxies," is empirically testable because the conditions that would make it true or false can be specified. The fact that we do not now have the means to test that statement does not make it unscientific. The following is an empirically untestable statement: "There is an invisible and intangible elf who sits on the president's shoulder. It never leaves a trace of existence, but it is there all the same." Since there are no means of verifying or falsifying this statement, it would be categorized as empirically untestable. This does not necessarily categorize the statement as senseless; it simply means that the statement is beyond the jurisdiction of science.

Perhaps more than any other scientific discipline, behavioral science has been plagued with what would be empirically classified as untestable statements. In the field of personality and clinical psychology, this shortcoming has been especially prominent. The closed system—one that does not specify the data that would have a bearing on it—has been all too prominent. The problems raised by neglect of scientific criteria are not nominal. Such systems, which present themselves as empirical or scientific, are often only speculative and do not benefit from the self-appraising feedback of experimental evidence. The only way to ensure the meaningfulness of statements about behavior is to compare the statements with the behavior in question. Modern behavioral science has incorporated the testability criterion into its framework, so that the speculative preoccupations of earlier times have been replaced by empirically testable assertions about behavior. This emphasis on testability and general scientific respectability is considered by some to be the most significant factor in the recent surge of progress made in behavioral research.

Objectivity and Operationism

Objectivity may be defined crudely as a nonpartisan approach to subject matter. It plays an enormously significant role in all science, and its utilization is perhaps more essential in behavioral science than in any other. The reason for this is that behavioral science is particularly susceptible to *subjective* observations and descriptions. Behavioral observers often have much in common with the objects of their observation, and reading in their own predictions and past experiences is very tempting. The best illustration of the difference between objective and subjective descriptions is given by Skinner (1963).

In a demonstration experiment, a hungry pigeon was conditioned to turn around in a clockwise direction. A final, smoothly executed pattern of behavior was shaped by reinforcing successive approximations with food. Students who had watched the demonstration were asked to write an account of what they had seen. Their responses included the following: (i) the organism was conditioned to *expect* reinforcement for the right kind of behavior; (ii) the pigeon walked around, *hoping* that something would bring the food back again; (iii) the pigeon *observed* that a certain behavior seemed to produce a particular result; (iv) the pigeon *felt* that food would be given it because of its actions; and (v) the bird came to *associate* his action with the click of the food dispenser. The observed facts could be stated, respectively, as follows: (i) the organism was reinforced *when* the behavior was of a given kind; (ii) the pigeon walked around *until* the food container again appeared; (iii) a certain behavior *produced* a particular result; (iv) food was given to the pigeon *when* it acted in a given way; and (v) the click of the food dispenser *was temporally related* to the bird's action. . . . The events reported by the students were observed, if at all, in their own behavior. They were describing what *they* would have expected, felt, and hoped for under similar circumstances. (pp. 955–956)

The contrast between the objectively presented facts and those that were subjectively reported is very dramatic. The reference to the organism's internal states will be discussed more thoroughly in the following chapter. For the time being, however, the reader should recognize the very important distinction between these two types of accounts. In more objective descriptions, the hard-core data are reported and a conscious attempt is made to avoid interpretations, inferences, or assumptions. Subjective descriptions, however, often abound with such nonobservable adornments. In a subjective account, many of the reported behavioral elements derive from the subject or observer, whereas in an objective account, the elements come from the object of observation. An illustrative exercise is to take some event and have several observers describe it. By comparing notes and discussing exactly which statements were observed and which were inferred, one can gain an appreciation of the desirability of objective accounts and the ease with which subjective statements can creep into a scientist's language. It should, however, be kept in mind that no observational account is ever totally objective. Even the most careful and conscientious scientist cannot avoid subtle assumptions and tacit biases in "seeing" something. Scientists work toward reducing subjectivity in observations (except when that is their focus—that is, the nature and patterns of human subjectivity). Absolute objectivity is an "impossible dream" but a worthy direction.

  The topic of objectivity is closely related to what has been called data language in behavioral science. As its name implies, *data language* is a type of scientific language that emphasizes objective facts. It is the cornerstone of empirical observation, since the evidence must be stated in a clear and communicable manner. Data language should be descriptive, not inferential. Because science is a search for order, it relies heavily on observation and experimentation. For observation to be useful, however, it must be as free as possible from inference and arbitrary interpretations. Inferences and interpretations are often very useful, but they must ultimately be linked to data. Data language points up the *public observability* characteristic of science. If the scientific community can agree on the description of some event, then that description is probably an objective one.[2] However, if controversy arises, it is probably because one or more observers have garnished the data with some subjective interpretations. The use of data language is one means of ensuring some agreement as to evidence in the scientific community. For example, one might wish to say that an individual had improved after being treated for a fear of heights. Such a description, however, is very subjective, since one researcher's definition of improvement may not correspond to another's. Translating such a description into data language, one would say that after treatment the individual was capable of climbing some specific number of feet up a ladder. The observable evidence is described in a form with which all observers could agree. Whether or not improvement took place would depend on a specified criterion for improvement.

Closely related to objectivity and data language is the topic of operationism. Broadly defined, *operationism* is an attempt to objectify scientific concepts by equating them with the operations used in their measurement. When a concept is operationally defined, it is defined in such a way that one knows what procedures are necessary to observe it. For example, an operational definition of the concept of intelligence would specify the operations needed to illustrate it. Thus, Boring (1923) defined intelligence as "what the (intelligence) tests test" (p. 35). Similarly, one might operationally define anxiety as an increase in heart rate, a change in respiration, or a particular score on some paper-and-pencil test. The particular operations involved in defining a concept can be arbitrary. One researcher might define psychotic behavior in terms of scores on a personality inventory; another might define it as the act of giving personality inventories. The point is that, regardless of how one defines a concept, if specific operations are outlined and described, there is little chance of confusion over one's evidence. For example, a researcher may report that a certain drug produced drastic improvement in institutionalized psychotics. Such a statement could (and often does) lead to serious misinterpretations unless improvement is operationally defined. The researcher might operationally define improvement as a change in the reported content of the patients' dreams. Since there are many other potential behaviors that might be relevant to improvement (for example, cessation of hallucinations, delusions, and bizarre behaviors), the criterion chosen could easily vary across researchers. Thus, it is important that the researcher specify precisely what is meant by certain concepts so that other workers can look at the data and the criteria used in defining a concept. Operational definitions and data language go hand in hand in helping to objectify scientific observations.

---

2. It is important to distinguish between objectivity and validity. As mentioned in our previous discussion of "facts," public consensus does not ensure accurate knowledge.

SCIENTIFIC SUBJECT MATTER VERSUS
SCIENTIFIC METHODOLOGY

A distinction frequently overlooked in behavioral science is that between scientific subject matter and scientific methodology. The former, of course, is comprised of those areas that are investigated by empirical methods. The latter is a loosely structured set of operations or procedures employed in those investigations. The distinction is an important one in that many misconceptions surround both subject matter and methodology.

With regard to scientific subject matter, it is often said that a particular topic is inherently unscientific. According to the characteristics of science discussed earlier, this is incorrect if the topic in question contains any empirically testable statements. For example, to say that the study of ESP or flying saucers is inherently unscientific is incorrect since there are many testable statements that could be generated in these two fields. If researchers do not generate such statements, then it is they who should be dubbed unscientific and not the subject matter. Keep in mind, however, that the term *unscientific* is not a pejorative label; it is a descriptive qualifier indicating phenomena or assertions that, for better or for worse, are outside the realm of contemporary science.

Misconceptions about scientific methodology often revolve around whether there exists a standardized set of techniques to be routinely employed in empirical investigations. Unless one were to define observation and experimentation as these techniques, no such storehouse exists. Scientific methodology consists of a diverse collection of techniques. The particular techniques are often designed for a specific subject matter and may be totally irrelevant for other avenues of investigation. Thus, there is no international standard of scientific methodology. If a particular technique can reveal lawful relationships to the scientific community, it is acceptable. A sophisticated apparatus, a microscope, or even a frequency counter are not inherent to the scientific endeavor.

To summarize, there is a distinction between scientific subject matter and scientific methodology. The former is virtually any topic about which testable statements can be made. The latter is a loosely structured collection of techniques that have been found useful in observing or describing lawful relationships among variables.

CAUSATION, CORRELATION, AND DETERMINISM

Although the reader may not immediately perceive any potential problems with the concept of causation, the fact of the matter is that it has constituted an area of philosophical debate for some time. The intricacies of "the problem of causation" would take us far afield from the present discussion, but a brief capsulation is both appropriate and beneficial. In behavior modification, as in all other scientific disciplines, the issue of causation is often a very significant one.

Perhaps the best way of summarizing the problem of causation is to describe it as an instance of inference rather than observation. Inference is a form of reasoning wherein one takes some assertion or bit of evidence and from it draws conclusions or makes speculations. Although it is unavoidable in scientific investigation, unwarranted inference is discouraged because it leads to problems of disagreement and ambiguity. How does one judge whether an inference is warranted or not? In western culture, the criteria for warranted inference are called the rules of logic—certain agreed upon restrictions on what makes sense and what does not.

One cannot *observe* causality; one must rather *infer* it. Perhaps a better way to put it is that one may observe *sequence* but not *consequence*. In searching for orderly relationships, one may observe all sorts of coordinated relations (or correlations) among variables. However, these observations can in no way guarantee a causal relationship. All that can be noted in the data language is that a change in the value of the IV was followed by a change in the value of the DV. Thus, for example, one may observe that shortly after sunrise there is an increase in temperature, or that the flipping of a light switch is followed by highly predictable changes in illumination. However, neither of these events has illustrated causation which, as we have explained, is not demonstrable. Our stubbornness in denying causality in these examples may seem strange to the reader, but the essential distinction we are making is between actually observed data and assumed or inferred relationships. To say that variable A caused variable B is to assert that the former was in some way instrumental in the occurrence of the latter. This is going beyond the scientific data, which may indicate only a frequent co-occurrence and a temporal priority (that is, event A always precedes event B). When two variables systematically vary with respect to one another, they are said to be *correlated*. Our argument is that the scientist can observe only correlation and not causation.

Perhaps a brief example will illustrate the need for scientific conservatism in drawing causal inferences from correlational observations. Consider the following hypothetical situation. Researchers have collected data over several years' time from a small community in an attempt to investigate the causes of drowning. After much data analysis and statistical exercise, it is reported that a very strong correlation exists between ice cream consumption and frequency of drownings. Based on these data, the researchers conclude that the drownings were in some way causally linked with ice cream consumption. Such a conclusion may seem partially justifiable. If children consume large amounts of ice cream just before swimming, it might be possible for them to develop cramps and drown. However, an alternative interpretation of the data is possible. Ice cream consumption is correlated with warm weather, which in turn is correlated with an increased frequency of swimming. Since the latter allows more opportunities for drowning, it is very possible that what our researchers have mistaken for a *causal* connection has only been a *correlational* one. That is, even though there is a systematic change in the two variables under study, such a change might be interpreted in terms of some third variable. Other examples of such unjustified jumps from correlational observation to causational inference are readily available.

The reader may well wonder how it is that science can make any progress if it is not allowed to make causal inferences. The fact of the matter is that scientists do make such inferences. Indeed, science is sometimes described as a search for causes. The reason for this seeming discrepancy is basically a pragmatic one. The constraints of everyday observation and direct communication often lobby for the use of some conceptual shorthand. It is much simpler to say that event A caused event B than that event B has followed event A 12,645,203 times. Moreover, the finer issues of scientific philosophy generally are not delved into in everyday experimentation. Even though a researcher may agree with the foregoing analysis of problems in causal inference, he or she may find it convenient and practical to informally conceptualize observations of A–B sequences in terms of causality.

The point of the foregoing has been to emphasize that (1) at a conceptual level causal descriptions always involve inference and should therefore be made conservatively, and (2) the practical demands of research and communication often encourage a loose usage of causal descriptions.

It cannot be stressed too strongly that stubborn conservatism is frequently necessary in correlation-versus-causation disputes (see Blalock, 1964). Selltiz, Jahoda, Deutsch, and Cook (1959) list the following as necessary to justify functional causal inferences: (1) evidence of concomitant variation; (2) evidence that the DV did not precede the IV; and (3) evidence ruling out other causal factors. The first two of these criteria are often very easy to fulfill. The third, however, constitutes a major problem in virtually every experimental investigation in behavioral science.

Our final point relating to this topic has to do with the term *determinism*. The concepts of causality and determinism are often considered to be equivalent in both meaning and implications. Science assumes that all events are uniformly determined, in the sense that, given two identical antecedent situations, there will be two identical subsequent events. A determined relationship is one that follows some lawful order (if A, then B). Note that there is no obvious necessity for the assumption of causality. However, partly because of pragmatic considerations, defenders of the deterministic viewpoint often wave the causality banner (see Boring, 1957; Grunbaum, 1952). The word *defenders* may have clued the reader to the fact that the assumptions of causality and determinism are not universally held. A long-standing philosophical controversy has raged over the issue of free will versus determinism. If every event is determined or caused, then how can one assign responsibility to individuals for their actions? Don't the assumptions of determinism and causality eliminate choice and free will from human behavior? These and related questions will be discussed further in Chapter 10.

To summarize, causation is an inferred relationship. It may never be observed and always involves going beyond one's immediate data. The scientist can observe sequence or correlation but not consequence or causation. However, practical considerations often lobby for an informal use of the term *causation* in science. The concepts of causality and determinism are frequently considered equivalent. However, determinism involves an assumption of lawful relationships in nature and does not require causative influence.

THE LIMITATIONS OF SCIENCE

The scientific rationale is not a universally agreed upon avenue for the pursuit of knowledge. Other avenues include mysticism, rationalism, and personalistic science. Mystics believe that they can attain knowledge via religious experiences, meditation, rituals, and so on. *Rationalists* believe that some or all of reality can be investigated by means of reasoning rather than experimental test. In prosaic terms, the rationalist believes that many truths are self-evident in that they are derivable from reasoning rather than experimentation. For example, some philosophers maintain that such propositions as "The shortest distance between two points is a straight line" can be intuitively recognized to be true. A humorous fable about the argument between rationalism and scientific empiricism goes as follows. The rationalist and empiricist were debating about which side of a buttered piece of toast would face upward if it were tossed into the air and allowed to fall. The rationalist said that it would obviously be the buttered side. The empiricist didn't know and said that an experimental test would be required. The toast was buttered, tossed into the air, and fell buttered side down. As the empiricist chuckled, the rationalist coolly remarked, "Obviously, the toast was buttered on the wrong side." This little story, which favors the empiricist's viewpoint, illustrates the issue of *a priori knowledge* (knowledge prior to experience) and *a posteriori knowledge* (knowledge subsequent to experience). The rationalist emphasizes the former and the empiricist, the latter. In actual practice, however, it is impossible to separate the rational (reasoning) and empirical (observational) elements of science. What scientists observe and how they interpret it can be dramatically influenced by preconceived notions and perceptual biases. For all practical purposes, then, the rationalist-empiricist debate is an intriguing one which can be argued but never completely resolved in favor of either extreme.

The *personalistic science* approach is yet another avenue of inquiry. It employs a loose scientific framework and emphasizes intrapersonal experiences. A considerable degree of inference and subjectivity is encouraged and strict adherence to rigorous scientific criteria is absent. Many of the more humanistically oriented psychologists exemplify the personalistic science approach (for example, Maslow, 1966). One of their contentions is that the richness and depth of human experience defy the constrictive methods of contemporary science. In recent years, the gap between hard-nosed laboratory science and personalistic science has become narrower, and the prospect of collaborative respect for different approaches to the subject matter seems to be looming on the horizon.

There are, of course, several other nonscientific approaches. The point is that the scientist does not have a corner on the knowledge market. All too often one hears the term *unscientific* applied in a condescending and critical manner. To say that a particular investigator is unscientific is not to label him or her as a quack or as some misguided wretch. Rather, it is simply to state that the person is not playing by the rules of that game called science (see Agnew & Pyke, 1969). The choice as to which game will be played lies solely with the individual, and intergame mudslinging would seem less than beneficial in our converging quest for knowledge.

At this point, the reader may want to interject that there must be reasons why so many individuals choose the science game over other approaches to knowledge. Before exploring the justification of the scientific approach, let us briefly delve into some of its major shortcomings.

First, science is deficient in the sense that it does not and cannot claim certainty. As pointed out earlier, the scientist can *approach* certainty by assigning higher and higher probabilities to some event. However, he or she can never claim to be absolutely sure about an experimental event. This is probably not a very devastating flaw, but it is nonetheless a limitation of the scientific approach.

Second, scientific "facts," methods, and principles are tentative and relative by nature. For example, the principles of operationism and testability have undergone considerable reformulation and modification since their inclusion in the scientific framework. Because of its self-appraising nature, science is constantly changing its framework to meet the demands of new problems and new evidence. The difficulty here is that there are always at least a few scientists who are working with outmoded facts or principles. Moreover, there is often a lack of agreement among scientists as to the appropriate procedure or correct principle. Many of these controversies can be witnessed in behavior-modification research. The scientist expects the most useful fact, method, or principle ultimately to win out by demonstrating its relative superiority. Meanwhile, however, there is considerable variability in the interpretation and application of the scientific approach. What is considered to be within the framework of science at one time may not be so considered at some subsequent time (see Kuhn, 1962).

Third, science is restrictive. Because of its stress on observable evidence, communicability, testability, and so on, science excludes many questions and problems that might be considered significant. Moral and religious issues are often considered beyond the province of scientific evaluation.

Note that each of these shortcomings is more a limitation than a flaw. The question remains as to why so many individuals choose the scientific approach. Are there any logical arguments that favor science over other approaches? The simple answer is no. Each approach to knowledge has as much logical justification as any other. Paradoxically, the assumption that science is the correct approach to knowledge would have to be classified by the scientist as untestable and unscientific since there are no finite tests by which to confirm or disconfirm it.

One might be tempted to conclude that science, mysticism, rationalism, and other approaches are supported by the faith of their adherents. However, one argument that does support the scientific approach is that of pragmatism. Scientists have shown their methods and principles to be useful in the attainment of knowledge. This reliance on practicality, of course, makes some assumptions about criteria for choosing from among the various approaches. The criterion of usefulness is probably no less justified than any other. Turner's (1967) comments regarding the justification of the scientific approach are a fitting capsulation. "Empiricism itself is culpable, yet we have found no reliable substitute for a knowledge supported by the fact of its public communicability" (p. 7).

SUMMARY

Behavior modification is characterized by an emphasis on the scientific approach to knowledge. Generally speaking, that approach may be described as an empirical search for order. It attempts to discover, describe, and utilize lawful relationships among events. For research purposes, events are often classified as independent and dependent variables. Confidence in the accuracy of a reported relationship is increased when that relationship can be replicated.

Science is a relative and approximate approach to knowledge. It denies finality and can never claim such absolute characteristics as certainty, truth, or proof. The only statements that can legitimately claim these characteristics are those dealing with the meaning and relationship among symbols. The rule of thumb for deciding whether a statement is analytic or synthetic is the principle of conceivable negation. If you can conceive of its being false, then it is synthetic.

As a continually open system of knowledge, science progresses through self-appraisal. Its facts are therefore only tentative. Among the generally conceded criteria of scientific research are those of testability and objective communicability. The relevance of science in any given area is determined by the satisfaction of these criteria.

A technical distinction can be made among the concepts of determinism, correlation, and causation. Determinism proposes that relationships among events are lawful. Correlation refers to an observed co-occurrence of events, while causation assigns responsibility to one or more of these events. Correlation may be observed but causation cannot be; it must be inferred. This technical distinction is sometimes overlooked in informal discussions.

Finally, science must be recognized as a fallible avenue of inquiry. It is not intrinsically superior to any other approach to knowledge. However, its demonstrated utility and self-appraising flexibility are advantages that lean heavily in its favor.

SUGGESTED READINGS

Kuhn, T. S. *The structure of scientific revolutions.* Chicago: University of Chicago, 1962.

Mahoney, M. J. *Scientist as subject: The psychological imperative.* Cambridge, Mass.: Ballinger, 1976.

Weimer, W. B. *Notes on the methodology of scientific research.* Hillsdale, N.J: Erlbaum, 1979.

CHAPTER 3

THE ROLE OF
INFERRED VARIABLES

This chapter is devoted to a controversial issue in behavior modification, namely, the usefulness and legitimacy of inferred variables in the explanation, prediction, and control of behavior. For our purposes, an *inferred variable* is one that has not been observed. For example, if one opens the refrigerator and finds that the last piece of pizza is missing, one may infer that a roommate or family member has consumed it. This conclusion is said to be inferential since the actual event was not observed. Note that the inferred event or variable connects or *mediates* a previous situation (the existence of the pizza) with a subsequent event (the pizza's disappearance). Like a clue in a murder mystery, the inferred variable often attempts to put things together and make sense of them. Because of this mediating function, inferred events are often called *mediational variables*. Lest the reader think that all inferred variables are alike, our discussion will begin with a brief consideration of some of the more important distinctions that have been made among inferred variables.

INTERVENING VARIABLES AND
HYPOTHETICAL CONSTRUCTS

Perhaps the most clear-cut distinction that can be made is that offered by MacCorquodale and Meehl (1948) between intervening variables and

41

hypothetical constructs. Although the distinction is somewhat complicated, we may summarize it briefly as follows. An *intervening variable* relates two events *conceptually*. Its existence as a physical object is not proposed. For example, one might say that rewarding an organism for responses in a particular setting will increase its tendency to respond in that setting. The inferred or intervening variable (the tendency) is a conceptual probability. We are not expected to operate on the organism and locate the source of the aforementioned tendency in its spleen. Rather, our statement refers to a conceptual variable that we may or may not find useful. Another example might be the case of a young child who refuses to come to the dinner table despite repeated pleading from a parent. In attempting to explain this situation, one might say that the child has a stubborn streak. The latter, of course, is not a presumed physiological variable but is rather a convenient conceptual mediator.

The intervening variable is to be distinguished from the *hypothetical construct,* which proposes the existence of an unobserved physical object or process to relate two or more events. For example, several contemporary theories hypothesize biochemical bases for schizophrenia. Such theories speculate about the existence of some inferred variables, such as hormone deficiencies, metabolic abnormalities, and so on. These hypothetical constructs are not merely conceptually useful. Rather, they are variables whose existence is hypothesized. They remain inferential only so long as they are unobserved. For example, let us return to the child who refused to come to the dinner table. We have a preceding event (the parents' pleas) and a subsequent event (the child's refusal). If these events are connected by a presumed conceptual element, such as a stubborn streak, then an intervening variable has been inferred. However, if a physical mediator, such as a stomach flu, is presumed, then a hypothetical construct has been inferred.

Intervening variables have been more common in psychology than have hypothetical constructs. Common examples may be found in the popular use of such terms as *self-concept, ego,* and *internal conflicts.* Indeed, the fields of personality theory and assessment are thoroughly imbued with such variables (see Mischel, 1968, 1976). Theoreticians and researchers use these inferential concepts as a means of relating environmental situations to behavioral events. They do not usually contend that these variables are potentially observable.

As pointed out earlier, both intervening variables and hypothetical constructs are mediating variables. However, this does not mean that all mediating variables, such as hypothetical constructs, must remain inferred. For example, Hilgard and Bower (1966) cite the hormone adrenalin as a variable which was originally hypothetical (unobserved). After being observed and described, it ceased being inferred, but it remains a mediating variable in the sense of our previous definition. Observed or inferred, a mediating variable occupies a position between input (stimulus) and output (response).

To summarize, an intervening variable is one that fills a conceptual role in relating behavioral events. A hypothetical construct, in contrast, proposes the existence of a physical object or process to relate such events. Both of these are inferred variables in the sense that they are unobserved mediating variables. The foregoing is a brief introduction to some of the distinctions made among inferred variables in behavioral science. We are now ready to explore some of the arguments for and against specific types of inferred variables. Then we will consider the utility of such variables in behavior modification.

MENTALISM VERSUS BEHAVIORISM

Psychology has always been filled with inferred variables. There are several reasons for this, not the least of which are the remnants of psychology's early preoccupation with "mental" states and processes. All mental events, such as love or hate, must be inferred from preceding situations and observed behaviors. One cannot see joy and anguish; these private experiences are inferred from a person's observable actions.

Mentalism

The earliest students of behavior were behavioral philosophers rather than behavioral scientists. Their interests were in the mind and its functions. Speculative views on the nature of the mind, soul, and life were very widespread. Consciousness was a frequent topic and its contents, form, and governing relationships became the subjects of early debates in behavioral philosophy. There were other debates on whether such a thing as mind exists and on the possibility of a relationship between mind and body. In general, those who argued in favor of the existence of the mind or made reference to mental states were called mentalists. For many years, mentalism was the convention in psychology. Indeed, its remnants can be observed in the everyday use of such mentalistic terms as *remind, slip one's mind, mental illness, mind over matter,* and so on. However, some very serious shortcomings in the mentalistic approach have become apparent during the last few decades. Although mentalism still predominates in some subareas of psychology, increasing attention is now given to behaviorism, which constitutes the foundation of concepts and research methods comprising behavior modification. Before discussing behaviorism, we will explore some of the shortcomings that have characterized the mentalistic approach to behavior.

One of the earliest objections to mentalistic hypotheses related to what has been called the mind-body problem, namely, how can a nonmaterial entity affect a material one, and vice versa? At first glance this may not appear especially devastating, particularly in a culture where a mind-body dichotomy is cultivated. However, upon further examination, the difficulty becomes more apparent. For the mind to be nonmaterial, it must, by definition, have no mass and occupy no space. However, the mind is typically posited as occupying the skull. Likewise, it is spoken of in terms of psychic energies and mental forces. In physics, a force is defined as an accelerated *mass,* and according to Einsteinian theory, mass and energy are interchangeable; thus, talk of psychic energy entails talk of potential mass. In sum, then, positing any sort of mind-body interaction is a weighty affair. It goes against the conservation of mass-energy principle of modern physics and raises some auxiliary problems, such as spatial location and site of interaction.

A second problem associated with mentalistic formulations relates to their highly inferential nature. A mentalist typically chooses some behavior, such as eating, and from that *infers* a mental state, such as hunger. Although such an inference may seem justified, it introduces difficulties of interpretation. There are many behaviors for which very different inferences might be made. The frequent disagreements of psychiatrists and psychologists regarding alleged mental events attest to the extremely subjective nature of many inferences. One psychiatrist or psychologist may attribute smoking to repressed sexual impulses, whereas another may see it as expressive of strong aggressive urges. As we say in Chapter 2, once a scientist leaves his or her data (for example, observed behaviors), there is wide room for personal speculation and subjectivity.

A third problem with mentalistic formulations lies in their occasional linguistic circularity. An explanation is circular or tautological when it fails to go beyond the definition of the event to be explained. For instance, one might wish to explain eating behavior by reference to an internal state of hunger. If, however, hunger is defined in terms of eating ("Hunger is a tendency to eat"), then a circularity results. The alleged explanation is a translation of "He eats because he is hungry" to "He eats because he has a tendency to eat." The circuitous journey began with a behavior, visited a mental way station, and ended up with the original behavior. The distinction between *describing* and *explaining* an event may be helpful here. It is easy to describe an event and thereafter assume that it has been explained.

Such an assumption not only is logically unjustified but also discourages further inquiry into the actual explanation. For example, one often hears or reads statements like, "He shot her *because* he hated her." If one were to ask, "How do you know that he hated her?" the typical answer would be, "Well, he shot her, didn't he?" The problem here, of course, is that the observed behavior (shooting) has been attributed to an inferred mental state (hate) which has in turn been inferred from the observed behavior (shooting). In this example, a behavioral description has illegitimately passed for a causal explanation. Since shooting is often classified as a hateful behavior, the situation has been described twice but not explained. Another example of such linguistic circularity is evident in the case of such inferred predispositions as hunger and thirst. To say, "She drinks *because* she is thirsty" is circular and meaningless if one uses drinking behavior as part of the definition of thirst. Further illustrations of this tautological trend in mentalistic hypotheses could be provided, but the central point is that the assumption of a mental event or state is both meaningless and unnecessary unless that event or state can be differentiated from observable behaviors. Otherwise, according to the behaviorist, one may as well stick to the observable behaviors.

One final objection to mentalistic formulations—and perhaps the most important to contemporary psychologists—is that they are often considered empirically untestable. Since mental events are, by definition, unobservable except to the person experiencing them, it is often difficult for an external observer to confidently test hypotheses about them. One may wish to make inferences about them, but the ultimate scientific data in such cases must be observable responses, whether it be verbalizations, psychological measurements, or whatever. There is no direct external means for getting at mental phenomena. Science can deal only with events that are *assumed* to be somehow related to mental events. Until recently, the scientific emphasis on public observability relegated most intrapersonal behaviors (thoughts, images, and so on) to an unscientific limbo. For some psychologists and philosophers, the fact that mentalistic propositions are often considered scientifically unrespectable indicates the shortcomings of science rather than the undesirability of mentalism.

Behaviorism

Having explored some of the major objections to mentalistic views of behavior, we may now proceed to a discussion of the behavioristic alternative. John B. Watson was the most outspoken critic of the mentalistic emphases of early psychology.

WATSONIAN BEHAVIORISM

Watson sought to establish a purely objective psychology grounded in natural science and based on the logical and evidential support of contemporary empiricism. He called that objectified psychology *behaviorism* since its basic data involved observable behaviors. Because Watson's approach was so radical and because he demanded abrupt changes of emphasis in psychology, his earliest formulation have come to be known as *radical behaviorism*. Among its propositions was the metaphysical contention that the mind did not exist. As noted in Chapter 1, a less radical and much more enduring contribution of Watson has been his influence on techniques and methodology in psychology, which has come to be known as *methodological behaviorism*. The difference might be conceptualized as one of subject matter versus methodology. In radical behaviorism, Watson was philosophizing about the nonexistence of the mind and the meaninglessness of mentalistic propositions. In methodological behaviorism, Watson was invoking an objectification of psychological research. The former has raised a lot of dust in both philosophical and psychological circles. The latter, however, has probably been one of the most significant contributions toward making psychology a productive and respectable science. Watson's emphasis on *behavior*—objective, observable, and quantifiable data—gave a new twist to the psychologist's task. Although radical behaviorism has remained a somewhat controversial issue in the philosophy of mind, methodological behaviorism has become a widely adopted approach among behavioral scientists. Before we explore some of the more contemporary offshoots of behaviorism, it might be worthwhile to examine Watson's radical and methodological behaviorism.

Watson maintained that the mind-body problem was a dead issue for the science of psychology. However, because he treated it at length in his early writings, he succeeded in focusing attention on the very issue that he considered dead. His main objection was that mental propositions were not scientifically legitimate. Watson (1924) considered consciousness "neither a definite nor a usable concept" (p. 2). He analyzed all behaviors in terms of muscular and glandular responses. Thus, thinking became an "implicit" verbal response. Early support for Watson's contention that thinking was implicit speech came from some experiments by Jacobson (1932) and Max (1935, 1937). Jacobson found that minute muscular responses could be detected in the vocal cords when individuals were instructed to think or imagine various tasks. Max followed these findings with some corroborative research on deaf-mutes. He found that these individuals showed some minute finger and arm movements during "abstract thinking" tasks. Since deaf-mutes communicate via hand signals, Max's findings accorded well with those of Jacobson. Finally, Shaw (1940) found that when individuals were instructed to imagine lifting various small weights, there were corresponding differences in the amount of recorded muscular activity.

These early findings, along with Watson's radical claims, raised no small amount of controversy. One reaction to the contention that thinking was implicit speech was to show that individuals whose vocal cords had been removed were still capable of thought. This implied an understandable misinterpretation of Watson's contention. He explicitly denied that laryngeal movement was equivalent to or necessary for thought (see Watson, 1924, p. 238). Nevertheless, his reduction of all behaviors to glandular and muscular responses would certainly lead one to believe that if thinking is indeed a behavior, it must be either glandular or muscular in nature. The misunderstanding arose from the assumed association between laryngeal movement and thought; as noted, although Watson had indicated that thinking may be muscular or glandular, he did not define it as laryngeal movement. This contention has fallen by the wayside in modern behaviorism.

A second characteristic of early, and especially radical, behaviorism was its almost exclusive emphasis on *learned behavior.* Watson was very critical of statements implying inborn or innate behaviors. He did acknowledge the existence of a group of *unlearned behaviors,* but beyond that he believed all behaviors, and especially complex ones, to be learned through conditioning. Indeed, much to the ire of ethologists and instinct psychologists, Watson (1924) advocated the total abandonment of the concept of instinct in psychology.

There are then for us no instincts—we no longer need the term in psychology. Everything we have been in the habit of calling an "instinct" today is a result largely of training—belongs to man's *learned behavior.*

As a corollary from this we draw the conclusion that there is no such thing as an inheritance of *capacity, talent, temperament, mental constitution* and *characteristics.* These things again depend on training that goes on mainly in the cradle. (p. 94)

Perhaps the most famous Watsonian quotation, and one of the most controversial, dealt with the role of learning or environmental conditioning in the development of individual behavior patterns.

I should like to go one step further now and say, "Give me a dozen healthy infants, well-formed, and my own specified world to bring them up in and I'll guarantee to take any one at random and train him to become any type of specialist I might select—doctor, lawyer, artist, merchant-chief and, yes, even beggar-man and thief, regardless of his talents, penchants, tendencies, abilities, vocations, and race of his ancestors." (1924, p. 104)

Watson readily admitted that such an ambitious statement went well beyond his data. However, such statements enlivened the controversy over the domain and dialogue of behavioral science. Watson incited a revolution in psychology. His radical statements about prevailing research topics and the techniques employed to study them set psychology to reassessing its subject matter and methodology.

Without doubt, Watson's most significant and lasting contribution to psychology was his emphasis on objectifying the methodology of behavioral research. In stating the behavioristic platform, Watson, (1924) stressed the need for empirical data. "Let us limit ourselves to things that can be observed, and formulate laws concerning only these things" (p. 6). His goal was to make psychology a natural science. His metaphysical statements on the nonexistence of mind and the meaninglessness of mentalistic propositions constituted an attempt to rid psychology of the many philosophical influences that had persisted since its inception as a discipline. However, his most notable contribution was his strong emphasis on *behavior* as the subject matter of psychology and on the *scientific method* as the means for studying that subject. Watson's conception of behavior was a very broad one and included thinking, feeling, talking, and imagining. All of these were to come under the purview of scientific investigation. Watson sought to put an end to armchair philosophizing about human behavior. Although he is probably better known for some of his more radical statements regarding the mind, conscious processes, and environmental influences, Watson's views on the subject matter and methodology of psychology laid the groundwork for modern behaviorism.

WATSONIAN BEHAVIORISM AND CONTEMPORARY BEHAVIORISM

The behavioristic movement has branched out in many directions since the era of John B. Watson. However, it continues to emphasize observable data, behavior as subject matter, and scientific methodology. Contemporary behaviorism is variously referred to as stimulus-response (S-R) psychology, neobehaviorism, and learning theory. Behavior modification represents a contemporary application of methodological behaviorism. Although taking several paths, the behavioristic movement is a growing and productive influence in modern psychology. Its effects on the tenor of behavioral science are almost inestimable. However, several modifications have been made in the behaviorist's outlook which justify the distinction between Watsonian behaviorism and contemporary or neobehaviorism. We will take the time at this point to explore these modifications.

In the first place, the mind-body problem has all but disappeared as an issue in behavioral science. There are several reasons for this. First, although writings in the philosophy of mind have continued, they have not reached most modern behaviorists. The mind-body problem can quickly become tiresome, and many contemporary behavioral scientists seem to have tired of its blind alleys. This may be an unjustifiable reason for ignoring an issue, but it does seem to be what has actually happened. Second, the area of linguistic analysis in philosophy has suggested that many mind-body dilemmas may be purely a matter of semantics (see Ryle, 1949). Finally, the fact that mentalistic propositions and mind-body assertions are often considered scientifically untestable has led many modern workers to classify them as meaningless and to ignore them. This has probably been the most significant factor in deterring behavioral scientists from pursuing the issue.

Early behaviorism also differs from contemporary behaviorism in its definition of behavior. Although there is no universally agreed upon definition for the terms *behavior* or *response,* the modern connotation of these terms is somewhat broader than that of the Watsonian era. Recall that Watson categorized all behaviors as muscular or glandular. The modern behaviorist would not be so restrictive. Indeed, the electrochemical firing of a single cell in the nervous system is now considered a discrete behavior.

Early behaviorism is distinguished from modern behaviorism in its emphasis on animal research and its views on the role of heredity. Although Watson's research dealt with humans, many of his immediate followers concentrated their research efforts in the animal laboratories. Since that time, the findings gathered in the animal laboratories have been applied to humans with remarkable success. However, the infrahuman emphases of early behavioristic research have led many to categorize all behaviorists as rat psychologists. The incongruity of such a generalization is readily apparent to any who familiarize themselves with the behavior therapy journals. As for heredity, contemporary behaviorism sees it in a much less negative light than did Watson. Although talk of instincts and inborn tendencies is still infrequent in behavioristic writings, it is not excluded. The current stance would seem to be that such concepts are admissible if they are useful.

Another distinction between early and contemporary behaviorism relates to the previously discussed dichotomy between subject matter and methodology. That behavior is and has been the subject matter of behavioral psychology since Watson's time can scarcely be denied. However, the emphasis on methodology that Watson initiated has become so extensive that some, including ourselves, equate contemporary behaviorism with methodological behaviorism. Karl Lashley, one of Watson's students, made some of the earliest attempts at specifying the requirements of methodological behaviorism. His efforts, and those of later behaviorists, have culminated in contemporary behavioral methodology. The modern standard places no restraints on the subject matter of behavioral science as long as it meets with the minimal criteria for empirical investigation.

One final characteristic distinguishing the old from the new behaviorism relates to the role of cognitive behaviors. Recall that Watson readily admitted the reality of such behaviors as thinking, feeling, and so on. However, his contention that only observable behaviors were amenable to scientific study placed such behaviors as thinking and feeling in a sort of empirical limbo. Unless such private events could be defined in terms of publicly observable physical responses, Watson and his immediate followers considered them beyond the scope of behavioral science. That view has been modified drastically by modern behaviorists, and this probably constitutes the most significant single characteristic distinguishing Watsonian from contemporary behaviorism. Partly because of developments in methodological behaviorism and partly because of the great need for research on cognitive behaviors, this area has received increasing attention from behavioral researchers (see Bandura, 1969; Mahoney, 1974a; Meichenbaum, 1977).

In cognitive behaviorism, research is done according to the following standard: *operationism and observable anchors*. This means that any talk of cognitive process must be defined in terms of the operation used to measure them (see Chapter 2) and that all cognitive behaviors must be anchored to publicly observable behaviors. For example, the cognitive behaviorist can deal with imagery by means of operationalizing the concept and anchoring it to observable data. Thus, *imagery* might be defined as that behavior in which an individual engages and later reports when asked to imagine something. The observable anchors in this instance are the experimenter's instructions and the subject's verbal report. An even more recent development in cognitive behaviorism is the possibility of using participant observation to make private events an area amenable to scientific inquiry. Homme (1965) noted that even though private events, such as thoughts, feelings, images, and sensations, are not publicly observable, they are not beyond the reach of scientific research. The individual who is experiencing publicly unobserved behaviors is certainly in a position to observe them and report on his or her observations. Thus, although we must add some cautions about relying on the accuracy and honesty of our participant observer, private events are within the boundaries of an empirical analysis of behavior (see Mahoney, 1974).

Despite the aforementioned modifications, contemporary behaviorism still carries with it many of the essential characteristics of early behaviorism, namely, the strong emphasis on *behavior* and on *scientific methodology*. To review and explore the many facets of contemporary behaviorism would be a monumental task. Suffice it to say that of all the schools and movements that have come and gone in psychology, behaviorism appears to be one that is here to stay. Its productive applications and its rapidly expanding approach to complex behaviors have made it one of the most popular and promising developments in behavioral science.

A Final Note

The foregoing account of the mentalism-behaviorism controversy has necessarily been superficial. There are many subissues and arguments whose discussion would take us far from our path. The relatively positive account of behaviorism given here would not be universally accepted. Numerous critiques of behavioristic philosophies are available (see Mahoney et al., 1974). Lest the reader think that antibehavioral critiques are extinct or that the behavioral approach is universally accepted, the following statement from Matson (1971) is provided.

Plainly, the differences between us must be very deep—not just technical or strategic or methodological but philosophical and perhaps moral. For my part, I believe that Skinner and his gentle friends state the case against their own philosophy so openly and candidly that one need only cry "Hark! See there? They are exposing themselves (the Grand Conditioner has no clothes)!" (p. 2)

INFERRED VARIABLES IN BEHAVIOR MODIFICATION

Thus far in this chapter we have examined the nature of inferred variables, some distinctions among them, and a few of the more common examples. We may now turn our attention to a discussion of their usefulness in the explanation, prediction, and control of behavior.

As we have pointed out, the role of inference has been a controversial one in behavior modification. Because of Watson's emphasis on observable behavior, early behavioral researchers were hesitant to engage in any inferential speculations.[1] Dealing with the observed behavior was deemed both necessary and sufficient. However, more recent trends in behavior modification have seen some cautious steps taken in the direction of controlled inference. Such inference is "controlled" in the sense that many sources of evidence are employed and observable anchors are required.

1. Exceptions to this were the early learning theorists (see Hilgard & Bower, 1966).

We might take a moment here to discuss the role of inference in everyday life so that the reader can discriminate between justified and unjustified inference. For example, one might see a newspaper on a doorstep and from that infer that the newspaper carrier had deposited it there. Such an inference would seem justified, for one frequently observes such persons depositing papers on doorsteps. Another example would be the motorist who looks at his or her fuel gauge and from the position of its needle infers the presence or absence of a certain quantity of gasoline in the tank. The actual fuel level is not observed, but only a needle designed to reflect that level. Such an inference is fairly well justified. Nevertheless, most of us probably have had the experience of making a faulty inference from a fuel gauge reading—and may also have suffered the inconvenience resulting from such a faulty inference. If the needle on such a gauge behaved erratically or never moved, then inferring fuel capacity from its position would be unjustified. The point is that an inference is justified only when it is based on sufficient evidence to make it useful in predicting or understanding events. If an inference helps establish or clarify a testable relationship, then it is justified. In science, just as in everyday life, an inference that does not pay off in the sense of aiding scientific goals is unjustified. Many of the more popular inferences in psychology have had dubious utility.

B. F. Skinner is probably the best-known critic of unjustified inferences and mediational accounts in the analysis of behavior. Many of his observations regarding the difficulties involved in inferential variables have already been previewed in our discussion of the problems of mentalism. For example, the problem of circularity is invoked. To say that an individual behaves strangely because of some inferred mental abnormality and then to justify one's inference of that abnormality by reference to the behavior is totally meaningless. John bites his nails because he is nervous. How do you know he is nervous? Well, he bites his nails. Such reasoning as this, although in much subtler form, pervades many theories of personality. It is circular, and it is often unnecessary. If to say that John bites his nails is equivalent to saying that John is nervous, one might just as well make only one of these statements. Another problem with inferred variables is that they often lead to premature conclusions. By allegedly explaining John's nail biting through reference to nervousness, one may come away thinking that the observed behavior has actually been explained rather than merely described in different terms. Such a premature conclusion may be dangerous if it discourages further analysis of the behavior.

Perhaps one of the most serious problems with inferential accounts of behavior is that of reification. *Reification* is a process whereby some concept gradually attains the status of an existing entity. For example, we have noted that many contemporary personality theorists make reference to various inferred variables. These are employed conceptually in explaining, predicting, and controlling behavior. However, these conceptual aids often become reified in the sense that they are talked about as if they were real-life entities (for example, hypothetical constructs). Terms such as *id, ego,* and *superego* were originally offered as conceptual variables by Freud. However, many researchers have fallen into the habit of considering such terms as names for real entities. Such reification might be conceptualized as an inadvertent shift from adjective to noun. One begins by saying, "George is exhibiting schizophrenic behavior." Later one may say, "George has schizophrenia." The change is obvious. We start by describing what George *does* and end by talking about what George *has.* Schizophrenia becomes a mystical demon or hypothetical illness within the individual rather than a descriptive label for bizarre behavior patterns.

It is problems like these that buttress Skinner's argument against the use of inferential and also mediational accounts of behavior. His contention is that lawful behavioral relationships can be described and utilized without reference to various intermediaries. One may roughly conceptualize an organism as being in an input-output relationship with the environment. So long as one can describe that relationship accurately without reference to "internal" variables, there would seem to be little use for them. Where other behavioral researchers might wish to posit a three-variable sequence (stimulus—mediating variable—response), Skinner emphasizes a two-variable sequence (stimulus—response). Note that he does not deny the existence or importance of mediating variables. He simply maintains that they may be unnecessary. Skinner's argument applies to noninferred mediating variables (for example, physiological processes, hormone levels, and so on) as well as inferred ones. Although the former are less susceptible to some of the difficulties outlined previously, Skinner asserts that they rarely aid and often impede the experimental analysis of behavior. His basic objection to mediational accounts of behavior—whether they involve hypothetical constructs, intervening variables, or observable intraorganismic processes—is that they often result in incomplete causal analyses. Skinner argues that the explanation of behavior by reference to some mediating variable is both useless and incomplete unless the latter can, in turn, be accounted for by some preceding external situation. Thus, to "explain" a child's aggressive behaviors by reference to an internal state of hostility is meaningless unless the conditions that give rise to that hostility are specified. Again, the input-output analogy is stressed. Given that certain variables feed into the organism and certain behaviors are emitted by that organism, it matters little what happens in between if one can lawfully predict the input-output relationship. The usefulness of the mediating variable in discovering, describing, and predicting that relationship is considered much more important than the nature of the variable itself. Indeed,

Skinner (1963, p. 958) states that "no entity or process which has any useful explanatory force is to be rejected on the ground that it is subjective or mental." His rejection of inferred variables thus stems from his opinion of their inutility rather then from the nature of such variables.

The role of inference in behavior modification might be compared to its parallel role in the physical sciences. Although the latter make use of inferential variables such as "atom" or "electron," they do so in a very conservative manner. The nonmediational argument, which criticizes both inferential and noninferential mediating variables, likewise emphasizes the utility or inutility of mediational variables in behavioral research. Thus, the role one assigns to inferred variables depends on one's opinion of their *utility* in research.

If it can be capsulated, the gist of Skinner's position is that mediational accounts of behavior are often troublesome and useless. The early history of psychology shows what a preoccupation with inferred variables can do. The issue, of course, has two sides. Just as Skinner has criticized mediational, and especially inferential, accounts of behavior, so have other workers criticized nonmediational accounts (for example, Breger & McGaugh, 1965; Dulany, 1968). Their main contention is that nonmediational accounts of behavior omit too much. As some have put it, "There is a lot going on in the dash between S and R." Critics of the nonmediational stance have accused it of oversimplifying behavior, especially at the human level. Although an input-output model might simplify our understanding of behavior, such a model is often sorely inadequate. Human beings do not passively register stimuli and then reflexively respond. Their actions are dramatically affected by intrapersonal variables—beliefs, perceptions, and self-statements—that are no less deserving of experimental scrutiny.

To summarize, the role of inferred variables in behavior modification has been a controversial one. Early behavioral researchers cautiously avoided inferential speculations. However, recent trends, such as cognitive behaviorism, have witnessed the introduction of controlled inferences in research. The majority of behavior modifiers continue to avoid inferential variables. However, noninferred mediational variables have received increasing attention from behavioral researchers so that intraorganismic behaviors have returned to the arena. Their comeback has been enhanced by methodological innovations which show the promise of establishing empirical bases for an experimental analysis of mediating behaviors. Likewise, the criterion of *utility* in evaluating mediating variables has allowed the behavior modifier to consider them as potential aids in the explanation, prediction, and control of behavior. But the byword in any scientific use of inferential variables is *caution*. Their potential usefulness in behavioral science must be qualified by the realization that inference is a conceptual step away from the data.

SUMMARY

An inferred variable is one that has not been observed. It is often used to mediate or connect observable input and output. Intervening variables and hypothetical constructs are two major categories of mediators in psychology. In general, the former perform conceptual functions and the latter are more empirical or physical in function.

The avoidance of inferred variables was stressed in John B. Watson's radical behaviorism. However, Watson's methodological behaviorism, which outlines the process rather than the content of scientific inquiry, is his enduring contribution to contemporary psychology. Although the essence of methodological behaviorism is still apparent in current behavior modification research, the same cannot be said of radical behaviorism.

Inferred variables, such as thoughts, feelings, and memories, have become increasingly popular in present-day efforts to understand human behavior. Mediating variables are admissible if they are operationally defined and observable. Even then, they are employed only if they are useful in the explanation, prediction, or control of behavior.

SUGGESTED READINGS

Mahoney, M. J. *Cognition and behavior modification.* Cambridge, Mass.: Ballinger, 1974.

Mischel, W. On the interface of cognition and personality: Beyond the person-situation debate. *American Psychologist,* 1979, *34,* 740–754.

Skinner, B. F. Behaviorism at fifty. *Science,* 1963, *140,* 951–958.

Watson, J. B. *Behaviorism.* Chicago: University of Chicago, 1924.

CHAPTER 4

DATA COLLECTION AND
RESEARCH DESIGN

The central feature of the scientific approach is the collection of data. Data refer to the information that serves as the basis for drawing inferences about relationships. Science seeks to understand orderly relationships among various phenomena. In experimental research, for example, some condition is altered to see whether changes are produced on a particular measure. The purpose is to demonstrate a relationship between the independent variable (the conditions that are altered) and the dependent variable (the measure that reflects the effects of the altered conditions).

Establishing relationships between independent and dependent variables is not as straightforward a task as it might seem. Special care needs to be taken to measure the outcome of an experiment and to arrange the conditions in such a way that conclusions can be drawn about what caused changes on the measure. The present chapter discusses some of the methods used to investigate behavioral treatment interventions.

DATA COLLECTION

Data collection is a form of scientific observation. The central characteristic of the information that is used as data is the objectivity of the assessment. Objectivity means that the information does not necessarily depend on any particular person but can be obtained in principle by others. Objectivity does not mean that the data are free from bias or subjective influences. Indeed, the data used in behavioral and social sciences are subject to all sorts of biases. For example, in survey research, people are asked their opinions about political candidates, tastes in food, and sexual practices. The opinions people provide are subjective. However, the information is usually collected in a consistent fashion and in such a way as to minimize the influences that observers have on the performance of those included in the survey.

It is not enough to accumulate piles of questionnaires that have surveyed the opinions of hundreds of persons. The information needs to be reduced so that quantifiable relationships can be drawn. For example, in a survey, the investigator may wish to compare young versus old, women versus men, rural versus urban residents, and so on. The information obtained on the questionnaires needs to be reduced in a quantifiable fashion, such as the percentage of respondents who indicated one answer rather than another to specific questions. Of course, the general requirements about gathering information and reducing the information to quantifiable dimensions pertain to scientific research generally. It is important to mention specifically the types of data that usually are utilized in behavior modification.

Classes of Behavioral Data

All behavioral data belong to one of four classes: (1) magnitude data, (2) temporal data, (3) frequency data, and (4) categorical data. *Magnitude data* include any measures that involve the strength or intensity of a response. For example, if one were to record the pressure exerted on the lever in a Skinner box, one would obtain a magnitude datum. Weight and height are also magnitude data. *Temporal data,* as the name suggests, involve measurement of time. The elapsed time between two events is an example of a temporal datum. Such measures as speed (distance divided by time) are here classified as temporal data; such measures include response latency, maze-running speed, and response duration. *Frequency data* involve discrete responses whose occurrences can be counted and used to make objective comparisons. Thus, such responses as the number of times a child hits herself on the head or bites her little brother, or the number of bar presses a laboratory animal makes, may be classified as frequency data. Note that frequency data often are temporally bound. For example, one may wish to report the number of occurrences of a particular behavior during some specified time period. For our purposes, the data would still qualify as frequency data. Thus, response rate, which is one of the most popular dependent variables in behavior modification, would be classified as a frequency measure even though it involves frequency divided by time. *Categorical data* involve measurements differentiating one response from another. In the simplest instance, such categorization may involve recording the presence or absence of a particular response. Likewise, recording whether response A or B occurred constitutes the accumulation of categorical data. Thus, for example, a right instead of a left turn in a maze would be a categorical datum. The presence of a bar press in situation A and its absence in situation B is another categorical datum.

The four data classes are not employed in a mutually exclusive manner. One may record whether a right or left turn occurred in a maze (categorical data), the number of right and left turns that were made (frequency data), and the running speed associated with each (temporal data). The foregoing data classification system is not intended as an ideal schema, but rather as a means of familiarizing the reader with the wide range of data types employed in the field of behavior modification.

Methods of Data Collection

An investigator must decide if he or she will collect data for the entire time period in which a target behavior may occur or collect data only for some portion of the time. This decision leads to the use of one of the two methods of data collection: continuous or sampling. In the *continuous* method, data are collected continuously over a period of time. In the *sampling* method (also known as *time sampling*), data are collected only for a portion of the total time. For example, one might want to know how many cars cross a particular intersection in one year's time. If the continuous method of data collection were used, the number of cars crossing the intersection would be recorded twenty-four hours a day for an entire year. Such an undertaking would, of course, be expensive, but it would provide complete data. A less expensive approach would be the sampling method. In the sampling method, one would choose a number of representative days or weeks and the number of cars crossing the intersection would be recorded only at those times. From the data obtained, one could generalize to the entire year by multiplying appropriately. Note that in the sampling method one gathers data only for some fraction of the total time during which the variable of interest is potentially recordable. Thus, one measures a sample of the total time in question.

Each of these methods of data collection has received extensive application in behavior modification. The continuous method is most often utilized when the time period in question is relatively short. The sampling method, on the other hand, is used in situations where the behavior of interest is evaluated over a relatively long time period. For example, one might wish to measure the amount of tantrum behavior emitted by a child in a month. The sampling method would be more useful, because the behavior of interest is to be measured over a long time period. It would be very expensive, if not impossible, to station an observer in the home for 720 consecutive hours.

There are several varieties of the sampling method. One can employ either *fixed* or *randomized* time samples. For example, one might sample the behavior in a classroom every day from noon until one o'clock. This would be a fixed time sample. A randomized time sample would entail sampling during randomly selected one-hour periods throughout the school day. The relative advantages of the latter method should be obvious. Unless one is interested in the behaviors that occur during some fixed time, the randomized method usually provides a more representative sample of the behavior in question. In the above example, it may well be that classroom behaviors between eight and nine o'clock are quite different from those between noon and one o'clock.

Both the continuous and the sampling methods have their relative advantages and disadvantages. The continuous method is more accurate since it entails full coverage of the behavior in question. The sampling method can be very misleading if one's choice of time samples is unrepresentative. For example, if one were to monitor the traffic at an intersection only on weekdays and from that generalize to the entire year, such a projection would probably be grossly inaccurate. Likewise, if one were to sample a student's studying behaviors only on weekends, an inaccurate representation might result. The advantage of the sampling method is that it is much less expensive than the continuous method. It is also very helpful in the measurement of nondiscrete behaviors. In general, the continuous method of data collection is to be preferred when it is practical. However, when correctly applied, the sampling method is also a very reliable means of data collection.

Data-Collection Formats

Within both the continuous and sampling methods a data-collection format must be chosen. Two of the most frequently used data-collection formats are *actual counts* of the behavior and an *all-or-none classification*. Actual counts refer to the recording of discrete units or instances of behavior. The occurrences of the behavior or unit of behavior are simply tallied. Actual counts of performance have been used to measure such responses as the number of social responses (instances of saying hello), self-stimulatory behavior (rocking), seizures, calories consumed, cigarettes smoked, and so on. Occasionally, counts are made of persons rather than specific responses. For example, behavioral interventions have been evaluated on the number of persons who litter, come to work on time, complete homework, and commit crimes.

All-or-none classification of behaviors refers to observations that are completed during a period of time. At the end of the period, performance is scored as occurring or not occurring. The time period is scored in an all-or-none fashion. Usually, performance is observed for several time periods (or intervals), each one of which is relatively brief (for example, fifteen seconds). If behavior occurs at all during the interval, the entire interval may be scored as an occurrence. This method, sometimes called *interval recording,* has been used to monitor many behaviors, such as whether persons are smiling, talking, working, or hitting others. Interval recording is well suited for ongoing responses that cannot be easily counted as single units. For example, a person may interact with others for fifteen minutes on one occasion and two minutes on another. The different durations make these difficult to score as simply two instances of the response. However, several brief time intervals could be scored in terms of the presence or absence of social behavior.

In summary, the process of data collection is perhaps the most significant single undertaking in behavioral research. It is only with objective data that meaningful scientific comparisons can be made. There are four basic classes of data in behavioral science: (1) magnitude data, (2) temporal data, (3) frequency data, and (4) categorical data. These classes often are used in conjunction with one another and testify to the variety of useful measures in behavioral research. Methods of data collection are generally of two types: continuous and sampling. There are several formats for data collection; two frequently used ones are actual counts and all-or-none classification.

RESEARCH DESIGN

In behavior modification, the collection of data allows one to determine whether behavior has changed. For example, treatment might be given to clients who have an intense fear of heights. Usually, data are collected before and after treatment to determine whether the fear has changed. In some behavioral interventions, data are collected while the treatment program is in effect as well as before and after treatment. For example, parents of a child with temper tantrums might observe the frequency of tantrums over several days prior to implementing a behavior-change program. Eventually a program might be implemented to eliminate tantrums. Data on frequency of tantrums would be collected while the program was in effect to see if there was a change. Assessment of behavior while a program is in effect allows one to alter the program if behavior is not changing. The collection of data is needed to evaluate behavior change.

Experimental Design

Data collection is a necessary but not sufficient means of treatment evaluation. Although data can determine whether behavior has changed, they can never explain *why* it has changed. Clients may improve in their performance on the dependent measures after receiving treatment or while treatment is in effect. Yet this does not mean that the treatment *caused* the behavior change.[1] To determine the cause of behavior change requires more than merely gathering data. The scientist must arrange a situation so that a causal relation can be demonstrated between certain conditions, such as treatment and behavior. The manner in which the situation is arranged in order to evaluate the effect of treatment intervention or some independent variable is referred to as the *experimental design*. The purpose of the experimental design is to structure the situation in such a fashion that the cause of behavior change can be unambiguously demonstrated. The importance and the essential features of the experimental design can be seen by examining a case study. A case study is not an experimental design but illustrates very clearly the need for experimental design.

The Case Study

In everyday experience, the case study is perhaps the most commonly relied upon source of information; many of our beliefs are based on practical notions derived from case material. The case study is a report of the events in a person's life that supposedly account for given behaviors.

People often make unwarranted conclusions about causal relations on the basis of events that happen to one or a few individuals in their experience. The problem is not so much with the number of individuals serving as a basis for information, but rather with the fact that the observations are

1. In this chapter, causal relationships will refer to causation as described in Chapter 2.

made in an uncontrolled fashion whereby unambiguous conclusions cannot be drawn. For example, octogenarians often attribute their longevity to one or more factors, such as hard work, clean living, piety, or good eating habits. Certainly, specific factors do cause longevity; yet the precise factors cannot be pinpointed on the basis of one individual's statements about what he or she *believes* those factors to be. These statements are unsubstantiated inferences based on uncontrolled observations. They cannot provide evidence for unambiguous relationships between events and consequences.

In psychology, case studies frequently are cited to posit that a given psychotherapeutic intervention is responsible for behavior change. An example of a case study can be seen in an interesting report of treatment for an eleven-year-old girl who suffered from insomnia (Weil & Goldfried, 1973). The girl took approximately two hours to fall asleep each night. To ameliorate her insomnia, an attempt was made to train the girl to relax while lying in bed. A therapist visited the child at home and attempted to relax her while she was trying to go to sleep. The therapist had the girl alternately tense and relax her muscles to develop deep muscle relaxation. The girl responded favorably and fell asleep within one hour rather than the usual amount of time. The therapist then made a thirty-minute tape recording of the relaxation instructions. The girl used the tape by herself for two weeks, typically falling asleep during the tape or immediately after its completion. Relaxation tapes of shorter duration were gradually introduced until a tape of only five minutes was used. Eventually, all tapes were eliminated and the girl was told to concentrate on self-relaxation (that is, giving herself instructions to relax). The parents indicated that insomnia still was no longer a problem six months after treatment had terminated.

This case study is interesting because it indicates that a person with a difficult problem was successfully treated. In the absence of objective data, such as the actual records of the onset of sleep, we cannot be certain of the precise extent of improvement. However, we can assume that there was some change. Certainly the implication from such a case study is that treatment was responsible for behavior change. Yet there is no way to determine whether treatment caused the change. A number of influences may have been responsible for change. Life events other than the therapy may have altered the significance of the problem or may have eliminated the sources of stress. Improvement may have resulted merely from meeting with a therapist, receiving reassurance, or from other factors. In short, in a case study, there is no way to determine whether change resulted from a specific treatment or whether it would have occurred in time without treatment.

In behavior modification, a variety of experimental designs are used to determine whether a given intervention is responsible for behavior change. Basically, two major design categories are used: *intrasubject* and *intersubject* designs. In an *intrasubject design,* the performance of an individual or group of individuals is compared across different conditions over time. Behavior of the individual or group is assessed under two or more conditions. For example, the effect of parental praise on the amount of time a child practices a musical instrument might be examined. The amount of time the child practices when the parents are providing praise would be assessed. The results would be compared with the amount of practice time when the parents are not providing praise. During alternating weeks, the parents might offer praise for practice and then withdraw praise for practice. The difference in the amount of practice time across these alternating conditions would reveal the effect of praise.

In an *intersubject design,* the performance of two or more groups, each of which is exposed to a different intervention, is compared. For example, the effect of praise upon child behavior might be evaluated by giving praise to one group of subjects for a particular response but not to another group of subjects. The effect would be evaluated by comparing the average performance of the two groups.

The two design categories do not represent uncompromising extremes; it is possible to combine these designs. The present discussion will focus on major versions of intrasubject and intersubject designs.[2] We will present various issues and will evaluate the several designs, but this does not imply that one design is inherently better and should always be used. An experimental design is a research tool and the experimenter should utilize the one that best helps to answer the posed experimental question.

Intrasubject Experimental Designs

REVERSAL OR ABAB DESIGN

In a number of programs, the effects of different procedures are evaluated by comparing the performance of an individual or several individuals under different experimental conditions. Specifically, data are collected on the frequency (or some other measure) of a certain behavior, such as tantrums, in a single individual or group. Observations are usually made for several days prior to any treatment intervention. The rate of behavior prior to treatment or intervention is referred to as the *baseline* or *operant rate.* The period during which the baseline rate of behavior is assessed is

---

2. Additional variations of these designs and design combinations may be obtained from the Suggested Readings.

referred to as the *baseline* or *A phase*. After a pattern of behavior emerges and performance is relatively stable, a particular program is implemented to alter behavior. The phase during which a program or treatment intervention is being implemented is referred to as the *treatment* or *B phase*. Data are gathered throughout baseline and treatment phases to determine whether behavior changes. If behavior changes after the program is implemented, this does not necessarily mean that the program was responsible for the change. Additional phases are required to determine what caused the change. After the program is in effect for some time and a consistent pattern is evident, the program may be withdrawn temporarily. This third phase is referred to as a *reversal phase* and is usually a reintroduction of the conditions that were in effect during the initial baseline phase. If behavior reverts to baseline levels when the program is withdrawn, this strongly suggests that the program was responsible for change. To increase the plausibility of this conclusion, the program is reinstated in the final phase of the experiment. If behavior again changes when the intervention is implemented, this is a clear demonstration that the intervention was responsible for the change. Of course, in an applied setting where one is attempting to modify an undesirable behavior, it is always essential to undertake this final phase.

The design is referred to as a reversal design because the phases are alternated or reversed; after baseline the program is first implemented, then withdrawn or altered in some fashion, and then implemented again. Behavior usually reverses as the phases are altered. The design is also referred to as an ABAB design because baseline (A) and treatment (B) phases are alternated to demonstrate that treatment was responsible for the observed change.

The reversal design can be illustrated by a program for a twenty-nine-year old mentally retarded woman who refused to comply with staff requests in an institution (Mansdorf, 1977). When the resident did not comply with requests, she would sit in the day room of the institution and watch television, listen to music, or go back to bed. A punishment procedure (time out from reinforcement) was used for instances of noncompliance. When the resident did not comply with a staff request, opportunities to engage in the above activities were removed for a brief period (five minutes). If she did not comply, television or music was turned off, peers were asked to leave the day room, and her bedding was removed. The reinforcers usually utilized by the resident were unavailable. The procedure was evaluated in an ABAB design. As shown in Figure 4.1, noncompliance decreased during the treatment phase and increased or decreased as treatment was withdrawn or reinstated, respectively. By the end of treatment, noncompliance was eliminated completely and remained at this level at a check six months later. The pattern of results in the ABAB

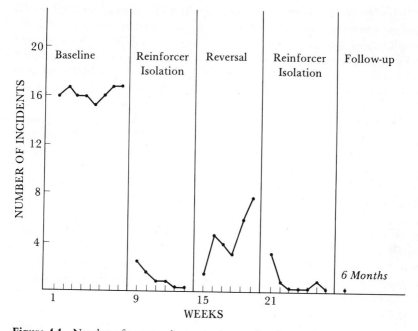

Figure 4.1   Number of noncompliant episodes per five-day work week, for each experimental condition.

Source: Reprinted with permission from *Journal of Behavior Therapy and Experimental Psychiatry*, 1977, *8*, 392, Mansdorf, I. J. Reinforcer isolation: An alternative to subject isolation in time-out from positive reinforcement. Copyright 1977, Pergamon Press, Ltd.

phases strongly suggests that the program was responsible for changes in the client's behavior.

Evaluation of the Reversal Design   The reversal design has been used extensively with single subjects and with groups, such as children in a classroom or patients in a psychiatric ward. Although the design can determine a causal relationship between behavior and an experimental intervention, there are some limitations in its use. First, changed behaviors sometimes do not reverse when the program is temporarily withdrawn. Behavior may remain at the level achieved during treatment. Thus, in the foregoing example, the patient might not have increased complaints when the program was temporarily withdrawn. If the behavior does not reverse or approach baseline when treatment is withdrawn or altered, it suggests that the program may not be responsible for the change. Behavior change may be a function of some event occurring simultaneously with the program.

Behavior may not reverse during withdrawal of treatment for another reason. Often, changes in behavior alter the environment in a way that supports and maintains the behavior change. For example, a child might be trained to interact socially with peers by receiving praise from a teacher or parent. When praise is withdrawn, this behavior may not reverse because the favorable consequences associated with peer interaction now maintain the behavior. Although teacher or parent praise may have been responsible for the initial behavior change, the behavior may now be maintained by consequences provided by peers. Because of failure of the behavior to reverse, a reversal design would not show what caused the behavior change.[3]

A second problem with the reversal design is that it is often undesirable or even unethical to show a reversal in a behavior even if a reversal can be achieved. For example, a program might be effective in altering extremely aggressive behavior in a child. However, few people would be willing to withdraw the program temporarily and permit an increase in aggressive behavior. There may be no clear justification for making the individual "worse" and possible endangering others by purposefully encouraging an increase in aggressive behavior.

Reversal designs have been used extensively in situations where a temporary reversal in behavior is not harmful to the individual. The reversal phase need not be long. Sometimes the program needs only to be altered or withdrawn for a few days. Once the behavior reverts toward baseline, treatment can be reinstated immediately. It should be emphasized that the purpose of the reversal design is to obtain causal knowledge about behavior change. This knowledge is essential for scientific validation of treatments. In many instances, temporary worsening of behavior must be avoided. Fortunately, there are a number of other designs that can be used when one of the aforementioned limitations causes an investigator to have reservations about employing a reversal design.

MULTIPLE-BASELINE DESIGNS

In multiple-baseline designs, a causal relationship between treatment and behavior is demonstrated by showing that behavior changes when treatment is introduced at several different points in time. However, this is accomplished without a reversal procedure.

There are several types of multiple-baseline designs, one of which is a

---

3. Procedures that increase the likelihood that a behavior will reverse have been outlined elsewhere (Hersen & Barlow, 1976; Kazdin, 1980a).

multiple-baseline design across behaviors. Baseline data are gathered across two or more behaviors in a given individual or group. After the behaviors have stabilized, a treatment may be introduced for the first behavior while baseline data continue to be gathered for the other behaviors. The first behavior should change while the other behaviors should not. If this is the case, the experimental intervention is introduced for the second behavior. Treatment for other behaviors is introduced at different points in time. Throughout the program, data are gathered on all behaviors. The treatment effect is demonstrated if each behavior changes only when the treatment intervention is introduced and not before then.

A multiple-baseline design across behaviors was used to evaluate the effectiveness of a reinforcement program for sixteen institutionalized male psychiatric patients (Nelson & Cone, 1979). The patients received tokens (colored tickets) which could be exchanged for a variety of commodities in a store on the ward, including hot and cold beverages, fruit, cookies, ice cream, records, toiletries, and other items. The tokens were delivered for several different behaviors included in four general categories: personal hygiene (for example, washing face, combing hair), personal management (dressing neatly, making bed), work on the ward (performing jobs like folding linens, dusting the dorm), and social skills (greeting staff, verbally participating in discussions). The program was evaluated in a multiple-baseline design by introducing the tokens for the different categories of behaviors at different points in time. Figure 4.2 shows that whenever treatment was applied to a particular behavior (implementation phase), the percentage of patients who responded increased. After the implementation phase, observations were discontinued, but the program remained in effect for all behaviors. When the observations were resumed (probe phase), the program still reflected changes. The pattern of results indicated that whenever the program was implemented, performance improved. Hence, it is likely that the program, rather than any extraneous variables, accounted for the changes in performance.

Another version of the multiple-baseline design is the *multiple-baseline design across individuals,* in which baseline data are gathered for a single behavior across two or more individuals. After data are gathered separately for each individual, treatment is applied to the behavior of one individual. Baseline observations are continued for the others. After the behavior of each individual shows a clear pattern, treatment is applied to another individual. The contingency is introduced to all other individuals at different points in time until everyone has been included in the program. For example, the multiple-baseline design across individuals might be used to alter the academic performance of three students. A recess privilege might be given to one student for high levels of academic performance while baseline conditions (no privilege) are continued for the other students.

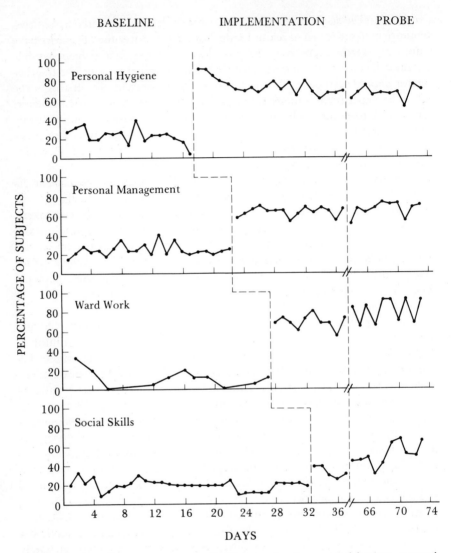

Figure 4.2 Overall mean percentages of subjects performing personal hygiene, personal management, ward work, and social-skills behaviors.

SOURCE: Nelson, G. L., & Cone, J. D. Multiple-baseline analysis of a token economy for psychiatric inpatients. *Journal of Applied Behavior Analysis*, 1979, *12*, 268. Copyright 1979 by the Society for the Experimental Analysis of Behavior, Inc.

Eventually, each student could earn the privilege contingent upon academic performance. The contingency would be introduced to each individual at a different point in time.

Another version of the design is a *multiple-baseline across situations*. In this version, baseline data are gathered across a given behavior for one individual or a group of individuals across two or more situations. After baseline data are obtained across all situations, treatment is introduced to alter behavior in the first situation. The program is introduced at different points in time for the remaining situations. For example, the recess privilege might be used to change academic behavior across two different class periods, namely, morning and afternoon class sessions. Baseline data would be gathered on academic performance during the morning and afternoon each day. Then the students would be informed that ten extra minutes of recess could be earned by a predetermined amount of improvement in academic performance during the morning. The privilege would initially be withheld from the afternoon session. Eventually it would be extended to the afternoon session. Behavior should change when and only when the recess privilege is introduced for each session.

Evaluation of Multiple-Baseline Designs   In the multiple-baseline design across different behaviors, individuals, or situations, a baseline phase is followed by a treatment phase. No reversal is required. A causal relationship is demonstrated if behavior changes when and only when treatment is introduced. Under some circumstances, the design may not demonstrate a causal relationship between treatment and behavior. This occurs when the introduction of the treatment has widespread effects and one behavior change in an individual alters other behaviors as well. For example, in one study, a preschool child was praised for using play equipment. Not only did this behavior increase, but social interaction with peers increased as well (Buell, Stoddard, Harris, & Baer, 1968). In such a situation, a multiple-baseline design across behaviors would not show clearly that the treatment caused the change.

Similarly, in a multiple-baseline design across individuals, altering the behavior of one individual may change the behavior of others. For example, it has been shown that providing attention to a child for appropriate classroom behavior sometimes increases the appropriate behavior of other students as well (Kazdin, 1979). In such situations, the multiple-baseline design across individuals would not show that the contingency resulted in the change in behavior.

Finally, in a multiple-baseline design across situations, behavior change in one situation sometimes carries over to other situations. For example, in a program with psychiatric patients, talking was increased in a restricted laboratory room. Even though the attempt to modify this behavior occurred only in a restricted setting, talking increased on the ward (Bennett & Maley, 1973). Use of a multiple-baseline design across settings would not have yielded clear results in this situation. Such problems with demonstrating a clear causal relationship between treatment and behavior in multiple-baseline designs do not occur often, however, The designs generally are quite useful, particularly in situations where a reversal phase could present problems or where behavior change is desired across different behaviors, different individuals, or different situations.

CHANGING-CRITERION DESIGN

Another intrasubject design to demonstrate the effect of treatment is the changing-criterion design. No reversal is required, nor are multiple-baseline data gathered across different behaviors. The design begins with a baseline phase at which time data are gathered for a single behavior. After the baseline rate is established, treatment is introduced, which may consist of rewarding a particular behavior. Early in the program the criterion for receiving the reward might be relatively lenient. As behavior changes, the criterion for earning the reward is changed. As further progress is shown, the criterion is continually changed. If behavior changes as the criterion for the reward is altered, one may conclude that the program is responsible for the change.

A changing-criterion design was used to evaluate a program aimed at reducing the caffeine intake of three persons who consumed excessive amounts of coffee each day (Foxx & Rubinoff, 1979). For example, one of the persons included in the study was a female schoolteacher who consumed on the average over one thousand milligrams of coffee each day (approximately the equivalent of eight cups of brewed coffee). To reduce her caffeine intake, a program was devised in which the subject provided a deposit of twenty dollars that was returned in small amounts if caffeine intake decreased. If a preset criterion was not met, part of the money was forfeited. To earn the money back, daily caffeine consumption needed to fall at or below a criterion level. The criterion was altered four different times. As shown in Figure 4.3, caffeine consumption decreased during each of the treatment phases. The pattern of the results suggests that changes in the criterion were associated with further reductions in caffeine consumption. Interestingly, after the program was terminated, caffeine consumption remained low up to ten months later.

Evaluation of the Changing-Criterion Design   The changing-criterion design provides a fairly clear demonstration of a causal relationship if a behavior

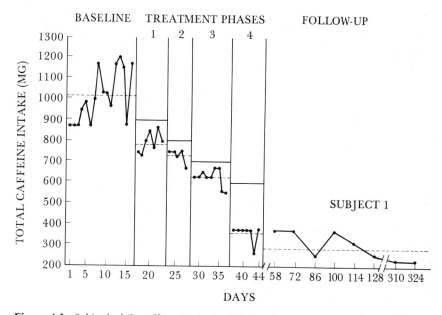

Figure 4.3 Subject's daily caffeine intake (mg) during baseline, treatment, and follow-up. The criterion level for each treatment phase was 102 mg of caffeine less than the previous treatment phase. Solid horizontal lines indicate the criterion level for each phase. Broken horizontal lines indicate the mean for each condition.

SOURCE: Foxx, R. M., & Rubinoff, A. Behavioral treatment of caffeinism: Reducing excessive coffee drinking. *Journal of Applied Behavior Analysis,* 1979, *12,* 339. Copyright 1979 by the Society for the Experimental Analysis of Behavior, Inc.

change correlates closely with changes in criterion as the latter is altered throughout treatment. The design is suited to those situations in which performance can be changed gradually and the final goal is reached in a series of steps. So that the performance criterion can be repeatedly altered, attainment of the goal must be gradual. Certainly, there would be a problem in the design if the performance criterion required a moderate change, such as reduction in the number of cigarettes smoked or alcoholic beverages consumed, but the behavior change was dramatic, such as the elimination of smoking or drinking. In cases where the behavior does not closely follow the criterion, it is possible that something other than treatment accounted for the behavior change. Even when the criterion is followed by the change in behavior, it is possible that some concurrent event is responsible for the change. If behavior changes in the desired direction during the program for reasons other than the program, it may appear to be following changes in the criterion. Thus, the changing-criterion design may not give the clearest demonstration of a causal relationship between the behavior and the program.

Intersubject Experimental Designs

An alternative to intrasubject experimentation is evaluation and comparison of groups. With *intersubject* designs, the effect of a given independent variable or treatment is evaluated primarily between groups rather than within subjects or groups over time. Usually, two or more groups receive different treatments. As with the intrasubject design, the goal is to arrive at a conclusion about the effects of treatment. However, the conclusion is reached by comparing a group that receives the treatment intervention with another group that does not. Of course, in order to conclude that any differences between groups are due to their differential treatment, the groups should be similar prior to treatment. To reduce the likelihood that groups differ prior to treatment, individuals are assigned *randomly* to groups. Assignment to groups must be unbiased. This may be accomplished by using numbers drawn from a random-numbers table, selecting numbers from a hat, and so on. If bias enters into the assignment of subjects to groups, then performance on the dependent measure might be due to the initial differences rather than to the effects of treatment.

CONTROL-GROUP EXPERIMENTAL DESIGN

The control-group experimental design includes at least two groups whose subjects have been randomly assigned. One group receives treatment; the other does not. Both groups are usually assessed before and after treatment on the dependent measure. The differences between groups at the end of treatment can then be evaluated to determine the effect of treatment.

If only a single group is used, any changes in its performance over time cannot be attributed to treatment. For example, a group of depressive clients may complete psychological measures of depression, undergo treatment for several weeks, and then undergo reassessment on the dependent measures. Posttreatment performance may reveal a substantial decrease in depression. Was treatment responsible for the change? The question cannot be answered in the situation described here. With the same amount of time between initial and final assessment, an untreated group might experience a similar reduction in depression. Having the group retake the test may have resulted in improved performance whether or not treatment was provided. A reduction in depression may occur for other reasons as well. Some individuals may be less depressed because they are no longer preoccupied with events that were once viewed with despair. Furthermore, events other than therapy, such as new social acquaintances, changes in employment, or world or local events, may influence performance. There are a number of other interpretations of such changes over time (see Campbell & Stanley, 1963; Kazdin, 1980b). The point remains that without a no-treatment control group, a single group measured before and after treatment is equivalent to the case study. The use of an equivalent control group excludes a variety of alternative interpretations of the results. To show the effects of treatment for depression, clients can be assigned randomly to the treatment or no-treatment control group. When the treatment subjects complete therapy, both groups are reassessed on the dependent measures. If there are differences in the reassessment data, it is likely that treatment accounted for the change.

The use of a control-group design for evaluating treatment is illustrated in an investigation designed to reduce the frequency of nightmares (Cellucci & Lawrence, 1978). College students who reported an average of two or more nightmares per week were assigned to one of three different treatments. One group received *systematic desensitization* which trained the subjects to relax and to not be bothered by the various themes and images that were raised in the nightmares. Relaxation was paired with images that were included in or provoked by the nightmares. A second group of subjects *discussed* nightmares, how they might be related to one's past and present activities, and their history. The third group simply recorded the frequency of nightmares and did not come for the individual treatment sessions given to the other two groups. The results can be evaluated by looking at changes in reported nightmares for subjects in each of the groups. As evident in Figure 4.4, subjects in the *record* group did not improve, whereas subjects in the other groups did. The greatest reduction in nightmares occurred in the desensitization group. The data suggest that the different treatments accounted for the results, because extraneous factors, such as group differences before treatment, exposure to the assessment procedures, and similar events, would not account for the pattern of results.

Evaluation of the Control-Group Design   The basic control-group design can determine a causal relationship between treatment and behavior change. However, it provides limited information. Additional groups are required to pose finer questions for investigation. Let us consider a therapy technique, nude group marathons, which is said to provide a wide range of therapeutic benefits (Bindrim, 1969). In nude group marathons, individuals discuss emotionally significant material (personal problems and sources of anxiety) and meet for an extended period of time (an entire weekend). During some portion of the marathon, individuals conduct their discussion while undressed.

An important question for investigation is whether nude marathons are

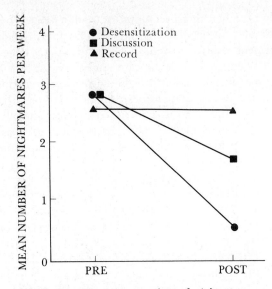

Figure 4.4 The mean number of nightmares per week by group for the baseline week and for the average of the last two weeks.

Source: Reprinted with permission from *Journal of Behavior Therapy and Experimental Psychiatry*, 1978, *9,* 112, Cellucci, A. J., & Lawrence, P. S., The efficacy of systematic desensitization in reducing nightmares. Copyright 1978, Pergamon Press, Ltd.

effective in reducing anxiety in social situations, one of the supposed therapeutic effects. This question might be answered by use of the basic control-group design with two groups, a treatment group and a no-treatment control group. Prior to the investigation, all individuals are assessed on interpersonal anxiety, the dependent measure. Assessment might take place during an interview in which various behaviors of the client, such as number of stutters or eye contact with the interviewer, could be measured. All individuals would be assigned randomly to one of the two groups. (To satisfy the requirements of the experimental design, the control group may not receive treatment initially, although they may receive treatment after the experiment is completed.)

At the end of treatment, let us suppose that clients in the nude marathon group show less interpersonal anxiety than clients in the no-treatment group. This demonstrates that treatment was more effective than no treatment. While this knowledge is important, it is limited. Was participation in nude-marathon therapy important or would *any* therapy have shown such a difference? When individuals *expect* to improve in therapy, they may improve independently of the actual technique to which they are exposed. Also, merely visiting with other individuals (not even under the guise of treatment) may have some therapeutic effect. Although treatment was better than no treatment, it is unclear whether (1) a specific ingredient in the nude-marathon session, (2) participation in treatment per se, or (3) the expectation of the therapist was responsible for the change. To answer more analytic questions such as these, the basic control-group design must be expanded.

The basic design can be expanded by adding groups to answer different questions. The major purpose of adding groups is to control for various events that may account for behavior change and to exclude rival interpretations of the results (Campbell & Stanley, 1963). Different groups can be used to determine which components of treatment are the crucial ingredients in altering behavior.

For example, nude marathons may consist of three important ingredients: (1) discussion of emotionally charged material; (2) participation in an extended session, perhaps for a few days; and (3) undressing during the session. Merely demonstrating that treatment is better than no treatment does not reveal whether it is something peculiar to nude marathons or some other specific ingredient that might be therapeutic. It would be useful to add various groups to the basic design of treatment and no-treatment groups. Perhaps in one control group, clients would be exposed to a procedure that excludes the crucial features of marathon therapy. Clients might merely come to therapy, discuss mundane events rather than personally significant problems, have a short session or sessions rather than a marathon, and stay clothed rather than undress. According to the rationale underlying nude-marathon therapy, this treatment should not be very effective. This control group is not provided with any of the supposedly essential treatment components. If this group improves, it probably would be due in part to changes that could be attributed simply to coming to therapy per se. In another control group, clients might receive ingredients 1 and 2 but not ingredient 3. This group would discuss emotionally valenced material for an extended period of time but would not undress. The progress made by this group would reveal the contribution of nudity in changing behavior. Another control group might receive ingredients 1 and 3 but not ingredient 2. These clients would discuss emotionally valenced material and undress but would have short sessions rather than an extended meeting. This group would control for the influence of the marathon feature of nude-marathon therapy. A final group might include ingredients 2 and 3 while omitting ingredient 1. These clients would meet for an extended period of time and undress, but would be permitted to discuss only mundane events rather than emotionally valenced material. At this point, we have added four groups to the basic control-group design. The groups include:

1. Nude marathon therapy (ingredients 1, 2, and 3)
2. Therapy sessions alone (none of the three ingredients)
3. Nude marathon without nudity (ingredients 1 and 2 only)
4. Nude marathon without extended meeting (ingredients 1 and 3 only)
5. Nude marathon without discussing emotional material (ingredients 2 and 3 only)
6. No treatment (none of the ingredients and no sessions of any kind)

Other groups could be added which would provide only one of the ingredients at a time. At the end of the marathon, when all subjects are reassessed, it is important to compare the different groups. It may be that all groups that receive some form of treatment would improve equally in reducing interpersonal anxiety and only the no-treatment group would experience no improvement. Such a result would suggest that nude marathons have no uniquely successful features. Merely spending time in a session discussing any material and expecting therapeutic change could account for the results.

Variations in control-group design are unlimited depending upon the questions the investigator wishes to ask. All possible control groups are not used; only those that help answer the questions that provided the impetus for the study are included.

FACTORIAL DESIGNS

In many instances, merely elaborating the basic control-group design will not answer all the questions of interest. Factorial designs are control-group designs in which two or more variables are examined simultaneouly, permitting evaluation of separate and combined effects of each variable. To continue the above example, the investigator may wish to evaluate the combined and separate effects of two independent variables, such as the length of time of the session (a few hours versus a few days) and material discussed in the session (emotionally significant material versus mundane topics). This would require four groups (see Figure 4.5). At the end of treatment, it will be possible to determine the effect of length of the marathon session alone by comparing groups 1 and 2 with groups 3 and 4. It will also be possible to examine the effect of the material discussed during the session by comparing groups 1 and 3 with groups 2 and 4. Finally, it

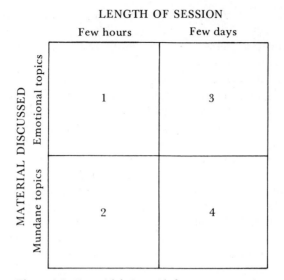

Figure 4.5   Factorial design with four groups examining the effect on treatment outcome of the topic discussed in therapy and the length of session.

will be possible to examine whether the effect of duration of the session depended on the kind of material discussed (that is, the combined or interactive effects). It may be that discussing emotionally significant material is helpful only when the session is long and individuals can resolve some of the problems and anxieties that are aroused. Thus, discussion of emotionally significant material might be helpful in group 1 but not in group 3. The groups must be compared to determine this.

Evaluation of Factorial Designs   Factorial designs are useful for two major reasons. First, they can determine the manner in which independent variables combine or interact to affect behavior. A variable that may seem important alone may depend for its effect upon other variables that are also operative. Second, the effects of several variables can be examined simultaneously in a single experiment. The experiment can answer a number of questions that would otherwise require separate experiments. In terms of utilization of clients, personnel, and time, a single study with several variables is more efficient than several individual studies. Because of these advantages, factorial designs are commonly used in psychological research.

SUMMARY

Data collection is a prerequisite to scientific research. In behavior modification, data collection can be accomplished in a variety of ways. Four classes of data are magnitude, temporal, frequency, and categorical data. Continuous data collection and sampling procedures are two methods of data collection. The format of data collection may vary; two frequently employed formats are actual counts and all-or-none classification. Data collected in behavior-modification programs tell the therapist whether behavior is changing. Because the goal of treatment is to alter behavior, careful assessment of change is essential. However, objective evidence of behavior change does not explain *why* behavior changes.

To assess the reasons for behavior change, an experimental design is necessary. Experimental designs are classified according to whether intrasubject of intersubject comparisons are made to infer a relationship between treatment and behavior change. Intrasubject designs include reversal, multiple-baseline, and changing-criterion designs. Intersubject designs include control-group and factorial designs. The purpose of these designs is to rule out factors other than the treatment intervention that could account for changes in behavior.

SUGGESTED READINGS

DATA COLLECTION

Bijou, S. W., Peterson, R. F., Harris, F. R., Allen, K. E., & Johnson, M. S. Methodology for experimental studies of young children in natural settings. *Psychological Record,* 1969, *19,* 177–210.

Ciminero, A. R., Calhoun, K. S., & Adams, H. E. (Eds.). *Handbook of behavioral assessment.* New York: Wiley, 1977.

Kazdin, A. E. *Behavior modification in applied settings* (2nd ed.). Homewood, Ill.: Dorsey Press, 1980.

RESEARCH DESIGN

Baer, D. M., Wolf, M. M., & Risley, R. T. Some current dimensions of applied behavior analysis. *Journal of Applied Behavior Analysis,* 1968, *1,* 91–97.

Campbell, D. T., & Stanley, J. C. *Experimental and quasi-experimental designs for research.* Chicago: Rand McNally, 1966.

Cook, T. D., & Campbell, D. T. (Eds.). *Quasi-experimentation: Design and analysis issues for field settings.* Chicago: Rand McNally, 1979.

Kazdin, A. E. *Research design in clinical psychology*. New York: Harper & Row, 1980.

Hersen, M., & Barlow, D. H. *Single-case experimental designs: Strategies for studying behavior change*. New York: Pergamon, 1976.

Underwood, B. J., & Shaughnessy, J. J. *Experimentation in psychology*. New York: Wiley, 1975.

CHAPTER 5

DATA ANALYSIS AND INTERPRETATION

As discussed in the last chapter, the collection of data is crucial for scientific research. But the collection of data alone does not ensure that the results can be interpreted unambiguously. One must be able to evaluate the meaningfulness of observational data or experimental evidence. Evaluation of the data derives from comparisons of the data obtained. These comparisons constitute the data analysis. Comparisons usually are made of performances at different points in time for an individual or group (intrasubject designs) or between different groups (intersubject designs). Once the comparisons are made or the data have been analyzed, the results must be interpreted.

Basically, two approaches to data analysis are used, namely, nonstatistical data analysis and statistical data analysis. A third type of analysis, which might be referred to as clinical evaluation, has recently emerged and is compatible with both nonstatistical or statistical evaluation. *Nonstatistical data analysis* is most frequently applied to intrasubject experimental designs. Conversely, *statistical data analysis* is usually applied to intersubject designs. The association of a particular type of data analysis with various designs is not fixed so that, for example, intrasubject designs occasionally rely on statistical analyses (Kazdin, 1976; Kratochwill, 1978).

NONSTATISTICAL DATA ANALYSIS

The fundamental characteristic of nonstatistical analysis is that it involves visual inspection of the data. The method, referred to as "criterion-by-inspection" (Sidman, 1960), is not as simple to apply as might be expected. Visual inspection involves comparison of graphic data in the form of lines (slopes) or the magnitude of performance under baseline and treatment conditions.

Criteria for Nonstatistical Method

The ability to apply visual inspection as a method of data analysis depends heavily upon special characteristics of the data. Perhaps the single most important feature is the *continuous assessment* of behavior over time. With extended observations, the investigator can see whether the data are stable before the intervention and whether performance subsequently varies as the intervention is implemented. The availability of multiple data points over time makes examination of the data through visual inspection less arbitrary than might be expected at first glance.

It is difficult to specify the criteria underlying visual inspection that determine whether the effects of the intervention are judged to be reliable. Indeed, objections to visual inspection are based in part on the difficulty in identifying the criteria so that they can be reliably invoked among different investigators. The effect of an intervention might be especially clear through visual inspection under various circumstances. First, performance during the treatment intervention, when plotted graphically, may not overlap with performance during baseline. For example, a treatment program may be introduced for a hospitalized psychiatric patient who makes frequent bizarre verbalizations. After baseline rates of bizarre verbalizations on the ward are assessed, some intervention may be introduced to decrease or eliminate them. Hypothetical data are plotted across the initial baseline and treatment phases in Figure 5.1(a). Note that the values of the data points in baseline do not approach any of the values of the data points during treatment. If these results were replicated over time with the same subject (reversal design) or across other subjects (multiple-baseline design), there would be little question that the treatment resulted in a behavior change.

A more typical, but less stringent, procedure for experimental evaluation is related to nonoverlapping slopes in baseline and treatment phases. This criterion emphasizes the trends in each phase. Usually, the baseline phase is not terminated if there is a trend toward improvement in the behavior that is to be changed. Since experimental evaluation depends on extrapolating how performance would be if no intervention were made, it is important to have a stable rate of behavior during baseline. If there is a trend, it should be opposite from the direction that is to be achieved with the intervention. In any case, baseline usually shows a relatively stable per-

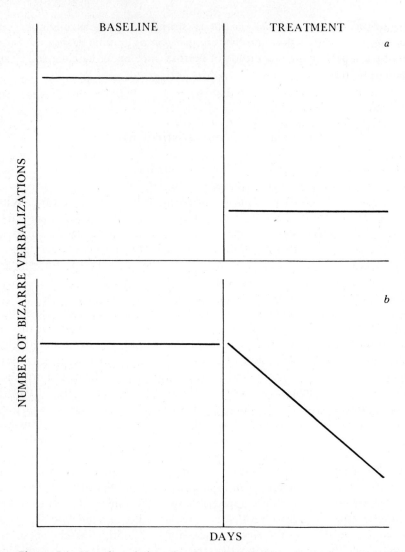

Figure 5.1 Hypothetical data showing nonoverlapping distributions (*a*) and changes in trend (*b*) across baseline and treatment phases.

formance rate with no particular trend. If we are to conclude that treatment had an effect, a definite trend should be evident indicating that behavior is changing from baseline. Figure 5.1(b) shows hypothetical data for the patient mentioned earlier. When treatment was introduced, the data began to show a trend that differed from the baseline trend. The data points during treatment overlap with those of baseline, although the trend during treatment reveals a marked change. Ordinarily, the intervention is continued until the trend is stable, indicating that continued intervention would bring behavior that is vastly different from baseline behavior. If baseline conditions are reimplemented for a reversal phase, the trend is likely to be in the opposite direction from that in the treatment phase. By alternating baseline and treatment phases, one can be convinced of the effect of the intervention even though the data points across phases may overlap.

The ease of evaluating data through visual inspection in intrasubject designs is a function of several factors including the magnitude of treatment effects, the presence or absence of trends in the data, the amount of variability in a given phase and across phases, and the duration of the individual phases. When the data in baseline are very stable and show little variability, smaller treatment effects are more easily detected through visual inspection during the treatment phase than when the data do not meet these conditions. For example, baseline data collected on one's duration of exercise may reveal a consistently low rate of performance with no variability, that is, zero minutes of exercise each day for two weeks. A small increase in exercise associated with an intervention would be easy to detect with this baseline pattern.

Of course, the ideal data conditions for visual inspection are not always met. But they do not have to be met to apply visual inspection effectively. The main criteria are stable rates of data with the absence of trend during baseline. Such a baseline provides an excellent basis for judging whether performance during the intervention phase departs from the level of performance expected if baseline were continued.

Possible Shortcomings

There are some possible shortcomings to the nonstatistical approach to data analysis. First, the changes that are referred to as reliable must be very obvious and dramatic. Although many regard this as an advantage of the nonstatistical approach, others consider the neglect of subtle variables that effect nondramatic but reliable changes as a disadvantage. Nondramatic but reliable changes represent variables that are relevant for a complete understanding of behavior. Also, variables that by themselves appear to have subtle effects may combine with other variables to produce marked changes in behavior (Kazdin, 1976).

A second potential problem is the lack of clear rules to establish when a finding is not reliable. In some cases, it is not clear whether there is a change over baseline or whether the change is sufficiently dramatic to conclude that the intervention was important (Jones, Vaught, & Weinrott, 1975). In cases of doubt, a finding is usually judged unreliable by the scientific community. Of course, a particular finding can often be subjected to statistical evaluation to determine whether it meets conventional statistical criteria. However, to individuals employing intrasubject designs, statistical proof generally is not regarded as relevant (Baer, 1977). The changes required to obtain a finding of applied significance make statistical proof a relatively weak test.

A final point worth noting is that the method of nonstatistical data analysis is often defended not so much because of its own merits, but rather because of the numerous shortcomings of its only competitor, statistical data analysis. This last point will be explored in the discussion of statistical analysis.

To summarize, data analysis involves comparing values on the dependent measures. In the nonstatistical approach, these comparisons usually involve visual inspection of the data. Evaluation depends on projecting from baseline data what behavior would be like in the future if an intervention were not implemented. When the intervention is implemented, performance may depart from this projected level and suggest that treatment was responsible for change. As the changes in performance are replicated over time or across behaviors, individuals, or situations, the plausibility of treatment as the source of change increases.

An important aspect of nonstatistical data analysis that should be mentioned here pertains to the clinical or applied significance of behavior change (Risley, 1970). Intrasubject designs are not concerned with merely demonstrating reliable changes alone but also with showing changes that are clinically important. Thus, the criteria for evaluating change in the nonstatistical approach are often quite stringent; and statistical evaluation is looked upon by many investigators as a much less stringent criterion. Typically, less behavior change is required to achieve statistical confidence than to demonstrate a change of clinical or applied significance. Evaluation of the clinical or applied significance of change in behavior modification is elaborated later in the chapter because it is used both in intrasubject and intersubject research.

STATISTICAL DATA ANALYSIS

The statistical approach to data analysis employs mathematical procedures in comparing dependent variable values. Although this approach is used predominantly with intersubject investigations, it is also applicable to intrasubject designs (Gottman & Lieblum, 1974; Kazdin, 1976). Because of the complexity of the subject matter, our discussion of statistical data analysis will be very rudimentary. The interested reader is urged to consult the Suggested Readings for reference to more comprehensive and detailed accounts.

Basic Statistical Method

Statistical data analysis involves probability. There are many real-life events that can be assigned a theoretical likelihood or *probability*. For example, when flipping a coin, the probability of obtaining heads is ½ or .50. This means that in the long run the coin will come up heads half the time. Now then, imagine a situation in which a friend comes to you with a coin and offers to bet you ten dollars per coin toss that the coin will come up heads. You might reason that if your friend always chooses heads and you always choose tails, you would both come out even in the long run. However, the fact that your friend is so anxious to begin the betting makes you suspect that the coin may not be fair. You inspect it and see that it has heads and tails. However, the possibility remains that the coin is loaded, or unevenly weighted. You might conceive the following hypothesis: "The coin is loaded in such a way that heads and tails do not come up equally often." The competing hypothesis would be that the coin is fair. Based on your knowledge of statistical data analysis, you might ask your friend to allow some experimentation on the fairness of the coin. You flip the coin 100 times and record the outcome (heads or tails) on each trial. If the coin is indeed fair, the theoretical value of the dependent variable (outcomes) is 50 heads and 50 tails.

As it turns out, the coin comes up heads 82 times and tails 18 times. You might conclude that the coin probably is loaded. If the ratio of heads to tails were 55/45 instead of 82/18, determining its fairness would be much more difficult. However, there are some statistical conventions that might help you in making such a decision. It is possible to assign a probability to the event of 82 percent heads. As you might expect, the probability of a fair coin coming up heads 82 percent of the time is very low.

As a matter of convention, psychologists often choose some standard level of improbability by which to guide their decisions. These levels, called critical significance or simply significance levels, may vary depending on researcher, subject matter, and so on. However, the most common level employed in psychology is 5 percent or .05. *Critical significance level* provides a standardized and objective criterion to evaluate comparisons. It is a means of ensuring that the data probably reflect some *real* difference in dependent variable values rather than some chance variation. In the coin-tossing example, the occurrence of 82 percent heads with a fair coin is very improbable. Note that it is not impossible, but only improbable. Indeed, the computed probability of such an occurrence is well below the critical significance level of .05. You are thus fairly well justified in concluding that the coin is not fair. There is a possibility that you are wrong and that the 82 percent heads was just a chance occurrence with a fair coin. However, you must choose some arbitrary cutoff point to guide your decision. If your reservations are strong enough, you can impose a more stringent critical significance level. Thus, you might require that the observed data (82 percent heads) be extremely improbable (for example, less than .01 or .001) before concluding that the coin is not fair. This would make you less open to the error of rejecting the fair-coin hypothesis when it is actually true.

The general paradigm in statistical data analysis may be conceptualized in terms of four stages.

1. A hypothesis is stated.
2. A critical significance level is chosen.
3. Relevant data are collected.
4. The data are analyzed (compared) and interpreted as being supportive, neutral, or nonsupportive of the hypothesis.

Each of these stages was illustrated in the coin-tossing example.

It should be noted at this point that statistical data analysis places considerable emphasis on variability in data. As we saw in the foregoing example, some variability in the 50/50 ratio was expected. A ratio of 52/48 or of 55/45 is possible. Perhaps a more meaningful illustration of the concept of variability would be helpful. Let us suppose that you are taking a daily record of your weight. You weigh in every evening at approximately the same time. However, you have noticed on past occasions that your bathroom scale does not always give consistent readings. You step on it and it registers 155 pounds. You step off, bite your lip in disbelief, and step back on the scale again. This time it might register 153.5! Bolstered by the apparently instantaneous weight loss, you step off and then back on again. Now it reads 156.5! This variation might be explained by a number of factors, such as weak springs or different foot placements. The important point is that there is an apparent variability in your data. The source might be called chance or uncontrolled variables. In either case, the variability persists and must be taken into account when conclusions about weight loss are entertained. Pursuing the example, you might weigh yourself the following evening and obtain recordings of 152, 153.5, and 151.5. Note that the previous night's data seemed to vary around a central point of 155 pounds. Can we conclude that this central point, your "real" weight, has changed on the second night? Well, the data from the second night also show variability, but their central point does seem to be lower (about 152 pounds). Thus, even taking chance variation into account, there does seem to be a decrease in weight from one night to the next.[1]

The concept of *statistical significance* deserves mention at this point. When a given outcome satisfies the critical significance level of improbability, then it is said to have achieved statistical significance at that level. For example, one might statistically analyze the weight data and find that the probability of a chance variation accounting for the divergent readings is less than .05. One could then state that a weight loss which was statistically significant at the .05 level had been observed. In essence, one would be asserting that the probability of such an observation being obtained as a function of chance is less than .05. In other words, the probability of obtaining two weight measurements that differ that much, if in fact you really weighed the same on both occasions, is less than .05. In our terms, the comparison of dependent variable values has revealed a statistically significant difference. A difference is statistically significant when it is greater than what might be expected because of uncontrolled variables and/or random variation.

The statistical approach to data analysis, then, relies heavily on mathematical probabilities, basic assumptions, variability, and critical significance levels. These combine in a way that gives the data analyst a numerical basis for data interpretation. Note that the process of *comparison* is still paramount. Whether the data analysis is statistical or nonstatistical, the core of the analysis involves comparison of specific dependent variable values. In one case, the comparison is made visually; in the other, the comparison is mathematical.

Possible Shortcomings

The use of statistical data analysis has been a controversial issue in behavior modification. Many researchers have criticized the statistical approach on several points. Let us explore a few of their arguments and rejoinders offered by statistically oriented behavior modifiers.

The first criticism relates to the obscuring of individual performance. Statistical data analysis is employed predominantly with groups. The

---

1. This illustration of variability ties in well with the concept of critical significance levels. It is possible that your real weight on the second night was identical to that on the first night. However, if you were allowed to make certain important assumptions (see Hays, 1963), you could assign a probability to the event of a registered average weight of 152 when your actual weight was 155. If that probability were less than the chosen critical significance level, then you could reject the hypothesis that the weights were the same on the two evenings.

argument against statistical measures is that they often summarize group performance without accurately representing any single individual's performance. A popular example is the census report. When the statistics of the U.S. Census Bureau indicate that the average family has 2.9 children, there can be little doubt that the statistical representation fails to coincide with any individual instance. Nine-tenths of a child is a rare occurrence! Although it is justified in some instances, this criticism usually meets the rejoinder that there are many situations in which a statistical measure may be representative of the individual performance. Moreover, statistical analyses may correct for the very deviant score of an atypical subject.

A second criticism of statistical data analysis is that it obscures "transition states" (see Sidman, 1960). Gradual changes or trends in behavior are often overlooked when traditional before-and-after (pretest to posttest) statistical analyses are made. Nonstatistical analyses often allow one to monitor moment-by-moment changes in behavior. The argument here is that a simple before-and-after comparison of dependent variable values is a very crude method of data analysis. Many relevant behavior changes occur between the pretest and the posttest. The statistician's rejoinder here might be that there are statistical measures that are sensitive to changes over time (Kratochwill, 1978). The fact that such measures are infrequently employed casts a reflection on the statistical analyst rather than on statistics per se.

A third criticism deals with the distinction between statistical and clinical or practical significance. It is possible and, indeed, common for a statistically significant result to be irrelevant for applied purposes (Hersen & Barlow, 1976). A reliable finding may not be of applied significance. This is especially true when extremely large numbers of subjects are employed. The larger the number of individuals used in an intersubject design, the smaller the actual differences required between the groups to achieve statistical significance. For example, we might wish to find out whether individuals in the United States who live east or west of the Mississippi River are the same height. If we measure an extremely large number of individuals in both locations, it is possible for a trivial difference in height, such as .001 inch, to be highly significant statistically. Although the results are statistically significant, they would not be useful in selecting an Olympic basketball team to compete against other countries. The failure of statistical significance to be necessarily of applied or practical significance is conceded by statisticians. Yet often, investigations employing statistical significance are testing predictions based on different theories. Although a particular statistically significant finding may not have applied significance, the ultimate consequences of supporting a given theory may be great.

A fourth criticism relates to the hallowed status of statistical techniques and statistical significance. You are probably aware of the great extent to which statistics are used and perhaps abused in modern advertising. The lay public frequently respects statistics as indisputable evidence. This glorification of statistics is also prevalent in some areas of behavioral science. Many journals will not publish experiments that fail to test for or demonstrate statistical significance. This bias prevents the publication of numerous experiments that may contain extremely important findings. Failure to obtain a statistically significant difference among dependent variable values may be a very important finding. Unfortunately, the professional emphasis on significance forces many researchers to "persevere until significance." That is, they may try dozens of statistical tests on the same set of data until something of statistical significance is found (Barber, 1976). Likewise, the resarcher may repeat an experiment over and over until significance is obtained. Recall that the use of a 5 percent or .05 critical significance level of improbability allows for 5 percent of one's "significant" results to occur by chance. Thus, it is possible that one out of every twenty articles in the statistically biased journals is actually reporting on a spurious or chance finding.[2] This criticism has been conceded by statistically oriented researchers (see Neher, 1967). (A journal that would publish negative results, or results that are not statistically significant, has been suggested to alleviate some of the foregoing problems.)

These, then, are some of the objections that have been raised regarding statistical data analysis.[3] A more complete understanding of these objections would entail elaboration of statistical methods. The interested reader is urged to consult the Suggested Readings for reference to some of the more comprehensive accounts of statistical data analysis.

To summarize, the statistical approach employs mathematical procedures in comparing dependent variable values. Basic assumptions, variability, probability, and critical significance levels play important roles in statistical data analysis. The role of statistics in behavioral research has been a controversial one (Kazdin, 1976). Some workers have emphasized the advantages of statistics in data analysis; these include objectivity, ability to use formalized mathematical systems, and ability to detect meaningful but

---

2. This assumes exact replication of each of those twenty studies. It does not mean that one of twenty *independent* studies should be so evaluated.

3. A fifth criticism, somewhat more complex than the others, relates to the important assumptions involved in the statistical approach. These are assumptions about the nature of the subject matter under study. When these assumptions are inaccurate, then the application of certain statistical measures is questionable. There are many examples of inappropriate statistical applications and failure of assumptions. The rejoinder to this argument is that there are many situations in which such assumptions are of considerably less importance. For example, when dealing with extremely large groups, a failure of assumptions is much less devastating. Furthermore, there are many statistical techniques that require few, if any, assumptions.

nonobvious differences in comparisons. Other researchers have enumerated the disadvantages of statistics, such as obfuscation of the individual performance, obscuration of transition states, failure of assumptions, the contrast between statistical and applied or practical significance, and the disproportionate emphasis placed on statisitcal results. Whether one uses the statistical or nonstatistical approach, however, data analysis always involves a comparison of dependent variable values.

CLINICAL EVALUATION

A definite limitation of statistical evaluation as usually applied is that it detracts somewhat from the question of the clinical or applied importance of behavior change. Visual inspection does not necessarily avoid the problem. Although visual inspection draws attention to the importance of achieving marked changes, it does not provide specific guidelines for evaluating whether the magnitude of changes are important. Recently, research has begun to invoke criteria to address the clinical significance of behavior change. Clinical significance refers to the practical value of the effect of the intervention, that is, whether the change makes a "real" difference to the client (Risley, 1970).

Occasionally, the clinical importance of the treatment changes is obvious. For example, treatment may reduce the head banging of an autistic child from 100 to 50 instances per hour. Such a change might be easily detected through visual inspection if observations were collected over several days. Also, statistical analysis might show a highly reliable effect. However, without virtual or complete elimination of the behavior, the clinical significance of the change can be challenged. Essentially, complete elimination of head banging probably would be needed to produce a change of clear clinical importance. Of course, in many areas of treatment, the presence or absence of a behavior is not necessarily the criterion for deciding whether an important change was achieved. Other criteria are necessary.

Basic Criteria

Two methods have been suggested for evaluating whether the effects of treatment are of applied significance (Kazdin, 1977a; Wolf, 1978). These methods consist of social comparison and subjective evaluation. The *social-comparison* method refers to comparing the behavior of the client before and after treatment with the behavior of nondeviant peers. The question asked by this procedure is whether the client's behavior after treatment is distinguishable from the behavior of his or her peers. To answer this question, persons who are considered to be functioning well but are similar to the client in such variables as age and gender are identified. The level of behavior of these latter persons can serve as a criterion for evaluating whether treatment with the clients has achieved an important level.

For example, one behavior program reduced the inappropriate eating behaviors of hospitalized mentally retarded persons who seldom used utensils, constantly spilled food while eating, stole food from others, and ate food previously spilled on the floor (O'Brien & Azrin, 1972). Through the use of prompts, praise, and food reinforcement, these behaviors were dramatically reduced. A dramatic reduction does not necessarily mean that the changes were clinically important. The investigators collected information on customers of a local restaurant by observing their inappropriate eating behaviors using the same observation system as that used with the retarded residents. Interestingly, the level of inappropriate mealtime behaviors among the retarded prior to training was much higher than the level of the normal sample. After training, inappropriate behaviors of the retarded fell slightly *below* the level of the normative sample. Thus, the magnitude of the changes achieved with training brought the residents to an acceptable level of performance for people functioning in everyday life.

In many behavioral programs using intrasubject and intersubject designs, the clinical significance of the changes has been evaluated with normative data. For example, applications have shown that the disruptive and unruly behaviors of children with conduct problems can be brought into the normative range after treatment and that social interaction of withdrawn, shy, or aggressive children and adults can be brought to the normative level of their peers.

Another method of evaluating the importance of behavior change is through *subjective evaluation*. This method refers to determining the importance of the treatment change by assessing the opinions of persons who are likely to have contact with the client. The question addressed by this method of evaluation is whether behavior changes are perceptibly different among persons with whom the client interacts. Persons who are in a special position to judge, either through expertise or as a result of their relationship with the client, evaluate whether changes in performance are important. Global ratings are used to make this evaluation.

For example, in one behavioral program for delinquent girls at a home-style facility, specific conversational skills were developed (Minkin, Braukmann, Minkin, Timbers, Timbers, Fixsen, Phillips, & Wolf, 1976). The girls were trained to engage in such behaviors as answering questions and attending to others during conversation. Persons with whom the delinquent girls might interact (for example, probation officer, teacher, counselor, social worker) rated tapes of conversation. These judges rated posttreatment conversation as superior to pretraining conversation. These results suggest that the concrete behaviors altered during training had implications for more general evaluations of overall conversation.

The subjective-evaluation method can be used for a variety of behaviors focused upon in treatment. Although specific behaviors may be changed, it may also be important to assess whether others with whom the client interacts see a change in performance. No matter how effective the program may be on specific behaviors, whether the client is viewed differently by others or whether the new behaviors can be detected in everyday performance may be important dimensions in their own right.

Possible Shortcomings

The use of normative data or global evaluations of client behavior represents an important step toward quantifying the extent to which the change produced in treatment is important. Of course, the methods of assessing the importance of behavior change raise problems of their own. For example, the social-comparison method is difficult to apply in many cases because the normative or comparison group may be difficult to identify. To whom should the severely retarded, chronic psychiatric patients, or prisoners be compared in evaluating treatment or rehabilitation programs? Developing performance so that it reaches normative levels of persons functioning adequately in everyday life may represent an unrealistic ideal, at least at this point in the development of treatment.

Even if a normative group can be identified, the range of behaviors that would be defined as acceptable is difficult to specify. It is relatively simple to identify deviant behavior that departs markedly from the behavior of "normal" peers. But as behavior becomes slightly less deviant, it is difficult to identify the point at which it falls within a normative range. A subjective judgment is needed to decide the point where behavior is acceptable.

The subjective-evaluation method raises problems as well. Relying on opinions of others for determining whether treatment effects are important has several risks. Subjective evaluations of behavior are much more readily susceptible to biases on the part of observers than are overt behavioral measures. It is possible that subjective evaluations will reflect change even when overt behaviors do not. Also, the fact that persons who interact with the client claim there is a difference in behavior does not necessarily mean that the amount of the client's change is clinically significant. A small change in behavior may be reflected in global ratings, but the clients' behaviors may still depart considerably from normative levels.

Although problems and potential limitations for determining the clinical or applied importance of behavior change can be identified, the methods point to a significant direction in treatment evaluation. The social-comparison and subjective-evaluation methods broaden the criteria usually used to evaluate interventions. And the methods can supplement nonstatistical and statistical criteria, as discussed earlier.

INTERPRETATION OF DATA

Once the data have been analyzed, they must be interpreted in terms of their implications for the topic under study. When the experiment has derived from a formal hypothesis, then the data must be evaluated in light of that hypothesis. When experimentation has been of purely exploratory nature, the data must be interpreted in terms of their meaning for behavioral research. Note, however, that data interpretation is sometimes less objective when hypothesis testing is involved. This may be because a researcher with a vested interest or a pet hypothesis is often biased toward viewing the data as being favorable to that interest. In a sense, he or she may be bending the data to fit a hypothesis. This is especially apparent when the data do not present a clear-cut directionality. To avoid personal biases in such instances, the researcher should either adopt very stringent criteria or allow an independent worker to analyze the data.

One might conceptualize the purposes of data interpretation as being twofold: (1) to evaluate the implications of the data for the particular situation from which they were drawn; and (2) to evaluate their implications for future and similar situations. These purposes correspond roughly to what has been termed internal and external validity (Campbell & Stanley, 1963). The first purpose is internal in that it deals with relationships within the experiment performed. The second, in contrast, pertains to the generality of such relationships.

The interpretation of data is a somewhat nebulous area. Except for the organizational outlines and decision procedures of statistical methods, no standard formula for data interpretation exists. This lack of an agreed upon standard often results in differing interpretations of the same data. Surprising as it may seem, it is not unusual to find researchers citing the same experiment in support of contradictory hypotheses. For example, many of the early studies on the effectiveness of psychotherapy were interpreted in opposite manners by researchers.

Perhaps the most important point to be stressed in data interpretation is the option of abstention. When the data are insufficient or ambiguous, the researcher should refrain from drawing conclusions. This emphasizes the importance of conservatism in the evaluation of evidence. The researcher should always be inclined to doubt the implications of data. Interpretations must be considered only in a tentative and cautious manner.

In summary, then, data interpretation involves the evaluation of evidence in light of a particular hypothesis or a particular subject matter. Interpretative biases are often encountered because of vested interests in the research. Thus, stringent criteria, objectivity, and conservatism should be emphasized, as they help eliminate ambiguities and contradictory interpretations. The scientific researcher should abstain from directional conclusions when data are either insufficient or ambiguous. Stubborn reluctance to accept premature conclusions is a scientific prerequisite in the interpretation of data.

SUMMARY

Data analysis requires making comparisons on the dependent measures to determine the effect of an independent variable. The approaches discussed included nonstatistical, statistical, and clinical evaluation.

Nonstatistical data analysis is usually associated with intrasubject designs. The criterion for evaluating an effect consists of visual inspection and is based on demonstrating marked changes in performance replicated over time or across behaviors, persons, or situations. The pattern of data, evaluated through graphical representation, is evaluated visually. Statistical data analysis is usually associated with intersubject designs. The analysis relies on comparisons between groups and on estimates of the probability that differences can be attributed to chance. Rules regarding probability levels help determine whether a particular difference between groups meets the criterion for statistical significance. A statistical criterion refers to the reliability of the finding.

Clinical evaluation is concerned with examining the clinical or applied importance of intervention effects. The issue is whether the changes produced in treatment make a difference to the client or to those with whom he or she may interact. Different methods currently are used to address this issue. The importance of the changes produced in treatment can be assessed by evaluating whether treatment brings the client's behavior to the level of a normative sample or whether other persons in everyday life subjectively view the client differently after treatment.

Data analyses, by whatever method, lead to interpretations about the investigation and its effects. Interpretations serve to evaluate the implications of the data. Conclusions are reached about the basis for the data given the particular experiment and the possible generality or lack of generality of the findings to persons, situations, and behaviors not included in the experiment.

SUGGESTED READINGS

NONSTATISTICAL ANALYSIS

Baer, D. M. Perhaps it would be better not to know everything. *Journal of Applied Behavior Analysis,* 1977, *10,* 167–172.

Michael, J. Statistical inference for individual organism research: Mixed blessing or curse? *Journal of Applied Behavior Analysis,* 1974, 7, 647–653.

STATISTICAL ANALYSIS

Hays, W. L. *Statistics for psychologists.* New York: Holt, Rinehart & Winston, 1963.

Kratochwill, T. B. (Ed.). *Single-subject research: Strategies for evaluating change.* New York: Academic Press, 1978.

CLINICAL EVALUATION

Kazdin, A. E. Assessing the clinical or applied significance of behavior change through social validation. *Behavior Modification,* 1977, *1,* 427–452.

Wolf, M. M. Social validity: The case of subjective measurement or how applied behavior analysis is finding its heart. *Journal of Applied Behavior Analysis,* 1978, *11,* 203–214.

CHAPTER 6

MODELS OF
BEHAVIOR CHANGE

Utilization of any set of procedures, such as psychotherapy or behavior modification, to alter personality or behavior assumes some model or conceptualization of the nature of human beings. The model includes assumptions about motivational forces, the processes that contribute to and shape attitudes and behavior, the degree to which various events influence an individual's life, and the degree to which the influence of such events can be modified. In addition, the model dictates the way in which behavior is viewed, the causes to which behaviors are ascribed, and the procedures considered appropriate to modify behavior.

Many models have been posed to explain behavior (see Hall & Lindzey, 1970). It is beyond the scope of this chapter to review the entire range of approaches. For our purposes, it is important to note the models that have had a major impact on the conceptualization of deviant behavior and psychological treatment procedures. Three models will be discussed; these include the medical, intrapsychic, and behavior models.

THE MEDICAL MODEL

The medical model of abnormal behavior is patterned after views adhered to in medicine. The medical model assumes that deviant behavior is the result of a disease. As in any disease, there is a specific group of symptoms (deviant behaviors) that go together, and each group of symptoms is the result of a specific disease which has a specific etiology or course of development. Such a cluster or group of behaviors is referred to as a *syndrome*. To explain the implications of such a position and the current form of the medical model, which is a source of controversy, we must discuss briefly the forms of disease in medicine. In medicine, at least three types of disease can be distinguished (Buss, 1966). First, there are *infectious diseases,* which are attributed to some pathogen such as a bacteria or virus (as in the common cold). Second, there are *systemic diseases,* which result from a failure or malfunction of a physiological system or organ. A particular organ may fail to function and cause a severe medical problem (for example, appendicitis). Third, there are *traumatic diseases,* which result from some external event, such as a physical blow or ingestion of a toxic substance. An example would be lead poisoning.

The conceptualization of the three types of diseases has been extended to the study of deviant behavior. The infectious-disease model advanced considerably with the discovery of the etiology of general paresis. Neural degeneration resulting from the syphilitic spirochete was found to be the cause of general paresis. Since some of the behaviors associated with general paresis resembled forms of mental illness (that is, psychoses), it was thought that other infectious causes might account for other deviant behavior. Generally, infectious diseases are not presently considered to be responsible for most deviant behavior, although various infectious diseases do have behavioral concomitants. Rather, it is the systemic-disease model that is used in research on deviant behavior. For example, some investigators are examining whether various forms of abnormal behavior, such as schizophrenia, represent a breakdown in bodily functions, such as a failure to metabolize certain substances, a lack of specific enzymes, or a malfunction of neurochemical processes. The traumatic-disease model has also been extended to abnormal behavior. Some deviant behaviors clearly result from externally induced trauma, including birth defects and severe head injury.

Within the realm of medicine and physiology, each of these approaches is useful and not a major source of contention. Investigating the physiological causes (infection, systemic defect, exogenous trauma) of correlates of abnormal behavior has led to important discoveries. However, for many behaviors considered deviant, there is no known organic cause, and in order to account for many of these behaviors, aspects of the medical model have been extrapolated and altered. Specifically, the model has been extended beyond the search for biological causes of deviant behavior. The current controversy focuses on the questionable utility of such a model in explaining deviant behavior that has not been shown to have a clear physiological basis. The medical model suggests that there must be some underlying disease to which the symptoms can be attributed. Thus, the model that posits that physical symptoms are due to underlying physical disorders has been extended to psychology where "psychological symptoms" are seen as resulting from "psychological disorders." In these cases, the supposed causal agent underlying "abnormal" or deviant behaviors is a set of "diseased" personality attributes. This extrapolation of the medical model, which utilizes the model but not its content, has been labeled the intrapsychic model or the quasi-medical model (Bandura, 1969).

INTRAPSYCHIC OR QUASI-MEDICAL MODELS

The quasi-medical model of abnormal behavior relies on personality and intrapsychic processes and includes assumptions that have been useful in physical medicine. First, it is assumed that there are "symptoms" (deviant behaviors) which result from some underlying "disease" process. The "psychological diseases," while not considered to be real entities, (except as a result of reification), function analogously to the systemic or traumatic disorders in the medical model. Second, to arrive at the root of the problem, treatment must focus on the underlying psychic state. To understand the extrapolation of the medical model to the realm of behavior disorders requires explanation of the intrapsychic or quasi-medical model in general and of psychoanalytic theory in particular.

The intrapsychic model focuses on psychological forces that are assumed to exist within the individual. A number of personality theorists have posited an assortment of such psychic forces, including drives, needs, impulses, motives, personality traits, and other attributes. The forces are assumed to propel behavior. There are many versions of the intrapsychic view; they differ on the precise forces and motives to which behavior is ascribed.

Psychoanalytic Theory

Sigmund Freud (1856–1939) provided an elaborate theory to explain the supposed motivational underpinnings of behavior. Freud emphasized those causes to which abnormal behaviors might be traced. Regarding psychological disorders, Freud accepted the structure of the medical model itself, but not its content. Psychological disorders were viewed as analogous to physical disorders; thus, failure of the personality to function appropriately would be analogous to systemic disease, while psychological trauma would correspond to traumatic disease.

Freud traced behaviors to psychological impulses, drives, forces, and unconscious processes occuring within the individual. According to psychoanalytic theory, all behavior can be traced to some underlying psychological process. The processes described by Freud are referred to as *psychodynamic processes* and the theory sometimes is referred to as a psychodynamic theory.[1] Freud's psychodynamic view of personality describes behavior in terms of psychological energies, or motivating forces, drives, and impulses, and their expression at various stages early in the individual's development.

Freud posed three structures of personality, the id, ego, and superego. The id is the reservoir of all instincts and is the source of psychic energy (libido) for all psychological processes and behavior. The ego interacts with the demands of reality and the need to fulfill instinctual wishes. Finally, the superego represents the internalization of social and parental standards and ideals of behavior. These personality structures are in constant conflict, which usually occurs at an unconscious level. Each structure contributes to determining whether an impulse will be expressed, and precisely when and in what form it will be expressed. The expression of psychic energy can be traced to different focuses for instinctual gratification as the child develops.

Freud delineated stages of psychosexual development through which everyone supposedly passes. At each stage, the focus or source of pleasure or instinctual gratification is associated with different areas and functions of the body. As the child develops, the expression of psychic energy invariably leads to conflicts with reality and within the structures of personality. Anxiety reactions, defense mechanisms, and alternate modes of behaving result from instincts not obtaining direct and immediate expression. Impulses, such as attraction toward the opposite-sexed parent, may not be resolved and may result in a breakdown of normal personality development. Normal behavior develops from the expression of impulses, wishes, and desires in socially appropriate ways. Deviant behavior, according to the psychoanalytic view, is due to an internal unconscious conflict resulting from the disruption of the normal development and expression of drives and needs, and their gratification. Psychological drives can fail and find expression in socially appropriate ways. Drives and unresolved conflicts may find symbolic expression in aberrant behaviors, which are considered symptoms of the real underlying problem. According to Freud's theory, normal everyday behaviors, as well as abnormal behaviors, can be traced to particular personality processes and the expression of psychic impulses. For example, cigarette smoking is not merely an unwanted or

---

1. Dynamics refers to a branch of mechanics in which phenomena are explained by referring to energy forces and their relation to motion, growth, and change in physical matter.

bothersome habit but also a reflection of an individual's need for oral gratification; it might result from insufficient or overindulgent stimulation early in life.

The intrapsychic model, and primarily the psychoanalytic approach, has had a tremendous impact on clinical psychology and psychiatry and, indeed, has dominated the field of mental health. This is evident in a variety of ways, such as the language associated with the development, occurrence, and amelioration of deviant behavior. Terms like *etiology, treatment, mental hospital, patient, clinic, psychopathology,* and *mental illness* reflect the carryover from the medical model.

Other Intrapsychic Approaches

Psychoanalytic theory has been referred to as an intrapsychic position because it posits that psychological forces within the organism account for behavior. There are a number of other intrapsychic views of personality and behavior. These views also explain behavior by looking to underlying psychological processes. In contrast to the psychoanalytic model, many of these models were designed to account for all of human behavior, normal and abnormal; much less emphasis, therefore, has been given to the development and alleviation of abnormal behavior.

In some theories, traits are posited as the psychological features that account for behavior. Behaviors are attributed to differential amounts of a given trait, such as kindness, or to different traits across individuals. In trait theories, an individual's behavior is explained by the dispositions or traits he or she possesses (see Allport, 1961). In other intrapsychic positions, the self-concept, or notion of the self, is believed to be an important basis for behavior (see Rogers, 1959). One's perception of oneself in relation to others and of various experiences in the world is assumed to dictate one's behavior. In yet another intrapsychic position, a taxonomy of needs is posited to account for behavior (see Maslow, 1966). The needs are internal psychological processes that give rise to overt behavior. Behavior can be traced to a diverse series of needs. Knowledge of the specific needs and the ways in which they are expressed is necessary in order to understand behavior. Although various forms of intrapsychic theories could be elaborated, knowledge of their unique features is not required in order to examine implications of the general approach.[2]

---

2. See the Suggested Readings for information regarding intrapsychic theories.

Implications of Intrapsychic Models

Adoption of the medical model and the intrapsychic models has significant implications not only for conceptualizing personality but also for psychological assessment and the labeling of behavioral problems (diagnosis) and for altering behavior (treatment).

The intrapsychic model has strongly influenced psychological assessment and diagnosis of behavioral disorders. Assessment focuses on underlying processes that explain behavior, and thus a client's overt behavior is not of direct interest. For example, an individual may seek therapy to overcome anxiety that arises in social situations. The focus is not on specific situations that appear to precipitate anxiety. Assessment focuses on the client's psychodynamics of personality attributes to which the anxiety is assumed to be traceable. Through psychodynamic assessment, the psychologist attempts to provide global descriptions of personality; to reconstruct the individual's psychological development; to determine how the person reacted to important psychological impulses, such as sex and aggression, in the past; to determine what defense mechanisms have developed; and to determine what basic characteristic traits or psychological defects account for behavior. Assessment searches for the psychological processes that are considered to be the sources of behavioral problems.

Projective tests are an example of the diagnostic tools of traditional personality assessment. These tests attempt to assess personality indirectly through reactions to ink blots, stories created in response to ambiguous stimuli, free associations, or other unstructured tasks. Projective tests provide the client with ambiguous stimuli onto which he or she must impose meaning and structure. The responses are considered as *signs* that reveal personality structure, psychodynamics, and unconscious motivation. Conclusions are reached by interpreting the meaning of the behavioral signs and inferring underlying processes. Interpretation of projective tests requires clinical judgment to extract meaning from responses. There has been serious criticism of the reliability and validity of these interpretations in predicting behavior. Individuals often disagree on the interpretation of test responses and about the psychological processes to which the responses are attributed. In fact, a number of authors have questioned the utility of projective tests (Lanyon & Goodstein, 1971; Mischel, 1968, 1979; Peterson, 1968; Sechrest, 1963).

There are many other psychological tests and inventories designed to assess aspects of the client's personality, character traits, and psychological needs, deficits, or defects (for example, tests of anxiety, paranoid tendencies, extroversion, impulsiveness, brain damage, intelligence). Psychological assessment with various inventories attempts to provide a profile of traits and to identify problem areas in personality or psychological development. In clinical use, the purpose of such tests is to help the clinician understand behavior and describe or diagnose personality.

A major task of diagnosis is to assign an individual a label that implies the underlying condition or defect responsible for the behavioral problem. Such labels include "schizophrenia," "neurosis," "mental retardation," "learning disability," "hyperactivity," "emotional disturbance," and numerous others which depict the motivational problem, inherent deficit, or "disease." Traditionally, the focus has been on identifying disorders and "symptom" patterns that go together, along the lines practiced in medicine (Phillips & Draguns, 1971). Once the disorders are clearly described, it is assumed that their etiology will be apparent.

Diagnosis attempts to describe the presenting problem, to isolate the conditions related to its occurrence, to proffer a therapeutic plan, and to predict the outcome of treatment (Stuart, 1970). Although these purposes have been fulfilled with many physical disorders in medicine, the traditional diagnostic approach to behavior problems has not fared well (Kanfer & Saslow, 1969; Zigler & Phillips, 1961a). For example, professionals who independently assign patients to diagnostic categories often disagree over the precise diagnosis. Moreover, there are great differences in the behavior of persons ascribed the same diagnosis as well as similar behaviors in individuals assigned diverse diagnoses. Psychological or psychiatric diagnosis seems to provide little information about behavior beyond that which was known when the diagnosis was made. Specifically, little information is given about the etiology, treatment of choice, and prognosis (Kanfer & Saslow, 1969; Mahoney, 1980; Zigler & Phillips, 1961b).

There is relatively little to recommend the general approach of the quasi-medical model in the way of treatment for individuals whose behavior is labeled abnormal. Psychological treatments based on the approach have not advanced as much as have medical treatments for physical disorders. Yet the promise of effective treatment is implicit in the development of psychiatric hospitals, outpatient clinics, and other facilities modeled after medical treatment. The efficacy of treatment for people labeled psychotics, neurotics, sociopaths, retardates, delinquents, emotionally disturbed children, and others has been severely questioned. Individual or group psychotherapy or counseling, which are conducted in outpatient and inpatient settings, are the general treatment strategies regardless of diagnosis or supposed personality problems (London, 1964; Stuart, 1970). Depending on the orientation of the therapist, a client receiving psychotherapy is usually required to relate aspects of experiences to the therapist to uncover the underlying personality. It is assumed that therapy can progress only when intrapsychic processes are revealed and altered.

Unfortunately, for many individuals, treatment may even be associated with deleterious effects. For example, psychotherapy with different types of patients (Strupp & Hadley, 1977) and institutional care for psychiatric patients (Goffman, 1961; Scheff, 1966) and the retarded (Kaufman, 1967; Schlanger, 1954) sometimes are associated with decrements in adaptive behaviors. When individuals are hospitalized for psychiatric treatment, they often must give up many of their responsibilities and rights as citizens. Thus, "treatment" sometimes further weakens the tie with society. The institution fosters dependency and lack of self-sufficiency, which may detract from the individual's subsequent adjustment to the community (Paul, 1969b). The stigma resulting from institutionalization ensures that post-hospitalization adjustment will be difficult.

The medical and intrapsychic models assume that problematic behaviors are symptomatic of some underlying disorder. In medicine, of course, internal conditions, such as infection or organ dysfunction, which are responsible for symptoms, such as fever or discomfort, are treated. But treatment of symptoms alone is insufficient if the underlying condition is not altered as well. In medicine, symptomatic treatment is employed and a disease is allowed to run its course only in cases where there is no acceptable cure for the underlying disorder, as with the common cold or a terminal illness. In these cases, symptoms may be ameliorated with decongestants or painkillers. However, in cases where a cure for the underlying physiological problem is known (for example, rabies, gallstones, ruptured appendix), symptomatic treatment alone is obviously inappropriate.

Within the medical and quasi-medical models, then, treatment focuses on the actual problematic behavior; the individual might not be cured. The notion of *symptom substitution* has been suggested as a possible consequence of symptomatic treatment. This notion suggests that if a maladaptive behavior is altered without treatment of the underlying disorder, another symptom might substitute for the problematic behavior. Symptom substitution is expected from a psychodynamic position because, according to this view, impulses, drives, and psychological forces not resolved through normal channels of behavior seek release through the formation of symptoms, such as anxieties, obsessions, tics, and so on. Alteration of the symptom through which release of a psychological impulse was sought will not alter the underlying impulse. So the impulse may seek re-expression in another form or another symptom. Cure can result only from the removal or reduction of the impulse, drive, or conflict that led to the maladaptive behavior.

There has been considerable dispute about symptom substitution. Disagreement has centered around these points: whether symptom substitution occurs, whether it can be assessed empirically, whether substitute symptoms can be predicted in advance, and whether its occurrence necessarily supports a psychodynamic position (Bandura, 1969; Cahoon, 1968;

Mahoney et al., 1974; Stuart, 1970; Ullmann & Krasner, 1975). At present there is little evidence indicating deleterious effects following treatment of specific behavior problems. Indeed, as discussed later, beneficial side effects frequently are associated with the alteration of specific behaviors.

Criticisms of Intrapsychic Models

One major historical benefit has accrued from the popularity of the quasi-medical models of deviant behavior. Prior to their presentation, deviant behavior was attributed to possession by demons, evil spirits, and supernatural forces. Ancient and medieval conceptualizations were based on the assumption that individuals were inhabited by evil spirits as retribution for their wickedness and sins. Exorcism was required to treat abnormal behaviors. Often, harsh and inhumane procedures, such as flogging and starvation, were used to make the body uninhabitable for the spirits. Recasting the deviant individual as "mentally ill" or "diseased" probably has contributed to increased sympathy and humane treatment (Ausubel, 1961b). Although the public still rejects and negatively evaluates individuals labeled mentally ill or associated with psychiatric treatment, current attitudes are more favorable and treatment is more humane than it previously was.

However, the quasi-medical or intrapsychic model has been faulted on several grounds. Some authors have noted that pessimism results from diagnosis and traditional formulation of the deviant behavior (Stuart, 1970). The problems clients express are reformulated in terms of personality or characterological defects, deficits, inabilities, or deeply rooted causes. The labels imply a permanent complex psychological state that is not readily alterable. Behavioral problems are attributed to defects in personality or psychological development. The defects are considered to be deeply rooted, making treatment an extremely elaborate endeavor. Of course, behavior change may never be a simple matter. Yet, attributing behavior to reified and complex inferred states makes behavior change even less straightforward than might otherwise be the case. Indeed, psychodynamic formulations of behavior probably have discouraged the direct alteration of behavior because of the inability to alter supposedly underlying causes in the individual.

The greatest and most frequent criticisms of the intrapsychic model have been leveled against Freud's psychodynamic position. Several authors have noted (1) the difficulty in scientifically establishing several of its propositions; (2) the inconsistencies within the theory itself and the therapeutic procedures derived from the theory; and (3) the lack of empirical support in many areas (for example, some features of child development) in which relevant research has been conducted (Bandura, 1969; London, 1964; Mischel, 1976; Stuart, 1970; Ullmann & Krasner, 1975). More lamentable, perhaps, is the relative sparsity of qualitative research on the viability of psychodynamic formulations. Some of its strongest supporters have noted their disappointment in this continuing scarcity of rigorous experimental evaluation (for example, Luborsky & Spence, 1978).

This being a textbook on behavior modification, it would be easy (and tempting) to render a lopsided evaluation—portraying psychodynamic approaches as misguided and unpromising while behavioral approaches are discussed with glowing optimism. Although tempting, such a polarity would be both inaccurate and misleading. Although some of the conjectures of Freud and his followers have not survived rigorous experimental scrutiny, it is equally clear that their enduring influence and stimulating hypotheses have been a major contribution to the field. Whatever else it may be, the enterprise of helping human beings is not a horse race between distinct ideologies. There are already signs of collaborative exchange and mutual respect between behavioral and psychodynamic theorists, and this may well be a promising sign of productive future integration (Garfield & Bergin, 1978; Garfield & Kurtz, 1976; Mahoney, 1979).

THE BEHAVIORAL APPROACH

The behavioral approach departs from the medical model and the intrapsychic views of behavior in a number of ways. As noted in previous chapters, some unique features of the behavioral approach are methodological, in terms of emphasis on assessment of behavior, objectification of concepts, evaluation of treatment interventions, and minimization of inferred variables. The behavioral approach tries to avoid unverifiable, unobservable inner states. However, it would be inaccurate to state that internal states are avoided altogether. Within the behavioral approach, various viewpoints differ on the extent to which inferred variables and inner states are utilized. For example, among operant conditioners, inferred variables are usually totally rejected. The focus is entirely on overt or publicly observable behavior. On the other hand, some behavior modifiers posit inferred or mediating variables to account for some overt behaviors. It is exceedingly important to distinguish the inferred variables posited by some behaviorists from intrapsychic notions. As noted in Chapter 3, inferred variables posited by behaviorists are amenable to objective assessment or have empirical ramifications. Anxiety, posited by some behavioral theorists (for example, Wolpe, 1958), can be assessed objectively, for example, through physiological means. Some behaviorists stress covert events, such as thoughts, self-verbalizations, and imagery, which mediate overt behavior. Yet the internal or private events are amenable to assessment, at least by the individual experiencing them. Moreover, overt procedures that alter private events can be observed publicly.

Despite differences among behaviorists, it is generally correct to state that the focus is on behavior rather than on underlying states. The inferred variables posited by behavior modifiers generally are more accessible both to the client who comes for treatment and to the therapist who undertakes a program of behavior change (Goldfried & Sprafkin, 1974; Rimm & Masters, 1979) than are psychodynamic states. For example, a client may wish to eliminate obsessive thoughts or undesirable urges. Although these are not overt behaviors, the behavioral focus would be on the occurrence of these thoughts or urges. Indeed, the client can observe the frequency of these thoughts to provide data for the therapist. The private event focused on here is accessible, at least to the client. Moreover, behavioral treatment will focus on the thoughts and urges themselves rather than on supposed sources of these covert events. In contrast, a psychodynamic view of the obsessional thoughts would hold that they reflect underlying dynamic processes; the thoughts would be considered signs of something else. They would not be taken as the problem itself.

The behavioral approach is concerned with the development, maintenance, and alteration of behavior. Abnormal behavior is not regarded as distinct from normal behavior in terms of how it develops or is maintained. Abnormal behavior does not represent a dysfunction or a disease process that has overtaken normal personality development. Rather, certain learning experiences or a failure to receive or profit from various learning experiences can account for behavior. Behavior develops according to the same principles, whether it is labeled normal or abnormal.[3]

Labeling behavior as abnormal is frequently based on subjective judgments rather than objective criteria (Bandura, 1969; Becker, 1963; Ferster,

---

3. This assumption, which is present in most variations of the behavioral model, has been much debated. Several alternative views have been suggested. The combining of the systemic medical model and a behavioral model is one example. Within such a model, schizophrenia may be viewed as a function of the interaction of a genetic predisposition with a particular type of environment. Unfortunately, with the vast majority of behavior disorders, research findings supporting such an approach are meager or nonexistent. Another point worth noting is that many psychologists successfully utilize behavior modification without making the assumption that the behavioral problem developed according to the same principles that are being used to change the behavior. Because reinforcement of a particular behavior leads to change in that behavior, one cannot argue that the behavior must have developed because it was reinforced; on the other hand, such a finding does not rule out the possibility that such a behavior developed because it was reinforced. This issue was raised in the example of the broom-holding woman in Chapter 1.

1965; Sarbin, 1967; Szasz, 1966; Ullmann & Krasner, 1965). A given behavior may be viewed by different people as abnormal or normal. For example, fighting among male children may be regarded as an expression of masculinity by peers and parents, but regarded as a sign of emotional disturbance by teachers and school counselors. Thus, the values of the individual who evaluates behavior play a major role in determining whether it is normal or deviant.

The social context is also important in determining whether a given behavior is regarded as deviant. Abnormal behavior is inferred from the degree to which behavior deviates from social norms (Mahoney, 1980; Scheff, 1966). Because social norms vary across cultures and across groups and settings within a given culture, it is difficult to posit objective criteria for abnormal behavior. For example, behaviors labeled by some as antisocial reflect patterns of behavior that are socially condoned and strongly supported in many peer groups where street fighting and theft are accepted activities. Labeling the behavior as antisocial and indicative of psychological disturbance is based on value judgments rather than on evidence of "diseased" psychological processes. There is no objective or value-free basis for claiming the behavior is "sick." Obviously, there are differences in behaviors across individuals. However, the differences probably reflect differences on a continuum rather than in terms of illness versus health.

The Behavioral Model and Learning

Behavior modification assumes that behavior, whether labeled abnormal or normal, depends to a great extent on environmental factors. The processes through which adaptive behaviors usually develop can explain the development of maladaptive or deviant behaviors as well. Moreover, therapeutic interventions involve training clients to engage in certain behaviors and not to engage in others, that is, to learn new modes of behaving. A goal of behavior modification is to provide learning experiences that promote adaptive and prosocial behavior.

To demonstrate how behavior is learned and how new behaviors can be taught, we will outline three types of learning which have played a major role in conceptualizing behavior and generating treatment techniques. The present discussion will merely outline them; in subsequent chapters, the various aspects of learning will be elaborated and additional processes that influence behavior will be discussed. As will be seen in Chapter 8, those factors and principles that affect the development and modification of behavior have been extended beyond the learning laboratory. Although behavior modifiers have historically drawn heavily from the learning area of psychology, current views are much broader, and it would be incorrect to assume that behavior modification is merely the application of principles of learning. However, for historical reasons and because of their widescale effective applications, we have incorporated basic learning principles in this chapter. A more comprehensive presentation of operant principles will be necessary for the applications discussed in Part Two.

Three types of learning have been considered important in explaining and altering behavior: classical or respondent conditioning, operant conditioning, and observational learning.

CLASSICAL CONDITIONING

Classical conditioning, extensively investigated by Ivan Pavlov (1848–1936), is concerned with stimuli that automatically evoke reflex responses. Some stimuli in the environment, such as noise, light, shock, and taste of food (referred to as unconditioned stimuli), *elicit* reflex responses (referred to as respondents). Respondents frequently are considered involuntary or autonomic responses that are not under control of the individual; this has recently become a much debated point. Examples of respondents include pupil constriction in response to bright light, flexion of a muscle in response to pain, or a startle reaction in response to loud noise. The relationship between the unconditioned stimulus and the response is automatic, or unlearned. A neutral stimulus, referred to as a conditioned stimulus, may be associated with the unconditioned stimulus that elicits the response. If a conditioned stimulus is paired with an unconditioned stimulus, the conditioned stimulus alone eventually elicits the response. *Classical conditioning refers to the process whereby new stimuli gain the power to elicit respondent behavior.* In classical conditioning, events or stimuli that *precede* behavior control a reflex response.

An example of classical conditioning has been provided by Watson and Rayner (1920), who demonstrated that fears could be learned. An eleven-month-old boy named Albert served as a subject. Albert freely played with a white rat without any adverse reaction. Prior to the actual conditioning, the investigators noted that a loud noise (unconditioned stimulus) produced a startle and fear reaction (unconditioned response) in Albert. To condition the startle reaction in response to the rat, the presence of the rat (neutral or conditioned stimulus) was immediately followed by the noise. When Albert reached out and touched the rat, the noise sounded and Albert was startled. Within a relatively short time, the presence of the rat alone elicited a startle reaction. The conditioned stimulus elicited the fear response (conditioned response). Interestingly, the fear generalized so that objects Albert had not feared previously, including a rabbit, a dog, a Santa Claus mask, a sealskin coat, cotton, and wool, also produced the fear reaction. This demonstrated that fears can be acquired through classical conditioning. (Of course, whether fears evident in everyday experience are in fact acquired through classical conditioning is difficult to say, because one rarely observes an individual at the time fears develop.)

OPERANT CONDITIONING

Much of human behavior is not involuntary or *elicited* by stimuli in the sense of reflexive reactions. Rather, behavior is *emitted* and is controlled primarily by the consequences that follow. Behaviors amenable to control by a change in the consequences that follow them are referred to as *operants,* because they are responses that operate on or have some influence on the environment and generate consequences (Skinner, 1953). Operants are strengthened or weakened as a function of the events that follow them. Most behaviors performed in everyday life are operants. They are not reflex responses elicited by stimuli. Operant behaviors include talking, reading, walking, working, smiling, or any response freely emitted. As will be apparent from reading the next two chapters, many complex human behaviors involve more than just emitting a response that has a consequence applied to it. Even from an operant standpoint, a more complex explanation is required; operant conditioning will be discussed in greater detail in Chapter 7.

DISTINGUISHING CLASSICAL AND OPERANT CONDITIONING

The distinction between classical and operant conditioning is obscure in many situations (Kimble, 1961). It has been thought that classical conditioning is restricted to involuntary behaviors whereas operant conditioning is restricted to voluntary behaviors. Yet a great deal of research has shown that such supposedly involuntary responses as heart rate, blood pressure, galvanic skin responses, intestinal contractions, and vasomotor reflexes can be altered through operant conditioning (Kimmel, 1967, 1974).

In everyday experience, the difficulty in distinguishing respondent and operant behaviors is evident. A response may be elicited (classical conditioning); it may also be controlled by the consequences that follow it (operant conditioning). For example, a child may cry in response to a painful fall. This crying is a respondent, or a reflexive response to pain. Once the crying begins, it may be sustained by its consequences, such as cuddling and effusive sympathy, and become an operant. It is sometimes difficult to separate operant from respondent crying.

This distinction between classical and operant conditioning seems vague also because operant behavior can be controlled by preceding stimuli. Operant behaviors are performed in certain situations with various cues present. When the consequences that follow behavior consistently occur in the presence of a particular set of cues, such as a certain person or place, the cues alone increase the probability that the behavior will be emitted. The stimuli that precede the response set the *occasion* for the response, or increase the likelihood that the response will occur. For example, the sound of music on the radio may serve as a stimulus for singing or dancing. This is not an example of classical conditioning because the preceding stimulus (music) does not *force* (elicit) the response (singing) to occur. In operant conditioning, the stimulus does not elicit or produce a response; it only increases the probability that the response will occur. The following major difference between classical and operant conditioning should be kept in mind. In classical conditioning, the primary result is a change in the power of a stimulus to *elicit* a reflex response. In operant conditioning, the primary result is a change in an *emitted* response.

Observational Learning

Observational or vicarious learning, or modeling (Bandura & Walters, 1963), includes both types of responses, respondents and operants. In observational learning, an individual observes a model's behavior but need not engage in overt responses or receive direct consequences. By observing a model, the observer may learn a response without actually performing it. Modeling can develop new responses and can alter the frequency of previously learned responses as well (Bandura, 1969; Rosenthal & Bandura, 1978).

To understand the effects of modeling, it is useful to distinguish *learning* from *performance*. The requirement for learning through modeling is the observation of a model. The modeled response is assumed to be acquired by the observer through a cognitive or covert coding of the observed events (Bandura, 1971). However, whether a learned response is *performed* may depend on response consequences or incentives associated with that response. The role of response consequences in dictating performance has been demonstrated by Bandura (1965). Children observed a film where an adult modeled aggressive responses (hitting and kicking a large doll). For some children, the model's aggression was rewarded; for others, aggression was punished; and for others, no consequences followed the model's behavior. When children had the opportunity to perform the aggressive responses, those who had observed the model being punished displayed less aggression than those who observed aggression being rewarded or ignored. To determine whether all children had *learned* the responses, an attractive incentive was subsequently given to children for performing aggressive responses. There were no differences in aggressive responses among the three groups. Apparently all groups learned the aggressive responses, but consequences to the model and observer determined whether they would be performed.

The effect of modeling on performance depends on other variables in addition to the consequences that follow the model's performance (Flanders, 1968; Rachman, 1972; Rosenthal & Bandura, 1978). Observers imitate models who are similar to themselves more than models who are less similar. Certain model characteristics also facilitate imitation. For example, greater imitation usually results from models who are high in prestige, status, or expertise. Imitation is also greater after observation of several models than after observation of a single model.

A classic example of modeling for purposes of treatment was reported by Jones (1924). A young boy, Peter, was afraid of a rabbit and several other furry objects (rat, fur coat, feather, cotton, wool). Peter was placed with three other children in a play situation in which a rabbit was present. The other children, who were unafraid of rabbits, freely interacted with the animal. Peter touched the rabbit immediately after observing others touching it. The example suggests the importance of modeling. However, other procedures were employed with Peter, such as associating the rabbit with the presence of food, so the precise contribution of modeling in reducing his fear is unclear.

The behavioral approach considers the majority of behaviors to be learned or alterable through the learning procedures outlined here. Attempts are made to alter behaviors that have been learned or to develop new behaviors rather than to alter psychological processes that traditionally have been assumed to underlie behavior. The behavioral view, like the medical model, has far-reaching implications for assessment and treatment of behavior problems.

Implications of the Behavioral View

The behavioral approach to assessment of behaviors departs from traditional diagnostic assessment (Arthur, 1969; Goldfried & Pomeranz, 1968; Mischel, 1968; Peterson, 1968), although they have some problems in common, such as reliability (Goldfried & Spraflin, 1974). The behavioral approach focuses directly on the behaviors that are to be altered rather than on the underlying personality. Although a problem may be described in vague or general terms (for example, hyperactivity), the behavior modifier seeks to observe the behavior that requires change and the events that prompted the diagnosis, the frequency of these behaviors, and the antecedent and consequent events associated with any outbursts. In short, assessment focuses on the behavior of the client as well as on environmental events. Assessment of the behavior to be changed (referred to as the *target behavior*) is essential to ascertain the extent of change that is required or the extent of the problem. Behaviors are not considered to reflect underlying psychological problems but are of direct interest in their own right. Sometimes the factors that precede and follow behavior are assessed. These factors may be useful in altering the target behavior. Events that precede behavior may include the presence of a particular person, instructions, and other cues in the environment that affect the response. This will be discussed in more detail in Chapter 9.

Behavior modifiers emphasize external events in the environment which can be used to alter behavior. This is not to say that events within the individual do not influence behavior. Indeed, internal events and covert behaviors, such as thoughts, feelings, and perceptions, can directly influence behavior. Behavior modifiers, however, disagree on the extent to which internal events are to be regarded as determinants of behavior.

It is important to distinguish the internal events sometimes focused on in behavior modification from the seemingly similar processes relied on by psychodynamic theorists. Psychodynamic theorists make inferences about underlying states that represent complex abstractions far removed from behavior. It is difficult and frequently impossible to verify that the internal state is or could be related to overt behavior. Few predictions can be made that could be subjected to scientific scrutiny. In contrast, behavior modifiers attempt to relate covert or underlying events closely to observable phenomena. In addition, predictions are made about the relationship between covert events and overt behavior. For example, some behavior modifiers believe that things people say to themselves privately ("I can't do that" or "I am incompetent") dictate performance. The influence of self-statements can be examined empirically by altering what people say to themselves and seeing whether this affects overt behavior (Craighead & Craighead, 1980; Meichenbaum, 1977). The role of such covert, cognitive, and mediational factors in behavior is discussed in Chapter 8.

It is considered unlikely that altering a problematic behavior will result in its replacement by another problem behavior, as in symptom substitution. Behaviorists do not consider problematic behavior a reflection of supposed psychic impulses that seek expression. In fact, behaviorists predict that once a particular problem behavior is altered for an individual, other aspects of his or her life and behaviors may improve as well. The beneficial effects of treating one behavior may *generalize* to other behaviors. If a stutterer is trained to speak more fluently, it can be expected that additional positive changes will result. The person may become more confident and extroverted, and less shy. Resolution of one problem may begin a series of favorable changes in a person's life. The notion of symptom substitution has little support. In contrast, several studies with diverse behavioral techniques confirm the generalization of beneficial effects to behaviors not originally included in treatment (Kazdin, 1973b; Mahoney et al., 1974). Of course, it is possible that a person who has one behavior altered will still have additional problems. However, this is far removed from the notion of symptom substitution. New problematic behaviors are not necessarily re-expressions of psychic conflicts. Treatment, whether medical or psychological in nature, is no guarantee against the development of further problems. For example, repairing a broken limb does not guarantee the absence of future injuries of a similar nature. Problematic behaviors may appear as a result of psychological treatment. It is possible, for example, that once deviant behavior is reduced, the person may have no appropriate response in his or her repertoire to take its place (Cahoon, 1968). The deficit may be evident in continued inappropriate social behaviors. If this occurs, it is frequently the result of poor assessment whereby all the problem areas are not evaluated, and thus the treatment program employed is inappropriate and too limited. This deficit can be corrected by a treatment program that develops appropriate behaviors while eliminating inappropriate ones.

SUMMARY

This chapter provides an outline of different models of behavior. The medical model can be broken down into three types: infectious, systemic, and traumatic. The quasi-medical or intrapsychic model is based on the systemic and traumatic medical models; however, it is only the structure of the medical model and not its content that is utilized. Thus, just as physical symptoms are considered to have underlying physical causes, the intrapsychic model assumes that deviant behavior has underlying psychological causes. The most popular intrapsychic model has been the psychoanalytic model proposed by Freud. In both assessment and treatment, the emphasis has been on the underlying psychological causes rather than on the deviant behavior.

The typical behavioral model assumes that all behaviors (those labeled normal as well as abnormal) develop according to the same principles. In both assessment and treatment the emphasis is on the problem behavior and the internal and external events associated with it. The importance of learning is stressed in the behavioral model. Learning is emphasized because it has in fact played a major role in behavior modification. However, as a general approach, behavior modification is not restricted to particular theories or orientations. The characteristic feature of behavior modification is the application of empirical findings for the purpose of behavior change. The content of behavior modification cannot be definitely specified because empirical findings and the science of behavior are constantly expanding. Nevertheless, subsequent chapters will detail the findings and principles currently included in the realm of behavior modification.

SUGGESTED READINGS

Hall, C. S., & Lindzey, G. *Theories of personality.* (2nd ed.). New York: Wiley, 1970.

Krasner, L., & Ullmann, L. P. *Behavior influence and personality: The social matrix of human action.* New York: Holt, Rinehart and Winston, 1973. Chapters 1–6.

Mischel, W. *Introduction to personality.* (2nd ed.). New York: Holt, 1976.

Sarason, I. G. *Personality: An objective approach.* (2nd ed.). New York: Wiley, 1972.

CHAPTER 7

PRINCIPLES OF
OPERANT CONDITIONING

Behavior modification relies on a body of established findings from psychology, many of which derive from the psychology of learning. In the previous chapter, types of learning were discussed. The present chapter describes the principles of operant conditioning in greater detail because several techniques of behavior modification have been based on these principles. In the next chapter, empirical findings from cognitive and other areas of psychology will be discussed.

The principles of operant conditioning describe the relationship between behavior and various environmental events (antecedents and consequences) that influence behavior. Although both antecedents and consequences can alter behavior, most applications of operant-conditioning principles emphasize the *consequences* that follow behavior. Behavior change occurs when certain consequences are *contingent* upon performance. A consequence is contingent when it is delivered only after the target behavior is performed.

In everyday life, many consequences are contingent upon behavior. For example, wages are contingent upon working and grades are contingent upon studying for exams. A *contingency refers to the relationship between a behavior and the events that follow the behavior.* The notion of contingency is important because behavior-modification techniques often alter behavior by altering the contingencies that control or fail to control a particular behavior.

Before we take a detailed look at the principles of operant conditioning, it may be helpful to clarify some common misconceptions by presenting an overview of the principles. In order to avoid confusion of terms, it is essential to distinguish between the label for an event or stimulus and the label for the principle that describes what occurs when an event or stimulus is used in a contingent manner. For example, the confusion surrounding the principle of negative reinforcement has largely resulted from the failure to distinguish between a negative reinforcer—that is, a stimulus or event—and negative reinforcement. Events or stimuli traditionally have been classified as positive reinforcers and negative reinforcers (aversive stimuli). Each class of stimuli or events may have different effects on the frequency of a behavior; the effect is determined by whether a stimulus or event is applied or removed following the occurrence of a behavior.

As can be seen in Figure 7.1, *positive reinforcement,* an increase in the frequency of behavior, occurs when a positive reinforcer is contingently applied or presented. *Negative reinforcement,* also an increase in the frequency of a behavior, occurs when a negative reinforcer is contingently removed. Thus, the *principle of reinforcement* always refers to an *increase* in the frequency of a response when it is followed by a contingent stimulus or event. Likewise, the *principle of punishment* always refers to a *decrease* in the frequency of a response when it is followed by a contingent stimulus or event. Again, as shown in Figure 7.1, there are two types of punish-

	APPLIED	REMOVED
POSITIVE REINFORCER	POSITIVE REINFORCEMENT	PUNISHMENT BY REMOVAL
NEGATIVE REINFORCER	PUNISHMENT BY APPLICATION	NEGATIVE REINFORCEMENT

Figure 7.1 Principles of operant conditioning based upon whether positive or negative reinforcers are applied or removed after a response is performed.

ment.[1] Several labels have been suggested for the two types of punishment; we prefer the following ones because they seem most clearly related to the procedures. *Punishment by removal,* a *decrease* in the frequency of a response, occurs when a positive reinforcer is contingently removed. *Punishment by application,* also a *decrease* in the frequency of a response, occurs when a negative reinforcer is contingently applied.

REINFORCEMENT

Reinforcement refers to the presentation of a positive reinforcer or the removal of a negative reinforcer after a response which increases the frequency of that response. The event that follows behavior must be contingent upon behavior. Again, we have noted there are two types of reinforcement: positive reinforcement and negative reinforcement.

Positive Reinforcement

Positive reinforcement refers to an increase in the frequency of a response that is followed by a positive reinforcer. It is important to distinguish the term *positive reinforcer* from *reward*. A *positive reinforcer* is defined by its effect on behavior. If an event follows behavior and the frequency of behavior increases, the event is a positive reinforcer. Any event that does not increase the behavior it follows is not a positive reinforcer. An increase in the frequency of the preceding behavior is the defining characteristic of a positive reinforcer. In contrast, *rewards* are defined as something given or received in return for service, merit, or achievement. Although rewards are subjectively highly valued, they do not necessarily increase the frequency of the behavior they follow. Many events that a person evaluates favorably may serve as reinforcers, yet this cannot be known on the basis of verbal statements alone. Moreover, there may be many reinforcers available for an individual of which he or she is unaware or which he or she does not consider as rewards. For example, in some situations, verbal reprimands inadvertently serve as positive reinforcers because they provide attention for a response. Behaviors followed by reprimands may increase

1. These distinctions regarding punishment and questions regarding whether punishment by removal is in fact punishment have been much argued. Because of the practical advantages and because much of the research has been based on the distinctions presented in Figure 7.1, we have chosen to present the material in this fashion.

(Madsen, Becker, Thomas, Koser, & Plager, 1968). Even though reprimands may sometimes serve as positive reinforcers, most people would
not refer to them as rewards. Thus, a reward is not synonymous with a
positive reinforcer. Whether an event is a positive reinforcer is empirically determined. Only if the frequency of a particular behavior increases
when the event immediately follows the behavior is the event a positive
reinforcer.

There are many examples of positive reinforcement in everyday life. (Of
course, rarely does anyone systematically measure whether a favorable
event that followed behavior increased the frequency of that behavior.) A
student who studies for an examination and receives an A is probably reinforced, and studying is likely to increase in the future because it was reinforced by an excellent grade. Winning money at a slot machine usually
increases the frequency of putting money into the machine and pulling the
lever. Money is a powerful reinforcer that increases performance of a variety of behaviors.

Positive reinforcers include any event that increases the frequency of the
behavior it follows. There are two categories of positive reinforcers,
namely, primary or unconditioned, and secondary or conditioned, reinforcers. Stimuli that do not require a person to learn their reinforcing
value are *primary reinforcers.* For example, food and water serve as primary
reinforcers to hungry and thirsty people. Primary reinforcers may not be
reinforcing all of the time. For example, food will not reinforce someone
who has just finished a large meal. However, when food does serve as a
reinforcer, its value is automatic, or unlearned, and does not depend on
previous association with any other reinforcers.

Some events that control behavior, such as praise, grades, money, and
completion of a goal, become reinforcers through learning. *Secondary reinforcers* are not automatically reinforcing. Events that once were neutral in
value may acquire reinforcing properties as a result of being paired with
events that are already reinforcing (either primary or other conditioned
reinforcers). If a neutral stimulus is repeatedly presented prior to or along
with a reinforcing stimulus, the neutral stimulus becomes a reinforcer. For
example, praise may not be reinforcing for some people; it may be a neutral
stimulus for them, rather than a positive reinforcer. If praise is to be established as a reinforcer, it must be paired with an event that is reinforcing, such as food or money. After several pairings of the delivery of food
with praise, the praise alone serves as a reinforcer and can be used to
increase the frequency of other responses.

Some conditioned reinforcers are paired with several other reinforcers
and are referred to as *generalized conditioned reinforcers.* Generalized conditioned reinforcers are extremely effective in altering behaviors because
they are paired with a variety of events rather than just one. Money is a
good example of a generalized conditioned reinforcer. It is a *conditioned* or

secondary reinforcer because its reinforcing value is acquired through learning. It is a *generalized* reinforcer because a variety of reinforcing events contributes to its value. Additional examples of generalized conditioned reinforcers include attention, approval, and affection from others (Skinner, 1953). These are generalized reinforcers because their occurrence is often associated with a variety of other reinforcing events. For example, attention from someone may be followed by physical contact, praise, smiles, affection, or delivery of tangible rewards, such as food.

In behavior-modification programs, generalized reinforcers in the form of *tokens* are used frequently (Kazdin, 1977b). The tokens may consist of poker chips, coins, tickets, stars, points, or check marks. Tokens serve as generalized reinforcers because they can be exchanged for other things or events which are reinforcing. For example, in a psychiatric institution, residents receive tokens for attending group activities, socializing with others, grooming, and bathing. The tokens may be exchanged for snacks, cigarettes, and privileges, such as watching television and attending social events. The strength of tokens derives from these reinforcers which back up their value. The events or stimuli that tokens can purchase are referred to as *back-up reinforcers*. Generalized conditioned reinforcers, such as money or tokens, are more powerful than any single reinforcer because they can purchase a variety of back-up reinforcers.

Reinforcing events include *stimuli,* such as praise, smiles, food, or money, which are presented to an individual after a response. However, reinforcers are not limited to stimuli. Allowing an individual to engage in certain *responses* also can serve as a reinforcer. Certain responses can be used to reinforce other responses. Premack (1965) demonstrated that behaviors that have a high probability of occurring can reinforce behaviors with a relatively low probability of occurring. If the opportunity to perform a high-probability response is made contingent upon performance of a low-probability response, the frequency of the lower-probability response will increase. It is important to note that Premack was speaking of high and low probability of behaviors and not high and low frequency of behaviors. The probability of a behavior is measured in a situation that is relatively free of extraneous contingencies. For example, if your choice of pizza over sirloin is not influenced by such factors as availability, your budget, or a friend's insistence, then your choice is contingency-free. Behaviors can be high in frequency without accurately reflecting your preferences; paying taxes, attending nonbehavioral lectures, and cleaning house are examples.

In ingenious laboratory experiments, Premack (1962) altered the probability of rats' drinking and running behaviors by depriving them of access to water or to an activity wheel. When rats were deprived of water (which made drinking a high-probability behavior), drinking would reinforce running (a low-probability response). When the animals were deprived of activity (which made running a high-probability behavior), running would reinforce drinking. In each case, a lower-probability behavior was increased or reinforced by following it with a high-probability behavior. At different times, drinking was the higher-probability response and running the lower-probability response, and vice versa.

On the basis of the foregoing laboratory work, the *Premack principle* was formulated as follows: *Of any pair of responses or activities in which an individual engages, the more probable one will reinforce the less probable one.* For example, for most children, playing with friends is more probable than completing homework. If the higher-probability behavior (playing with friends) is made contingent upon the lower-probability behavior (completing homework), the lower-probability behavior will increase.

Mitchell and Stoffelmayr (1973) applied the Premack principle to increase the activity of psychiatric patients who were inactive on the hospital ward. The patients usually sat or paced on the ward rather than engage in some of the work activities that were available. The two behaviors relevant for the Premack principle were inactivity, or sitting, (higher-probability behavior) and working on a task, wire stripping (lower-probability behavior). To increase work, sitting was made contingent upon doing some work. A criterion was set for completing work before patients earned the opportunity to sit down. The amount of work required to earn the opportunity to sit was increased gradually. Work increased when it was followed with sitting in this fashion.

A variety of behaviors, such as engaging in recreational activities, hobbies, going on trips, or being with friends, are relatively more probable responses and usually can serve as reinforcers for other behaviors. To employ the Premack principle, the target response must be of a lower probability than the behavior used to reinforce that reponse.

Antecedent as well as consequent events affect the occurrence of behaviors. Antecedent stimuli serve as cues signaling that the reinforcer will follow a behavior. Such a stimulus, which marks or indicates the time and place that a response will be reinforced, is called a discriminative stimulus or an S^D. Such stimuli affect our lives every day. One needs only to visualize the grocery market to see how buying behavior is affected by the stimuli that precede it; for example, think of the cookie shelf or the check-out counter. Both contain stimuli that are likely to increase buying responses.

Negative Reinforcement

Negative Reinforcement refers to an increase in the frequency of a response following removal of a negative reinforcer (aversive event or stimulus) immediately after the response occurs. An event is a *negative reinforcer* only if its removal after a response increases performance of that response. Events that appear to be annoying, undesirable, or unpleasant are not necessarily negative reinforcers. A negative reinforcer is defined solely by its effect on behavior.

It is important to note that reinforcement, whether positive or negative, always *increases* a behavior. Negative reinforcement requires an ongoing aversive event which can be removed or terminated after a specific response occurs. A familiar example of negative reinforcement is putting on a coat while standing outside on a cold day. Putting on a coat (the behavior) usually terminates an aversive condition, namely, being cold (negative reinforcer). The probability of wearing a coat in cold weather is increased. Similarly, taking medicine to relieve a headache may be negatively reinforced by the termination of pain. Of course, whether negative reinforcement occurs in the foregoing examples depends on whether or not the behavior that terminates the undesirable condition increases.

An interesting example of a negative reinforcement was reported in a study with a socially withdrawn psychiatric patient (Fichter, Wallace, Liberman, & Davis, 1976). The purpose of treatment was to increase the patient's voice volume and duration of his speech because he spoke inaudibly and only for brief intervals. Nagging was the aversive event and consisted of staff constantly reminding the patient to speak louder or for longer periods during conversations with them. If the patient did not comply within three seconds, he was nagged again. From the patient's perspective, the appropriate behavior (louder and longer speech) avoided further nagging. Thus, avoidance of the aversive event was the basis for changing behavior. The results showed that each of the behaviors that the staff nagged the client to perform increased with the avoidance contingency.

Negative reinforcement requires some aversive event, such as shock, noise, or isolation, which is presented to the individual before he or she responds. The event is removed or reduced immediately after a response. As with positive reinforcers, there are two types of negative reinforcers: primary and secondary. Intense stimuli, such as shock or loud noise, which impinge on the sensory receptors of an organism serve as *primary negative reinforcers*. The aversive response to them is unlearned. Secondary negative reinforcers, or *conditioned aversive events,* become aversive by being paired with events which already are aversive. For example, disapproving facial expressions or saying the word *no* can serve as aversive events after being paired with events that are already aversive (Lovaas, Schaeffer, & Simmons, 1965).

One type of negative reinforcement occurs when an individual *escapes* from an aversive situation. Both classical and operant conditioning may be involved. An aversive stimulus or event may elicit an escape response (classical conditioning) that serves to terminate the aversive stimulus or event (operant conditioning). Escape behaviors gradually occur earlier and earlier as the individual approaches the aversive stimuli, and eventually the individual avoids the aversive situation. This avoidance response is maintained and the individual stays out of the aversive situation. Escape and avoidance responses may be learned by a combination of a number of the factors we have summarized to this point. In everyday life, various secondary negative reinforcers may gain the power to elicit escape responses and therefore lead to avoidance responses. These factors interact in simple ways at some times and in complex ways at other times.

As with positive reinforcement, antecedent or discriminative stimuli may affect behavior. Such stimuli signal the individual that negative reinforcement will follow a response; that is, if the response occurs a negative reinforcer will be terminated. Thus, a camper who hears a bear growl may make an avoidance response, or a new mail carrier who sees your "beware the dog" sign may not deliver your mail. Several other examples from everyday experience show that avoidance behavior is under the control of antecedent stimuli, such as air raid sirens, screeching car tires, threats, and traffic signals.

PUNISHMENT

Punishment refers to the presentation of an aversive stimulus or event or the removal of a positive event after a response which decreases the probability of that response. This definition diverges from the everyday use of the term, in which punishment refers merely to a penalty imposed for performing a particular act. For an event to meet the technical definition of punishment, the frequency of the response must decrease (Azrin & Holz, 1966). Because of the negative connotations frequently associated with punishment, it is important to dispel some stereotypic notions that do not apply to the technical definition of punishment. Punishment does not necessarily entail pain or physical coercion. Punishment is neither a means of retribution nor a retaliation for misbehaving. Sometimes in everyday life, "punishment" is employed independently of its effects on subsequent behavior. For example, children are "taught a lesson" for misbehaving by undergoing a sacrifice of some kind. Similarly, criminals may receive penalties that do not necessarily decrease the frequency of their criminal acts. In the technical sense, punishment is defined solely by its effect on behavior. Punishment is operative only if the frequency of a response is reduced.

There are two types of punishment. First, an aversive stimulus can be applied after a response; this is *punishment by application*. Familiar examples include being reprimanded or spanked after engaging in some behavior, or being burned after touching a hot stove. Whether these examples from everyday life qualify as punishment depends on whether they decrease the frequency of the preceding response. Second, a positive reinforcer can be removed after a response; this is *punishment by removal*. Examples include losing privileges after staying out late, losing money for misbehaving, and having one's driver's license revoked.

There are a variety of conditions that may influence the effectiveness of punishment. As you will see, the satisfaction of these conditions in nonlaboratory applications of punishment is often quite difficult. Generally, each of the following enhances the suppressive effects of punishment:

1. *Immediate* application or removal of the contingent stimulus after the undesired response
2. Punishment of each and every occurrence of the response
3. Introduction of the contingent punishing stimulus at maximal intensity, rather than with gradual increases in severity
4. Removal of motivation for the undesired response
5. Training of an alternative, acceptable response, especially when the motivation for the undesired response cannot be eliminated
6. Reinforcement of responses that are incompatible with the punished response
7. In humans, a description of the punishment contingency

Aside from the question of its effectiveness, there are a number of side effects from punishment that have caused its use in applied settings to be questioned. Some of these side effects are (1) increased emotional responding, (2) avoidance of the punishing agent, and (3) imitation of the use of punishment. (In many instances, positive side effects have also been reported, however.) It is frequently argued that, whenever possible, positive reinforcement of a behavior incompatible with the one to be decreased should be employed. Another alternative to punishment is the use of extinction. However, there are some situations that require the use of punishment. For example, head banging must be decreased quickly, and punishment is frequently employed. Even then, positive reinforcement programs for alternative behaviors should be used concurrently with punishment procedures.

To summarize, behaviors are affected by contingent consequences. Reinforcement refers to procedures that increase the frequency of a response, whereas punishment refers to procedures that decrease a response. There are two kinds of reinforcement: positive and negative. There are two kinds of punishment: punishment by application and punishment by removal. It is important to note the distinction between negative reinforcement and punishment. The Premack principle demonstrates that a high-probability response may be used to reinforce a low-probability response. Behaviors may also increase as a function of their antecedents, that is, stimulus control.

OPERANT EXTINCTION

Operant extinction refers to a reduction in response frequency following the cessation of reinforcement. A previously reinforced behavior will decrease when it ceases to produce positive reinforcers or to terminate negative reinforcers.[2] Technically speaking, extinction is the process of "disconnecting" the prior relationship between a response and its consequences. It is common, however, for people to use the term in reference to its effects. When this occurs, the term *extinction* may be inappropriately used as a synonym for *reduction*. For example, parents might say that they "extinguished" their child's swearing behavior. This usage is misleading for two reasons. First, it overlooks the fact that other procedures, such as punishment, also reduce behavior, but would hardly be called extinction. Bear in mind that in punishment, a response is followed by the presentation or removal of a stimulus. In extinction, no such change occurs—the response is not followed by any contingent environmental change.

Extinction should also be kept distinct from *recovery*. Recovery refers to the increase in behavior that may occur with a cessation of punishment. A previously punished response may increase when it ceases to produce negative stimuli or to cause the removal of positive stimuli. For example, in the absence of any other changes, the suspension of fines for speeding may increase the frequency of that behavior. Recovery undoubtedly occurs in applied settings, but usually there is an attempt to minimize its effect. On the other hand, extinction is a widely used principle upon which several clinical procedures are based.

In everyday life, the most common use of extinction is ignoring a behavior that may have been reinforced previously with attention. A parent may ignore a whining child. A physician may ignore the complaints of a hypochondriac. A teacher may ignore children who talk without raising their hands. A therapist or counselor may ignore certain self-defeating statements made by the client. In each of these examples, the prior reinforcer (attention, approval, or sympathy) for the response is no longer

2. The situation described here is one in which a response has previously terminated an ongoing negative reinforcer. In extinction, the negative reinforcer would be ongoing, but the previously learned response would no longer terminate it. This should not be confused with the situation wherein the organism, by totally avoiding the negative reinforcer, precludes the opportunity for extinction to occur.

presented. The following are additional examples of extinction: putting money into vending machines (the behavior) will cease if gum, food, or drink (the reinforcer) is not forthcoming; turning on a radio will cease if the radio no longer functions; and attempting to start a car will extinguish, if the car will not start. In these examples, the consequences that maintain the behavior are no longer forthcoming. The absence of reinforcing consequences reduces the behavior. In clinical applications, the stimuli or events that previously reinforced the behavior must be identified so that their occurrences can be controlled. It is important to note that extinction frequently results in a temporary increase in the behavior and a subsequent decrease. However, such an extinction burst, or temporarily increased response rate, does not always occur when extinction is employed.

In clinical applications, the stimuli or events that previously reinforced the behavior must be identified so that their occurrence can be controlled. Once the reinforcer is withheld, a temporary *increase* in behavior may occur. This increase, referred to as a *burst* of responses, usually subsides quickly and behavior decreases. For example, Wright, Brown, and Andrews (1978) treated a nine-month-old girl who constantly engaged in ruminative vomiting (regurgitating food after eating). The girl weighed only eight pounds, even though normal weight for her age would be about twenty pounds. The girl received little nourishment from her meals because of her excessive vomiting. Constant attention was provided to the girl for her vomiting. An extinction contingency was initiated in which the staff was instructed to leave the child's presence and not to attend to her when she began to vomit. At the beginning of extinction, there was an increase in episodes of vomiting. Fortunately, the burst lasted only two days and was followed by a decrease in vomiting and an increase in weight. The gains achieved in treatment were evident over a year later when follow-up information was obtained.

REINFORCEMENT SCHEDULES

Reinforcement schedules are the rules describing the manner in which consequences follow behavior. Reinforcement is always administered according to some schedule. In the simplest schedule, the response is reinforced each time it occurs. When each instance of a response is reinforced, the schedule is called *continuous reinforcement.* If reinforcement is provided only after some instances of a response but not after each response, the schedule is called *intermittent reinforcement.*

Continuous- and intermittent-reinforcement schedules produce important differences in performance. These differences are most apparent at three stages in learning. First, during the initial development of a response, continuous reinforcement is preferable because it accelerates this early performance and produces higher rates of responding. At the second stage, however, when response maintenance is an important consideration, intermittent schedules of reinforcement result in dramatically higher performance rates. Although continuous reinforcement is more efficient during response acquisition, intermittent reinforcement is generally preferable for response maintenance. Another advantage of intermittent reinforcement becomes apparent in the third stage (extinction). When a previous response-reinforcer relationship is terminated, extinction will occur fairly rapidly if the response was on a continuous-reinforcement schedule. If the response was maintained by intermittent reinforcement, however, the rate of extinction will be much slower. That is, the individual will respond more frequently and for a longer period of time. This phenomenon is often expressed by saying that intermittent-reinforcement schedules increase *resistance to extinction*. The advantages of that resistance will become more apparent as we discuss clinical applications.

The different effects of continuous and intermittent reinforcement are apparent in everyday experience. Examples of relatively continuous reinforcement might be opening the refrigerator (assuming that it always contains goodies) or placing a favorite album on a stereo turntable. Examples of intermittent reinforcement include casting a fishing line into the water (which does not always result in a fish) or entering a lottery (which seldom results in winning a prize). The different effects of continuous and intermittent reinforcement are well illustrated by looking at responses made in the presence of vending and slot machines. Vending machines require a response (placing coins into a slot and pulling a lever) that is reinforced with a stimulus (cigarettes or candy) virtually every time. Thus, there is continuous reinforcement. When a reinforcer is no longer provided for putting in coins and pulling a lever, rapid extinction follows. As soon as the reinforcer, or the product, is no longer delivered, performance most likely stops immediately. Few individuals would place more coins into the machine. Behaviors associated with slot machines reveal a very different pattern. The response (putting money into a machine and pulling a lever) is only intermittently reinforced with "jackpot" money. If money were never delivered, the response would eventually extinguish. With an intermittent schedule, and especially one in which the reinforcer is delivered very infrequently, responding may continue for a long time.

Although the major emphasis in schedules research has been on reinforcement, it is worth mentioning that punishment can also be scheduled in the same ways as reinforcement. There are some differences in the resulting performances, but in general what we have written about reinforcement schedules can be inverted and applied to punishment schedules.

Most relevant, perhaps, is the generality that intermittent punishment tends to increase resistance to recovery; that is, it suppresses the undesired response for longer periods than does continuous punishment. Since our current understanding and application of schedules is considerably more extensive for reinforcement than for punishment, we will restrict our focus to that area.

Intermittent reinforcement can be scheduled in a variety of ways. First, reinforcers can be delivered after the emission of a certain *number* of responses. This type of delivery is referred to as a *ratio schedule* because the schedule specifies the number of responses required for each reinforcement. Second, reinforcers can be delivered on the basis of the *time interval* that separates available reinforcers. This is referred to as an *interval schedule,* meaning that the response will be reinforced after a specified time interval.

The delivery of reinforcers on either ratio or interval schedules can be *fixed* (unvarying) or *variable* (constantly changing). Thus, four simple schedules of reinforcement can be distinguished, namely, fixed ratio, variable ratio, fixed interval, and variable interval. Each of these schedules leads to a different pattern of performance.

A *fixed ratio schedule* requires that a certain number of responses occur prior to delivery of the reinforcer. For example, a fixed ratio 2 schedule (FR:2) denotes that every second response is reinforced. A *variable ratio schedule* also requires that a certain number of responses occur prior to delivery of the reinforcer. However, the number varies around an *average* from one reinforcement to the next. On the average, a specific number of responses are required for reinforcement. For example, a variable ratio 5 schedule (VR:5) means that on the average every fifth response is reinforced. Over 10 trials, the required number of responses for reinforcement might be as follows: 2, 4, 7, 5, 3, 3, 9, 8, 5, 4. If you calculate the average of these numbers, it will be 5. On any given trial, however, the organism does not know how many responses are required.

Performance differs under fixed and variable ratio reinforcement schedules. On fixed schedules, typically there is a temporary pause in response after reinforcement occurs and then a rapid rise in response rate until the number of responses required for reinforcement is reached. The length of the pause after reinforcement is a function of the ratio specified by the schedule. Larger ratios produce longer pauses. In contrast, variable ratio schedules lead to fairly consistent performance and relatively constant response rates. Because of the unpredictable schedule, performance rates tend to be relatively high.

Interval schedules can be either fixed or variable. A *fixed interval schedule* requires that an unvarying time interval must pass before the reinforcer is available. The first response to occur after this interval is reinforced. For example, in a fixed interval 1 schedule (FI:1), where the number refers to minutes, reinforcement is produced by the first response occurring after 1 minute has elapsed. An interval schedule requires that only one response occur after the interval elapses. Any responses occurring before the interval elapses are not reinforced. With a *variable interval schedule,* the length of the interval varies around an average. For example, in a variable interval 4 schedule (VI:4), reinforcers might become available after the following number of minutes: 6, 4, 4, 2, 7, 5, 4, 1, 3, 4. Notice that the average is 4 minutes. The interval units may vary from seconds to weeks, depending on the organism and the response. The first response after the interval elapses is reinforced.

Performance differs under fixed and variable interval schedules. Fixed interval schedules tend to lead to marked pauses after the reinforcer is delivered. Unlike the pattern in fixed ratio schedules, responding after the pause is only gradually resumed—the organism often learns to wait until the interval is almost over. After extensive training, fixed ratio and fixed interval performances may look very similar. With variable ratio schedules, pauses are usually absent and performance is more consistent. In general, the rate of response is higher for variable than for fixed interval schedules.

Among the four simple schedules, it is worth noting that higher rates of response usually are achieved with ratio rather than interval schedules. This is understandable because high response rates do not necessarily speed up the delivery of reinforcement in an interval schedule as they do with ratio schedules. Moreover, variable schedules tend to produce more consistent response patterns, that is, they are not marked by the all-or-none pauses and response bursts of fixed schedules.

The various intermittent schedules are important for developing resistance to extinction. Variable schedules are particularly effective in prolonging extinction. As performance is achieved under a particular schedule, the schedule can be made "leaner" by gradually requiring more responses (ratio) or longer periods of time (interval) prior to reinforcement. With very lean schedules, few reinforcers need to be delivered to maintain a high level of performance. The shift from a "dense" or more generous schedule to a lean one, however, must be made gradually to avoid extinction.

Examples of reinforcement schedules are not difficult to find in everyday experience. Individuals who fish, hunt, gamble, enter lotteries, or work for commissions are familiar with variable ratio schedules. Each response is not reinforced. These behaviors are under ratio reinforcement schedules because the reinforcer—if it follows at all—will come only after numerous responses. A number of situations demonstrate interval scheduling. For example, television programs, buses, and wages frequently occur at particular intervals that are relatively fixed. Performance under fixed interval schedules is often marked by all-or-none patterns, such as last-minute cramming for exams and postexamination pauses. (For a more detailed discussion of reinforcement schedules, the reader is referred to the Suggested Readings.)

SHAPING

New behavior cannot always be developed by reinforcing a response. In many cases, the desired response may never occur. The behavior may be so complex that its component elements are not in the repertoire of the individual. For example, developing appropriate eating behavior requires, among other things, selecting and using appropriate utensils, which may not be in the repertoire of very young children. *Shaping* refers to reinforcing small steps or approximations toward a terminal response rather than reinforcing the terminal response itself. Responses that resemble the final response or that include components of that response are reinforced. Through reinforcement of *successive approximations* of the terminal response, the final response is gradually achieved. Responses that are increasingly similar to the final response (goal) are reinforced and they increase, while those responses dissimilar to the final response are not reinforced and they extinguish.

One of the most familiar examples of shaping is training animals to perform various tricks. If the animal trainer waited until the tricks were performed to administer a reinforcer, the reinforcer might never be delivered. However, by shaping the response, the trainer can achieve the terminal goal. Initially, food may be delivered for running toward the trainer. As that response becomes stable, the trainer may reinforce running up to the trainer when he or she is holding the hoop. Other steps closer to the final goal would be reinforced in sequence, such as walking through the hoop on the ground, jumping through the hoop when it is slightly off the ground, and jumping through the hoop when it is high off the ground. Eventually, the terminal response will be performed with a high frequency, whereas the unnecessary responses or steps developed along the way will have extinguished.

Shaping requires reinforcing behaviors that resemble the terminal response or approximate the goal. As the initial approximation is performed consistently, the criterion for reinforcement is altered slightly so that the next response resembles the final goal more closely than did the previous response. This procedure is continued until the terminal response is developed.

CHAINING

Behaviors can be divided into a sequence of responses referred to as a *chain*. The components of a chain represent individual responses which may already be in the behavioral repertoire of the individual. The unique feature of a chain is that individual responses are ordered in a particular sequence. The behavior of attending a party illustrates the ordering of component responses in a chain. Going to a party may be initiated by a call from someone or by a written invitation. Once the behavior is initiated, several responses follow in sequence, including getting dressed for the party, leaving the house, entering a car, traveling to the party, parking the car, entering the house, and eating, drinking, and socializing. The response sequence unfolds in a relatively fixed order until the chain is completed and the last response is reinforced (eating, drinking, and socializing may serve as the reinforcers). Later responses in the chain (entering the house where the party is) are preceded by a series of responses (traveling in the car and so on). The order is fixed so that early responses must precede later ones. Each response in the chain does not appear to be reinforced. Only the last response (the response immediately preceding eating, drinking, and socializing) is followed by the reinforcers. Because a reinforcer alters or sustains only the behavior that immediately precedes it, it is unclear what maintains the entire chain of behaviors leading to the final response. However, there are many chains of responses that are maintained in everyday experience. For example, mastering a musical instrument or preparing for athletic competition both require a series of intermediate responses before the final reinforcing event is achieved. The major question is what maintains all the intermediate responses that precede achievement of the final goal. The answer requires explanation of the factors that link the response components of a chain.

An important concept which is basic to understanding chains is that an event or stimulus that immediately precedes reinforcement becomes a cue or a signal for reinforcement. As noted earlier, an event that signals reinforcement for a particular response is referred to as a discriminative stimulus (S^D). An S^D sets the *occasion* for behavior; that is, it increases the probability that a previously reinforced behavior will occur. Yet, an S^D serves another function as well. An S^D not only signals reinforcement but eventually becomes a reinforcer itself. With frequent pairing of an S^D and a reinforcer, the S^D gradually develops reinforcing properties of its own. This procedure was mentioned in the discussion of conditioned reinforcement. The discriminative-stimulus properties of events that precede reinforcement and the reinforcing properties of these events, when they are frequently presented prior to or paired with reinforcers, are important in explaining how chains of response are maintained.

Consider the chain of responses involved in going to a party, described previously.[3] A phone call may signal the first response to go to the party. All the behaviors in the chain of responses are then performed, ending in positive reinforcement (eating, drinking, and socializing). The final response in the chain before reinforcement is entering the house. This response is directly reinforced with food and drink. Yet, any event that preceded reinforcement becomes an S^D for reinforcement. In the chain, the last response (entering the house) becomes an S^D for reinforcement, because this response signals that reinforcement will follow. The constant pairing of an S^D with a reinforcer (food and drink) eventually results in the S^D becoming a reinforcer as well as a discriminative stimulus. Hence, the response that precedes direct reinforcement has become an S^D for subsequent reinforcement and a reinforcer in its own right. The response serves as a reinforcer for the previous link in the chain of responses. The response (entering the house) becomes a reinforcer for the previous behavior (parking the car). Since parking the car now precedes reinforcement, it too becomes an S^D. As with other responses, the pairing of the S^D with reinforcement results in the S^D becoming a reinforcer. The process continues in a *backward* direction, so that each response in the chain becomes an S^D and a reinforcer. Each component response is both an S^D for the next response in the chain and a reinforcer for the previous response in the chain. Even the very first response becomes an S^D, but it does not reinforce a prior response. Although the sequence appears to be maintained by the reinforcers at the end of the chain of responses, the links in the chain are assumed to take on conditioned-reinforcement value. The building of response chains requires training from the last response in the sequence, which precedes direct reinforcement, back to the first response. Since the last response in the sequence is followed immediately and directly by the reinforcer, it is most easily established as a conditioned reinforcer that can maintain other responses.

The differences between shaping and chaining may appear unclear. Generally, shaping is used to develop new behaviors. Cues, such as instructions and gestures, may be used as discriminative stimuli combined with direct reinforcement, such as praise, for responses that approach the terminal goal. In contrast, chaining is usually employed to develop a sequence of behaviors, using responses that are already present in the individual's repertoire. To obtain a chain of responses consisting of discrete behaviors, shaping may be used first to develop component behaviors. The clearest difference between the procedures is that chaining proceeds in a backward direction beginning with the last response and linking together prior

3. Of course, the chain could be further divided into several components smaller than those mentioned.

behaviors, whereas shaping works in a forward direction. Furthermore, shaping focuses on developing a particular terminal response; the behaviors performed during training for the terminal response may not be evident when shaping is completed. In chaining, behaviors developed early in training are still evident when training is completed.

PROMPTS

Antecedent events, such as cues, instructions, gestures, directions, examples, and models, can facilitate development of a behavior. Events that help initiate a response are referred to as *prompts*. Prompts precede a response. When the prompt results in the response, the response can be reinforced. When a prompt initiates behaviors that are reinforced, the prompt becomes an S^D for reinforcement. For example, if a parent tells a child to return from school early and the child is reinforced for doing so, the instruction or prompt becomes an S^D. Instructions signal that reinforcement is likely when certain behaviors are performed. Eventually, instructions alone are likely to be followed by the behavior. As a general rule, when a prompt consistently precedes reinforcement of a response, the prompt becomes an S^D and can effectively control behavior.

Developing behavior can be facilitated in different ways using various kinds of prompts, such as physically *guiding* the behavior, *instructing* the child to do something, *gesturing* to the child, and *observing* another person (a model) performing a behavior (such as watching someone play a game). Prompts play a major role in shaping and chaining. Developing a terminal response using reinforcement alone may be tedious and time consuming. If the person is prompted to begin the response, more rapid approximations to the final response can be made.

Although prompts may be required early in training, they can be withdrawn gradually or faded as training progresses. If a prompt is abruptly removed early in training, the response may no longer occur. But if the response is performed consistently with a prompt, the prompt can be progressively reduced and finally omitted. Gradually removing a prompt is referred to as *fading*. To achieve behavior without continued dependence on prompts requires fading of prompts and reinforcement of responses in the absence of cues or signals. For example, prompts may be used to train children to feed themselves. Initially, a trainer may guide the child's arm to help the child place a spoon into the food and bring the food to the mouth. At the beginning of training, prompts may be essential to initiate performance of the appropriate behavior. The completion of the behavior, even though accompanied by prompts, is reinforced. Gradually, guidance by the trainer is reduced. Perhaps the trainer will exert less physical strength in initiating movement of the spoon to the food. Eventually, the trainer may fade all touching of the child and merely point or say to the child, "eat." Ultimately, the trainer may eliminate prompts and merely reinforce the child for completing the eating sequence. Thus, although prompts may figure heavily in the development of the behavior, at the end of training they may be omitted. It is not always essential to remove all prompts or cues because much of ordinary behavior is controlled by such cues. For example, it is important to train individuals to respond to the presence of certain prompts, such as instructions, that exert control over a variety of behaviors in everyday life.

DISCRIMINATION AND STIMULUS CONTROL

The discussion of prompts and discriminative stimuli reveals the importance of antecedent events in controlling behavior. It is important to elaborate the role of antecedent events and explain how they acquire control over behavior.

In some situations or in the presence of certain stimuli, a particular response may be reinforced, whereas in other situations or in the presence of other stimuli, it is not. When a response is consistently reinforced in the presence of a particular stimulus and consistently not reinforced in the presence of another stimulus, each stimulus signals the consequences that are likely to follow. The stimulus present when the response is reinforced signals that performance is likely to be reinforced. Conversely, the stimulus present during nonreinforcement signals that the response is not likely to be reinforced. As mentioned earlier, a stimulus whose presence has been associated with reinforcement is referred to as an S^D. A stimulus whose presence has been associated with nonreinforcement is referred to as an S^Δ (S delta). The effect of differentially reinforcing behavior in different stimulus conditions is that eventually the reinforced response is likely to occur in the presence of the S^D but unlikely to occur in the presence of the S^Δ. The probability of a response can be increased or decreased by presenting or removing the S^D. The S^D occasions the previously reinforced response or increases the likelihood that the response will occur. When the individual responds differently in the presence of different stimuli, he or she has made a *discrimination*. When responses are differentially controlled by antecedent stimuli, behavior is considered to be under *stimulus control*.

Instances of stimulus control pervade everyday life. For example, the ring of a telephone signals that a certain behavior (answering the phone) is likely to be reinforced (by hearing someone's voice). Specifically, the ring of the phone is associated with the voice of someone on the phone (the reinforcer). The ring of the phone (S^D) increases the likelihood that the receiver will be picked up. In the absence of the ring (S^Δ), the probability of answering the phone to hear someone's voice is very low. The rings of a doorbell, telephone, alarm, and kitchen timer all serve as discriminative stimuli and increase the likelihood that certain responses will be reinforced. In social interaction, stimulus control also is important. For example, a greeting or gesture from someone is likely to occasion a social response, such as initiation of conversation. Whereas a greeting serves as an S^D, or signals that reinforcement is likely to follow a social response, a frown serves as an S^Δ, or signals that reinforcement is not likely to follow a social response.

The notion of stimulus control is exceedingly important in behavior modification. In many behavior-modification programs, the goal is to alter the relationship between behavior and the stimulus conditions in which the behavior occurs. Some behavior problems stem from a failure of certain stimuli, such as instructions, to control behavior although such control would be desirable. Other behavioral problems occur when certain behaviors, such as overeating or smoking, *are* under control of antecedent stimuli when such control is undesirable.

GENERALIZATION

The effect of the contingencies on behavior may *generalize* across either the stimulus conditions beyond which training has taken place or across the responses that were included in the contingency. These two types of generalization are referred to as stimulus generalization and response generalization, respectively.

Stimulus Generalization

A response that is repeatedly reinforced in a particular situation is likely to be repeated in that situation. Situations and stimuli often share common properties. Control of behavior exerted by a given stimulus is shared by other stimuli that are similar or that share common properties (Skinner, 1953). Thus, a behavior may be performed in new situations similar to the original situation in which reinforcement occurred. If a response reinforced in one setting also increases in other settings, even though it is not reinforced in these other settings, this is referred to as *stimulus general-*

ization. Stimulus generalization refers to the transfer of a response to situations other than those in which training has taken place.

Numerous examples of stimulus generalization can be seen in everyday life. For example, a child may develop fear in response to a physician because of an association of the physician with pain from an injection. The avoidance and fear responses that occur in the presence of the physician may also occur in the presence of dentists, nurses, and milk deliverers. To the child, the fear may generalize to any individual wearing a white uniform. Until the child has different contingencies associated with different uniforms across different settings, the fear response may remain across diverse types of uniforms. The example entails generalization because the fear was acquired in a specific stimulus context but generalized to other similar contexts.

Stimulus generalization is the opposite of discrimination. When an individual discriminates in performing responses, the response fails to generalize. Conversely, when a response generalizes across situations, the individual fails to discriminate in performing the response. The degree of stimulus generalization is a function of the similarity of a new stimulus or situation to the stimulus under which the response was trained (Kimble, 1961). Over a long period of time, a response may not generalize across situations because the individual discriminates that the response is reinforced in one situation but not in others.

Stimulus generalization represents an important area in behavior modification. Although training takes place in a restricted setting, such as an institution, special classroom, hospital, day-care center, or home, it may be desirable that the behaviors developed in these settings generalize or transfer to other settings.

Response Generalization

An additional type of generalization involves responses rather than stimulus conditions. Alteration of one response can inadvertently influence other responses; this is referred to as *response generalization.* For example, if a person is reinforced for smiling, the frequency of laughing and talking might also increase. The reinforcement of a response increases the probability of other responses that are similar (Skinner, 1953). To the extent that a nonreinforced response is similar to a reinforced one, the probability of the similar response is also increased.

Alteration of one behavior is sometimes associated with alteration of other behaviors. For example, in one study, inappropriate verbal behaviors, such as shouting, whining, using profanities, and complaining, were suppressed in a ten-year-old retarded boy (Jackson & Calhoun, 1977). Each verbal outburst was followed with two minutes of isolation. Not only did verbal behavior change but appropriate social behaviors, such as joining in activities and starting conversations with others, increased as well. In many instances, such as this particular case, it is unclear precisely how change in one behavior affects other responses.

SUMMARY

Although behavior modification has borrowed extensively from a number of other areas of psychology, it has relied most heavily on the psychology of learning, including classical conditioning, operant conditioning, and observational learning (modeling). Classical conditioning and modeling were presented briefly in the last chapter, and modeling will be discussed again later. The present chapter outlines the principles of operant conditioning, which have served as the basis for several behavior-modification techniques.

Contingent consequences affect behavior. There are two reinforcement procedures that increase the frequency of a response: the application of a positive reinforcer (positive reinforcement) and the removal of a negative reinforcer (negative reinforcement). There are two punishment procedures that decrease the frequency of a response: the application of a negative reinforcer (punishment by application) and the removal of a positive reinforcer (punishment by removal). Extinction refers to a reduction in response frequency following the cessation of reinforcement. Reinforcement may follow a continuous or intermittent schedule. Four types of intermittent schedules were discussed: fixed ratio, variable ratio, fixed interval, and variable interval.

Shaping refers to reinforcing small steps or approximations toward a terminal response. Chaining refers to the linking together of responses within an individual's repertoire; this is done in a backward direction. Prompts are events that precede a response and help to initiate it; prompts may gradually be faded.

Antecedent stimuli or events may also affect behavior. When this occurs a response is under stimulus control.

There are two types of generalization: stimulus and response. Stimulus generalization refers to the transfer of a response to situations other than those in which training has taken place. Response generalization refers to the altering of other responses in addition to the response that has been trained. Discrimination is the opposite of generalization.

SUGGESTED READINGS

Holland, J. G., & Skinner, B. F. *The analysis of behavior*. New York: McGraw-Hill, 1961.

Kazdin, A. E. *Behavior modification in applied settings* (2nd ed.). Homewood, Ill.: Dorsey Press, 1980.

Logan, F. A. *Fundamentals of learning and motivation*. Dubuque, Iowa: William C. Brown, 1969.

Rachlin, H. *Introduction to modern behaviorism*. San Francisco: W. H. Freeman, 1970.

Williams, J. L. *Operant learning: Procedures for changing behavior*. Belmont, Calif.: Brooks/Cole, 1973.

CHAPTER 8

COGNITIVE INFLUENCES IN BEHAVIOR MODIFICATION

As noted in the previous chapter, behavior modification attempts to rely on research from general psychology. Thus, findings culled from diverse areas may be relevant to achieving behavior change. It is difficult to specify all the available findings that might be employed to alter behavior for clinical purposes. In the main, findings from the psychology of learning have generated the largest number of ideas and techniques.

Recently, however, cognitive psychology has been utilized in behavior modification. Several investigators have emphasized the role of cognitions (perceptions, thoughts, beliefs) on behavior (Bandura, 1969; Ellis, 1962; Kanfer & Phillips, 1970; Mahoney, 1974a; Meichenbaum, 1977). The cognitive position emphasizes the role of mediation in learning, or the cognitive and symbolic processes that influence behavior. The effects of variables in these areas have been evaluated according to the demands of scientific investigation as discussed in Part One. The processes include perception and interpretation of environmental events, belief systems, verbal and imaginal coding systems, thinking, planning, problem solving, and others. These processes are crucial to understanding the interrelationship between the individual and environmental events. Understanding either cognitive processes of the individual or the environmental events alone without understanding their interaction provides an insufficient account of many behaviors. The importance of environmental consequences of behavior was emphasized in the previous chapter. In the present chapter, the importance of an individual's interpretation and cognitive organization of environmental events assumes greater importance. An individual's perception of environmental events rather than the events themselves often accounts for behavior. Two individuals exposed to an identical situation respond differently, depending in part on the interpretations and meaning that they place on the situation.

COGNITIVE PROCESSES AND
ENVIRONMENTAL EVENTS

Bandura (1969) and Mahoney (1974a) have discussed four cognitive processes and environmental events that influence behavior. These include attention, mediation, component behaviors, and incentive or motivational conditions. These will be outlined briefly.

Attention refers to those conditions that enhance an individual's awareness of specific environmental events. Because a person is confronted with many events, attention is selective. The events to which individuals attend determine behavior. In a given situation, different individuals attend to diverse stimuli. Attentiveness to different events accounts in part for differences in behavior. For example, individuals taking an ocean cruise may attend to different stimuli associated with the cruise. One individual may be struck by the peaceful nature of the surroundings. Another might attend to the extreme isolation and lack of touch with the mainland. Yet another may attend to the hazards, real and imagined, of ocean travel. The behaviors in which these individuals engage, such as relaxing on the deck, letter writing, or remaining in the cabin, respectively, may in part be determined by the events to which they attend. In everyday life, as well as in therapy, knowledge of the stimuli to which individuals attend is important in explaining behavior. In the treatment of clinical problems, a great deal of emphasis often is placed on the stimuli to which the individuals attend.

Mediation refers to those processes that account for coding or cognitive representation of events upon which attention has been focused. Material to which we attend is stored in memory and subsequently influences behavior. To effect enduring behavior change, it may be important to ensure that observed or learned material has been coded in some fashion. Various procedures, such as symbolic coding operations in the form of verbal or imaginal rehearsal, can influence retention of learned material (Bandura, 1971). For example, observational learning is facilitated by having the observer code the model's behavior. Individuals who observe a model and symbolically code the observed material through either imaginal or verbal representation (that is, describe verbally to themselves what the model did) are better able to reproduce the material than individuals who have not engaged in the coding processes (for example, Gerst, 1971).

The manner in which events are mediated or coded is relevant to the understanding of diverse forms of maladaptive behavior. Mediational phenomena, such as anticipation of outcomes of courses of action, superstitions, expectations, and misperceptions, may be related to maladaptive behavior (see Rotter, 1954). For example, an individual's expectation of failure may lead him or her continually to avoid various situations.

Component behaviors or response repertoires of an individual must also be considered in explaining behavior. Attention to environmental events and symbolic coding of these events do not ensure performance of a given behavior (Bandura, 1969). Attentiveness to and perception of environmental events are preconditions for certain kinds of performance, but they are not sufficient in themselves; a person must also possess the specific skills required to behave in a particular fashion. Exposure to environmental events may not result in behavior change if an individual has severe response deficits. For example, a socially inept individual may not show behavioral improvement merely by watching another perform in an adept fashion. Being socially adept requires a number of skills and responsiveness to a variety of nuances which are not quickly learned. For someone who has very few or none of the initial response components in his or her repertoire, behavior change may require building of individual responses. In such cases, shaping procedures may have to be employed to teach the final, target behavior.

Motivational or incentive conditions also dictate performance. The control that external consequences exert over behavior was detailed in the discussion of operant-conditioning principles in Chapter 7. For understanding and altering behavior, one should know the consequences associated with a particular behavior in a given environment and what consequences can be used to influence behavior.

Aside from focusing on the actual consequences of behavior, the cognitive position focuses on an individual's thoughts about and perceptions of the consequences. Anticipation of consequences occurs in many situations and plays a role in a variety of behaviors, such as entering lotteries, carrying an umbrella, and leaving a sinking ship. Indeed, the anticipation of consequences probably plays a major role in behaviors assumed to be indicative of self-control, such as following the law, refusing a final drink when offered the proverbial "one for the road," refusing an extra dessert, and maintaining a rigorous exercise regimen. Anticipation refers to imaginally bringing delayed consequences closer in proximity to the behavior that will eventually produce the consequences. Anticipation is the symbolic (verbal or imaginal) representation of the consequences that might result from the behavior. Cognitive representation of consequences determines many of the behaviors that we undertake, complete, or terminate.

The foregoing discussion outlines the importance of perceptions and cognitions (attention, mediation, anticipation of consequences), the behavior of the individual (component responses), and environmental events (incentive conditions) in explaining and changing behavior. These factors provide an expanded account and different points of emphasis from those outlined in the previous chapter.

CONTRIBUTIONS OF COGNITIVE PSYCHOLOGY

A number of areas in behavior modification pertain to an individual's perceptions of or cognitions about events. A number of covert events mediate behavior change. In the following discussion, significant areas of research that are drawn upon in behavior modification will be sampled. The discussion provides an overview of various cognitive influences. In some ways, this information expands upon the discussion of cognitive factors or processes examined in the previous section.

Attribution

One area of research that appears relevant for behavior modification is the area of attribution. *Attribution* refers to explanations of and perceptions about the cause of particular events. The causal agents to which events are attributed account for many behaviors. The role of attribution in behavior modification is particularly interesting because it points out the importance of cognitions or thoughts regarding observed events. The importance of cognitions is readily apparent when an environmental event receives differing interpretations from different people. For example, a simple sound, such as the ticking of a clock, may be interpreted by one person as a harmless clock and by another person as a time bomb. Such attributions placed upon events may dictate different behaviors.

A classic experiment in the area of attribution was performed by Schachter and Singer (1962). These authors demonstrated that an individual's emotional state depends on physiological arousal plus cues in the environment to which this arousal might be attributed. In their experiment, some subjects received an injection of epinephrine (adrenalin), which results in physiological arousal, and others received placebo injections of salt water. One-third of the subjects in each group received correct information regarding the effects of epinephrine (for example, that heart rate increases), one-third received incorrect information (about irrelevant effects, such as itchy feet), and one-third received no information. After the injection, subjects were exposed to someone who was behaving in either an euphoric or an angry manner. These individuals were confederates actually working for the experimenter. The euphoric confederate appeared elated and played games, such as throwing crumpled paper into the wastebasket, sang, and so on. The angry confederate made nasty remarks and appeared generally upset. The main issue was the reactions of subjects exposed to the euphoric or angry confederates. The results indicated that those who received the injection of epinephrine and had no clear explanation for their arousal described their feelings in terms of the cues available to them, that is, in terms of the actions of the confederate. Thus, the attributions made about their own feelings were dictated not only by a physiological state but by interpretations of the environment.

The clinical relevance of attribution may be potentially great although it has not been completely evaluated. One study (Davidson & Valins, 1969) explored the role of attribution in maintaining behavior change after drugs are withdrawn. Individuals whose behavior is altered with the use of drugs may show behavior change only while the drugs are administered. Once the drugs are withdrawn, the gains may no longer be maintained. Quite possibly, individuals attribute changes in their own behavior to the drugs rather than to themselves. Such attribution may account for whether or not behavior is maintained once the drugs are withdrawn. An important question in understanding behavior change is the effect of having individuals attribute behavior change to themselves rather than to extraneous events.

Davison and Valins gave subjects a series of shocks and then administered a placebo drug. Subjects were then given a series of milder shocks and led to believe that they were now able to tolerate more pain. The implication, of course, was that the drug helped the individuals tolerate greater pain. After this, some subjects were told that the drug actually was a placebo. Those who were led to believe in the power of the drug were told that the real effects of the drug were wearing off. During the final series of shocks, these two groups differed in their pain tolerance. Those subjects who attributed their increased tolerance to the drug did not tolerate as much pain as did those who attributed their increased tolerance to themselves. In short, the putative increased tolerance of some subjects could not be attributed to the drug, for they were told that it was only a placebo. These individuals, in fact, were able to tolerate more pain subsequently because of the self-attribution.

In clinical practice, attribution may play a major role in behavior change. As part of therapy, individuals may learn to alter the attributions that they impose upon themselves, others, and events in their environment. Individuals may learn to attribute to themselves greater control over their own behavior and view themselves as agents who can affect the world rather than as passive objects victimized by environmental fiat. This is, in fact, one of the focal issues in Bandura's (1977a) *self-efficacy theory*. Self-efficacy is one's perceived capacity to meet some challenge or perform a particular response. According to Bandura,

expectations of personal efficacy determine whether coping behavior will be initiated, how much effort will be expended, and how long it will be sustained in the face of obstacles and aversive experiences (p. 191).

Self-efficacy is a mediational variable that attempts to refine our prediction and understanding of the processes by which humans change. Whether it can achieve these goals is an issue that has received increasing attention and stimulated considerable debate (Bandura, 1978; Borkovec, 1978; Eysenck, 1978; Kazdin, 1978b; Lang, 1978; Poser, 1978; Rosenthal, 1978; Teasdale, 1978; Wilson, 1978c; Wolpe, 1978).

Placebo Reaction and Demand Characteristics

A phenomenon related to attribution is the placebo reaction. Within medical circles, *placebo reaction* refers to a psychological, physiological, or psychophysiological effect of a drug which is independent of its specific pharmacological effect (Shapiro & Morris, 1978). The placebo reaction is a general response to a procedure per se rather than a reaction to any specific chemical. For example, patients may show improvements in a particular physiological symptom as a result of taking medicine per se (that is, any medicine) whether or not the medicine is pharmacologically active. The term *placebo* has been employed in psychology with much the same meaning; within psychology, the reaction usually refers to a response to some psychological procedure rather than to a drug.

Historically, several concoctions under the guise of medical treatment have succeeded as curative agents. Often, it has subsequently been established that the curative procedures were placebos because the agents or drugs themselves did not possess sufficient pharmacological powers to alter the disorder. The importance of placebo reactions is widely recognized. Research has shown the effectiveness of placebos in treating pain, migraine headaches, anxiety, colds, and a host of other disorders (see Shapiro & Morris, 1978). In the area of psychotherapy and behavior modification, the importance of placebo effects is well recognized (Frank, 1973). Individuals participating in psychotherapy often show some improvement independently of the specific treatment being provided. Indeed, as noted in Chapter 5, it is important to separate placebo reactions from specific treatment effects when evaluating therapy. To evaluate therapy, it is not sufficient to compare clients who receive treatment with those who do not receive treatment. Any changes in behavior as a result of treatment may be due to the actual therapeutic effect of a specific treatment, to placebo effects, or to their combination. Research often employs placebo control groups to control for the *nonspecific* effects that are due to participation in treatment per se. For example, clients in a placebo control group may receive a procedure that seems effective from the client's standpoint. That is, the rationale for the procedure is reasonable and the client is likely to expect therapeutic change; however, the placebo treatment is designed so that it does not have a specific ingredient that should result in behavior change (Paul, 1969a).

Clinically, placebo effects may play an important role in treatment. Indeed, for the benefit of the client, it may be wise to maximize placebo effects when a veridical treatment is provided. If the treatment is one that is likely to work, it still may be useful to maximize the client's belief in its curative powers. This is not deception in the sense that a useless or inert treatment is portrayed as effective. Rather, an effective procedure may be enchanced by increasing a client's expectations for improvement. Because placebo effects have been shown to be important in altering behavior, they must be considered as an important means of behavior change. Indeed, placebo effects are so well established that the burden of proof is placed upon any new therapy technique to demonstrate that something other than placebo effects is operative.

Placebo reactions are referred to when nonspecific effects occur in a therapeutic context. An analogous effect in an experimental setting is referred to as the *demand characteristics* of the situation (Orne, 1962). Demand characteristics refer to an individual's responsiveness to cues in an experimental setting. Cues in the setting convey to the individual how he or she is to behave and thus affect performance in the experimental situation (see Weber & Cook, 1972). A number of investigations have shown that in psychological experiments, individuals can be induced to perform in a particular way depending on the manipulation of extraneous cues. For example, Orne and Schiebe (1964) conducted an experiment on meaning deprivation in which individuals were to be isolated and deprived of stimulation in a manner similar to that used in sensory-deprivation investigations. Experimental subjects were treated in an elaborate fashion to provide cues suggesting that certain kinds of behaviors were expected of them. These subjects were given an initial interview in a hospital setting by someone wearing a white coat, had their medical histories taken, and viewed drugs and equipment displayed conspicuously on an "emergency tray." Experimental subjects were instructed to note any unusual or hallucinatory experiences (which have been reported in sensory-deprivation experiments). Finally, subjects were shown an "emergency alarm" they could press to escape from the situation. In contrast to the elaborate treatment provided for experimental subjects, control subjects were merely told they were a control group for a sensory-deprivation study. They were not led to believe that anything unusual would happen. All subjects were then placed in an isolation room for a few hours. At the end of the task, experimental subjects demonstrated greater impairment on cognitive and perceptual tasks (behavior associated with sensory deprivation) than did control subjects. Moreover, the experimental group reported a greater number of bizarre experiences. These results were interpreted to reflect the effect of the cues to which subjects were exposed rather than of the isolation itself.

Placebo reactions and demand characteristics reveal the importance of suggesting to individuals in a subtle fashion that their behavior is going to change in a particular direction. Situations in treatment and experimentation often lead to behavior change because of the meaning subjects place upon various events rather than because of the events themselves.

Problem Solving

Traditionally, behavior modification has focused on discrete responses for therapeutic change in a given client. Yet many of the problems individuals encounter are not discrete or easily specifiable in advance. In everyday life, individuals meet a number of situations ranging from minor sources of frustration to major traumas. Experience suggests that some individuals usually handle diverse situations rather effectively, whereas others, for whatever reason, experience difficulty in coping with a variety of situations. Individuals sometimes seek therapy and counseling in unmanageable situations, such as the death of a relative, marital discord, extreme anxiety, or hopelessness.

Frequently, individuals in therapy are trained to resolve a particularly difficult situation. However, it is not uncommon that a person so trained is not able to use that particular skill to deal with additional problems. Recently, then, some attempts have been made to teach individuals problem-solving skills so that they not only can manage the reported problem situation but also can apply the learned problem-solving skills to many other situations (D'Zurilla & Goldfried, 1971).

Problem solving has been defined as "a behavioral process, whether overt or cognitive in nature, which (a) makes available a variety of potentially effective response alternatives for dealing with the problematic situation, and (b) increases the probability of selecting the most effective response among these various alternatives" (D'Zurilla & Goldfried, 1971, p. 108). The goal in developing problem-solving skills is to train an individual in how to resolve new problems as they arise rather than merely to solve a single problem. It is assumed that through training the client will develop a strategy to manage or cope with virtually all problems encountered. This does not mean that a client will effectively solve all problems, but only that he or she will have the skills to develop and select solutions.

D'Zurilla and Goldfried (1971) divide problem solving into five stages or components. To resolve a problem, an individual must

1. develop a general orientation or set to recognize the problem;
2. define the specifics of the problem and determine what needs to be accomplished;
3. generate alternative courses of action that might be used to resolve the problem and achieve the desired goals;
4. decide among the alternatives by evaluating their consequences and relative gains and losses; and
5. verify the results of the decision process and determine whether the alternative selected is achieving the desired outcome.

Problems may arise in everyday life if any of these steps is not utilized. A person may not recognize that there is a problem and may even deny its presence; may not recognize specific features of the problem which, if noted, might be more manageable; may not generate viable solutions to the problem; or may pursue unsuccessful courses of action without recognizing their futility. For example, a student may have deficits in social skills in relation to the opposite sex. Rather than recognizing the real problem (failure to interact at all), the individual may think of it as simply undue shyness. Even if the individual recognizes the problem, it might well be that he or she does not know which specific encounters are problematic or how to formulate alternative courses of action to remedy the problem.

Individuals who show response deficits or inhibitions that transcend a single situation might be trained in problem-solving skills. Training is accomplished by progressively shaping problem-solving skills in the client. Simulated and actual problems can be introduced in therapy, and the requisite component skills outlined above can be gradually developed. Initially, minor problems can be introduced for practice while the problem-solving approach is being developed. The final goal is to train the individual to approach all problematic situations with the problem-solving strategy. Training proceeds by developing each of the five components. The client focuses on recognizing problems and on controlling impulsive reactions that short-circuit the entire problem-solving sequence. After the general problem is formulated, specific aspects of the problem are focused on. By identifying specific features of the overall problem—that is, external events that account for the problem and internal reactions that contribute to its status as a problem—the client finds solutions more readily available. An explicit definition of the problem also helps to clarify goals. Once the goals are clear, the alternatives for specific action may be posed. Then the individual, in conjunction with the therapist, weighs the consequences associated with each alternative. The long- and short-term advantages and disadvantages of each alternative are evaluated. Next, one alternative is selected in light of its likely consequences. Once a specific plan is decided upon, the client tries to develop concrete procedures for implementing the plan. When the plan is finally implemented, the client must evaluate whether the intended effect is achieved and whether he or she is satisfied within the constraints of the available alternatives.

The problem-solving strategy is demonstrated in the following example. A female college senior may be in conflict about two aspects of her future. Specifically, she may be indecisive about an impending marriage because of the possibility that it will interfere with her graduate work and career plans. The general problem must be specified as carefully as possible. The abstract problem of conflict and indecisiveness must be clarified by an expression of the goals the client wishes to accomplish and their relative value. Of course, selecting alternative goals that are desirable but potentially incompatible is difficult. However, the student may decide she wishes both to marry and to continue her education. Once deciding on the specific goals, the student can generate alternative plans to attain them. One might be to marry and temporarily leave her husband (who might already be committed to a job) to attend graduate school. Another plan might be to postpone marriage until graduate work is completed. A third plan might be to marry her fiance only if he agrees to accompany her to graduate school. Assume for the sake of the example that the last alternative is selected as the most viable solution. The final step of the problem-solving approach is determining whether the course of action selected satisfies the original goals. It might well be that, once the student enters graduate school accompanied by her spouse, school and a dissatisfied spouse make living conditions deplorable. The goals of completing graduate work and having a reasonably happy marriage might not be compatible. Thus, an alternative plan is selected and implemented. The procedure of selecting alternative plans and evaluating their utility continues until the problematic situation is resolved.

It should be clear from this example that the stages of problem solving outlined earlier are not discrete steps that one follows in an unvarying sequence. In everyday situations, the conflict of goals makes selecting alternative plans difficult. Sometimes decisions must be made before there is a clear, unequivocal commitment to a goal or before the consequences of alternative sources of action can be predicted. Nevertheless, the problem-solving strategy helps specify the different features of a problem that must be approached to reach a solution.

The therapeutic strategy emphasizes the client's cognitive abilities for handling problems. The therapist serves to develop individual component skills and to help the client use the processes which will lead to resolution of problems. Thus, the therapist is likely to help the client weigh the alternative plans for action, enumerate the range of consequences associated with alternative plans, and later assess the effect of a particular course of action.

An interesting feature of the problem-solving approach, consistent with various behavior-therapy techniques, is that it encourages experimentation with oneself. When alternative courses of action are selected, their efficacy in achieving the anticipated outcome is evaluated. If the course of action is not achieving its purpose or is inefficient for reaching a goal, it can be altered. Part of the problem-solving training is to give the individual experience in trying out new courses of action.

Some components of problem solving and the role of these skills in behavior change have been studied in a therapeutic context. (Mahoney, 1974a; Mahoney & Arnkoff, 1978). Although the data are still preliminary and more rigorous methodologies are needed, the available evidence suggests that training in problem solving may be a valuable component in treating a wide range of behavior problems and personal concerns.

Verbal Mediators of Behavior

The role of language in controlling behavior has long been recognized in psychology. Obviously, individuals respond to language in the form of instructions, commands, and rules that govern behavior. However, there are more subtle means, such as in self-verbalizations, through which language influences behavior. It is important to outline some forms of verbalization that may control behavior.

INSTRUCTIONS

One area of interest pertains to the influence of instructions in controlling behavior. As noted earlier, an individual's perceptions of various environmental events dictate reactions to the events. One way to alter a person's perception is to provide instructions. In this context, *instructions* refers to statements describing the relationship between events. Several investigations have shown that instructions can alter an individual's responsiveness to external events in a conditioning situation. For example, the development and extinction of classically conditioned responses are enhanced by informing subjects about the events that are to occur (Bridger & Mandel, 1964, 1965; Grings & Lockhart, 1963; Notterman, Schoenfeld, & Bersh, 1962). Similarly, in laboratory investigations of operant conditioning, instructions about the contingencies markedly affect the level and pattern of acquisition (for example, Dulany, 1968; Kaufman, Baron, & Kopp, 1966; Merbaum & Lukens, 1968). Related research, mostly in the area of verbal conditioning, has emphasized the importance of awareness in learning. Individuals who are aware of reinforcement contingencies, or of the relationship between the target response and consequences, perform at a higher rate than those who are unaware (see Bandura, 1969; Kanfer, 1965).

The importance of instructions about the reinforcement contingencies has been demonstrated in applied settings. In one investigation (Kazdin, 1973c), the role of instructions and reinforcement was examined with elementary school children. Some children were told that they could earn tokens exchangeable for a variety of rewards for appropriate classroom behavior, such as paying attention to the lesson, sitting in their seats, and so on. Thus, individuals were led to *believe* that they were reinforced for appropriate behavior. However, tokens were delivered noncontingently on a predetermined random schedule. Students received tokens on the basis of their eye color, sex, and place of the first initial of their name in the alphabet. Instructions and the noncontingent delivery of reinforcement improved the behavior of a number of children in the three-week period during which tokens were administered. Thus, tokens did not have to be delivered contingently to improve behavior as long as individuals were led to believe that reinforcement was delivered contingently. The procedure did not alter the behavior of students who were particularly disruptive. Yet evidence was provided that the students' perceptions of the contingency partially dictated performance.

Other studies have shown that reinforcement can be enhanced by the use of instructions. Ayllon and Azrin (1968) trained psychotic clients to use utensils instead of their hands when eating meals. Providing a reinforcer (extra dessert) for the use of utensils was not very effective in improving their behavior. However, providing instructions stating the relationship between the desired behavior and the consequences enhanced performance tremendously. Instructions or rules about behavior in a given situation by themselves, on the other hand, do not always control behavior. This, of course, is obvious from the violation of laws in everyday life. Several studies in applied settings have demonstrated that instructions alone, when not backed by consequences for behavior, do not lead to consistent behavior change (Herman & Tramontana, 1971; Kazdin, 1973d; O'Leary, Becker, Evans, & Saudargas, 1969; Packard, 1970). Yet, much behavior is controlled by instructions in both verbal and written form. Warnings like weather reports of impending disasters or signs that note "Beware of Dog" demonstrate the importance of instructions in controlling what individuals believe and how they behave in various situations. Instructions can be used similarly to enhance behavior change in therapeutic contexts. For example, placebo effects and expectations for improvement can be altered by verbal suggestions about the efficacy of various procedures.

Self-verbal Mediators

Individuals frequently make comments to themselves that may influence their own behavior. For example, young children can be seen to speak out loud to describe what they are doing while playing. Similarly, adults may covertly make comments to themselves. For example, in preparing to ask an employer for a raise, individuals may verbally rehearse and direct themselves in how to make the request. Of course, saying something to oneself prior to or while performing a particular behavior does not necessarily mean that the self-verbalizations cause the behavior. *Self-verbalizations* refer to concomitants of behavior or to actual guides of behavior.

Various therapy techniques are based on the assumption that self-instructions guide or control one's behavior. For example, Albert Ellis's (1962) *rational emotive therapy* assumes that psychological disorders derive from irrational patterns of thinking. The irrational patterns of thinking are represented in what individuals say to themselves in explicit or implicit self-verbalization. Ellis maintains that a variety of specific irrational ideas may cause and maintain maladaptive behavior. One irrational idea is the notion that because some past event has strongly influenced one's life, it should indefinitely affect it (instead of the notion that one can learn from one's past experience but not be a victim of it). Another irrational idea is that it is essential for an adult to be loved by everyone for every action (instead of focusing on self-respect, and on loving rather than being loved). There are several additional irrational beliefs that have been detailed elsewhere (Ellis, 1962, 1970; Ellis & Harper, 1961). The main point of Ellis's position is that thought patterns are responsible for most problems in everyday experience. The actual events that one encounters, such as rejection by a loved one, are not themselves traumatic except insofar as one's assumptions, ideas, and interpretations of them make them catastrophic. Even inevitable events that one might argue are traumatic (for example, death) affect individuals differently, depending on the interpretations placed on such events. Although there are some differences, Beck's (1976) *cognitive therapy* also presumes that distressing patterns of feeling and action often stem from irrational or distorted beliefs about real-world contingencies.

From the standpoint of effecting behavior change, both rational emotive and cognitive therapy attempt to make explicit those cognitions and self-verbalizations that account for one's feelings and actions. Essentially, therapy focuses on restructuring the cognitions that have led to problems. The therapist helps the client recognize the illogic of the premises and self-verbalizations that are implicit in the client's actions. Therapy provides the client with insight into the source of the problems and trains the client to examine the belief system under which he or she operates. The premises under which an individual acts are shown to relate directly to various negative emotions, such as feelings of failure, rejection, and self-denigration. The therapist emphasizes that certain events, such as being rejected by a lover, do not necessarily entail irrational conclusions, such as that one is worthless. As a function of therapy, the individual supposedly eliminates self-defeating thoughts and verbalizations and develops constructive verbalizations in their place. Rational emotive and cognitive therapy have been increasingly employed in recent years. The available evidence suggests that they may hold particular promise in the treatment of anxiety and depression (see Craighead, 1980; Ellis & Whiteley, 1979; Foreyt & Rathjen, 1978; Kendall & Hollon, 1979; Mahoney & Arnkoff, 1978). Research on their effectiveness in other areas is also rapidly accumulating (see Meyers & Craighead, in press).

Cognitive and rational emotive therapy include a number of components, although self-instructions and self-verbalizations are most strongly emphasized. The role of self-verbalizations has received a great deal of attention in its own right. Laboratory investigations, for example, have evaluated the impact of saying things to oneself to control various behaviors. For example, in one investigation, elementary school boys earned prizes by working on a task (O'Leary, 1968). The likelihood of earning a prize could be enhanced by "cheating," or at the inappropriate time, taking tokens exchangeable for prizes. All children were made aware of the "right" and "wrong" behaviors. Some children were told to tell themselves whether they *should* make a response before actually doing so. Other children were not told to instruct themselves in this fashion. The children who self-instructed made fewer transgressions, or "wrong" responses, than those who did not self-instruct; thus, self-instruction controlled behavior. A variety of other investigations have also shown that self-instruction enhances performance across diverse tasks (Craighead, Craighead, & Meyers, 1978; Meichenbaum, 1977).

Indeed, *self-instructional training* has recently been systematically investigated as a behavior-modification strategy for therapeutic purposes. For example, in one project (Meichenbaum & Goodman, 1971), impulsive and hyperactive children were trained to administer self-instructions. Prior to training, the children made frequent errors on various tasks because of their rapid and careless performance. During self-instructional training, the experimenter modeled how to perform various tasks, such as coloring figures and copying lines. While performing each task, the experimenter described its performance. By talking, the experimenter modeled thinking out loud and verbally reinforced himself for working carefully. An example of the verbalizations modeled by the experimenter for the line-drawing task was:

Okay, what is it I have to do? You want me to copy the picture with the different lines. I have to go slow and be careful. Okay, draw the line down, down, good; then to the right, that's it; now down some more and to the left. Good, I'm doing fine so far. Remember go slow. Now back up again. No, I was supposed to go down. That's okay. Just erase the line carefully. . . . . Good. Even if I make an error I can go slowly and carefully. Okay, I have to go down now. Finished. I did it. (Meichenbaum & Goodman, 1971, p. 117)

The children were trained to instruct themselves out loud while performing the task. Eventually, they were trained to instruct themselves covertly without talking but only by moving their lips, and finally without lip movements. Individuals who were trained to instruct themselves on how to perform were more methodical in their work than individuals who practiced the experimental task but did not receive self-instructional training.

Self-instructional training has been successful with a number of behaviors and populations. In analogue studies, which focus on behaviors considered to resemble clinical problems, self-instructional training has decreased test anxiety and fear of snakes. Individuals who are trained to verbalize statements that facilitate adaptation to anxiety-provoking situations can substantially reduce their anxiety (Meichenbaum, 1972). A recent demonstration of self-instructional training was completed by Meichenbaum and Cameron (1973) with clients diagnosed as schizophrenic. In two experiments, these authors demonstrated the effect of training the schizophrenic clients to "talk to themselves" in improving performance on perceptual and cognitive tasks.

Another interesting research finding is that changes effected with self-instructional training seem to generalize. For example, training individuals to cope with one anxiety-provoking situation or to perform on one task results in beneficial effects in other situations (Meichenbaum, 1973). Moreover, effects achieved with self-instructional training appear to be maintained over time. These two features of self-instructional training, if borne out by future research, will provide further support for the notion that self-instructional training makes alterations in general cognitive strategy rather than effecting isolated changes in specific target behaviors (Craighead & Craighead, 1980).

Imaginal Mediators of Behavior

Increasingly, the role of imagery has been recognized as an important influence on behavior. Indeed, in everyday life, imagery is frequently relied on to direct one's behavior; examples are envisioning the outcome of a task or vividly recalling a pleasant event or experience. Research has shown that imagined stimuli appear to elicit reactions similar to those elicited by actual events (Mahoney, 1974a). Of course, this is known to anyone who has awakened frightened from a nightmare.

A number of behavior-therapy techniques depend on the similarity of responses evoked by imagined and by real-life cues (Bauer & Craighead, 1979). For example, *systematic desensitization* relies on imagery to alleviate anxiety. Typically, individuals imagine a graded hierarchy of anxiety-provoking stimuli. If relaxation is associated with the images of anxiety-provoking situations, anxiety in the actual situations abates. Therapeutically, anxiety is alleviated in the presence of imagined stimuli only, rather than in the situations themselves. Thus, behavior change is achieved by engaging a person's imagination.[1]

Aside from desensitization, a series of techniques referred to as *covert conditioning* (Cautela, 1972) rely extensively on imagery. Covert conditioning techniques are characterized by having individuals imagine themselves performing behaviors that they wish to change or develop and then imagine certain consequences directly following from the behaviors. One technique, referred to as *covert sensitization,* is used in attempts to decrease maladaptive-approach behaviors, such as overeating, excessive alcohol consumption, drug abuse, and sexual deviance. Individuals imagine themselves engaging in the behaviors they wish to decrease or eliminate. When the behavior is clearly imagined, the individuals are instructed to imagine

1. On occasion, systematic desensitization is conducted in the actual situations rather than with imagery; this is known as in vivo desensitization.

highly aversive events. The aversive events are designed to suppress the behaviors. As treatment progresses, individuals are told to imagine themselves resisting performance of the deviant behavior and feeling relieved as a result. For example, in treating overeating, a scene used to suppress eating desserts might be as follows:

I want you to imagine you've just had your main meal and you are about to eat your dessert, which is apple pie. As you are about to reach for the fork, you get a funny feeling in the pit of your stomach. You start to feel queasy, nauseous, and sick all over. As you touch the fork, you can feel food particles inching up your throat. You're just about to vomit. As you put the fork into the pie, the food comes up into your mouth. You try to keep your mouth closed because you are afraid that you'll spit the food out all over the place. You bring the piece of pie to your mouth. As you're about to open your mouth, you puke; you vomit all over your hands, the fork, over the pie. It goes all over the table, over the other people's food. Your eyes are watering. Snot and mucus are all over your mouth and nose. Your hands feel sticky. There is an awful smell. As you look at this mess you just can't help but vomit again and again until just watery stuff is coming out. Everybody is looking at you with shocked expressions. You run out of the room, and as you run out, you feel better and better. You wash and clean yourself up, and it feels wonderful.[2]

As treatment progresses, the scenes become less dramatic and focus on individuals' successful resistance to temptation. For example, later in therapy, the following scene might be imagined in the session:

You've just finished eating your meal and you decide to have dessert. As soon as you make the decision, you start to get that funny feeling in the pit of your stomach. You say, "Oh, oh; oh, no; I won't eat that dessert." Then you immediately feel calm and comfortable.[3]

Across several sessions clients imagine a variety of situations until they are no longer attracted to the previously desired stimuli. Clients are asked to employ the scenes outside of treatment so that control over behavior can be achieved in the actual situations as well as in the therapy session (Cautela, 1967, 1969).

Recently, a number of covert techniques have been derived from operant-conditioning principles. For example, one technique referred to as *covert reinforcement* requires an individual to imagine engaging in some

2. Reprinted with permission of author and publisher from Cautela, J. R. Covert sensitization. *Psychological Reports*, 1967, *20*, 459–468.
3. Reprinted with permission of author and publisher from Cautela, J. R. Covert sensitization. *Psychological Reports*, 1967, *20*, 459–468.

response he or she wishes to increase, such as speaking up in a group. After the response is imagined, the individual imagines some reinforcing event taking place, such as skiing down a mountain. The procedure is designed to increase the probability that the client will engage in the imagined target behaviors. There are additional covert techniques, such as *covert extinction, covert punishment,* and *covert modeling,* which are conducted entirely in imagination. With each technique, the imagery of the client is guided by instructions from the therapist.

Covert techniques have been applied in a number of clinical cases to alter alcohol consumption, sexual deviance, drug abuse, social skills, overeating, and diverse fears, to name a few major applications. Unequivocal evidence for the efficacy of given techniques has been sparse, in part because of the recency of the procedures. Also, some of the research that has been completed in support of various covert techniques has been criticized on methodological grounds (Mahoney, 1974; Mahoney & Arnkoff, 1978).

SUMMARY

This chapter outlines several areas relevant to behavior change which reflect research in the cognitive tradition. The processes posed to account for behavior (attention, mediation, component behavior, and incentive conditions) and the specific areas of research included (attribution, placebo reactions, demand characteristics, problem solving, and verbal and imaginal mediators of behavior) broaden the areas from which behavior modification can draw principles. Cognitive influences go beyond external environmental events. To account for behavior, both cognitive and environmental influences should be considered. However, these influences should not be considered as exhausting those factors that control behavior, because they exclude other obvious factors, such as sociological and genetic influences. Nevertheless, for the purpose of achieving behavior change in therapeutic contexts, findings from general psychology, particularly in the areas of learning and cognition, have proven heuristically valuable.

It is important to reiterate that the domain of behavior modification cannot be described definitively by its current content. Indeed, it may not be meaningful to refer to a specific domain since the field is defined by applying experimental findings to behavior change. Not all of the experimental findings that might be relevant for altering behavior are known. Thus, the domain of behavior modification is always expanding. For example, social and physical features of the environment are known to affect behavior and are included in the realm of findings that might be relevant for changing behavior in a clinical context. In this book, those findings pertaining to human learning and cognition are stressed because of the role they currently play in many behavior-modification techniques. However, it is important to keep in mind that the general area of behavior change is much broader.

SUGGESTED READINGS

Foreyt, J. P., & Rathjen, D. P. (Eds.). *Cognitive behavior therapy: Research and application.* New York: Plenum, 1978.

Kendall, P. C., & Hollon, S. D. (Eds.). *Cognitive-behavioral interventions: Theory, research, and procedures.* New York: Academic Press, 1979.

Mahoney, M. J. *Cognition and behavior modification.* Cambridge, Mass.: Ballinger, 1974.

Meichenbaum, D. *Cognitive-behavior modification: An integrative approach.* New York: Plenum, 1977.

Meyers, A. W., & Craighead, W. E. (Eds.). *Cognitive behavior therapy with children.* New York: Plenum, in press.

CHAPTER 9

ASSESSMENT AND TREATMENT
STRATEGIES

Behavior modification has broad applications, ranging from the home to the mental hospital; however, it has received its most extensive utilization in individual clinical work. In this chapter, we will discuss general guidelines for the application of behavior modification, and we have chosen as our example the individual therapy setting. These guidelines are equally applicable in other clinical settings involving the application of behavior modification and even extend to broader community problems (Kazdin, 1980a; Chapter 24 this volume), although specific practical details may vary from setting to setting. This chapter is not intended as a how-to-do-it cookbook, but as a general model for experimental/clinical intervention.

Issues regarding assessment procedures have received increasing attention from behaviorally oriented clinicians and researchers. The focus has largely been on traditional issues of personality assessment, such as reliability and validity of the assessment procedures (Goldfried & Sprafkin, 1974; Wiggins, 1973). This increased interest is demonstrated by the recent appearance of two new journals which focus exclusively on behavioral assessment. Many of these issues will be discussed and empirical findings will be presented in Part Two. This chapter will focus on the clinical situation.

In the typical clinical situation, a person with a problem comes to a therapist. Ullmann and Krasner (1969) have described that situation as follows:

An individual may do something (e.g., verbalize hallucinations, hit a person, collect rolls of toilet paper, refuse to eat, stutter, stare into space or dress sloppily) under a set of circumstances (e.g., during a school class, while working at his desk, during a church service) which upsets, annoys, angers, or strongly disturbs somebody (e.g., employer, teacher, parent, the individual himself) sufficiently that some action results (e.g., a policeman is called, seeing a psychiatrist is recommended, commitment proceedings are started) so that society's professional labelers (e.g., physicians, psychiatrists, psychologists, judges, social workers) come into contact with the individual and determine which of the current set of labels (e.g., schizophrenic reaction, sociopathic personality, anxiety reaction) is most appropriate. Finally, there follow attempts to change the emission of the offending behavior (e.g., institutionalization, psychotherapy, medication). (p. 21)

All the behaviors in this sequence of events may be analyzed from an experimental standpoint. Each person and his or her behavior plays a functional role in this sequence, and each behavior may be analyzed and modified.

Since this chapter is concerned with what a behavior therapist does in the clinical setting, let us focus on the role of the therapist. The traditional role of the therapist in this sequence has been to make a diagnosis. However, because of the relative lack of reliability and validity of traditional diagnostic categories and because of data indicating that the treatment that follows may be unrelated to the differential diagnosis, most experimentally oriented clinicians have discontinued such diagnoses. This change in the therapist's role was reflected in the models presented in Chapter 6. Our experimental clinician is unlikely to utilize traditional assessment devices to look for underlying problems but rather will attempt to discover what the client has done, thought, or said to upset someone. The behavior therapist's job is to help the client change that behavior and alleviate its accompanying distress by means of some clinical intervention.

As the behavior therapist, where would you look for a general model to serve as your guideline for clinical intervention? The thesis of this book is that the appropriate guide is the general scientific or experimental model. Even in clinical work, the scientific method is basic in a behavioral approach.

EXPERIMENTAL/CLINICAL MODEL

The scientific model provides both the general objectives and the methodology for the experimental/clinical model of therapeutic intervention. As explained in earlier chapters, the objectives of the scientific approach of methodological behaviorism are the explanation, prediction, and control of behavior. These objectives find their counterparts in the clinical activities of assessment (explanation), development of a treatment strategy (prediction), and implementation of a treatment program (control). Thus, the overall objectives of the scientific endeavor correspond to the overall objectives of the therapeutic endeavor. The means of accomplishing those therapeutic objectives also may be derived from the scientific model. Just as the experimenter at times engages in activities that are difficult to fit within the conceptual model that specifies what he or she is supposed to do, so will the clinician at times engage in behaviors that are difficult to fit within this model. However, it is maintained that therapeutic effectiveness will most readily be obtained by the therapist who submits his or her endeavors to this experimental/clinical model.

The experimental/clinical model suggests that the methodology applied in the laboratory experiment should also be employed in the clinical setting. The ingredients of the experimental methodology outlined in earlier chapters become the ingredients of the clinical methodology proposed here. There are, of course, many empirically verified procedures that the clinician may employ, but we are speaking here of general guidelines for clinical intervention and not of specific behaviors to be employed in the therapy session.

As we have seen, the ingredients of the experimental methodology are the identification or definition of independent and dependent variables, the collection of data within an experimental design, the analysis of data, and data interpretation. The identification of dependent and independent variables is important to the clinician in two ways—the first in assessment and the second in treatment development and evaluation. "At its heart, the goals of behavioral assessment are to identify meaningful response units and their controlling variables (both current environmental and organismic) for the purposes of understanding and altering behavior" (Nelson and Hayes, 1979, p. 1). Within the experimental/clinical model, the therapist's first job is defining the problem behavior (dependent variable) and the factors maintaining that behavior (independent variable). In other words, the therapist as an empirical scientist attempts to develop with the client a clear definition of the presenting problem and what is causing it. This is referred to as the *functional analysis of behavior,* although the more traditional label of *assessment* may also be used. Next, the therapist must develop a treatment strategy; essentially he or she must design an experiment and in so doing must go about defining dependent and independent variables as well as carrying out the rest of the experimental methodology. The therapist must decide what behavior(s) needs to be changed. This behavior(s) is frequently called the target behavior, because it is the focus or target of change in the treatment program. In the analogy we are using, the target behavior is the dependent variable. The therapist must define what variable or treatment strategy (independent variable) will be employed in an effort to affect the dependent variable. The experimental clinician will want to utilize all the other steps of the scientific method in order to assess the treatment's effectiveness. The clinician will choose a research design, a method of data collection and analysis, and a means of data interpretation. Although the clinical situation may make such an ideal difficult to achieve, it is an ideal toward which the clinician should constantly strive. It is posited that the more closely a clinician comes to this ideal, the more effective he or she will be.

From the foregoing it can be seen that the clinical endeavor is comparable to the experimental endeavor—hence the label, *experimental/clinical model.* With these guidelines, we can now look at some of the specific activities in which a contemporary behavior modifier might engage while doing clinical work.

CLINICAL ASSESSMENT

When an individual asks for professional help, that individual has said, thought, or done something upsetting and is seeking this means of alleviating the distress associated with the behavior. The first job of the behavioral-change agent is to identify the upsetting behavior (the dependent variable) and what is causing and maintaining that behavior (the independent variable). This means that the clinician must conduct a functional behavioral analysis of the client's present life situation, specifically in regard to the behavior the client reports as a problem. By functional analysis, we mean that the therapist identifies dependent and independent variables that have led the client to seek therapy.

Model for Assessment

Many behavior modifiers, especially those with an operant bent, have described the assessment process in terms of an $A \rightarrow B \rightarrow C$ model. The change agent first identifies the problem behaviors (B) or responses that are to be changed. These are sometimes labeled the target behaviors. The change agent proceeds to identify those events or stimuli that immediately precede the target behavior (antecedent stimuli, A) and those events that immediately follow the target behavior (consequences, C). Within the operant framework, these variables are viewed as being outside the body. They are called environmental variables and thus, in the very strict operant sense, are external to the human body. Although there may be a few internal variables, such as physiological ones, which may be measured directly, even these internal responses have frequently been excluded from consideration. This model for assessment serves some valuable functions. Occasionally, the problem is rather simple and straightforward, and this type of assessment is adequate. This is most likely to be true with cases involving small children and severely retarded residential populations for whom cognitive activity seems to be of less significance. However, even when this model is inadequate to account for human behavior, it frequently serves to teach the client the language that will be employed in the therapy situation.

As noted in Chapters 1 and 8, this model has been expanded; variables inside the organism are considered important and should be included in the assessment process. These internal variables may be difficult to measure, but if they are important in understanding, predicting, and modifying human behavior, they must be assessed. At the most basic level, this is a measurement rather than conceptual problem. At the present time, except for some physiological measures, the therapist is dependent on self-report as a measure of internal variables. However, refinements are presently being made in the means of assessment and modification of these internal variables (Kendall & Korgeski, 1979). As will be seen in Part Two, there is considerable promise in the clinical data derived from studies that have attempted to modify behavior via the modification of internal cognitive processes.

Although the $A \rightarrow B \rightarrow C$ assessment model may still serve a practical purpose in the functional analysis of behavior, its primary utility lies in the sequencing and the correlation (in a literal sense of the word) of events. Within the behavioral model presented in this book, any of the As, Bs, or Cs may be inside or outside the organism. Variables may range from simple, external reinforcers, to reasonably far-removed variables of nutritional deficiencies, to a sequence of internal self-reinforcing statements. For example, the internal biofeedback self-reinforcement sequence following an autistic child's self-stimulatory behavior may far exceed the strength of punishment from an external source. Thus, assessment should be as broad and exhaustive as possible. *Every variable that the experimental psychology literature has delineated as being important in a problem area should be assessed via the best available procedures. An experimental clinician should not just learn operant conditioning, but should also know the general psychology literature.* Other factors being equal, the more the clinician knows or the broader the experimental base, the more effective her or his clinical interventions are likely to be.

Settings for Assessment

The appropriate settings for behavioral assessment are determined by several of its defining features or characteristics. One of those is the behavior therapist's conceptual view of the client's problem. For the behavior therapist, the behavior is the problem. Whether observed by the therapist or reported by the client, each specific event is considered a *sample* of the problem behavior. This contrasts with traditional assessment where the problem behavior is viewed as a *sign* of an underlying or intrapsychic conflict. Consequently, the behavior therapist attempts to gather as much information as possible from diverse settings in order to conduct a functional analysis of the problem behavior. Some problems may necessitate direct observation, whereas others may be more appropriately described in a clinical interview.

A second characteristic of behavioral assessment is that in addition to providing an understanding of the problem, it provides information for the development of a treatment program. This contrasts with traditional assessment where the primary purpose is producing a differential diagnosis or classification of the "mental disorder." Since the assessment provides the information for the development of the treatment program, the therapist needs to know about the relevant behavioral repertory of the client in several different settings.

A third characteristic of behavioral assessment is its emphasis on current level of functioning. Although the behavior therapist may inquire about the historical development of a problem and that information may be critical to the development of the treatment program, the actual data or dependent variable is the client's current responding. The focus is on behavior to be changed in the "here and now." The setting for assessment will be determined by the behavior to be changed and when and where it occurs.

A fourth characteristic of behavioral assessment is that it is continuous throughout therapy. The initial assessment has as its purposes the gathering of information and the development of a treatment program, but as we have noted repeatedly, the behavior therapist also evaluates the effectiveness of therapy by *assessing* the effects of the treatment program on the target behavior. Again, the setting is determined by the target behavior, which may range from physiological laboratory monitoring of sexual arousal, to a deviant fantasy, to self-monitoring of the number of calories eaten per day.

Given the possible settings for information gathering, it may come as some surprise that most behavior therapists base their assessment on information obtained via verbal clinical interviews. As just noted, how the clinician views and utilizes the information differs from the purposes of assessment in traditional therapy, but much of the information in both approaches is obtained in the same manner. However, because of the nature of behavioral assessment, behavior therapists are more likely to also use nontraditional assessment procedures, such as real-life observations and self-monitoring data. The setting and type of assessment procedure will be determined by the type of problem and the data needed to meet the purposes of the assessment.

Empirical data regarding the assessment practices of clinicians have been recently summarized by Swan and MacDonald (1978) in their survey study of 353 behavior therapists. Their findings regarding the setting and procedures for assessment and the percentage of clients for whom each procedure is employed is reported in Table 9.1. These data support the notion that the behavior therapist's primary source of information in an outpatient therapy setting is the clinical interview. It might be argued that such information may be inaccurate and misleading. In fact, that frequently is the case, especially when the client's distortions of the environment are part of the problem. It is precisely because of the problems with the validity of self-report that the behavior therapist frequently engages in other assessment practices, such as asking the client to monitor some behavior, observing the client in real life, interviewing others, engaging in role playing, and so on. Thus, there are several settings from which data may be obtained for the therapist's assessment purposes. Specific examples of how assessment occurs in many settings will be presented in the applications section of this book.

At this point, let us return to our clinician who was ready to begin outpatient therapy assessment when we digressed in order to discuss the model and setting for clinical assessment. We now know that the therapist is ready to do a functional analysis of the client's problem and offer an experimental treatment program and, furthermore, that it is most likely that

Table 9.1   Assessment settings and procedures used by behavior therapists.

Setting and Procedure	Percent of Clients Treated with Setting and Procedure
1. Interview with identified client	89%
2. Client self-monitoring	51
3. Interview with identified client's significant other	49
4. Direct observation of target behaviors in situ	40
5. Information from consulting professionals	37
6. Role play	34
7. Behavioral written self-report measures	27
8. Demographic questionnaires	20
9. Personality inventories	20
10. Projective tests	10

SOURCE: Based on data from Swan, G. E., & MacDonald, M. L. Behavior therapy in practice: A national survey of behavior therapists. *Behavior Therapy*, 1978, *9*, 799–807.

the client will be seen for a clinical interview. However, before the interview begins, the therapist must decide what type of information he or she will seek about the presenting problem. What are the aspects of the problem and its causes that the therapist will need to know? What general areas will the therapist need to assess?

Areas of Assessment

There are three general areas of assessment that the experimental clinician should consider. First, there is the area for which behavior modifiers have been best known: the *somatic-motor responses*. These are most often referred to as *behaviors*—they are the actual overt responses of the organism. Second, there is the area of *physiological responses,* which has received some consideration by behaviorists, especially with problems traditionally labeled as anxiety and mental retardation. These variables need to be assessed with as much expertise as the behavioral-change agent can develop. Where necessary and appropriate, professional consultation or collaboration should be employed (for example, a gynecological examination in orgasmic dysfunction, or nutritional consultation in obesity). Third, there is the area of *self-report measures.* Traditionally, self-report measures referred to questionnaires, but for the behavior therapist, the self-report measures usually focus on thoughts or feelings in a specific situation, such as rating on a 10-point scale one's fear of riding on an airplane. More recently, behavior therapists have used self-reports of the client's internal thinking or imagery in both assessment and treatment. This has become such a common practice that the assessment of self-report has become almost synonymous with the assessment of *cognitive responses.* Frequently one sees the three areas of behavioral assessment referred to as overt behaviors, physiological responses, and cognitive responses. Cognitive responses have increasingly become more central to the clinical practice of the behavior therapist. What is going on in the client's head? What does the client think about in certain situations? How are these cognitive variables related to external behavior? These are legitimate questions for the behavior modifier. There is a possible fourth area for consideration, emotional responses. These refer to the client's feelings. Certainly the feelings or emotions are more than the client's self-report of them, but since the therapist can only know the client's emotions by his or her self-report, emotional responses are usually classified as self-report measures by the behavior therapist. These variables may be difficult to measure and quantify, but if they are important and essential in the explanation, prediction, and control of behavior, they must be considered.

Like most clinicians, a behavioral-change agent does not begin assessment sessions by simply asking straightforward questions regarding these areas of consideration. The interview begins with an attempt to establish rapport and a good working relationship with the client. The therapist behaves in a manner that would be described as warm, friendly, empathetic, reassuring, and kind. The therapist is aware that such attention and behaviors will affect client output. The behavioral-change agent expects to obtain the information necessary for an adequate assessment by covering many areas of life and yet maintaining awareness of the client's three response classes (somatic-motor, self-report [cognitive], and physiological) in a broad spectrum of situations. The therapist is attuned to both verbal and nonverbal cues from the client during the interview process.

The therapist may follow an outline of potential problem situations in the client's life. Outlines that we have found useful in clinical practice and in training graduate students in assessment are included in Figure 9.1 and 9.2.[1] Figure 9.1 is for an initial interview only; Figure 9.2 covers the entire assessment process. These serve as general guidelines of how assessment might be conducted and are used with great flexibility. More extensive examples are presented by Peterson (1968), Lazarus (1972), and Gottman and Lieblum (1974).

The information garnered from the assessment process must be synthesized and ordered so that the change agent may identify the dependent variables (client's problem behaviors) and independent variables (causing and maintaining factors). Once this assessment is completed, it is presented to the client, and then the clinical experiment (treatment program or behavior-modification program) is explained to the client and is subsequently implemented. In clinical practice this summary presentation of the assessment is often referred to as a *summary interview*.

This same assessment model may be utilized in working with children at home or in a residential treatment center. The specific outline followed or procedures employed may vary from situation to situation, but the experimental/clinical *model* of assessment remains the same.

TREATMENT STRATEGIES

Following presentation of the summary clinical assessment to the client, the therapist explains the proposed treatment strategy. This treatment

1. These outlines reflect the impact of a number of our professional mentors. It is not possible to recall who added what to the outline, but undoubtedly each will recognize his or her contribution and should be blamed accordingly.

Initial Interview Outline

I. Objectives
  1. Establish good relationship with the client.
  2. Obtain adequate information to identify dependent and independent
     variables of client's problem.

II. Assessment session
  1. Opening question: "Why are you here?"
     a. Begin by introducing self, confidentiality, and clinic policies.
     b. Invite client to tell about problem as client sees it, by asking the
        opening question.
     c. Find out how and why the decision to come in was made.
     d. Use of "reflection and clarification" to keep client talking about how
        he sees his problem.
  (Depending on what is said in response to the opening question, go on to either
  2 or 3 below.)
  2. Inquiry into assets and liabilities.
     a. Socioeconomic situation. (How is the situation financially?)
     b. Job situation. (Does he or she have a job? What?)
     c. Work situation. (What is the relation to others on the job?)
     d. Educational background.
     e. Religious background.
     f. Peer relations. (What are relations to the same and the opposite sex?)
     g. Relationship with spouse.
     h. Relationship with in-laws.
     i. Relationship with children (each specific child).
  (Gaining information in these areas will allow you to: (1) develop a better
  understanding of the client; (2) determine strengths and weaknesses; and (3)
  determine if and how problems in these areas may be related to the problem
  presented in Section I.)
  3. Set clear definition and specification of problem areas (dependent variables)
     and the associated independent variables.
     a. Identify and define each distressing problem.
     b. Presence and absence of positive and negative eliciting and discriminative
        stimuli (internal and external).
     c. Presence and absence of reinforcement and punishment (internal and
        external).
     d. To whom it is distressing.
     e. Timing and frequency.
     f. Circumstances under which behavior occurs (focus on specific situations).
     g. What happens afterward.
     h. What client says to himself before the behavior.
     i. What client says to himself after the behavior.
     j. What is currently being done about problem.
     k. Availability of reinforcement.
  4. Objectives of therapy.
     a. What do you want to be different at end of therapy?
     b. Just a beginning in formulating objectives.

III. Closing first interview
   Give a nebulous statement with regard to helpfulness of the information and
   your feelings of being able to help the client with his problem. Inform the client
   that you need more information to complete the assessment (if such is, in fact,
   the case) and that you need to look at the information already gained. TELL
   THE TRUTH, BUT BE AS POSITIVE AS POSSIBLE.

Figure 9.1   Initial interview outline.

Behavior Assessment Form

Date _____

Therapist _____

Name _____ Address _____

Phone _____ Age _____ Occupation _____

Marital Status _____ Children _____

Previous Therapy _____

    Outcome _____ Orientation _____

    Current expectancies _____

Known Medical Problems _____

    Most recent exam _____ Current drugs _____

Atypical Background or Experiences _____

    _____

Average Hours of Sleep per Night _____ Regular? _____

Eating Patterns _____

Physical Description _____

    _____

Social & Interview Behaviors _____

    _____

Self-Description: (Aver.)

1. Physical condition   (V. Poor) 0 1 2 3 4 5 6 7 8 9 10 (Athletic)
2. Intelligence   (Stupid) 0 1 2 3 4 5 6 7 8 9 10 (Bright)
3. Physical looks   (Ugly) 0 1 2 3 4 5 6 7 8 9 10 (Attractive)
4. Assertiveness   (Shy) 0 1 2 3 4 5 6 7 8 9 10 (Aggressive)
5. Likeability   (Disliked) 0 1 2 3 4 5 6 7 8 9 10 (Well liked)
6. Self-confidence   (Inferior) 0 1 2 3 4 5 6 7 8 9 10 (Confident)
7. Coping style   (Anxious) 0 1 2 3 4 5 6 7 8 9 10 (Relaxed)
8. Personal worth   (Bad) 0 1 2 3 4 5 6 7 8 9 10 (Good)

             Sum = _____ Mean = _____

9. Name some of the particularly good things about yourself (assets, talents, etc.): _____ (space is provided for answer) _____

10. Name some of the particularly bad things about yourself (faults, deficiencies, etc.): _____ (space provided) _____

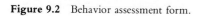

Figure 9.2   Behavior assessment form.

2

Presenting Problem(s):

1. Definition & description:_____ (space provided)_____

2. Historical development (recency, etc.):_____ (space provided)_____

3. Current state & correlates:

   a. Frequency/intensity_____

   b. Situationality_____

   c. Temporal distribution_____

   d. Antecedents (environmental & cognitive)_____

      _____

   e. Consequences (social & self-presented)_____

      _____

4. Atypical or complicating factors:_____ (space provided)_____

5. Comments:_____ (space provided)_____

Tentative Treatment Program:

1. Modification targets:_____ (space provided)_____

2. Assessment methods:_____ (space provided)_____

3. Probable determinants:_____ (space provided)_____

4. Tentative treatment strategies:_____ (space provided)_____

5. Auxiliary topics or comments:_____ (space provided)_____

Figure 9.2 (*cont.*)

strategy is again based on the experimental/clinical model. The therapist and/or the client is going to conduct an experiment.

The objectives of the clinical experiment have been developed from the assessment process. The client has informed the therapist why he or she has sought professional help and what he or she expects to gain from the treatment sessions. These objectives provide the basis for the development of the experimental/clinical hypothesis. They serve the same function as in the development of an experimental hypothesis in the laboratory setting. The objectives allow the clinician to determine what directions the treatment strategies will take, and they provide the basis from which the criteria of success can be drawn. When it seems likely that the therapy process will be lengthy or difficult, or if client motivation is low, intermediate objectives may be formulated and utilized. These are especially helpful in providing feedback to the client regarding progress. (Such feedback may not hurt the therapist's motivation either!)

How does a behavior-modification therapist decide what treatment strategy to employ? We return to the experimental/clinical paradigm for the initial answer to this question. Given the assessment of the ongoing situation in the client's life and the formulation of therapeutic objectives, the therapist must design an appropriate clinical intervention project. First, the dependent variable must be identified. In many cases, this will be the one identified as the problem behavior during the assessment process, and the one that will be directly modified in the treatment program. Many times there is more than one dependent variable. In some cases, additional dependent variables may be identified and focused on during the treatment program; for example, the therapist may decide to decrease one dependent variable by increasing the frequency of another, incompatible dependent variable.

Once the behavior (dependent variable) to be changed has been clearly identified, the therapist must decide what treatment procedures will be employed in the effort to change that dependent variable. This treatment constitutes the independent variable. As will be seen in examples later in this chapter in Part Two, several procedures are often combined in one treatment package. Although the therapist may be able to evaluate the overall effectiveness of such a treatment program, he or she cannot identify which components of the treatment package are responsible for the package's effectiveness.

Thus we have seen that the therapist's task in developing the treatment strategy is to identify dependent and independent variables. The dependent variables have been derived in one way or another from the assessment sessions, but from where does the therapist derive independent variables? Ideally, they originate from the presently available experimental literature. The procedures derived from that literature are continually being expanded and improved upon by new findings. The present findings in the clin-ically relevant literature were presented in summary form in Chapters 6 through 8. It is from these findings and from empirical evaluations of their effectiveness in clinical situations (as presented in Part Two) that the therapist draws the procedures or treatment strategies that will be em-ployed in a given clinical situation. Fortunately, the experimental/clinical literature is a burgeoning one, and the clinician increasingly can look to that literature for direction. However, at our current level of knowledge, the experimental clinician must frequently rely on past experience and clinical hunches, since there may not be a directly applicable experimental literature. As a result, the clinician, either from practical necessity or ex-perimental creativity, must often decide on a new independent variable. As always, however, the effects of such a variable must be evaluated. One advantage of this approach to clinical intervention is that the experimental clinician not only can draw upon the experimental/clinical literature, but also may contribute to it through systematic evaluation of intervention procedures.

Once the dependent and independent variables are selected, the therapist must decide what data to collect and what research design to employ in evaluating the clinical experiment. These would be determined by refer-ring to the guidelines presented in Chapters 4 and 5. The client's objectives will allow the therapist to decide these issues in accordance with the suggestions for research design, data collection, and data analysis.

One of the hallmarks of behavior therapy is the interactive relationship between assessment and treatment. The treatment program is developed directly from the information gained during assessment. However, assess-ment does not end with the beginning of treatment, but rather continues over the course of treatment. This ongoing assessment allows the behavior therapist to evaluate the effectiveness of the therapy regimen. Further, it allows the therapist to alter the treatment program as new and pertinent information may be reported, as often happens during therapy.

The foregoing description refers to an individual therapy program, but the general treatment model is applicable in all treatment situations. As with assessment procedures, the specifics may vary widely across differ-ent situations in which an experimental approach to clinical intervention is used.

EXAMPLES OF EXPERIMENTAL/CLINICAL
APPROACHES

The following case study demonstrates the utilization of the experimen-tal/clinical method of clinical assessment and treatment. In some cases, such as this one, the exigencies of clinical intervention make it impossible to specify which particular treatment procedure is responsible for the treatment's effectiveness. Several treatment procedures that have been shown to have clinical promise are included in an overall treatment package. Furthermore, the design does not permit any clear causal statements to be made. However, it does demonstrate the value of defining independent and dependent variables and evaluating the effect of the independent variables (clinical procedures) upon the dependent variable. Of course, with the limited design, other factors may be responsible for the behavior change.

The following example was chosen because it represents the clinical utility of the "classic" behavior-therapy procedure of training in progressive muscular relaxation (Wolpe, 1958). It was also chosen because frequently in a clinical setting, a client will report a specific problem that precludes utilization of an intrasubject design. Although it might have been possible to employ an ABAB design, clinical exigencies precluded the use of a reversal procedure. The method of evaluation in this case study is an improvement over reliance on clinical intuition. At least the therapists would have known if the program had not had an effect.

The client (Mrs. W.) was a forty-one-year-old woman with a history of asthma since the age of seven. Her breathing difficulties had become quite severe during the preceding three years. Medical treatments ranging from desensitization shots to cortisone therapy had resulted in only minor improvement, and the client's performance of routine daily activities was seriously jeopardized. Prior to behavior therapy, the client was consuming medically contraindicated amounts of prescription drugs, including ephedrine-based bronchodilators, corticosteroids, and phenobarbital, in order to maintain marginal respiratory functioning. A portable nebulizer, or Bronkometer, prescribed only for the alleviation of severe attacks, was being used extensively. Since chronic heavy dosages of such medication can result in serious pulmonary impairment, reduced consumption became a major focus of therapy. The client was therefore instructed to self-record the daily frequency of her Bronkometer use (Sirota & Mahoney, 1974).

The foregoing information was gained from an interview based on one of the assessment formats presented earlier. Additionally, it was determined that the client's breathing difficulties not only were caused by diagnosed reactions to typical allergies, but also occurred in anxiety-eliciting situations. For example, being physically separated from the Bronkometer would elicit a near panic reaction followed by an asthma attack. Such upsets as a family squabble or noisy children would also precipitate the onset of an asthma attack. The dependent variable thus was the frequency of Bronkometer use. Since the client always used it when an attack occurred and since this level of usage was contraindicated, it was chosen as the target behavior to be changed. The series of events leading to the utilization of the Bronkometer was broken down into a sequence of small steps. Treatment was then introduced as early as possible in each behavioral sequence in order to break the chain and prevent a full-blown attack.

The client was trained in the use of deep muscle relaxation as a coping response for stress and anxiety. This procedure includes sitting quietly and alternately tensing and relaxing sixteen different muscle groups throughout the body (Bernstein & Borkovec, 1973). She was instructed to practice relaxation at home twice daily for one week with the aid of a cassette tape. After a brief (thirteen-day) baseline study of self-monitored Bronkometer use, an immediate treatment intervention was deemed advisable. The client was given a portable timer that she was to carry at all times. For the first five days of treatment, she was instructed to set the timer for semi-random intervals averaging thirty minutes in length. When the timer buzzed, the client was to perform a brief muscle inventory, noting her anxiety level and relaxing away any incipient tension. This technique was intended to help interrupt anxiety chains and to encourage spontaneous and natural self-monitoring of performance. The timer interval was subsequently lengthened to one hour.

An additional treatment strategy (began on day 9) involved brief postponement of Bronkometer use. Any time the client experienced breathing difficulty and wanted to use her inhalant, she was told to set the timer for three to four minutes, practice abbreviated relaxation, and then employ the Bronkometer if it was still necessary. Systematic desensitization, the systematic pairing of visualizations of stressful situations with deep muscle relaxation, was begun along two hierarchies (Bronkometer separation and domestic situations), but it was terminated before completion because of dramatic decreases in the use of the Bronkometer. A total of nine therapy sessions were conducted.

The results of the study are presented in Figure 9.3. As can be seen, the client was using the Bronkometer an average of nine times per day during baseline. During the course of treatment, the use of the Bronkometer gradually decreased and by day 14 of treatment it was not being used at all. It was not used through the rest of the treatment period. Data were not taken during the time between termination and follow-up, but at the five-day follow-up six months later, the client still was not using the Bronkometer. Additionally, during treatment the client had terminated cortisone therapy, reduced ephedrine-based broncodilators by 80 percent, and reduced or eliminated all remaining asthmatic medications.

The utilization of several clinical procedures does not allow us to determine which factors may have resulted in the behavior change, and the design does not allow us to draw any causative conclusions regarding the entire treatment package, although treatment does seem to have been the cause of the change. More definitive conclusions and the isolation

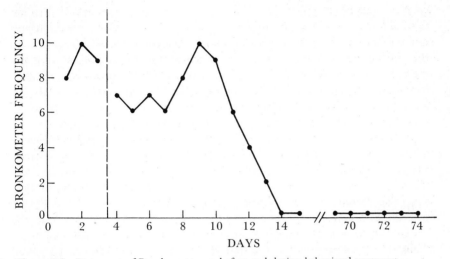

Figure 9.3   Frequency of Bronkometer use before and during behavioral treatment.

Source: Sirota, A. D., & Mahoney, M. J. Relaxing on cue: The self-regulation of asthma. *Journal of Behavior Therapy and Experimental Psychiatry*, 1974, *5*, 65–66. Reprinted by permission of Pergamon Press Ltd.

of the effective treatment components might occur in additional research. Mrs. W. felt that the early identification of tension and the ability "to relax it away" had been very important in the alleviation of her asthma attacks. She also reported that the ticking of the timer eventually became a cue that helped her to remain calm.

The reader should be cautioned that not all clients present problems that can be dealt with in only nine sessions. In fact, many clients have more complex problems requiring more complex interventions over much longer periods of time. It is also important to note that not every intervention is so effective. But if the experimental clinician evaluates what is done, at least he or she will know whether or not it is effective even if, as in this study, one cannot specify exactly why.

Our second example is chosen because it demonstrates a clinical application of recently developed cognitive behavior approach to treatment. This example by Rush, Shaw, and Khatami (1980) reports the treatment of a commonly reported clinical problem, depression. The client was a thirty-three-year-old married woman, who was the mother of four children. She reported having been depressed for the past 4½ months and having had three previous depressive episodes of approximately 4 months each. Her husband was described as an overly solicitous but easygoing professional, who rarely expressed feelings.

The client exhibited many of the thinking and behavioral patterns characteristic of depression. For example, she felt she was a burden to her family and that she was a worthless person. She discounted her children's expressions of affection, and in fact, felt guilty about her interactions with the children. She was unable to express her positive feelings toward her husband and children and generally was unassertive. She had poor parenting skills. She had gotten to the point that she desired to avoid social contacts, including visits from her parents and in-laws.

Since so much of the problem involved the interaction between the client and her husband, the therapy included both spouses. The clients participated in twenty-two sessions over a sixteen-week period, two sessions per week for six weeks and one session per week for ten weeks. The authors collected follow-up data at weeks 24 and 30, but did no further therapy. The therapy process was divided into the following three steps: (1) recording cognitions; (2) identifying cognitions and behaviors within the couple's system; and (3) correcting cognitive distortions. Although the actual data are not presented, the first step of recording cognitions allowed the client and the therapist to have self-monitored data of the client's negative thought processes and their relationship to her depressive feelings and behaviors. For example, she was able to see that she continually read rejection into her family's behavior by recording twenty-seven instances of "no one really cares for me" in one day.

The second step of the program was implemented by tape-recording the treatment sessions and having the couple review the tapes between sessions. The basic purpose of these sessions and the analysis of the tapes was to get the couple to see the relationships between their thoughts, feelings, and behaviors. A typical communication pattern is presented in Table 9.2.

The final phase of treatment consisted of correcting both the personal cognitive distortions of the client and those of the couple during their interactions.

Therapy sessions focused on her automatic thought that "no one cares." A meeting was held to clarify family roles and expectations. The husband's notion that she simply has to work her way out of depression ("just do things and you'll be happy") was identified and challenged. He recognized the paradox between his previously unstated expectations of her and his fear of "putting too much pressure on her," and agreed to work on his verbal and nonverbal communications. In fact, as the patient recognized that her husband didn't want only a "house-cleaner," she began to reconsider some of her own ideas. She realized that her behavior was geared toward "cleaning house to get approval."

Each member of the couple began to ask, "What do I want, what does my spouse want, how can we achieve our goal?" Communication generally improved as the couple learned about each other's thinking styles. The patient became more confident and less dependent by learning to directly verbalize her needs. On the

Table 9.2 An illustrative interaction of a depressed client and her husband.

	Wife's Responses		Husband's Responses	
Situation	*Affect*	*Cognition*	*Affect*	*Cognition*
She wants to go shopping. He agrees but starts to work on another project.	Anger	First, he promises to go shopping and then he lets me down. He doesn't really care.	Happiness	I'm glad she is feeling good today. I'll finish up this job and then we'll handle the shopping.
She withdraws to bedroom. He continues working.	Sadness	Nobody cares about what I want. I don't really deserve to go because he has more important things to do. I shouldn't make requests of him. I'm too selfish.	Anxiety	She's going into one of her moods again. I wonder what upset her? I'd better leave her alone or she'll lose her temper.
She sits upstairs. Having finished the other job, he makes coffee for the couple.	Guilt	I don't deserve to be his wife. I'm just a burden on him. It would be better if I were dead.	Anxiety	I'd better make the dinner tonight to take off some pressure.
He makes dinner.	Sadness	He doesn't even need me to cook anymore. The kids didn't even notice I wasn't around. I'm totally useless to my family.	Anger	Well, if she's going to pout all night, I'm going out for a beer.

SOURCE: Rush, A. J., Shaw, B., & Khatami, M. Cognitive therapy of depression: Utilizing the couples system. *Cognitive Therapy and Research,* 1980, *4,* 109. Reprinted by permission of Plenum Press.

other hand, her husband appreciated the clear messages and willingly recognized that she did not have to follow his prescriptions for coping with depressed feelings. (Rush, Shaw, & Khatami, 1980, pp. 109–110)

In addition to the just described clinical report, the authors evaluated the effectiveness of their therapy on the Beck Depression Inventory. This inventory is a self-report of the severity of the thoughts, feelings, behaviors, and physiological responses characteristic of depression (Beck, 1967), and it is widely accepted as a research and clinical measure of depression. Moderate depression is indicated by a score of 17 to 25 and severe depression is indicated by a score of 26 or greater. The data for the Beck Depression Inventory scores for the client are reported in Figure 9.4. In general, the data indicate that the client showed a decrease in reported depression over the

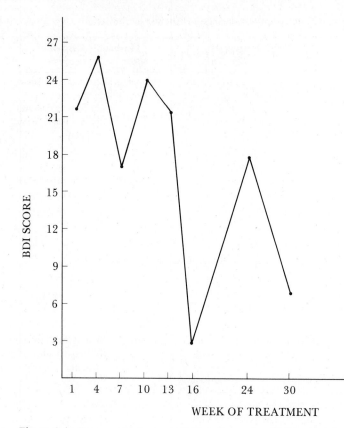

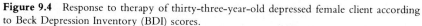

WEEK OF TREATMENT

Figure 9.4   Response to therapy of thirty-three-year-old depressed female client according to Beck Depression Inventory (BDI) scores.

SOURCE: Rush, A. J., Shaw, B., & Khatami, M. Cognitive therapy of depression: Utilizing the couples system. *Cognitive Therapy and Research,* 1980, *4,* 103–113. Reprinted by permission of Plenum Press.

course of teatment. By the end of treatment, her depression scores were in the "normal" range. Of course, from a scientific standpoint, these data must be cautiously interpreted. The study is a case report, and as such, did not employ one of the single-subject designs noted in Chapter 4. the increase in depression at week 24 makes the data difficult to interpret; unfortunately, in the case report, the authors did not offer any explanation for the week 24 data.[2] It would also have been nice to have had follow-up

2. A personal communication from Brian Shaw indicated that the BDI for the twenty-fourth week resulted from a short-lived (approximately four days) episode during which the client became very concerned about the changes associated with therapy. Because of her doubts about the types of changes produced in therapy, she suffered this temporary depressive episode. He also reported that the client has remained essentially depression-free for the three years following treatment.

data, but sometimes this is not possible in the clinical setting. It would have been better to have included additional behavioral measures or some data on the direct effects of the cognitive therapy on the frequency of the self-monitored cognitions (see Craighead, 1980). However, as reported, this case illustrates nicely the value of conducting an ongoing evaluation and assessment of the effectiveness of treatment. The therapist was not dependent on some "clinical intuition" about the effects of the therapy, but rather had some objective data by which to evaluate its effect.

The third example of an experimental/clinical approach to therapy is chosen for several reasons. It clearly demonstrates the value of ongoing evaluation of the treatment program, and how a therapist may alter the treatment program on the basis of the obtained data. It also demonstrates how the clinician may employ procedures that have been demonstrated empirically to be effective with a problem, as this clinician based his treatment program on previous research. It also illustrates one of this book's central themes, which is that the clinician should use as many procedures from as broad a perspective as possible to help the client make the desired changes.

This clinical example described the behavioral treatment of anorexia nervosa (Ollendick, 1979), a relatively infrequent disorder. Anorexia nervosa is characterized by refusal to eat sufficient food with a resultant serious weight loss; there is an association death rate of over 15 percent. The client was a sixteen-year-old male (Rick), who was referred by his family physician after two extensive physical evaluations had revealed no apparent physical causes for his refusal for food, vomiting when forced to eat, and extreme weight loss (39 percent during the six months preceding treatment). Information from his parents and teachers indicated that his refusal to eat had resulted from peer criticism for being overweight and from required attendance in a physical education class where the peer criticism was apparently severe. Behavioral observations at school and home indicated "that anxiety associated with weight gain and negative peer criticism were the primary factors maintaining his maladaptive behavior" (Ollendick, 1979, p. 127).

The following treatment program (independent variables) was followed with Rick over a three-year period.

Feedback and Desensitization I. Rick was seen for a total of 24 sessions over an eight-month period. At the beginning of each session, he was weighed under standardized conditions and received informational feedback by recording his weight on the chart and by acknowledgment from the therapist. During the first two weeks, he was seen for six sessions of deep muscle relaxation training; for the next 14 weeks he was seen for weekly sessions of systematic desensitization (Wolpe, 1973), employing a 10-item hierarchy related to weight gain and peer criticism. Specifically, following relaxation training, he was instructed to imagine hearing the word "food," seeing food on the table, being called to the table, being seated at the table, eating nutritious food, enjoying the food, weighing himself and noticing that he was gaining weight, a stranger commenting on his weight, family members commenting on his weight, and, finally, peers commenting on his weight. Upon attaining a safe weight of 160 pounds, he was seen for four additional monthly sessions of informational feedback and desensitization training.

Feedback I. Systematic desensitization was discontinued, but Rick was seen on a monthly basis for four months. During these sessions, he was weighed under the standardized conditions and received informational feedback by recording his weight on the chart and by acknowledgment from the therapist.

Feedback and Desensitization II. Rick was seen for a total of 24 sessions over an eight-month period. At the beginning of each session, he was again weighed under the standardized conditions and provided informational feedback. Further, he was seen for six sessions during the first two weeks for reinstruction in deep muscle relaxation training and then for 14 weekly sessions of systematic desensitization employing the same hierarchy previously used. Upon reattaining the safe weight of 160 pounds, he was seen for four additional sessions on a monthly basis.

Feedback II. Again, systermatic desensitization was discontinued, but Rick was seen on a monthly basis for four months. During these sessions he was weighed under standardized conditions and continued to receive informational feedback.

Feedback and Cognitive Restructuring. Rick was seen for a total of 24 sessions over an eight-month period. Again, weight was recorded under standardized conditions and informational feedback was provided. He was seen for six sessions during the first two weeks to instruct him in the use of the cognitive strategies and then for 14 weekly sessions of cognitive restructuring (Beck, 1976; Mahoney & Mahoney, 1976b). Specifically, the five categories of weight-relevant thoughts proposed by Mahoney and Mahoney (1976b) for obese individuals were adapted for Rick: (1) thoughts about pounds gained (e.g., "I've tried to eat that food but haven't gained a pound"), (2) thoughts about capabilities (e.g., "There's no way I can gain weight again"), (3) excuses (e.g., "If those kids liked me, I could gain weight"), (4) standard setting (e.g., "I threw up this morning, there's no use to try. I may as well quit"), and (5) thoughts about how peers would perceive him (e.g., "Nobody will like me if I gain weight"). He monitored and recorded "self-talk" thoughts related to weight gain and peer criticism between sessions; during sessions this "homework" was reviewed and the inappropriate thoughts were analyzed and restructured. On attaining a safe weight he was once again seen for four sessions on a monthly basis.

Feedback III. During this phase, cognitive restructuring was discontinued, but Rick was seen for the standardized weight measurement and informational feedback each month for four months.

Extended Follow-Up. Rick was seen for follow-up measurements at 6 months, 12 months, 18 months, and 24 months. He was again weighed under standardized conditions and continued to receive informational feedback.[3]

The dependent variable for this therapy program was weight gain. The results of the treatment program are presented in Figure 9.5. The data indicate that it was likely that the systematic desensitization resulted in the initial weight-gain; since systematic desensitization always occurred in conjunction with information feedback, it is possible that it was the combination of treatments that produced the weight gain. It seems unlikely that informational feedback alone would have resulted in the weight gain, because each time the therapy was reduced to informational feedback alone, the client lost the weight he had gained during the combined treatment. Since the weight gained with the systematic desensitization and informational feedback combined was not maintained over time, the therapist altered his strategy and engaged the client in a cognitive restructuring and informational feedback program. This therapy program produced weight gain which was maintained up to eighteen months. Although the client had begun to lose weight at a two-year follow-up (month 60 in Figure 9.5), this was quickly reversed.[4]

Since the cognitive restructuring program followed systematic desensitization therapy, it will be up to future research to determine whether cognitive restructuring with feedback is adequate to produce weight gain in anorexic clients, or if it must be offered in a particular sequence with systematic desensitization to produce weight gains that are maintained. However, by collecting data in a systematic fashion, Ollendick was able to develop an effective therapeutic program for Rick. Furthermore, the study strongly suggests that the therapy program should be matched to the client's problem, which in this case included an anxiety and a cognitive component. After the client was offered therapy for both the anxiety (systematic desensitization) and the maladaptive cognitive responses to peer criticism (cognitive restructuring), the therapeutic gains were maintained. Thus, this use of the experimental/clinical approach not only was valuable to the client but offers support for an important issue in research, suggests an important therapeutic strategy change for anorexic clients, and suggests some interesting hypotheses for future research in the treatment of anorexia nervosa.

3. This excerpt from "Behavioral Treatment of Anorexia Nervosa" by Thomas H. Ollendick is reprinted from *Behavior Modification,* Vol. 3, No. 1. (January 1979), pp. 124–135 by permission of the publisher, Sage Publications, and the author.
4. A personal communication from Thomas Ollendick indicated that data at month 61 showed that the client's weight had stabilized at approximately 145 pounds. At that point the client was seen for two sessions per week for two weeks. The therapy was cognitive restucturing, since the assessment at that point indicated the weight loss had stemmed from the increased frequency of maladaptive thoughts. The client was then seen once a month for three months for check-up sessions to review progress and to be weighed. During this time his weight increased to 170 pounds, and it has maintained at that level for the past 2½ years.

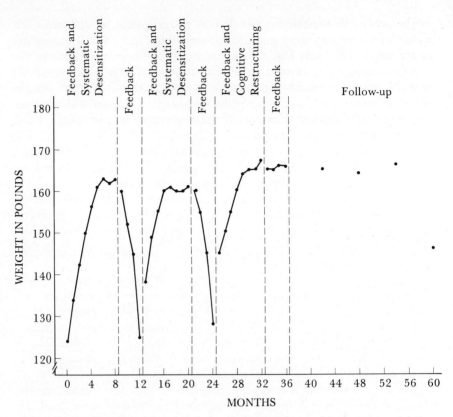

Figure 9.5 Rick's weight in pounds during the various phases of the experimental design. While not shown here, data obtained following the submission of this manuscript indicate that with the reinstitution of maintenance sessions, rapid weight gain resulted.

SOURCE: Ollendick, T. H. Behavioral treatment of anorexia nervosa: A five year study. *Behavior Modification,* 1979, *3*(1), 131.

A FINAL NOTE

Up to this point we have seen the behavior modifier as a person who designs a clinical experiment to allow for the modification of a behavior (as broadly defined in this book) that is upsetting or annoying someone. The overall objective of that modification is to make the upset or annoyed person feel better and thus in a small way contribute to making this a better world. As will be seen later in the book, these same methodologies and procedures may have broad social applications and implications. This broad application and the evaluative statement regarding "making the world a better place" direct our thoughts to ethical questions. Better for whom? Better for what? Who will modify whose behavior? These issues have become of such significant importance that they are discussed in detail in the next chapter and will appear intermittently throughout the chapters in Part Two.

SUMMARY

This chapter presents the experimental/clinical approach to the assessment and treatment of behavioral problems. The experimental/clinical model represents the use of methodological behaviorism in applied settings. Our example is the individual-therapy setting, but the model is equally appropriate for all areas of behavior modification.

Experimental/clinical assessment is frequently done within an operant paradigm in which the clinician identifies the behavioral problem (B) and its antecedent (A) and consequent (C) stimuli. Even when the therapist goes beyond the operant model, it may be advisable to conceptualize the assessment in operant language. In assessment the clinician needs to evaluate somatic-motor, physiological, and cognitive behaviors.

Experimental/clinical intervention or the use of treatment strategies is also seen within the model of methodological behaviorism. The clinician and the client conduct an experiment. The target behavior is seen as the dependent variable and the treatment program becomes an independent variable. Ideally, the program's effectiveness is evaluated within an intrasubject design, though in clinical settings, this may be difficult. The cases of the asthmatic, depressed, and anorexic clients illustrate the practical utilization of the experimental/clinical model.

SUGGESTED READINGS

Bernstein, D. A., & Nietzel, M. T. *Introduction to clinical psychology*. New York: McGraw-Hill, 1980. Chapters 4, 5, 6, and 7.

Goldfried, M. R., & Sprafkin, J. N. *Behavioral personality assessment*. Morristown, N.J.: General Learning Press, 1974.

Gottman, J. M., & Lieblum, S. R. *How to do psychotherapy and how to evaluate it.* New York: Holt, Rinehart and Winston, 1974.

Peterson, D. R. *The clinical study of social behavior.* New York: Appleton-Century Crofts, 1968.

CHAPTER 10

ETHICAL AND LEGAL ISSUES

The prediction and control of behavior are basic goals in the science of psychology. These goals, of course, are based on the assumption that human behavior is systematic, that it obeys functional relationships. Substantial research evidence supports the notion that some complex human actions can be accurately predicted and controlled. Psychologists are far from being capable of such prediction and control with all or even most behaviors, but their progress over the last decade has been quite impressive.

The existing information on human behavior raises a variety of issues. Several ethical implications follow from development of a technology of behavior change or behavior control. If human performance can be reliably modified, who should choose the "desired" behaviors? Who controls whom? Related to the ethical issues is the possibility that persons who cannot act on their own behalf may be exposed to abuses of technology. Legal issues arise in implementing behavior-change procedures that may infringe upon a person's rights. The present chapter discusses ethical and legal issues raised by a technology of behavior change and suggests guidelines for protecting clients who receive treatment.

ETHICAL ISSUES
Free Will, Determinism, and Responsibility

Scientific prediction and control require the assumption of *determinism*. Recall from Chapter 2 that the principle of determinism states that all

183

events must have a cause or causes. Phenomena are determined in the sense that they obey a lawful functional relationship; they consistently follow a preceding set of circumstances. For example, when one billiard ball strikes a second one, the latter's reaction is determined: it will move in a predictable direction at a predictable speed for a predictable distance. This consistency is necessary for accurate prediction. If the reactions of the second billiard ball were not determined, then it would show no consistent relationship to preceding events and its movements would be said to occur by chance rather than in response to specific forces acting upon it.

An alternative explanation of order and consistency is contained in the assumption of free will. Philosophically, free will is one's alleged ability to initiate or alter a causal chain. Although individuals frequently may be influenced by learning history or environmental events, the free will doctrine asserts that they can moderate and alter their actions in various ways through "will power." This capacity for free will is usually reserved for humans (one seldom observes a self-determined rat or turtle). Usually its mechanism is vaguely described: individuals somehow step in and override the influences that are impinging on them. For centuries, philosophical debate has centered around the issue of free will versus determinism. Religious philsophers have been particularly interested in demonstrating that humans are free to determine their own destiny. However, the overwhelming consensus among philosophers, logicians, and scientists has been in favor of determinism. Several attempts have been made to salvage some artifacts of freedom, unpredictability, or randomness in physical events (for example, the principle of indeterminacy in physics). Many of these arguments have been based on inadequacies inherent in our measurement systems (see Mahoney et al., 1974). In the last few decades, psychological research has amply demonstrated that the assumption of determinism is both justified and essential in dealing with human behavior. Although only a small minority of the cause-effect relationships in human performance have been identified to date, these modest beginnings have indicated that we are on the right track. Complex human performances are a function of complex variables, and it is the task of the behavioral scientist to identify and describe those functional relations.

Before we discuss the implications of determinism for human behavior, an important distinction should be made. There is a critical difference between the assumption of determinism and notions of *predeterminism*. The latter term refers to a fatalistic predestination of cause-effect chains. Let us consider any two related events, A and B. Determinism states that event B is caused or determined by event A; this relationship allows one to predict with some probability that whenever event A is encountered, event B will soon follow. Predeterminism, on the other hand, states not only that event A causes event B but also that event A is going to happen no matter what.

This is a more sweeping and ambitious prediction. While the determinist is stating, "If event A occurs, I predict that event B will follow," the predeterminist says, "Event A must occur and will be followed by event B." Most scientists adopt only the assumption of determinism.

If human performance is composed of many complex behavioral events, the assumption of determinism states that those events are determined and therefore predictable, at least in principle. The fact that we cannot now accurately predict 100 percent of a person's actions is assumed to be a result of our ignorance rather than the capriciousness or randomness of the behavior. We have not yet identified the elements that comprise event A.

Most individuals will admit that to some extent their current performances are influenced by preceding events, such as childhood experiences, praise for previous performance, and so on. However, at a gut level, many people feel that they are not walking billiard balls, predictably pushed and pulled by environmental forces. Most of us feel that we play some role in determining our future—that our actions are influenced by our hopes, aspirations, and expectations. The determinist would agree and add, however, that one's hopes, aspirations, and expectations are themselves determined by previous events. You are pursuing a college degree because you "want" to. Yes, but your "want" has been caused by a complex learning history of modeling from others, praise and/or pressure from family, stimulating instructors, and so on. One cannot override the causal chain—if a person rebels against the predictions of the determinist, in principle that rebellion is predictable from previous experience. The Russian novelist Dostoyevsky once stated that man would go to great extremes to avoid being predictable. As a last resort, he stated that an individual would go mad just to maintain independence from determinism. Skinner has pointed out that Dostoyevsky's prediction closed all possible routes of escape from deterministic predictability; by stating that man would go mad to avoid being predictable, Dostoyevsky himself had made a prediction!

If our actions are totally determined by preceding events, then they are in a sense out of our hands, aren't they? This question raises the issue of responsibility. If environment or learning history is the cause of a criminal behavior, is it not both futile and unethical to hold a person responsible for it? Many determinists have adopted this view. According to Skinner (1971), an individual should not be held responsible for either positive or negative accomplishments; the environment has been the cause of both. What is overlooked in this contention is that the act of holding people responsible or making them accountable for their behavior is in itself a very important environmental event. To neglect to thank a person for a kindness because it was only the environment that caused it is to dramatically alter that environment. Praise and blame are environmental events. If holding someone responsible for behavior means that a systematic relationship will be enforced (for example, behavior A will be rewarded; behavior B will not), then the behavioral scientist is both justified in assigning and obliged to assign responsibility to the person. In this sense, the term *responsibility* does not try to isolate a cause. Instead, it predicts a consequence. We are not responsible in that we cause or will ourselves to do something. In determinism, there can be no single or first cause: event B was determined by event A, which, in turn, was determined by a preceding event, and so on into infinity. However, we are responsible in the sense that we usually have at least two alternative response options to choose from, and frequently we know what the consequences of those various responses are. If those consequences are removed, a significant element of our controlling environment is eliminated. One is reminded here of a utopian community that was patterned after Skinner's *Walden II* (1948). The inhabitants of this community decided that an individual would neither be thanked nor criticized for performance since it was the environment rather than the person which was responsible. This arrangement led to a great deal of personal stress because most of the community residents were accustomed to receiving evaluative feedback on their actions. When this feedback was eliminated, a critical element in their environment had been removed.

Despite the rather overwhelming logical and scientific support for the assumption of determinism, the fact remains that most individuals *believe* that they are free, self-determining beings. Thus, efforts to demonstrate and convince them otherwise may be ill-aimed. As Kanfer and Karoly (1972) point out, the important issue is not whether free will or determinism is in fact valid, for the fact of the matter is that most individuals function under the assumptions of freedom and personal responsibility. These beliefs become important variables in the prediction and control of behavior.

Behavior Control and Countercontrol

Most discussions of behavioral determinism highlight the fact that human performance is controlled by environmental forces. The individual is portrayed as a mindless robot, passively responding in a reflexive fashion to surrounding environmental forces. This rather unsavory portrayal has unfortunately been encouraged by some behavioral scientists. However, just as there is no first cause of a specific response, *the influence process between environment and behavior is not a one-way street*. The existing psychological evidence does strongly support the notion that environmental events exert control over behavior. However, there is equally strong evidence illustrating that *behaviors exert control over environments* (Bandura, 1977b). For example, one might argue that rewarding a rat with food pellets for pressing a lever has exerted an influence: the environment (the food dispenser) has determined the rat's behavior. On the other hand, one is equally justified in pointing out that the environment, or at least the rate of food pellet delivery, is being determined by the rat's behavior. The influence process is reciprocal in that it works both ways. Environments influence behavior; behaviors influence environments. Which comes first? The question is, of course, unanswerable. The relationship between environment and behavior is an interdependent one; that is, each influences the other in such a complex manner that it is both meaningless and inaccurate to assign one the primary role in the relationship. It should be noted that the term *environment* as used here includes those significant private events (thoughts, feelings, images) that play such an important role in complex human performance. Phenomena in this internal environment can exert a tremendous influence on behavior (Mahoney, 1974a). They thus become significant elements in the endless reciprocity.

This *reciprocal determinism* between behavior and environment has tremendous significance for human performance and the issues of personal freedom, responsibility, and choice. Since environments are a function of behavior, the individual can take an active role in self-determination. That is, one can arrange one's environment to produce or eliminate specified behaviors. Does this reintroduce the concept of free will? No; the act of taking an active role in engineering one's personal environment is determined by previous environmental influences (which may, in turn, have been determined by previous behaviors). However, the interdependence of behavior and environment points up the fact that we are not passive recipients of environmental influence; our performance is a critical determinant of that environment.

One popular issue that arises in a discussion of behavioral control is a political one. Given that human performance can be reliably predicted and controlled, *who will control whom?* Who will be the controllers? Who will be the controlled? A frequent assumption here is that one person or a small group of sophisticated behavioral engineers will condition the masses. Visions of a mad scientist manipulating herds of humans are implied. There are three basic misconceptions here. To begin with, even if behavior control were a one-way street, there is little reason to believe that it would entail a totalitarian system. One could envision a democracy in which citizens elected persons to engineer their environments. Indeed, this is the underlying assumption in contemporary Western democracy. We select representatives who we think will implement contingencies like laws, taxes, and response opportunities that are to our liking. Members of congress, law enforcement officers, and the like are paid by us to control us. We, of course, attempt to control them, which brings us to the second major misunderstanding in the issue of behavior control.

The question is not just one of who shall control whom because the influence process is *reciprocal*. A does not simply control B; B also controls A. As many a parent or teacher will attest, adults do not have a monopoly on behavior-influence processes. Controllers are also controllees, producing changes in others' behavior which may, in turn, have a dramatic influence on their own actions. In some instances, this reciprocal system is highlighted by the phenomenon of countercontrol. If individuals object to the behavior-change efforts directed toward them by others, they may respond in a negative or opposite-to-prediction manner. For example, the rebellious adolescent frequently bucks the system and performs contrary to prevailing expectations or contingencies. In so doing, he or she is countercontrolling, that is, exerting an influence on the person or persons who are attempting to control his or her behavior. Research on the phenomenon of countercontrol has suggested that it may be influenced by such variables as the magnitude of incentives, the subtlety of the behavior-change influences, and the availability of choice (alternate responses) to the individual (Davison, 1973; Mahoney, 1974a).

The phenomenon of countercontrol points up a third aspect of the behavior-control issue. In a classic debate, Rogers and Skinner (1956) discussed the desirability of investigating and refining behavior modification techniques. According to Rogers, the dangerous and dehumanizing menace of those techniques warrants their avoidance. He contended that we should not research techniques of behavior change because of their potential use for unethical purposes. Skinner, on the other hand, pointed out that we have an obligation to study and identify the principles and processes involved in human behavior. The issue is not whether we should control behavior; behavior is always controlled. Your actions at this very moment are being influenced by a variety of factors. The point is that much of the environmental control that currently prevails is haphazard and detrimental. Investigating the principles of behavior will not produce behavior control; it will refine and improve the control that now exists. It is not as if psychological research is introducing an element of determinism that did not previously exist. One's behaviors are always determined. However, until its determinants are identified, one's performance and perhaps happiness may be left to haphazard influences rather than to systematically planned and managed ones. Skinner pointed out that part of Rogers's objections to the development of a behavior technology may have stemmed from the assumption that to engineer a culture or performance is bad. Humanity's development and culture are best left to "natural evolution," according to this view. However, the dangers of such passivity are readily apparent in the contemporary dilemmas of overpopulation, aggression, and obesity. Sexual productivity, physical aggressiveness, and high calorie consumption are patterns that persist in part because of their survival value during the dawn of the species. However, we are currently facing an early demise of the species unless these naturally evolved behavior patterns are modified through extensive systematic planning and management. The gross trial-and-error aspect of "natural" developments often makes them expensive and time consuming. By taking an active part in one's own behavioral and cultural evolution, it is possible to enhance and refine its course. Indeed, recent limited efforts employing this approach to social change have been promising (Meyers, Craighead, & Meyers, 1974).

Another objection to Rogers's argument that we terminate research on applied behavioral principles relates to the previously discussed phenomenon of countercontrol. If we are to take an active part in our own development, we must be familiar with the behavior change techniques that others may be directing toward us. To remain ignorant of the laws governing behavior is to encourage a one-way influence process; it effectively reduces our own chances of having an impact on the environmental events that influence us. Evidence on consumer and voting behavior illustrates that extensive behavior-change efforts are being continually directed at the public. Many of these efforts are both sophisticated and effective. An informed public—one familiar with the principles and techniques of behavior change—would be better equipped to identify and influence these efforts.

Behavioral Freedom and Humanistic Issues

Another frequently encountered objection to behavioral approaches to human performance is that they are simplistic and stultifying. A complex and intricate being is analyzed down into discrete responses. Humans are funneled into a composite of stimuli and responses; the human essence is sacrificed and creativity is abandoned.

This funnel effect, if it does exist, is a reflection of specific applications of behavior technology rather than any deficiencies in the technology itself. That is, behavior principles and the technology that has developed around them are neither good nor bad in and of themselves. Atomic energy is similarly amoral. However, any technology can be put to appropriate or inappropriate uses. If a teacher uses behavior-change principles to elicit docile and uncreative responses from students, the error lies in the application of those principles and not in the principles themselves.[1] In one sense, we may be near the Los Alamos stage of behavioral research. Some very powerful techniques have been developed for the prediction and control of performance. How those techniques are applied will be partially determined by the extent to which they are understood and influenced by the public. The same principles that may be inappropriately used by one teacher to produce docility may be applied by another to encourage creativity and personal growth in students. As a matter of fact, Skinner (1971) has recommended the programming of innovative and diverse responses because of their beneficial role in the accelerated evolution of improved performance and cultures. By designing a learning environment that encourages creative problem solving, the teacher can increase the likelihood of those responses that often become landmarks in the progress of civilization—new conceptual systems, inventions, and so on.

One final ethical issue relates to the question of behavioral freedom. Earlier we discussed the concept of free will and self-determination in human performance. Behavioral freedom refers to the number of response options available to us at any given time. To the extent that we have a wide range of behaviors to draw upon, we are free to react with diversity to environmental influences. This behavioral freedom plays a significant role in personal adjustment and growth. Mahoney and Thoresen (1974) discuss the relevance of behavioral technology as a means for attaining humanistic ends. If individuals are trained to become their own behavioral engineers, they can take an active part in the direction and development of their own lives. This behavioral humanism represents a new and exciting avenue of psychological research. Familiarity with the processes and principles of human performance allows individuals to enter into their own behavioral equation. Instead of being mere recipients of environmental influence, they become significant factors in the form and direction of that influence. The pursuit and refinement of behavioral research may thus become a uniquely humane endeavor.

LEGAL ISSUES

The discussion of ethical issues of behavioral control and individual freedom raises important issues about the influence that technology might exert on individual persons. The issues pertaining to behavioral control

---

1. The scientific method does not presently seem applicable to the question of the determination of goals or objectives. To what *ends* the findings of scientific investigation will be directed is not a question to which the scientific method itself has been addressed.

and individual freedom have received increased attention in recent years in the context of legal matters pertaining to the rights of persons who receive treatment. The courts have entered increasingly into matters related to treatment, rehabilitation, and education wherein a person's rights might be infringed.

The United States Constitution grants persons a variety of freedoms. Restricting individual's rights for their own welfare and the welfare of society raises a host of legal issues. For example, institutionalized populations, such as psychiatric patients, prisoners, and the retarded are usually involuntarily confined. Questions have arisen about the extent to which treatment and rehabilitation can abridge individual rights that normally are granted outside of institutional life. It should be noted at the outset that these issues, as noted for the ethical issues considered earlier, are not raised by behavior modification only but apply to treatment in general. However, the present discussion reviews several issues that have implications for the implementation of selected behavioral techniques.

Environmental Restraint

Much of the attention of the courts in cases of treatment and rehabilitation pertain to the restraints that can justifiably be placed upon a person. The courts have adopted a policy referred to as the *least restrictive alternative doctrine* (Ennis & Friedman, 1973). The doctrine states that a person is entitled to the least restrictive conditions of confinement that will achieve the purposes of treatment. Thus, a person who might be considered for institutionalization in a psychiatric hospital is entitled to the least restrictive conditions necessary for treatment purposes. Hospitalization may not be allowable if the person could function adequately without confinement. A hospital may be more restrictive than necessary.

The least restrictive doctrine requires an institution to justify its actions with respect to the care given a patient. Also, the doctrine applies to the conditions provided to a person if they are eventually institutionalized. In many treatment institutions, patients or retarded residents may be restricted in their movements on the ward. Deprivation of access to hospital grounds or restrictions on the movements of patients within the hospital may be used as a basis for providing reinforcing consequences for behavior. For example, a patient may be required to perform such activities as attending therapy or socially interacting with others to have access to the hospital grounds. Yet, such deprivation may be unnecessarily restrictive under the least restrictive alternative doctrine.

The courts have ruled that institutionalized populations are allowed to have access to a variety of privileges and activities and that these cannot be withheld for use as reinforcers. The decisions have been relatively recent and have important implications for behavioral programs in institutionalized settings. Psychiatric patients, the mentally retarded, institutionalized delinquents, and other populations are entitled by right to a variety of activities, such as receiving visitors, interacting socially with others, and engaging in recreation. These rights have been important in behavioral programs where positive reinforcers are sought which can be utilized to alter behavior. Reinforcement programs cannot withhold events and activities to which patients are entitled by right. Instead, reinforcers that ordinarily are not available must be used. Hence, there are some specific legal protections concerning infringements on individual freedoms that have been addressed only generally in the discussion of ethical issues.

Use of Aversive Procedures

An obvious area where persons can be mistreated is in the application of aversive events. Behavior modification programs rely more heavily on positive reinforcement than on negative reinforcement and punishment. Yet aversive techniques have been used and have come under the purview of the courts. In fact, the courts have a long history of evaluating punishment, particularly for prisoners, because of the protection provided by the Constitution against "cruel and unusual" punishment.

As might be expected, most of the court rulings apply to relatively severe procedures, such as the use of corporal punishment, physical restraint, and inhumane conditions, that are not part of behavioral techniques. However, some of the court rulings have implications for behavioral procedures. For example, one form of punishment often used is referred to as *time out from reinforcement*. The technique consists of withdrawing opportunities for positive reinforcement for a brief period of time immediately after an undesirable behavior has been performed. In an institution, for example, a psychiatric patient may be placed into a room isolated from others for ten minutes after performing an aggressive act. Although the use of brief periods of time out usually is not an issue, occasionally programs have placed persons in seclusion for extended periods with the justification that it is a form of time out. The courts have ruled that only brief periods of isolation are allowed, and these can be used only for severe behaviors, such as those leading to physical harm or destruction of property.

In behavioral programs, usually a variety of techniques are available, and options exist, even when using punishment, that need not infringe on a person's rights. For example, several variations of time out exist that do not require isolation at all. In some variations, time out consists of a brief period of time in which the person cannot earn reinforcers that otherwise would be provided. In such cases, the person is not isolated at all and continues to have access to normal activities even during the time-out period.

Severe forms of punishment occasionally are used in behavioral programs. For example, brief electric shock is sometimes resorted to because it can completely eliminate performance of a dangerous behavior. Children who engage in severe self-injurious behavior have occasionally received contingent shock for instances of self-injury, and this has resulted in rapid elimination of the behavior. The courts have recognized that in extraordinary circumstances such as these, shock might be applied, but only when other procedures have proven unsuccessful. Most forms of punishment used in behavioral programs have not come under the purview of the courts. Techniques like taking tokens away or having persons practice desirable performance are relatively mild from the standpoint of the courts.

Informed Consent

Many of the problems that might be raised by implementing programs with involuntarily confined clients can be alleviated if persons provide consent for receiving treatment. For consent to be informed, the person who provides consent must be *competent,* have *knowledge* about the nature of the treatment, and provide consent of his or her own *volition* (Martin, 1975). Competence refers to a person's ability to make a well-reasoned decision and to understand the alternatives available. These conditions are difficult to achieve with some treatment populations, such as children, the mentally retarded, or severely debilitated psychiatric patients, in which cases others (for example, guardians, parents) must provide consent for the person.

Consent must also be based on the client's knowledge which includes understanding the nature of treatment and its potential risks and benefits. A potential problem in meeting this condition is that complete information about many treatments is unavailable, so that the risks and benefits are not entirely known. Thus, a client, or therapist for that matter, cannot make a truly knowledgeable decision but selects treatment based on what seems to be the likely or potential risks and benefits. Another aspect about the knowledge upon which consent is based is that the client must be aware that he or she does not have to give consent and that once consent is given, it can later be revoked if the client changes his or her mind.

The final ingredient of informed consent is volition, or the client's agreement to participate without duress. The client must be able to decide to participate or not participate without pressures from those who provide treatment. For example, a patient may feel compelled to participate in a behavioral or other program because of the pressure from staff. Agreement under such duress would not meet the requirements for informed consent.

Informed consent raises a host of issues for treatment in general rather than just for behavioral procedures. It is easy to see how some aspects of consent could interfere with conducting certain types of programs. For example, a reinforcement program in a hospital might use a variety of events (for example, special recreational privileges, activities) that normally are provided as reinforcers. These events could be withheld for treatment purposes if the client initially provided consent. Yet, if, on a given occasion, the patient did not earn the reinforcer, he or she might immediately withdraw consent and nullify the program.

The purpose of informed consent is to increase the protection of the client. The consent procedures emphasize that the patient must be as informed as possible or as is reasonable in light of the proposed treatment. Only when the client has access to all of the available or relevant information can consent be truly informed.

Protecting Client Rights

The ethical and legal issues suggest that cases can arise in which individual rights are unnecessarily sacrificed, particularly for persons who are involuntarily confined. Legal rulings by the courts do not by themselves provide sufficient protection for client rights. Indeed, by the nature of the rulings, the courts typically enter into the problems of treatment *after* questions are raised about specific practices. Guidelines need to be developed to help handle the ethical and potentially legal dilemmas *before* treatment is provided.

In fact, a large set of guidelines and safeguards have been developed and include international codes, national guidelines, and codes of ethics by various professional groups (see Kazdin, 1978c). A recently developed set of guidelines, provided in Table 10.1, illustrates the questions that need to be raised in treatment. The questions pertain to many of the concerns mentioned in the discussion of legal issues, such as informed consent. The guidelines are *not* uniquely relevant for behavior modification procedures. Behavior change procedures, independently of their conceptual origin,

Table 10.1 Ethical issues for human services.

The questions related to each issue have deliberately been cast in a general manner that applies to all types of interventions, and not solely or specifically to the practice of behavior therapy. Issues directed specifically to behavior therapists might imply erroneously that behavior therapy was in some way more in need of ethical concern than non-behaviorally-oriented therapies.

In the list of issues, the term "client" is used to describe the person whose behavior is to be changed; "therapist" is used to describe the professional in charge of the intervention: "treatment" and "problem," although used in the singular, refer to any and all treatments and problems being formulated with this checklist. The issues are formulated so as to be relevant across as many settings and populations as possible. Thus, they need to be qualified when someone other than the person whose behavior is to be changed is paying the therapist, or when that person's competence or the voluntary nature of that person's consent is questioned. For example, if the therapist has found that the client does not understand the goals or methods being considered, the therapist should substitute the client's guardian or other responsible person for "client," when reviewing the issues below.

A. Have the goals of treatment been adequately considered?
1. To insure that the goals are explicit, are they written?
2. Has the client's understanding of the goals been assured by having the client restate them orally or in writing?
3. Have the therapist and client agreed on the goals of therapy?
4. Will serving the client's interests be contrary to the interests of other persons?
5. Will serving the client's immediate interests be contrary to the client's long term interest?

B. Has the choice of treatment methods been adequately considered?
1. Does the published literature show the procedure to be the best one available for that problem?
2. If no literature exists regarding the treatment method, is the method consistent with generally accepted practice?
3. Has the client been told of alternative procedures that might be preferred by the client on the basis of significant differences in discomfort, treatment time, cost, or degree of demonstrated effectiveness?
4. If a treatment procedure is publicly, legally, or professionally controversial, has formal professional consultation been obtained, has the reaction of the affected segment of the public been adequately considered, and have the alternative treatment methods been more closely reexamined and reconsidered?

C. Is the client's participation voluntary?
1. Have possible sources of coercion on the client's participation been considered?
2. If treatment is legally mandated, has the available range of treatments and therapists been offered?
3. Can the client withdraw from treatment without a penalty or financial loss that exceeds actual clinical costs?

D. When another person or an agency is empowered to arrange for therapy, have the interests of the subordinated client been sufficiently considered?
1. Has the subordinated client been informed of the treatment objectives and participated in the choice of treatment procedures?
2. Where the subordinated client's competence to decide is limited, have the client as well as the guardian participated in the treatment discussions to the extent that the client's abilities permit?

Table 10.1   Ethical issues for human services. (*cont.*)

> 3. If the interests of the subordinated person and the superordinate persons or agency conflict, have attempts been made to reduce the conflict by dealing with both interests?

E. Has the adequacy of treatment been evaluated?
> 1. Have quantitative measures of the problem and its progress been obtained?
> 2. Have the measures of the problem and its progress been made available to the client during treatment?

F. Has the confidentiality of the treatment relationship been protected?
> 1. Has the client been told who has access to the records?
> 2. Are records available only to authorized persons?

G. Does the therapist refer the clients to other therapists when necessary?
> 1. If treatment is unsuccessful, is the client referred to other therapists?
> 2. Has the client been told that if dissatisfied with the treatment, referral will be made?

H. Is the therapist qualified to provide treatment?
> 1. Has the therapist had training or experience in treating problems like the client's?
> 2. If deficits exist in the therapist's qualifications, has the client been informed?
> 3. If the therapist is not adequately qualified, is the client referred to other therapists, or has supervision by a qualified therapist been provided? Is the client informed of the supervisory relation?
> 4. If the treatment is administered by mediators, have the mediators been adequately supervised by a qualified therapist?

SOURCE: Association for Advancement of Behavior Therapy. Ethical issues for human services. *Behavior Therapy*, 1977, *8*, v–vi.

raise similar ethical and legal issues. The questions address issues that need to be raised in order to guide those who provide any form of treatment.

Although the same questions might be raised about treatment in general, certainly some procedures warrant more careful scrutiny than others in protecting client rights. Hence, guidelines have suggested that distinctions might be made on the basis of whether the treatments are conventional and routine or whether they are controversial and warrant especially careful monitoring. For example, a well-known proposal, referred to as the Florida guidelines, was developed in response to a program that engaged in several abuses of mentally retarded, delinquent, and emotionally disturbed boys. Severe physical punishment, forced sexual acts, and deprivation were used as "treatment." The abuses resulted in the formation of a task force designed to develop specific guidelines for treatment that would take into account legal considerations, such as those outlined above (May, Risley, Twardosz, Friedman, Bijou, & Wexler, 1976).

The guidelines developed a three-level system for evaluating treatment procedures. The levels were based on the specific techniques that were proposed and the behaviors they were designed to alter. The *first* level consisted of treatments that are generally routine and applied to behaviors that are not particularly controversial. For example, using praise, attention, and feedback to alter self-help skills would not threaten the rights of clients. Procedures and behaviors at the first level are generally standard, widely practiced, and do not seem to propose a serious threat to a client's rights.

The *second* level included slightly more controversial procedures. The procedures that might be included at this level would be justified only if procedures at the first level had not produced the desired changes. Mildly aversive techniques might be included here, such as fines or time out from reinforcement. The behaviors might be the same as those included in the first level.

The *third* and final level included behaviors and procedures that might be very controversial and worthy of extremely close scrutiny. Behaviors included in this level might be patterns of sexual deviance in which the direction of change or change itself could be questioned. Procedures might consist of last-resort techniques, such as electric shock. The nature of the behaviors and severity of the techniques might warrant close review. The Florida guidelines suggested that committees closely review treatment applications in the third level to ensure that the client's rights are fully taken into account. A review committee could include a legal counselor, a behavioral scientist, lay persons, and others who would represent different interests in behalf of the client.

In general, a variety of guidelines have been developed to ensure that treatment practices are more carefully evaluated than has been the case in the past. However, the means of protecting clients that are proposed, including the specific ones sampled here, are only guidelines. Careful control and close monitoring of what is actually done in treatment are difficult to enforce. However, the guidelines have increased the sensitivity of practitioners as well as clients to the sorts of treatments that are appropriate and the kinds of questions that can be raised.

SUMMARY

The assumptions and applications of behavior modification have increased concern in the last few years. Apprehensions about the abuse of behavioral principles have been apparent. Many of these ethical objections, however, seem to be based on inaccurate views and invalid inferences regarding the behavioral perspective. The assumption of determinants of behavior, for example, does not strip humans of choice or responsibility. Also, fears that a small group of individuals may gain totalitarian behavior control are unwarranted. Development of behavior modification does not necessarily interfere with human choice, responsibility, or freedom and, indeed, can increase these for the individual who recognizes the determinants of behavior.

Legal issues involved in treatment have received increased attention in recent years. The issues arise in response to concerns about protecting individual rights in cases where persons do not have the opportunity or resources to influence what is done to or for them. Legal rulings have addressed important issues, such as the least restrictive alternative doctrine and abuses of aversive procedures. Also, the conditions of informed consent have been elaborated to help ensure that clients are more aware of their options and are more informed about their ability to decide whether to elect one procedure rather than another.

The protection of client rights raises a variety of issues beyond informed consent. For many of the decisions that need to be made, the therapist, investigator, practitioner, or others must critically evaluate practices that are being considered for treatment, and they must have others provide independent evaluations about the merit and appropriateness of treatment. Selected guidelines have been developed to help protect client rights.

SUGGESTED READINGS

Budd, K. S., & Baer, D. M. Behavior modification and the law. Implications of recent judicial decisions. *Journal of Psychiatry and Law,* 1976, *4,* 171–244.

Kazdin, A. E. *History of behavior modification: Experimental foundations of contemporary research.* Baltimore: University Park Press, 1978.

Krapfl, J., & Vargas, E. (Eds.). *Behaviorism and ethics.* Kalamazoo, Mich.: Behaviordelia, 1977.

Mahoney, M. J. The sensitive scientist in empirical humanism. *American Psychologist,* 1975, *30,* 864–867.

Mahoney, M. J., Kazdin, A. E., & Lesswing, W. J. Behavior modification: Delusion or deliverance? In C. M. Franks & G. T. Wilson (Eds.), *Annual review of behavior therapy: Theory and practice* (Vol. 2). New York: Brunner/Mazel, 1974.

Martin, R. *Legal challenges to behavior modification: Trends in schools, corrections, and mental health.* Champaign, Ill.: Research Press, 1975.

Wexler, D. B. Reflections on the legal regulation of behavior modification in institutional settings. *Arizona Law Review,* 1975, *17,* 132–143.

APPLICATIONS OF
BEHAVIOR
MODIFICATION

PART TWO

So far we have talked primarily about conceptual and ethical issues and the laboratory research from which the principles of behavior change have been developed. It has been repeatedly emphasized that a familiarity with these conceptual and experimental foundations is essential for an adequate understanding of therapeutic applications. We are now ready to explore some of those applications. The chapters that follow represent a sample of contemporary uses of behavioral principles. The topics and authors were selected to provide a broad overview of both well-established and relatively recent applications. These chapters presume an understanding of the fundamental principles covered in the preceding sections.

Within the model of this book, the scientific approach to the study of human behavior—including its assumptions as set forth in Chapters 1 through 10—reigns supreme. It is through this model of methodological behaviorism that we can most expediently and efficiently come to an understanding of behavior. As indicated earlier, this model and its resulting empirical data have been derived from the experimental laboratory. The real contribution of behavior modification has been in the application of that model or approach to clinical and social problems. Part One came first so that you would have a grasp of the rationale, assumptions, and methodology of behavior modification, as well as an understanding that behavior modification does not represent an arrived-at body of knowledge or set of procedures.

Let us review briefly what we have said thus far. In the opening sentences of this book, it was stated that behavior modification is "one of the most exciting and promising developments in contemporary behavioral science." The paragraph goes on to laud the versatility, popularity, expansiveness, and success rate of behavior-modification applications. To any but the most avid supporters, statements like these probably sound more like television commercials or drug advertisements than objective descriptions of some development in behavioral science. Ironically, there is some truth to both the opening statements and the television commercial analogy. The behavior-modification approach has received increasing attention and application during the last decade. Its success rate, although far from perfect, has been very rewarding, especially when compared with those for prevailing models of clinical intervention. Converts to behavior modification have ranged from traditionally oriented psychotherapists to grandmothers. There have, of course, been a few defectors. Thus, while there is some deserving praise to be accorded behavior modification, the unfortunate aura of a "school" has developed around it. It is often spoken of as if it were a miracle cure, the ultimate in our search for behavioral therapeutics, and with the same awe and reverence that the peddler used in selling brain pills and bust developers. To be sure, the success rates have often encouraged enthusiastic predictions and exaggerated inferences; Skinner has noted that one of the characteristic features of the behavior modifier is his or her enthusiasm. However, many behavior modifiers have fallen into the unfortunate habit of considering learning theory–based behavior modification to be both centrally and exclusively true. The rest of psychology is often talked of as if it were a deranged psychotic whose only glimpses of reality are provided by the behavioral model. A particular set of principles and procedures is often stretched far beyond its limits—not to mention its data—in an attempt to explain virtually every aspect of behavior. Although this tendency to deify and consecrate scientifically the area of behavior modification is fortunately not as widespread as it once was, its continued presence is still an impediment to the field because it encourages premature smugness in the face of behavioral ignorance. It likewise creates both inter- and intradisciplinary animosities which discourage the free interchange of ideas and information.

The foregoing may have left the reader somewhat puzzled as to our intent. This is supposed to be a book that presents the rationale and methodology of research in behavior modification. It presumes an interest in or acceptance of the behavioral frame of reference. Now, however, we have presented several criticisms of behavior modification. This possibly puzzling act actually stems from our concern for and support of behavior modification. We hope that this book will provide the reader with an appreciation for conservative modesty and caution in the execution and interpretation of behavior-modification research.

The purpose of research—as well as of science in general—is to discover functional relationships among events. The unparsimonious glorification of behavior modification or any other area discourages continuing and expanding research. The mark of a good scientist lies not solely in his or her ability to speculate or explain, but also in the ability modestly to admit the limitations of a field's knowledge. Finality is one thing that science denies. However, when one describes a field in such glowing terms that it appears to be the ultimate answer, then finality is implied. Such closed-mindedness impedes progress in any field of research. If assumptions are erroneously accepted and remain unresearched, they may misguide and retard the delineation of behavioral principles and methods of behavior change. Similarly, if data are squeezed into a specified behavior modification framework (rather than the latter being modified to fit the former), knowledge will again be eluded. If an effective technique is avoided or de-emphasized because it does not fit comfortably into the present behavioral view of things, then behavioral science has been cheated.

It is our intent, then, to point out the ever present need for evaluative research. The evaluation and re-evaluation of various techniques, the modification of these techniques according to experimental findings, and the generation of new research ideas are all integral parts of that "exciting and promising" development called behavior modification. An understanding of the rationale behind research, the various methods available to researchers, and the limited but meaningful interpretations obtainable from such research provides the reader with a valuable anchor in the evaluation and appreciation of behavior modification.

This approach to the study of behavior change allows us to evaluate what we do in attempting to solve clinical and social problems. One does not appeal to a theory as justification for actions; one appeals to data, which will allow for corrective feedback. This approach should be the hallmark of the behavior modifier, underscoring the necessity of understanding the scientific method and how to utilize it in applied settings. If one is to understand, employ, or be the recipient of behavior modification, then it is imperative that its scientific underpinnings be understood.

Perhaps the question most frequently asked regarding any clinical approach or technique is "Does it work?" As you know by now, the behavioral researcher attempts to answer that question by relying on the principles of methodological behaviorism; the experimental clinician asks for an empirical evaluation of procedures. Although this may not always be achieved, it is the ideal toward which researchers aspire. Because of our commitment to this ideal, we requested that the authors of the following chapters present data-based material. By that we did not mean that all the numbers and statistical probabilities for each reported study should be cited, but rather that the authors review the evidence bearing on each area of application. In addition, the authors were invited to present the issues and findings with freedom of style and opinion. Some authors have presented an overall evaluation of treatment procedures, others have focused on conceptual and treatment issues, and still others have examined specific treatment or clinical research programs. It is hoped that these different styles and emphases will provide the reader with a working knowledge of the current state of the science in applied behavior modification. This area of applied research is continuing to grow rapidly in both volume and perspective. A textbook on the topic of applied behavior change will probably look very different a decade from now. This commitment to continual growth and refinement is a critical element in clinical science and an exciting aspect of the mental health helping professions.

CHAPTER 11

ANXIETY MANAGEMENT

Douglas A. Bernstein

University of Illinois at Urbana Champaign

The bulk of this chapter deals with behavioral or social learning approaches to the reduction or elimination of anxiety. Before specific techniques are discussed, however, we should be sure to understand what it is that we are attempting to reduce or eliminate. Dealing with the concept of anxiety is a lot like dealing with the idea of "class." Many people feel that having class is good, but everyone has a slightly different idea of what it is and there is considerable disagreement on how to tell when someone has it.

Similarly, most people would probably agree that "having anxiety" or "being anxious" is bad, unpleasant, and to be avoided if possible, but no universally accepted definition of anxiety is available. This lack of consensus is reflected in the fact that there are at least 120 specific procedures available that purport to measure anxiety (Cattell & Scheier, 1961). The main problem with trying to define anxiety is that it is not a single entity like an arm or leg which a person does or does not have. Rather, it is a shorthand term which originally referred only to a painful, choking sensation in the throat (Sarbin, 1964), but which, primarily because of the influence of Freud's emphasis on *Angst* (translated as "anxiety") in the development of behavior and behavior disorders, has come to have much broader meaning.

DEFINITION AND MEASUREMENT OF ANXIETY

Today, the word *anxiety* refers to a complex and variable pattern of behavior which occurs in response to internally (cognitively) or externally (environmentally) produced stimuli and which can show up in three dimensions, or response channels. The first of these is the subjective or *self-report* channel, in which an individual may indicate informally as in "I was scared to death!" or formally through psychological test scores the degree of anxiety he or she experiences, either as a rule (trait anxiety) or in response to specific situations (state anxiety). Various general-purpose and specialized paper-and-pencil tests are available to measure this aspect of anxiety (Levitt, 1967; Spielberger, 1972), but their results must be interpreted cautiously, since individuals' responses to self-report measures may be subject to intentional or unintentional bias of many types (Azrin, Holtz & Goldiamond, 1961; Mischel, 1968; Sundberg, Tyler, & Taplin, 1973). Some individuals may report lower levels of anxiety than they actually experience in order to please a therapist or to appear "mentally healthy"; others may spuriously inflate their reports in an effort to give responses they think are desired by an experimenter or as a means of gaining attention.

The second response channel is that of *psychological arousal,* primarily involving activity of the sympathetic branch of the autonomic nervous system. Persons showing anxiety in this channel display changes in one or more indices of arousal, including galvanic skin responses (GSR), heart rate, blood pressure, blood volume, respiration, muscle tension, pupillary response, and the like. Many technical problems make accurate, unbiased measurement of the physiological component of anxiety difficult. Temperature, movement, body weight, diet, cognitive activity, and the presence of drugs are just a few of the factors that may affect physiological responses (for example, Borkovec, Weerts, & Bernstein, 1977). It is not enough to measure anxiety through only one index of physiological activity, such as heart rate; each individual's arousal may appear in a slightly different way (Lacey, 1967; Lacey & Lacey, 1968), thus necessitating the use of multiple response measures.

The third anxiety response channel involves overt *somatic-motor behavior,* such as trembling or stuttering, which occurs either as an observable consequence of physiological arousal or as a means of escape from or avoidance of certain stimuli. Assessment of anxiety through this channel usually consists of direct observation of an individual's avoidance and/or performance during what is, for that person, some kind of stress, such as giving a speech, taking an exam, climbing a ladder, touching a snake, or whatever. Observations are quantified through the use of an approach scale or other rating system (for example Paul, 1966) that allows each subject's overt behavioral responses to be compared in standard fashion with those of any other subject. However, this approach to anxiety measurement is also vulnerable to a certain amount of bias, mainly through social/situational factors. For example, subjects who are not strongly encouraged to perform a stressful task may display more overt behavioral anxiety than they would if the test situation clearly demanded fearlessness (for example, Bernstein, 1973; Bernstein and Nietzel, 1973; Blom & Craighead, 1974; Rosenthal, Hung & Kelley, 1977; Smith, Diener, & Beaman, 1974).

The problem of defining anxiety is further complicated by the fact that the three channels of anxiety response often do not correlate well with one another (Lacey, 1959; Lang, 1968). A person who is anxious in relation to a particular stimulus situation may display strong reactions in only one channel, for example, in self-report but not in overt behavior or physiological activity. Such discrepancies are due mainly to the fact that the appearance of anxiety in each channel is a function not only of the target stimulus situation, such as a dentist's office, but also of other variables as well. For example, a male college student may show strong physiological arousal and a great deal of overt avoidance behavior in relation to large dogs, but because he does not wish to appear foolish or unmasculine, he may vigorously deny any discomfort. A person who is learning to skydive may display clear physiological arousal and some avoidance behavior before a jump, but that arousal may be interpreted by the individual as excitement (Schachter, 1964; Schachter & Singer, 1962), and thus no anxiety is reported. Finally, an individual who reports strong anxiety in relation to dentistry and displays clear autonomic arousal in the dentist's chair may show no overt avoidance behavior because of the anticipated positive consequences of receiving treatment (Kleinknecht & Bernstein, 1978).

Obviously, whether or not a person is labeled as anxious, fearful, phobic, or the like depends to a great extent on (1) which anxiety channel is assessed and (2) what social/situational, cognitive, consequential, or other factors are operative. Many researchers in the field now recognize this problem and seek to base statements about anxiety on measures that reflect all three channels and that minimize the influence of artifacts. In fact, because of the complexity, multidimensionality, and elusiveness of the anxiety construct, some social-learning theorists and practitioners (for example, Bandura, 1969; Krasner & Ullmann, 1973; Ullmann, 1967; Ullmann & Krasner, 1975) hardly use the term *anxiety,* referring instead either to the external or internal stimulus conditions that result in behaviors labeled as anxiety or to some specific components of anxiety, such as emotional arousal or avoidance behavior. This approach is based on the notion that the theoretical construct called *anxiety* provides little in the way of specific information about behavior, and that it has become reified and used as an explanation of maladaptive, irrational, or unusual behavior when, in fact, it provides only a description. Krasner and Ullmann (1973) put it succinctly.

We have to deal not with . . . anxiety, but with the conditions giving rise to anxiety. . . . The concept of anxiety is superfluous in dealing directly with people rather than with theories. In a clinical interaction we deal with what is being avoided, with what a person needs to learn or unlearn or relearn. . . . [The concept of anxiety] makes us think we know something when we do not and should be looking harder. (pp. 98–99)

Consistent with this kind of thinking, the behavioral or social-learning approach to anxiety and anxiety measurement focuses on clear specification of stimulus conditions and on objectively quantified responses to those stimuli rather than on use of psychological tests designed to measure the presence of or changes in a generalized trait or construct. This has resulted in the development of anxiety-management techniques that are designed not to eliminate anxiety, but to alter individuals' maladaptive overt and cognitive response patterns to specific classes of stressful stimuli. The success of these treatment procedures is evaluated in terms of the magnitude of desirable changes in specified traget behaviors (often in all three anxiety channels), which are assessed before and after treatment.

NATURE AND DEVELOPMENT OF ANXIETY AS A CLINICAL PROBLEM

Everyone experiences negative emotional arousal and/or displays behavioral avoidance in relation to stressful stimulus situations. In fact, a certain degree of arousal or activation is a prerequisite to adequate everyday functioning; a totally nonaroused person would be in a coma twenty-four hours a day. However, too much activation can also be debilitating (Hunt, 1961); when response patterns referred to collectively as anxiety reach high levels of intensity, frequency, duration, and generality, the individual and those around her or him experience severe discomfort, and disruption of adaptive behavior occurs. For example, an individual whose arousal is too high before and during an academic examination or a date may experience physical discomfort and draw a blank when attempting to answer test questions or think of conversation topics. Such experiences may make future tests or dates even more stressful, thus adding to the discomfort and further disrupting performance.

In addition, overaroused individuals may engage in behaviors that seem irrational or bizarre to others but which are merely attempts to escape or avoid stimuli that they find strongly aversive. Thus, a salesperson who is upset by driving might refuse to deal with customers except on the telephone or in the home office. If he or she refused to explain the basis for this behavior, and especially if he or she were hostile and defensive about it, such actions might ultimately result in loss of employment. If intense arousal continues for extended periods of time, other results, such as depression, exhaustion, and even actual tissue damage (ulcers, for example), may appear (for example, Selye, 1956, 1969).

Thus, when anxiety becomes a clinical problem, the client's presenting complaints may involve clearly defined and recognized maladaptive responses in one or more of the three anxiety channels discussed earlier, or they may reflect the consequences of those responses. The clinician must always be alert to the possibility that anxiety responses may be involved in cases that at first glance appear to be of a totally unrelated nature.[1]

In developing intervention procedures applicable to anxiety, the behavioral or social-learning approach begins with the assumption that maladaptive response patterns that produce client discomfort are learned on the basis of the same principles as is most other behavior, adaptive or maladaptive (for example, Ullmann & Krasner, 1975; see also Chapters 6, 7, and 8 in this volume). This assumption is based on and supported by a great deal of research, the results of which can only be summarized and illustrated here (see Bandura, 1969, for details).

Suppose that you are holding a four-year-old child on your lap while two other four-year-olds play on separate areas of your living room floor and that, as child A gently pets your English sheepdog, child B inserts a butter knife into an electrical outlet. Everyone would learn something from this incident. Because it was directly associated with severe, unexpected pain and accompanying autonomic arousal, child B would learn to avoid using wall sockets as knife holders and possibly to stay away from electrical outlets altogether. Child A might learn, or at least begin to learn, to avoid the sheepdog or dogs in general. When child B suddenly screamed and cried, it startled child A, and since the occurrence of any strong, sudden, unexpected, and novel stimulus produces autonomic arousal, the harmless dog was associated with a strong, unconditioned response to a stressful stimulus.[2] Depending on the focus of his or her attention at the time, the child on your lap might later display avoidance of

1. We shall refer to this point again later, but see Paul and Bernstein (1973) and Borkovec, Weerts, and Bernstein (1977) for a fuller discussion of the issues.
2. Watson and Rayner (1920) produced the same effect over several trials by suddenly producing a loud noise while a small child played with a tame white rat.

wall sockets (if he or she was watching child B), of dogs (if he or she was watching child A), or of you. Incidentally, since many of the principles of learning apply to both humans and animals, it is also possible that the sheepdog may subsequently try to avoid children.

This somewhat oversimplified example illustrates several important points. First, strong arousal in relation to specific stimuli or classes of stimuli can be learned. Second, learned arousal can be attached to harmless stimuli in the same way as it can to those that are objectively dangerous. Third, an individual may acquire anxiety responses on the basis of observation of another person's behavior and its consequences, thus underscoring the role of cognitive activity in the development and maintenance of such responses. Finally, learned anxiety responses may be adaptive ("rational") or maladaptive ("irrational"), a distinction that is very important in making clinical treatment decisions.

Obviously, when anxiety responses are appropriate and adaptive, as when an individual faces a clearly hazardous situation (for example, walking across the Grand Canyon on a greased clothesline), the clinician is unlikely to suggest or implement treatment; but when such responses are inappropriate or maladaptive, intervention is both reasonable and beneficial. As we shall see later, most of the anxiety-related problems dealt with by clinicians involve inappropriate reactions or attempts to avoid or escape stimuli which are by and large harmless.

TARGETS OF ANXIETY MANAGEMENT

Clinical interventions that employ the social-learning approach are aimed at two broad categories of anxiety-related target problems. The first of these involves situations in which an individual's overarousal occurs as an appropriate reaction to actual stress conditions which themselves occur partly as a function of the person's own behavior. As an example of this target category, called *reactive anxiety,* consider the person who reports strong arousal related to parties and other social gatherings as a result of having been ignored or insulted by others in those situations in the past. If the individual actually elicits these consequences by displaying obnoxious social behavior, we have an instance of reactive anxiety. In these cases, treatment focuses first on alteration of the behaviors that bring about negative consequences from others, not on elimination of anxiety responses to those consequences. When skill deficits and/or behavioral excesses are eliminated, the likelihood of pleasant social interactions is increased, thus reducing reactive anxiety (see Chapter 13 in this volume for a discussion of some of the techniques involved).

If after successful social skills training, the person continues to respond to social situations *as if* they were threatening, we have an example of the second category of target problems: *conditioned, inappropriate anxiety responses*. Such responses may develop in other ways than from a prior deficit in skills. We will discuss four subtypes of such problems and the intervention tactics available to deal with them.

1. *"Simple" conditioned anxiety.*   In these cases, the client responds with strong arousal to stimulus classes that are not objectively threatening. Usually, the client clearly reports anxiety as the main problem and pinpoints the stimulus or class of stimuli, auch as public speaking, air travel, or elevators, that results in discomfort. Sometimes, however, overarousal may have generalized to the point that discomfort occurs in relation to such complex stimulus patterns, or in extreme cases, to so many stimulus conditions (both external and cognitive) that the client is unable to specify the nature of the problem. Depending on severity, this situation has been called free-floating anxiety, nervous breakdown, or even acute psychotic episode.

2. *Psychosomatic or psychophysiological disorders.*   Anxiety responses that occur in the physiological channel, especially if they are of long duration and are focused in specific response systems, can result in actual tissue damage, such as ulcerative colitis or peptic ulcer. When this occurs, the intervention tactics described in this chapter are often effective in reducing and preventing learned, inappropriate arousal, but the physical disorders themselves must be dealt with medically. In other cases, physiologically expressed anxiety may take the form of physical symptoms which do not necessarily involve obvious damage, but which are nonetheless uncomfortable or potentially dangerous. Tension and/or migraine headaches, high blood pressure, asthma, and chronic fatigue are examples of physical problems that may be based on conditioned, inappropriate anxiety responses and that may disappear when those responses are reduced.

3. *Breakdown of complex behavior.*   When too much arousal occurs, disruption of performance, especially of the type that involves complex tasks, may result. When this happens, the client may not complain of anxiety but rather of inability to concentrate, poor memory, confusion, cognitive "flooding," breakdown of physical skills, such as typing or other motor behaviors, or lack of fluency in speech. Sexual functioning, a complex combination of physiological, cognitive, and motor responses, may also be disrupted, resulting in reports of impotence, ejaculatory incompetence, orgasmic dysfunction, vaginismus, or other problems (Masters & Johnson, 1970).

4. *Development of appropriate or inappropriate escape or avoidance behaviors.*   It is rare that an individual has no opportunity to escape or avoid

stressful stimuli, and most escape or avoidance behaviors do not qualify as clinical intervention targets. However, when a person seeks to avoid or escape stimuli that result in anxiety responses by engaging in behaviors that are either socially appropriate but restricting or socially inappropriate and thus problematic in themselves, clinical intervention may be helpful. Examples of the former include avoidance of air travel, parties, public places, elevators, escalators, and other stimulus situations that can be circumvented but only by causing considerable inconvenience for the client or others. If escape or avoidance is successful, clients' complaints usually do not include reports of strong, everyday discomfort (because they do not allow themselves to be exposed to feared stimuli), but they focus instead on dissatisfaction with or depression over the lengths to which they must go to remain at ease. Often, clients fail to display or report the problem until some change in their life situation necessitates contact with stressful stimuli, as when a high school student who avoids unfamiliar surroundings must leave home to attend college. In other cases, clients' escape or avoidance strategies take forms that are not only inconvenient but also very obviously maladaptive, inappropriate, and even bizarre. Examples may include various classical "neurotic" or even "psychotic" behaviors, such as amnesia, obsessions and compulsions, delusions, "hysterical" paralyses, or other "conversion reactions." In addition, some cases of alcoholism, drug abuse, problematic sexual behavior, and criminal activity can be related to attempts to avoid stressful stimulus situations.

BEHAVIORAL APPROACHES TO ANXIETY MANAGEMENT

There is insufficient space in a brief chapter to present in detail every one of the many intervention strategies that have been developed within the behavioral or social-learning framework for dealing with the broad array of anxiety-related problems brought to the clinician. What follows, therefore, is a general description of two of the most important and frequently employed treatment packages, each of which is altered and adapted somewhat in clinical practice to meet the specific needs of each client (for more detailed coverage, see Bandura, 1969; Kanfer & Phillips, 1970; Leitenberg, 1976; Morris, 1975; Rimm & Masters, 1979; Wolpe, 1973). It should be understood that each of the procedures to be discussed is not employed in a single, ritualized fashion as if all clients were identical but rather is implemented within the context of a positive and trusting therapeutic relationship. The client is viewed as an important and active participant in a cooperative educative process designed to bring about not only unlearning of maladaptive behaviors but also acquisition or reacquisition of more appropriate and adaptive behaviors. The clinician is thus a sort of teacher and assistant who acts not as an all-knowing judge or manipulator of behavior but as a consultant whose expertise lies in analysis of human behavior problems and in planning and implementing strategies for change.

The most influential of these strategies are systematic desensitization and modeling. They share the assumption that maladaptive anxiety responses are based on learning, but each approaches the task of producing unlearning and/or relearning with a slightly different emphasis.

Systematic Desensitization

The set of anxiety-reduction techniques known as *systematic desensitization* has been employed informally for many years (for example, Jones, 1924a, 1924b) but did not achieve the status of a clearly recognizable treatment package until publication of Wolpe's volume, *Psychotherapy by Reciprocal Inhibition,* in 1958. As the title indicates, the approach is based on what Wolpe called the reciprocal-inhibition principle, which was derived from laboratory research by Wolpe and others on the nature of the automatic nervous system and on mechanisms involved in the learning and unlearning of anxiety responses by both animals and humans. Wolpe (1958) stated that "if a response antagonistic to anxiety can be made to occur in the presence of anxiety-evoking stimuli so that it is accompanied by a complete or partial suppression of the anxiety responses, the bond between these stimuli and the anxiety responses will be weakened" (p. 71). In simplest terms, this means that since a person cannot be anxious and nonaroused at the same time, one can break the learned link between a particular stimulus and the anxiety response it evokes by seeing to it that the stimulus occurs while the anxiety response is prevented from occurring.

Wolpe identified several behaviors that are incompatible with anxiety responses. Some of these, such as sexual arousal, eating, or assertion (that is standing up for one's rights and/or clearly expressing one's feelings),are somewhat specialized in that they are employed therapeutically only when anxiety-eliciting stimuli are directly related to them. However, the most generally applicable and commonly employed anxiety-inhibiting response or state is deep muscle relaxation, which Wolpe induced first by hypnosis and later by means of waking-state procedures called *progressive relaxation* (Jacobson, 1938). At first glance, systematic-desensitization procedures appear to be relatively simple, but actually they are quite complex and require a great deal of technical skill. As dictated by the reciprocal-inhibition principle, the clinician's task is to expose the client to anxiety-provoking stimuli without producing an anxiety response. Three steps are required. First, a behavior incompatible with anxiety responses must be established. When muscle relaxation is chosen, this requires several weeks of specific training and at-home practice (Bernstein & Borkovec, 1973; Paul & Bernstein, 1973). Sometimes, biofeedback of muscle tension (EMG) is used instead of or in combination with progressive relaxation to produce desired reductions in arousal (for example, Gatchel & Price, 1979; Reeves & Mealiea, 1975; Townsend, House, & Addario, 1975).

Second, care must be taken that the stressful stimuli presented to the client are weak enough that relaxation can effectively prevent discomfort. This is done by breaking up feared stimulus classes into graded *hierarchies,* ordered from least to most distressing. As an example, the hierarchy for a person who expresses fear of closed spaces (claustrophobia) might begin with easy items like sitting in a comfortable chair in a large, well-lit living room and progress in many small steps to much more threatening items, such as standing in a crowded elevator. Some hierarchies are *thematic* in the sense that their items progress along an increasingly distressing theme (for example, being in a room with one small dog; being in a room with three small dogs; being in a room with five large dogs), whereas others are *spatial-temporal* in the sense that they vary along space and/or time dimensions (for example, buying an airline ticket; checking your baggage; boarding the plane). In many cases, thematic and spatial-temporal hierarchies are combined to form a *mixed* hierarchy.

Third, hierarchy items must be presented to the client in some way while anxiety responses are inhibited. The most commonly employed means of doing this is to ask the client to visualize each hierarchy item, beginning with the least threatening, while deeply relaxed. Because only weak versions of stressful stimuli are presented at first, anxiety responses to them will easily be prevented by relaxation, thus diluting their ability to provoke discomfort.[3] As each item is desensitized, the item above it in the hierarchy becomes a little less threatening and can be dealt with in the same way. Ideally, the client never experiences anxiety in relation to any hierarchy item because (1) each represents only a small and easily tolerated

3. Whether this reduction in potential for anxiety elicitation occurs because a new response, such as relaxation, actually replaces anxiety (the counterconditioning hypothesis) because the client simply learns that no adverse consequences follow imagination of feared stimuli (the extinction hypothesis), or as the result of such additional factors as social reinforcement by the therapist, self-reinforcement by the client, or changes in expectations or other client cognitions is not entirely clear. The question has resulted in much research and debate (for example, Benjamin, Marks, & Huson, 1972; Cooke, 1968; Davison, 1968; Davison & Wilson, 1973; Kazdin & Wilcoxon, 1976; Lader & Mathews, 1968; Wilson & Davison, 1971), but resolution of the issue is of academic rather than practical importance (Craighead, 1973).

increase in threat value over the one prior to it, and (2) no new item is visualized until the one below it no longer causes discomfort. If arousal is encountered, the item causing it is either diluted (for example, by presenting it again for a shorter time or by changing it slightly to make it less threatening) or a new one is inserted which requires a smaller step up from the last successfully completed stimulus.

Since each visualized hierarchy item provides a symbolic representation of actual stressful stimuli, the client's ability to imagine these items without discomfort transfers to real life. Thus, when the client actually encounters previously feared stimuli, the weakening of the learned link between those stimuli and anxiety responses which took place in treatment results in a greatly if not completely reduced level of arousal. If transfer does not occur as desensitization progresses, the clinician seeks out and corrects any procedural or other problems that may be evident and makes other necessary changes in the intervention program. Sometimes these alterations take the form of new or revised hierarchy items, additional relaxation training, or practice at item visualization. Whatever the specifics, the goal is to adjust and readjust the treatment program until it becomes effective in eliminating the clients' maladaptive anxiety responses.

The standard systematic-desensitization package has been subjected to increasingly intense research since about 1960, and for the most part, it has received high marks (see reviews by Borkovec, 1970; Lang 1969; Paul, 1969c, 1969d; Rachman, 1967). Paul (1969d) summarized his review by noting, "For the first time in the history of psychological treatments, a specific therapeutic package reliably produced measurable benefits for clients across a broad range of distressing problems in which anxiety was a fundamental importance" (p. 159). Although some doubt and considerable controversy exists regarding the mechanisms through which desensitization produces its effects (for example, Borkovec, 1972; Brown, 1973; Davison & Wilson, 1972, 1973; Goldfried, 1971; Kazdin & Wilcoxon, 1976; Morgan, 1973; Wilkins, 1972, 1973, 1976), it is agreed that the effects themselves are strong.

In some cases, the use of systematic desensitization alone and in its standard form constitutes an incomplete approach to maladaptive conditioned-anxiety responses. In addition to helping clients unlearn inappropriate behaviors, the clinician must also assure that adaptive alternative behaviors are available.[4] If clients are unskilled at or unfamiliar with behaviors appropriate to previously avoided stimulus situations, unsupplemented systematic desensitization may only temporarily weaken conditioned arousal,

---

4. Because humans and animals are constantly behaving, when one response pattern changes, another always replaces it. The question is simply whether the new pattern is desirable or undesirable.

which is subsequently relearned. For example, a child's unrealistic fear of dogs may easily return following successful desensitization unless steps are taken to assure that the child has the knowledge and skills necessary to maintain friendly relations with dogs, control their behavior, and recognize potential danger. As Bandura (1971a) has noted, "No psychological methods exist that can render an organism insensitive to the consequences of its actions" (p. 693).

So that the development of appropriate and adaptive behaviors following desensitization is not left to chance, behavioral theorists and therapists have added variations, supplements, and alternatives to the basic and well-established package. An important example is called *in vivo desensitization* (Wolpe, 1969). The procedures involved parallel those of imaginal desensitization with several important exceptions. First, the hierarchy stimuli are not imagined but presented live (in some cases, slides, films, audio tapes, and video tapes are employed). Second, although progressive relaxation or variations on it, such as conditioned or differential relaxation (Paul & Bernstein, 1973), may be enlisted as an anxiety-inhibiting influence, the calm and reassuring presence of the therapist (along with careful hierarchy gradations) is often used to serve the same function. Third, and perhaps most important, the client is allowed to actually deal with (rather than merely be exposed to) feared stimuli and thereby to develop or reacquire requisite skills while unlearning maladaptive responses.

Thus, a person who is overaroused while speaking to a group may first present a short, simple talk to an audience of one (perhaps the therapist), then to two, three, and so on until no disruptive discomfort is experienced while addressing relatively large groups. Later, the length and spontaneity of the talk may be varied to assure generalization to a wide variety of situations. Some research (for example, Garfield, Darwin, Singer, & McBreaty, 1967; Goldstein, 1969; Hamilton & Schroeder, 1973; Sherman, 1972) and many case reports (for example, Gurman, 1973; Kohlenberg, 1974; Weidner, 1970) confirm the utility of this approach. It is obviously the treatment of choice when unassertiveness or sexual dysfunction are treatment targets, but it is also applicable whenever stressful stimuli can be graded and presented live in a controlled fashion.

Another set of variations on systematic desensitization emphasizes teaching the client to develop and use particularly relevant anxiety-inhibiting *cognitions* (or thoughts) to suppress and ultimately overcome maladaptive emotional responses to imaginal or in vivo stimuli. The idea here is that if clients can learn to say calm, rational, and constructive things to themselves in the face of previously upsetting circumstances, they will not only combat overarousal but will also be in a better position to use whatever more adaptive and constructive responses they may have (or may have learned from the therapist). In one version of this approach,

Meichenbaum (1974, 1975a) has combined systematic desensitization with training in corrective self-statements, similar to those utilized in Ellis's rational emotive therapy (see Chapter 8 in this volume). With the early items in the hierarchy the client visualizes the scenes as in systematic desensitization, but if in the latter part of the hierarchy, the client experiences anxiety, rather than having the scene altered to weaken it, the client visualizes himself or herself making adaptive and coping self-statements until the experienced anxiety is successfully handled. These self-statements (for example, "You can handle the situation"; "Just think rationally") not only may facilitate the person's approach to a previously feared situation, but may also be used as coping responses in that and other situations. In some cases, clients are given special opportunities to practice and perfect their self-instructional training by using it under therapist-controlled stress conditions (for example, mild, but unpredictable electric shock, anxiety-provoking films, or social embarrassment). This procedure is called *stress inoculation* (Meichenbaum, 1977).

Another, even more elaborate type of cognitively oriented desensitization, called *systematic rational restructuring,* has been described by Goldfried (Goldfried, Decenteceo, & Weinberg, 1974; Goldfried & Goldfried, 1975). Here, the client is asked to visualize an anxiety-provoking scene from a graded hierarchy, become aware of the cognitive as well as autonomic components of the resulting arousal (for example, "I feel afraid I'll make a fool of myself"), try out more adaptive and rational thoughts (which may initially be suggested by the therapist), and notice the consequent reduction in discomfort. As each item is dealt with, there is a dialogue between the therapist and the client as they work together to identify and refine those thoughts that will be of maximum use in combating stress and promoting more functional behavior (see also Goldfried & Davison, 1976). The value of using cognitively oriented versions of desensitization to help clients to think straighter about the situations and stimuli that upset them has been supported by a number of experimental investigations (for example, Holroyd, 1976; Meichenbaum, Gilmore, and Fedoravicius, 1971; Weissberg, 1977).

Modeling

Some of the basic ideas behind systematic desensitization are employed by behavioral therapists in *modeling,* a related intervention approach that capitalizes on the fact that human beings can learn by observation as well as by direct participation. Our behavior is strongly influenced by what we observe and/or hear about other individuals' behavior and its consequences.[5] Modeling techniques seek to reduce anxiety responses by providing a programmed learning experience which emphasizes such vicarious processes. In simplest form, the clinician who uses modeling arranges for the client to observe other people, usually of the client's age and sex, as they fearlessly and successfully deal with increasingly threatening versions of the stimuli that frighten the client. The graduated nature of the stimuli and the use of relaxation or other anxiety-inhibiting factors, such as physical distance or the presence of a reassuring therapist, during the demonstration act to suppress the client's anxiety responses and thus increase attention to the model's behavior. In some situations, someone other than the therapist may serve as the calm and reassuring person, such as a parent with a child or a cooperative sexual partner in sexual dysfunction (Fischer & Gochros, 1977; Meyers, Farr, & Craighead, 1976).

The modeling display may be live or symbolic (that is, filmed, videotaped, or even imagined) and contains at least two beneficial elements. First, it provides the client with information. For example, by watching a film depicting others playing with a dog, a person who fears dogs can learn much about both the animal's behavior and the human skills needed to deal with it. Second, it demonstrates that an encounter with feared stimuli can have a positive outcome. The filmed models experience no discomfort; they smile, laugh, enjoy themselves, and of course, are not harmed or threatened by the dog in any way. These elements combine to reduce both maladaptive cognitions relating to the feared stimulus and, in turn, the emotional arousal stemming from such thoughts. This reduction in self-produced arousal increases the likelihood that the client will be able to approach the feared stimulus and practice the adaptive thoughts and behaviors displayed by the models.

The effectiveness of modeling for anxiety reduction is well supported (for example, Bandura, Grusec, & Menlove, 1967; Bandura & Menlove, 1968; Bandura, Blanchard, & Ritter, 1969; Geer & Turtletaub, 1967; Meichenbaum, 1971), but as with desensitization, the original modeling package did not include procedures that allowed clients actually to deal with feared stimuli under controlled circumstances, and thus it was incomplete. When this feature was added (for example, Bandura, Jeffery, & Wright, 1974; Ritter, 1969), it substantially enhanced the effectiveness of the intervention (Bandura, Blanchard, & Ritter, 1969; Blanchard, 1970). For instance, instead of simply giving snake-fearful clients a demonstration of other people's interaction with snakes, an elaborated modeling approach,

5. This can be very fortunate since it spares us the necessity of actually experiencing disastrous consequences (for example, being hit by a truck) in the process of learning to avoid danger, but it can also result in the acquisition of emotional arousal and avoidance behaviors in response to stimuli that are not dangerous (for example, because of what they have heard, some women respond to all men as if they were sex maniacs, when this is not always true).

called *participant modeling,* goes on to invite the client to emulate each gradual step of the model. The model thus acts as a teacher who not only shows what to do but how to do it and, in addition, provides physical assistance, reassurance, encouragement, and praise while the client unlearns anxiety responses and acquires adaptive alternative behaviors (see Bandura, Jeffery, & Gajdos, 1975).

Especially when anxiety responses are related to relatively concrete physical or social stimuli that can be presented in a controlled graduated manner, treatments that combine the principles of in vivo desensitization with those of vicarious learning and then add specific training in and practice of adaptive alternative behaviors are more effective than approaches employing any one of these components in isolation (for example, Bandura, Blanchard, & Ritter, 1969; Bandura, Jeffery, & Gajdos, 1975; Blanchard, 1970; Hersen, Eisler, Miller, Johnson, & Pinkston, 1973; McFall & Twentyman, 1973; Ritter, 1969).

Flooding and Implosion

So far, we have been considering anxiety-management techniques that involve graded presentation of stressful stimuli under conditions designed to produce little or no discomfort. Two alternative approaches, both based on the principle of extinction (see Chapter 7), are also available. Though not used or researched as extensively as desensitization or modeling, they have nevertheless generated considerable clinical interest. These techniques are called *flooding* and *implosion,* and though they differ in procedural details, each stems from the notion that responses that are not reinforced will ultimately disappear, or extinguish (Masserman, 1943; Solomon, Kamin, & Wynne, 1953; Solomon & Wynne, 1954). It is assumed that an individual's continued overarousal to stimuli that are not objectively dangerous, such as domestic cats, is maintained in part by the fact that they can escape or avoid such stimuli (Mowrer, 1939). In other words the escape or avoidance behavior of a person who never stays around them long enough to discover that cats are harmless is continually rewarded by thoughts and feelings of relief and relaxation at having prevented what he or she assume would be disastrous consequences.[6]

Flooding and implosion both seek to disrupt this maladaptive learning

6. An old joke is relevant here. A woman sits on a park bench in New York City watching a man sticking small pieces of toilet paper on his nose and then blowing them away. After some time, she asks the man for an explanation of his strange behavior and is told, "It protects me from attack by rogue elephants." When the woman points out that there are no rogue elephants in New York City, the man says, "It works great, doesn't it?"

by preventing escape or avoidance and by keeping the client in contact with strong versions of stressful stimuli until the arousal they cause finally disappears. Flooding simply involves repeated presentation, usually in imagination but sometimes in vivo, of highly distressing stimuli (for example, "You are in a telephone booth with twenty-two cats"); implosion, an approach developed by Stampfl (for example, Stampfl & Levis, 1967), goes several steps further. Clients receiving implosive therapy are asked not only to visualize strongly arousing stimuli but also, because maximum arousal is desired, to imagine the most terrifying consequences. The therapist provides a more or less continuously running monologue designed to describe and intensify the horrors of each scene. (For example, "You are in a small room with no doors or windows, when suddenly hundreds of cats emerge from the walls and begin attacking you. You scream as they tear at your flesh, and your blood begins to cover the floor." [7]

The nature of these interventions, especially implosion, has forced behavioral theorists and practitioners to question whether clients actually benefit from the approach, and if so, whether equivalent improvement can be brought about through less stressful means. In a recent review of literature on the effects of flooding and implosion, Morganstern (1973) concluded that there is at present "no convincing evidence of the effectiveness of implosion or flooding with human subjects nor is there any evidence that the techniques are superior to systematic desensitization" (p. 318). Others (for example, Bandura, 1969; Wolpe, 1969) have expressed concern over possible detrimental consequences of implosion, but its proponents (for example, Levis, 1974) feel that this concern is unfounded.

Unfortunately, the methodological quality of research on the effects and possible dangers of flooding and implosion has been inconsistent (for example, Levis & Hare, 1977; Marshall, Gauthier, & Gordon, 1979; Morganstern, 1973), thus precluding firm evaluative conclusions about these techniques at present.

Further, implosion and flooding focus almost entirely on extinction of anxiety responses and not at all on fostering development of adaptive alternative behaviors. In this sense, these approaches appear incomplete and certainly less useful clinically than the other more comfortable and comprehensive treatment packages that are available.

SOME CONCLUDING COMMENTS

As indicated earlier, the development of behavioral procedures for anxiety management, such as systematic desensitization, modeling, and the dozens

7. Sorry about that, but reading this example may give some idea of the feelings produced during implosion.

of variations on each of them (see Bandura, 1969; Kanfer & Phillips, 1970; Lazarus, 1971, 1972; Meichenbaum, 1974; Paul & Bernstein, 1973; Rimm & Masters, 1979; Wolpe, 1969; Yates, 1970), has stimulated a great deal of research activity aimed both at evaluation of these techniques and at their refinement into more streamlined packages. On the basis of this research and a mountain of case reports, it can now be stated with considerable confidence that, in most cases, the social-learning or behavioral approach to the problem of maladaptive anxiety responses provides an effective solution, which not only brings about initial changes in behavior but also promotes the generalization and durability of those changes. At the risk of sounding like a television commercial, it can be said that today no one need endure the discomforts of strong, disruptive, maladaptive anxiety responses.

Yet behavioral theorists and practitioners are far from having all the answers about the development, maintenance, and elimination of these problems. Their most notable initial achievements came in dealing with a fairly restricted set of anxiety-related difficulties, such as specific phobias and performance disruptions, and the knowledge gained from the research and practice of the last twenty years is constantly being applied to new and diverse targets. In addition, innovations, such as self-administered treatment and automated treatment, continue to appear (for example, Lang, Melamed, & Hart, 1970; Rosen, Glasgow, & Barrera, 1976). Paralleling these developments is increased attention, in both research and clinical practice, to the role of cognitive factors in the development and modification of anxiety responses. Much more needs to be learned about those combinations of client, therapist, and treatment characteristics that result in the greatest and most rapid reductions in various presenting problems.

In short, it is not enough to know that social-learning approaches to anxiety management are effective; rather we must deal with what Paul (1969a) called the "ultimate question." "What treatment, by whom, is most effective for this individual with what specific problem, under which set of circumstances, and how does it come about?" (p. 44) Working on the answer to this question and those that follow from it will keep researchers and clinicians very busy for many years to come.

SUMMARY

This chapter deals with social-learning approaches to the reduction or elimination of anxiety. It was shown that the concept of anxiety does not reflect a "thing" but rather constitutes a shorthand term which refers to a complex and variable pattern of behavior which occurs in response to internal or external stimuli and which can be measured in self-report, physiological, and overt motor channels.

It was noted that a certain amount of anxiety or arousal is necessary to maintain everyday functioning, but that overarousal can produce disruption in behavior and may even promote the appearance of "neurotic" or "psychotic" symptoms. When this happens, anxiety becomes a clinical problem.

From the social-learning perspective, anxiety is seen as primarily a learned phenomenon which can be dealt with through a variety of learning-based therapy techniques. These techniques include systematic desensitization, modeling, implosion, and flooding. The basic procedures involved in each of these techniques (and several variations on them) were described. It was noted that, as a group, social learning–based interventions have been highly successful in the modification of clinically problematic anxiety.

CHAPTER 12

BEHAVIORAL TREATMENT OF DEPRESSION

Peter D. McLean

University of British Columbia

Clinical depression has only recently attracted significant attention in the field of behavior modification. Depression is not easily operationally defined and can be a profoundly covert experience. The fact that the study and manipulation of covert events has become increasingly sanctioned by behaviorists has, no doubt, been responsible for a major part of this new interest in depression. Perhaps more important in the building of interest in depression has been the realization that it ranks as one of the two most frequent mental health disorders in North America and that this frequency has been on the increase relative to other mental health disorders since the early 1950s. Frequently referred to as the common cold of mental disturbance, depression is an experience that no one escapes, even if only in its mild form.

DIMENSIONS OF DEPRESSION
Definition and Assessment of Depression

First and foremost, depression is a mood disorder characterized by pervasive dysphoria. Depending on the severity of this negative mood and

223

the manner in which it has developed, dysfunctional thoughts and overt behavior as well as physiological complaints may be present. Typically, the order of development of the symptom complex is, first, negative thoughts; second, dysfunctional overt behavior; and finally, the appearance of physiological symptoms in direct proportion to overall severity. Depression can be best understood by noting the changes that occur in three response modes—cognitive, overt behavior, and physiological—when someone is depressed compared to the person's normal state.

The *cognitive* habits of depressed individuals are the opposite of those required for adaptive coping. High-frequency, automatic thoughts of hopelessness, helplessness, and negative expectations for the future are experienced routinely (Beck, 1967). This glum outlook does not apply to others or to the world in general, but is anticipated as the course of one's own future; it stems from the depressed person's belief that he or she is personally incompetent (Garber & Hollon, 1980). This and other systematic negative distortions fosters an acute sensitivity to negative information, such as criticism (Lewinsohn, Lobitz, & Wilson, 1973), and paints a bleak outlook in general. The perceived aversiveness of this state of affairs is testified to by the high rate of suicidal ideation in clinically depressed populations. We found, for example, that of a group of two hundred clinically depressed outpatients, 43 percent gave serious consideration to suicide several times a month for over 1.5 hours each time. In contrast, less than 2 percent of a matched, nondepressed population thought about suicide during the month, and when they did, they reported changing the topic of thought in less than five minutes.

Over time and with increased severity, these negative thoughts and feelings generalize and affect *overt behavior*. Depressed individuals withdraw from opportunities for social interaction, procrastinate freely, disengage themselves from pleasant activities (Lewinsohn & Libet, 1972) and simply do less but despair more. In social situations, depressed people complain more about themselves (Lewinsohn, 1974) and are more often visibly distraught (for example, crying, agitated) than are nondepressed people.

As depressed cognitive- and overt-behavior habit patterns progress, many, but not all, depressed individuals begin to experience *physiological* symptoms which usually become the center of focus and serve to confirm the "illness" in the mind of the symptom bearer. Such complaints as sleep disturbance and agitation are most common, followed by gastrointestinal disturbance and weight change.

In attempting to define and assess depression, several factors complicate our efforts. First of all, depression is episodic in nature, with the average clinical episode lasting three to six months. Approximately half of those who experience an episode of clinical severity never have another, and the other half have two or more episodes spaced out over years. The second complicating factor is that the manifestation of symptoms between the three response modes is poorly correlated. As a result the "typical depression" is difficult to define because each case has some but not all of the characteristics at any given time. Unqualified, the label *depression* is a stereotype which communicates very little.

There are several ways to try to focus the clinical picture more clearly. Psychiatric nomenclature, in keeping with the medical model, construes depression into a *subtype classification* system as a function of symptom description, course characteristics, and presumed cause. Each diagnostic subcategory is considered to be unique, and progression of severity can occur within but not between diagnostic subcategories. The traditional diagnostic distinction has been between reactive depression (a reaction to known events) and endogenous depression (appears to occur in the absence of precipitating circumstances and is thought to be biochemically, and perhaps genetically, mediated). The Diagnostic and Statistical Manual of Mental Disorders (DSM-II), produced by the American Psychiatric Association in 1968, included a number of subcategory diagnoses under the more general headings of neuroses and psychoses. In a proposed revision, the DSM-III lists nine subtype depression diagnostic categories which are distinguished on the basis of whether episodes of depression are recurrent, unipolar (depression only) or bipolar (depression and manic phases), a personality disorder, or atypical (includes both unipolar and bipolar conditions). Unlike its predecessor, the proposed DSM-III recommends rating individual cases on five axes (clinical psychiatric syndrome, personality disorders, physical disorders, severity of psychosocial stressors, and highest level of adaptive functioning in past year). This multiaxial classification system in effect uses a checklist criteria-rating method in which each level is operationally defined in terms of severity, but not frequency or duration of occurrence. A major difficulty of this classification system is that the assumed biochemical processes responsible for depression in some of the diagnostic subcategories remain entirely hypothetical. Furthermore, because of the complexity of both the classification system and the symptom patterns of depression, assignment of clients to one category or another is no easy matter. Interclinician agreement ratings on subcategory assignment are notoriously low (Presly & Walton, 1973; Zubin, 1967), making this classification of relatively little value to behavioral science. Other classification systems are less complex. For example, Wolpe (1979) advocates a three-drawer classification system: normal, neurotic, and endogenous depression. Also, there are a number of commonly used disorder-criteria checklists (for example, Feighner, Robins, Guze, Woodruff, Winokur, & Munoz, 1972) which are designed to reduce subject heterogeneity in research studies by specifying entrance and exclusion criteria. But again, we are dealing with qualitative differences that do not account for frequency and duration of symptoms.

The search for clinical subtypes has been conducted on the empirical front as well, but the results to date are mixed. Paykel, Prusoff, Klerman, Haskell, & Dimascio (1973) classified depressed clients using multivariate statistical procedures into four subgroups on the basis of twenty-nine psychopathology-related questionnaire items. They were then able to predict treatment response to antidepressant medication on the basis of subgroup membership. On the other hand, a subsequent study (McLean & Hakstian, 1979) using a broader questionnaire base not surprisingly found different subgroups, but in this case, treatment response and group membership were not related. Clinical experience suggests there are at least two depression subtypes: short-term reactive depression and a depressed life-style pattern. Nonetheless, delineation of subtypes is an empirical matter and awaits the development of more sophisticated measurement technology.

The alternate method of describing individual differences in depression is the *dimensional approach* in which clinical differences are viewed as only variations in degree of severity. Quantitative differences between normal, everyday blue moods and severe depression are described in terms of global-scale scores. Popular self-report global measures of depression include the Beck Depression Inventory (Beck, Ward, Mendelson, Mock, & Erbaugh, 1961), the Depression Adjective Checklist (Lubin, 1965), and the Zung Self-Rating Depression Scale (Zung, 1965). Similar global measures of depression severity can be completed by the therapist during the course of an interview (for example, Grinker, Miller, Sabshin, Nunn, & Nunally, 1961; Hamilton, 1960). The advantages of using these instruments are the ease of administration, the simplicity of a single score, and the lack of causal assumptions. The major disadvantages are that these measures describe only a single dimension of depression and overrepresent mood items to the relative neglect of the overt-behavior-response category.

The behavioral clinician when assessing a depressed client will be interested in a wide range of information in addition to a global depression-severity score in order to plan a treatment strategy. A review of client functioning in each of the three response modalities together with any problems the client mentions provide the basis for further exploration and description during the behavioral interview. The clinician will then want to define the frequency, duration, intensity, antecedents, and consequences of problem behaviors (that is, thoughts and actions) and symptoms. Information about the client's strengths (social resources, in particular), expectations, goals, and stressful demands, as well as his or her personal understanding of the development of the depression, is also critical. With this information at hand, the behavioral clinician can then begin to evolve and confirm a flow chart of events, symptoms, behaviors, beliefs, circumstances, and expectations as they interrelate and influence the experience of depression. What we have from this sort of assessment is a wealth of treatment-relevant information and the basis for treatment-progress evaluation, both in terms of problem reduction and goal attainment.

Individual Differences in Vulnerability to Depression

How do some people maintain their mood and preserve their performance under prolonged and negative circumstances, whereas others under mild provocation become fully depressed? An interaction of personal skills and external conditions seem responsible for these major individual differences. The three demographic factors that are statistically most associated with high risk for clinical depression are (1) being female; (2) being married, separated, widowed, or divorced; and (3) having children (McLean, 1976). Presumably, cultural and economic conditions associated with the experience of marriage and children disadvantage women compared to men. Brown and Harris (1978) in a large epidemiological study in England identified the following four factors which render women vulnerable to depression: (1) low intimacy (availability of husband or boyfriend as a valued confidant), (2) unemployment, (3) having three or more children at home under the age of fourteen years, and (4) loss of mother before eleven years of age. In another study, Brown, Harris, and Peto (1973) established a causal link between the volume of life-stress events sustained during the six months prior to hospitalization and the onset of clinical depression. These life-stress events, however, are likely to be less contributory to depression than is one's ability to influence interpersonal encounters and to avoid maladaptive cognitive habits, such as permitting a self-stimulating train of negative thoughts to run on unchallenged. For example, one of my depressed clients once made a suicide attempt half an hour after burning two pieces of toast on a morning which, the client reported, had been otherwise going quite well. She had forgotten to pop the toaster and the smoke literally engulfed the kitchen. Her immediate conclusion was, "My God, I can't even make toast."

It seems that people who are predisposed to clinical depression function normally over time, rising periodically over the clinical threshold as a function of their inability to cope successfully with a particularly large concentration of environmental or imagined stressors, before returning to their functional prestress baseline. Behavior therapies, in contrast to other verbal interventions and medical treatments, hold considerable promise in reducing vulnerability to depression, since treatment is aimed at teaching self-management skills. In this manner, clients can learn to avoid depression-related circumstances and behaviors altogether and to reduce their impact through skillful coping when they cannot be avoided.

UNITARY THEORIES AND TREATMENT METHODS

Behavioral theories of the development and treatment of depression are primarily distinguished from other formulations by their detailed focus on cognitive and physical performance. They share the belief that depressed people can learn to interact more constructively with their cognitive and interpersonal environments. Three prominent behavioral theories have been selected for review. These are unitary theories inasmuch as the formulation of depression is accounted for by a single process (Craighead, 1980) in each theory.

Insufficient-Reinforcement Theory

Depression, according to the operant-reinforcement model, is the natural consequent of a sustained reduction in the amount of reinforcement an individual receives. Ferster (1965) originally pointed out that the most notable feature of depression was a general reduction in specific adaptive responses which could be positively reinforced. Failure to produce adaptive behavior may be the result of any number of reasons, including (1) sudden environmental changes which require the establishment of new reinforcement sources, such as a job transfer and residential relocation; (2) engaging in aversive interpersonal exchanges which preempts the opportunity for positive reinforcement, as in the case of marital conflict; and (3) failure to attend to the environment in sufficient detail to interact in a socially appropriate manner, thereby receiving relatively little positive feedback. In effect, the position is that reinforcement follows appropriate behavior and if there is no contingency relationship between adaptive behavior and positive reinforcement, or if depressive behavior is inadvertently reinforced out of sympathy, the behavioral conditions for establishing and maintaining depression are present.

Lewinsohn (1974), who with his University of Oregon colleagues made the major contribution to the development of this theory, identified three assumptions upon which this behavioral formulation of depression rests. They were (1) depressive behaviors and dysphoric feelings are elicited as a result of a low rate of response-contingent positive reinforcement; (2) this relatively low rate of response-contingent reinforcement is sufficient to account for the occurrence of other components of the depression symptom complex; and (3) the total amount of response-contingent reinforcement received by anyone is a function of the number of events that are potentially reinforcing to the individual, the number of potentially reinforcing events available in the individual's environment, and the individual's ability to engage in behaviors that elicit positive reinforcement in this environment.

During the past ten years, the Lewinsohn group has pursued the rate-of-reinforcement concept in depression by directing its activities in two areas: determination of the relationships between pleasant and unpleasant mood-related events and depression; and the functional relationship between social competence (that is, means of influencing social reinforcement) and depression.

In order to help identify standard events having reinforcing properties, MacPhillamy and Lewinsohn (1971) developed the Pleasant Events Schedule. This schedule consists of 320 items which are considered by a large sample of the normal population to be sources of pleasure. Each of the 320 events is rated by frequency of occurrence and subjective enjoyability, reflecting the recent rate of reinforcement and potential reinforcement value for each event. Subsequently, Lewinsohn and Talkington (1979) developed a 320-item Unpleasant Events Schedule in order to measure the occurrence of, and subjective value attached to, events generally considered to be aversive. These questionnaires have demonstrated good psychometric qualities and are correlated with mood (Lewinsohn & Amenson, 1978). They sidestep many of the practical problems of attempting to determine which events have positive and negative reinforcing properties by means of extended interviews or observation.

The *low-rate-of-response-contingent-positive-reinforcement model* has been evolved by Lewinsohn and his colleagues through systematic investigation. They have found that compared to normal control subjects, depressed subjects exercise less skill in social interactions, receive less response-contingent reinforcement, and engage in fewer pleasant activities; the rate of positive reinforcement received by depressed subjects has been shown to increase with clinical improvement.

The role of cognitive appraisal and both positive and negative self-statements is not addressed by Lewinsohn. One does not know if cognitive mediation of depressed actions and inactions is considered untenable or whether Lewinsohn regards private events to be beyond the realm of acceptable standards of measurement.

Such inattention to cognitive behavior becomes conspicuous when the variable nature of specific reinforcers is considered. The boyfriend of a graduate student, for example, who has just had her thesis proposal rejected by her supervisor for the third time may have lost his reinforcer effectiveness, as have other friends, activities, and personal fantasies. Yet the

potential reinforcement effectiveness of the supervisor has increased because of his exalted position as judge in a universe of decreasing possibil-
ities. A major problem in the treatment of depression is that previous reinforcers have lost their attractiveness because they are diminished by more
pressing problems. How attractive can dinner at a five-star restaurant be if
you are considering suicide?

Much of the work done in the development of Lewinsohn's theory is
correlational in nature—depressed feelings and withdrawal from pleasant
activities go together—and a cause-and-effect relationship has been inferred rather than demonstrated. Indeed, Lewinsohn and Graf (1973) were
unable to demonstrate a significant relationship between changes in activities on one day and subsequent changes in mood one or two days later,
using cross-lagged correlations.

Treatment Studies

Results of attempts to increase the rate of positive reinforcement that
depressed clients experience, either by increasing the number of pleasant
activities engaged in or by improving the quality of their social interactions via therapeutic instruction or training, has been mixed. Basing a
study on Lewinsohn's theory, Padfield (1976) treated a group of rural
women for twelve sessions by getting them to increase their rate of pleasant activities. A control group of women received nondirective counseling. Multivariate analysis of a variety of outcome measures failed to
show an overall significant difference in treatment effect between these
two groups. This finding may be due to the fact that the theory really was
not tested in the first place, since the pleasant-activities manipulation did
not distinguish between the two groups—women in the behavior-therapy
group did not increase their rate of pleasant activities beyond that of the
control group.

Hammen and Glass (1975) asked mildly depressed college students to
increase their rate of pleasant activities as part of an experiment. Although
these subjects did increase their rate of pleasant activities compared to control groups, they ended up feeling more depressed. Hammen has raised
the possibility that self-attribution, rather than just raising the rate of participation in positive activities, may be the critical factor in reducing depression. In a study, again with depressed students, Hammen, Rook, and
Harris (cited in Blaney, in press) found that students who had a chance to
choose from a list their own pleasant activities in which to participate became less depressed than did a comparison group of students who increased their rate of participation in pleasant activities selected by the
experimenter.

The single positive finding in support of the increased-rate-of-positive-activities solution to the low-rate-of-response-contingent-positive-reinforcement problems was reported by Turner, Ward, and Turner (1979). These investigators assigned depressed clients to one of four groups: activity-increase, fitness-exercise, client-centered, and self-monitor (daily activities and mood) groups. Treatment consisted of five sessions over a one-month period. Clients in the activities group did increase their rate of activities and, relative to the other groups, did prove to be less depressed after treatment. The fact that there was an effort to individually tailor pleasant activities to each client may account for the positive outcome in this study.

Rate of participation in activities typically considered to be reinforcing has been found to be inversely correlated with depressed mood, when both participation and type of activity have been elective. There is little evidence to show that assigned activities at specified rates are reinforcing. Again, a problem for Lewinsohn's theory is that what is reinforcing under normal circumstances is likely to be of little importance when a person is depressed, compared to the crush of other personal problems which beg for resolution.

Learned-Helplessness Theory

On the basis of animal experimentation and human analogue studies, Seligman (1975) proposed that depression is the result of a generalized belief that responding is useless. Dogs exposed to inescapable electrical shocks do not take advantage of avoidance opportunities when subsequently placed in a situation in which they clearly could avoid shocks. Instead, they passively absorb the punishment. This phenomenon is dramatically attenuated depending on the dogs' previous experience with punishment avoidance in similar conditions. Presumably, both dogs and humans learn that responding and consequences are independent, thereby fostering the belief that they have no control over their circumstances. As Blaney (1977, p. 207) has noted, however, "the essence of helplessness is generalization." Few novice skiers, for example, who feel helpless on the summit and who have no control over their descent, similarly feel helpless in other domains of their lives. And if they did, how likely would the perception of noncontrol on the ski slopes be contributory? Traumatic exposure to helplessness is probably not the manner in which most depressed individuals acquire their sense of helplessness. Insidious domestic environments or the combination of unassertive social skills, self-consciousness, and an insensitive environment can presumably produce the same effect.

To be viable, the learned-helplessness model has to demonstrate that a depressed mood can be manipulated by the perception of control over external events. Because of obvious limitations on human experimentation, Seligman and others have pursued a series of laboratory analogue studies to investigate this relationship. The results are not clear-cut. Klein, Fencil-Morse, and Seligman (1976), for example, reported that depressed subjects who successfully participated in a problem-solving exercise showed a significant improvement in mood compared to controls. This finding is in contrast with Miller and Seligman's (1975) study which showed that depressed subjects exposed to noxious but controllable noise marginally increased their negative mood, although depressed subjects did show less task persistence and learning compared to nondepressed subjects, as would be predicted by the theory.

Seligman suggests that traumatic induction is not necessary for the perception of noncontrol in humans in the development of helplessness and consequently depression. People poorly equipped to cope with stress and those with poor social skills do have less control over their environment. At this point, however, the argument is indistinguishable from that of Lewinsohn's. For both theories, noncontingent reinforcement is central. From the point of view of common sense and clinical experience, the helplessness hypothesis has strong appeal. But many theoretical and practical questions remain unanswered. The unique feature of Seligman's theory is the perception of noncontrol leading to a belief in helplessness. The challenge facing Seligman's theory is to account for the hypothetical generalization process across a variety of functional areas of one's lifestyle (for example, marriage, work, child management, social interactions, personal competence in sport, hobbies, cultural endeavors, or other interests).

TREATMENT STUDIES

Virtually all of the developmental work done on the helplessness model has been done in analogue studies using students as subjects. In the single exception, Glass, as cited by Blaney (in press), designed a therapy procedure to field-test Seligman's theory. Twenty-nine moderately depressed students were assigned to either one of two treatment groups or a no-treatment control group. Helplessness treatment consisted of identifying areas of personal functioning in which helplessness was debilitating and of promoting the belief in control by prompting clients to remedy the problem by using responses already in their repertoire. Comparison treatment involved clarification of feelings, group support, and self-monitoring. By and large, the helplessness group did best, although on a measure of the cognitions of helplessness, the groups were not differentiated.

Seligman's theory suggests no specific means of inducing a sense of mastery or personal effectiveness within a treatment context, aside from assertion training, antidepressant medication and, ironically, electroconvulsive shock therapy. Graded-task assignment, problem solving, and self-esteem building are universal to almost all verbal treatments of depression. In terms of treatment utility, the learned-helplessness theory remains conceptual rather than empirical and must generate clinical data consistent with the theory.

Cognitive-Distortion Theory

Depression has traditionally been considered to be a cognitive and affective disorder. The lack of motivation and the characteristic manner in which depressed people construe their world, frequently in the absence of any external evidence, invite confrontation on the part of friends in an attempt to dissuade them from their pessimistic beliefs. Beck (1967, 1974) has systematically reviewed the thematic content and thought distortions of clinically depressed people and has concluded that depression, etiologically and therapeutically, is a cognitive problem. He considers negative affect and motivation to be the result of negative conceptualizations, particularly those revolving around loss—irrevocable loss of valued relationships, attributes, and opportunities. Sensitized by unfavorable circumstances, depressed people are thought to become predisposed to overreact to related life circumstances later on. Subsequent experiences of loss are then liable to be misinterpreted or exaggerated. Beck identifies four cognitive distortions, or errors: *arbitrary inference* (unwarranted conclusions); *selective abstraction* (not considering all aspects of a situation); *magnification/minimization* (major errors in judgment in either direction, when considering the significance of events and behavior); and *overgeneralization* (jumping to general conclusions based on minimal information). These cognitive distortions work to promote the assignment of personal cause with the result that low self-esteem and self-criticism, apathy, and sadness follow. The treatment task is to identify particular cognitive distortions, misconceptions, and maladaptive assumptions and to systematically "test their validity and assumptions" through verbal interactions while encouraging the client to search for alternative interpretations and solutions.

The cognitive-distortion theory has been subjected to very little empirical investigation, and in treatment, relatively little use is made of more recent behavioral techniques to measure and manage the frequency of thoughts (Mahoney, 1974; Meichenbaum, 1973). Furthermore, the application of this theory to depressions not induced by cognitive distortions is unclear. A depressed person may have a very accurate assessment of his or her circumstances which are themselves punitive and restrictive. This model seems to assume that the problem lies in the *perception* of one's circumstances, rather than in the manner in which the individual *interacts* with the environment.

TREATMENT STUDIES

In the last several years a number of treatment-comparison studies have been reported, which utilized cognitive techniques ranging from the cognitive-distortion approach of Beck to the behavioral management of particular thoughts as suggested by Mahoney and Meichenbaum. Rush, Beck, Kovacs, and Hollon (1977) found their cognitive treatment to be superior to antidepressant medication, which has been considered the treatment of choice by physicians for many years. Cognitive therapy has also been shown to be temporarily superior to both nondirective and behavior (increased positive activities, behavioral rehearsal) therapies (Shaw, 1977) and, when combined with behavior therapy, superior than either treatment alone (Taylor & Marshall, 1977). Finally, in a well-designed study, Zeiss, Lewinsohn, and Munoz (1979) found cognitive treatment to be indistinguishable in results from treatment focused on building interpersonal skills or from a third treatment aimed at increasing pleasant activities.

Caution is required in the interpretation of several of these studies since the same therapist delivered all of the verbal treatments within the same study (Shaw, 1977; Taylor & Marshall, 1977). These treatment studies provide inconsistent support for the efficacy of cognitive intervention, compared to alternative verbal interventions.

There have been other behavioral-treatment studies that are not easily classified. Fuchs and Rehm (1977) reported the effects of a successful group treatment modeled after self-control concepts (Rehm, 1977). This same study has also been classified as a pleasant-activities treatment (Biglan & Dow, in press) and as a cognitive treatment (Hollon & Beck, 1979). Several other studies have focused on social skills or on a wide combination of behavioral treatments and will be discussed later.

So far we have seen that there is no consistent support for any one of the behavioral theories, regardless of whether they concentrate on cognitive or physical behavior. Labeling of treatments is fairly arbitrary, and many treatments include procedures that are quite universal (for example, self-monitoring) which may work to make results between groups and studies more homogenous. Most of the studies have used very small sample sizes and at least half have used only mildly depressed students as subjects, all of which limit their interpretation and the generalization of their results.

How significant are the treatment results that have been attained, and how does the behavioral clinician select between treatment choices? Those studies that did include a waiting-list control group have shown behavior-treatment-group superiority over the waiting-list control (that is, compared to the natural course of the disorder). But the fact that these treatment groups were so similar in terms of their results suggests that either nonspecific treatment effects are very significant or that theoretical differences are not reflected in treatment procedures in important ways, or both. If the difference between the before-and-after-treatment measures of the worst treatment group (assuming the treatment did no harm) or of an attention control group were compared to the difference between the end-of-treatment measures of this same group and the end-of-treatment measures of the best performing group in any treatment-comparison study, one would have a comparison of the magnitude of nonspecific-treatment effects and specific-treatment (that is, active ingredient of treatment is known) effects. Such computations typically show that nonspecific-treatment effects far outweigh specific-treatment effects. The challenge to behavioral theory is to account for more of the nonspecific-treatment effect.

MULTICOMPONENT THEORY AND TREATMENT METHODS
Rationale

The multicomponent theory assumes that there are more causes of depression than can be explained by any of the unitary theories (Biglan & Dow, in press; Craighead, 1980; McLean & Hakstian, 1979). The treatment procedures advocated by the unitary theories are not unique to their parent theory, and each unitary theory at best represents a necessary but insufficient condition for the universal evolution of depression. The common factor in the various accounts of depression is that stress results from disappointment. More than anything else, depression seems to represent a *common side effect* of a large variety of problems (for example, marital discord, unemployment, physical illness) which, when severe enough, becomes functionally autonomous; symptoms and their effects stimulate more depressed cognitions, actions and physiological reactions. Frequently, the source of stress is evident, as in the case of bereavement, marital discord, or illness. But more often, personal stress is not obvious to the external observer and consists of high-frequency losses or disappointments occurring at the rate of ten to eighty per day. Together, and in the absence of compensating positive events and thoughts, these stressors provide a major and chronic impact. Critical looks between spouses, constant self-appraisal resulting in negative conclusions, realization that lifestyles portrayed by the media and modeled by attractive people are beyond one's grasp, selective recall of previous failures, and the setting of unrealistic work schedules—all are the sort of stressors that are grist for the depression mill. Of course, nondepressed individuals report these stressors as well, but the critical difference is that they report the experience of a compensating number of positive events and thoughts within the same time period which effectively offsets the impact of routine stressors. *It is the ratio of negative to positive events and outcomes that is decisive for mood determination.* Common sources of stress associated with depression are (1) unrealistic goals and performance criteria; (2) personal disuse, due to lack of goals; (3) life-stress events (that is, more major than daily stressors); and (4) inadequate coping techniques.

The major advantage of a multicomponent approach to treatment is that the therapist can tailor the treatment techniques to the individual needs of the client. This is likely to add credibility to the treatment program, which should, in turn, be reflected in increased treatment compliance and efficacy.

Treatment Assembly

The remainder of this chapter will present the essential components of a multicomponent, behavioral treatment program which draws heavily on my own clinical experience, although the techniques and the manner in which they are used are common to many behavioral programs. Treatment consists of ensuring satisfactory performance in three functional areas—social interaction, behavioral productivity, and cognitive control. Goal-attainment, self-monitoring, reinforcement, and a focus on adaptive coping are considered to be the four common objectives of the treatment process.

During the process of assessment, the behavioral clinician will elicit an operationally defined list of three to five prominent problems brought on by the depression (for example, *sleep disturbance,* gets four to five hours of intermittent sleep per night compared to a regular seven hours; *social withdrawal,* does not initiate more than three conversations at work per day and goes out at night with someone two times per month, compared to one to two times per week; etc.). Similarly, the therapist will elicit treatment goals which act as client criteria for improvement. These goals are stated in very specific (measurable) and positive language. The therapist can construct a serial hierarchy of treatment targets based on this information as well as information about the client's expectations, living circumstances, resources, and immediate capabilities. In doing so, treatment tasks are arranged so that there is immediate payoff to the client. That is, the therapist selects initial minigoals which are well within the capability of the client and are relevant to his or her concerns. Wherever possible, initial treatment tasks involve social activities because inherent task demands of such activities make it less likely that the client will be able to indulge the habit of negative rumination. Finally, working on about three to four meaningful tasks at once seems to be optimal for most clinically depressed clients and ensures that they are not under- or overchallenged by homework assignments between treatment sessions. Keeping in mind the principle of graduated practice, the therapist assembles a treatment program for individual clients, drawing treatment goals from, first, the social-interaction and behavioral-productivity areas and, finally, from the cognitive-control area.

SOCIAL INTERACTION

A tendency of depressed people is to become increasingly self-absorbed to the mutual exclusion of interpersonal interaction. Often, but certainly not always, the individual lacks social skill, in which case remedial training is necessary. The rationale for promoting quality social interactions is straightforward. Other people, particularly significant others, are more potent sources of reinforcement to the depressed individual than the individual is to himself or herself. This is due to the pervasive self-critical attitude held by depressed people. In addition to the opportunity for positive recognition from others, social interaction affords the scope for feedback from others on a host of issues, including problem solving. This is particularly relevant given that content analyses of depressed clients' treatment goals, as well as the problems that led to their depression in the first place, have repeatedly shown that the top items on both goal and problem lists are of a social nature. Finally, social interactions are incompatible with destructive self-preoccupations and provide a concrete measure of personal activity, both of which are considered to be therapeutic.

The idea is to mobilize clients to a reasonable rate of social interaction across a variety of social situations. Typically, great care is directed to detailed planning here. The number and types of social instigations are planned, conversations are role-played (Zeiss et al., 1979) if necessary, and clients are prompted not to complain or disclose their negative feelings or cynicism. An initial roadblock, of course, is that none of this makes sense to the client, who is operating with the opposite strategy in mind, saying "When I feel better, then I'll be fit for human consumption." We explain to clients, for example, that their depression is normal given their social withdrawal, physical inactivity, and negative outlook, and that normal mood *follows* sustained and normalized social activity, behavioral productivity, and cognitive control. In the meantime, depression symptoms (for example, lack of motivation, feeling down, tension, and sleep problems) are best treated as annoying, but temporary side effects of behavioral mismanagement. A redundant but important task of the behavioral therapist is to focus and motivate the client towards the achievement of behavioral goals while otherwise ignoring or redirecting attention away from symptomatic complaints. Clients with a history of social withdrawal when they are not depressed will likely need help in locating activities available in the community and will need to understand that most friendships evolve from shared activities.

Clients deficient in assertive social skills require graduated task assignments in this area, particularly in initiating and maintaining conversation, dealing constructively with criticism, and making requests of others. Zeiss et al. (1979) had their clients read *Your Perfect Right* (Alberti & Emmons, 1974); Rehm, Fuchs, Roth, Kornblith, and Romano (1979) used a role-playing format (refusing unreasonable demands, making requests, expressing criticism and disapproval, and expressing approval and affection) to teach assertion skills to their depressed clients.

If depression stems from aversive marital exchanges, communication training and behavioral contracting are recommended techniques to use early in the treatment program. Aversive marital control represents an attempt to influence one's spouse and tends both to punish the weaker member and reduce the total amount of verbal communication. The reduced rate of communication frustrates domestic management and easily generalizes from contested topics to other topic areas, so that communication eventually involves only terse discussion of administrative issues. It has been found in one study, for example, that married couples (one spouse clinically depressed) negatively cued each other 61 percent of the time during domestic discussions when using electronic cue-boxes that flashed color-coded approval/disapproval signals (McLean, Ogston, & Grauer, 1973). An analysis of domestic conversations with couples in the behavior-therapy group of the same study further showed that when the ratio of positive to negative verbal interactions was significantly increased as a function of treatment (feedback training and behavioral contracting), depression was reduced relative to a treatment comparison group. To enhance domestic interchanges, couples with a depressed member are typically asked to spend twenty minutes per day reviewing the day and talking about any topic while (a) avoiding criticism and (2) premeditating and monitoring their individual interactions to ensure that their contributions are constructive and are likely to be received positively.

The therapist will have many early opportunities to help depressed clients structure, rehearse, review, and further plan constructive social interactions. The objective is to take full advantage of the powerful influence of social reinforcement, helping the client become a demonstrably valued, skilled, and frequent participant in a range of social interactions, rather than being a passive observer or victim.

BEHAVIORAL PRODUCTIVITY

Poor motivation and self-preoccupation combine to produce dramatic levels of procrastination or deterioration of work performance in most clinically depressed clients. Further, this highly visible complaint serves to reinforce the client's negative self-concept. It does not occur to most depressed clients that successful performance will improve mood, and dysphoric mood is typically used as the excuse for inaction. The belief that successful performance is a powerful antidepressant has its origins both in the law of effect and in self-efficacy theory (Bandura, 1977a). Behavioral productivity encourages self-reinforcement and allows obstacles to successful performance to be identified. Almost all behavioral programs utilize some form of behavioral productivity, ranging from the recording of tasks to pleasant-event schedules. My approach has been to elicit goals in accordance with the client's criteria for feeling better, which then become operationally defined and calibrated into graded task assignments. Such goals are usually pragmatic in nature ("Be up by 7 A.M."; "Spend one hour a day with the children"; "Find a half-time job"; "Work at my accounting course"; etc.). The behavior therapist's task is to (1) divide performance goals into tasks, small enough to ensure completion; (2) ensure that the goals are relevant to the client's needs and are not perceived as contrived busy work; (3) negotiate daily task assignments and ask clients to monitor daily goal attainment; and (4) encourage positive recognition for successful performance.

COGNITIVE CONTROL

Depression impairs cognitive functioning through judgment distortion and the intrusiveness of high-frequency negative thoughts. These thought processes in turn impair memory recall and ability to make decisions. Interestingly, many depressed people justify their introverted style and tendency to be relatively absorbed in past events by claiming to be looking for the reason for—the key to explain—their depression. The predictable result is an intensified negative mood, because the key is not in the past.

The behavior therapist will, in the same circumstances, direct the client in a search for *solutions instead of causes.*

Few people fully appreciate the consequences of their thought content and assume they are harmless unless acted upon. Teasdale and Bancroft (1977), in contrast, have demonstrated that thinking negative thoughts has the sinister effect of inducing negative moods and increasing electromyographic activity. Negative thoughts, because they occur at such high rates, present many opportunities for the trained client to control them. Suggested procedural steps for cognitive control are to (1) teach clients to detect and label depressed though patterns before they develop any momentum; (2) ask clients to disrupt depressive thoughts and substitute instead task-oriented, coping thoughts or positive scanning (that is, a quick inventory of opportunities, personal assets, strengths, and behavioral accomplishments); (3) model verbal feedback, which should accompany cognitive coping strategies (that is, teach clients to pace performance by talking supportively to themselves); (4) ask clients to avoid unscheduled personal and program evaluation; and (5) ask clients to follow a geographic, stimulus-control procedure (that is, faithfully go to a predetermined area, such as a particular chair or position in the room, to have depressed thoughts) when they are unable to suppress depressed cognitions through thought substitution or interruption.

In contrast to early behavioral-treatment studies in which treatments were designed around a single-cause theory of depression, increasingly more behavioral clinicians are using multicomponent treatments tailored to the specific problems and goals of the client, which represents a step in the direction of making treatment more relevant to the client. Although in published studies the emphasis has been on self-management, the recommended coping techniques seem always to be therapist-developed—the implicit assumption being that the client's coping skills are deficient. But are therapist-derived coping techniques the same as those used by depressed and normal populations? Using a market-research approach, we asked 142 recently treated clients and 48 matched normal control subjects who had no history of any clinical depression to detail their five most successful coping techniques used in dealing with depression. A content analysis grouped the responses into eleven categories, and the proportion of times members of both groups chose a category as their number one coping technique is listed in Table 12.1. The top three specific (that is, excluding "other") coping techniques for the treated population corresponded completely to the recommended treatment-focus areas previously described, although only one quarter of this group had received behavioral treatment in which these coping techniques were promoted. It is also interesting to note that the normal group endorsed thought control twice as often as did the treated group. In way of further explanation derived from

Table 12.1 Favorite coping technique used to deal with depressed moods on the part of depressed clients in remission and normal control populations.

Coping Technique	Depressed (N =142)	Normal (N =48)
1. Increasing one's activities	24%	19%
2. Changing one's routine	7	4
3. Confiding in others	6	17
4. Socializing	14	2
5. Religion/meditation	4	2
6. Physical exercise	5	2
7. Positive thought control	13	25
8. Withdrawal (e.g., sleep, daydream, cry)	6	15
9. Selective avoidance (i.e., avoid people/situations that stimulate depressed mood)	3	2
10. Problem analysis (i.e., try to solve it)	4	10
11. Other (e.g., drugs, help others, etc.)	14	2

interviews, members of the normal group tended to confide in others (category 3) for shorter periods of time, albeit more often, and solicited advice (that is, treated it as a consultation) more frequently than did those in the treatment group. Further, when those in the normal group withdrew (category 8), they reported feeling "refreshed" afterwards more often and tended to "do it and get it over with." Finally, the low endorsement of socializing (category 4) as a coping technique on the part of the normal group may be accounted for by their relatively high base rate of social activity.

SUMMARY

There is as yet no reliable basis on which to divide depression into subclassifications. However, a working distinction between depressed lifestyle (low grade and chronic) and depressed episode (acute and time limited) will likely prove useful. An exception can be made in the case of manic depression which may prove to be largely biochemically mediated.

During the last two decades, the treatment of choice for clinical depression has been antidepressant medication, psychotherapy, or both. Intensive development of behavioral technology in the field of mood management has progressed to the extent that behavioral intervention with clinically depressed outpatient adults has proven to be significantly more effective than antidepressant medication (Rush, et al., 1977) and psychotherapy (McLean & Hakstian, 1979).

A number of unitary behavioral theories have been developed to account for the etiology and maintenance of depression, but these theories
fail to account for the development of all depressions and typically use
common treatment techniques, making differential clinical evaluation difficult, if not impossible. Depression is more likely to be a common side effect of stress resulting from a number of life problems and their interpretation. Accordingly, multicomponent treatments designed to tailor specific
intervention techniques in order to atain individual-client-performance
goals in the areas of social interaction, behavioral productivity, and cognitive control are likely to be most effective. Of the three factors that influence treatment outcome, namely, course characteristics (outcome, independent of treatment), identified treatment effects (known active
ingredient of treatment), and nonspecific treatment effects, the nonspecific
effects remain uncomfortably large in treatment-outcome studies. Nonspecific treatment effects in behavioral-treatment programs for depression
are likely due to the high treatment structure of behavioral programs, the
emphasis on a social-learning rather than a disease-model rationale, and
their sustained focus on increasing constructive social interactions and
other external interests.

CHAPTER 13

SOCIAL-SKILLS AND ASSERTION TRAINING

James P. Curran

Veterans Administration Medical Center
Brown University Medical School
Providence, Rhode Island

SOCIAL-SKILLS TRAINING

In order to obtain a clear picture of what we mean by social skills, let's eavesdrop on the following telephone conversation. Rick and Beth are two college students. Rick has called Beth with the intention of asking her out on a date for the upcoming weekend.

Rick Hi. You probably don't remember me, I'm Rick. I sat in back of you in sociology class last semester.

Beth Oh yes, Rick. How are you?

Rick Fine. Look, I was wondering if you were busy this weekend.

Beth What do you mean?

Rick Well, I guess a girl as popular as you are has dates lined up for every weekend.

Beth I do have a date for Saturday night.

Rick I guess I should have called sooner. Well, look, maybe if you have nothing to do Friday night, we might go out.

Beth What did you have in mind?

Rick I didn't have anything planned. I just thought if you weren't doing anything and I wasn't doing anything, we could get together, but if you don't want to, that's okay.

Beth Well, actually my sister will be visiting me Friday, and I feel responsible for showing her the campus.

Rick I understand. Thanks anyway. 'Bye.

Beth 'Bye, Rick.

I think we would all agree that Rick could have handled himself more skillfully in this interaction. He took a defeatist posture from the beginning, put himself down, was vague with respect to his intentions, and had no firm suggestions regarding potential dating plans. The inept manner in which Rick attempted to arrange a date with Beth might have been responsible for his failure to achieve his objective. He certainly could have presented himself to Beth in a more positive manner and could have proposed more attractive dating options. There is no guarantee that if Rick had behaved more skillfully, he would have been successful in arranging a date. However, a better presentation might have increased his probability of success.

This example illustrates the basic premise of social-skills training, which is that some style of social interactions are more likely to result in rewarding social outcomes than other styles. Many types of social interaction (for example, arranging for a date, applying for a job, criticizing a friend, saying no to an obnoxious salesperson, and so on) are difficult and problematic for individuals. Social-skills training is a systematic attempt to teach individuals to cope with these social situations. Goldsmith and McFall (1975, p. 51) described social-skills training as

a general therapy approach aimed at increasing performance competence in critical life situations. In contrast to the therapies aimed primarily at the elimination of maladaptive behaviors, skills training emphasizes the positive educational aspects of treatment. It assumes that each individual always does the best he can, given his physical limitations and unique learning history in every situation. Thus, when an individual's best effort is judged to be maladaptive, this indicates the presence of a situation specific skill deficit in the individual's repertoire . . . Whatever the origin of this deficit (e.g., lack of experience, faulty learning, biological dysfunction), it often may be overcome or partially compensated through appropriate training in more skillful response alternatives.

Social-skills training involves the application of behavioral procedures, such as modeling, behavioral rehearsal, and others, in order to teach skillful response alternatives. Social-skills training techniques have been used with many different populations (for example, children, psychiatric patients, married couples) and for a wide variety of problematic social situations (for example, job applications, consumer situations, marital encounters). The use of social-skills training techniques with psychiatric patients is reviewed by Hersen & Bellack in Chapter 18 of this book, and consequently, this review will be limited to a nonpsychiatric population. Furthermore, although social-skills training techniques have been used for a variety of problematic social situations, because of space limitations this chapter will focus on the two most researched areas (dating and assertive situations).

Prevalence of Dating Concerns

Dating appears to be a problem and a genuine concern for many college undergraduates. Glass, Gottman, and Shmurak (1976) had undergraduates rate various social situations with respect to difficulty level. Dating situations were rated as difficult by 54 percent of the males and 42 percent of the females. Martinson and Zerface (1970) reported that problems in dating relationships were the most frequent complaints voiced by undergraduates utilizing a college counseling center. Borkovec, Stone, O'Brien, and Kaloupek (1974) found that approximately 15 percent of the males and 11 percent of the females surveyed in a two-year study reported some fear of being with members of the opposite sex, and 32 percent of the males and approximately 38 percent of the females expressed some fear when meeting someone for the first time. In another survey, Pilkonis (1977) reported that 41 percent of the undergraduates surveyed reported being shy, especially in a dating situational context.

In addition to the concern over dating, there is some indirect evidence that problems with dating may be a precursor of later social malfunctioning. For example, Bryant, Trower, Yardley, Urbieta, and Letemendia (1976) reported that socially inadequate psychiatric outpatients were likely to have had a history of poor mixing with others and to have experienced failure in dating situations. These patients reported considerable difficulty in a wide range of social situations, including starting up friendships, being in a group of the opposite sex, going to parties, and meeting strangers. One should not draw the conclusion that all people with concerns over dating will later exhibit psychopathology but only that some psychiatric patients report having had difficulties in dating encounters.

Poor Social Skills and Dating Problems

As mentioned previously, a social-skills-training-treatment approach assumes that an individual's inadequate social performance is due to situation-specific skills deficits. An individual may never have learned appropriate ways to act and talk on a date and/or learned inappropriate dating behavior, and this is the basis of the dating problem. Individuals with social-skill deficits will often exhibit anxiety in dating situations as a result of their inadequate performance. Because of their lack of requisite dating skills, dating-deficient individuals will not cope with the demands of the dating situation adequately and, therefore, will often experience aversive consequences which can in time elicit anxiety. The anxiety experienced is viewed as a natural response to the aversive consequences resulting from the skills deficits.

There are data which would indicate that skills deficits play a role in dating anxiety and frequency. Borkovec et al. (1974) compared high and low socially anxious males in a simulated social situation and found differences between these groups on global ratings of social skills. Arkowitz, Lichtenstein, McGovern, and Hines (1975) found differences between high- and low-frequency male daters not only on overall skills ratings but also on more specific behavioral measures, such as total talk time, speech latency, and number of silences. Rhyne, MacDonald, McGrath, Lindquist, and Cramer (1974) found that judges perceived differences in social-skills performance on a role-play test between volunteers who had been accepted for treatment for dating problems and other college students.

In general, differences between contrasted groups (that is, high- and low-frequency daters, high and low dating, anxious subjects, and so on) have been established on global ratings of social skills, but the search for more specific behavioral indicators of skills between contrasted groups have been by and large disappointing (Curran & Fischetti, in press). Several reasons may account for this finding. Fischetti, Curran, and Wessberg (1977) cautioned that investigation may have been too simplistic with respect to the specific indicators that have been used in the past. Most of these have been frequency counts (that is, number of smiles) which ignore the interactive nature of social situations. Fischetti et al. (1977) demonstrated that although high-socially anxious/low-skilled and low-socially anxious/high-skilled males did not differ with respect to the frequency of a response, they did differ with respect to the timing and placement of their responses in a social interaction. A second reason for the failure to find differences between comparison groups suggested by Perri, Richards, and Goodrich (1978) is that insufficient attention has been placed on developing assessment instruments. They noted that little care has been used in the development of many of the assessment procedures, and that perhaps with more careful development of these assessment procedures, more specific behavioral differences would be established. A third reason is that many of the specific indicators used in the past were selected on the basis of their face validity with little empirical justification given for their use. In a pair of complementary studies, Conger, Wallander, Mariotto, and Ward (in press) and Conger and Farrell (1980), a more empirical approach was taken and better results achieved. In the Conger et al. study, 135 undergraduates viewed videotapes of competent and incompetent males in a simulated dating situation. The investigators asked the undergraduate judges to rate the social-skills level of the subjects (which they were able to do with a good deal of success). In addition to having the judges make overall ratings, the investigators also had them nominate the cues they used in order to determine their ratings. A large number of cues were generated and grouped in a hierarchical classification system. In the Conger and Farrell study, some of the cues that were nominated in the Conger et al. study were operationalized, and the tapes were rerated for these more specific indicators. A list of components was generated which was found to be highly related to the overall-skills rating. The most important component with respect to the overall skills rating was total talk time. Other indicators that were related to overall social-skills ratings were gaze, smiles, and gestures.

More research is needed to isolate components of social skills so that we may more efficiently teach these components in our training programs and measure them in our assessment protocols. Although the search for specific components of social skills continues, it does appear that dating anxiety and poor dating performance may, in part, be due to social-skills deficits. Unfortunately, however, from an assessment perspective, dating anxiety and poor dating performance may be due to numerous other factors in addition to social-skills deficits.

Cognitive, motivational, and emotional factors may all contribute to inadequate dating performance. This may be the case even when an individual possesses the necessary behavioral repertoire to do well in a dating situation. Let us examine how these other factors may lead to inadequate dating performance. Emotional states, such as anxiety, may be so overwhelming that they may interfere with the smooth application of skillful performance even when an individual possesses the necessary dating skills. There exists ample evidence that anxiety states may be conditioned to previously neutral situations through a classical conditioning process. That is, if a previously neutral stimulus has been paired with an aversive stimulus, this neutral stimulus may also come to evoke a fear response. A dramatic scenario of a potential conditioning episode which could lead to dating anxiety and poor dating performance would be the case of a female who has been sexually assaulted on a date. This traumatic experience may cause her to feel a great deal of anxiety in any dating encounter, and this anxiety may interfere with her social-skills performance. The fact that systematic desensitization, a treatment technique based on the classical conditioning model, has been demonstrated (Curran, 1975; Curran & Gilbert, 1975) to have some success in both reducing anxiety and increasing skills performance is indirect evidence that poor social performance may be the result of anxiety interference.

Arkowitz, Lichtenstein, McGovern, and Hines (1975) speculated that dating anxiety and problems are not the result of inadequate skills repertoires, but rather that they are caused by faulty cognitive processes. In one study, Clark and Arkowitz (1975) found no differences between high-socially anxious and low-socially anxious males with respect to their performance in a simulated dating situation. However, high-socially anxious male subjects significantly underestimated their amount of skill in comparison to objective judges' ratings while low-socially anxious subjects overestimated their performance. Clark and Arkowitz reasoned that it was not the lack of skills that was responsible for the subjects' anxiety but rather their cognitive interpretation of their performance. In another study, O'Banion and Arkowitz (1977) demonstrated that after a simulated social interaction, high-socially anxious females remembered negative feedback and criticism better than low-socially anxious females, although they had received identical feedback. In an experiment by Smith and Sarason (1975), high-socially anxious subjects perceived the same feedback as more negative and evoking a more negative emotional response than low-socially anxious subjects. As Curran (1977) noted, numerous cognitive factors may be responsible for dating problems and anxiety, including unrealistic criteria, misperception of social cues, overly negative evaluation of performance, negative self-statements, insufficient self-reinforcement, and so on. Some of these cognitive factors may directly effect skill performance in dating situations (for example, misperception of social cues), and others may indirectly effect performance by eliciting high levels of anxiety (for example, negative self-evaluation).

It is quite likely (Curran, 1977) that the basis of poor heterosexual-social performance is different for different individuals and that the poor performance exhibited by any one individual may be the result of a combination of skills deficits, conditioned anxiety, and faulty cognitive appraisal systems. In order to illustrate the difficulty in determining the factors involved in poor dating performance, consider the character portrayed by Woody Allen in the recent movie, *Play It Again, Sam*. Poor Woody could certainly be characterized as behaving unskillfull in dating encounters. He tripped over chairs, knocked over funiture, and said inane things to his dates. But was his inappropriate dating behavior due to an actual skills deficit? You could also make a case for some conditioned-anxiety components. He had been divorced from a wife who rudely told him that he was one of the most unimaginative and boring individuals that she had ever met in her life. After the breakup of his marriage, Woody was on a date, when members of a motorcycle gang tried to move in on his date. Woody was severely beaten by the members of the gang, and his date left with them. On the other hand, maybe Woody's inadequate performance was due to the anxiety he generated himself by his cognitive self-statements. He lacked self-confidence and thought that no girl in her right mind would go out with him ("I wouldn't want to go out with any girl who would want to go out with me").

Diagnostically, it would seem important to determine the etiological and maintaining factors underlying inadequate performance because of the possible interaction between the source of the poor dating performance and treatment strategies. If social-skills deficits are responsible for poor dating performance, dating anxiety, and dating problems, then procedures to teach more effective responses are the treatments of choice. Poor dating performance due to conditioned anxiety or to cognitive factors should theoretically (Curran, 1977) be more efficaciously handled by counterconditioning or by cognitive restructuring treatment procedures, respectively. Unfortunately, to this date, no assessment procedures are available that allow us to differentiate precisely the various sources of poor dating performance. A sampling of the assessment strategies used to measure dating skills will now be reviewed.

Assessment of Dating Skills and Anxiety

Because of the relationship between social skills and social anxiety, very often both these constructs are measured. Numerous assessment strategies to measure both constructs have been employed in the literature; however, because of lack of space, we will not review all of the techniques but just highlight a few which exemplify the types of assessment strategies generally used.

SELF-REPORT QUESTIONNAIRES

The most frequently used questionnaires to measure heterosexual-social anxiety have been the Social Avoidance and Distress Scale (Watson & Friend, 1969), the Fear of Negative Evaluation Scale (Watson & Friend, 1969), the Situation Questionnaire (Rehm & Marston, 1968), and the Survey of Heterosexual Interaction (Twentyman & McFall, 1975). The Social

Avoidance and Distress Scale is a twenty-one-item true-false scale which measures both social anxiety and avoidance behavior in a wide variety of social situations, not only dating situations. The Fear of Negative Evaluation Scale is also a true-false scale which measures the degree of anxiety experienced when receiving negative evaluations from others. The Situation Questionnaire consists of thirty situations which are rated for anxiety on a seven-point scale. Here, the items appear to be specific to dating situations. The Survey of Heterosexual Interaction consists of twenty items specific to heterosexual-social interactions. Subjects rate each item on a seven-point scale with respect to their ability to carry out these interactions. Unfortunately, each of these scales appears to measure somewhat different constructs. Wallander, Conger, Mariotto, Curran, and Farrell (in press) administered these four scales to sixty-seven undergraduate males. The correlations between the questionnaires was generally low to moderate, and knowing the status of a subject on one scale was not very helpful in predicting his status on one of the other scales. Of all the self-report questionnaires used in the Wallander et al. study, the Survey of Heterosexual Interaction appeared to be the best instrument. Not only did scores on the Survey of Heterosexual Interaction correlate best with the other self-report questionnaires, but these scores were related to the subject's degree of dating experience and frequency, and skill ratings from judges who viewed the subjects in simulated social situations.

SELF-MONITORING

Subjects in dating-anxiety studies have often been asked to self-monitor their own responses in naturalistic situations. Subjects have been requested to keep behavioral diaries in which they record variables, such as number of dates, frequency, range, and duration of heterosexual interactions. Although self-monitoring procedures are versatile, they have been demonstrated to be reactive, and their accuracy has been questioned (Nelson, 1977). In addition, variables, such as dating frequency, are only indirect measures of skill acquisition and performance (Curran & Gilbert, 1975). Dating frequency is a function of many other variables (for example, opportunities to date) in addition to dating skills. Although dating frequency is at best a crude measure of social skills, Galassi and Galassi (1979) still argue for its use because an increase in dating frequency is very often one of the aims of dating-skills training programs.

SELF-RATINGS

Self-ratings of dating anxiety and dating skill have been obtained in both naturalistic settings (Christensen & Arkowitz, 1974) and in simulated social interactions (Curran, 1975). In most cases, these self-ratings consist of one global rating of anxiety and/or skill, although at times more detailed questionnaires are used (Curran & Gilbert, 1975). Self-ratings are extremely versatile measures and can be used in a variety of settings; however, their validity is questionable. Farrell, Mariotto, Conger, Curran, and Wallander (1979) obtained self- and observer-ratings of anxiety and social skills in two simulated dating interactions. Three different methods of self-ratings were used. Subjects were first given written descriptions of the two simulated dating situations in which they were to participate and asked to rate their degree of expected anxiety and skill in these situations. Subjects then completed similar anxiety and skills ratings immediately after participating in these simulated interactions. Two weeks after their participation in these interactions, subjects viewed the videotapes of their own interactions and again made similar ratings. Self-ratings from these three assessment strategies were only moderately related to each other, and little relationship was found between self-ratings and the ratings of trained judges. In other words, the subjects' own self-ratings were not only not related to the trained judges' ratings but differed depending on whether they were made before, during, or after the simulated social situation. In addition to the other usual problems associated with self-ratings (for example, faking good or faking bad), the fact that the construct of social skills is such a novel construct little understood by subjects probably contributes to the invalidity of self-report skill ratings.

Others' Ratings

The two most common types of others' ratings in the dating-skills literature are untrained judges in naturalistic settings and trained judges in simulated social interactions. Untrained judges have been asked to rate subject skill and anxiety levels in naturalistic dating situations or to report on the number of opposite-sex contacts initiated by the subjects. For example, in some studies, investigators (Christensen & Arkowitz, 1974; Christensen, Arkowitz, & Anderson, 1975) arranged dates between male and female subjects as a part of the treatment program. After these arranged dates, both male and female subjects rated each other on a number of scales including global measures of skill and anxiety. As with self-ratings, the accuracy of ratings made by untrained others are suspect, and since, in most cases, different individuals are rating differnt subjects, there is no comparability in the rating process.

Because of the logistical and ethical problems involved in utilizing trained judges in naturalistic settings, trained judges are used most commonly in simulated dating interactions. The types of simulated interactions used have varied greatly along a number of dimensions, but perhaps the most salient dimension has been the discrete-versus-continuous-interchange nature of the simulations. Discrete simulations generally consist of a narrator setting a scene, a prompt issued by a confederate, and a subsequent reply by a subject. An example of one of these discrete simulations is taken from Perri and Richards (1979).

> *Narration*   A girl in one of your classes telephones you to ask about a class assignment. You would really like to get to know this girl better. While on the phone, you answer her questions about school but would like to get a personal conversation started before she hangs up. She says:
>
> *Confederate*   "Thanks for the information about the assignment, you were very helpful."
>
> *Subject*   Response of subject.

Perri and Richards developed items for this discrete simulation test using Goldfried and D'Zurilla's (1969) behavioral-analytical assessment model. This model is an empirically based approach to surveying problematic stimulus situations, generating and sampling potential responses to these stimulus situations, and establishing empirical criteria to evaluate the effectiveness of potential responses. A number of these discrete simulations comprised Perri and Richards's (1979) Heterosocial Adequacy Test which has been shown to differentiate dating-adequate from dating-inadequate males. The advantage of discrete simulation tests like these is that it is relatively easy to devise objective scoring criteria for such tests in comparison to more continuous simulations. However, the give-and-take of natural conversations are neglected in these discrete tests and potentially important variables, such as the timing and sequencing of responses, cannot be assessed.

The more extended interaction simulations by necessity are performed using live confederates. Confederates are programmed by investigators to behave in a similar fashion, although the degree to which confederates actually conform to these instructions may be a confound. An example of a longer extended interaction may be found in a study by Curran, Gilbert, and Little (1976). Subjects in the study were told to imagine that they and the confederate attended a movie and that this was their first date. They were now seated in a pizza parlor awaiting their pizza. Subjects were also told to imagine that an organization to which they belonged was sponsoring a dance and they would like to ask the confederate to attend. Subjects were instructed not to ask for the date until a light went on behind the confederate. The light went on 3½ minutes into the 5-minute role play. Confederates were programmed to appear somewhat detached and to provide minimal responses. If no conversation occurred in a fifteen-second time period, the confederate was instructed to ask brief questions.

Scoring of these extended interactions are generally more subjective than in the discrete situations, although simulated interactions appear to be more realistic than discrete simulations. Wessberg, Mariotto, Conger, Conger, and Farrell (1979) provided data which indicated that ratings from extended simulations similar to the one described above were related to ratings of skills in a more naturalistic waiting-room situation in which the subjects did not realize they were being rated. More data need to be obtained for all of the above-mentioned assessment strategies with respect to how adequately they reflect the subjects' behavior in the natural environment.

None of the assessment strategies nor instruments in the social-skills area has been sufficiently validated. The fact that these instruments have been insufficiently validated should be kept in mind when evaluating the results of the dating-skills-treament studies in the following section. Until conclusive evidence is provided that any of these strategies or instruments are valid, then the use of multiple-assessment procedures is urged. Consistency of results across multiple-assessment procedures can strengthen our confidence regarding the effectiveness of social-skills training programs.

Dating-Skills-Acquisition Programs

A Description

The description of the dating-skills-acquisition treatment program that follows was taken from the work of Curran and his colleagues (Curran, 1975; Curran & Gilbert, 1975; Curran, Gilbert, & Little, 1976). Other dating-skills programs may differ on a number of parameters; however, despite the differences, there exists a fair amount of similarity between dating-skills programs with respect to both content and teaching strategies. Consequently, the Curran program can be taken as fairly representative of the other dating programs. The Curran program is a group-based program utilizing male and female cotherapists. Treatment sessions consist of eight weekly sessions of ninety minutes duration. The program includes

instructional presentation, discussion of skills, modeling via videotape, behavioral rehearsal, group and videotape feedback, homework assignments and social reinforcement. Skills that were presented as segments of the program included the giving and receiving of compliments, feeling talk, listening skills, assertion, nonverbal methods of communication, techniques to handle periods of silence, training in planning and asking for dates, ways of enhancing physical attractiveness, and approaches to physical intimacy problems. One or two of these skills was concentrated on in each weekly group session.

The full training sequence and the approximate time devoted to each section of the training program was as follows: (a) Co-therapists presentation and group discussion of a skill (10–15 min). During the discussion the group leaders would define the behaviors involved, elaborate on the importance of such behavior and ask the group members to relate instances in their own life illustrating the impact of such behavior. (b) Videotape presentation of models (10–15 min). Subjects first viewed a videotape sequence which depicted a model deficient in a particular skill. The co-therapists then asked the subjects to comment on how the model could have handled the situation more appropriately. Immediately after this discussion another videotape sequence of the same model in the same situation was shown, but this time the model performed in a more skillful manner. (c) Behavioral rehearsal plus group and videotape feedback (30–40 min). After viewing the modeling tape each subject was presented a situation to roleplay in which the subject was to attempt to implement the particular skill being emphasized. These roleplays were videotaped while they were being enacted and were presented to the group for both group and co-therapists feedback. Following the feedback it was left to the discretion of the co-therapists as to whether another roleplay was needed for the subjects to integrate the skill. (d) Homework assignments (10–15 min). At the close of each group session, the co-therapists distributed homework sheets to the group members. On these sheets the individual group members were to record incidents in their daily lives in which they had attempted to use the ability they had learned in the group. Subjects were also to record on these sheets the outcome of these incidents and provide an evaluation of their performance in implementing these skills. (e) Homework reporting and social reinforcement (10–15 min). At the beginning of the following session the co-therapists had a discussion based on the homework sheets and praised those individuals for appropriate attempts at implementation of the skill. (Curran & Gilbert, 1975, pp. 513–514)

It should be noted that although the focal point of this treatment package is on skills acquisition, there are components within the program that involve both cognitive restructuring techniques (group discussion regarding realistic performance expectations and evaluations) and counterconditioning procedures (practice exercise in the natural environment). Consequently, those subjects whose primary dating problems center around conditioned anxiety or faulty cognitive processing may also benefit from this program, although it would be expected that these individuals would be more efficaciously treated in programs that more directly address these problems.

TREATMENT RESULTS

The Curran program just described has been shown to lead to self-reported decreases in dating anxiety on questionnaires, to decreases in self-ratings of anxiety and increases in self-rating of skills after participation in simulated extended social interactions, and increases in self-reported dating frequencies. Judges, after observing the subjects' behavior in extended simulated social interactions, concurred with the subjects' self-report (that is, perceived the subjects as less anxious and more skilled after treatment than before treatment). The changes exhibited by subjects in the dating-skills programs were significantly greater than changes exhibited by subjects in waiting-list control groups and attention-placebo groups. Changes were demonstrated to be maintained at a six-month follow-up. When the dating-skills program was compared to a systematic-desensitization approach (Curran & Gilbert, 1976), both programs appeared to be equally effective in decreasing anxiety, although there was some evidence for the superiority of the skills-training approach over the desensitization approach with respect to increases in social skills at follow-up. When compared to a sensitivity-training program (Curran, Gilbert, & Little, 1976), the dating-skills program demonstrated superiority on both self-ratings and judges' ratings of anxiety and skills as well as evidencing significantly greater increases in dating frequency.

Bander, Steinke, Allen, and Mosher (1975) also compared the relative effectiveness of a dating-skills-acquisition program to a sensitivity program and also to a program combining dating-skills acquisition and systematic desensitization. Two control groups, a minimal-contact control and a nonspecific-therapy control were also included. Results indicated that all three treatment programs (dating-skills acquisition, sensitivity training, and dating-skills acquisition plus desensitization) proved superior to control groups on self-report measures indicating decreases in anxiety. The data also indicated the superiority of both programs that included dating-skills acquisition over the sensitivity program on the judges' ratings derived from an extended simulated interaction. No significant differences were found between the group that received dating-skills acquisition and the group that received dating-skills acquisition as well as desensitization. The authors attributed this lack of increased effectiveness for the group that received both dating-skills acquisition and desensitization to the fact that the dating-skills-acquisition program incorporated components (for example, practice exercise) with demonstrated success in reducing conditioned anxiety.

Twentyman and McFall (1975) evaluated the effectiveness of a dating-skills-acquisition program on a wide variety of dependent measures. An assessment-only group was employed as a control. The results indicated (1) significant group differences in favor of the dating-skills-acquisition group at posttest on the Survey of Heterosexual Interaction; (2) decreased physiological anxiety (pulse rate) during a social simulation task; (3) less avoidance behavior on certain behavioral tests; (4) increases in skill and decreases in anxiety as perceived by judges during simulation tasks; and (5) increases in the number of interactions with females at posttest (however, increased interaction was not maintained at a six-month follow-up assessment).

Two types of dating-skills programs (one including and one excluding practice assignments outside of the treatment sessions) were compared by MacDonald, Lindquist, Kramer, McGrath, and Rhyne (1975). Attention-placebo and waiting-list controls were also employed. Both dating-skills-acquisition groups and neither of the control groups were judged by trained raters as demonstrating decreased anxiety and increased skills on a discrete simulated dating-interactions task. Both dating-skills-acquisition groups and neither of the controls showed significant improvement on some but not all self-report questionnaires administered. At a six-month follow-up, the dating-skills-acquisition group that received extra-session practice showed a significant increase in dating behavior.

Glass, Gottman, and Shmurak (1976) compared the relative effectiveness of a dating-skills-acquisition approach, a cognitive self-statement-modification approach, and a combined dating-acquisition/cognitive-modification approach. The major dependent measures consisted of trained judges' ratings of the subjects' anxiety and skill level on a series of discrete simulated dating-interaction tasks. Some of these discrete simulations were used in the treatment programs for training in behavioral rehearsal and were labeled as trained, whereas others were not used during the treatment programs and were labeled as untrained, and served as a measure of generalization. Another dependent measure was a phone-call task wherein the subjects were requested to telephone female undergraduates to get to know them. These females had agreed to participate in the study and to rate the subjects with respect to their interpersonal adequacy on the phone-call task. All the treatment groups performed significantly better than a waiting-list control at posttest and at six-month follow-up on the discrete-simulation tasks on which they had received training. The dating-skills-acquisition group and the combination group were significantly superior to the cognitive-modification group on the trained tasks. However, the cognitive-modification and combined groups proved significantly superior to the skills-acquisition group on the untrained tasks at posttest and at follow-up. The cognitive-modification group also made more phone calls and were rated as being more impressive than the other groups at posttest, although these differences disappeared at follow-up. The data also suggested that men who had never dated or almost never dated benefited most from the combined approach, whereas the more frequent daters benefited most from the cognitive approach. The results suggest that it is possible that low-frequency daters both lack adequate skills and have faulty cognitions, whereas the more-frequent daters possess adequate skills, but their performance is inhibited by faulty cognitions.

Although the conclusions drawn from these studies must of necessity be tentative because each of them contains some methodological flaws (Curran, 1977), these studies taken as a group generally support the effectiveness of a dating-skills-acquisition approach. The majority of these studies demonstrated significant treatment effects when compared to various control groups (assessment-only, attention-placebo, and so on). The majority of studies indicated increases in social skills and a reduction of anxiety on both self-report measures and in ratings by others. In the one study (Twentyman & McFall, 1975) in which a physiological index of anxiety was obtained, a significant reduction of pulse rates was found. Several studies (Curran & Gilbert, 1975; Curran, Gilbert, & Little, 1976) demonstrated an increase in dating frequency.

The fact that the subjects employed in these various studies had, in all probability, heterogeneous dating problems (that is, different etiological and maintaining factors) needs to be emphasized. Subjects were selected for these studies by utilizing a vast number of criteria, including dating frequency, self-report of dating anxiety, self-report of inadequate dating performance, and so on. The major focus of dating-skills-acquisition programs is on skills acquisition, and in all likelihood, some of the subjects in these studies already possessed an adequate skill repertoire. As mentioned previously, dating problems may exist even though no skills deficits are evident; in fact, poor dating performance may be evident even when no actual skills deficits exist. The fact that the majority of these studies demonstrated the treatment effectiveness of a dating-skills-acquisition program, even though in all likelihood many subjects in these programs may have been inappropriately assigned, speaks to the robustness of the treatment effect. What is needed is more sophistication with respect to the assessment of the etiological and maintaining factors regarding dating problems so that subjects may be assigned to treatment modalities that would be maximally effective for them and the types of problems they are facing.

BEHAVIORAL ASSERTION TRAINING

Assertion training has taken a variety of formats, some of which are clearly nonbehavioral. This review, in keeping with the theme of this book, will cover only those approaches that are behavioral and that follow a response-acquisition format (that is, behavioral rehearsal, feedback, and so on). This review will also be rather brief since the training format and the research problems in the assertion-training literature resemble closely those in the dating-skills-acquisition literature.

The origins of assertion training may be found in the work of Salter

(1949) and Wolpe and Lazarus (1966), who viewed assertion training as a procedure for decreasing the anxiety individuals experience in social situations. Assertive responses were seen as incompatible responses, and it was assumed that the continued application of assertive responses would eventually lead to the inhibition of anxiety. Since its introduction, assertion training has gone beyond its original formulation as an inhibitor of anxiety and has been used with a variety of populations whose major problematic behaviors have not been primarily anxiety related. The rise of the women's rights movement gave special impetus to the application of assertion-training procedures. Consequently, many studies concentrate on female populations, although other groups have also been studied (for example, adolescents and psychiatric populations).

Assertion training has sometimes been equated with the more general construct of social-skills training, although assertion training should be more properly ascribed only to those training programs that concentrate on assertive responses. Defining what is meant by an assertive response is an extremely complex problem. Linehan and Eagan (1979) reviewed the numerous definitions proposed in the literature and found many to be overly broad, nonspecific, and at times conflicting. They proposed a series of general characteristics which they felt represented the manner in which the concept is generally used in the literature, although freely admitting that other investigators might not agree with these proposed characteristics. To paraphrase Linehan and Eagan (1979, p. 245–246), assertion generally involves self-expressiveness and standing up for one's rights. The style of an assertive response is usually direct and open but not coercive or aggressive. Assertive responses are socially acceptable, appropriate for a given situation, and chosen to maximize effectiveness. Assertive responses often occur in situations in which someone is trying to get a person to give in to a demand or do a favor at the person's own expense, is insulting or inconsiderate, or in which someone could do something the person would like, but only at the person's initiation. The identification of a response as assertive depends on a complex value judgment. Linehan (1977) noted that the effectiveness of any given assertive response can be evaluated from one of three points of view: (1) its effectiveness in achieving the objectives of the response; (2) its effectiveness in maintaining a relationship with other persons in the encounter; and (3) its effectiveness in maintaining the self-respect of the assertive person. Quite often, situations occur in which these various types of effectiveness may be in conflict with each other. Even when there is no conflict in effectiveness criteria, there appears to be judgmental problems in labeling a response as assertive. For example, some individuals judge assertive responses as aggressive, causing them to dislike the perpetrator of the assertive response (Ford & Hogan, 1978). This appears to be especially the case when females act assertively. Rose and

Tryon (1979) had forty-eight male and female college students view video-tape enactments of various assertive situations. These scenarios were en-acted by male and female actors. Both male and female judges gave higher, more aggressive, ratings to scenes in which the female actors were responding than to scenes in which male actors were responding, even though the male and female actors practiced until they performed in a sim-ilar manner. These definitional issues as well as the value judgments in-volved create problems for both assessment and treatment.

Etiological and Maintaining Factors

As with dating competency, an individual's behavior is judged as assertive on the basis of performance. As noted earlier, an individual's performance, although dependent on his or her skills repertoire, is also affected by numerous emotional, motivational, and cognitive factors. For example, Fiedler and Beach (1978) demonstrated that an individual's perception of the outcome of a potential assertive response influences the emittance of assertive actions. Eisler, Frederiksen, and Peterson (1978) found that as-sertive subjects expected more favorable consequences from others in so-cial situations than did unassertive subjects. In the Eisler et al. study, high- and low-assertive subjects were shown various video-tape enactments of alternative responses (assertive, nonassertive, and aggressive) to an asser-tive-type situation. They were asked to pick those responses that they felt were the best way of handling the situation. Before indicating their prefer-ences, subjects had been placed in the same simulated situations and asked to respond. Their responses were categorized by trained judges for each of the three categories: assertive, nonassertive, and aggressive. There was a good deal more correspondence for the high-assertive subjects between what they felt was the best way to handle the situation and their own be-havior. In situations in which the low-assertive subjects selected an assert-ive response as being the most appropriate, their performance was judged to be assertive only 55 percent of the time. Two possible reasons were suggested for this discrepancy. First, because unassertive subjects expected less positive consequences from assertive actions, they did not exhibit as-sertive behaviors. A second possibility was that the low-assertive subject were, in part, deficient in assertive skills and had difficulty exhibiting as-sertive behaviors.

As in the dating-skills literature, three major hypotheses have been pro-posed to explain inadequate assertive behavior: the skills-deficit, condi-tioned-anxiety, and faulty-cognitions models. It is likely that all three con-tribute to the lack of assertive behavior in various individuals. As of yet, no assessment protocols exist that can accurately differentiate these factors, and consequently, subjects in treatment groups are again in all probability heterogeneous with respect to these factors. Various types of treatment programs are based on these three models as they were in the dating-skills literature. This review will concentrate only on those treatment programs based on the skills-deficit model emphasizing a response-acquisition approach to treatment.

Assessment of Assertive Behavior

Three of the more commonly used self-report measures of assertive behavior are the College Self-Expression Scale (Galassi, DeLo, Galassi, & Bastien, 1974), the Conflict Resolution Inventory (McFall & Lillesand, 1971), and the Rathus Assertiveness Schedule (Rathus, 1973). In general, most of these measures possess adequate reliabilities (both split-half reliability and test-retest reliability). However, evidence for concurrent and predictive validity has been less impressive (Hersen & Bellack, 1977). For example, Galassi and Galassi (1974) found a correlation of $r = .33$ between College Self-Expression Scale ratings made by male and female undergraduate dormitory residents and ratings made by their resident hall counselors.

As in the dating-skills literature, the primary assessment strategy in the assertion literature is judges' ratings made on the basis of subjects' performances in simulated (both discrete and extended) social situations. One of the more carefully developed discrete simulation tests is the College Women's Assertion Scale (CWAS) by MacDonald (1978). Items from the CWAS are presented on audio tape. An example of an item is as follows:

Last week you bought a pocket calculator and resolved not to ever loan it since it cost so much. A very good girl friend calls and says, "I have a take home statistics quiz I just can't finish by hand, and it's due tomorrow. Can I borrow your new calculator? I'll be really careful with it.'

Subjects' responses to these items are audio-taped and then scored by judges using preset criteria. Both the items themselves and the scoring key were determined on an empirical basis. Scores on the CWAS have been shown to be significantly related to self-report measures; however, these correlations were only in the moderate range (MacDonald, 1978).

There has been greater use in the area of assessment of assertive responses (as compared to dating-skills assessment) of extra laboratory measures of an unobtrusive nature. That is, there has been more frequent use of contrived situations in which the subjects did not realize they were being evaluated. For example, McFall and Twentyman (1973) measured assertive behavior by means of a bogus telephone call. A research assistant pretended to be another student in the subject's class and proceeded to make a graded series of seven unreasonable requests involving borrowing the subject's notes before an examination. More recently, Higgins, Alonso, and Pendleton (1979) contrived a situation in which they announced to the subjects their intention to withhold well-deserved experimental credits for their participation in an experiment in order to evaluate the subjects' assertive behavior in such a situation. Although the objective of the evaluation of the subjects' behavior in a natural environment is worthwhile, the deceit required raises ethical concerns. In summary, the assessment strategies and instruments employed to measure assertion have, in general, not been adequately validated. As in the dating-skills literature, the lack of validation makes conclusions drawn from outcome studies tenuous.

Treatment and Outcome

A response-acquisition approach to the training of assertive behaviors in a nonpsychiatric population has generally contained the same components found in the dating-skills-acquisition programs (that is, modeling, coaching, behavior rehearsal, feedback, and in vivo response practice). Most of this training is group based. The content usually consists of direct, brief responses in which one stands up for one's rights in interpersonal situations. As Linehan and Eagan (1979) have pointed out, no one seems to question whether indeed there are ways to be assertive other than by using direct and unembellished statements. In fact, Linehan and Eagan cite data which would seem to suggest that these direct, brief replies may not be the most effective replies.

Response-acquisition, assertive-training programs have been demonstrated to be effective with college female and male students (Galassi, Galassi, & Litz, 1974; Rathus, 1972). Linehan, Walker, Bronheim, Haynes, & Yevzeroff, (in press) found no differences in treatment effectiveness between a group-based assertion-training program and an individual-based program. Thorpe (1975) and Linehan, Goldfried, and Goldfried (1979) found no differences between a cognitive-restructuring program and a response-acquisition program with respect to increasing assertive responding and increasing comfort in assertive situations; both were equally effective. Linehan et al. found some suggestive but far from conclusive evidence that a combined package of cognitive restructuring with response acquisition was somewhat more effective than either alone.

Behavioral-assertion-training programs appear to be effective as measured by our current assessment techniques. However, more research on these techniques is required if we are to be confident that assertive-training programs do, in fact, lead to increases in assertive behaviors in the natural environment. More sophisticated assessment instruments are also needed to differentiate etiological and maintaining factors underlying the lack of assertive behavior in order that we may construct treatment programs wherein we may directly remediate these factors.

SUMMARY

Social-skills and behavioral-assertion training represent a response-acquisition approach to treatment. They assume that an individual's maladaptive responses are due to a situation-specific skills deficit. The aim of the training programs is to increase performance competence by teaching skillful response alternatives. Training usually involves instructional presentation, modeling, behavioral rehearsal, feedback and coaching, and in vivo practice. Assertion training refers to training programs that concentrate on assertive responses; social-skills training refers to training many different response classes and not exclusively assertive responses. The formats for social-skills and assertion training are similar as are the research issues and problems in both areas.

An individual is judged as unskilled or unassertive on the basis of social performance. Unfortunately, from an assessment perspective, social performance, although dependent on a skills repertoire, is also affected by numerous emotional, motivational, and cognitive factors. Three primary hypothesized sources for poor social performance are proposed in the skills-deficit, conditioned-anxiety, and cognitive models. Evidence exists supporting all three models, and any and all of them might contribute to an individual's inadequate performance. Current assessment protocols do not allow for the precise differentiation of the various sources of poor social performance. Consequently, it is likely that subjects in treatment-outcome studies are heterogeneous with respect to the source of their inadequate performance which presents an experimental problem and makes interpretation of results difficult.

Numerous self-report questionnaires, self-monitoring indexes, and self-rating scales have been used to assess social skills and assertive behaviors. It appears that many of these self-report indexes are measuring somewhat different constructs and the relationship between self-report measures and other types of ratings and behavioral measures is at best only moderate. The primary assessment strategy used has been the observation of subjects in simulated social interactions (either discrete or extended). Although it is a promising assessment strategy, more research needs to be done demonstrating that a subject's behavior in a simulated situation is an adequate representation of his or her behavior in a naturalistic situation. The use of untrained observers in naturalistic situations, in most cases, precludes comparability of ratings, and the use of contrived situations raises ethical problems. The use of multiple-assessment procedures and strategies is encouraged with consistency of results across assessment instruments strengthening our interpretation of results.

Response-acquisition programs, in most cases, have been demonstrated to lend to an increase in the skills taught and to changes in other constructs of interest (for example, decreases in social anxiety, increases in dating behavior, and so on). Response-acquisition programs have been demonstrated to produce significantly greater changes than various control programs, and when compared to other therapeutic strategies (for example, sensitivity groups), response-acquisition programs have been demonstrated to be equal or better than these treatment alternatives. As promising as response-acquisition programs appear to be, however, our enthusiasm should be tempered, because of the methodological flaws in the studies and the lack of convincing evidence regarding the adequacy of the assessment procedures employed.

CHAPTER 14

ALCOHOLISM AND DRUG DEPENDENCE: COGNITIVE SOCIAL-LEARNING FACTORS IN ADDICTIVE BEHAVIORS

G. Alan Marlatt and Dennis M. Donovan

University of Washington

"It's all in the mind . . . if you want to get addicted, you will. . . ."
–A twenty-one-year-old occasional heroin user (Powell, 1973, p. 587)

Humanity has a long history of drug use. Early accounts have attested to both the virtues and the vices associated with a variety of psychoactive or consciousness-altering substances. The pervasive theme of such accounts is that the use of certain drugs in moderation is an acceptable practice. However, if one's consumption of a particular drug repeatedly exceeds the socially, culturally, or legally defined boundaries of moderation, the individual's behavior and motivation for using the drug are brought under scrutiny. A distinction is made between appropriate use and misuse of a particular drug. All drugs appear to have a potential to be misused or abused (Brecher, 1972; Irwin, 1971; Ray, 1972; Weil, 1972). Weil (1971), for example, has described the use of a commonly employed kitchen spice, nutmeg, as an intoxicant and hallucinogenic drug. Although the vast majority of mind-altering drugs have the potential for abuse, not all appear equally capable of producing addiction. The two drugs most frequently associated with addiction are alcohol and the narcotics (including opium, morphine, heroin, and methadone).

The word *addiction* has traditionally been defined as a strong dependence, both physical and psychological, on a habit-forming drug (Sarason, 1976). The addicted individual is viewed as one who has lost the power of self-control in relation to the drug. Addiction typically has been defined in terms of a constellation of physiological and psychological characteristics (Irwin, 1971; Marlatt & Rose, 1980; Ray, 1972). The first is an increase in *tolerance,* which has been traditionally defined as the development of body or tissue resistance to the effects of a drug. The same dose of the drug, after repeated use, is no longer capable of producing the same effects, thereby causing the user to increase the dosage in order to obtain effects equivalent to those obtained with smaller doses. A second component is *physical dependence,* or an altered physiological state or body equilibrium brought about by continued drug administration over a long period of time. The most notable feature of physical dependence is the development of *withdrawal distress* (for example, general physical discomfort, sweating, tremors) when the drug is discontinued. Irwin (1971) indicates that the magnitude of physical dependence and the severity of withdrawal distress vary directly with the amount, frequency, and duration of drug use. A third aspect is *psychological dependence*. Here, the individual comes to rely on the emotional effects produced by the drug. The individual anticipates that the drug will produce pleasure or will reduce discomfort. Drug use is substituted for other, more appropriate types of adaptive behaviors. The individual is assumed to develop a *craving* for the drug, defined as an overpowering subjective desire for the drug and its anticipated effects. Finally, there is a tendency to *relapse,* or return to drug use, even after a prolonged period of abstinence. The expectation is that "once an addict, always an addict."

The order in which these component features develop in the process of addiction is not clear. Often the individual develops a psychological dependence on a drug prior to the development of physical dependence. Furthermore, it is not clear whether it is the psychological or the physical component which exerts a greater degree of control over drug-taking behavior. There is no doubt that drugs, such as heroin and alcohol, exert powerful pharmacological influences in the body. However, the individual's perception of and expectations about a drug's effects, and the attribution of these effects to the drug's pharmacological action, all appear to influence behavior (Schacter, 1964; Schacter & Singer, 1962). Thus, it appears that both physiological and psychological factors frequently interact as determinants of drug use, and it is often difficult to determine the relative contributions made by these two sets of factors.

Recent research on the determinants of addiction has begun to tip the balance toward a conceptual model that places increasing emphasis on cognitive and psychological factors as they influence the acquisition and maintenance of drug abuse and dependence. Eddy, Halbach, Isbell, and Seevers (1970) suggest that a state of mind characterized by a desire to continuously administer drugs to produce pleasure or avoid discomfort is the most powerful of all the factors involved in chronic intoxication by psychoactive substances. The physical dependence that accompanies certain drug use serves to reinforce the user's psychological reliance on the anticipated effects. Evidence showing the potency of expectations and placebo effects as determinants of drug use and its associated behavioral correlates strongly suggests that cognitive factors must be taken into account in the conceptualization of addictive disorders (Marlatt and Rose, 1980). It has been demonstrated empirically that cognitive expectancies appear to override the pharmacological effects of alcohol for a variety of human behaviors in which one's beliefs about alcohol play an important role (Marlett, 1978; Wilson, 1978a). Similar investigations showing that both the initial effects of heroin and the withdrawal syndrome may be greatly influenced by learned conditioning processes (for example, Davis & Smith, 1976; O'Brien, 1976) also suggest the importance of environmental and psychological factors in the use of narcotic drugs.

It may be, as indicated by the quotation of the occasional heroin user in the opening of this chapter, that becoming addicted is "all in the mind." The psychological processes involved may exert a common influence across various addictive drugs. There appear to be several parallels, for instance, between alcoholism and heroin addiction. These are noted in such factors as the comparable expectations individuals have about the ability of these drugs to produce pleasure and reduce discomfort (Crowley, 1972; Marlatt, 1978); the nature of the learning processes that underlie alcoholism and heroin addiction (Ludwig & Wikler, 1974; Wikler, 1973); the pattern of emotional changes with the chronic use of either drug (McNamee, Mello, & Mendelson, 1968; McNamee, Mirin, Kuehnle, & Meyer, 1976); and the situational factors most commonly associated with relapse after voluntary abstinence from either drug (Marlatt & Gordon, 1979). Because of the number of such shared behavioral commonalities between a variety of drugs, Solomon (1977) has suggested that all addictive behaviors are mediated by a form of learned or acquired motivation.

Previous research concerning drug abuse has been criticized because of its fragmentation. Braucht, Brakarsh, Follingstad, and Berry (1973) have noted that a number of interesting and potentially relevant psychosocial variables related to drug use have been studied in isolation. There has been a failure to integrate these variables into a coherent explanatory model. Further, these investigators have criticized researchers who focus on a particular drug for failing to appreciate the commonalities that appear to underlie substance abuse in general, regardless of the particular drug. The present chapter represents an initial, tentative step to rectify these shortcomings. The purpose of the chapter is to examine the cognitive, psychosocial, and behavioral factors that appear to influence addictive behaviors. The general theoretical model employed is a cognitive social-learning approach, an approach that is best able to encompass the many components of the addictive process. The focus will be placed on those factors that appear to underlie the acquisition and maintenance of addiction to alcohol and heroin. Parallel processes involved across these two drugs will be examined within the framework of acquired motivations. Finally, the implications for the treatment of these two addictive behaviors will be discussed.

A COGNITIVE SOCIAL-LEARNING MODEL OF ADDICTION

The basic assumption of the present approach is that addictions represent learned behavioral disorders with multiple determinants (Marlatt & Donovan, in press; Ray, 1972). These disorders can be understood best through the empirically derived principles of social learning, cognitive psychology, and behavior therapy. The focus of this approach is on the observable aspects of drug-taking behavior, including the frequency and duration of drug-taking episodes, the quantity of drugs used, and the problems associated with excessive use. Particular interest is paid to the determinants of drug-using behavior. These include situational, environmental, and emotional factors, the individual's past learning history, prior experiences with alcohol or heroin, and cognitive processes and expectancies concerning the effects of these drugs. Such factors serve as *antecedents* or cues that often precipitate the use of these substances. An equal emphasis is placed on the *consequences* of drug use which serve to maintain the behavior. Such consequences provide information concerning the potential reinforcing effects of these drugs. Also included as reinforcing variables are the social and interpersonal reactions experienced by the drug user. This perspective is consistent with the position presented by Ray (1972). He suggests that addiction is a learned phenomenon, indicating that:

(1) learning to be an addict is a separate and distinct stage from being an addict; (2) learning to be an addict can result from either an approach to pleasure or an escape from discomfort; (3) being an addict has multiple motivations and rewards; and (4) the same nonspecific factors that help determine other forms of drug-taking operate in determining addiction. (p. 202)

Acquisition of Drug Use

It appears that the processes involved in the initial experimentation with alcohol and heroin differ from those responsible for continued use and eventual addiction (Bandura, 1969; Feldman, 1976; Platt & Labate, 1976; Solomon & Marshall, 1973). The factors that appear to initiate and reinforce drug use are primarily *social* in nature. An important prerequisite is the ready availability of and access to the drug (Ausubel, 1961; Bourne, 1974). Robins (1974), for instance, indicated that many American servicemen in Vietnam reported that, among other reasons, heroin was used because it was often cheaper and easier to obtain than Coca Cola. Alcohol, although not less expensive than soda, is equally accessible. From personal experience, it often seems quite easy for individuals to find others to purchase alcohol or other drugs if they are not able to "score" themselves.

A second important factor is the influence of *cultural and subcultural norms* that define the reinforcement contingencies governing the use of drugs (Bandura, 1969). These norms are to a large extent transmitted vicariously through modeling behavior of parents and peers. The literature on the family background of both alcoholics and heroin addicts depicts a picture of generalized stress, emotional upheaval, and strained interpersonal relationships (for example, O'Leary, O'Leary, & Donovan, 1976; Salmon & Salmon, 1977). In addition, at least in the case of those individuals who are later labeled as alcoholic, the parents fail to provide a model for appropriate social drinking (O'Leary et al., 1976). They often are either rigid abstainers or heavy drinkers or alcoholics themselves. Frequently, no middle ground is found between these two extremes. If the offspring begin to drink, there are no appropriate parental norms or guidelines against which to judge the frequency or quantity of consumption. In those cases where one or both parents are alcoholic, there is often either implicit or explicit approval of the child's drinking. Bandura (1969) noted that exposure to excessive parental drinking across a variety of circumstances, including the use of alcohol as a means of coping with stress, may result in the transmission of a similar pattern of drinking to the children. This exposure may also serve to shape the individual's expectations concerning alcohol use as a primary source of reinforcement.

The influence of parental modeling on heroin use is less well documented (Platt & Labate, 1976). However, the available evidence suggests that from approximately 20 percent to 25 percent of heroin addicts have addicted family members (Hekimian & Gershon, 1968; Valliant, 1966). Brown, Gauvey, Meyers, and Stark (1971) found that only a relatively small percentage of addicts attributed their first experimental use of heroin to parents or relatives. Although it appears that there exists a differential parental influence on initial drinking and heroin use, the importance of *peer modeling* and *social pressure* seems comparable across both drugs (Huba, Wingard, & Bentler, 1979). Ball (1966), for example, found that more than 85 percent of his male subjects reported that they were introduced to experimental heroin use by addicted friends. Brown et al. (1971) found that their addicted subjects rated the influence of friends as the most important factor in initial heroin use. As subsequent use continues, the individual progressively tends to restrict his or her circle of friends to peers and adults who use the same drug (Beckett, 1974; Feldman, 1976; Huba et al., 1979). The friends of addicts are more likely to have used heroin than the friends of nonaddicts (Kaplan & Meyerowitz, 1970). O'Leary et al. (1976) also noted that problem-drinking adolescents tend to select heavy drinkers as friends. Such gravitation toward those utilizing the same drug appears to have at least two influences. First, it produces a subculture which makes the use of the particular drug normative. Second, with peer-group affiliation contingent on drug use, there is strong social pressure to continue drug-taking behavior.

The influence of peer modeling and implicit social pressure on drinking behavior has been demonstrated empirically by Caudill and Marlatt (1975). Heavy social-drinking males took part in a task where they were to rate three varieties of wine along a number of taste dimensions (for example, bitter, sweet, dry, and so on). They were to drink as much of each wine as necessary to make accurate judgments. The actual purpose of this taste-rating task was to nonobtrusively measure the amount of alcohol consumed. Two subjects were to work on the ratings at the same time. Unknown to the real subject under observation, the second person was a confederate of the experimenter who acted as a drinking model. In the two modeling conditions of the experiment, the confederate played the role of either a heavy or light social drinker. In the heavy-drinking condition, the model consumed the equivalent of a full bottle of wine (700 ml.) over a fifteen-minute period. In the light-drinking condition, the confederate drank 100 ml. of wine. A third group of subjects, completing the rating task alone without a model, served as a control group. The results indicated that peer modeling exerts a significant degree of control on the amount consumed. Those subjects who were exposed to the heavy-drinking model drank twice as much wine as the no-model control subjects;

those exposed to the light-drinking model evidenced a further drop of 22 percent in the amount consumed relative to the control condition.

Predisposition for Continued Drug Use

Although a relatively large number of individuals may initially experiment with alcohol or heroin, not all of these first-time users will eventually become addicted (Ausubel, 1961a; Bourne, 1974). The National Institute on Alcohol Abuse and Alcoholism (1971, 1974, 1978) has summarized the results of a number of national surveys on drinking practices. These reports indicated that in the mid 1970s approximately 68 percent of the adult American population (eighteen and older) drank alcoholic beverages at least occasionally; however, only about 7 percent of the adult population were considered to be problem drinkers (including alcoholics). Similarly, in a follow-up of servicemen who initially began using heroin in Vietnam, Robins (1974) found that only 7 percent were still using heroin one year following their return home. Thus, in addition to the external factors described above as important components in the initiation of drug use, other variables may predispose an individual toward dependence. It has been suggested that such predispositions represent internal personality structures that enhance the attractiveness of the pharmacological properties of the drug, particularly as a means of adjustment (Ausubel, 1961; Wikler, 1953).

A number of investigators have searched for the typical "addictive personality" within both alcoholics and heroin users (for example, Hoffman, 1976; Platt & Labate, 1976). Variables, such as depression, dependency, psychopathy, sociopathy, anxiety, and neuroticism, have been explored as potential predisposing variables. By and large, such attempts to find a homogeneous constellation of personality traits which reliably differentiates addicts from nonaddicts have not been particularly fruitful. Rather, it appears that populations of substance-dependent individuals are relatively heterogeneous, composed of a number of different subtypes (Berzins, Ross, English, & Haley, 1974; Donovan, Chaney, & O'Leary, 1978; O'Leary, Donovan, Freeman, & Chaney, 1976). It appears that a potentially more productive approach would be to focus on the individual's behavioral competencies and associated cognitive processes (Bandura, 1977a, 1977b; Mischel, 1973). Such factors include the person's ability to deal effectively with interpersonal situations, the availability of adaptive coping skills to allow a satisfactory resolution of problem situations, the perceived ability to utilize these skills when needed, and the resultant sense of personal control experienced within the situation.

SOCIAL-SKILLS DEFICITS

All of us live in a world that places demands upon us. We must deal with others. We are confronted by a variety of problems from a wide range of sources. An important predisposition in the area of addictive behaviors is the availability of appropriate social skills, interpersonal competencies, and general problem-solving abilities to deal effectively with stressful situations as they arise. It appears that individuals who later become either alcoholics or heroin addicts have significant deficits in those social skills that might increase their accessibility to desired and reinforcing outcomes (Beckett, 1974; Bowden, 1971; O'Leary et al., 1976; Tsoi-Hoshmand, 1976). Alcoholics and addicts have been shown to be deficient in their interpersonal problem-solving ability (Appel & Kaestner, 1979; Intagliata, 1978; Platt, Scura, & Hannon, 1973). Furthermore, such individuals have also been found to be less able than nonaddicted persons to express their feelings in an open, constructive, and assertive manner (for example, Callner & Ross, 1976, 1978; Chaney, O'Leary, & Marlatt, 1978). In those cases where no difference exists between alcoholics and nonalcoholics in assertive behavior, it appears that the alcoholics experience a greater level of anxiety or discomfort (Hamilton & Maisto, 1979). This tendency is most pronounced when alcoholics are confronted with situations requiring the expression of negative emotions.

Although the relationship between social-skills deficits and actual heroin use has not been directly investigated, experimental analogue studies have examined the influence of problems in assertiveness on drinking behavior. It has been found that complex interpersonal situations requiring the use of well-developed social skills may produce social anxiety; in the absence of more adaptive responses, drinking may serve as a means of coping (Hamburg, 1975; Kraft, 1971). Miller, Hersen, Eisler, and Hilsman (1974) found that in a nonstressful situation, there was no difference between the amount of alcohol consumed by alcoholics and nonalcoholics. However, when both groups were criticized concerning the inadequacy of their responses in a variety of social situations requiring assertive behavior, the alcoholics drank significantly more. This was the case even though physiological measures indicated that this stressful condition led to equivalent levels of emotional arousal in both groups. This increase in drinking appeared to be related primarily to the inability to express negative feelings (Miller & Eisler, 1977). Marlatt, Kosturn, and Lang (1975) also found that heavy social drinkers who were provoked to anger without the opportunity to express these feelings tended to significantly increase the amount they drank relative to subjects who were not angered. However, when subjects were given the opportunity to openly express their anger after being provoked, they drank even less than those who had never been angered.

PERCEPTIONS OF CONTROL AND SELF-EFFICACY

The previous findings suggest that when the person is capable of producing an adaptive behavioral response appropriate to the social demands of the situation, there is an increase in the person's perception of control. As a result, by means of effective assertiveness and emotional problem solving, there is a reduced need to rely on alcohol as a means of coping. The issue of control, both perceived and experienced, appears to be an important factor in the development and maintenance of addictive behaviors (Donovan & O'Leary, 1975, 1978, in press; Manganiello, 1978). Naditch (1975), for example, found that a lack of perceived control over the outcome of significant life events was related to increased drinking among young men. In general, those studies utilizing appropriate matching techniques among subjects have found alcoholics and heroin addicts to have lower levels of perceived control than nonaddicted subjects (Manganiello, 1978; Rohsenow & O'Leary, 1978). Such findings suggest that in the absence of adaptive social skills, the addiction-prone individual will experience a decrease in personal control within stressful situations.

Bandura (1977a) has recently developed a theoretical formulation based on the construct of perceived self-efficacy. An efficacy expectancy represents the individual's belief that he or she either can or cannot successfully execute the behavior required in a particular situation in order to produce a desired outcome. The ability to deal with these situations requires skills, such as assertiveness and interpersonal or emotional problem solving. The level of self-efficacy thus appears to depend on an interaction between one's appraisal of the behavioral requirements of the situation and the perceived availability of adaptive coping skills within one's repertoire. A lowered level of personal efficacy, or the lack of perceived or experienced control, within a stressful situation will lead to a failure on the person's part to attempt to exert control. It will also cause the situation to be perceived as more stressful or anxiety provoking (Lazarus, Averill, & Opton, 1970). The attribution of such failures to cope effectively to personal inadequacies leads to an increase in the level of depression and a decrease in both self-esteem and motivation to exert control in similiar situations in the future (Abramson, Seligman, & Teasdale, 1978).

The apparent lack of general behavioral competencies, including interpersonal skills and awareness, role-appropriate responsible behaviors, problem-solving skills for dealing with the demands of daily living, and the ability to evaluate the consequences of one's behavior (Tsoi-Hoshmand, 1976), appear to characterize individuals who are predisposed to repeated use of heroin or alcohol. These deficits lead to a perceived lack of control and a reduced sense of personal efficacy. The individual experiences increased levels of anxiety and depression and a decrease in self-esteem. This constellation of related behavioral and cognitive factors appears to enhance the probability that alcohol or heroin will represent an attractive alternative means of dealing with an otherwise uncontrollable situation (Bowden, 1971; Kaplan & Meyerowitz, 1970; Manganiello, 1978; Marlatt, 1976; Marlatt & Donovan, in press).

Maintenance of Continued Drug Use

The initial social factors that serve to reinforce experimental use appear to be supplanted to an increasing extent by the reinforcement attributed to the pharmacological effects of the drugs themselves. This is particularly true among individuals who are predisposed in the manner described earlier. Crowley (1972), for instance, suggests that there are certain persons who are more susceptible to the reinforcing effects of heroin than others. As a result of their past experience, they have come to believe that they cannot exert control over reinforcement from their environment. They perceive heroin use as a source of reinforcement that is more completely under their personal control.

LEARNING AND REINFORCEMENT

Both alcohol and heroin have strong reinforcing qualities which appear to be qualitatively similar in nature (Crowley, 1972). The current cognitive-behavioral position views addiction to heroin and alcohol as a learned behavioral pattern that is maintained by a variety of *antecedent* cues and *consequent* physiological, psychological, and social reinforcers (Copemann, 1975; Gøtestam & Melin, 1980; Marlatt & Donovan, in press; Miller & Barlow, 1973; Solomon & Marshall, 1973). Both classical (Pavlovian) conditioning and operant (Skinnerian) learning principles contribute to the maintenance process.

The reinforcement derived from drug use may be either positive or negative (Cahoon & Crosby, 1972; Crowley, 1972). Positive reinforcement represents desirable consequences which increase the probability of a particular behavior being repeated. A primary factor in addiction, particularly to heroin, is the *euphoria* produced by the drug (Ausubel, 1961a; Cahoon

& Crosby, 1972; McAuliffe & Gordon, 1976; Senter, Heintzelman, Dorf-muller, & Hinkle, 1979; Wikler, 1948). The euphoric sensations produced by both drugs are subjectively experienced as a high, a calm, an inner peace, a lift, a sense of relaxation. These sensations are interpreted posi-tively by the user. Ausubel (1961) has suggested that the euphorogenic properties of opiates are causally related to the development of depen-dence. As for alcohol, recent research (Senter et al., 1979) has also inves-tigated the difference in the perceived pleasantness of drinking between al-coholics and social drinkers. Alcoholic subjects rated their first drinking experience as significantly more pleasant and positive than social drinkers. Furthermore, the alcoholics reported subsequent drinking episodes as pro-ducing more euphoric affective consequences than did the social drinkers. These results suggest that the high degree of euphoria produced by alcohol on the first and subsequent occasions of drinking produce strong reinforc-ing expectancies that may influence the development of dependence. In ad-dition to the primary drug effects, continued use is further maintained by secondary, social reinforcement. Sources of such reinforcement include continued affiliation with and acceptance by one's peer group, an increase in the range (although not necessarily the appropriateness) of social behav-ior, and attention from family and friends (Cahoon & Crosby, 1972; Crowley, 1972; Miller & Barlow, 1973).

Negative reinforcement refers to a process whereby a behavior that serves to remove an unpleasant or aversive state will subsequently be more likely to occur. Within the area of the addictions, negative reinforcement appears to operate on both a psychological and a physiological level. An early theoretical formulation within the area of alcoholism is the *tension-reduction hypothesis* (for example, Conger, 1956; Kepner, 1964; Kingham, 1958; Kraft, 1971). This hypothesis assumes that alcohol serves to reduce tension, stress, or arousal and to minimize the experience of negative emo-tional states, such as anxiety and depression, and that the reduction of these feelings reinforces the drinking response. A corollary of this hypoth-esis assumes that the initial experience of arousal will increase the probabil-ity of subsequent drinking (Cappell & Herman, 1972; Marlatt, 1976). This hypothesis is consistent with many typical reasons given by heavy social drinkers, alcoholics, and heroin addicts for their drug use.

In line with the tension-reduction hypothesis, Ogborne (1974) found two general types of continual heroin users. The first type was labeled *enhancers,* whose use is motivated primarily by a desire to enhance self-es-teem. The second group was characterized as *avoiders,* whose primary mo-tivation is escape-oriented. Deardorff, Melges, Hout, and Savage (1975) and Tamerin (1975) found that feelings of depression, anxiety, and anger enhanced both the desire to drink and actual drinking among problem drinkers and alcoholics. Such reliance on alcohol and heroin as a means of coping with negative arousal states increases the probability that a behaviorally predisposed individual will become psychologically dependent on the drug and its anticipated effects.

As the individual becomes more dependent and tolerance develops, the initial social reinforcement and euphoric effects appear to play a decreasingly significant role in the maintenance of continued drug-taking behavior (Cahoon & Crosby, 1972; Copemann, 1975; Lindesmith, 1968; Solomon & Marshall, 1973; Wikler, 1953, 1965, 1973). The individual begins to experience *withdrawal distress* when he or she stops taking the drug or the concentration of the drug in the blood drops below a certain critical level. This phenomenon is often subjectively experienced as "coming down" or "losing the high" and is often felt physically as acute discomfort or sickness. Alcohol and heroin again serve a negative-reinforcement function by allowing the individual to delay the onset of or escape from these noxious consequences by taking the drug. This represents a primary source of reinforcement. Further, as drug taking becomes well established, there is a subsequent shift in reinforcement from the reduction of *actual* withdrawal symptoms to the removal of *anticipatory* withdrawal stimuli (Solomon & Marshall, 1973).

The latter point suggests one of the many roles that antecedent cues may play in the maintenance of drug-taking behavior. Wikler (1953, 1965) has suggested that previously neutral stimuli, both physiological and environmental, which have been associated closely in time with the onset of withdrawal eventually acquire the ability to elicit withdrawal-like symptoms. Thus, if individuals are confronted by former drug-using friends or find themselves in the solitary confines of a hotel room resembling a previous drug-taking setting, they may experience the incipient stages of a subclinical withdrawal syndrome. The anticipation of withdrawal will motivate drug usage as a means of preventing the onset of further withdrawal.

A similar classical-conditioning hypothesis has been developed by Ludwig and his colleagues to explain the influence that drinking-related cues have on the experience of craving and relapse among alcoholics (Ludwig & Wikler, 1974; Ludwig, Wikler & Stark, 1974). Furthermore, through the process of generalization, other forms of negative arousal states may also come to be interpreted as components of impending withdrawal and thus promote heroin use or drinking. The avoidance of either an actual or anticipated withdrawal syndrome will reinforce and increase the likelihood of continued use.

One difficulty with this position is that those cues that are most closely associated with actual withdrawal experiences should be most likely to precipitate subsequent drug use. However, the social and environmental cues found in detoxification and treatment centers, which theoretically should be prepotent, appear to be less influential antecedents than those cues associated with prior use of the drugs. Miller (1976) has suggested that such antecedent cues represent *setting events,* or environmental stimuli that set the occasion for drinking to occur. A similar position has been presented by Meyer and Mirin (1979) for heroin use. Cues, such as negative mood states, including depression, anxiety, loneliness, boredom, and perceived personal failure, as well as situational cues, such as the presence of drinking acquaintances or a barroom setting, have been associated so frequently with the reinforcement derived from excessive drinking that they have acquired secondary reinforcing properties. The mere presence of such cues may serve to initiate drinking (Ludwig et al., 1974; Miller, Hersen, Eisler, Epstein, & Wooten, 1974). It appears that the drinking behavior of social drinkers is controlled by a much narrower range of alcohol-related cues than is the drinking of alcoholics, whose drinking is more generalized and less controlled by situational variables (Miller et al., 1974).

The previous review suggests that much of the addictive process is learned. Drug usage is motivated by the person's desire to achieve a state of euphoria, to reduce the experience of negative emotions, or to avoid the onset of a withdrawal syndrome. These consequences, in addition to related social and interpersonal variables, serve to reinforce continued usage. Cues previously associated with drug-taking or withdrawal serve as antecedents which precipitate drinking or heroin use. The individual has developed a dependence on the drug. He or she is hooked into an addictive circle of antecedents and consequences that tend to perpetuate and maintain the use of drugs.

The Emotional Paradox

An interesting paradox appears to occur on an emotional level with continued chronic use of both alcohol and heroin. As noted above, individuals frequently report that they use these drugs to experience a high or to avoid feeling low. But with repeated use, a reversal takes place. The emotional states that the individual expects to feel under the influence of these drugs do not always correspond to the moods they actually experience when intoxicated. The euphoria becomes less pronounced or is no longer present. The negative emotions that the person hoped to reduce are enhanced instead. Alcoholics, for example, report that they expect to feel more relaxed, more comfortable, and less depressed prior to a prolonged period of experimental intoxication. However, following intoxication these same individuals experience an increase in dysphoria and tension, effects that are directly opposite of those that they had anticipated (McGuire, Mendelson, & Stein, 1966; McNamee et al., 1968; Nathan, Titler, Lowenstein, Solomon, & Rossi, 1970). Similarly, chronic opiate administration among addicts has been found to produce a generalized dysphoric state characterized by increased levels of anxiety, depression, and hostility (McNamee et al., 1976; Meyer & Mirin, 1979; Mirin, Meyer, & McNamee, 1976).

Such findings, along with a variety of other evidence, seriously question the validity of a strictly interpreted tension-reduction hypothesis. In fact, recent reviews within the area of alcoholism have failed to support the assumption that alcohol has an inherent tension-reducing quality or that individuals consume alcohol for its tension-reducing effects (Cappell, 1975; Cappell & Herman, 1972; Marlatt, 1976). The discrepancy between the expected and actual mood states associated with alcohol and heroin may be related to an underlying biphasic response to these drugs, similar to an opponent-process reaction assumed to mediate the effects of all psychoactive drugs (Solomon, 1977). Recent reviews (Marlatt, 1976, 1978; Mello, 1968) describing the biphasic reaction suggest that at low doses alcohol leads to increased physiological arousal. This aroused state is subjectively experienced and cognitively labeled by the drinker as feelings of excitement, euphoria, increased energy, and perceptions of the self as more powerful. As time passes and the amount consumed increases, the initial feelings of euphoria are transformed to feelings of increasing dysphoria. These resultant negative affective states tend to exert a minimal influence on reducing subsequent drinking since their onset is delayed in time. Rather, such increases in subjectively experienced tension and dysphoria may lead instead to an increase in drinking. This would be expected, given the individual's belief that alcohol *should* reduce tension and/or his or her attempt to regain the high previously experienced at lower doses.

Solomon (1977) suggests that an equivalent model applies both to alcohol and to heroin addiction. Individuals are again hooked into a cycle in which they use drugs to minimize the negative emotions that in actuality result from their continued use. The attempt to regain the euphoria previously experienced at lower doses and to reduce dysphoria may lead to the increase of drug dosage characteristically associated with tolerance. This assumption is consistent with recent findings from animal research that suggest that tolerance to both alcohol and opiates can be accounted for in terms of learning processes (in example, LeBlanc, Gibbins, & Kalant, 1975; Parker & Skorupski, in press; Siegal, 1975, 1977). Also consistent with this position is the finding of McAuliffe and Gordon (1976) that addicts' use of "deluxe doses" of heroin (for example, the use of heroin over and above the amount required to suppress withdrawal) was motivated primarily by an attempt to experience euphoria.

Cognitive Expectancies in the Maintenance of Drug Use

The previous discussion indicates the important role that learning processes, both classical and operant conditioning, play in the maintenance of drug-taking behavior. It may be, as suggested by Schuster and Villareal (1968), that reinforcement effects are more critical to the addictive process than are factors associated with physical dependence. The central role of physiological factors has been questioned by a series of recent findings, including the acquired nature of withdrawal from opiates (for example, Wikler, 1973), demonstration of the learned components of tolerance (for example, LeBlanc et al., 1975; Parker & Skorupski, in press; Siegal, 1975, 1977), the ability of certain alcoholics to return to controlled drinking (for example, Lloyd & Salzberg, 1975; Miller & Caddy, 1977; Pattison, Sobell, & Sobell, 1977), and the low rate of addiction to heroin among some individuals who have used this drug for prolonged periods of time (for example, Powell, 1973; Robins, 1974).

As mentioned earlier, the pharmacological effects of drugs appear to exert some influence in maintaining drug taking. If continued use of both alcohol and heroin leads to a predictable reduction in euphoria and an increase in negative moods, however, what other factors motivate this repeated drugtaking? Strict principles of reinforcement seem somewhat deficient in explaining this phenomenon. Recent research has indicated that the inclusion of cognitive factors, such as the users' expectancies and beliefs about the effects of these drugs, appear to play an important role in the maintenance of addictive behaviors (Copemann, 1975; Donovan & Marlatt, in press; Lindesmith, 1968; Marlatt, 1976; Marlatt & Donovan, in press; Wilson, 1978a).

An important belief or expectancy that influences continued and/or increased drug use is that use of the drug *should* result in increased euphoria and reduced tension, anxiety, and depression. The individual frequently *believes* this to be the case even though the actual outcome is often just the opposite. This expectancy appears to develop during the early use of these drugs, prior to the onset of the more negative component of the opponent process. The more immediate pleasurable effects of the initial phase of alcohol's or heroin's biphasic response curve appear to have the greatest influence on learning and on shaping the individual's expectations about these drugs as tension-reducing agents. Furthermore, it appears that it is these *anticipated* positive effects, rather than the actual effects, that mediate the reinforcement for drinking or heroin use.

The role of expectancies concerning the tension-reducing properties of alcohol has been demonstrated in a series of recent experimental analogue studies. These studies are based on a revision of the tension-reduction hypothesis, taking into account the cognitive processes of the individual (Marlatt & Donovan, in press). It is likely that the probability of drinking will increase in those situations which the individual perceives and personally defines as stressful, and for which he or she expects alcohol to reduce the experience of tension or stress. In one relevant study, for example, Higgins and Marlatt (1975) found that heavy-drinking males who anticipated that they would be rated by a group of females along selected dimensions of personal attractiveness drank significantly more than those in a low-interpersonal-threat group. Wilson and Abrams (1977) extended this research by employing a balanced placebo design (Marlatt & Rohsenow, 1980) to determine the relative contribution of both cognitive expectancies and alcohol's pharmacological effects to the reduction of interpersonal anxiety. In the balanced placebo design (Marlatt, Demming, & Reid, 1973), as employed in the Wilson and Abrams study, half of the male subjects were led to believe that they were consuming vodka in a tonic base while the other half were told that they were receiving only tonic. Within each of these two conditions, half the subjects actually received alcohol (vodka and tonic) while the other half received only tonic. All the subjects were told that they were participating in a study on the effects of alcohol on interpersonal communication patterns. They were to make as favorable an impression as possible in a conversation with a female stranger. The findings indicated that only those subjects who *believed* that they had consumed alcohol, regardless of the actual content of their beverage, evidenced significantly less increase in heart rate and a lower level of self-reported anxiety during this interpersonally stressful interaction than those who believed that they had consumed only tonic.

A second important expectancy, particularly for individuals having deficient social skills and low self-efficacy, is that alcohol or heroin will enhance the person's perception of personal control or power (for example, Bowden, 1971; Donovan & Marlatt, in press; Donovan & O'Leary, in press). McClelland and his coworkers have found that the consumption of moderate doses of alcohol among male social drinkers was associated with increased perceptions of personal power (McClelland, Davis, Kalan, & Wanner, 1972). McClelland's findings suggest that for some individuals, drinking may be a response to needs for personal control (Deardorff et al., 1975). Kaplan and Meyerowitz (1970) and Ogborne (1974) also suggest that heroin may be used as a means of enhancing self-esteem or of avoiding self-derogatory attitudes. These results are consistent with those of a number of clinical and experimental analogue studies which demonstrate that alcohol consumption or heroin use increases in those situations in which the individual perceives himself or herself as powerless or as having low levels of personal efficacy (Callner & Ross, 1976; Manganiello, 1978; Marlatt et al., 1975; Miller et al., 1974; Miller & Eisler, 1977; Tsoi-Hoshmand, 1976).

A final set of expectancies may be more related to alcoholism than to heroin addiction. An important defining characteristic of alcoholism is the *loss-of-control* phenomenon, in which the consumption of only small amounts of alcohol is assumed to trigger continued drinking. Traditional theorists, such as Jellinek (1960), suggest that this phenomenon is based on relatively permanent physiological changes associated with addiction to alcohol. However, the results of Marlatt et al. (1973) indicate that loss of control may result instead from the *belief* that if an alcoholic drinks alcohol, he or she *will* lose control. Marlatt et al. (1973) involved alcoholics and heavy social drinkers in a rating task in which they were to judge taste dimensions of a variety of beverages. The balanced-placebo design was employed in a taste-rating task procedure. Half the subjects were led to believe that they were drinking vodka mixed with tonic, while the other half believed that they were drinking only tonic. Half of the drinks in these two conditions contained vodka while the other half contained no alcohol. The measure of interest was the amount of beverage consumed under the differing conditions in the taste-rating task. It was found that both alcoholics and heavy social drinkers drank more when they *believed* that the beverage contained alcohol; the actual presence or absence of alcohol exerted no influence on drinking rates. These findings suggest that loss of control is primarily determined by the drinker's belief system which serves as a form of self-fulfilling prophecy.

AN INTEGRATIVE MODEL OF DRUG USE

The expectancies that one has about the euphorogenic and/or tension-reducing properties of alcohol or heroin, the relative deficits in one's adaptive social skills, and the resultant lowered level of personal efficacy and perceived control all represent factors that appear to operate interactively to influence substance use. The present model (Marlatt, 1976, 1979; Marlatt & Donovan, in press) predicts that the probability of excessive drinking or heroin use will vary in a particular situation as a function of the following factors:

1.   The degree to which the drinker feels controlled by or helpless relative to the influence of another person or group (for example, social pressure to conform, peer-group modeling, personal evaluations or criticisms by others, or being frustrated or angered by others), or by external environmental events that are perceived by the individual as beyond personal control. Such situations, which threaten the user's perception of control, represent high-risk situations.

2.   The availability of an adequate coping response as an alternative to drinking or drug use in these high-risk situations. If the person is unable to perform an appropriate coping response to resolve the situation because of deficits in the repertoire of behavioral competencies, perceived self-efficacy

is lowered resulting in a further reduction in perception of control, an increase in perceived stressfulness of the situation, and an increased sense of personal helplessness.

3.   The availability of alcohol or other drugs and the constraints upon their use within the particular situation.

4.   The user's expectations about the potential effects of alcohol or other drugs as one means of attempting to cope with the situation. To the extent that environmental, interpersonal, physiological, or emotional cues associated with prior usage are present, the stronger will be the situationally specific expectancies concerning the drug effects and the perceived reinforcing value of their use.

If through past experience the individual has developed the belief that drinking or other substance use will increase feelings of personal power and perceived control as well as decrease negative states of emotional or physical arousal, these drugs become prepotent sources of reinforcement. When the user is confronted by a situation that is personally defined as stressful and for which there is no adequate coping response available, the individual will experience a decrease in perceived control and self-efficacy. If the user expects alcohol or heroin to be an effective means of decreasing the perceived stress and enhancing a sense of control, the probability of drinking or heroin use will be high.

CRAVING AND THE RELAPSE RESPONSE

Craving and relapse back to drug use following prolonged periods of drug abstinence are two defining features of addiction. A common assumption has been that craving and relapse resulted from metabolic or physiological changes within the body following prolonged excessive use of alcohol or heroin. However, recent research has questioned the physiological underpinnings of these phenomena (for example, Engle & Williams, 1972; Maisto, Lauerman, & Adesso, 1977; Marlatt, 1978; Meyer & Mirin, 1979; Mirin et al., 1976). Instead, it appears that cognitive factors, such as expectancy, are integrally involved in both the experience of craving and relapse.

Isbell (1955) made an early distinction between two forms of craving: physical craving and psychological or symbolic craving. With respect to alcoholism, it was felt that symbolic craving, based on the anticipated effects of alcohol, accounted for the first drinking experience and subsequent relapse after a period of abstinence. Ludwig and Wikler (1974) and Wikler

(1973) similarly view craving as a psychological or cognitive representation of a subclinical withdrawl syndrome which may be evoked by physiological arousal, negative mood states, or environmental cues previously associated with drinking. An important component of the development of craving is the way in which the user interprets these interoceptive and exteroceptive cues. Those situations that have been associated with former use or that suggest the availability of the drug increase the probability that negative arousal states will be perceived as craving for the drug (Ludwig & Wikler, 1974; Meyer & Mirin, 1979). Thus, craving appears to represent the individual's cognitive labeling of a strong desire for the anticipated reinforcing effects of alcohol or heroin in potentially high-risk situations (Lindesmith, 1968; Marlatt, 1978; Meyer & Mirin, 1979).

A number of specific high-risk situations have been found to precipitate relapse among both alcoholics and heroin addicts (Brown et al., 1971; Chaney, O'Leary, & Marlatt, 1978; Litman, Eiser, Rawson, & Oppenheim, 1979; Marlatt & Gordon, 1979; Ray, 1976; Waldorf, 1976). It is interesting to note that the relapse rates, as well as the precipitants of relapse, are quite comparable in both alcohol and heroin addiction (for example, Hunt, Barnett, & Branch, 1971; Marlatt & Gordon, 1979). The three predominant high-risk situations for relapse with both drugs include coping with negative emotional states, such as depression, anxiety, or boredom; coping with interpersonal conflicts in which the person becomes frustrated or angered without directly expressing these feelings; and inability to resist social or peer pressure to resume substance use. Marlatt and Gordon (1979) found these three categories accounted for approximately 75 percent of the relapses for both alcoholics and heroin addicts. However, the relative importance of these factors appears to differ somewhat between these two groups. Social pressure was the most influential among heroin addicts, whereas negative emotional states represented the most frequent reason for relapse among alcoholics.

Lindesmith (1968) indicates that when addicts are taken off drugs, they do not lose their belief in their efficacy. A variety of unpleasant experiences of almost any sort therefore constantly remind the abstainer of the potency of the drug. It appears that the addicted individual often is lacking in the appropriate social skills to deal with these high-risk relapse situations, with a resultant feeling of perceived helplessness (Litman et al., 1979). The individual may cognitively interpret and label the strong desire for the anticipated reinforcing effects of alcohol or heroin as a state of craving. Within this situational context, along with the individual's beliefs about these drugs as a means of coping, the likelihood of relapse is enhanced.

When an alcoholic or heroin addict has the first drug experience following a prolonged period of voluntary abstinence, the probability of continued use, or loss of control, is increased. For alcoholics this appears to be facilitated by the *belief* that even a single drink will trigger loss of control (Marlatt, 1978). A similar belief—"once a junkie, always a junkie"—is involved in relapse among heroin addicts (Ray, 1976). On a cognitive-affective level, relapse may result in an *Abstinence Violation Effect* or *AVE* (Marlatt, 1978). The intensity of this effect is a function of the individual's prior degree of commitment to abstinence and the duration of abstinence achieved. The AVE is thought to be mediated by two primary cognitive processes. The first is a *cognitive-dissonance effect,* in which the individual's resumed drug-taking behavior is perceived as discrepant with the cognition of the self as an abstainer. Such cognitive dissonance often results in a negative state of arousal involving depression, guilt, and lowered self-esteem. Continued drug use would seem likely given the individual's belief that alcohol or heroin will ameliorate negative emotions. Subsequent drug-taking behavior would also serve to modify the person's cognitions and self-image to be consistent with no longer being abstinent (for example, Ray, 1976).

The second component process of the AVE is a *personal-attribution effect,* in which the individual attributes the return to drinking or heroin use to internal weakness and personal failure (for example, lack of will power) rather than to external or situational factors. Such attributions concerning the failure to control important outcomes are often associated with further feelings of dysphoria and helplessness with a resultant decrease in one's motivation to exert control (Abramson et al., 1978). The attribution of failure to one's personal deficiencies also leads to a decrease in the individual's perceived self-efficacy. Again, given the addicted individual's belief about alcohol or heroin as a means of coping and of enhancing the perception of control, such internal attributions concerning the causes of the initial relapse would be predicted to increase the probability of continued use.

IMPLICATIONS FOR TREATMENT

The previous review has indicated that a major component of the addiction process is based on learning and reinforcement principles. A variety of behavior-therapy techniques have direct implications for the treatment of addictive behaviors (Callner, 1975; Droppa, 1973; Gøtestam & Melin, 1980; Marlatt, 1979; Marlatt & Gordon, 1979; Miller, 1973; Miller, 1976; Miller & Mastria, 1977; Tsoi-Hoshmand, 1976). A number of areas are of particular relevance. The first involves the acquisition of generalized social skills and behavioral competencies. This involves training in assertive skills important to the expression of negative emotions and to the resistance of peer pressure to use alcohol or heroin (Callner & Ross, 1978). The individual should also be given training in constructive problem-solving skills (Intagliata, 1978) and in specific behavioral alternatives to high-risk situations (Chaney et al., 1978). Such treatments should increase the range of adaptive coping skills available to the individual when confronted by interpersonally stressful situations, thus reducing the need to rely on alcohol or heroin as a primary means of coping. The availability of these behavioral skills will also tend to increase the person's self-efficacy and self-image with a corresponding decrease in depression (Bandura, 1977a). The drug user's perception of personal control has also been found to be enhanced by more generalized intervention strategies, such as meditation and relaxation training (for example, Marlatt & Marques, 1977).

A second area of treatment should focus on the cognitive factors that are involved in the maintenance of drug use. A variety of recently developed cognitive behavior-therapy techniques could be employed to challenge the addict's belief and expectancy system as they relate to drug use (for example, Ellis & Grieger, 1977; Mahoney, 1974a; Meichenbaum, 1974). A final area of attention involves the restructuring of the individual's community-reinforcement system. The addict's environment typically is more supportive of continued drug use than of abstinence. Although this represents a much more difficult and time-consuming process, programs that have systematically rearranged the environment in such a way as to reinforce abstinence appear relatively effective in reducing subsequent drug usage (Hunt & Azrin, 1973).

SUMMARY

An individual's first experience with alcohol and other psychoactive drugs is frequently social in nature, dependent on peer pressure and the modeling of drug use by friends and relatives. However, not all individuals who initially experiment with these drugs continue use or eventually become addicted. It appears, however, that a smaller percentage of experimental drug users are behaviorally predisposed toward repeated usage. These individuals are characterized by a relative deficiency in appropriate social skills and interpersonal problem-solving abilities necessary to deal effectively with problem situations as they arise. They often have a negative perception of themselves, characterized by low self-efficacy, a lack of perceived control, and an increased sense of personal helplessness. These predisposing characteristics appear to enhance the attractiveness of the pharmacological effects of alcohol or heroin, particularly as a means of adjustment.

The primary effects of these drugs which appear to motivate continued use include the production of euphoria and the reduction of negative emotional states. These positive effects, associated with relatively short-term use of low to moderate doses, represent a powerful source of reinforcement. However, with chronic use there is a characteristic change in mood. The drugs no longer tend to produce euphoria, but instead lead to increased levels of dysphoria and negative arousal. Continued use at this point appears to be motivated by the belief that these negative states can be reduced with increasing drug doses, thus setting up a perpetuating cycle that may contribute to the tolerance effect. Drug use is further maintained by attempts to escape or avoid actual or anticipated withdrawal distress.

The experienced user develops a set of powerful cognitive expectancies about the possible effects of heroin or alcohol. These expectancies are shaped primarily from the reinforcing effects produced by these drugs during early use. Three expectancies appear to be particularly salient: (1) alcohol or heroin reduces tension and minimizes negative mood states; (2) alcohol or heroin produces an increase in feelings of personal power and control; and (3) "once an addict, always an addict." When confronted by high-risk situations, these beliefs appear to be evoked and enhance the probability of continued drug use or relapse. The strong subjective desire for the anticipated positive effects of the drug is experienced as a sensation of craving; these subjective sensations are stronger in those situations containing cues associated with previous drug use. Relapse results in an Abstinence Violation Effect. The two primary cognitive components of the AVE, cognitive dissonance and personal attribution of failure, increase the likelihood that drug use will continue following an initial relapse.

Addiction is a complex process which appears to involve a multitude of psychological and physiological determinants. The present position advocates that addictive behaviors can best be understood within the framework of cognitive social-learning theory. However, one should not unduly minimize the role played by alcohol and heroin and their pharmacological effects. Lindesmith (1968) argues that neither cognitive nor physiological factors alone are sufficient to explain addiction. Rather, addiction appears to be an interactive product of learning in a situation involving physiological events as they are interpreted, labeled, and given meaning by the user. Both the cognitive and physiological elements are indispensable features of the total experience and serve to shape the behavioral, attitudinal, and expectancy patterns found in the addiction process.

CHAPTER 15

BEHAVIORAL INTERVENTIONS FOR WEIGHT REDUCTION AND SMOKING CESSATION

Linda Wilcoxon Craighead

The Pennsylvania State University

Kelly D. Brownell

University of Pennsylvania

John J. Horan

The Pennsylvania State University

Smoking and obesity have been considered to be respectively the number one and number two preventable health-risk factors. Refraining from smoking, eating less, and exercising more are three (supposedly simple) steps a person can take that will have a substantial payoff in improved health. Millions of Americans successfully initiate such behavior changes each year without professional assistance. Unfortunately, there are millions more who either do not make such attempts or are markedly unsuccessful on their own. To help these individuals, behavioral researchers began experimenting with various techniques that had been successful in other problem areas. Their methodological skills have been applied to develop and critically evaluate clearly specified treatment programs for weight loss and smoking cessation.

The high incidence and demonstrated health risks indicate that smoking and obesity deserve serious clinical consideration. Thirty percent of men and 40 percent of women between the ages of forty and forty-nine are at least 20 percent overweight. Although many become overweight as adults, 10 to 15 percent of young children are obese, and by adolescence, the proportion reaches 30 percent (Brownell & Stunkard, 1978). Eighty percent of these overweight children subsequently become overweight adults. Although estimates have suggested that some 29 million Americans have given up smoking (Mausner, 1973) in light of the 1964 Surgeon General's Report (USPHS, 1964), data from 1970 indicated that 31 percent of women and 42 percent of men are still smokers (American Cancer Society, 1974). In fact, the 1979 Surgeon General's Report (USPHS, 1979) presented alarming new evidence attesting to the recently accelerating use of cigarettes by young women, which was clearly accompanied by an increase in smoking-related diseases among them.

The 1979 Surgeon General's Report concluded that the use of cigarettes is *causally* linked to lung cancer. There is also evidence of a direct relationship between smoking and other problems, such as heart disease and chronic bronchitis. In the medical community, it is clearly accepted that smoking is harmful to one's health; however, some individuals choose to believe otherwise or at least to believe it is not true for them. In addition, pregnant women who smoke increase the risk to their unborn children (USPHS, 1979). Cigarette smoke can have deleterious effects on others, ranging from eye irritation and loss of visual acuity (Johansson, 1976; Steinfield, 1972) to serious symptom exacerbation in individuals having heart and lung impairments (USPHS, 1975). Many nonsmokers simply find the smoke irritating. Thus, smoking is becoming a public concern as well as a personal choice.

Obesity is associated with a number of serious medical disorders, including insulin insensitivity, diabetes mellitus, impairment of pulmonary and renal function, surgical risk, greater risk with anesthesia, and complications during pregnancy (Bray, 1976). The most serious medical complication of obesity is its association with coronary heart disease. Obesity plays an important role in heart disease, probably through its influence on blood pressure, blood lipids, and carbohydrate intolerance (Kannel & Gordon, 1979). Weight loss can result in improved glucose tolerance, decreased blood pressure, and decreased cholesterol and triglycerides. Alexander and Peterson (1972) found that every parameter of cardiovascular functioning improved in obese patients after weight loss. Epidemiology studies estimate that if everyone were at optimal weight, there would be 25 percent less coronary heart disease and 35 percent fewer episodes of congestive heart failure and brain infarctions.

The psychological hazards of obesity are often overlooked in favor of the more apparent medical hazards. However, the psychological perils of obesity can be disabling and permanent. Body-image disturbance is one of the most common correlates of obesity. Many obese persons feel their bodies are grotesque and detestable and are certain that others view them with contempt (Stunkard & Mendelson, 1967). This feeling is particularly common among persons who have been overweight since childhood and can lead to shyness, withdrawal, and social immaturity.

The obese person who senses negative reactions from others may have accurate perceptions. The social bias against obesity is surprising in both its strength and its early development. The labels used to characterize obese persons are uniformly negative and connote blame. These include *lazy, sloppy, self-indulgent, ugly,* and *stupid.*

MANAGEMENT OF OBESITY

Obesity is one of the most puzzling problems of modern society. The remedy is simple: the obese person needs to eat less, exercise more, or both. Nonetheless, if *cure from obesity* is defined as reduction to ideal weight and maintenance of that weight for five years, a person is more likely to recover from cancer than from obesity. Obesity is a complex phenomenon with genetic, biological, psychological, and environmental origins (Bray, 1976; Stunkard, 1980; Wooley, Wooley, & Dyrenforth, 1979). Despite this, the public holds strongly to several beliefs: (1) obesity is so prevalent because food is abundant and people are lazy; (2) obesity is due to gluttonous overindulgence; and (3) weight reduction is a simple task, and failure in this regard results from lack of will power and poor self-esteem. Fortunately, science has advanced beyond these biases.

There are multiple causes of obesity in animals, and the same is probably true of humans. Even the basic mechanisms of hunger and satiety are surprising in their complexity. A thorough discussion of these factors can be obtained from several sources (Bray, 1976; Bray, 1979; Brownell & Venditti, in press; Stunkard, 1980).

Body weight is clearly a function of the balance between energy intake and energy expenditure, but there has been considerable debate over whether obesity is primarily due to excessive intake or restricted expenditure. Early studies by Mayer and others suggested that obese persons eat no more than thin persons but are far less active (Mayer, 1968). Subsequent studies with adults have confirmed these findings, but for children, the picture is less clear. In reviewing the research, Brownell and Stunkard (1980) conclude that obese children may be as active as thin children, but obese adults appear to be less active than thin adults. These findings suggest that physical inactivity may be more a consequence of obesity than its cause, but more carefully controlled study is needed to resolve the issue.

As the study of obesity becomes increasingly more sophisticated, the list of etiological factors becomes longer and more complex. Biological factors may play a major role in obesity. Many researchers feel that humans and animals have a *set-point* for body weight, that is, a specific body weight that the organism is set to defend (Keesey, 1978). When body weight deviates from the set-point, the organism experiences physiological and psychological changes that encourage movement back to the original weight. Each organism may have a different set-point so that, for some, obesity may be the ideal physiological state. This theory has not been proven, but it does illustrate the possible contribution of physiological factors.

Social, environmental, and psychological factors also influence obesity. The likelihood that an individual will be obese is best predicted by social class, ethnic group, religious affiliation, and the weight history of the family. One of the more extensively studied psychological hypotheses suggests that obese persons are more sensitive to environmental cues, such as the sight or taste of food, while individuals of normal weight rely more on internal physiological cues (Schacter & Rodin, 1974). Thus, obesity has many contributing factors, and attributing obesity to a lack of will power is a gross oversimplification.

The treatment of any problem depends on the results of assessment. A comprehensive plan for assessment is necessary to define treatment goals, to evaluate a client's physiological and psychological functioning, and to test the effectiveness of treatment procedures (Brownell, 1980). Initial medical screening is recommended to rule out contraindications for caloric restriction or exercise (Bray, 1976), and where there is any concern, a client's health should be carefully monitored. Several sources are available for a thorough discussion of assessment issues (Bray, 1976; Brownell, 1980). Perhaps the major point at this time is that obesity researchers have relied almost exclusively on simple measures of actual body weight (that is, pounds lost). LeBow (1977) notes that fatness (as measured, for example, by skinfold measures taken from several places on the body) is not exactly synonymous with pounds overweight, although they are at least moderately correlated. This is of particular concern in assessing exercise programs, since subjects may lose fat but not much weight. At least as far as health is concerned, it may be important to assess fatness and physical fitness as well as pounds lost. A second point relates to the assessment of adherence to the prescribed program. It is necessary to carefully assess eating and exercise behaviors before, during, and at the end of treatment in order to determine how they relate to each other and to weight loss and physical fitness measures. In addition, few researchers and clinicians assess changes in the very factors that prompt obese persons to lose weight (health risks and psychological and social problems).

Overview of Behavioral Interventions

One of the first published reports of a behavioral intervention program for the treatment of obesity was presented by Ferster, Nurnberger, and Levitt (1962) and suggested the utility of self-monitoring plus various stimulus control procedures. These initially positive findings were strongly substantiated in a subsequent case-study report by Stuart (1967) detailing the effects of an intensive, multifaceted behavioral program with eight women. These subjects were seen individually over a one-year period and demonstrated an average weight loss of thirty-seven pounds. The losses were clinically significant, and in addition, many subjects reported improved marital and social relationships.

In the next few years, a large number of studies with experimental-group designs were conducted to evaluate the behavioral approach more carefully and to examine the many different techniques that comprised the comprehensive self-control program. The results strongly supported the overall effectiveness of the behavioral approach but, unfortunately, rarely matched the clinically significant weight losses reported by Stuart. This may be at least partly related to two of the major criticisms discussed by Abramson (1977). The programs were of much shorter duration (typically eight to twelve weeks) and the subjects were less clinically obese (frequently college students recruited for the experiment). Nonetheless, there were sufficient studies to establish behavior therapy as the treatment of choice, at least for mild to moderate obesity. Harris (1969) demonstrated that a behavioral program was superior to a no-treatment control group. Wollersheim (1970) reported group behavior therapy was also significantly more effective than a social-pressure treatment based on a commercial self-help approach and a nonspecific group that focused on unconscious motives and personality factors (though both these groups did better than the no-treatment control). Penick, Filion, Fox, and Stunkard (1971) provided further evidence that the strength of the program was the specific behavioral techniques. Traditional group therapy led by seasoned psychotherapists (who believed their therapy would be effective) did not lead to as much weight loss as did the behavioral program, even though those groups were led by less experienced therapists.

Behavior therapy has since become a very popular treatment for obesity. Weight Watchers, the largest self-help organization, has incorporated behavior therapy into its standard program. Behavior therapy clinics can be found in many cities, and self-help books have been written by many researchers in the field. Numerous reviews of the research are available (Abramson, 1977; Foreyt, 1977; Leon, 1976; Stunkard & Mahoney, 1976; Wilson, 1978b), and these generally conclude that behavioral programs are effective and are more effective than other treatments to which they are compared.

For a more comprehensive picture of the overall effectiveness, Jeffery, Wing, and Stunkard (1978) reviewed twenty-one controlled studies of behavior therapy and found that the average weight loss after eight to twelve weeks of treatment was 11.5 pounds. The same authors studied 125 patients in the twelve-to-twenty-week program of the Stanford Eating Disorders Clinic; the average weight loss was 11.04 pounds. The consistency of results is remarkable; subjects in behavioral programs average 1 to 2 pounds lost per week. Programs longer than the usual eight to twelve weeks do produce a somewhat larger total loss, but the weekly rate of loss drops significantly when treatment is extended beyond the initial ten weeks. Although there have been many new variations, these do not seem to have significantly increased effectiveness. The best average weight losses (16 to 22 pounds) have been demonstrated by multifaceted, longer treatments (sixteen to twenty-five weeks) conducted with more clinically obese clients (Brownell, Heckerman, Westlake, Hayes, & Monti, 1978; Craighead, Stunkard, & O'Brien, 1978; McReynolds, Lutz, Paulsen, & Kohrs, 1976).

Despite the predominately positive findings, behavioral programs are still in need of further development. Many subjects become discouraged with the slow rate of loss even though this is the stated goal of the program. Drop-out rates typically range from 10 to 30 percent, sometimes higher in programs that do not request an initial monetary commitment (deposit) (Hagen, Foreyt, & Durham, 1976). Because of the slow rate of loss and the further slowing after ten weeks, programs would have to be extraordinarily long if clinically obese clients were to achieve goal weight by the end of the program. In present programs, only a few subjects do reach goal weight during treatment. Since clients are supposedly learning adaptive habits to use the rest of their lives, they are expected to continue using the procedures to eventually reach goal weight. As the section on maintenance will indicate, this has not occurred. Another problem is that the techniques are not effective for all clients. There is a large variability in client response to the program which cannot be accounted for by any known subject or program characteristics (Jeffery, Wing, & Stunkard, 1978).

Components of the Behavioral Package

Although there are many variations of what is frequently referred to as the standard behavioral package, considerable agreement exists about the major components or techniques that are to be taught. A number of manuals or texts are available that describe the clinical application of these techniques: Ferguson, 1975; Jeffrey and Katz, 1977; Mahoney and Mahoney, 1976a; and Stuart, 1977.

In his 1977 review, Abramson classifies such treatments as *complex self-control* programs and notes that since overall effectiveness has been generally upheld, researchers have focused on systematically evaluating the various components. Each of these components will be briefly described and the relevant research discussed. Although we now know a great deal more about the techniques, Abramson's 1977 summary statement is still the most appropriate. "In view of the conflicting evidence, it is not yet possible to draw any firm conclusions regarding the relative merits of the various techniques" (p. 359). No one technique seems to be indispensable nor does any particular technique seem to be sufficient by itself. Manipulating certain variables, however, often results in statistically significant differences which may be theoretically, if not practically, important.

A major problem in evaluating studies on the various techniques is that there is very little data on whether subjects actually apply the techniques that the programs are designed to teach. Few studies include even self-reports of program adherence. Studies that have assessed how well subjects carried out the designated program assignments have found few behaviors that were significantly related to weight loss, and in general, reports of behaviors accounted for only a small part of the variance in weight loss (Brownell et al., 1978; Brownell & Stunkard, 1978; Jeffery et al., 1978; Stalonas, Johnson, & Christ, 1978). However, these self-reports generally indicate a high level of adherence which may be inaccurate.

That so many variations work and that researchers cannot yet explain how or why the procedures work suggest that more general or nonspecific factors may be largely responsible for the success of the behavioral programs. However, as noted earlier, behavior therapy has clearly been more effective than a number of placebo or comparison therapies. Stalonas et al. (1978) have suggested a possible hypothesis which has not been tested. These researchers noted that most behavioral programs demand an extremely large amount of out-of-therapy time (for example, to record, graph, monitor) as compared to other weight-reduction regimens. Thus, the procedures may be effective because they continuously prompt the client's (and others') attention to weight loss.

CONTINGENCY MANAGEMENT

The techniques of contingency management as applied to weight control refer to procedures designed to alter the consequences for certain events related to weight in order to modify the probability of future responses. Reinforcement procedures are typically used to increase desirable eating or activity habits; punishment procedures to decrease inappropriate responses are less frequently used.

Contingency management may be utilized by the person involved, in which case it becomes a self-control procedure, or it may be enforced by an external source, such as a therapist. Several early studies compared self-control programs with therapist-controlled reinforcement. Typically, subjects earned back money they had deposited with the therapist at the beginning of treatment. Results from such studies indicate that both methods are about equally effective during treatment (Abrahms & Allen, 1974; Hall, Hall, DeBoer, & O'Kulitch, 1977). In Jeffrey (1974), subjects who were self-reinforced were more successful in maintaining weight loss after treatment. Israel and Saccone (1979) found that reinforcement by a therapist did not significantly enhance a basic stimulus-control program, whereas reinforcement by a significant other did. In addition, this group maintained their losses better at follow-up. Self-control, or internal contingency management, is a rather complex process but typically involves three basic steps: self-monitoring, self-evaluation, and self-reinforcement. Typically, the procedures are used to alter eating habits, as discussed in the next sections. Researchers have looked carefully at many subtle variations of self-control procedures.

Self-Monitoring Simple self-monitoring of eating habits (Mahoney, Moura, & Wade, 1973; Mahoney, 1974b) appears to have only a small, temporary effect on weight. Two studies reported on very brief, four-week programs, but during that time, simple, daily self-recording of weight and caloric intake was as effective as a behavior management program or a combined approach (Romanczyk, Tracey, Wilson, & Thorpe, 1973; Romanczyk, 1974). Bellack, Rozensky, and Schwartz (1974) found that timing of the recording might be important. Premonitoring (recording immediately before eating) was slightly more effective than postmonitoring (after eating) which, by itself, was not more effective than the no-monitoring control group. Green (1978) then examined both the type and timing of monitoring. Self-monitoring of caloric intake was the most effective, and the follow-up data suggested that premonitoring was helpful in this group.

Self-evaluation   This strategy is often considered an implicit part of the self-reinforcement procedure, although recent research points out its critical role. In Bellack, Glanz, and Simon (1976) and Carroll, Yates, and Gray (1980), subjects' general self-evaluative style (assessed on nonweight-related tests) correlated with weight loss during treatment. Subjects who were more likely to evaluate themselves positively (self-reinforce) did better in behavioral programs. Rozensky and Bellack (1976) found that such subjects lost more weight in a self-control program than in one with therapist-controlled reinforcement, whereas it made little difference for subjects who scored low on this self-reinforcement test.

Self-reward   Several studies found that self-monitoring was enhanced by the addition of self-reward procedures (Mahoney, Moura, & Wade, 1973; Mahoney, 1974b). These subjects awarded themselves money from a deposit given to the experimenter; in Bellack (1976), they gave themselves a grade for each instance of eating. The first study demonstrated that self-punishment was not as effective as self-reward, but these results were not replicated in a later study (Castro & Rachlin, 1980). In this study, there were no differences between subjects who self-monitored but paid for sessions noncontingently and subjects who either earned money (self-reinforcement) or paid money for each pound lost. The authors suggested that all these procedures serve simply as feedback to the person who wants to lose weight, and the use of money makes it more salient. Mahoney (1974b) found that self-rewards based on changing eating habits were more effective than when they were based simply on amount of weight lost. The Israel and Saccone (1979) study supported this last finding in that reinforcement for eating-behavior change promoted better weight loss and maintenance than reinforcing weight loss.

General Problem Solving   Mahoney and Mahoney (1976a) refined the basic self-control procedures, presenting them to clients as a seven-step "personal-scientist" model. In this approach, the client gathers data to identify idiosyncratic problem areas, determines a strategy tailored to the problem, and assesses the results to determine if revised solutions are needed. Thus, each person becomes his or her own problem solver. Clinically, the approach seems highly desirable, even though total weight loss appears to be similar to that achieved in more traditional programs (Mahoney, Rogers, Straw, & Mahoney, 1977).

Modifying Eating Behaviors

The following procedures are utilized to modify undesirable eating patterns so that an overweight person develops an appropriate, controlled eating style. There is conflicting evidence regarding whether an "obese" eating style is truly characteristic of overweight persons and to what extent this causes their weight problem. Nonetheless, most programs have assumed this to be the case, and certainly there is a wealth of clinical evidence that clients find such procedures useful. Typically, programs teach clients some or all of these procedures in a systematic fashion to be utilized within the overall self-control framework just discussed. Most of them have not been independently evaluated, so it is impossible to assess how much each contributes to the effectiveness of a total program.

Pace of Eating   The purpose is to slow down the rate of eating so the person will eat less. The extra time allows the person to sense the feeling of fullness and to stop before feeling stuffed. In addition, the person avoids the temptation to nibble while waiting for others to finish. Clients are instructed to put down their fork completely between each bite. They stretch out the mealtime by introducing short (two-minute) delays in which they just socialize. Including foods with high bulk or that take a long time to eat (for example, salads, artichokes) also contributes to an earlier sensation of fullness.

Timing of Eating   Clients are instructed to avoid skipping meals and subsequently eating when starved, when they are more likely to eat too fast and too much before they will feel full. Regular, planned meals and snacks promote controlled eating.

Focusing on Internal Cues   Clients deliberately practice leaving a small amount of food on their plate to overcome the habit of automatically eating whatever is in front of them. The purpose is to get clients to attend to internal cues to regulate their eating rather than to external cues. In addition, clients practice asking themselves, "Am I really hungry?" whenever they feel an urge to eat impulsively. They learn to discriminate externally cued impulses and to eat only in response to internal cues.

Altering Behavioral Chains   Once clients have learned to discriminate environmentally cued eating, they practice substituting alternative, competing (not eating) responses when this occurs. Clients make lists of activities (for example, dusting, taking a walk, taking a bubble bath) that will get them out of the situation or distract them until the urge subsides. Another method is to set a timer for ten minutes to introduce a delay; frequently the urge subsides. As clients become more sophisticated in their ability to look for and analyze behavioral patterns (for example, *a*ntecedents, *b*ehaviors, *c*onsequences), they learn to intervene early in a chain of behaviors to avoid situations that are particularly likely to lead to eating. It is far easier to substitute early in a chain that to wait until the urge actually occurs.

Typical problem behavior chains involve eating when tired (a better alternative is a fifteen-minute snooze), bored, depressed, or anxious. It is a widely held assumption that obese people are more likely to eat in response to negative emotional states. However, the experimental evidence relating anxiety or boredom to eating is contradictory (see Abramson & Stinson, 1977; Reznick & Balch, 1977). Leon and Chamberlain (1973) found that 25 percent of both obese and normal subjects reported eating when lonely or bored. However, eating in response to negative emotional states may become more of a problem for the obese even if it is not initially causally related to their being overweight. Since behavioral interventions for obesity are usually conducted in groups within an educational framework, clients with serious or recurring personal problems would be referred to other professionals to deal with those issues.

Refusing Food Offers   Clients often feel uncomfortable refusing food in social situations. Clients may be taught how to refuse food assertively using behavioral rehearsal and are asked to eat only food that they have specifically requested. The purpose of this is to have clients totally control their intake (based on internal cues) rather than letting other people or situational cues control their eating.

STIMULUS CONTROL: MODIFYING THE ENVIRONMENT

A number of different stimulus control procedures have also been developed to use within the more general self-control framework. *Stimulus control* refers to modifying the environmental cues so that a particular, undesirable response will be less likely to occur or a particular, desirable response will be more likely to occur. Used in a self-control framework, it refers to something that a person does ahead of time to alter the probability of subsequent events. The use of these procedures in controlling obesity is based on the assumption that the obese person is responding to environmental cues. Thus, the procedures are designed to eliminate cues for impulsive, uncontrolled eating and to introduce new cues that will promote controlled eating. Clients learn to monitor and self-reinforce for making these self-controlling responses.

Eliminate Extraneous Visual Food Cues   Clients do not have tempting foods available. All food is stored away in opaque containers. Extra food is put away before starting to eat and is not left on the table.

Narrow the Range of Cues Associated with Eating   Clients are asked to designate specific places to eat and to eat only in these approved places (not all over the house). Clients are not allowed to pair other activities (such as TV) with eating, since the activities become discriminative stimuli for eating.

Minimize Contact with Food   Clients eliminate any unnecessary exposure to food (for example, extensive baking/cooking). Often other people are enlisted to prepare food and/or clean up. Leftover food or tempting food gifts are immediately thrown out or given away. Clients are encouraged to shop and prepare foods ahead of time (when they are not feeling hungry).

Introduce Cues to Eat Less   Clients use graphs, signs, and other cues to remind themselves to use new eating habits. A special placemat or set of dishes (small dishes are best) can serve as new cues (and make small portions appear larger).

Preplan   Clients are asked to plan their meals and snacks ahead and to write down their plan so they will be more likely to stick with it. This is done the day before; then clients monitor their actual intake, correcting the plan when they do not adhere to it. The continuous feedback for planning enhances the client's control over his or her intake. It is particularly useful in handling parties, dinners out, or other special occasions, when a person is more likely to overeat if not committed to a particular plan. Frequently, clients not only preplan but also pre-prepare snacks in the specified amounts to decrease the probability of eating more than was planned.

RESEARCH ON SELF-CONTROL COMPONENTS

Modifying the environment and eating habits constitute the major components of complex self-control packages. Little research is available to evaluate the specific impact of any particular technique. However, a simple self-control program, called the mouthful diet, was developed which focused on reducing the actual number of bites taken. Subjects recorded each bite taken on a wrist counter and systematically reduced their number of bites per day until a satisfactory rate of weight loss was obtained. Two comparisons of this simple program with more complex self-control programs indicated that both were equally effective and were better than control groups (Fowler, Fordyce, Boyd, & Masock, 1972; Hall, Hall, Hanson, & Borden, 1974). However, the total loss was small and a follow-up in the latter study indicated that neither group maintained their weight loss after treatment.

McReynolds et al. (1976) compared a complex self-control package with a program that focused exclusively on stimulus-control procedures. Both programs were equally effective during treatment and produced substantial weight losses averaging about sixteen pounds. Although both groups maintained most of this loss, there was a significant difference in favor of the simpler, stimulus-control program at the three- and six-month follow-ups.

A subsequent study by Stalonas et al. (1978) supported the importance of the self-managed contingency-component procedures. The addition of very specific self-reinforcement procedures for applying the strategies did not enhance the effectiveness of the standard behavioral program (which included self-monitoring) during treatment, but groups receiving this contingency component were more successful in maintaining weight loss during follow-up.

Role of the Therapist

The role of the therapist in a self-control behavioral program has been the subject of numerous investigations. Supposedly, the specific procedures are the critical components, and thus the therapist's primary function is to maintain interest and participation in the program. The following studies varied the amount of therapist contact from the typical weekly lecture and discussion groups to various types of bibliotherapy (manuals) presented with little or no contact with the therapist. Minimal contact with a therapist might be provided by mail, a brief visit(s), or phone contacts (Bellack et al., 1974; Hagen, 1974; Hanson, Borden, Hall & Hall, 1976). In fact, the trend in the last study cited suggested that groups receiving less contact maintained their losses better. The benefits of reduced reliance on a therapist were upheld in a subsequent study (Carter, Rice, & DeJulio, 1977), which found a program in which the therapist was faded-out to be more successful than the standard program, both at the end of treatment and at follow-up. However, it should be noted that these programs were relatively short (eight to ten weeks) and did not produce the more clinically significant weight losses achieved by some of the longer, combination programs that are reported later in this chapter. In addition, Brownell, Heckerman, and Westlake (1978) found that group therapy was more effective than bibliotherapy, which produced only negligible weight losses. In the one study investigating increased therapist contact, Jeffery and Wing (1979) found that subjects contacted three times a week (one visit and two phone contacts) lost more weight than the standard weekly contact group. No follow-up data were available.

The therapist's role may be more important than initially recognized, especially in clinical populations. Most studies do not find differences due to a particular therapist, but in an evaluation of a large-scale program reported by Jeffery, Wing, and Stunkard (1978), average weight loss was better in groups led by therapists who had had experience with at least two previous groups. Additional evidence suggests also that the therapist's training positively effects client outcomes (Levitz & Stunkard, 1974).

Additions of Diet and/or Exercise

Although the initial behavioral interventions focused on eating habits and environmental control, this approach was soon expanded to incorporate nutritional/dietary information and programmed exercise (Stuart, 1971). The importance of increasing energy expenditure as well as decreasing caloric intake in order to balance appropriately the energy equation was acknowledged, as was the value of eating a nutritionally sound diet instead of simply decreasing amounts eaten. Nonetheless, the issue of energy balance is clearly complex. One recent outcome study (Jeffery & Wing, 1979) found that self-reported caloric intake was the best predictor of weight loss, but self-report of energy expenditure was not significantly related to weight loss. Although the specific contribution of nutrition/diet information cannot be isolated from the overall effectiveness of complex programs, the most effective programs reported have included extensive nutrition/diet information (Craighead, Stunkard, & O'Brien, 1978; McReynolds, Lutz, Paulsen, & Kohrs, 1976). Flexible, exchange-type programs rather than rigid diets are typically recommended, since the goal of such programs has been to develop an adaptive long-term eating style rather than one promoting short-term losses.

Promising results were reported by the Dietary Rehabilitation Clinic (Musante, 1976) for an intensive behavioral program combined with a nutritionally sound but very restricted, standardized 700-calorie diet. Two hundred twenty-nine clinically obese clients were treated in an outpatient program in which all meals were provided in a supervised dining area. Treatment was individualized and of varying lengths, which makes comparisons to other studies difficult, but substantial weight losses were reported. Over half of the patients lost more than twenty pounds and a quarter lost more than forty pounds. Although follow-up data were not available, it appears that an intensive program can be initially successful, even for obese patients who have been considered refractory (unsuccessful in many previous programs). The potential of such a restricted diet to improve the initially slow rate of loss associated with behavioral programs deserves further empirical evaluation. Clinical reports (Katell, Callahan, Fremovw, & Zilterer, 1979; Lindner & Blackburn, 1976) suggest that a combination of fasting and behavior therapy may be one way to lose large amounts of weight initially and then to maintain the loss.

Increasing exercise behavior is also a procedure that is very compatible with the general orientation of behavioral interventions. Thus, it is somewhat surprising to note in a recent review (LeBow, 1977) that 80 percent of the 105 reports surveyed did not teach clients to increase energy output, and none actually assessed changes in physical fitness. Three studies (Dahlkoetter, Callahan, & Linton, 1979; Harris & Hallbauer, 1973; Stalonas et al., 1978) that specifically investigated the role of exercise found that combined programs were slightly, but not significantly, better than more traditional behavioral programs or an exercise program alone. However, results at follow-up indicated that subjects in groups receiving exercise were more likely to continue losing or to maintain their weight loss. The Dahlkoetter et al. study did assess physical fitness. Groups receiving exercise demonstrated improved fitness (on heart rate after exercise, resting pulse, sit-up rates) compared to the other groups (which had lost similar amounts of weight). All treated groups evidenced decreased blood pressure.

Modifying Cognitions Related to Eating

Another expansion of the standard behavioral package involved focusing specifically on the cognitions or thoughts of the obese person. It was assumed that obese subjects were more likely to think about food and that their subsequent internal monologues were maladaptive since they did not reliably lead to restraint. There is considerable clinical evidence attesting to the negative and self-defeating thoughts verbalized by overweight people attempting to lose weight, but little data to suggest that such cognitive factors are causally related to obesity. Nonetheless, outcome data suggest that cognitive procedures may still be useful in treatment programs.

The earliest cognitive procedures reported were variations of *coverant-control therapy*. Horan and Johnson (1971) and Horan, Baker, Hoffman, and Shute (1975) found they were effective in short-term programs, but concluded they would only be useful as part of a more comprehensive package. Subjects used eating stimuli as cues to read their coverant cards, which was reinforced by "highly probable" behaviors. The use of positive coverants focusing on the desirable attributes of normal weight was significantly more effective than negative coverants focusing on the aversive aspects of being overweight.

Cognitive restructuring procedures have also been applied to cognitions about eating. The program developed by Mahoney and Mahoney (1976a) included a unit of "cognitive ecology," in which subjects learned to monitor their thoughts and to replace their maladaptive internal dialogues with more appropriate and encouraging self-talk. Problematic thoughts often concerned rigid, unrealistic goals, negative evaluations of personal capability to lose weight, justifications (excuses) for eating, inability to distract from food thoughts, and impatience with slow rates of loss.

Some preliminary evidence exists that suggests that adaptive cognitions may be related to success in weight control. A self-report scale developed by the Mahoneys and their colleagues to assess cognitions relevant to eating correlated significantly with final weight loss in two outcome studies (Craighead et al., 1978; Mahoney et al., 1977). In another study, Steffen and Myszak (1978) used a pretherapy induction procedure to assess their clients' cognitions regarding their ability to succeed using self-control strategies. Groups receiving this brief pretreatment training continued to lose weight during follow-up while the other groups did not.

Maintenance of Weight Loss

Although it was clear that clients were not reaching goal weight during treatment, it was initially assumed that clients would learn the techniques and continue to lose on their own once treatment was terminated. Many of the early studies did not even include long-term follow-ups to determine if this occurred. Reviews of the long-term efficacy of the behavioral approach have been disappointing in that regard (Brightwell & Sloan, 1977; Jeffery et al., 1978; Stunkard & Penick, 1979). These summaries indicate there is moderate evidence that weight loss is maintained but certainly no evidence of continued weight loss. Two more recent programs with substantial initial weight losses have confirmed that the most effective programs demonstrate good maintenance as long as a year afterward (Beneke, Paulsen, McReynolds, & Kohrs, 1978; Craighead et al., 1978). Nonetheless, even in these studies, few subjects achieved their goal weight during treatment, so they in fact needed to lose more, not just maintain.

Booster sessions designed to provide additional training and social support after treatment is terminated were suggested as possible procedures to enhance maintenance. Early reports (Hall, Hall, Borden, & Hanson, 1975;

Kingsley & Wilson, 1977) indicated that boosters might be helpful under certain conditions. However, four subsequent studies found that booster sessions did not improve maintenance (Ashby & Wilson, 1977; Beneke & Paulsen, 1979; Craighead et al., 1978; Wilson & Brownell, 1978). Thus, it appears that new procedures still need to be developed if long-term weight control is to be achieved.

Combining Behavior Therapy and Pharmacotherapy

Pharmacological treatments for obesity have been in disrepute because of their short-lived weight losses and the abuse potential of many drugs. However, it may be possible to utilize such interventions to produce initially more rapid loss in combination with behavioral interventions to produce subsequent long-term adherence to modified patterns of diet and exercise (which would maintain the initial weight loss). An initial investigation (Craighead et al., 1978) assessed the utility of combining behavior therapy and fenfluramine (a mild appetite suppressant with sedative rather than stimulant properties). Results of a twenty-five-week program indicated that this medication did significantly enhance the effectiveness of the behavioral package (by an average of eight pounds) for a total loss of about thirty-one pounds. However, a combination of medication and supportive therapy (with self-monitoring and nutrition counseling) was just as effective. The long-term benefits of behavior therapy were expected to be demonstrated in follow-up. In fact, the standard behavior therapy group demonstrated excellent maintenance at one-year follow-up. However, the combination group that had received medication with supportive therapy gained weight during this period and, surprisingly, the combination group with medication and behavior therapy did no better. Thus, at one year, the trends had reversed; the standard behavior therapy group now showed a total loss of about twenty pounds, which was somewhat better (but not statistically significant) than the two combination groups, which had maintained a loss of only about twelve pounds.

A second study (Craighead, 1979) investigated methods designed to prevent, or at least diminish, this relapse phenomenon. Two different sequences of medication and behavior therapy designed to determine when the medication might be used most effectively were carried out. During treatment, subjects lost more weight when they were taking medication, regardless of the sequencing. The most successful sequence was behavior therapy for eight weeks followed by a combination of behavior therapy with medication for eight weeks; this group lost 20.7 pounds, significantly more than either behavior therapy or medication alone. Unfortunately, by four-month follow-up, the relapse phenomenon was demonstrated in all the combination treatments despite the new sequencing. The group receiving only behavior therapy maintained their loss, regaining significantly less weight than any other group. The sequence of combined behavior therapy and medication (eight weeks) followed by behavior therapy alone (eight weeks), designed to provide continued support while medication was terminated, was effective in preventing relapse during treatment but not more effective in preventing relapse during follow-up. Thus, the combination of behavior therapy and pharmacotherapy appears to be a promising new development, but the problem of relapse has not been solved.

Behavior Therapy and Social-Influence Intervention

Eating and dieting occur within a constellation of social interactions. The social forces operating through the family, the work environment, religious groups, fraternal organizations, the community, and so forth may be powerful motivators of behavior change. Utilizing such powerful, "natural" reinforcement systems may be a very effective (and perhaps more efficient) way to ensure that therapeutic gains are maintained.

FAMILY INTERVENTIONS

Many social interactions involving food occur within the family, and family members may play an important role in aiding or hindering the dieter. Wilson and Brownell (1978) carried out the first systematic trial of family intervention. All subjects received the standard behavior therapy package; half of the subjects attended sessions alone, while the other half attended sessions with a family member. The family members were taught behavioral principles and were taught to be encouraging. There were no significant differences between the groups, but the investigators concluded they may not have provided sufficiently specific instruction to the family members so that they could be helpful.

A highly structured couples intervention was then tested by Brownell, Heckerman, Westlake, Hayes, and Monti (1978). With the couple as the focal point of treatment, subjects and spouses were instructed in a variety of techniques, including stimulus control, modeling, reinforcement, and mutual monitoring. Subjects and spouses had their own treatment manuals with corresponding lessons to emphasize that behavior change was required of both parties. This couples condition was compared with two other conditions: a cooperative-spouse–subject-alone condition in which spouses agreed to take part in the program but did not actually participate, and a noncooperative-spouse condition in which spouses refused to participate. At the end of treatment, subjects in the couples group lost an average of twenty pounds which was nonsignificantly more than the other two groups. However, by the six-month follow-up, the couples group had lost thirty pounds which was now significantly more than the other two conditions, nineteen and fifteen pounds, respectively. The results of the Brownell et al. study were striking, because the weight losses were nearly triple those reported in most studies of behavior therapy of this length, and because nearly one-third of the total weight loss in the couples condition occurred *after* weekly treatment sessions ended.

WORK-SITE TREATMENTS

Many adults spend a large part of their day at the work place. The naturally occurring social forces inherent in this situation may be useful for mobilizing changes in health behaviors. In addition, treatment may be cost-effective at the work site because large numbers of potential subjects can be treated together. Stunkard and Brownell (in press) conducted the first controlled clinical trial of work-site treatment for obesity. The program was carried out with employees of Bloomingdale's and Gimbel's retail department stores in New York. The subjects met for a sixteen-week behavioral program, were treated by professional therapists or by fellow employees, and were scheduled for four weekly meetings or the traditional once-weekly treatments. Two measures were used—attrition and weight loss. Attrition rates were lower in groups led by nonprofessional therapists than in professionally led groups and were lower for subjects meeting four times weekly than for subjects meeting only once weekly. There were no differences in weight loss among the conditions, probably because of the small sample size. Thus, work-site treatment is feasible but must be investigated more fully before the extent of its potential can be realized.

SELF-HELP TREATMENTS

Persons with a problem often join together for mutual assistance. The most widely known of these groups is Alcoholics Anonymous, but many obese persons also seek help from such groups. Weight losses reported from most groups average around fifteen pounds; however, these reports usually come from the groups themselves and include only those subjects who are the most reliable participants. Attrition appears to be the major problem confronting self-help groups. Levitz and Stunkard (1974) carried out a large-scale trial to evaluate the use of behavioral interventions within a self-help group. The effectiveness of the standard TOPS program was greatly enhanced by behavior therapy, resulting both in larger weight losses and decreased attrition. Thus, behavior therapy and self-help treatments may be natural partners.

SMOKING CESSATION

One's first inhalation of cigarette smoke can be a terribly noxious experience involving, for example, feelings of disequilibrium and nausea. Why then do people try smoking, let alone allow it to become a deeply ingrained habit? Most answers to this question are long on theory and short on data. Cigarette smoking has a number of well-established psychosocial correlates (Smith, 1970; USPHS, 1979, chaps. 17 & 18), and the tendency to label them as *causal* is attractive if not unwarranted. Especially convincing are the relationships between an individual's use of cigarettes and the smoking behavior of peers (Levitt & Edwards, 1970; Newman, 1970a, 1970b; Palmer, 1970), older siblings (Palmer, 1970), and parents (Borland & Rudolph, 1975; Palmer, 1970; Wohlford, 1970). These data patterns lend themselves well to speculative hypotheses involving the behavioral principles of modeling and social reinforcement, but such processes are only part of a complex process that has not yet been clearly defined.

Given that smoking behavior persists beyond the exploratory stage, a variety of theoretical models have been offered to account for maintenance of the habit. Pomerleau (1979), for example, offers a complex operant analysis which indicates that smoking eventually provides a wide variety of positive and negative reinforcers independent of those that initially elicited exploration. Other authors have formulated classification systems which essentially try to represent (via factor analysis of questionnaire data) different categories of smokers (Best & Hakstian, 1978; Coan, 1973; Ikard, Green, & Horn, 1969; McKennell, 1968; Tomkins, 1968). For example, some individuals reportedly smoke to relieve negative affect, others to elicit positive affect. If such typologies were truly consistent, the implications for differential (and successful) treatment programming would be profound. Unfortunately, there may be little or no congruence between classification systems based on self-report data and actual smoking behavior (Adesso & Glad, 1978). Finally, the role of nicotine in maintaining the smoking habit is illustrated by the work of Schachter (1978) and his colleagues (Schachter, Silverstein, Kozlowski, Perlick, Herman, & Liebling, 1977). They view nicotine deprivation as an aversive state which one can avoid (or escape from) by smoking. Jarvik (1977), however, concluded that nicotine is a necessary but insufficient condition for maintenance of a smoking habit. A diverse array of other etiological theories have appeared in the literature, but most have few implications for the design of more effective treatments.

Assessment Procedures

The overwhelming majority of smoking treatment programs rely on unverified self-report for evaluating effectiveness. Such data are usually expressed in terms of the subjects' estimated number of cigarettes smoked per day prior to and after treatment. However, self-report data are highly suspect because, for example, of the pervasive problems of digit bias and differential demand. Digit bias refers to the tendency of subjects to express their smoking rates in terms of half-packs or multiples of five cigarettes. The accuracy of self-report can probably be enhanced by continuous tallying as opposed to retrospective estimation and by requesting that subjects provide the evaluator with the name of another person (roommate, relative, and so on) who will agree to verify the reported usage.

Biological assays, however, provide the best collaborative evidence. Smoking is hazardous because it introduces chemical toxins into the body; it is possible to quantify smoking behavior by examining these residual compounds directly. For example, in the lungs of a smoker, carbon monoxide has a higher affinity for hemoglobin in the blood than does oxygen; it reacts very quickly to form a compound known as carboxyhemoglobin (COHb). Smokers invariably have much higher concentrations of COHb in their blood than do nonsmokers. Similarly, heavy smokers have greater amounts of COHb than light smokers.

There are essentially two major methods for measuring COHb. The first requires laboratory tests of blood samples drawn from each subject; the second relies on the fortunate fact that COHb is directly related to expired air concentrations of CO. A subject's smoking behavior can be quickly and conveniently assessed by a simple breath test. Nonsmokers will rarely exhale more than a few parts per million (ppm) CO; smokers, on the other hand, typically range from 30 to 80 ppm. Expired air CO correlates quite well with self-reported indices of smoking behavior (Horan, Hackett, & Linberg, 1978; Lando, 1975). COHb may be a better index of health risk than frequency counts of cigarettes; the latter, even if absolutely correct, do not take into account factors like puff frequency or depth of inhalation. The principal difficulty with using COHb as an index of smoking behavior is its relatively brief half-life of about five hours. Thus, after a day or two, it may be impossible to distinguish a smoker from an abstainer on the basis of CO alone. Since most smokers do not typically abstain for prolonged periods of time, the half-life phenomenon is not as problematic as it might appear (Horan et al., 1978). Nevertheless, other biological assay options exist. Thiocyanate concentrations in blood, urine, and saliva can reliably reflect smoking behavior (Brockway, 1978). These concentrations have a far longer half-life than COHb (up to fourteen days) but, unfortunately, may be influenced by dietary factors (USPHS, 1979). Finally, smokers can be distinguished from nonsmokers on the basis of a urinalysis for nicotine (Paxton & Bernacca, 1979). Apart from the utility of biological assays in their own right, we strongly suspect that their use increases the accuracy of self-report measures.

Although program success can be defined in terms of reduced smoking frequency and lowered quantities of biochemical compounds, abstinence provides the most meaningful test of treatment efficacy. Complete elimination of the habit is the goal sought by most smokers undergoing treatment; this is a wise choice as those who simply reduce their consumption level eventually return to baseline (Lichtenstein & Danaher, 1976). Moreover, abstinence represents the ultimate reduction of health hazard. For research purposes, abstinence data generate the most confidence. In the first place, subjects can discriminate whether they are smoking or not with greater accuracy than rate estimation allows, regardless of the self-monitoring format employed. Likewise, the person in the environment nominated by the subject to verify the self-report can more readily do so with abstinence rather than with rate-reduction criteria. Finally, abstinence is easier to verify than lowered consumption level with biological assays.

Overview of Behavioral Interventions

Initial attempts to develop behaviorally based treatment programs were not much more successful than unaided attempts to quit. Extensive reviews of the literature (Bernstein & McAlister, 1976; Hunt & Matarozzo, 1973; Lichtenstein & Danaher, 1976; Schwartz, 1969; USPHS, 1979) detail the many types of interventions that were initially investigated. These reviews support McFall and Hammen's (1971) conclusions (based on a summary of ten studies) that virtually any program can be expected to produce low-moderate success rates (26 percent abstinence) which will inevitably decay to practical insignificance (13 percent abstinence) if a six-month follow-up is conducted. It is perhaps not surprising when one considers that clients usually attend such programs as a last resort, having failed in many attempts to quit on their own. However, it is notable that programs specifically designed as placebos (just giving structured attention) were just as good as many behavioral interventions.

The following sections describe some of the more successful programs that have produced results better than the base rates just described. In view of the assessment issues already delineated, there are several methodological criteria which must be considered in initially evaluating the effects of such programs. At a minimum, treatment studies must present abstinence rates (including all dropouts) that are independently verified (preferably by biological assays) both at posttreatment and at six-month or longer follow-up. Studies that produce success rates of 70 to 90 percent at posttest and 40 to 60 percent at follow-up can be considered exemplary, given the current state of the art.

RAPID SMOKING

The single most effective treatment technique to appear in the literature over the past decade is an aversion-conditioning strategy known as *rapid smoking*. This technique was first mentioned by Lublin (1969), but Lichtenstein and his associates are credited with most of the procedural refinement and validation (Lichtenstein, Harris, Berchler, Wahl, & Schmahl, 1973; Schmahl, Lichtenstein, & Harris, 1972). Rapid smoking essentially consists of having cigarette users take a normal inhalation every six seconds until they are no longer able to do so. Each trial usually lasts about five minutes during which time an average of four or five cigarettes are smoked. Two or three trials punctuated by five-minute rest periods are given in each of eight to twelve treatment sessions. Subjects are instructed not to smoke between sessions, and initial sessions are scheduled daily. Initial studies found that rapid smoking alone produced 60 percent abstinence rates (verified by independent informants) six months after the end of treatment. However, multiple year follow-ups of these early studies on rapid smoking have shown some disappointing relapse (Lichtenstein & Rodrigues, 1977). Current investigations have also produced less impressive results. Danaher's (1977) exhaustive review points out that many of the failures to replicate may be due to changes in the standard treatment format.

The actual role of an aversion-conditioning mechanism underlying the effectiveness of rapid smoking is not clear. Favorable evidence (Hackett, Horan, Stone, Linberg, Nicholas, & Lukaski, 1977; Norton & Barske, 1977) is at best tentative, and it pales in light of a finding that the technique may lose much of its effectiveness when administered apart from the context of a warm, supportive counseling relationship (Danaher, 1977; Lichtenstein & Danaher, 1976). Thus, cognitive and social-reinforcement factors may play a much larger role than initially hypothesized.

The principal drawback to the rapid-smoking procedure involves a controversy concerning medical risk. Rapid-smoking is specifically designed to induce physiological discomfort. It does so through bodily absorption of greatly increased quantities of tobacco smoke which contains particularly reactive ingredients like nicotine and carbon monoxide. Since larger doses of these compounds can severely strain one's cardiovascular system, the rapid-smoking procedure is absolutely unsuitable for individuals with coronary or pulmonary diseases (Hall, Sachs, & Hall, 1979; Horan, Hackett, Nicholas, Linberg, Stone, & Lukaski, 1977; Horan, Linberg, & Hackett, 1977, 1980; Lichtenstein & Glasgow, 1977; Miller, Schilling, Logan, & Johnson, 1977; Russell, Raw, Taylor, Feyerabend, & Saloojee, 1978). Although the technique is probably safe for normal smokers, the question of which screening criteria are adequate for routine clinical practice has not been satisfactorily answered, and consultation with a cardiologist is highly recommended.

Risk-free Alternatives to Rapid Smoking

Normal-paced-aversive smoking (NPAS) (Danaher & Lichtenstein, 1978) and focused smoking (Hackett & Horan, 1978, 1979) are very promising risk-free alternatives to the rapid smoking procedure. Although both procedures were independently conceived and developed, they continue to evolve in the same direction. NPAS was distilled from an attention-placebo treatment involving Bantron (a nicotine chewing gum). Focused smoking initially resembled an in vivo form of covert sensitization (that is, horror images pertaining to the potential consequences of smoking experienced during the act of smoking), but over the course of several unpublished pilot investigations, realistic images and experiences began to be emphasized. Both NPAS and focused smoking are now sufficiently similar to permit the following common description.

The general rationale and context are similar to rapid smoking. Subjects sit facing a blank wall and smoke at their normal rate while being cued by the experimenter to focus on the discomforts of smoking. These include, for example, a bad taste in the mouth, a burning in the throat, and feelings of lightheadedness and nausea. As treatment progresses other negative sensations reported by the subjects are incorporated, for example, shakiness, sweating, dull headaches, difficulty in breathing, and an uncomfortable, heavy, tired feeling. Reminders to concentrate only on the effects of smoking are repeatedly provided. Hackett and Horan (1978, 1979) report that the procedure is comparable to rapid smoking in terms of reported discomfort and treatment success (verified abstinence 40 to 60 percent after six months), yet all of the medical risks associated with rapid smoking are avoided.

Satiation (doubling or tripling one's daily consumption of cigarettes prior to abstinence) is another alternative to rapid smoking. While not innocuous, this procedure is probably less hazardous than rapid smoking. As a sole treatment, satiation is of questionable utility; however, multicomponent treatment packages which include satiation have shown considerable promise (Best, Owen, Trentaclue, 1978; DeLahunt & Curran, 1976; Lando, 1977).

COMPREHENSIVE PROGRAMS

Comprehensive treatment programs for smoking have assumed a variety of formats. Some seek to enhance the effects of rapid smoking (Flaxman, 1978; Hackett & Horan, 1977; Hackett et al., 1977; McAlister, 1976) or its less risky alternatives (Best et al., 1978; Hackett & Horan, 1978, 1979; Lando, 1977) by incorporating additional techniques, which may include cognitive restructuring, contingency contracting, covert sensitization, cue-controlled relaxation, stimulus control, systematic desensitization, and thought stopping. Each such technique has at least minor theoretical relevance to certain aspects of the smoking problem. For example, if some individuals smoke when anxious, learning how to relax might prove helpful. It has been thought that additional techniques might better address individual reasons for smoking and should enhance maintenance once treatment was terminated.

Hackett and Horan (1979) compared focused smoking with a comprehensive program alone and with a combination of the two. Although all programs were highly effective after eight sessions (80 to 90 percent abstinence verified by carbon monoxide tests), the programs that included focused smoking were more effective than the comprehensive program alone at follow-up. Surprisingly, adding more techniques did not enhance the simple focused smoking procedure. The authors suggest that these alternate approaches may be useful for clients who do not respond to focused smoking, or that they may be developed in some way to enhance maintenance, once abstinence has been achieved.

Other comprehensive programs do not involve the rapid smoking technique or its alternatives. The Pomerleau and Pomerleau (1977) approach (cf. Horan, 1978) is based on an operant analysis of smoking behavior and is designed to bring about gradual self-control of smoking over an eight-week period. During the first week, subjects simply record their smoking behavior (self-monitoring). The goal for week 2 is reduction to a daily average of between fifteen and twenty cigarettes; this may be accomplished by eliminating low-priority cigarettes or by letting a preset timer dictate the occasions for smoking. Several additional stimulus control techniques are introduced during weeks 3 and 4 as the smoking-rate goal tapers to less than five cigarettes per day. Total abstinence is expected during the fifth week. Subjects are encouraged to reflect on the positive reinforcers resulting from smoking cessation; they are also taught a procedure similar to covert sensitization designed to combat the urge to smoke. During the final two weeks, maintenance of a nonsmoking lifestyle is fostered through cognitive restructuring and other self-control procedures. Early reports indicated about 33 percent abstinence at follow-up.

Blittner and Goldberg (1978) evaluated a similar program that emphasized self-control training by the application of stimulus control. In addition to the gradual reduction (easiest situations first), subjects were taught to discontinue pairing smoking with other activities (for example, reading, TV) which were associated with urges to smoke. Results at follow-up were quite poor (11 percent abstinence) but were significantly better (33 percent) for a group that was continuously given feedback that they demonstrated special capacities for self-control.

Flaxman (1978) also provided a comprehensive self-control program and found that an abrupt-cessation strategy—subjects prepared for two weeks and then quit on a designated target date—was more effective than gradual tapering off or quitting cold turkey. However, follow-up results were poor and were not verified by any means. Such findings suggest that it may be useful to attend to cognitive factors associated with decisions to quit smoking. In addition, there were some interesting differences between men's and women's responses to the various strategies, which may bear further investigation.

SUMMARY

High incidence rates and demonstrated health risks of both obesity and smoking have led behaviorally oriented clinicians to design treatment programs for weight reduction and smoking cessation to help those who have not been successful through their own efforts. In both cases, the focus of treatment is refraining from a behavior that is immediately gratifying but has long-term negative consequences. Both of these problem behaviors have usually become strong habits by the time treatment is sought. Because such habits are embedded in a person's working and socializing patterns, change is exceedingly difficult and may necessitate more general changes in lifestyle if new pattens are to be maintained. The contributions of physiological/biological factors related to weight loss and nicotine withdrawal have not been clearly assessed, but future developments in these areas may have implications for treatment.

Although many of the same behavioral interventions have been useful in both problem areas, there are important differences. The goal in one case is controlled eating, while in the other, it is total abstinence. Efforts to teach controlled smoking have had only temporary effects, and obviously, one cannot totally abstain from eating. This difference may account for the differential success of the various techniques. Aversive conditioning procedures have been extremely successful in initially producing abstinence from smoking and at least moderately successful at follow-up. Adding other techniques has not enhanced its effectiveness, at least at this time. On the other hand, comprehensive self-control programs emphasizing stimulus control and change in eating habits have been the most successful weight-reduction strategies. Aversive conditioning procedures were initially investigated, but were soon dropped as they contributed little and were temporary when used alone. Since weight loss is slow, most people do not reach goal weight by the end of a program, even though most will lose some weight (anywhere from five to sixty pounds). In the most effective programs, people do maintain their weight losses at follow-up, but there is little evidence of continued weight loss.

Behavioral interventions have shown considerable promise in both these problem areas, and their effects are significantly stronger than more traditional treatments. More effective methods are needed to maintain abstinence from smoking and to maintain continued weight loss until goal weight is achieved and then to maintain goal weight. Recent efforts to identify subtypes of clients within each group may make it possible to match clients and treatments. There appear to be many different reasons why clients smoke and/or eat excessively. As indicated in earlier chapters, the behavioral clinician always conducts a complete initial assessment, tailors the strategy to the client problem, and evaluates the effects of the strategy. The research presented in this chapter describes many strategies that have been successful, but the clinician must rely on his or her assessment to guide the choice of which strategy or group of strategies to employ.

CHAPTER 16

TREATMENT OF SEXUAL DYSFUNCTION

Bruce Richards Reed and Joseph LoPiccolo

State University of New York at Stony Brook

In 1954 William Masters began a systematic program of research on the physiology of human sexuality and five years later added to it an experimental sex-therapy program. Though many of the techniques he, Virginia Johnson, and their colleagues used had been described before (for example, Hastings, 1963; Semans, 1956; Wolpe, 1958), the publication of *Human Sexual Inadequacy* (1970), an account of their therapy and its results, was a landmark event. There followed an extraordinary increase of therapists specializing in treating sexual dysfunctions; most adopted Masters and Johnson-type techniques. Thus a new psychotherapeutic speciality, sex therapy, was created.

Nearly any therapeutic technique can be explained from a variety of theoretical perspectives. Systematic desensitization is a behavioral technique, and yet the dynamically inclined can argue that the reason it works is that it builds the client's powers of introspection and self-description. A behavioral counter might be that when insight therapy succeeds in reducing anxiety, it is because the therapist's interpretations have succeeded in having the client repeatedly imagine his or her fears in a graduated fashion while relaxed. That is, the insight therapist has *really* performed desensitization. Practitioners often use techniques from different theoretical schools,

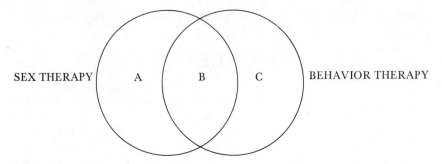

Figure 16.1   Relationship between sex therapy and behavioral treatment of sexual dysfunction.

though in doing so they may supply their own rationale and alter some procedural details.

Masters and Johnson described their therapy in rather atheoretical terms, and the new sex therapists who adopted and adapted their techniques represented a wide variety of theoretical bases. Although sex therapists share a core of techniques which can be characterized as cognitive-behavioral methods (Heiman, LoPiccolo, & LoPiccolo, 1979), sex therapy is not a subset of behavior therapy. First, most of the major techniques of sex therapy were not developed by self-designated behavioral psychologists. Second, although many techniques were developed in a research context, it would be inaccurate to state that they were derived from experimental psychology. Finally, there are some techniques and theoretical concepts commonly used by sex therapists that cannot be reasonably described as behavioral. At the same time, there are behavioral techniques for the treatment of sexual dysfunctions that are not commonly used by sex therapists. The relationship between sex therapy and the behavioral treatment of sexual dysfunctions can be diagrammatically expressed, as shown in Figure 16.1.

In this chapter, we will focus on what might be called behavioral sex-therapy techniques (B). Other behavioral methods, less consistently used in sex therapy (C) will be given less attention, and we will try to convey at least some sense of why and when clinicians "stray" into the nonbehavioral realm (A). Before discussing treatment, however, we will describe the sexual dysfunctions and offer a brief discussion of etiology.

THE SEXUAL DYSFUNCTIONS

This is not the context for an extended discussion of the issues involved in the classification of sexual dysfunctions (see Davison & Neale, 1978; Lo-

Piccolo & Hogan, 1978). However, it is important to at least be aware of the major issues, especially in reviewing a classification scheme that has so pervaded the media as to perhaps appear uncontroversial.

Classification schemes are neither true nor false; they are constructed, ideally for specific purposes, and hence need to be evaluated in terms of their utility. Any number of systems can be constructed using different combinations of the myriad variables associated with human behavior. All current nosologies of sexual dysfunctions are typologies, systems principally organized around present, overt aspects of sexual behavior (for example, latency to ejaculation, frequency of orgasm). Whether it is better to focus on these characteristics, the etiologies of these behaviors, or still other variables, is in large part an empirical question for which we have no answer. Perhaps there is no best system: different users, for instance, clinicians and researchers, may need different nosologies.

It is important to remember that concepts of sexual normality and dysfunction are culturally influenced. Our ideal of sexuality has changed rapidly through the last century, and with it have changed our ideas of dysfunctional sexuality (J. LoPiccolo & Heiman, 1978). Sex therapists now prescribe masturbation as a treatment, but 150 years ago U.S. physicians thought that masturbation led to insanity (LoPiccolo & Lobitz, 1972). Interestingly, in present day People's Republic of China, physicians hold that same view, and sex therapy is unheard of (Butterfield, 1980).

No single nosology currently dominates the field (LoPiccolo & Hogan, 1978). Different professionals use identical terms to refer to different behaviors, use different terms to refer to the same behaviors, disagree on which behaviors are dysfunctional, and even use identical terms to refer to identical behaviors. Thus, comparing reports from different groups can be difficult, and one should always pay careful attention to definitions when reading the literature.

Below is a simplified version of the diagnostic system now in use at the Sex Therapy Center at Stony Brook (Schover, Friedman, Weiler, Heiman, & LoPiccolo, 1980). It is presented as an illustration of a typology as well as a specific guide to the sexual dysfunctions.

In this system, the dysfunctions are organized into five categories. Three categories correspond to phases of the sexual-response cycle (the desire, arousal, and orgasm phases), and two are groupings of conceptually similar disorders not associated with any particular phase of the cycle. Each dysfunction is further classified according to its pattern of onset and degree of situational specificity. A dysfunction is classed as *lifelong* if it has always been present but as *not lifelong* if it was preceded by normal functioning. Situation-specific dysfunctions (that is, those present only with a specific form of stimulation or a particular partner) are termed *situational* while those present in all situations are termed *global*. It is critical to remember these two dimensions—lifelong versus not lifelong and situational versus global—while reviewing the dysfunctions. For example, a woman who has never experienced orgasm presents a very different clinical challenge than a woman who is orgasmic with masturbation but is no longer orgasmic with her husband.

Desire-phase dysfunctions include low sexual desire and aversion to sex and can be diagnosed for both males and females. "Low desire" is an absence or decline in one's desire for sexual activity, coupled with a low frequency of sexual activities (including masturbation). "Low frequency" is defined as less than once every two weeks, but a higher rate of sexual activity due to partner pressure would not rule out this diagnosis. Although this criterion may be controversial, the diagnosis is often obvious. For example, it is not uncommon for a client to desire sex once a year or less. Low sexual desire is an increasingly frequent diagnosis. "Aversion to sex" covers those cases in which sexual activity elicits strong negative emotional reactions, such as fear, anxiety, shame, or guilt. Aversion to sex by definition includes low sexual desire and is differentiated from low sexual desire alone by the presence of an active aversion as opposed to a lack of positive interest.

The *arousal-phase dysfunctions* are erectile failure and impaired female physiological arousal. *Erectile failure* is diagnosed when a male frequently fails to achieve an erection of sufficient rigidity for intercourse and/or loses his erections before ejaculation can occur. Pleasure and psychological arousal may or may not be impaired, and as previously noted, the dysfunction can be current or lifelong and situational or global. Some practitioners still use the term *impotence* to refer to these disorders. Impotence is a poor term for several reasons, one being that it is imprecise, having been used to refer to virtually every type of male sexual dysfunction. Also, inasmuch as impotence connotes the inability to father children, it may be incorrect, since men can ejaculate without an erection. Finally, the word has highly negative, unfounded connotations regarding the male's personality and general competence. Erectile failure is a common sexual problem.

Frigidity has been used in an analogous way to refer to female sexual dysfunctions. It too is an unfortunate term. It is no more precise, appropriate, or kind than is impotence and hence is best not used. One dysfunction once labeled frigidity is "impaired female physiological arousal," a disorder analogous to male erectile failure. This dysfunction is characterized by difficulty in achieving or maintaining physiological states, such as genital vasocongestion and vaginal lubrication, which normally accompany sexual stimulation. This lack of physiological arousal may or may not be accompanied by reduced pleasure and psychological arousal. The relative frequency of impaired female physiological arousal is hard to estimate since it has not often been distinguished from other disorders.

Next are the *orgasm-phase dysfunctions*. The female dysfunctions in this group involve either the total absence of orgasmic response (anorgasmia) or orgasmic response that is confined to some limited form of stimulation (for example, vibrator, self-stimulation, or noncoital partner stimulation). Some argue that the failure to attain orgasm in coitus should not be labeled dysfunctional if the woman is orgasmic with other types of partner stimulation. We list *infrequent coital orgasms* as a dysfunction because some couples find this situation quite distressing. We do not imply that the ability to have orgasms in coitus without manual stimulation is a criterion of sexual health.

Latency to ejaculation is the key variable defining the major male dysfunctions of the orgasm phase. Latencies too brief characterize *premature ejaculation*. How to operationally define *too brief* is a perennial problem. The normative data on ejaculatory latency is only suggestive rather than definitive because different investigators report widely varying figures (Hunt, 1974; Kinsey, Pomeroy, & Martin, 1948). Masters and Johnson (1970) skirt the question by proposing that the ejaculatory latency is too short if the woman fails to climax at least half the time. Though creative, this proposal confuses the issue by confounding the diagnosis of premature ejaculation with the female's capacity to reach orgasm rapidly. It should be noted that a substantial proportion of women regularly experience coital orgasm with a coital duration of under one minute (Gebhard, 1966). We decided, somewhat arbitrarily, that latencies consistently less than three-minutes duration are usually dysfunctional and that latencies between three and seven minutes can be considered dysfunctional if the clients are dissatisfied with his degree of ejaculatory control. Recognizing premature ejaculation is not always as hard as defining it: some clients usually ejaculate before entering the vagina and latencies of less than thirty seconds are not uncommon.

When the ejaculatory latency is unusually long or ejaculation is absent despite adequate sexual stimulation, the condition is referred to as *ejaculatory incompetence* or *retarded ejaculation*. Typically, these males ejaculate with normal latency with masturbation but not at all during intercourse (situational retardation), though the inability to ejaculate can be absolute (global retardation). In contrast to the female orgasmic problems and premature ejaculation, retarded ejaculation is rarely seen clinically.

The fourth category of disorders is those involving *coital pain*. *Dyspareunia* is diagnosed when either the male or the female experiences pain during intercourse. It is a broad term, covering pain of all types and sources other than those distinguished below. *Vaginismus* is diagnosed when involuntary contractions of the outer third of the vagina prevent penile penetration. Though it is not intrinsically painful, pain usually results if attempts at intercourse are pursued. Pain on or after ejaculation that is not necessarily confined to intercourse is another dysfunction in this group.

The last category is comprised of two conditions which, strictly speaking, are not dysfunctions. *Frequency dissatisfaction* is diagnosed when either partner feels that his or her level of sexual activity is significantly higher or lower than he or she desires.

Thus far, nothing has been said about the frequency of sexual dysfunctions in the general population. In point of fact, there are no data that enable reasonable estimates of the incidence or prevalance of particular dysfunctions to be made. As a group though, sexual dysfunctions seem to be quite common. In a survey of one hundred, mainly white, high socioeconomic status (SES), happily married couples—couples one might expect to be functioning well sexually—Frank, Anderson, and Rubinstein (1978) found 63 percent of the females and 40 percent of the males reported having recently experienced sexual problems. Transient episodes of sexual dysfunction are probably almost universal among those who are sexually active. That is, ejaculating too quickly, failing to get an erection, not having an orgasm, and infrequently desiring sex are things most people experience occasionally. Obviously, not everyone needs treatment. Although the question of who should seek therapy and when is not simple, a reasonable rule is that evaluation for sex therapy is warranted when the dysfunction is persistent, distressing, and refractory to the individual's own remedial efforts.

THE ASSESSMENT OF SEXUAL DYSFUNCTION

The goals of clinical assessment are to gain a detailed description of the problem and to identify the factors contributing to its existence with the purpose of formulating a treatment plan. Every case is a potential morass of facts. Which of all the features of any situation are to be selected as meaningfully describing the problem? Which of the endless number of hypothesizable causal factors are to be explored? Clinicians must have some conceptual bases for guiding their searches. One such basis is the therapist's theoretical model of psychological problems. A behavioral model directs one to describe the problem and its determinants differently than does the psychodynamic model or a systems model. A second basis is empirical results. If research demonstrates the significance of a descriptive feature or causal factor, then the clinician should assess these variables. A third basis for guiding the assessment is clinical lore—the educated guesses of therapists. Individually and as a group, therapists hold ideas about what to assess which are neither deduced from theory nor supported by research. These are ideas based in clinical experience and observations of which factors appear to have been significant or helpful in past cases. Clinicians have been repeatedly warned of the perils of using these impressions, but where data are sparse and theory lacking, clinical lore has great influence. Such is the case with sexual dysfunctions.

Areas for Assessment

The nosology presented above guides assessment by indicating many of the parameters thought to be important in describing sexual dysfunctions. Below we review those parameters which are assessed because therapists believe they are common causal factors. No attempt will be made to detail the basis for the assumption that these factors are causal, except to note that most are based largely in clinical experience.

One current controversy concerns the relative contribution of physiological and psychological factors in the etiology of sexual dysfunction. We believe that the two sets of factors are interdependent and each can influence the other. Further, it seems that dysfunctions are caused by multiple variables interacting in complex ways (Hogan, 1978; Kaplan, 1974). Hence, the question of whether a dysfunction is organic *or* psychogenic is an inappropriate one, and we group factors under physiological and psychological headings for heuristic purposes only.

Behavioral discussions of etiology stress the distinction between the historical variables that initiated the dysfunction and those variables that currently maintain it, a distinction that Masters and Johnson's (1970) well-known model includes. However, in that model, most factors can function only as historical variables, and only "performance anxiety" and "spectatoring" serve as maintaining variables. Many clinicians disagree with that formulation, however. The assumption here is that any of the variables described in the following sections can act in either role.

PHYSIOLOGICAL FACTORS

Physiological and anatomical factors can produce or contribute to any of the sexual dysfunctions. What follows is a list of the major types of such factors and some illustrative examples. For a comprehensive review, consult Kaplan (1974).

Anatomical Defects   Normal sexual functioning relies on the major genital structures being intact. If, through defective development or trauma, these structures are absent or damaged, sexual functioning can be impaired. For instance, occasionally a child is born with external female genitalia but no vagina. A more common problem is dyspareunia due to scarring as a result of giving birth.

Circulatory System Problems   Dysfunctions can result from an insufficient supply of blood to the genitals. This is most often seen in cases of erectile failure and is often a result of diabetes or arteriosclerotic disease.

Nervous System Defects   Injury or disease of either the central or peripheral nervous system can influence sexual response. For instance, spinal cord injuries can (but do not necessarily) impair erectile, ejaculatory, and orgasmic capacity (Higgins, 1978). Diabetes frequently produces neuropathy and may inhibit sexual response (Ellenberg, 1971).

Hormone Levels   Sexual functioning is not linked to sex hormone levels in any simple way, but levels outside of a broad normal range do seem to impair sexual response. Occasionally, for example, a tumor will reduce male sexual functioning by causing excessive amounts of female sex hormones to be produced.

Nonspecific Effects of Disease   One's sexual interest and responsivity may decline any time one is weakened, fatigued, or in pain. Therefore, nearly any illness can interfere with sexual functioning (Kaplan, 1974).

Drugs   A wide variety of drugs are known or suspected causes of sexual dysfunctions (Segraves, 1977). To mention only a few: many antihypertensive medications cause erectile failure, antiadrenergic drugs can stop ejaculation, and CNS depressants (alcohol, barbiturates) immediately reduce arousability and responsivitiy and eventually reduce sex drive (Kaplan, 1974).

It is important to note that although physical variables *can* contribute to sexual dysfunctions, the frequency with which they actually do so is not known. As a rule, the effects of these variables are unpredictable. Drug effects vary considerably from person to person, the same disease can have different sequelae, and very similar injuries or deficits may be associated with quite different sexual capacities. The discovery of physical problems does not, of course, eliminate the possibility that other factors are influential.

PSYCHOLOGICAL FACTORS

Again, no attempt at being comprehensive will be made; rather, major types of variables will be listed and illustrated.

Affective States   Anxiety is the most frequently cited psychological cause of sexual dysfunction (Heiman, LoPiccolo, & LoPiccolo, 1979). It is thought that anxiety can inhibit sexual responding whether it is elicited by the sexual stimuli or by stimuli distant from the sexual situation. Fear, a closely related construct, is also frequently identified as a cause of dysfunction. Fear of failure to perform sexually and fear of being physically or psychologically hurt by sexual activity are thought to be especially important. Most people probably find anger incompatible with sexual activity. One of the generally recognized effects of depression is diminished sexual interest and responsivity.

Evaluative Beliefs   Several types of cognitions affect sexual functioning. One of the most important types is evaluative beliefs—attitudes and other value-expressing thoughts. One such set of beliefs is those regarding the propriety and consequences of sexual activity. Sexual functioning may be compromised if one believes that it is wrong, bad, dirty, or immoral. Ideas that sexual activity will make one a bad person or be physically harmful may also be inhibiting. Another important set of evaluative beliefs is those a client has regarding his or her partner(s). Examples of such harmful cognitions include "she's ugly," "I can't trust him," and "I want to marry a good woman, and good women don't like sex."

Knowledge Deficits   Another example of how cognitions affect sex is that ignorance of sexual physiology, functioning, and technique may impair sexual performance. For instance, an older man may experience erectile failure because neither partner knows that older men tend to need more direct genital stimulation to be aroused. Even if their general sexual knowledge is adequate, a couple may face sexual problems if either is ignorant of the other's sexual preferences. In such a case, knowing the reason for the ignorance is important. It may result from fears of being sexually aroused or from beliefs about the partner's trustworthiness or intentions. Or it may be that the couple cannot communicate effectively.

Skills Deficits   When considered closely, it is difficult to tell whether skills deficits are really knowledge or motivational deficits, or vice versa. We include the category to stress the importance of the clients' overt behavior. Regardless of attitude or knowledge, a couple must *do* certain things to function well sexually. Poor communication skills are frequently cited as contributing to sexual dysfunction. Inadequate communication may affect sexual functioning directly if the partners are incapable of telling each other what excites them. It may indirectly affect sexual functioning by creating marital discord. Marital discord is associated with many of the negative affective states and harmful beliefs mentioned above. Another area where skills deficits are damaging is that of sexual technique. To extend the example from above: knowing that the older male needs direct genital stimulation may not help if the woman is sexually unskilled.

To summarize, the implications of current thinking regarding etiology are that physiologic and anatomical factors should be assessed in every case. The client's affective state needs to be explored as does the influence of his or her belief system. Sexual knowledge, sexual technique, and communication skills should be assessed. Because of its wide-ranging influence, the quality of the couple's relationship merits close examination. And of course, a detailed description of the couple's current behavior must be obtained.

Methods of Assessment

SEX HISTORY INTERVIEWS

The therapist's basic source of information is usually the sex-history interview. *History* is a bit of a misnomer since current behavior and events are usually inquired about as well. Typically, these interviews are long (two to eight hours), semistructured, and conducted with each member of the couple separately by a therapist of the same sex (cf. Hartman & Fithian, 1972; L. LoPiccolo & Heiman, 1978; Masters & Johnson, 1970). The drawbacks of interview data are substantial (see Linehan, 1977); however, there is no good alternative. Sex therapists are handicapped in this respect, for the best alternative to the interview, namely direct observation, is an extremely problematic way to assess sexual behavior. Some therapists think otherwise. For example, Serber (1974) argues for observing clients' sexual behavior by video-taping it, and Hartman & Fithian (1972) use a "sexological exam," a quasi-medical exam in which the therapist sexually stimulates the client to test for and demonstrate sexual responses. The major arguments against these practices are, first, that direct observation may be an unusually reactive assessment method because of the highly emotional and private nature of sex. Second, many couples probably would refuse to be observed. Finally, the potential for therapists to exploit direct observation is obvious (LoPiccolo, 1977b). Both the American Psychological Association and the American Association of Sex Education, Counselors and Therapists (AASECT) officially consider sexual contact between therapist and client to be unethical.

SELF-REPORT INVENTORIES

Using self-report inventories is the main alternative to the interview. They do not present any unusual ethical problems but are of limited utility. The best of them, the Sexual Interaction Inventory (LoPiccolo & Steger, 1974) and the Sexual Arousal Inventory (Hoon, Hoon, & Wincze, 1976), provide detailed description and useful summary statistics on the couples' current behavior. Both are limited in scope though (the SAI is for females only) and are best used adjunctively with interviews.

Setting Goals

Selecting a treatment strategy depends not only on the initial assessment (what is the problem and its determinants) but on the goals of therapy. It is hard to know how to proceed unless you know both where you are and where you want to be. Clients propose a basic goal merely by requesting sex therapy: they would like to be more satisfied with their sex life. By accepting them for therapy, the therapist acknowledges that that will be one of the goals of treatment. However, the way in which that goal will be met always needs to be clarified. When someone is dissatisfied, there is a discrepancy between what they think should be happening and what they perceive to be happening. So, to increase their satisfaction, one can either change what is happening, change their perception of what is happening, or change their ideas of what should happen.

The most common choice is to attempt to increase sexual satisfaction by improving sexual functioning. For instance, if premature ejaculation is dissatisfying, then the goal of therapy would likely be to increase the latency to ejaculation. On occasion, however, it is more appropriate to change the couples' ideas of what ought to happen. One such occasion is when expectations are unrealistic. If a couple is distressed because the female does not consistently experience orgasm during intercourse without manual stimulation, the goal of therapy might be to convince the couple that her sexual functioning is normal and healthy and that to expect coital orgasm every time is unrealistic. Another instance when beliefs rather than behaviors are targeted for change is when functional changes are impossible. A diabetic who has lost his erectile capacity may still be accepted for sex therapy with the proviso that one aim of therapy would be to change his concept of good sex. Changing the clients' perception of their sexual activity is more often a goal late in therapy after changes start to occur, since behaviors often change faster than the cognitions they support.

It is important to realize that nonsexual behaviors are often the targets of change in sex therapy. Marital issues and communication practices often affect sexual behavior; hence they may be worked on in therapy. Treatment of individual problems, such as depression or lack of assertiveness, may also be goals of sex therapy.

TREATMENT

Sex therapists use the same core procedures in most cases. Added to this base are some techniques that are routine but specific to the particular dysfunction, and others that vary case by case according to the therapist and clients participating in therapy.

Core Procedures

The first sessions of sex therapy are quite structured. The therapist is active and directive and expressly controls the types of sexual activities the couple may engage in through restriction and by giving them "homework assignments" (exercises to be done at home). For instance, a routine first step is for the therapist to forbid the couple to attempt sexual intercourse. As therapy proceeds, the therapist becomes more passive, shifting control to the clients. The emphasis on homework continues throughout therapy, but by the end, the clients are generally giving themselves the assignments and are free to do whatever they enjoy.

Several of the early assignments given by the therapist are likely to be *sensate-focus* exercises. Sensate focus (Masters & Johnson, 1970) consists of a graded series of massage-like exercises. The couple is told to spend about an hour undressed, taking turns touching each other in ways the partner enjoys. While doing the touching, the task is to give physical pleasure to the other. While being touched, the task is to concentrate on the sensations and, without reciprocating, communicate to the other what feels best. Genital touching is forbidden at first, allowed later on, and finally assigned as homework. The emphasis throughout is on sensual rather than merely sexual pleasure. Clients are encouraged to drop their sexual-achievement orientation and to physically explore each other.

The sensate-focus exercises are a good example of a therapeutic technique that can be explained from a variety of perspectives. It can be considered an instance of in vivo desensitization, or it can be seen as a sexual-skills-training exercise or as a communications-training exercise. Regardless of the rationale, sensate-focus exercises are basic to sex therapy.

Dysfunction-Specific Techniques

As the couple continues with the sensate-focus exercises, techniques specific to the dysfunction are introduced and eventually integrated with them. For ease of presentation, we will group the treatments according to whether they are for male-centered, female-centered, or other dysfunctions. We use the qualifier *centered* to stress that the nonsymptomatic member of the couple often plays an important role in maintaining the dysfunction.

MALE-CENTERED DYSFUNCTIONS

Premature Ejaculation   The major technique used in the treatment of premature ejaculation is to first stimulate the male until he is on the verge of ejaculating. The stimulation is then interrupted until his level of arousal subsides, and then stimulation is resumed. This sequence is repeated a number of times before ejaculation is allowed (Semans, 1956). The interruption of sexual stimulation can be done in different ways. The pause technique simply involves stopping direct stimulation of the penis. The squeeze technique involves manually squeezing the penis either immediately below the glans or at its base. We do not know which technique works best for whom, so current practice is to teach the couple both and have them use whichever is most effective. Couples using the squeeze technique need to be warned to release the penis should ejaculation begin. If ejaculation occurs with the squeeze applied, it is possible to rupture the seminal vesicles. There is a sequence to the types of sexual stimulation used in this procedure. Masturbation is used first, then manual and oral stimulation by the partner, then intercourse in stages beginning with motionless vaginal containment of the penis. These exercises are practiced over several weeks with the goals of increasing the amount of stimulation and reducing the number and duration of the interruptions. In contrast to some "home remedies" for premature ejaculation, the emphasis is on attending to the sensations and on making sex maximally pleasurable. Rather than fading out these exercises altogether, many couples incorporate some variation of them into their sexual routine after active therapy ends.

Erectile Failure   There is no circumscribed set of techniques used in the treatment of erectile failure. Rather, treatment varies widely according to the etiology. In general, the aims of treatment are to reduce anxiety and to provide the male with adequate sexual stimulation. Obviously, the sensate-focus exercises contribute toward those ends. One common addition is the "tease technique" (Masters & Johnson, 1970) in which stimulation is stopped when an erection occurs and resumed only after the erection is gone. Presumably, this reduces anxiety about losing erections and demonstrates to both partners that an erection can be regained if lost. Another technique to reduce performance anxiety is to have the couple begin inter-course with the woman stuffing the flaccid penis into her vagina. The therapist may try to improve the couple's sexual technique through discus-sions, readings, films, and by encouraging the couple to use more and dif-ferent types of foreplay.

Couples often assume that erectile failure is the result of low arousal or desire, and that low arousal and desire reflect a lack of affection for the partner. The failure to get an erection is then interpreted as more than a sexual problem. Once made, this interpretation can be self-validating, as each member responds in hurtful ways to what he or she perceives (cor-rectly or incorrectly) as hostile acts by the other. Even without such infer-ences, erectile failure obviously can be a very frustrating dysfunction for the woman. Her demands for sexual performance and the anger that may result usually only make matters worse. Couples often have interactional patterns which seem to maintain the problem, whether or not they con-tributed to its emergence. The erectile failure is then essentially a rela-tionship problem and is attacked in a variety of ways, just as are other sorts of destructive interactions (see Chapter 19 for a discussion of marital therapy).

Retarded Ejaculation   The treatment of retarded ejaculation is similar to that of erectile failure, inasmuch as the couple is instructed in effective techniques of sexual stimulation and efforts are made to reduce anxiety about sexual performance. In addition to instructing the woman in sexual techniques and the man in how to communicate his desires to her, the man is taught ways of psychologically arousing himself and of physically triggering orgasm. As in the treatment of premature ejaculation, different types of stimulation are used sequentially. First, the man is taught to ejac-ulate with self-stimulation, then with non coital partner stimulation, and then with various degrees of coital stimulation.

FEMALE-CENTERED DYSFUNCTIONS

Orgasmic Dysfunction   The distinction between orgasmic problems that are lifelong and global and those that are not lifelong or situational is quite im-portant when it comes to treatment. For women who have never had an orgasm, treatment is relatively uniform and straightforward. One ap-proach is to begin with a program of masturbation training (Heiman, LoPiccolo, & LoPiccolo, 1976; LoPiccolo & Lobitz, 1972). Over several weeks, the woman performs a series of exercises designed to teach her how to stimulate herself to orgasm. She begins by becoming comfortable looking at and touching her genitals, then does touching for pleasure and touching for sexual arousal. She is encouraged to try different types of physical stimulation, including electric vibrators, and different types of psychological stimulation, including erotica and fantasy. She is taught to physically trigger orgasm when she is highly aroused (for example, by tensing muscles).

Along with the masturbation program, the woman is asked to do the Kegel exercises (Kegel, 1952). The Kegel exercises are designed to strengthen the pubococcygeus muscle, which encircles the bladder and part of the vagina. It is thought that a well-toned pubococcygeus increases a woman's orgasmic capacity.

Once the woman has orgasms with masturbation, the task becomes one of generalizing that response to partner stimulation. To do this, she is asked to show or tell her partner what feels best in a variety of sexual activities, including intercourse. Couples are discouraged from setting as their goal coital orgasms without manual stimulation. Some therapists do not use the masturbation program but instead use a graded series of activities involving both members of the couple from the start (for example, Masters & Johnson, 1970). These two approaches seem roughly equal in their overall effectiveness.

The man has a more important role in the treatment of orgasmic dysfunction than the description so far implies. Even during the masturbation portion of the program, his reaction (approval, disgust) to her masturbation and to the prospect of change (is he afraid that he will not be able to satisfy an orgasmic woman?) can greatly influence her progress. His importance is obvious in the portion of treatment that involves her communication of and his response to her desires.

Selecting the treatment is not as routine when the presenting problem is current, or situational orgasmic dysfunction. As with erectile failure, this dysfunction often seems to be entwined in the larger interactional patterns of the couple. Treatment techniques are quite varied, and there is no standard approach that is uniformly used. If the woman is orgasmic only within a narrow range of stimulation (for example, thigh-pressure masturbation), a modified version of the masturbation program described above may be used. If, however, the woman is orgasmic with varied sorts of stimulation, or with other partners, or was once orgasmic with this partner, treatment will focus on the couple's interaction. The sensate-focus exercises may help to reduce performance demands and sexual anxiety, and teach the couple better ways of communicating and more effective sexual technique. In addition, the couple's response to the assignments can reveal, and provide a vehicle for working on, relationship problems which may be interfering with their sexual pleasure. Some of the more common problem areas are the expression of affection, the division of tasks, and the exercise of control.

Vaginismus   Vaginismus is treated by physically dilating the vagina gradually over a number of sessions. There are graduated dilators which are designed especially for this purpose, but fingers can be used just as well. Sometimes the procedure is begun at the gynecologist's office, and sometimes it is done entirely at home. Although the procedure itself is simple and fast, the change it effects in a couple's sexual life is drastic, and the couple often needs help adjusting. Months or years of unsuccessful attempts at intercourse can teach the couple that sex is an anxiety-ridden, frustrating, and painful experience. Given such a history, it takes more than the penis in the vagina to transform sex into a truly intimate, loving act.

OTHER DYSFUNCTIONS

Low sexual desire, aversion to sex, and discrepancies between desired and actual frequency of sexual activity can be grouped together for purposes of discussion. None of these dysfunctions have well-developed, specific treatment techniques. They often accompany other dysfunctions, such as erectile failure or anorgasmia, and the specific treatments for those dysfunctions may serve as the outline for therapy. Frequently they appear to be maintained as functional parts of larger patterns of interactions between the couple. Thus, treatment may borrow heavily from marital therapy. The general techniques of sex therapy remain useful for enhancing the couple's sexual pleasure and reducing anxiety and inhibition, and may be the main intervention.

Additional Techniques

Even in treating the dysfunctions for which there are specific, well-developed techniques, sex therapy varies from case to case. Sexual behavior is controlled by the same diverse factors that control other behaviors. Not surprisingly then, sexual dysfunctions are treated by the same diverse techniques found useful in the treatment of other problems. Which techniques are used in any given case depends on the persuasions of the therapist and the characteristics of the clients. Every client presents a unique pattern of dysfunctional behaviors and etiological factors, and sex therapists come from many different schools of thought. The techniques of sex therapists most often are behavioral, are sometimes drawn from the other schools of therapy, and are sometimes medical procedures.

Behavioral Techniques

Nearly all of the major behavioral techniques are used in treating sexual dysfunctions. Perhaps the most frequently used are those we will term *direct-anxiety-reduction techniques*—those reducing anxiety by means other than changing mediating cognitions or behaviors. Of these, the most common procedures are various forms of desensitization. It was noted earlier that some consider the sensate-focus exercises to be a form of in vivo desensitization. Specifically targeted in vivo hierarchies may be used, for example, to treat fears of semen or of vaginal containment. Imaginal desensitization has been used to treat many different sexual fears and anxieties. Other variants used include video desensitization (the distressing images are visually presented) and desensitization with relaxation induced via fast-acting barbiturates. The efficacy of desensitization as a treatment for all types of sexual dysfunction has been demonstrated in experimental as well as case studies (Hogan, 1978). However, the literature also suggests that the effects of desensitization may be confined to anxiety reduction.

Guided imagery, flooding, and implosion are three closely related anxiety-reduction techniques which have been reported as effective in case studies (Frankel, 1970; Wolpin, 1969). Guided imagery involves having the client imagine a continuously evolving scene instead of a hierarchy of discrete scenes. Flooding varies the desensitization paradigm by having the client retain the distressing image even after anxiety is evoked until the anxiety is extinguished. Implosion does the same thing by presenting the client with evolving images often incorporating psychodynamic themes.

A second major group of adjunctive behavioral techniques are those we will term *cognitive-change techniques.* Some of these are intended to change attitudes and personal beliefs which interfere with sexual enjoyment by producing anxiety, guilt, or by stopping the client from engaging in sexual activities. Rational restructuring, the name for such procedures, is essentially persuasion and can be done in many ways. One of the best-developed systems is Ellis's (1971) rational emotive therapy (RET). Ellis has identified sets of what he thinks are common, irrational beliefs about interpersonal relationships and sex, such as "I am a completely worthless person if everyone does not agree with me all of the time." He proposes that these beliefs can be changed and their emotional sequelae relieved through repeated, forceful verbal confrontation.

Other cognitive techniques give clients strategies for coping with problems. One way of coping with a problem is to solve it, and training in problem-solving strategies are a frequent part of therapy. For instance, a couple's sexual relationship may suffer because of mutual hostility produced by their repeated failures to satisfactorily divide household responsibilities. Such a couple might be taught to define the problem, brainstorm for solution, assess and select a solution, implement it, and assess the result in a manner after that proposed by D'Zurilla and Goldfried (1971). Another coping strategy is to anticipate the situation and plan out one's actions. Therefore, some clients are taught to cognitively rehearse situations. Preselected self-statements are another coping aid. For example, teaching a male to think "She still respects me even when I don't get an erection" at times when he fails to get an erection can help to break the vicious cycle of failure, negative consequence, anxiety, and failure.

Relabeling is a useful technique. For instance, a woman having problems reaching orgasm might be incorrectly labeling the sensations that accompany sexual stimulation as distress-produced tension. Knowing that they are actually sexual feelings might help her to become even further aroused. Couples often make harmful causal attributions for each other's behavior. For example, if a man believes that his anorgasmic wife would be orgasmic if she loved him, she may feel under such pressure to perform sexually that it is impossible for her to do so. If, on the other hand, he is persuaded that her anorgasmia results from performance anxiety stemming from an intense desire to please him (because she loves him), the consequences of her failure to climax may be quite different.

Finally, there are cognitive techniques intended to change the client's knowledge of sex (educational techniques). To this end, the therapist may use discussion, assigned readings, charts, models, and films LoPiccolo, 1977a; Mikulus & Lowe, 1974).

A third major group of behavioral techniques includes those that involve *modeling*. The therapist inevitably is a model for the clients. Throughout therapy, he or she demonstrates a way of talking about sex, an attitude toward sex, a way of discussing problems, and a way of solving problems. If there is a cotherapist, the pair model features of a heterosexual relationship. Therapists may use modeling systematically to teach communication skills. Within the bounds of professional ethics, they may also demonstrate some sexual techniques. For instance, the squeeze used in treating premature ejaculation can be taught using plastic models. Films and video tapes are useful for illustrating sexual techniques, showing relaxation in sexual situations and modeling taking pleasure in sex.

Our final set of behavioral techniques is *direct-behavior-change techniques*. This consists mainly of operant techniques which are used by therapists to get clients to change and are taught to clients so that they can help themselves change. Therapists often give directives or advice based on operant principles (for example, "When he does X which you like, do Y which he likes"). The intentional use of reinforcement can increase the likelihood that advice will be followed, as for example, when the clients are praised for doing their homework or acting differently. Some therapists use a formal-contingency structure, such as requiring a monetary deposit which is returned only if homework is done (Lobitz & LoPiccolo, 1972), as a way of influencing client behavior. A plainly operant intervention is the behavioral-exchange contract (see Chapter 19). In which specific consequences follow targeted behaviors of each member of the couple. Sometimes clients are taught the principles of reinforcement, extinction, and punishment so that they can better control their own lives. (Incidentally, note that these principles can be used to relabel behavior patterns. "She's ignoring me because she's mean" invites retaliation, but "She's ignoring me because I extinguish her attentive behavior" suggests change).

Skills training is another direct-behavior-change intervention. Several specific procedures for skills training have been proposed. In general, they involve specifying the desired behavior, modeling it, rehearsing or role-playing it, and shaping it with feedback from the partner or the therapist. Sexual technique, communication skills, and assertion are three skills commonly taught in the course of sex therapy (Lobitz & LoPiccolo, 1972; LoPiccolo, 1977a; Masters & Johnson, 1970; Wolpe & Lazarus, 1966).

Nonbehavioral Techniques

Most practicing therapists describe themselves as eclectically oriented (choosing their ideas and techniques from a variety of theoretical schools), and there is no reason to think sex therapists are an exception. "Eclectically oriented" is, of course, a motley category, so there is tremendous variety in the ideas sex therapists bring to therapy. Although the field is dominated by behavior therapy, other schools, including the psychodynamic (Kaplan, 1974), general-systems theory (Steinglass, 1978), gestalt, and humanistic/existential (Lobitz et al., 1974), have contributed important concepts and techniques to sex therapy (for integration, see Heiman, Lo-Piccolo, & LoPiccolo, 1979; Hogan, 1978). Since this text presumes no background in those orientations, it is impractical to review their contribution here. To briefly note a few: behavior may be usefully relabeled using psychodynamic or systems concepts; gestalt therapy has contributed sensory-awareness exercises; the psychodynamic concept of defense mechanisms is often useful in assessing and predicting client behavior as are psychodynamic concepts of resistance; systems-theory concepts often prove useful in understanding couple's interactional patterns, and many communications concepts and interventions come from systems theorists.

Medical Techniques

The medical treatments we will consider are of two types, surgical and pharmacological. The most common surgical treatments of sexual dysfunction are those for erectile failure. These operations can be separated

into two groups: implant procedures and circulation-improving procedures. Implant procedures involve placing a prosthesis in the penis which
makes the penis sufficiently rigid for intercourse. The prostheses are of
two types. One is a permanently implanted semirigid plastic rod and the
other is an inflatable device which the man fills using a small permanently
implanted pump. Neither device restores true erection, or improves sensation, or arousal or ejaculatory ability. In addition, the usual dangers of
implant surgery (infection, expulsion, displacement) are present. In contrast, circulation-improving procedures may, in some cases, restore normal erectile functioning. Initial case studies show that an artery-transplant
procedure (Britt, Kemmerer, & Robison, 1971) and an operation facilitating venous outflow (Wagner & Ebbehej, 1978) are promising. At best,
these will benefit only certain men, and more outcome studies are needed
to assess their potential.

Less common and more questionable are surgical procedures designed
to improve female orgasmic capacity. One such operation is the freeing of
"adhesions" between the clitoral shaft and hood. Since it has been proposed that coital orgasm results from stimulation of the clitoral shaft by
the clitoral hood (Masters & Johnson, 1966), the operation seems conceptually sound. However, its logic has been undermined by recent work
questioning the relationship of these (possibly common) adhesions to
orgasmic capacity (Graber & Kline-Graber, 1979). Outcome data for the
operation have not been reported. Vaginal reconstruction surgery, in
which the angle of the vagina is changed and the clitoris repositioned so
that it is directly stimulated by the penis during intercourse (Burt & Burt,
1975) also lacks outcome data. This operation changes the muscular support system of the pelvis and may cause urinary incontinence and complications in childbearing.

Many drugs have been tried as treatments for various sexual dysfunctions, and a few do seem to be useful. For example, exogenous testosterone may help in cases of male low desire or erectile failure *if* endogenous levels are grossly low. It does not appear useful where
testosterone levels are within normal limits. Though testosterone is effective in increasing female sexual interest and responsivity, its use is contraindicated because of strong masculinizing side effects. Estrogen creams
are often effective in treating dyspareunia resulting from vaginal dryness in
postmenopausal women. However, their use is controversial: present indications are that their use increases the risk of cancer for some women but
may also lower the risk of cardiovascular disease.

No drug has been demonstrated to increase sexual desire in healthy people. There are some, though, that are reported to increase subjective sexual
pleasure. Most are illegal, and some are very dangerous, ruling them out
as routine treatments. Alcohol is a possible exception. Alcohol can reduce

anxiety and inhibitions. That, along with the effects of our expectations regarding its effects (Wilson & Lawson, 1976; 1978), may combine to enhance sexual pleasure. Physiological arousal, though, seems to be impaired by alcohol (Wilson, 1977). Alcohol abuse may irreversibly alter secondary sex characteristics and diminish sexual desire and capacity.

When drugs cause sexual dysfunction, an obvious treatment is to switch the medication hoping to lose the undesired side effects. Sometimes the side effects are the desired outcome of treatment. For instance, delaying ejaculation is the goal in treating premature ejaculation and is a side effect of some major tranquilizers. However, the main effects of such drugs (for example, sedation) are so severe that their use in treating sexual dysfunction alone is precluded.

There is some evidence that tranquilizers, including alcohol (Brady, 1966; Dengrove, 1971; Kraft, 1969a, 1969b), can be useful adjuncts in the treatment of erectile failure or orgasmic dysfunction associated with severe anxiety. Another sometimes effective use of drugs is that of antidepressants in the treatment of low sex drive associated with severe depression.

MODES OF THERAPY

In Masters and Johnson's (1970) highly influential treatment program, male-female therapy teams conduct conjoint therapy (see both members of the couple in each session) every day for two weeks. The obvious drawbacks of this system—namely, the expense of two therapists, the problem of treating clients without partners, and the inconvenience of two weeks of intensive therapy—have made particularly salient questions regarding the optimal format of therapy. One question is whether two therapists are better than one. Despite some very sensible reasons why this might be the case, comparative studies (Mathews et al., 1976) have failed to demonstrate the superiority of mixed-sex therapy teams. There are many reports of successful treatment by lone therapists (Kaplan, 1974). Dysfunctions for which there are well-defined treatment programs may respond well to written self-help programs involving little or no therapist contact (Heiman, LoPiccolo, & LoPiccolo, 1976; Lowe & Mikulus, 1975).

Another question is whether conjoint therapy is necessary. We know that a variety of procedures can be effective with individual clients (Barbach, 1974; Ellis, 1971; Husted, 1972; Kockott, Dittmar, & Nusselt, 1975). Therefore, a partner need not always be involved in therapy. However, we do not know what the optimal therapy unit is. There is some evidence that conjoint may be superior to individual therapy (Cooper, 1969; Prochaska & Marzilli, 1973). This may be especially true when relationship issues are important, since a consistent finding in the marital-therapy literature is that conjoint formats are superior to individual formats (Gurman & Kniskern, 1979). Group therapy has been used to treat erectile failure (Lazarus, 1968), premature ejaculation (Kaplan et al., 1974), and lifelong global orgasmic dysfunction (Schneidman & McGuire, 1976) with encouraging results. We do not know how group therapy compares in effectiveness with individual and conjoint therapy.

Another question of format is what is the optimum number and rate of sessions? There is no evidence to suggest that open-ended therapy is superior to time-limited therapy. Most sex therapy is time limited, using a fixed number of sessions ranging from ten to twenty in different programs. Sessions are usually held weekly and there are no data suggesting any advantage in more frequent meetings.

It should be noted that the evidence bearing on these questions consists of very gross comparison. It may be that which format is best depends on the clients, the dysfunction, the nature of their sexual and romantic relationship, and the type of treatment used.

THE EFFECTIVENESS OF SEX THERAPY

Sex therapy enjoys a reputation for being highly effective. Unfortunately, that reputation is not as firmly supported as one might wish. Though there are reports of very high success rates, several concerns temper the conclusions one may draw. One is the fact that most of the reports are single case studies, multiple-case "demonstrations" of treatment effectiveness, or badly confounded clinical studies (Hogan, 1978). Another is that studies assessing behavior both pre- and posttherapy with measures of demonstrated validity are rare; usually only the therapist's own global-outcome rating is reported. The better studies remedy these faults, but they have been generated by very small numbers of therapists and must be more widely replicated before one may conclude that it is the techniques, rather than the therapists, that are effective.

Sex therapists sometimes group the dysfunction into those easy to treat and those hard to treat. The "easy" group consists of premature ejaculation, lifelong global orgasmic dysfunction, and vaginismus. Success rates of 85 to 95 percent are usually reported for premature ejaculation and vaginismus (Hogan, 1978; Kaplan, 1974; Masters & Johnson, 1970). Success rates for orgasmic dysfunction are equally high if orgasm by any means is the criterion for success. If orgasm in coitus is the standard, success rates drop to between 30 and 50 percent. The "difficult" dysfunctions are erectile failure and the other female orgasmic dysfunctions. Lifelong global erectile failure is successfully treated 40 to 60 percent of the time. Other erectile failures have a slightly better prognosis, with therapy-success rates of 60 to 80 percent. It is hard to assess the success rates for orgasmic dysfunction because the different types are poorly differentiated in the literature. Overall, though, it seems that with therapy 70 to 80 percent of these women successfully achieve orgasm in heterosexual activity, although only 30 to 50 percent will experience coital orgasm. Retarded ejaculation is so rare that success rates are tentative. Reports are that between 50 and 80 percent of these clients are successfully treated.

Perhaps reflecting the lack of well-developed techniques, low sex drive, aversion to sex, and desired-versus-actual-frequency-discrepancy disorders do not appear to respond as well as the other dysfunctions. All are recently recognized disorders for which success rates have not been established.

SUMMARY

Sex therapy emerged in the early 1970s as a distinct psychotherapeutic specialty. It is typically short-term therapy using active interventions aimed directly at changing the distress-producing behaviors. As such, it may be termed a behavioral therapy, although therapists from other schools engage in sex therapy and have contributed useful ideas and techniques.

Current diagnostic classification systems for sexual dysfunctions are typologies. The common dysfunctions are premature ejaculation, erectile failure, anorgasmia, dyspareunia, vaginismus, and low sexual desire. Whether the dysfunction is global or situational and lifelong or not lifelong has major implications for treatment.

Sexual dysfunctions seem to be caused by the interaction of multiple variables both physical (for example, neuropathy, hormone deficiencies, circulatory problems) and psychological (for example, negative affective states, knowledge and skills deficits). The sex-history interview and specific medical tests are the major means of assessing sexual dysfunctions, since alternative methods are unethical or of questionable validity. Usually the goal of therapy is to improve sexual functioning, but at times therapists select changes in cognitions or perceptions as the major goals. Treatment is highly structured and the therapist very directive, especially at first. The sensate-focus exercises are a part of most treatments, regardless of the dysfunction. Specific techniques have been developed for some dysfunctions—for example, the pause technique for premature ejaculation, or masturbation training for anorgasmia—and are used when appropriate. Additional techniques are used at the therapists' discretion to attack specific client problems. Many of these are behavioral techniques; desensitization is effective in reducing anxiety, rational restructuring can change beliefs, skills training and educational techniques impart knowledge, and operant principles help change behavior in session and out. Sex therapists often use nonbehavioral techniques and concepts as well. Surgical and drug treatments are of value in some cases.

Although it has been demonstrated that sex therapy can be effective in a variety of formats (for example, conjoint or single therapy, one therapist or two, daily or weekly sessions), questions regarding the optimal format are unresolved. Sex therapy is reported to be highly effective for some dysfunctions, but more high-quality research is needed to substantiate these claims and to identify its effective components.

CHAPTER 17

RECENT DEVELOPMENTS IN ASSESSMENT AND TREATMENT OF PARAPHILIAS AND GENDER-IDENTITY DISORDERS

David H. Barlow

State University of New York at Albany

Gene G. Abel

*College of Physicians and Surgeons,
Columbia University*

Ways of thinking about sexual disorders change over the years, and these ideas often find their way into new methods of classification and new approaches to treatment. This has certainly been true in the area of sexual disorders. For many years a group of sexual disorders that shared as the common component unwanted or undesired sexual arousal were lumped under the heading of *sexual deviation*. Reflecting changes in public attitudes and advances in clinical science, the new Diagnostic and Statistical Manual

Preparation of this chapter was supported in part by Research Grant MH 33553 from the National Institute of Mental Health.

of the American Psychiatric Association (DSM-III) has broken these problems down under somewhat different labels. As indicated in the title of this chapter, disorders like pedophilia, exhibitionism, fetishism, and so on, are now grouped under the label *paraphilia,* which refers to sexual arousal to nonhuman objects, to humans involving real or simulated suffering or humiliation, or to nonconsenting partners. A somewhat different group of disorders is now labeled *gender-identity disorders.* This refers to a state of affairs in which the gender with which one identifies psychologically (amount of maleness or femaleness) differs in some degree from one's anatomical sex to an extent that serious psychological discomfort results.

Homosexuality, on the other hand, is not considered a classifiable psychiatric disorder unless homosexual-arousal patterns are distinctly disturbing to the client at hand. This is a major revision of a system that heretofore held that homosexuality was inherently pathological.

With the emphasis on sexual deviation, as it was labeled until recently in classification systems, treatment approaches during the last several decades stressed the reduction or elimination of this unwanted arousal. Some of the interest in behavior-therapy approaches during the 1960s was a result of the treatment of sexual deviation by what were then the newly developed techniques generally labeled *aversion therapy,* which were designed to decrease undesired arousal. The fact that these were new and more successful than traditional psychotherapeutic approaches had much to do with increased interest in behavior approaches at that time.

Although early controlled studies indicated that aversion therapy was successful in eliminating unwanted arousal in up to 60 percent of clients (for example, Feldman & MacCulloch, 1971) as compared to 10 to 30 percent with more traditional approaches (for example, Bieber, Bieber, Dain, Dince, Drellich, Grand, Grundlach, Kremer, Wilber, & Bieber, 1963; Curran & Parr, 1957; Woodward, 1958), the results were not as clinically impressive as they might have been. Further research into aversion therapy indicated that there was very little of an automatic conditioning nature about it. It seemed essentially to be a self-control procedure (Barlow, 1978), and the treatment could be effectively applied totally in imagination, which therefore avoided the use of painful but harmless electric shocks or nausea-inducing drugs so commonly used in the sixties (Brownell, Hayes, & Barlow, 1977; Callahan & Leitenberg, 1973). A more important consequence of the emphasis on reducing sexual deviation, however, was the preclusion of careful assessment of the multiple-behavioral excesses and deficits which comprise sexual deviation and reveal the complexity of the problem. In fact, reducing excesses in unwanted arousal, which is the major goal of aversion therapy, comprises only a small part of the treatment as it has evolved, and sometimes no part at all (Barlow, 1973).

It is a hallmark of behavior therapy that faith in individual procedures gives way in the face of accumulating empirical evidence to the contrary. As behavior therapy matured and it became clear that aversion therapy alone was, at best, an inadequate treatment of sexual deviation, treatment approaches changed radically. The key to this change was a more thorough and detailed behavioral assessment of the various problems found in sexual deviation. The major finding was that sexual deviation, whatever its object, was far more complex than heretofore assumed. Although the emphasis may be on unwanted arousal or behavior (for example, pedophilia) it is very seldom indeed that a client who complains of unwanted sexual arousal does not present associated behavioral excesses or deficits. Often these associated problems are the major concern of the client. For example, a transvestite may not be concerned about cross-dressing, but rather complains of inability to become aroused with females. Thus, throughout this chapter, *deviant arousal* will not refer to a diagnostic label or classification, but will be synonymous with unwanted or undesired arousal, and the terms will be used interchangeably.

There are at least three associated problems that may accompany deviant arousal:

1. *Deficiencies in heterosexual arousal.*   Undesired arousal may or may not be associated with absence or minimal levels of heterosexual arousal. Occasionally, a client may have frequent heterosexual arousal and behavior with a wife or girlfriend and still engage in deviant sexual behavior. The "true" bisexual and some fetishistic clients are included here. Often, however, unwanted sexual arousal is accompanied by diminished heterosexual arousal.

2. *Deficiencies in heterosocial skills.*   Deviant arousal may or may not be accompanied by deficiencies in heterosocial skills necessary for meeting, dating, and relating to persons of the opposite sex. Clients who complain of deviant arousal may also have adequate heterosexual arousal but may be unable to act on this arousal because of inadequate heterosocial skills. On the other hand, a client with deviant arousal may have adequate heterosocial skills but experiences no sexual arousal to the opposite sex.

3. *Gender-role deviation.*   Finally, a client with deviant arousal may have some degree of gender-role deviation in which opposite-sex-role behaviors are present and some preference for the opposite-sex role is verbalized. This is most common in some homosexuals and transvestites. When opposite-sex-role behavior is completely adopted and the client consistently thinks, feels, and behaves in the opposite-sex role, this mistaken-gender identity is called transsexualism (Green & Money, 1969). These clients usually request sex-reassignment surgery.

In addition to the conceptual issues in classification, recent findings from our laboratory (for example, Abel, Blanchard, Barlow, & Mavissakalian,

1975) indicate that patterns of deviant arousal cannot be glibly categorized under our traditional headings of exhibitionism, pedophilia, and so on. Although this is still suggested by the labels subsumed under *paraphilia,* our data suggest such classification is inappropriate, since the type of stimuli or behavior that arouses one pedophiliac may be entirely different from the stimuli or behavior that arouses a second client also called a pedophiliac.

The increased precision in assessment of the various problems associated with sexual deviation has also modified our treatment strategies. As Bergin and Strupp (1972) note, more accurate assessment of the various problems comprising any diagnostic category will lead to the construction of specific treatments aimed at specific components of a problem. In paraphilias or gender-identity disorders, no client is the same; each has some combination of behavioral excesses and deficits mentioned above, and each requires individual assessment and construction of a specific treatment package suited to his or her own goals. For this reason, any chapter on behavior therapy for sexual problems or any behavior disorder cannot retain the typical division between diagnostic categories on the one hand and treatment considerations on the other. In behavior therapy, where assessment and treatment are often one process, a meaningful description of these procedures must be intermeshed (cf. Chapter 9 of this volume). Thus, this chapter will dispense, for the most part, with a description of various labels ascribed to parphilias, such as pedophilia, and will concentrate on problems that cut across the various categories, such as deficiencies in heterosexual arousal, and so on.

The remainder of this chapter will outline assessment and treatment strategies, using various cases from our own files as examples. The issue of assessment of patterns of sexual arousal will be discussed in some detail, followed by a discussion of assessment and treatment of various components of sexual deviation, using one particularly complex case as an example.

ASSESSMENT OF PATTERNS OF SEXUAL AROUSAL

Since behavioral techniques rely heavily on valid, objective measures of the course of treatment, it is not surprising that with the advent of behavior therapy rapid advancements in the areas of assessment measures have been made. This is of critical importance, for as we shall see, the development of better assessment allows further behavioral treatments to be developed. Prior to the use of behavioral-treatment techniques, clinicians and researchers relied heavily on assessment by either verbal report or attitudinal measures.

Verbal Report

Verbal report is information provided by clients or members of their environment regarding their clinical course, for example, if male, does he still expose himself, or is the pedophiliac patient interacting with children and what is the nature of that interaction? Such global information is rather easily obtainable and has been one of the major evaluative tools of other therapeutic approaches, such as dynamically oriented therapy. Unfortunately, verbal report is easily invalidated by clients, and many times it is difficult for them to assess adequately their own course, since their perception of their behavior is unintentionally distorted for various reasons. Recent evidence demonstrates that under certain conditions clients will say they are sexually aroused when they are not (Barlow, Agras, Leitenberg, Callahan, & Moore, 1972) or report that they are aroused by one stimulus when in fact another is responsibile for the arousal (Abel, Blanchard, Barlow, & Mavissakalian, 1975). In these cases, the client attempts to report accurately but fails. To complicate matters further, some sexual deviates, such as voyeurs, exhibitionists, and so on, carry out behaviors contrary to prevailing legal standards, which may lead to their arrest. Verbal report is very likely to be at variance with behavior under these circumstances in order to avoid legal contingencies. These factors make verbal report a poor means of assessing patterns of sexual arousal.

Attitudinal Measures

Additudinal measures, the second major category of assessment techniques, attempts to quantify patients' sexual attitudes and beliefs concerning their arousal patterns. This usually involves scaling written statements along a continuum. Repeated scaling of the same statements allows a quantitative comparison of a client's attitudes with his or her prior ratings or ratings made by other groups. Older global measures of sexual orientation or arousal, such as the masculine-feminine scale of the Minnesota Multiphasic Personality Inventory or the Rorschach tests, have been cast aside as too vague. More recent attitudinal measures have attempted to pinpoint the specific attitude the therapist is attempting to alter. Feldman, MacCulloch, Mellor, and Pinschoff's (1966) measure of male or female preference, or card-sort techniques constructed specifically for each individual client (Barlow, Leitenberg, & Agras, 1969) are examples of such recent attitudinal measurement.

In sexual assessment, all such attitudinal measures have two limitations. First, since it is the client who does the rating, attitudinal measures like verbal report are easily distorted by the client. Secondly, behavioral programs do not primarily attempt to alter inner attitudes or verbal reports, although such changes enhance the validity of client improvement. The primary goal of treatment is behavior change; that is, the client's deviate behavior stops and nondeviate behavior begins or continues. Often, however, attitudinal changes *follow* behavioral changes and these measures can provide valuable information when used in conjunction with more objective measures.

Physiological Measures of Sexual Arousal

Since an objective measure of sexual arousal is so necessary for the assessment of any behavioral treatment, it should not be surprising that the greatest advancements in recent years have been made in this area. Masters and Johnson (1966) have pioneered physiological measures of sexual arousal during the actual sexual act. Vaginal lubrication, elevation of blood pressure, tachycardia, and muscular contraction are but a few of the objective physiological changes that occur during female and/or male orgasm. Most paraphiliacs, however, have problems of sexual arousal that precede the act of sexual intercourse. A male pedophiliac, for example, may be able to have sexual intercourse with an adult female, reaching orgasm without difficulty. He may accomplish this feat, however, by fantasizing that he is actually having sexual relations with a child. In reality, those events that precede the act of intercourse with a female—such as being attracted to the woman's personal characteristics, her sexual features, the social interactions that are the antecedents of intercourse, his fantasies of social and sexual interactions with the woman—are very alien and non-arousing to the patient. In other words, most of his problems occur very early in the chain of events leading to sexual intercourse. Thus, the necessary measurement must be a measurement of *early* sexual arousal. Many deviates likewise lack a sexual partner; that is, they do not have a wife or a girlfriend. Since their very problem includes their avoidance of adult women, measures that require the client to interact sexually with an adult female cannot always be used with these clients.

Types of Measures

Zuckerman (1971) reviewed the available literature regarding physiological measures of early sexual arousal, such as galvanic skin response, cardiac rate, respiration, and so on. Many of these physiological measures change considerably during sexual arousal, but other emotional states, such as fear, anger, and pain, can cause similar changes and these measures are subsequently not specific to sexual arousal. Penile erections, however, appear to be the one objective physiological measure specifically correlated with sexual arousal in males,[1] and subsequently several pieces of apparatus have been developed to calibrate changes in penile size. Because penile measurement has become such an integral part of the assessment technique for behavioral treatments and since penile measurement itself has given us considerable new insight into the nature of sexual arousal, these methods will be reviewed in some detail.

Penile Measures of Arousal

Two types of penile measurement apparatuses are currently available.

Circumference Measurement   A number of authors describe the use of mercury-filled tubing (Bancroft, Jones, & Pullan, 1966) or strain gauges (Barlow, Becker, Leitenberg, & Agras, 1970) that encircle the penis. As penile size increases, the electrical properties of these gauges change. Such changes, when compared with those of a full erection, enable the client's erection to be expressed as a percentage of full erection. Sexual arousal thus becomes quantifiable. The advantages of circumferential apparatuses is that they are relatively small, lightweight, and their use does not cause major stimulation of the penis during the measurement process. More importantly, these apparatuses measure within a functional and thus clinically relevant range of sexual arousal, for example, 25 to 100 percent full erection.

Volumetric Measurement   Freud, Knob, and Sedlarcek (1965) pioneered the use of the penile plethysmograph, a volumetric device that encloses a significant portion of the penis, measuring even minute changes in penile volume, which are frequently so small they are beyond the client's awareness. The advantage of this apparatus is its marked sensitivity to such small changes. Disadvantages include its bulky size causing considerable penile stimulation during application, its expense, and the fact that most studies using the apparatus deal with erection values less than 10 percent of a full erection, that is, erections far outside a functional range for the patient. Each apparatus, however, appears to have advantages for specific types of studies.

1. Exceptions are apparent in certain pathological conditions wherein erections may be present without the client being sexually aroused (priapism), or sexual arousal may be present without concomitant erections (impotence, or following spinal cord transsections).

USES OF PENILE MEASURES

Feund (1963, 1965, 1967), using a plethysmograph, has presented to groups of males still pictures of men, women, and children. Relying on small subliminal changes measurable by the volumetric device, he has successfully categorized these subjects as homosexuals, heterosexuals, and pedophiliacs on the basis of their erection responses alone. Such results illustrate our current ability to objectify sexual preferences by means of this physiological measure.

Further understanding of the concept of paraphilia has resulted from investigations of subliminal arousal patterns with the volumetric device. Freund, McKnight, Langevin, and Cibiri (1972) isolated specific body parts of various age females (5 to 26 years old) and recorded normal heterosexual males' erection responses during such stimulus presentation. Results indicated that nondeviates responded to such female stimuli along an age continuum, with greatest erection responses to adult women and smaller but still significant erection responses to very young, prepubertal girls. These findings suggest that our current division of adult heterosexuals from pedophiliacs on the basis of erection responses to adult females versus female children may be more of a quantitative difference than a qualitative one, since even normal males responded to stimuli depicting young girls. Such results from improved instrumentation are contributing considerably to ever expanding appreciation of patterns of sexual arousal.

To determine patterns of sexual arousal in our laboratories, we most often use audio-taped descriptions of erotic scenes (Abel, Levis, & Clancy, 1970; Abel et al., 1975), since this method is capable of pinpointing idiosyncratic patterns of arousal. Typically, during a two-minute description of an erotic scene, certain portions of the auditory description will produce erection blips (B and C, Figure 17.1), while other content will not be correlated with erections. Often subjects will admit that the content during some blips was highly erotic, but occasionally they will deny arousal at these points. The content under each of the erection blips is then discussed with the patient and elaborated in a second description; content not correlated with erection responses during the first description are dropped during this second description (D). The second description usually generates even larger erection responses (E and F) when played back to the subject. The content under these larger blips is discussed further with the subject and elaborated in greater detail in the final description (G); the content in the second description (D) not correlated with erections is excluded. The final taped description (G) will elicit marked erections, sometimes depicting sexual material that the patient denied as sexually arousing (see Abel et al., 1975), and Brownell & Barlow, 1980, for examples). These

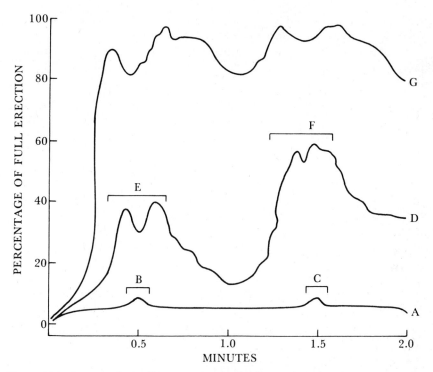

Figure 17.1   Patterns of arousal to two minutes of audio-taped erotic scenes.

SOURCE: Barlow, D. H., & Abel, G. G. Recent developments in assessment and treatment of sexual deviation. In W. E. Craighead, A. E. Kazdin, & M. J. Mahoney (Eds.), *Behavior modification: Principles, issues, and applications.* Boston: Houghton Mifflin Co., 1976.

studies demonstrate the importance of obtaining behavioral as well as self-report data.

A major advantage of the audio-tape method is the capacity to control stimulus content presented to the client during penile measurement. One case where this would be important is in determining transsexual-arousal patterns. A transsexual, unlike a homosexual, is one who entirely identifies with the opposite sex, for example, a transsexual male will think, feel, and act as a female. Like a homosexual, the transsexual male will be attracted to males, but only if he fantasizes himself in the role of a female, an important distinction. Attempting to measure what is erotic to a transsexual male client, for example, might include measuring his erection while he views a heterosexual videotape depicting a couple engaged in sexual intercourse. The client's marked erection to such a scene may lead the therapist to conclude that the client has marked arousal to female cues. Questioning the client may reveal that he is imagining himself as the woman in the scene, and his arousal actually reflects his arousal to the male from the vantage point of his identification with the female.

To illustrate this procedure, actual descriptions used with a client who presented mixed transsexual and homosexual features follows. To determine the specific erotic cues, we constructed a four-minute audio-taped description that alternated every minute between descriptions of transsexual scenes and homosexual scenes. The first two, 1-minute segments of the audio description were as follows:

It's in the evening time and you're with George. You're a woman, you're a woman and you're in bed with him and you're having intercourse. He really loves you and he's right on top of you there. You can feel the weight of his body. George is right on top of you. You see his face, beard. He's right on top of you and he's got a stiff erection. You can feel his erection, it's right in your vagina. He's moving up and down on top of you. He's whispering that he loves you, whispering that he loves you and you can feel his penis right in you. Deep in you, he's got his penis deep into your vagina, he's really excited and just losing control of his sexual arousal. He's really stimulated. You can feel his penis right in your vagina. (End of first minute of audio description, with patient as a woman.)

Now you're a man, he's having intercourse with you, you're a man and he's having anal intercourse with you. He has his arms around you. He really loves you and cares for you and is really excited by your body. You're a man and he's having anal intercourse with you. You can feel his penis in you. You can feel his penis in you, deep in you, and he's really penetrated you deep. You're a man and he's holding on to you, he has his arms around you. You can feel his arms around you. He's holding you very closely, he really cares about you. He's a man. He's really attracted by your body. He says he loves you, you can hear him, he says he loves you. His arms around you, he has penetrated you deep, deep into your rectum. He's having intercourse with you. He's really enjoying you, he's really excited. (End of second minute of description, with patient as a homosexual.)

The client's erection response (see Figure 17.2) to the successive minutes of transsexual followed by homosexual scenes demonstrate tumescence to transsexual cues and detumescence to homosexual cues, suggesting that the client's sexual-arousal patterns are transsexual, not homosexual. This case reflects the necessity of precisely controlling the stimuli presented and not leaving to chance the client's interpretation of the stimuli he's experiencing. These procedures have also been used to determine the erotic fantasies of dangerous rapists (Abel, Barlow, Blanchard, & Guild, 1977).

Once patterns of arousal are determined, erection measures are used in two ways during treatment. First, the client's erections to sexual cues can be used as an integral part of treatment. For instance, some techniques to accelerate heterosexual responsiveness (Barlow & Agras, 1973; Brownell &

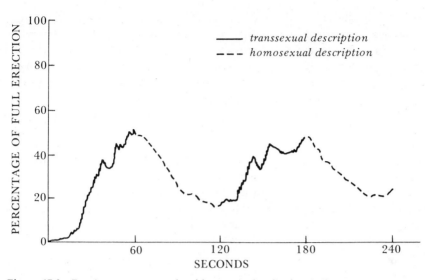

Figure 17.2 Erections to transsexual and homosexual audio descriptions.

Source: Barlow, D. H., & Abel, G. G. Recent developments in assessment and treatment of sexual deviation. In W. E. Craighead, A. E. Kazdin, & M. J. Mahoney (Eds.), *Behavior modification: Principles, issues, and applications.* Boston: Houghton Mifflin Co., 1976.

Barlow, 1980) involve contingencies applied to erection responses while viewing erotic stimuli involving adult females. Similarly, erections to deviant stimuli may be used in constructing an aversive procedure. The second and most common use of erection responses is to assess patterns of arousal as treatment proceeds. This allows the therapist continually to sample the client's sexual responses to determine the effectiveness of any treatment procedure.

NEW DEVELOPMENTS IN TREATMENT OF SEXUAL DEVIATION
Development of Alternative Treatments

Although assessment of heterosexual and undesired patterns of arousal is essential before the construction of a treatment package suited to a particular client, equally important is proper assessment both of social skills in heterosexual situations and of deviation-in-gender role. At the beginning of the chapter, we noted that problems in these areas may or may not accompany deviation in patterns of sexual arousal, since these problems appear to be relatively independent of one another. Although it is not common to find all four major components of sexual deviation present in one case, there is one clinical entity where this does occur with some consistency. This behavior disorder is called transsexualism, or the gender-dysphoric syndrome, and is the most severe problem among the sexual deviations. As noted above, transsexualism occurs when a biologically and genetically normal male or female thinks, feels, and behaves as a member of the opposite sex. Many such clients will say something like "I am a woman trapped in a man's body" (Green & Money, 1969).

The usual treatment for this condition to date has been sex-reassignment surgery. The purpose of this surgical procedure is to modify a patient's primary sexual characteristics to those of the opposite sex. For a male-to-female transsexual, castration is followed by creation of an artificial vagina. To qualify for surgery, the patient must live in the opposite-sex role for at least one year. During this period, administration of hormones facilitates development of secondary sexual characteristics as well as breast development in men. This radical procedure has been relatively successful in synchronizing patients' bodies with their gender identity, which in turn enables them to lead a more normal life. Recently, we have approached this problem from the psychological rather than the surgical point of view (Barlow, Reynolds, & Agras, 1973; Barlow, Abel, & Blanchard, 1979). Employing newly developed behavior-therapy procedures, the four basic components of sexual deviation were modified one by one, resulting in a change in gender identity. Since this condition does contain all four components of sexual deviation, examples of newly developed behavior-therapy procedures for each component will be presented in the context of treatment of this transsexual. From this description, one may extrapolate a typical treatment program for other paraphiliacs or gender-identity disorders with fewer components of the problem, since the basic treatments, as they are now developed, are similar. For instance, a pedophiliac may demonstrate marked pedophilic arousal, deficits in heterosexual arousal, and inadequate heterosexual skills on assessment, but evidence no signs of gender-role deviation. In this case, treatments to be described for the transsexual would be administered to the pedophiliac in these three areas only, although some modification would be necessary to adapt these treatments to the particular individual.

Example of Behavioral Treatment

The client was a seventeen-year-old male and the last of five children. He was a keen disappointment to his mother since she desired a girl. Nevertheless, he became her favorite child. His father worked long hours and had little contact with the boy. For as long as the client could remember, he had thought of himself as a girl. Spontaneous cross-dressing, as reported by the client and confirmed by his parents, began before the age of five years and continued into junior high school. During this period, his mother reported that he developed an interest in cooking, knitting, crocheting, and embroidering, skills he acquired by reading an encyclopedia. His older brother often scorned him for his distaste of "masculine" activities, such as hunting. The client reported associating mostly with girls during this period, although he remembered being strongly attracted to a "boyfriend" in the first grade. In his sexual fantasies, which developed at about twelve years of age, he pictured himself as a female having intercourse with a male.

Upon referral, he was moderately depressed, withdrawn, and attending secretarial school where he was the only boy in the class. He reported a strong desire to change his sex. Since surgery was not possible at his age, he agreed to enter a treatment program designed to change his gender identity on the premise that it might at least make him more comfortable and that surgery was always possible at a later date.

The first step, as in any behavioral treatment, was a thorough assessment of the behavioral excesses and deficits comprising the four major components of sexual deviation. This assessment revealed that the client was strongly aroused by transsexual fantasies, had no heterosexual arousal, demonstrated grossly inadequate social skills, and presented severe gender-role deviation, the most obvious manifestation being extremely effeminate behavior.

Changing Gender Role

Experience with this case, as well as other evidence (Barlow, 1974), indicated that inappropriate gender-role behavior had to be modified before treating other components. Thus the client's effeminate behavior, which was causing much scorn and ridicule from his peers, was chosen as the first target for treatment. To this end, a behavioral check list of gender-specific motor behaviors was developed (Barlow, Hayes, Nelson, Steele, Meeler, & Mills, 1979). Males and females were observed over a period of time in the natural environment, and characteristic ways of sitting, standing, and walking were chosen on the basis of uniqueness to sex. Four male characteristics and four female characteristics of sitting, walking, and standing were chosen to form the scale. For example, one of the behavioral components characteristic of sitting in males is crossing the legs with one ankle resting on the opposite knee. One of the female behaviors is legs crossed, closely together, with one knee on top of the other (see Barlow et al., 1979).

Direct modification of sitting, standing, and walking was then attempted by modeling and video-tape feedback. The effect of this feedback was experimentally analyzed in a multiple-baseline design in which the modification of only one category of behavior was attempted while measures of all three categories were collected. After completion of work on the first category, modification of the second category was attempted, and so on.

In the experimental treatment phase, daily measures of masculine and feminine components of sitting, standing, and walking were taken (by a rater who was not aware of changes in the treatment program) as the client came into the waiting room before his session. One thirty-minute session was held daily. After five days of baseline procedures in which no treatment was given, modification of sitting behavior was begun. In each session, the constellation of appropriate behavior was broken down and taught piece by piece. Each behavior was modeled by a male therapist and then attempted by the client. Priase for success and verbal feedback of errors was administered. The last trial of the day was video-taped and shown at the beginning of the following session. When the client was sitting appropriately in the session and reported feeling comfortable, treatment was begun on walking.

Pretreatment measurement showed that this client's motor behavior was almost exclusively and regularly feminine with only an occasioal instance of masculine behavior. During treatment, he learned to behave in a more flexible manner while sitting, standing, and walking. Furthermore, the experimental design demonstrated that the treatment was responsible for these changes, since male and female behaviors comprising sitting and walking did not change appreciably until treated. That is, treatment of sitting produced changes in that category but not in walking behavior, which in turn improved when treatment was administered directly to walking.

Few clients or people in general will demonstrate such a predominance of rigid female behavior. The extent of gender-role deviation observed in this client is most often found only in the male-to-female transsexual (Barlow, Mills, Agras, & Steinman, in press). Nevertheless, some degree of gender-role deviation is present in many clients. Recently, Freud, Nagler, Langevin, Zajac, and Steiner (1974) discovered that gender-role deviation for homosexuals is on a continuum from masculine to feminine. Most homosexuals are entirely masculine in their gender identity and behavior. Other homosexuals, however, may be found at any point along the continuum from entirely masculine to entirely feminine. Although data are not available, clinical evidence indicates that the same may be said for transvestites who dress in clothing of the opposite sex for sexual pleasure only. In all of these clients, the available evidence (Barlow, 1974) indicates that modification of deviant gender-role behavior must be the first stage in any treatment approach if treatment is indicated.

When this treatment phase was completed, the client reported that he enjoyed his more flexible or "androgynous" motor behavior since people did not stare at him so much and the severe ridicule experienced from his peers had decreased substantially. No changes were noted, however, in his patterns of sexual arousal, which remained strongly transsexual with little or no heterosexual arousal. In addition, the client remained withdrawn and socially inadequate.

Increasing Heterosocial Skills

Accordingly, the next component requiring therapeutic attention was social skills appropriate to a heterosexual orientation. Treating sexual deviation by teaching new heterosocial skills is not a new idea. From the descriptions of case reports, this approach often constitutes a major part of the psychoanalytic-oriented psychotherapeutic treatment of sexual deviation, with individuals or groups. Although procedures are seldom specified, several case reports illustrate this process.

Ovesey, Gaylin, and Hendin (1963), in approaching homosexuality from the traditional analytic viewpoint of heterosexual phobia, stated: "Psychotherapy of homosexuality is essentially that of any phobia. Sooner or later the homosexual patient must make the necessary attempts and he must make them again and again." Insight in the approach is a means to an end. They then describe successful treatment of three homosexuals, each of whom seemed gradually to learn more effective heterosexual-approach behavior. Ovesey et al. also stated: "The patient must become more masculine by learning appropriate patterns of assertion and increasing his self-sufficiency. In some cases merely an increase in non-sexual assertion may prove sufficient to initiate and maintain heterosexual behavior" (p. 22).

It is interesting to note that this is precisely the approach advocated by Wolpe (1969) working within a behavioral framework. Several cases of sexual deviation have been successfully treated by assertive training (Edwards, 1972; Stevenson & Wolpe, 1960) wherein clients were taught non-sexual assertion, which presumably enabled them to be more successful in heterosocial situations, which in turn led to heterosexual relations. In many of these cases it seems that deviant responsiveness dropped out once heterosexual behavior was established.

In a group-psychoterapy approach, Birk, Miller, and Cohler (1970) reported that a female cotherapist was most useful during therapy in that homosexuals had opportunities to learn to relate to the female in a heterosocial way. Their newly learned feelings and behavior then generalized to other heterosocial situations, based on reports of the clients.

A similar procedure within a behavioral framework was reported by

Cautela and Wisocki (1969). Their homosexual clients actually rehearsed such heterosocial behaviors as asking for a date with a young female therapist before being sent out to attempt these steps. Treatment for our client followed a similar pattern, although the first step in behavior rehearsal involved learning to relate to the males in his environment since his skills were also quite deficient in this area. An additional procedure for this client was voice retraining, since like many transsexuals, he had affected a high-pitched, effeminate voice.

Behavior rehersal enabled the client to acquire the social skills necessary to interact with males and females in his environment. Such behavior as eye contact, appropriate affect in social situations, content of conversation (how to make small talk, and so on) were all taught in a painstaking step-by-step process. Practice in lowering his voice was also successful after instructing him to place his finger on his thyroid cartilage (Adam's apple) while speaking. As the thyroid cartilage lowers, so does pitch. When this phase was completed, the client reported he was quite capable socially and was getting on well with his peers. A subsequent fantasy-retraining phase (Barlow, Reynolds, & Agras, 1973) removed the last vestige of mistaken gender identity so that he now acted like a male and believed he was a male. Continuing assessment of patterns of sexual arousal, however, revealed that he was still strongly attracted to males and demonstrated no heterosexual arousal. In other words, he could now be called a homosexual. At this point, his homosexual arousal contained no signs of transsexual fantasies in which he would imagine himself as a female making love to a male. His arousal, measured by penile-circumference measures described above, was now typically homosexual.

INCREASING HETEROSEXUAL AROUSAL

With treatment of gender-role deviation and heterosocial deficits complete, intervention in a third component, deficits in heterosexual arousal, was instituted. Several procedures have been devised to increase heterosexual responsiveness. However, because of the emphasis on aversion during the 1960s, most techniques are still in a preliminary stage of development (Barlow, 1973; Brownell & Barlow, 1980). This is surprising when one examines the prevailing theories on the etiology of deviant sexual behavior in general. Both psychoanalytic and behavioral theories emphasize the importance of avoidance of heterosexuality in the genesis and maintenance of deviant behavior (for example, Rado, 1949; Wolpe, 1969). This notion finds some support in two surveys. Bieber et al. (1963) noted that 70 of the 106 clients in their survey reported fear of or aversion to female genitalia. Ramsey and Van Velzen (1968) in a survey of homosexuals, heterosexuals, and bisexuals, found that both homosexuals and heterosexuals had strong negative emotional feelings concerning sexual practices with the nonpreferred sex. Freund, Langevin, Cibiri, and Zajac (1973) obtained similar results with homosexuals and heterosexuals on attitudinal and penile-response measures. Most recently, Masters and Johnson (1979) found significant heterosexual anxiety in a large group of homosexuals seeking treatment.

Clinically, the best course is to increase heterosexual arousal before decreasing deviant arousal. There are two reasons for this. First, providing alternative patterns of sexual arousal is sometimes sufficient treatment in that deviant arousal then decreases without any direct attempt to accomplish this (for example, Herman, Barlow, & Agras, 1974). If this does occur, then treatment is shortened considerably, since it can be terminated at this point and the complications of an aversive procedure are avoided. Second, decreasing deviant arousal before providing the client with alternative arousal leaves the client with no arousal for a time and thus no sexual outlet. Since sexual arousal is a major pleasure or reinforcer, removal of this may lead to severe depression. An exception to this occurs in the treatment of dangerous child molesters or rapists whose deviant arousal must be brought under control as soon as possible (Abel, Barlow, Blanchard, & Guild, 1977).

Among the several procedures to increase heterosexual responsiveness recently tested is a classical-conditioning procedure (Herman et al., 1974). Although this technique successfully increased heterosexual arousal in our client, further testing revealed that the many procedural difficulties with this technique precluded widespread application. An alternative new behavior-therapy technique that seems more successful has been described recently by Barlow and Agras (1973). Derived from the work on errorless discrimination in the laboratories of experimental psychology (Terrace, 1966), this procedure concentrates on "fading in" heterosexual stimuli during periods of sexual arousal in an effort to change stimulus control of sexual responsiveness. This technique has been investigated in a series of three controlled, single-case experiments with homosexuals designed to develop heterosexual arousal. In this procedure, one male and one female slide were superimposed on each other. Through the use of an adjustable transformer, a decrease in the brightness of the male slide resulted in a simultaneous increase in the brightness of the female slide. During treatment, the female stimulus was faded in, contingent on the subject maintaining 75 percent of a full erection as measured by a strain-gauge device, through a series of twenty steps ranging from 100 percent male brightness to 100 percent female brightness. A reversal experimental design was utilized and consisted of fading, a control procedure where fading was reversed or stopped, followed by a return to fading.

The first homosexual completed the fading procedure in that he became sexually aroused to the female slide alone in six sessions. This arousal generalized to female slides in separate measurement sessions and to reports of heterosexual behavior. In a control phase, when fading was reversed, heterosexual arousal and reports of heterosexual behavior dropped considerably. When the female slide was faded in once more, heterosexual arousal increased. Homosexual responsiveness remained high throughout the experiment.

In the second experiment, heterosexual arousal rose during the initial fading, continued rising, but then dropped sharply during a control phase in which fading was stopped at the halfway point and the slides shown separately. Heterosexual arousal rose once again when fading had dropped sharply after termination, *without* therapeutic attempts to accomplish this goal, at follow-ups of one and three months. This experimental procedure and result were replicated on a third homosexual.

This procedure can seemingly also be used on fantasy where gradual reinforced changes in erotic fantasies are followed by changes in arousal pattern (Annon, 1975; Brownell & Barlow, 1980). Finally, Masters and Johnson (1979), using their standard two-week heterosexual-training procedures, reported failure on developing significant functioning heterosexual arousal in only 20 percent of a large series of male and female homosexuals desiring these objectives. All homosexuals brought an opposite-sex partner with them for the two-week period.

Decreasing Deviant Arousal

To return to our client, three components of sexual deviation—gender-role deviation, inadequate heterosocial skills, and deficits in heterosexual arousal—responded to treatment. As noted above, treatment often stops here because deviant arousal sometimes decreases "spontaneously" or because the client does not want to eliminate deviant arousal, as is the case with many homosexuals. In this particular case, homosexual arousal remained strong, and the client was quite adamant about eliminating this source of sexual arousal.

At this point, and at this point only, it is appropriate to consider aversion therapy. Because of the early popularity of aversion therapy described in the beginning of the chapter, these procedures have undergone more development and testing in clinical situations than treatments directed at other components of sexual deviation. Evidence cited in the beginning of the chapter and elsewhere (for example, Barlow, 1974) demonstrate that aversive techniques can be effective if the treatment goal is the narrow one of decreasing deviant arousal. Although electrical aversion has been the most popular aversion technique, covert sensitization (Cautela, 1966, 1967) in which the patient imagines both the chain of events comprising the deviant behavior as well as the aversive situation also is effective (Barlow, Leitenberg, & Agras, 1969). In fact, as noted above, recent evidence indicates that this procedure may be more effective than electrical aversion in some instances (Callahan & Leitenberg, 1973). Also, Maletzky (1980) has reported success with up to 86 percent of 186 exhibitionists, using covert sensitization as one of the major components of his treatment package, with follow-ups approaching nine years. This is a very impressive series.

In the transsexual case, a combination of electrical aversion and covert sensitization successfully eliminated deviant arousal. Treatment of this fourth and last component marked the end of formal intervention in this case. At this point, the client had adequate heterosexual arousal, little or no deviant arousal, or gender-role deviation, and ample heterosocial skills. Follow-up visits continued sporadically for several months, consisting mostly of support and advice on new situations that arose. At a six-year follow-up, the client was attending college and dating regularly, with an exclusive heterosexual orientation. Two other adult transsexuals were treated in a similar way, and each demonstrated reversals of gender identity. Unlike the first one, however, these clients chose to retain homosexual arousal and are now well-adjusted homosexuals (Barlow, Abel, & Blanchard, 1979).

Despite the success with this case, we are a long way from the development of a treatment package that can be routinely applied to every client. Increased sophistication in assessment procedures should pinpoint additional aspects of sexual deviation requiring therapeutic intervention. Treatments now in use will most likely become obsolete as future clinical research uncovers more effective procedures. Wide-ranging individual differences among patients, previously thought to be similar based on our artificially imposed diagnostic schema, will only ensure increased complexity in our research efforts as we seek to answer the major questions concerning abnormal human behavior. But the scientific underpinnings of the behavior-therapy approach provide the necessary base to build a truly cumulative set of principles unencumbered by dogma or blind adherence to unproven assumptions. As these principles and facts emerge through painstaking research, we should begin to realize more fully our goals of relieving human suffering and enhancing human functioning.

SUMMARY

Recent developments in the classification of sexual disorders are reviewed, in particular, the DSM-III categories of paraphilias and gender-identity disorders. Although early behavioral approaches to the treatment of sexual deviation concentrated on aversive procedures, recent research has indicated that this was a narrow approach which concentrated only on unwanted sexual arousal. At least three associated problems may accompany unwanted arousal and require assessment treatment. These are: (1) deficiencies in heterosexual arousal, (2) deficiencies in heterosexual social skills, or (3) gender-role deviation. Recent developments in the assessment of these problems are reviewed, including methods of collecting reports of the behavior as well as attitudinal measures. The most important development in assessment in the last several years, direct physiological measures of sexual arousal, is reviewed and examples are given of their use.

The most up-to-date treatments in each of the four major areas encountered in paraphilias or gender-identity disorders are reviewed and examples of their use are given in the context of the treatment of a complex case of a seventeen-year-old transsexual boy.

CHAPTER 18

TREATMENT OF CHRONIC MENTAL PATIENTS

Michel Hersen

Western Psychiatric Institute and Clinic
University of Pittsburgh School of Medicine

Alan S. Bellack

University of Pittsburgh

More than one decade ago, Gordon Paul (1969b) clearly pointed out to the mental health community that chronic psychiatric patients tended to remain hospitalized in spite of the then general increase in discharge rates for those with more acute disturbances. Despite the advances in pharmacological and psychological approaches over the last two decades (cf. Baldessarini, 1977; Hersen & Bellack, 1978; Kazdin, 1977), the inpatient treatment, disposition, and subsequent aftercare of the chronic patient still remain a major challenge for mental health practitioners. Indeed, Talbott (1979), chairperson of the American Psychiatric Association Ad Hoc

Preparation of this chapter was facilitated by Grant MH 32182-02 from the National Institute of Mental Health.

Committee on the Chronic Mental Patient, refers to this situation as a "national disgrace." Similarly, the American Psychiatric Association (1979) has issued a position statement that represents "a call for action" on behalf of the chronic mental patient. Recommendations touched on a variety of areas, including research training, community and provision of services, financial needs, administrative issues, and civil rights.

Before going on to a description of the behavioral strategies that have been implemented with the chronic patient, let us first define what we mean by *chronic*. Also, we will consider the diagnoses and characteristics of the individuals who comprise this group.

Although most practicing clinicians would agree about the specific behaviors that typify chronicity in the psychiatric patient, an examination of the research literature indicates that there is some variation in definition. Generally, however, there is a period of continuous hospitalization. For example, Goldstein and Halperin (1977) operationally defined their chronic patients (long-term) as follows:

If the patient was hospitalized for a minimum of a complete year prior to administration of the neuropsychological tests, he was classed as a long-term patient. Subjects who were not hospitalized for a complete year but who had multiple admissions during the years preceding testing amounting to a year or more of hospitalization were also included in the long-term group. (p. 36)

In addition to the duration of hospitalization, there is a fair amount of deterioration in the chronic patient's overall behavior. He or she tends to be apathetic, socially withdrawn, irresponsible, unkempt, dependent on the mental institution (for example, the large state mental hospital or long-term Veterans Administration facility), and quite fearful of venturing outside of the institutional confines for any length of time. That is, the chronic mental patient feels alienated from the outside world and usually has not kept up with world events and the changing mores and dress characteristic of extra-hospital living. This deterioration and dependency on the hospital has been termed the *social-breakdown syndrome* (SBS) (Gruenberg, 1967).

As argued by Bellack and Hersen (1978), "Regardless of theoretical orientation and idiosyncratic associations, there is almost undoubtedly a single common element in the images of all readers: the chronic patient looks and acts in an anomalous manner" (p. 169). Indeed, even when attempts are made to reintegrate the chronic patient into the general community, it is clear by his or her actions and/or dress that he or she does not possess the requisite social skills for effective functioning (see Hersen & Bellack, 1976b). Thus, the chronic patient, even if temporarily returned to the natural environment, often may experience such marked social stress that a readmission to the hospital will be indicated (cf. Zubin, 1976). That is, psychiatric symptoms previously under apparent control (for example, hallucinations, delusions) become increasingly evident and interfere with the individual's adjustment and acceptance by the community.

Most patients designated as chronic bear the diagnosis of schizophrenia and either have had a few very prolonged hospitalizations or multiple hospitalizations with successively decreased time periods in the community between each admission. Other diagnoses associated with chronicity include bipolar depression (manic-depressive disorder), paranoid states, psychotic depression, alcoholism, and a variety of organic brain syndromes. Many of the remaining patients in large institutions who are labeled chronic are over sixty-five years of age and have in some instances been hospitalized for periods exceeding forty years. Also, a good number of these patients suffer from medical disorders in addition to their psychiatric symptomatology. Thus, given the nature of their disorders, the effects of institutionalization, the social disintegration, the length of institutionalization, and the presence of significant organic problems (cf. Goldstein & Halperin, 1977), it is understandable why treatment and eventual disposition for the chronic psychiatric patient represent enormous difficulties, irrespective of the clinician's theoretical perspective.

Behavior therapists have made important inroads in the treatment of chronic psychiatric disorders (cf. Hersen & Bellack, 1978; Kazdin, 1977b; Paul & Lentz, 1977). In this chapter we will describe some of the strategies that have been carried out in this direction. Included in our survey will be discussion of wardwide and individual token economies, other individual operant techniques, social-skills-training approaches, and the synergistic effects of drugs and behavior therapy.

THE TOKEN ECONOMY

The token economy is one of two behavioral strategies that initially received widespread attention from behaviorists and nonbehaviorists alike (cf. Bellack & Hersen, 1977, chap. 8). Although the token economy has been used effectively in a number of rehabilitative environments (see Kazdin, 1977b), its initial application was designed to motivate chronic psychiatric patients in large mental institutions (for example, Atthowe & Krasner, 1968; Ayllon & Azrin, 1968). In discussing the mounting popularity of such programs, Kazdin (1978a) notes:

Ward-wide reinforcement programs have been designed to operate within the constraints of institutions, including the low staff-patient ratio. Also, many reinforcement programs can function within the financial constraints of institutional care because they depend upon restructuring many of the existing resources (e.g., privileges and activities for patients) rather than providing new resources. The ability of reinforcement programs to operate within traditional treatment and rehabilitation practices explains why they have been so widely implemented in institutions for psychiatric patients, the mentally retarded, drug addicts, alcoholics, delinquents and prisoners, geriatric residents, and other populations . . ." (p. 91)

As a motivating environment, the token economy rearranges the psychiatric unit so that most aspects of the chronic patient's life are delivered on a contingent basis. That is, with the exception of the necessities of life (that is, food, drink, shelter, medical care), the patient is expected to earn his or her privileges (for example, more luxurious accommodations, such as a private room, ground privileges, passes outside of the hospital, recreational opportunities, such as television program of choice or attending a movie off the ward). In exchange for these "privileges," the patient is required to perform behaviors that are more consistent with life in the community rather than with institutional living (for example, good grooming, neat appearance, being on time for appointments, actual work in the institutional setting, evidence of social skills, and so on). The theoretical notion here is that if these aforementioned behaviors can be elicited and reinforced within the confines of the institution, then the possibility for returning and maintaining the patient outside of the hospital in community-based facilities (for example, halfway houses, foster homes) is enhanced.

Before going on to a discussion of the efficacy of the token economy, let us consider its basic characteristic features. Included in this discussion are brief definitions of tokens, back-up reinforcers, rate of exchange, banking hours, response cost, and pinpointing of behaviors.

Features of the Token Economy

Tokens

Tokens simply are used as a medium of exchange as is money in the natural environment. Tokens have different forms, shapes, or colors, depending on the particular program (cf. Carlson, Hersen, & Eisler, 1972). Also, in some programs, points serve as the medium of exchange (for example, Hersen, Eisler, Smith, & Agras, 1972). Basically, the token or point, administered contingently to the patient when appropriate behavior is performed, bridges the delay between the targeted behavior and the patient's access to privileges and goods. Thus, the token is a secondary reinforcer.

BACK-UP REINFORCERS

Back-up reinforcers are the privileges and commodities that may be purchased by patients when they earn a sufficient number of tokens or points. For example, in the Ayllon and Azrin (1965) program, a personal cabinet cost two tokens per day, a trip to town with an escort one hundred tokens, attendance at a movie on the ward one token, and reading and writing materials two to five tokens. Most well-organized token-economy programs have a large array of reinforcers to prevent the patients from becoming satiated for any one. Again, this is to ensure continued motivation and performance of targeted behaviors.

RATE OF EXCHANGE

Rate of exchange, as in the real world, refers to the number of tokens needed to purchase a given privilege or item. This, then, represents an economic principle. That is, if prices are too low, the patient may accumulate too many points and stop being productive. By contrast, if prices for privileges are too high, the patient may give up inasmuch as the goal may seem unattainable. In the well-designed economy, prices of privileges and goods and number of tokens awarded for specified behaviors are balanced so that excessive savings are not accumulated by the patient. This again is to ensure the continued motivation of the patient.

BANKING HOURS

Banking hours are those specified times when patients exchange their tokens or points for privileges and material goods. During banking hours, there are opportunities to prompt and reinforce patients' social interactions. In addition, banking hours can be used to teach patients (in simulated fashion) how to plan and organize a budget.

RESPONSE COST

Most of the principles governing the token-economy system are of a positive nature. However, as in the real world, fines are imposed (that is, response cost) when rules and regulations of the system are broken. For example, in one token economy, Winkler (1970) showed that the use of fines served effectively to reduce noise and violence on that psychiatric unit.

PINPOINTING OF BEHAVIORS

In the token-economy system, precise descriptions of targeted behaviors are provided to patients and staff to ensure that tokens are administered in reliable and equitable fashion. As noted by Bellack and Hersen (1977), "Thus, the vagueness usually associated with large scale psychiatric treatment is counteracted" (p. 278). For example, in a recent report of a token-economy program, Nelson and Cone (1979) described "cleaning a bed drawer" as "all objects stacked or placed in orderly fashion; all clothes folded; no obvious dirt or dust," and "greeting staff" as "initiating an appropriate verbal greeting, such as 'Good morning,' 'Hello,' or 'How are you?' within 30 minutes of the director or assistant's arrival on the ward" (p. 258). With such precision, there should be little question as to whether the behavior occurred or not.

Research Studies of Token Economy

Token-economic techniques as applied to psychiatric patients have received periodic review in the literature (for example, Carlson et al., 1972; Hersen, 1976; Kazdin, 1977b, 1978a). A variety of studies have been carried out to assess the effects of the token economy with chronic psychiatric patients, including (1) demonstrational studies, (2) within-subject designs, (3) individualized programs, (4) controlled-group studies with no follow-up, and (5) group-outcome studies with follow-up. Generally, these studies indicate that targeted behaviors can be elicited and reinforced using token-economic methods, that overall social functioning of the chronic psychiatric patient can be improved, that the token economy, when compared to ward controls, leads to greater discharge rates, and that the token economy is somewhat superior to "milieu" approaches in increasing discharge rates and maintaining patients in the community.[1]

Let us consider recent examples of these studies in some detail. Fullerton, Cayner, and McLaughlin-Reidel (1978) describe the results of a study conducted with chronic psychiatric patients who had an average hospital stay of ten years. Of 174 patients treated, 125 patients completed the program. Diagnoses included schizophrenia, affective disorders, organic brain syndrome, and personality disorders. The program was organized on a

---

1. Milieu therapy is a nonbehavioral approach for treating chronic inpatients. Featured in this approach are: emphasis on responsibility, group participation, group decision making, confrontation of the individual by the group, patient task forces, and patient government. This is accomplished together with staff, but of course staff do have veto power over potentially unwise patient decisions.

system of four progressive levels, with discharge purchased by the patient with one thousand points. Patients discharged were followed up for an average of three years. At the time of follow-up, 72 percent (91) of the patients were still living in the community. More impressive, however, is the fact that 60 percent of the patients who completed the program and who were residing in the community were employed. Data indicate that best results were obtained with patients who had been hospitalized for less than ten years and whose IQs exceeded 80. Fullerton et al. point out that the extraordinarily successful posthospital community stay may be attributed, in part, to the aftercare received by the patients from the community treatment team.

In another recent study, Gershone, Erickson, Mitchell, and Paulson (1977) compared how patients behaved on a token economy and on a standard-psychiatric-treatment unit. The token-economy unit was arranged so that patients received points for meal attendance, grooming and self-care, and participation in ward activities. Also, response-cost procedures were carried out for property destruction and remaining in bed during prescribed activities. In addition to the general ward-point system, individualized programs involving extra points and contractual arrangements were carried out. By contrast, the standard-psychiatric-treatment unit involved group discussion of problems, individual and group therapies, and "emphasis in a community environment." Both units offered somatic therapies and were similar in physical appearance.

Results of the study showed that token-economy patients attended activities more frequently, were better groomed, made fewer negative (distress) comments, and stayed in bed less frequently during activities; however, they tended to smile less often. There were no significant differences between the groups with regard to socialization and meal attendance. Gershone et al. (1977) concluded that ". . . . the results demonstrate that token economies can be differentiated from more traditional psychiatric programs by observed patient behaviors" (p. 384).

In still another recent study contrasting token economy with a standard-psychiatric-ward approach for chronic schizophrenics (albeit relatively young in age), the superiority of the behavioral approach was documented (Miller & Dermer, 1979). The token economy was a three-level program that incorporated all aspects of the "traditional units" but in addition reinforced adaptable behaviors. These included work skills, grooming, self-help skills, ward and conversational abilities, and appropriate use of leisure time. Also, response-cost procedures were applied to undesirable behaviors, such as stealing, fighting, and inattendance to scheduled activities.

In a complicated statistical analysis, it was demonstrated that token-economy subjects had significantly better posthospital-release data than their traditional-ward counterparts. That is, the token-economy program appeared to reduce days hospitalized per month during the thirty-month follow-up period. Miller and Dermer (1979) argue that ". . . these data suggest that a token-economy program, designed to enhance response generalization and including a conventional treatment program, may be more effective at maintaining patients in the community than conventional treatment alone" (p. 627).

The most ambitious evaluation of the token economy for chronic psychiatric patients has been carried out by Gorden Paul and his colleagues over a period of several years. Many publications have emanated from this massive undertaking, with the entire program and resulting data presented in book form (cf. Paul & Lentz, 1977). The basic study involved a comparison of three matched units: (1) token economy, (2) milieu therapy, and (3) ward controls receiving standard psychiatric-inpatient treatment. Pre- to posttreatment changes during the inpatient stay were evaluated in addition to postdischarge adjustment and staff attitudes. As indicated by Paul and Lentz (1977), "Intensive aftercare, on a declining-contact schedule was provided for twenty-six weeks postrelease for patients in all groups and as needed thereafter. Rehospitalization, when necessary, was to the place of release" (p. 15).

At the end of the study, 89.3 percent of patients from the token-economy ward were improved; this is contrasted to only 46.4 percent for milieu-unit patients. At eighteen months posthospital discharge, 92 percent of the token-economy patients and 71 percent of the milieu patients were living in the community. However, only 10.7 percent of these patients could be described as independent and self-supporting. Most were housed in board-and-care facilities, with 20 percent functioning at a lower level than before experimental treatment had been initiated. Somewhat similar results had earlier been reported by Hollingsworth and Foreyt (1975), who noted that only 11 percent of token-economy patients returned to the hospital as contrasted to 27 percent of the patients who had received standard inpatient treatment. However, in an earlier study contrasting token economy and a token-economy program combined with milieu principles, Greenberg, Scott, Pisa, and Friesen (1975) found that the combined group was more successful in that patients spent a significantly greater number of days outside of the hospital than their token-economy counterparts. In this study, it would appear that milieu principles added to the token economy facilitated posthospital generalization. Thus, at this point, we cannot state that the token economy, in itself, is unequivocally superior to all other therapeutic approaches.

Despite the fact that data generally support the superiority of the token-economic approach, there are indications that some patients *do not* respond to the inpatient phase of treatment (cf. Kazdin, 1972, 1973a). Moreover, even if a patient responds to the general inpatient wardwide economy, there is no guarantee that the results will naturally generalize to extra-hospital living.

Let us consider a case where the token economy by itself was not sufficient and where an additional behavioral strategy (behavioral contracting) was required to ensure maintenance of inpatient-treatment gains into the home. Frederiksen and Williams (1977) describe the pharmocological and behavioral treatment of a forty-one-year-old chronic undifferentiated schizophrenic. Because the patient refused to take pills, he was given intramuscular injections of 25 mg of prolixin enanthate every two weeks. This was effective in controlling psychotic symptoms. To increase the patient's rate of social interaction, an experimental analysis indicated that a program of social praise in combination with points was effective in maintaining high levels of his performance. However, once the patient was ready to be discharged from the hospital, the therapist and the patient's sister targeted several behaviors which were to be reinforced in the home. A behavioral contract between the patient and his sister was negotiated, specifying number of points to be earned (awarded by the patient's sister) for performance of targeted behaviors. Points earned were redeemable for money. Results of the outpatient phase of this single-case study clearly shows that behavioral contracting was a useful technique for extending the results of the inpatient token economy into the patient's home environment. Thus, it is important for generalization of gains seen during hospitalization to be specifically programmed in the postrelease phase.

INDIVIDUALIZED APPROACHES

Token-economy programs are most notable for their efficiency as ward management procedures. A single token system can be devised to govern an entire ward, an entire building, or an entire hospital. Generally, the more patients and settings involved, the more complex the system. At a minimal level, a few behaviors can be consequated in one setting, such as a classroom. Large-scale programs can cover everything from grooming to socializing to behavior on work assignments. Regardless of their extent, most token programs are designed to deal with relatively common behaviors. It is impossible to include a rule to cover all possible behaviors of all participants. Consequently, there frequently are specific problem behaviors which are not affected by the general token system. In such cases, individually tailored interventions must be applied.

One way of dealing with such problem behaviors is to develop individualized contingencies within the token system. For example, assaultive behavior and fighting generally are controlled by response cost. But some patients may need idiosyncratic programs to bring these behaviors under control. Thus, a differential reinforcement of other behavior (DRO) contingency might be applied, in which the patient receives token reinforcement for engaging in prosocial (nonaggressive) activities. Similarly, some regressed patients may require extensive shaping to reinstitute speech or self-help behaviors. This can be accomplished by superimposing an individualized token-reinforcement program on the wardwide token economy.

There are other behavior problems which do not generally respond to token systems. In this section, we will examine strategies that have been employed to deal with some of the most difficult and common problem behaviors exhibited by chronic schizophrenics: hallucinations and delusions. We will also briefly consider treatment strategies for two nonpsychotic but severely incapacitating disorders: anorexia nervosa and obsessive-compulsive disorder.

Hallucinations and Delusions

A classic symptom of schizophrenia is hallucinations: seeing things that are not there or hearing voices. The customary treatment for these phenomena is antipsychotic medication. But some patients do not respond to medication, and a variety of conditioning strategies have been employed. Most typically, hallucinatory experiences have been followed with some noxious event. Some early success was reported with the use of self-administered electric shock (Bucher & Fabricatore, 1970). However, a controlled outcome study involving forty-five patients failed to find any difference between self-administered shock, a placebo group, and an untreated control group (Weingaertner, 1971).

Somewhat more positive results have been reported for experimenter-administered aversive stimuli. Although experimenter control is not portable, it has the advantage of consistency and reliability (that is, contingency). An example is provided in a single-case experiment by Turner, Hersen, and Bellack (1977). The patient was a thirty-three-year-old woman complaining of disturbing auditory hallucinations. She had an eleven-year history of schizophrenia, with ten inpatient hospitalizations.

The experiment entailed ten phases:

1. *Baseline 1.* During this phase the patient sat in a reclining chair and simply raised her right index finger whenever she heard the "voice." She dropped her finger when the voice ceased. This allowed a measure of frequency and duration of hallucinations during the twenty-minute sessions.

2. *Social disruption.*   In this phase, a research assistant engaged the patient in conversation unrelated to her symptoms.

3. *Baseline 2.*   Same as previous baseline.

4. *Social disruption.*   Same as phase 2.

5. *Stimulus bell.*   During this phase, a loud bell was sounded whenever the patient reported hearing voices.

6. *Baseline 3.*   Same as previous baselines.

7. *Stimulus bell.*   Same as phase 5.

8. *Baseline 4.*   Same as previous baselines.

9. *Electrical shock*   Annoying but nonharmful electric shocks were administered to the patient's left wrist as long as she reported hallucinations.

10. *Baseline 5.*   Same as previous baselines. Follow-ups were conducted at twenty-two- and twenty-five-week intervals.

The results are presented in Figure 18.1. The data suggest that the bell had the greatest effect on the extent of hallucinations. However, these effects were temporary, reversing during the return to baseline. Conversely, the effects of electric shock were less marked, but persisted through the subsequent baseline and follow-up period. Although these data suggest that shock was effective, it may well be that the patient simply ceased reporting hallucinations in an effort to avoid the shock. Unfortunately, the presence of hallucinations can only be ascertained by self-report. Thus, actual effect of shock is unclear. This uncertainty, coupled with the ethical problems in using such aversive procedures, limit the use of shock except in unusual circumstances.

Like hallucinations, delusions and associated irrational speech are also treated most frequently by antipsychotic medication, but a number of operant strategies have been employed for cases in which medication was ineffective. A variety of punishment procedures have been utilized in an effort to suppress delusional speech. For example, Davis, Wallace, Liberman, and Finch (1976) applied time out (TO) contingent on delusional verbalizations (for example, "I have black goo running out of my brains") in a thirty-three-year-old schizophrenic woman. The patient was engaged in a series of five-minute conversations with a staff member. During treatment phases, any instance of delusional speech was immediately followed by a fifteen-minute period in a time-out room. Such punishment resulted in marked decreases in irrational speech. However, the effects did not generalize to other situations and did not persist in the experimental setting after the contingency was terminated. In general, punishment appears to be effective in suppressing overt manifestations of hallucinations and delusions, but it is unlikely that it actually reduces patient distress. In fact, there is some suggestion that punishment has negative side effects, including increased hostility and discomfort (Gomes-Schwartz, 1979).

An alternative to punishment is positive reinforcement of rational or

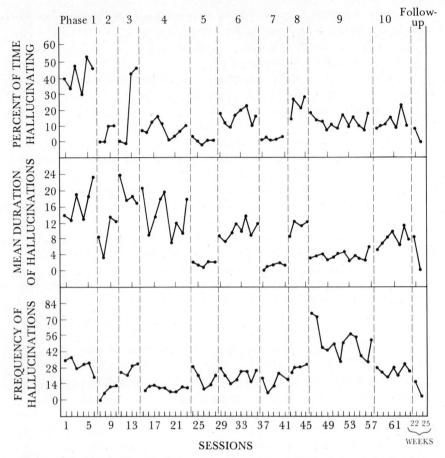

Figure 18.1   Percent time, mean duration, and frequency of hallucinatory behavior during probe sessions and follow-up in a chronic schizophrenic patient.

SOURCE: Turner, S. M., Hersen, M., & Bellack, A. S. Effects of social disruption, stimulus interference, and aversive conditioning on auditory hallucinations. *Behavior Modification*, 1977, *1*, 254.

nondelusional speech. In addition to avoiding the negative side effects of punishment, this approach has the advantage of increasing a socially desirable and incompatible alternative response. Several studies have demonstrated the effectiveness of token reinforcement (for example, Patterson & Teigen, 1973; Wincze, Leitenberg, & Agras, 1972). Liberman, Teigen, Patterson, and Baker (1973) demonstrated that attention and social reinforcement could have a dramatic effect on the rational quality of speech. Subjects were four chronic paranoid schizophrenics. Each subject was given a ten-minute interview with a staff member four times per day, and participated in a thirty-minute chat (with snacks) with a staff member in the evening. During treatment, length of the evening chat was made contingent upon the amount of rational conversation during the interviews. Thus, subjects were positively reinforced by attention for nondelusional speech. The results are presented in Figure 18.2. As can be seen, there was a marked increase in rational talk by each patient after the contingency was applied. However, there was limited generalization and maintenance of these changes.

The literature suggests that contingency procedures can modify the extent of overt hallucinatory and delusional activity. But these effects have not been shown to generalize, to maintain once contingencies are removed, or to reduce the actual occurrence of the phenomena. Further research is needed in order to identify more clinically useful strategies. Interestingly, little attention has been paid to the antecedent of these problems: the internal and/or external stimuli that precipitate their occurrence. A strategy that reduces the frequency with which these stimuli occur or that modifies their impact (for example, by reducing anxiety) might be more effective than approaches that attempt only to consequate them.

Obsessive-Compulsive Disorder

Obsessive-compulsive disorder has traditionally been classified as a neurosis, suggesting that it is only of moderate severity. However, severe forms of the disorder can be as debilitating as schizophrenia, causing marked impairment. It is not uncommon for a severe compulsive to spend six to eight hours per day washing in a ritualistic fashion, sometimes until the skin is raw. Bedtime checking rituals can entail one to two hours of systematically checking every entry point into the home for signs of gas leaks. In some cases, the person's entire life is given over to performing rituals. Such extreme cases generally do not respond to the low intensity of outpatient treatment. Rather, a period of inpatient hospitalization is often required.

The most promising treatment for obsessive-compulsive behavior is flooding with response prevention. Rachman (1976) has suggested that the disorder is characterized by a phobiclike dread of something (the obsession), which is reduced by ritualistic avoidance or undoing (the compulsion). Treatment thus requires extended exposure to the feared stimulus (flooding) under conditions in which the avoidance or undoing response cannot occur (response prevention).

An example is provided by a study conducted by Turner, Hersen, Bellack, and Wells (1979). The patient was a sixty-six-year-old woman with a

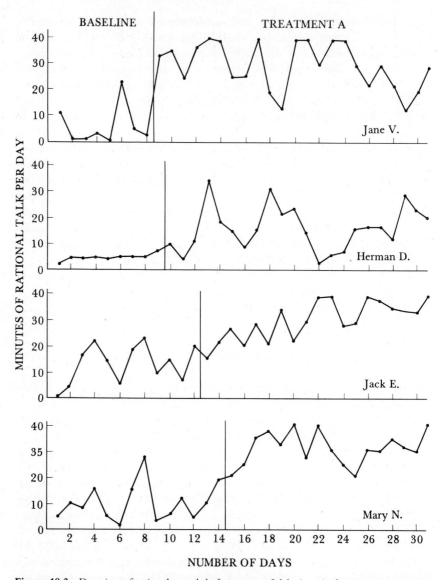

Figure 18.2   Duration of rational speech before onset of delusions in four ten-minute interviews under baseline and contingent social reinforcement (Treatment A) conditions.

SOURCE: Liberman, R. P., Teigen, J., Patterson, R., & Baker, V. Reducing delusional speech in chronic, paranoid schizophrenics. *Journal of Applied Behavior Analysis*, 1973, *6,* 61.

forty-year history of excessive washing and checking. On admission, her rituals consumed the entire day, preventing her from working or doing housework. She would spend an extensive amount of time visually checking a room before entering and performed an elaborate washing ritual each time she touched another person or anything that had been touched by someone else. The flooding component of treatment involved both the washing and checking urges. The patient was directed to repeatedly touch a host of objects she ordinarily avoided, including garbage, doorknobs, and other people. For the checking urge, her room and possessions were repeatedly handled by nursing staff and left in disarray. Throughout flooding therapy, she was prevented from washing or ritualistically rearranging her possessions. In addition, she was placed under twenty-four-hour per day observation and prevented from engaging in rituals at any time. Prevention entailed instruction, requests, and distraction; no physical force was ever required. Results are presented in Figure 18.3. Treatment was quite successful across a variety of behaviors. The effects were maintained when response prevention was terminated and persisted through a two-month follow-up. Although generalization training in the home was not conducted in this case, it is probably necessary in most cases if the changes are to transfer out of the hospital.

Anorexia Nervosa

Anorexia nervosa is a life-threatening condition which is characterized by self-starvation. Anorectics eat extremely small amounts of food or refuse to eat at all. Malnutrition is common, and mortality estimates range from 3 percent to 25 percent. Anorexia is also accompanied by a variety of physical symptoms and disturbed family relationships. Not surprisingly, the life-threatening aspect of the disorder frequently necessitates hospitalization.

Numerous single-case studies have been reported in which a variety of operant strategies have rapidly re-established eating and produced sizable weight gains. The typical procedure includes hospitalizing the patient, ignoring complaints and worries about food and weight gain (patients generally worry about becoming obese!), and providing positive reinforcement for eating and/or weight gains. Blinder, Freeman, and Stunkard (1970) made access to exercise contingent on a daily weight gain of ½ pound. Halmi, Powers, and Cunningham (1975) limited patient access to a variety of social reinforcers, such as receiving visitors and telephone calls. These reinforcers could be earned by a weight gain of 1.1 pounds over five

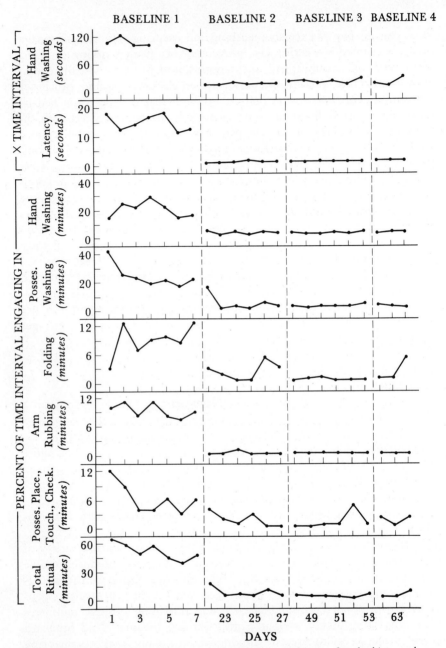

Figure 18.3 Mean time engaged in handwashing, mean latency for checking, and percentage of observation intervals engaged in handwashing, possession marking, folding, arm rubbing, possession touching, placing-checking, and total rituals.

SOURCE: Turner, S. M., Hersen, M., Bellack, A. S., & Wells, K. C. Behavioral treatment of obsessive-compulsive neurosis. *Behaviour Research and Therapy*, 1979, *17*, 102.

days. Agras, Barlow, Chapin, Abel, and Leitenberg (1974) found that re-inforcement combined with precise feedback about the number of calories consumed was more effective than reinforcement alone.

It is clear that operant procedures can rapidly restore eating and produce weight gain. However, the durability of these changes is suspect. It is not unusual for patients to be rehospitalized after a short return to the commu-nity. This should not be surprising as these operant strategies do not deal with the etiological factors that produce the maladaptive behavior or the factors that maintain it (Bellack & Williamson, in press). For example, in some cases, the eating problem is the patient's sole means to gain the atten-tion of parents. Operant procedures are probably most useful as the first stage of a comprehensive program. They are not apt to be sufficient by themselves.

Social-Skills Training

Perhaps the most pervasive problem manifested by chronic psychiatric pa-tients is an inability to deal with the social environment. Chronic patients look different and act differently than most nonpatients. They generally cannot develop and maintain adequate interpersonal relationships. Con-sequently, they have poor marital, work, and school histories. These three areas of functioning comprise what Zigler and Phillips (1960, 1961) refer to as *social competence*. Premorbid social competence is the best predictor of posthospital adjustment for chronic patients.

From a behavioral perspective, social competence and interpersonal functioning depend on the person's repertoire of *social skills*. These are a complex set of learned responses which govern the nature and quality of performance in interpersonal encounters. There are both *expressive* and *receptive* skills. Expressive skills include (1) speech content, or what we say to others; (2) paralinguistic aspects of speech, including such things as speech rate, voice tone, and pitch, which provide emphasis to speech con-tent; and (3) nonverbal features, such as facial expression, posture, and eye contact. Our impact on other people and what we communicate are func-tions of the manner in which these various elements are combined. The socially skilled individual is successful because he or she has learned to use these responses properly and in appropriate combinations (for example, you do not smile when offering condolences or expressing anger).

Receptive features of social skill are referred to as social perception, the ability to "read" social cues and respond accordingly. This skill includes paying attention to the appropriate cues, being able to decode them, and knowledge of social mores. Research has shown that social skills are situationally specific; behavior that is appropriate in one context may be entirely inappropriate in another. Also, subtle differences in performance are frequently required in related but slightly different situations (for example, disagreeing with an employer versus a friend). Consequently, the socially skilled individual must be able to carefully monitor the situation and adjust his or her own behavior accordingly.

As indicated above, most chronic psychiatric patients have marked social-skill deficits. In some cases, they never learned the appropriate responses. In the case of patients with histories of long hospitalizations, skills may have been lost through disuse. Finally, anxiety or depression can interfere with social performance despite the presence of an adequate response repertoire. Social-skills training has been found to be an effective intervention strategy for patients with any of these three etiological patterns (Bellack & Hersen, 1978; Hersen & Bellack, 1976b).

The first step in social-skills training is to conduct a thorough assessment and determine the precise pattern of skill deficits. This includes identifying specific responses that are deficient or performed in excess and the situations in which the problems occur. A preliminary analysis can be achieved by an interview, by informal observation on the ward, and by securing an interpersonal history. The general information secured in this manner is then examined in a more detailed manner with the use of a behavioral role-playing test. A series of eight to sixteen social scenarios of relevance to the patient is identified. The patient then role-plays each scenario with a staff member, who portrays someone in the environment (for example, parent, employer). The Behavioral Assertiveness Test—Revised (Eisler, Hersen, Miller, & Blanchard, 1975) is a standardized role-play test to assess assertion skill. A representative scenario is as follows: "You're in a restaurant with some friends. You order a very rare steak. The waitress brings a steak to the table which is so well done it looks burned." A role model portraying a waitress then says, "I hope you enjoy your dinner, sir." The patient's response to the role model is video-taped and then rated on the various expressive-response dimensions. Problem areas are then targeted for treatment.

Social-skills training is a didactic procedure which includes five elements: instructions, modeling, role playing, feedback, and practice. Each element is systematically applied to each target behavior in each targeted situation.

1. *Instructions.*   The therapist first defines the target behavior and specifies why it is important. The patient is then given precise directions for how to perform the behavior. Instructions are kept brief. For example: "It is important that you look at people when you speak with them. If you

don't, they think you're not interested and they feel uncomfortable or angry. I want you to look at my face while we speak. Look at my eyes for a few seconds, then my forehead, then my mouth, then back to my eyes."

2. *Modeling.*   Instructions alone are rarely sufficient to teach a new behavior. The patient must see what the correct response looks like. Consequently, after giving instructions, the therapist models the response, either with the patient or a cotherapist. This is accomplished in a brief role-play scenario like those used in the role-play assessment tests.

3. *Role playing.*   Social skills are much like motor skills (for example, bicycle riding, roller skating). They cannot be learned solely by instruction and observation, but they must be repeatedly practiced. Thus, the heart of social-skills training is role playing. The therapist and patient jointly enact relevant scenarios again and again until the targeted response can be performed in an acceptable manner.

4. *Feedback.*   Following each enactment, the therapist provides feedback. This is always couched in positive terms and includes social reinforcement for positive features of the performance. For example: "Very good! You really showed some improvement there. Let's try it again and this time try to look at my face for a little bit longer." Once performance reaches acceptable levels, training shifts to the same behavior in a different scenario or to the next target behavior.

5. *Practice.*   The limited amount of practice that can be accomplished within sessions is generally not sufficient to overcome a lifelong deficit. In addition, role-playing with the therapist is a lot easier than performing in the natural environment. Consequently, the effects will not be maintained or generalize without in vivo practice. When possible, the therapist should escort the patient into the community to direct real-life practice experiences. Whether or not this is possible, the patient is given a specific homework assignment after each training session. The assignments are designed to ensure success and are very explicit. For example: "Each day until our next session I want you to say 'Hello' to the person behind you in the lunch line, and at the table make a comment about the food."

Social-skills training can be applied individually or in groups of four to eight patients. Individual training has the advantage of being more intensive; it allows training to be precisely tailored to the patient's needs. Group training is more economical and allows the patient to interact with a number of other individuals. This might be an important factor to increase generalization. Patients are directed to role-play with one another and to give each other feedback. This facilitates training in social-perception skills and provides greater input about the diverse response styles that will be encountered in the community.

Of course, group training must deal with common themes having relevance to most patients. Our own program includes two therapists for four to six patients. Training consists of twenty-four 50-minute group sessions over twelve weeks. In addition, each patient is escorted into the community twice a week to practice skills covered in the previous group session. Training involves three general areas for four weeks each: conversational skills, assertion, and special problem areas. Conversational skills include starting conversations with acquaintances and strangers, maintaining conversations, and gracefully ending conversations. The section on assertion covers both positive and negative assertion. The former includes expression of such positive feelings as affection, approval, and appreciation. Negative assertion includes standing up for one's rights, avoiding mistreatment, expressing complaints, and compromising. The section on special problems varies with the needs of the particular group. Generally, it includes dating skills, job interview skills, and interactions with medical staff about medication (for example, complaining about negative side effects).

Social-skills training has been shown to be effective in a number of studies. Hersen and Bellack (1976a) and Bellack, Hersen, and Turner (1976) presented a series of single-case analyses in which a variety of specific target behaviors were effectively modified (for example, eye contact, speech duration, response latency, speech content). Williams, Turner, Watts, Bellack, and Hersen (1977) demonstrated the effectiveness of a group social-skills-training program. Several comparative outcome studies have shown social-skills training to be more effective than a variety of other procedures (Argyle, Bryant, & Trower, 1974; Goldsmith & McFall, 1975; Percell, Berwick, & Beigel, 1974).

Currently, social-skills training appears to be one of the most promising treatments for the chronic patient. There is little doubt that it can produce marked changes in a variety of specific behaviors. However, three critical questions have not yet been answered. *First,* do changes in specific behaviors have a significant impact on the overall quality of the patient's social performance? That is, can improvements in four or six or ten molecular response components, such as eye contact and the use of gestures, really alter the person's social competence? *Second,* do the effects of training generalize to the natural environment and are the effects maintained over time? *Third,* do the specific effects of social-skills training improve the patient's adjustment in the community and decrease the frequency of rehospitalization? The ultimate utility of the procedures depends on the answers to these questions.

DRUGS AND BEHAVIOR THERAPY

Researchers in pharmacology (drugs) and behavior therapy, although obviously operating from different perspectives, have one common feature: concern with hard data. In the last few years, interest in combining the two approaches for treating difficult psychiatric disorders has increased (cf. Greenberg, Altman, & Cole, 1975; Hersen, 1979; Liberman & Davis, 1975; Zitrin, Klein, & Woernes, 1978). In our estimation, this collaboration has proved fruitful in terms of the individual and the combined effects of each therapeutic strategy.

In general, with disorders like schizophrenia and bipolar depression, drugs (for example, the phenothiazines and lithium) have proved most successful in reducing psychotic symptoms, such as delusions, hallucinations, agitation, thinking disorders, and flight of ideas. However, in teaching chronic patients newer and more adaptive behaviors, drugs in the absence of specific behavioral strategies so targeted are insufficient (cf. Paul, Tobias, & Holly, 1972). On the other hand, token-economy techniques and social-skill approaches appear to be efficacious in teaching chronic patients behaviors that may enable them to make the transition into the community (Hersen & Bellack, 1976b; Paul & Lentz, 1977). When such requisite behaviors are not part of the patient's repertoire, there is the likelihood that environmental stress will result in deterioration and a return to the hospital. Therefore, working in concert with one another, drug maintenance after discharge protects the patient from a return of major psychotic symptoms while the behavioral approach increases social competency.

Recently, the usefulness of maintenance antipsychotic drugs in preventing relapse of chronic psychiatric patients has been questioned (for example, Tobias & MacDonald, 1974). However, in our opinion, there is fairly substantial evidence suggesting that in the absence of drug maintenance, the behavior of chronic patients deteriorates significantly (cf. Baldessarini, 1977; Davis, Gosenfeld, & Tsai, 1976; Detre & Jarecki, 1971). Indeed, there is evidence that some patients will not respond to the demands of a token economy unless properly medicated (Agras, 1976). Also, in our own work, we have found that chronic schizophrenics will not respond to social-skills training unless the psychotic features of their disorder are controlled with medication (Bellack, Hersen, & Turner, 1976). Finally, in a recent clinical report, it was found that lithium improved the cognitive and affective responses in patients with severe organic brain syndromes, making them more responsive to behavioral intervention (Williams & Goldstein, 1979).

SUMMARY

In this chapter we briefly examined the behavioral approach to the treatment of chronic mental patients. The social significance of this problem was outlined, and definitions of chronicity were presented. Next we discussed the widespread application of wardwide token economies for managing and treating chronic patients. This was followed by presentation of more individualized treatment regimes for patients labeled psychotic and neurotic. The growing importance of teaching social skills to chronic mental patients then was highlighted. Although social-skills training appears to be a very promising technical advance, the definitive long-term value of the approach has yet to be determined. Finally, the important interactions between the behavioral and pharmacological approaches in the comprehensive treatment of the chronic psychiatric patient was considered. In our estimation, such collaboration in the future should continue to prove useful in combating chronicity in psychiatric patients.

CHAPTER 19

HELPING MARRIED COUPLES IMPROVE THEIR RELATIONSHIPS

Neil S. Jacobson

University of Washington

Mercedes Dallas

University of Iowa

Behavioral therapy has grown quite ambitious with age. Rather than being content with the treatment of fairly discrete target behaviors, such as smoking or obesity, it has also become interested in seemingly amorphous problems, such as marital distress. The recent interest in treating marital distress is easily justified by examining some disturbing facts: 40 percent of all marriages end in divorce; marital distress is associated with problems such as depression and spouse abuse; 28 percent of all murders are perpetrated by family members; and 20 percent of all police deaths occur during interventions in family quarrels (Doherty & Jacobson, in press; Patterson, Weiss, & Hops, 1976).

Unfortunately, marital distress does not easily lend itself to a behavioral analysis. *Relationship satisfaction* is not a specific response that can be easily measured; rather, we use the term *marital satisfaction* as a summary label, or construct, for an *amalgamation* of both observable and unobservable behaviors. Given that marital satisfaction is not a thing but a construct, we need an operational definition of the construct. By identifying the observable events that are associated with marital satisfaction and distress, we learn which of the many areas of marital interaction to assess, what problems to treat, and how to treat them. Theory, assessment, and treatment research are interdependent. The more sophisticated the theory, the more effective the treatment will be. Measures for assessing distress help to test the theory and evaluate treatment outcome. Finally, treatment efficacy provides some indirect evidence that our theoretical model is on the right track. In short, the study of marital distress is multifaceted, with research related to theory, assessment, and therapy each enhancing one another and continuously leading to a more thorough understanding of the construct.

In this chapter, we will be discussing the behavioral theory, assessment, and treatment of marital distress. The first two sections briefly review theoretical underpinnings of behavioral marital therapy (BMT) and its assessment devices. In the third section, the major treatment strategies are considered.

THEORETICAL UNDERPINNINGS OF BMT

BMT focuses not only on the observable behaviors that transpire in marital relationships, but also on the private beliefs and feelings experienced by each spouse. Marital distress refers both to behavioral and cognitive events. Simply stated, unhappy couples both feel and behave differently than their nondistressed counterparts. The role of BMT is then one of examining the environmental events that lead to, and maintain, both the subjective and objective components of marital satisfaction, since both are thought to be a function of the reinforcers available in the relationship-relevant social environment. By *relationship-relevant social environment* we mean all aspects of the social environment capable of dispensing reinforcements and punishments relevant to the marital relationship. In a marriage, the primary social environment of each member is the partner since it is he or she who is capable of providing or withholding the major source of marital gratification. The tendency for a spouse to behave pleasantly or unpleasantly in a relationship and his or her feeling of satisfaction with the relationship are primarily functions of the environmental consequences provided by the partner. In other words, the major influence on how a person feels and behaves in a relationship is exerted by the behavior of the partner. For example, if the husband reinforces positive wife behavior, she is likely to continue behaving positively toward him and feeling happy with the relationship. That this is largely true can be seen by perusing the available empirical data; Wills, Weiss, and Patterson (1974) and Jacobson, Waldron, & Moore (in press) have found that a spouse's subjective feeling of relationship satisfaction as well as her or his tendency to behave positively or negatively toward the partner on a given day are strongly related to the number of rewards and punishments received from the partner on that day.

If relationship satisfaction is a function of the amount of reinforcement and punishment provided by the spouse, it follows that marital distress is maintained by a scarcity of positive reinforcement and/or an overabundance of punishment. Since punishing and reinforcing relationship behaviors are independent (Wills et al., 1974), marital unhappiness can result from either a high rate of punishment, a low rate of reinforcement, or both. Indeed, numerous studies have found that distressed couples exchange fewer rewards and more punishments than happy couples (Birchler, Weiss, & Vincent, 1975; Gottman, Markman, & Notarious, 1977; Vincent, Weiss, & Birchler, 1975), and one important study has provided data to suggest that these reinforcement patterns precede and therefore may be causally related to marital distress (Markman, 1979).

One variable that affects the precise relationship between spouse-provided reinforcement and relationship satisfaction is the partner's appraisal of such behavior, based on the latter's idiosyncratic preferences. The level of positive reinforcement necessary for a given spouse to feel satisfied may be very different from that of another spouse. The same is true of punishment: spouses may differ in their tolerance for punishing behavior; at some point, punishing behaviors produce a decline in subjective satisfaction. In short, different folks need different strokes.

Low reinforcement rates and excessive punishment are viewed as antecedents as well as maintainers of marital distress. The pervasive state of dissatisfaction has several consequences, among which is an oversensitization to aversive spouse-emitted behaviors (Jacobson & Margolin, 1979).

Unhappy couples are more responsive to negative as opposed to positive spouse behaviors. Subjectively, members of distressed dyads are happiest on days when they receive few negative behaviors from their spouses and least happy on days when they receive many. Positive spouse behaviors affect them very little. Happy couples present an almost diametrically opposed picture: happiest on days when there is an abundance of reinforcing spouse-emitted behaviors and least happy when there is a dearth of reinforcement. They are little affected by aversive partner behaviors (Jacobson et al., in press). Behaviorally distressed couples are also more sensitive to aversive behaviors from their partners, being more likely than their nondistressed counterparts to reciprocate partner-initiated negative behaviors (Gottman et al., 1977; Wills et al., 1974). In conclusion, members of distressed dyads are subjectively and behaviorally more responsive to negative partner behavior than are nondistressed couples.

Thus far we have focused on the satisfaction of one spouse as a function of the behavior of the partner. However, causality in a marital relationship is bidirectional and circular, rather than unidirectional and linear. The behavior of one spouse is both *caused by* some antecedent behavior on the part of the partner and *the cause of* some subsequent behavior on the part of the partner. Thus, levels of marital satisfaction result from the cumulative series of sequential transactions that occur between spouses over a period of time. This interdependence has been described by a principle known as *reciprocity* (Patterson & Reid, 1970), which hypothesizes that spouses reinforce and punish each other at approximately equal rates. Reciprocity describes a lawful relationship between marital partners, regardless of their level of distress. Behaviorally, positive reciprocity refers to an equivalence in the exchange of positive reinforcement, whereas negative reciprocity refers to an equivalence in the exchange of punishing behaviors.

At the behavioral level, many studies have found evidence for both positive and negative reciprocity in both distressed and nondistressed dyads (Gottman et al., 1977; Wills et al., 1974). As we mentioned earlier, however, distressed couples are more reactive to aversive spouse behavior, and thus negative reciprocity is more characteristic of unhappy than happy couples.

Thus far, we have focused exclusively on the formal characteristics of marital satisfaction and distress from the perspective of reinforcement theory without speculating on the processes from which these characteristics emerge. Both predictions have met with empirical support; at the behavioral level, negative reciprocity is more characteristic of unhappy than happy couples. But there are many paths to marital distress as well as many paths to marital success. Anything that affects the quality of punishment or reinforcement in a relationship will affect marital satisfaction. Since the reinforcers and punishers in relationships are highly idiosyncratic, among the important developmental precursors of marital distress are deficiencies in problem solving, or conflict resolution skills. Unhappy couples are often deficient in their ability to handle conflicts effectively and in their ability to bring about changes in the behavior of each other when such changes are desirable. More specifically, distressed couples are thought to rely primarily on aversive-control tactics to bring about relationship change. That is, they rely on punishment and negative reinforcement rather than on positive-control techniques, such as positive reinforcement, to promote changes in the behavior of their partners. Positive-control techniques are thought to be more characteristic of happy couples. Several researchers have found that distressed couples exhibit more behaviors associated with poor conflict-resolution skills when attempting to solve their problems (Birchler et al., 1975; Gottman, 1979). However, whether these conflict-resolution skills are antecedents, maintainers, or simple by-products of marital distress remains to be seen. Communication deficits, which encompass a more general class of behavior than do problem-solving skills, have been found to be antecedents of marital distress. Markman (1979) found that a spouse's ratings of partner-emitted communication predicted marital distress 2½ years later.

More generally, the behavioral model conceptualizes a successful relationship as requiring a series of skills; deficits in any one of a number of areas can produce marital conflict. These areas include the physical expression of caring (sex and affection), communication, child rearing, and household, domestic, and financial management.

In addition, *reinforcement erosion* is a common antecedent of marital distress (Jacobson, 1979a; Jacobson & Margolin, 1979). Over time, spouses' ability to gratify each other is often reduced, simply because of habituation. Behaviors that were once very reinforcing gradually lose their potency as the partners become accustomed to them. Although this erosion process occurs to some extent in all relationships, it does not inevitably produce severe problems. Many couples successfully cope with the erosion process by expanding their behavioral repertoires and finding new ways to reinforce one another.

ASSESSMENT

Pretherapy and ongoing assessment are an integral part of BMT. Since there are numerous ways in which a couple can reinforce and punish each other, there are numerous possible antecedents and maintainers of a given couples' distress. Although the BMT model offers a set of hypotheses regarding the possible antecedents and maintainers of the current dysfunctional interaction, the role of assessment is essentially an individualized one. Through the process of assessment, these general hypotheses are tested for their application to the couple in question. The role of pretherapy assessment is to identify the specific factors responsible for the difficulties a couple is experiencing. Therapeutic strategies are derived from this information. Assessment does not stop here but is rather an ongoing process designed to evaluate the effectiveness of our interventions.

It is far from an easy task to conduct a behavioral analysis of a distressed relationship. Couples are frequently vague when describing their problems, expressing their discontent in very general terms, such as "feelings of emptiness." It is often extremely difficult to pinpoint the relationship behaviors that are upsetting them. For one thing many spouses are reluctant to view their problems in behavioral terms. The therapist must convince the couple that neither the partner nor the therapist can do much with "feelings of emptiness," but that all of them can work together to change the specific behaviors responsible for creating their dissatisfaction. To obtain a thorough picture of the relationship, the therapist asks a specific set of questions to provide the necessary information; researchers have developed a specific set of instruments to answer these questions (cf. Weiss & Perry, 1979). The choice of both has been guided by theoretical assumptions regarding the importance of certain skills for relationship success, as well as by an emphasis on multidimensional assessment, which includes the evaluation of both objective and subjective sources of data. The questions the pretherapy assessment attempts to answer are: (1) what are the beliefs each spouse holds about the relationship? (2) what is the nature of their day-to-day interaction? (3) what factors contribute to the central relationship problems? (4) what are the major strengths of the relationship? and (5) how do spouses attempt to bring about change in their relationship? The set of skill areas evaluated for their possible contributions to current distress include the ability of the couple to discuss relationship problems; their current reinforcement value for each other; their general competencies in the areas of child rearing, communication, sex, and financial management; their strategies and personal preferences for utilizing their leisure time in a satisfying manner; the distribution of roles and decision-making responsibilities; their ways of showing affection; the social environment of each spouse; and the individual functioning of each member.

The strategies employed for obtaining the necessary information for the development of a treatment plan include the interview, self-report measures, spouse-observation techniques, and direct observation of problem solving and communication. The specific instruments used have all received some empirical validation. We will now turn to discussion of the strategies and instruments typically used in the assessment of relationship distress.

Interview

Unlike other behavioral and nonbehavioral approaches that utilize interview material as the major source of assessment information, BMT de-emphasizes the interview as a means of data collection. Our standard intake interview focuses primarily on gathering a developmental history of the relationship, asking questions like How did they meet? or What qualities about each of them made them attractive to one another? The interview also provides the therapist with a firsthand view of how the couple interacts with each other and how they present themselves as a couple to a third party.

We also use various questionnaires and inventories to gather information regarding specific complaints, global satisfaction with the relationship, and a variety of other areas (Jacobson, Elwood, & Dallas, in press; Jacobson & Margolin, 1979; Weiss & Perry, 1979).

Spouse Observation

Marital assessment has the unique advantage of having an observer present in the home—the spouse. A lengthy check list, the Spouse Observation Checklist (SOC) (Weiss & Perry, 1979) has been developed to measure the number of rewarding and punishing behaviors received from the partner on a daily basis and provides a picture of the couple's day-to-day interactions. The SOC contains four hundred punishing and rewarding spouse behaviors which fall into twelve topographical categories, including communication, affection, child rearing, sex, and household management. Spouses fill out the SOC on a daily basis, indicating the occurrence of each partner behavior and sometimes indicating how pleasurable or displeasing the behavior was. In addition, a nine-point daily-satisfaction scale is included, where spouses indicate their personal satisfaction with the relationship each day.

The SOC is an extremely useful instrument. In addition to providing information about the couple's day-to-day interaction, it is possible to correlate behavioral frequencies with daily-satisfaction ratings and uncover the most reinforcing behaviors for each spouse. Throughout therapy, the SOC is employed to monitor progress.

Direct Observation of Problem-Solving and Communication

As part of our assessment, the couple is asked to discuss several relationship problems while being observed and video-taped by the therapist. Strengths and deficits in their attempts at conflict resolution are assessed at this time. The research clinician sometimes employs formal coding systems and uses this observational data as a pre- and posttherapy outcome measure. The couple may later be shown video tapes of their problem-solving attempts as part of the assessment feedback.

Assessment generally lasts three weeks, at the end of which the therapist should have a complete picture of the couple's major problems and of the factors that maintain the problem behaviors. Then an interpretive session is devoted to assessment feedback and treatment recommendations. It is at this point that a therapy contract is agreed upon if both parties wish to begin therapy. The contract specifies a number of weekly sessions, generally from eight to twelve, depending on the particular couple. At the end of this time period progress is evaluated, and a decision to continue or terminate is made.

THERAPY

BMT might include the application of several standardized techniques, such as communication training, contingency contracting, and the application of reinforcement principles to increase positive behavior. The extent to which all or any of these techniques are applied, however, depends on the specific deficits a couple is exhibiting. For example, communication training is a general treatment strategy based on the observations that (1) many distressed couples have faulty communication patterns (for example, Vincent, Weiss, & Birchler, 1975) and (2) communication is a major determinant of marital satisfaction (Jacobson et al., in press; Markman, 1979). However, whether communication training is indeed employed depends on the specific deficits the assessment process has revealed.

Although BMT encompasses a series of seemingly unrelated interventions, there are various themes which cut across the major treatment techniques. A discussion of these themes will add conceptual unity and clarity to the various available treatment options.

Themes of BMT

Positive Tracking

Relationship strengths are emphasized throughout the entire therapy process, and treatment is characterized as a way to build on these strengths rather than as a way to eliminate the weaknesses of the relationship. Positive tracking is aimed at shifting a couple's bias from an almost exclusive focus on the negative aspects of the relationship (Robinson & Price, 1980). This negative bias, often accompanied by a belief that "everything is awful in the relationship" leads to a negative cycle of hopelessness, frustration, and a reluctance to work at improving the relationship. Positive tracking aids in the reversal of this self-defeating cycle by showing couples that there are positive aspects to their relationship and that they can be hopeful about the relationship becoming more reinforcing.

Empirical evidence exists to support an emphasis on increasing the positive aspects of the relationship. First of all, positive and negative relationship behaviors are independent (Jacobson et al., in press; Wills et al., 1974), which implies that decreasing the amount of negative relationship interaction does not affect the rate of positive interaction. Secondly, there is some evidence that negative behaviors decrease in frequency during the course of marital therapy without much direct attention being paid to them; positive behaviors, on the other hand, are not increased without specific intervention strategies designed to that end. Finally, since the satisfaction of happy couples is largely determined by positive events (Jacobson et al., in press), it seems unlikely that simply decreasing negative behaviors will lead to the maintenance of relationship satisfaction.

Positive Control

Positive control refers to the use of positive reinforcement rather than punishment as a means of altering the behavior of the partner. Distressed couples often employ aversive control strategies involving punishment and negative reinforcement in their ineffectual attempts to bring about change in the relationship. Although in the short run, aversive control strategies are very effective since they often produce immediate compliance, in the long run they are highly ineffective. Coercion begets coercion, and eventually the spouses find themselves involved in a highly coercive pattern of interaction which acts to exacerbate their distress. Therapy attempts to reverse this highly coercive pattern of interaction by teaching spouses positive control strategies for bringing about desired changes in the behavior of the partner. Problem-solving training and behavior exchange procedures, discussed below, are examples of positive control strategies.

Reciprocity

A major implication of the principle of reciprocity is that marital unhappiness is a function of the behavior of both partners. Many distressed couples shun all personal responsibility for their relationship problems, while placing all the blame on their partners. Therapy attempts to demonstrate that each partner plays a role in maintaining the distress, and consequently, that both partners need to change if the relationship is to improve. Acceptance of the reciprocity principle has an added advantage: each spouse stops feeling powerless and begins to believe that he or she may have some control over what happens to the marriage. As much of the social psychological literature has demonstrated, the perception of control has a number of beneficial effects, among them sustained effort in the face of traumatic events.

Focus on the Learning of Relationship Skills

Therapy is based on the teaching of various skills necessary for relationship success. As such, the technology employed for skills training and for the programming of generalization and maintenance must be closely followed. Examples of the technology for teaching skills are the use of behavior rehearsal, instructions, therapist feedback, and practice in the natural environment. The conceptualization of relationship problems as skill deficits also helps couples to accept therapy more readily; they are not "crazy" or "neurotic" people who need to be treated by a "shrink," but rather people who lack certain skills.

The Beginning Stages of Therapy

The initial stages of therapy have several specific goals: (1) the creation of positive outcome expectancies; (2) the development of a collaborative set; and (3) the provision of some immediate relief from distress. These three goals are interdependent with success in one enhancing the likelihood of success in the other.

The creation of *positive outcome expectancies* refers to a cognitive change on the part of spouses, wherein each begins to believe that marital therapy will lead to improvement in the relationship. These cognitive changes reduce their feelings of anxiety and hopelessness and also enhance the likelihood that they will comply with homework assignments (Jacobson, in press). A *collaborative set* similarly refers to each spouse's tendency to work together to view the problems in the relationship as mutual. The relationship will not improve unless spouses work collaboratively. Positive expectancies facilitate the development of a collaborative set. However, since distressed couples seldom initiate therapeutic contact in a collaborative spirit, such a set must be developed by the therapist. Much of the initial therapy contact is aimed at the challenging task of developing a collaborative set.

The goals of the initial therapy stages are illustrated in the first actual therapy session, when the therapist summarizes findings from the pretreatment assessment and renders treatment recommendations. The general principles of BMT are explained to the couple in a highly personalized fashion, employing a framework that emphasizes reciprocal and mutual causality. Spouses' mutual contributions to the relationship problems are emphasized, and the necessity for collaboration is explained. Here is an example of how a therapist introduces the principle of reciprocity and the importance of a collaborative set:

Each of you ignores your own role in making it difficult to solve your problems. You each have a theory of your relationship which says that your partner is causing all the problems. Pam, you think that the relationship is in bad shape because Dennis is withdrawn, and he doesn't talk to you. Dennis, you think that the problem exists because Pam nags you and spends too much time on outside activities. Well, let me give you an expert opinion . . . You are both responsible for the problem. Your (to the wife) verbal intimidation and nagging lead him to not want to talk to you. And your (to husband) withdrawal makes her feel rejected, and because of that she jumps down your throat . . . (Jacobson & Margolin, 1979, p. 119)

Once therapy begins, the goal of the initial treatment phase is to provide the couple with some immediate therapy benefits, thereby increasing the reinforcement power of the relationship. Rather than teaching new skills, this stage of therapy helps couples increase the benefits that they already offer to each other but that are not occurring at a satisfactory rate. Behavior exchange procedures involve pinpointing behaviors that, if increased, would improve the quality of the relationship, and inducing increases in the frequency of those behaviors. Major relationship problems are not dealt with at this time; they are left for later stages of therapy when a collaborative set has been firmly established, and the reinforcement value of the relationship has increased.

Behavior exchange procedures come in many forms. At times, spouses agree to engage in a greater number of shared recreational activities. In other cases, the receiver identifies pleasing behaviors he or she would like to experience more frequently. For example, a husband may enjoy it when his wife surprises him with plans for an exciting evening; he may than ask her to increase the frequency of these behaviors. In still other cases, the giver may select target behaviors which please her or his spouse. Thus, a wife who notes that her husband likes it when she calls him at work to say hello may decide to increase these behaviors. A variation of this procedure is often employed: each spouse is told to please the other as much as possible during a specified period of time. In most cases, it is best that the giver select the target behaviors to be increased. First of all, this self-selection process allows for internal attributions to be made; both the giver and the receiver feel that the former is choosing to change a specific behavior rather than being ordered to do so. Secondly, it forces the giver to become more sensitive to the partner in order to identify behaviors that the latter finds reinforcing. Finally, when both spouses have the freedom to decide how they want to go about pleasing the partner, there is less danger that they will resist the enactment of those behaviors.

Another way of producing behavior changes is to have each spouse sign a written contract in which the nature of the changes is specified. Contracts come in two forms, one being the *quid pro quo* in which the behavior each spouse agrees to perform is made contingent on the partner's behavior. For example, if the husband has agreed to do the evening dishes and the wife to take the children to school in the mornings, the quid pro quo contract establishes a contingency between these two behavior change agreements. The husband does the evening dishes only if the wife has taken the children to school in the morning. Likewise, she takes the children to school in the morning only if he did the dishes the previous evening. Alternatively, couples may form *parallel,* or *good faith,* contracts in which each agrees independently to enact some behavior change without a specific contingency linking the two pledges (Weiss, Birchler, & Vincent, 1974). Each spouse independently agrees to increase the frequency of certain behaviors. Since the two forms of contracting are equally effective (Jacobson, 1978), it is up to the clinician to evaluate the relative usefulness of each for the specific couple involved. Some couples may react unfavorably to the idea of an explicit contingency, whereas others, perhaps because of a lack of trust in the partner, may demand it. Recording the agreement in writing serves several important factors: it constitutes a public commitment to change; it decreases the likelihood of forgetting; and it prevents each spouse from retrospectively distorting the terms of the agreement.

Throughout this initial stage in therapy, spouses are also trained to become more aware of the impact their behavior has on their partner. By examining the relationship between their enactment of various behaviors and their partner's daily satisfaction rating, they can determine whether their efforts at pleasing one another have been successful. With the help of the therapist, they also use the SOC to examine the behavioral classes which covary with the daily-satisfaction ratings of the partner, thereby identifying the effective reinforcers for the latter.

When introducing behavior exchange procedures, the therapist requests that each member temporarily focus on pleasing the partner. Often the task is presented as a challenge, wherein each spouse is encouraged to demonstrate her or his capacity to please the partner. The therapist may say something like

We find in our work with couples that they often lose touch with how to make each other feel happy. They think they know exactly how to please the partner but it turns out that they are wrong. Let's see how you two go about it.

Even if the initial attempts at pleasing each other are made grudgingly, soon the couple will reap the newly acquired benefits and begin to feel better about the relationship. As relationship satisfaction increases, the enactment of pleasing behavior will occur with greater spontaneity, and each will be more likely to view his or her partner's efforts as spontaneous. Behavior exchange procedures are ideally suited for the initial stages of therapy, for they demand relatively little from both partners: the behaviors to be increased are already in their repertoire, costly behavior changes are avoided, and the changes can be implemented in the absence of a collaborative set. These procedures also facilitate collaborative behavior, partly because the relationship becomes more attractive and partly because spouses obtain objective evidence of their power to affect the behavior of their partners. If a couple enters therapy having forgotten how to please each other, behavior exchange procedures force them to attend closely to these effective reinforcers and to use this knowledge to make the partner happier. Finally, couples begin to learn two lessons that are crucial for the more demanding stages of therapy. First, each spouse must verbalize what he or she wants from the partner, rather than expecting the partner to know intuitively what is needed. Second, a successful relationship requires that each spouse devote time and effort to pleasing the other, and at times behaviors must be performed for that reason and that reason alone.

Behavior exchange procedures are typically employed for the first three to five sessions of therapy. The extent to which couples benefit from these procedures determines the next stage in therapy. Some mildly distressed couples find that their problems have been solved; in these cases, therapy comes to an end. More often than not, however, couples need our advanced technology. These couples enter the next stage of therapy.

The Middle Stages of Therapy: Communication and Problem-Solving Skills

Communication and problem-solving training generally comprise the middle stages of therapy. Couples have learned some of the basic premises of the model. They are feeling happier with the relationship, and a spirit of collaboration has begun to emerge. The couple is thus prepared for the increased demands of the middle phase when the existence of a collaborative set is of supreme importance.

Communication is the primary vehicle for the exchange of rewards and punishments. As previously mentioned, the quality of communication has been found to predict relationship satisfaction 2½ years later (Markman, 1979). Rewards and punishments in the area of communication are likewise the best predictors of marital happiness on a day-to-day basis for both distressed and nondistressed couples (Jacobson, Waldron, & Moore, in press). The importance of communication for short-term and long-term marital happiness, coupled with the fact that distressed couples exhibit deficits in this area (Birchler et al., 1975; Vincent et al., 1975), make communication and problem-solving training necessary treatment interventions.

Although communication training is part of most marital therapies regardless of their theoretical orientation, communication training from a behavioral perspective can be distinguished both by the content of skills taught and by the procedures used to teach them (Jacobson & Margolin, 1979). In problem-solving training, couples are taught specific skills to heighten the effectiveness of their efforts to bring about relationship changes. The ultimate goal is to achieve conflict resolution in the form of behavioral change, and focusing on the process of communication is considered to be the most expedient means of achieving this end. The procedures used to teach these skills are similar to those employed in other skills-training programs: instructions, behavior rehearsal, and therapist-provided feedback.

Problem-solving training focuses on both process and content. The focus of training is on the process of communication; the specific skills couples learn are aimed at facilitating this process. The content of the problem-solving discussions consists of the couple's most significant relationship problems, problems not amenable to change through behavior-exchange procedures. Thus in the process of learning how to solve conflicts more effectively, the couple is also solving their relationship problems.

Problem-solving training attempts to break the habitually coercive and ineffective patterns of communication distressed couples typically exhibit and to replace these with more effective and reinforcing ways of communicating. Breaking an established habit and teaching new skills are both difficult endeavors, requiring effort, repeated practice and, very importantly, structure. Because of these demands, problem-solving is described to couples as "structured interaction between two people designed to resolve a particular dispute between them" (Jacobson & Margolin, 1979, p. 215). As a specialized and structured activity, problem solving has a specific set of rules the couple is to follow. First, dates and times for use are specified: the couple sets aside two weekly times to problem solve; attempts at solving problems are made only at these times. The emotional flare-up that could easily accompany the discussion of the problem were it brought up at the time of its occurrence is greatly diminished by this strategy.

Second, problem solving has two distinct stages: a problem definition phase and a problem solution phase. During the first phase, a clear and very specific definition of the problem is agreed upon by both partners. In the next phase, there is no further discussion of the problem; the focus is exclusively on attaining a resolution.

Third, there are specific guidelines for the couple to follow while the problem is being discussed. Three sets of rules are recommended: general guidelines for problem solving, guidelines for defining problems, and guidelines for solving problems.

General Guidelines

1. *Only one problem is to be discussed at a time.*
2. *Paraphrase each other's remarks.* Every remark made by the speaker is summarized by the listener. Although seemingly artificial, this strategy forces the couple to listen carefully to each other.
3. *Do not make inferences about the other person's behavior.* Couples are taught to focus exclusively on the observable aspects of each partner's behavior.
4. *Be neutral.* Verbal abuse of any kind is actively discouraged, especially the use of derogatory adjectives or nouns, such as *stupid* or *incompetent*.

Guidelines for Problem Definition

5. *When stating a problem, begin with something positive.* The way a problem is first stated sets the tone for the entire discussion. It is difficult to accept criticism, and being reminded that there are aspects of one's behavior that are likable softens the impact of the criticism. For example, compare the impact of "I like it when you hold me while we watch TV, but I feel rejected when you aren't affectionate in other situations" with "I

feel rejected by you because you are seldom affectionate." The former communicates appreciation for behaviors the partner is already emitting; the person is being reminded that it is only one aspect of his or her behavior that is being criticized.

6. *Be specific when defining problems.*   Compare the impact of "You seldom ask me questions of how my day at work went and sometimes walk away when I'm telling you about it" with "You refuse to acknowledge my existence as an individual outside of this relationship." *Trait labels,* such as *stubborn* and *lazy,* interfere with the specific operationalizing of problems, as do overgeneralizations, such as "You never show appreciation for things I do well." Problems defined in specific behavioral terms are more amenable to change; they are also easier for the partner to accept. Problems expressed in global terms tend to alienate the partner; the latter often feels criticized for who she or he is. Specific, discrete complaints are less likely to have this effect; they convey the message, "I found one aspect of your behavior unacceptable, but I still love you as a person."

7. *Feeling expressions are encouraged.*   Spouses are encouraged to accompany the behavioral description of the problem with a statement about its psychological impact. The complainer generally feels better when he or she is able to communicate the way a problem makes him or her feel, and the listener is better able to understand and empathize.

8. *Both partners should acknowledge their role in the maintenance of the problem.*   This rule applies to both the complainer and the complainee. The complainee should admit to engaging in the given behavior; if the problem has been pinpointed, there should be little disagreement as to its occurrence. Acknowledging the occurrence of a given behavior does not necessarily imply a commitment to change it. The complainer should also admit to a role in the problem, since by definition it takes two for a problem to exist. For example, if the wife wants the husband to spend more time with the children, she may admit to some responsibility for the problem by acknowledging, "I know that I sometimes interfere when you are playing with the kids . . ." If the complainer carefully searches, it is almost certain that she or he can identify personal behaviors that exacerbate the problem under discussion.

9. *Problem definitions should be brief.*   When defining a problem, there is no need to give example after example of its occurrence. Similarly, once a problem is defined, no further discussion of its psychological roots or meaning are necessary. Psychologizing, intrinsically rewarding but irrelevant to the goal of solving a problem, is best left for outside the problem-solving arena. The essence of problem-solving training is its solution focus: the definition phase is only a preliminary.

Examples: A well-defined problem includes a description of the undesirable behavior, a specification of the situation in which the problem occurs, and the consequences of the problem for the partner who is distressed by it, as shown in the following:

a. When you let a week go by without initiating sex, I feel rejected.
b. The problem is that although we have been talking a lot more lately, you still don't talk to me about your feelings. That makes me feel distant from you.

Problem Solution

10. *Focus on solutions.* The discussion now centers around what can be done about the problem. A technique called *brainstorming* helps maintain a solution-oriented discussion. When brainstorming, couples list many possible solutions to the problem, disregarding the quality of the solutions; the final solution is chosen from this list. By specifically instructing the couple to disregard the quality of the solutions, both members are less inhibited about proposing possible solutions; they need not fear scorn, anger, or any other disagreeable reaction from each other.

11. *Behavior change should include mutuality and compromise.* In the spirit of collaboration and mutual responsibility for problems, the final agreement should involve change in both partners. The complainer should offer to change some aspect of his or her behavior in order to help the partner change. In addition, spouses learn that they cannot always get exactly what they want when they want it; compromising is often necessary.

12. *Final agreements should be in writing.* They should be specific and spelled out in clear behavioral terms. Cues reminding both spouses of the changes they have agreed to make should be included when possible.

Example: Don will actively listen and reflect Laura's verbalization of her depression. He will not offer suggestions unless asked to do so, nor will he express anger and frustration with Laura. Laura will refrain from asking for suggestions unless she really wants to hear them.

The couple is encouraged to generalize problem-solving skills—in particular those designed to enhance the positiveness of verbal exchanges—to their day-to-day communication. In addition, more basic communication skills, when they are lacking, are taught in this phase of therapy. Examples include empathy and listening skills, expressing feelings, or appropriate anger expression.

The Final Stages of Therapy: Concerns with Maintenance

Therapy approaches an end when (1) the couple has mastered the various skills they initially lacked, and (2) they have resolved their major problems. The therapist's main concern at the end of therapy is with the maintenance of therapeutic gains. Inherent in BMT is programmed generalization, since couples are continuously practicing the skills taught in therapy in the natural environment of their homes. In addition, as therapy termination approaches, the therapist becomes less directive, allowing the couple to carry a greater burden of the session. Finally, a fading out of therapy procedure is employed; weekly sessions are switched to biweekly and then to monthly sessions. The therapist is able to assess the extent to which the couple has generalized the skills learned in therapy when regular contacts with the therapist no longer occur. Therapy sessions often function as discriminative stimuli for the adherence to the newly learned procedures, and a fading-out process allows the couple to slowly become accustomed to employing their skills without frequent therapist contact. Maintenance of treatment gains is often the most difficult phase of any therapy, and thus careful follow-up procedures are of supreme importance.

Effectiveness of BMT

There have been four controlled outcome studies with clinical populations, which meet the required methodological criteria for internal validity. Three of these have been conducted in our laboratories (Jacobson, 1977, 1978, 1979b).

In the first study (Jacobson, 1977), behavior exchange and problem-solving procedures were found more effective than a no–treatment control procedure on both observational and self-report measures. One year after termination, 90 percent of the spouses in the BMT group reported scores within the normal range of marital adjustment, whereas before therapy only 20 percent had reported scores in this range. In the second study (Jacobson, 1978), BMT was found to be more effective than a very credible placebo control condition; these differences were maintained at a six-month follow-up.

The above two studies employed moderately distressed couples and two components of BMT, behavior exchange procedures and problem-solving training. In the third study (Jacobson, 1979b), severely distressed couples were treated with problem-solving training. Six couples were studied as separate single-subject experiments, with data collected by spouses in the home serving as the primary criterion for change. This procedure allowed for functional relationships between specific therapy interventions and behavior changes to be established. For each couple, problem-solving training was compared to a control procedure, where couples were simply instructed to increase the frequency of pleasing behaviors. All six couples improved during therapy although in only three cases could improvement be specifically attributed to problem-solving. At follow-ups ranging from six months to a year, five of the six couples had maintained their improvement.

Whether BMT is more effective than other forms of marital therapy cannot be ascertained at this time. The only comparative study, conducted by Liberman, Levine, Wheeler, Sanders, and Wallace (1976), attempted to compare an insight-oriented approach with a behavioral one. Couples in both groups improved from pre- to posttherapy on self-report measures, although only the behavioral group showed improvement on problem-solving observational measures.

SUMMARY

In this chapter, we have discussed theoretical, assessment-related, and clinical aspects of BMT. The main theoretical premise is that marital satisfaction is a function of spouse-emitted reinforcers and punishments. The precise relationship between reinforcements and punishments and marital satisfaction is mediated by several factors. Data are consistent with this major premise. The principle of reciprocity takes into account the circular causality in a dyadic relationship and states that couples will reinforce and punish each other at equivalent rates. Empirically, the predictions from reciprocity theory have been supported, although negative reciprocity is more characteristic of unhappy than happy couples. There are numerous antecedents to marital distress, since there are many factors which affect the level of reinforcement and punishment exchanged in a relationship. Consequently, BMT emphasizes critical skills for relationship success, communication and problem-solving skills being considered the most important.

The assessment of marital distress is aimed at identifying the major relationship problems and the factors maintaining these problems. Assessment is broad-based and relies on interview, self-report, spouse-observational data, and direct observation of problem-solving behavior. Throughout therapy, the assessment process is continued in order to evaluate the effectiveness of therapy interventions.

Therapy interventions are dictated by both assessment information and specific technologies. Four themes are common to the various technologies the behavioral therapist can employ: positive tracking, positive control, reciprocity, and a focus in the learning of relationship skills. The initial stages of therapy are devoted to the creation of positive outcome expectancies, the development of a collaborative set, and the provision of some immediate relief from distress. These three interdependent goals are thought to greatly enhance the effectiveness of our technology.

The first active intervention employs behavior exchange procedures which serve as an expeditious way of providing the couple with some initial therapy benefits. Behavior exchange procedures attempt to exploit the reinforcement power already existent in the relationship by identifying pleasurable behaviors each spouse already receives and increasing these behaviors.

Once the couple is feeling happier about their relationship and have developed a collaborative set, the middle stages of therapy begin. Problem solving and communication training are employed to help the couple solve major difficulties requiring discussion and compromise. Problem-solving training focuses on the process of communication as an efficient way of achieving the ultimate goal of behavioral change. Through instructions, rehearsal, and therapist feedback, the couple is taught a number of specific rules which facilitate the solution of problems. The major concern of the final stages of therapy is the maintenance of therapeutic gains.

BMT has been established as a successful treatment strategy for mildly as well as severely distressed couples. Its effectiveness relative to alternative marital treatment strategies remains a goal for further research.

CHAPTER 20

BEHAVIORAL AND COGNITIVE-BEHAVIORAL APPROACHES TO OUTPATIENT TREATMENT WITH CHILDREN

Philip C. Kendall and Carolyn L. Williams

University of Minnesota

The treatment of behavior disorders in children has been a part of the behavioral literature since its inception. In fact, the person considered to be the founder of behaviorism, John B. Watson, utilized a study on the conditioned emotional response of an eleven-month-old child as an experimental test of his theories (Harris, 1979). The conditioning of little Albert, first described by Watson and Rayner (1920), is one of the most famous, widely cited, and unfortunately, misquoted studies in the psychological literature (Harris, 1979; Prytula, Oster, & Davis, 1977). Interestingly, Harris (1979), after examining the methodology and results of the little Albert study and how the details of the study changed over the years, concluded that "by itself the Albert study was not very convincing proof of the correctness of Watson's general view of personality and emotions" (p. 158).

Watson's interest in children was not limited to the little Albert study. His works included several articles and books on child rearing that were prepared for the general public (for example, Watson, 1927, 1928a, 1928b). Watson also served as an adviser to Mary Cover Jones, a child therapist who conducted treatment studies on the elimination of children's fears.

Jones's most well-known client was Peter, a child with fears very similar to those Albert was conditioned to have. Watson and Jones saw an opportunity to extend the work with little Albert by demonstrating with Peter that children's fears could be "unconditioned" (Jones, 1924a), just as Watson claimed that he could condition them (Watson & Rayner, 1920). Peter's treatment contained procedures that closely parallel those of today's desensitization and modeling. Jones decided to work directly with Peter's fear of rabbits, the fear that seemed to be the strongest. The first treatment program consisted of bringing Peter into the laboratory with three other children who were chosen because of their lack of fear of rabbits. The children played in the laboratory with the rabbit while Peter was present. After a period of time, Peter's fear "progressed from a great fear of the rabbit to a tranquil indifference and even a voluntary pat on the rabbit's back when others were setting the example" (Jones, 1924a, p. 312). At this point, his treatment was interrupted and when Peter returned, his fear was described as being at its original level.

Jones decided to begin another method of treatment she called *direct conditioning*. Peter was brought into the laboratory, seated in a high chair, and given his favorite food as the rabbit was brought closer and closer in a wire cage. The rabbit was brought as close as possible as long as it did not interfere with Peter's eating. Occasionally, other children who were not afraid were brought in to assist with the treatment. Jones (1924a) concluded that her treatment of Peter's fear of rabbits was very successful. She further concluded that the treatment generalized such that Peter was no longer fearful of cotton, a fur coat, or feathers. A modern-day reader of this study would find the methodology weak (for example, the modeling and desensitization procedures were confounded, and the observational techniques were inadequate), but the study nonetheless provided the framework for future treatments of both children and adults.

In Jones's subsequent research (1924b), she treated the fears of seventy children ranging in age from three months to seven years. Jones described seven different methods of treating children's fears and presented case-study results on their effectiveness. She concluded that only two, "direct conditioning" and "social imitation," produced "unqualified success" (p. 390). According to Jones, direct conditioning "associated the fear object with a craving object, and replaced the fear by a positive response. By the method of social imitation we allowed the subject to share, under controlled conditions, the social activity of a group of children especially chosen with a view to prestige effect" (Jones, 1924b, p. 390). Again, though the methodology was lacking, the treatment procedures she described are still widely used today (Johnson & Malamed, 1979).

There are several other studies in the early literature which forecast later developments in treatment techniques. Weber (1936) combined techniques similar to those used by Jones (1924a) with parental involvement. His client was a nineteen-month-old girl with a strong fear of her shadow. This case is one of the earliest in the behavioral literature in which a child's parent was actively involved in the treatment. The girl watched the therapist cast shadows of a doll, a ball, and her own hands on the wall while her father held her. Gradually, she moved from her father's arms to the floor and eventually played with the toys and watched their shadows with no outward signs of fear. This all occurred in one session, and her parents subsequently reported that she was no longer fearful at home as well. Another successful behavioral treatment for a common childhood problem, bed wetting or enuresis, was described by Mowrer and Mowrer in 1938. Their treatment introduced a device now known as the urine alarm, or bell and pad, which is still used in the treatment of enuresis (Doleys, 1977).

The early behaviorists focused on applying the principles of learning to the treatment of directly observable problem behaviors. The primary emphasis was on altering the antecedents and consequences of the observable behaviors and thereby modifying these behaviors. Thoughts or cognitive processes were siad to be unimportant to the change process. Gradually, over the years, a shift in emphasis occurred to include a much broader model of behavior modification. This broader model, often referred to as *cognitive behavior modification* (Mahoney, 1974a; Meichenbaum, 1977), allowed for the inclusion of thoughts or cognitive processes as behavior that could (and should) be studied and modified (Craighead, Wilcoxon-Craighead, & Meyers, 1978; Kendall, 1977). Two other shifts in behavior therapy with children can also be identified. Behavior therapists are beginning to treat much more complex behaviors, such as social skills (Combs & Slaby, 1977) or the behavior patterns of families, for example, juvenile delinquents (Tharp & Wetzel, 1969). Parents are also increasingly being included in their children's behavioral treatments, often in the role of cotherapist (Graziano, 1977).

This chapter serves as an introduction to the behavioral and cognitive behavioral treatment approaches typically utilized for outpatient children. The material is presented in two major sections—one covering the behavioral treatments and the other covering the combined cognitive behavioral approaches. These sections roughly parallel the time line along which treatments for children have progressed. Within each of the major sections, the material is organized around common childhood problem behaviors.

BEHAVIORAL TREATMENTS
Fears and Phobias

Studies of large numbers of children reveal that fears are very common in childhood. A classic developmental study by MacFarlane, Allen, and Honzik (1954) found that 90 percent of their sample had at least one specific fear between the ages of two and fourteen years. Lapouse (1966) reported that 40 percent of the children (ages six to twelve) he studied had seven or more fears. Although the incidence of fears in normal children appears to be quite high, the limited information on the prevalence of clinically significant fears or phobias suggests their incidence to be low, with the exception of school phobia (Graziano, DeGiovanni, & Garcia, 1979). School phobia is by far the most common childhood fear described in case studies in the behavioral literature, followed by reports on fears of animals, noise, and bodily injury. The controlled experimental investigations of fear reduction in children typically study children who have mild to moderate fears of animals, bodily injury, darkness, test anxiety, and social isolation (Graziano et al., 1979).

The most widely used behavioral treatments for children's fears are desensitization procedures (also referred to as counterconditioning), modeling techniques, and operant procedures (Johnson & Melamed, 1979). The desensitization techniques used today are strikingly similar to the procedures described by Jones (1924a, 1924b). Basically, desensitization involves the gradual exposure of the child to the feared stimulus while the child engages in behavior that is incompatible with the response of fear. With adult clients, muscular relaxation is often paired with the feared stimulus. Behavior therapists working with children have also used muscle relaxation as well as other techniques, such as feeding the child a favorite food, playing with the child, or having the child imagine a favorite hero while the feared stimulus is presented (Johnson & Melamed, 1979).

Modeling, like desensitization, was also foreshadowed by Jones (1924a, 1924b). The typical procedure for modeling involves having the fearful child watch a nonfearful playmate (the model) cope and interact with the feared stimulus. The child is then encouraged to imitate the model's behavior (see Bandura, 1969). The model may be either live or presented on film. Graziano et al. (1979) suggested an interesting use of modeling techniques for preventive purposes. They suggested that televised symbolic modeling may be used to "immunize" large numbers of children for common fears, such as entering school or stressful medical or dental procedures.

The operant procedures for fear reduction focus on rewarding the child's approach behavior to the fear stimulus and ignoring expressions of fear (Johnson & Melamed, 1979). Kennedy's (1965) treatment of school phobia is a good example of the use of operant procedures. This procedure requires that the school-phobic child be identified as early as possible and immediately forced to return to school. The child's parents are instructed to ignore all the child's complaints, including ones of physical symptoms. Regardless of how difficult it is to get the child to school in the morning, the parents are instructed to praise him or her for going to and staying at school when he or she returns in the afternoon. This procedure seems to be the most effective with younger children at the first onset of the symptoms. Kennedy (1965) reported successful results for all fifty of the school phobics he treated with this procedure.

Many of the studies on the effectiveness of the various treatments for childhood fears have been fraught with methodological problems. Two basic problems are the procedures used to identify children who have severe enough fears to warrant treatment and the assessment devices used to indicate whether the treatment was effective. Johnson and Melamed (1979) report that although a variety of assessment devices have been developed, very few have reported adequate reliability and validity. And without adequate assessment devices, it is difficult to determine treatment effectiveness. A recent review of desensitization procedures with children concluded that there was no clear evidence in the literature of their effectiveness because of methodological problems with the studies (Halzenbuehler & Schroeder, 1978). Graziano et al. (1979) concurred with that conclusion, but added that the research literature does support the effectiveness of the modeling techniques.

Enuresis and Encopresis

Children who wet their beds or soil their clothes past the age when other children are using the toilet properly cause considerable problems for themselves and their parents and are often referred to psychologists for treatment. The clinical terms for wetting and soiling are enuresis and encopresis, respectively. Of the two, nocturnal enuresis (referred to as enuresis throughout this chapter) is by far the more widely researched and treated by behavior therapists. However, Wright (1973) suggests that the problem of encopresis is rich in its behavioral implications and warrants further study.

Although it is true that most children who are enuretic at age five will "grow out of it" by adolescence or adulthood, no one can predict whether or not a specific child will do so (Doleys, 1977). For this reason, the younger child is treated in order to spare him or her the possible later in-convenience or embarrassment. There is a wide variety of available treat-ments for the enuretic child, ranging from psychoanalysis to surgery or medications to behavioral treatments (Doleys, 1977, 1979b).

Perhaps the most researched behavioral treatment for enuresis is the urine alarm, first described by Mowrer and Mowrer in 1938. The urine-alarm device is placed on the child's bed before he or she retires at night. Upon wetting, a sensing mechanism activates an alarm which awakens the child. The child can then get up and finish urinating in the toilet. Doleys's (1977) summary of the experimental studies on the urine alarm indicated a success rate of 71 percent, an average treatment duration of five to twelve weeks, and a relapse rate of 32 percent with use of the divice. Several vari-ations in the method, such as more frequent consultation and supervision of the parents (Dische, 1973), an overlearning period in which the child is required to maintain nighttime dryness while also drinking up to two pints of liquid one hour before bedtime (Young & Morgan, 1972), and an intermittent (instead of continuous) schedule of alarm presentation (Finley, Besserman, Bennett, Clapp, & Finley, 1973) have all resulted in either higher success rates or lower relapse rates or both (Doleys, 1977).

Azrin, Sneed, and Foxx (1974) used a urine alarm in their dry-bed train-ing program. In addition to the urine alarm, Azrin et al. added such fea-tures as training in inhibiting urination (retention-control training), posi-tive reinforcement for correct urination, training in rapid awakening, increased fluid intake, increased social motivation to be dry, self-correction of accidents (full-cleanliness training), and practice in correct toileting (positive practice). As a result, the dry-bed training program is a rather complicated and time-consuming method. However, all twenty-four chil-dren treated in the Azrin et al. study became dry in a shorter period of time than with the urine alarm alone. Again, as with the urine alarm, there was a 30 percent relapse rate after six months.

Bollard and Woodroffe (1977) utilized a parent-administered dry-bed training procedure and found results similar to those of Azrin et al. In a replication by Doleys, Ciminero, Tollison, Williams, and Wells (1977), fewer children met the dryness criteria and a longer treatment period was needed than in the Azrin et al. study. A two-year follow-up of the chil-dren treated by Doleys et al. revealed that 38 percent of the sample had relapsed (Williams, Doleys, & Ciminero, 1978).

The diversity of procedures utilized in dry-bed training has also been used singly, as have several other procedures with varying degrees of suc-cess (Doleys & Ciminero, 1976). Many of them (for example, positive re-inforcement for correct urination) are much easier to implement than the urine alarm or dry-bed training. Unfortunately, assessment techniques are not yet sophisticated enough to predict which procedure works best with which child. Therefore, Doleys and Ciminero suggest that a hierarchy of treatments be designed for each child. For example, the therapist might begin with having the child self-record his or her dry nights (this also serves as a baseline), then implement staggered awakenings (Creer & Davis, 1975), and finally use the urine alarm or dry-bed training, if necessary.

Encopresis, in spite of its frequency (approximately 3 percent of the population) has not received as much attention in the behavioral literature (Doleys, 1979a) despite several case studies (for example, Balson, 1973; Conger, 1970; Doleys & Arnold, 1975) that demonstrate the effectiveness of reinforcement and punishment contingencies in the elimination of the behavior. A problem often encountered by the behavior therapist in treating encopresis is that the child is not engaging in appropriate toileting at all, making it impossible to reinforce. Suppositories have been used to elicit elimination in toilet (for example, Ashkenazi, 1975; Wright, 1975; Wright & Walker, 1978). The child is given a suppository by the parent and placed on the toilet to defecate. The child is then rewarded if a defecation in the toilet occurs. Wright (1975) further recommends an enema if the suppository is ineffective and also suggests a mild punishment (for example, loss of television privileges for the day) when soiling occurs. The use of the rewards, suppositories, and punishments are gradually faded out of use in both procedures. Both Wright and Ashkenazi report successful outcomes with these procedures, although further well-controlled research studies are needed.

One additional consideration in the treatment of encopresis is Wright's (1973) description of a reinforcer that appears to be consistently effective with the encopretics he has treated and observed. The reinforcer of earned time with parents seems to be uniformly applicable. This effect is in keeping with other authors' hypothesis that soiling is used as a means of acquiring parental attention (for example, Balson, 1973; Conger, 1970).

Conduct Disorders

Children's problem behaviors included in the category of conduct disorders are much more complex than those previously described. In treating conduct-disordered children, behavior therapists can no longer specify a single, discrete behavior to be changed, but must work with a class of behaviors (for example, aggressiveness, juvenile delinquency, vandalism, disobedience) and very often the child's total social environment. Because of these considerations, many behavior therapists work directly with persons in the child's natural environment, such as parents and teachers. This shift represents a change from traditional psychotherapy in which the child is usually treated alone for a few hours per week in the therapist's office (for example, Axline, 1947).

Several different treatment strategies have been introduced in the research literature on conduct disorders. The most widely researched behavioral treatments have been those involving parent-training techniques, although evidence is also being accumulated on home token economics and contingency contracting (Wells & Forehand, in press). The major assumption behind the use of the parent-training procedures is that since children's maladaptive behavior is learned in their natural environment, the best way to treat it is by modifying that environment through changes in the parent's behavior (Graziano, 1977).

Patterson and his colleagues (for example, Patterson, 1974; Patterson, Cobb, & Ray, 1973; Wiltz & Patterson, 1974) and Forehand and his associates (for example, Forehand & King, 1974, 1977; Peed, Roberts, & Forehand, 1977) have described and utilized two of the more widely researched parent-training programs. Patterson's program focuses on children ages five to thirteen, whereas the program utilized by Forehand is designed for children age two to eight. Most often it is the mother who is trained with either program.

Patterson's program contains three parts (see Patterson, Reid, Jones, & Conger, 1975). Parents must complete the requirements in each part before proceeding to the next. The first part involves teaching the parents the basic principles of social-learning theory as applied to children. The parents are assigned a programmed text (either Patterson, 1971, or Patterson & Gullion, 1968) and must pass a written test on the material before continuing. The parents are then taught to apply the general principles to their particular child by learning how to define precisely and record their child's behavior. The parents are asked to define and monitor two prosocial and two deviant behaviors of their child for three days in the home during this second phase. In the last phase of the program, the parents are taught how to design specific intervention programs for the behaviors they recorded during the second phase. The interventions taught involve a point system which includes the provision of points for prosocial behavior and loss of points for deviant behaviors, the use of social reinforcers (for example, praise), and the use of a time-out procedure (five minutes of isolation).

The program utilized by Forehand and associates, although similar to Patterson's, has also some important differences. As mentioned earlier, the children treated by Forehand are typically younger. In addition, Forehand focuses on a more general parent-child interaction style rather than discrete behaviors, trains parents in the clinic with the child present, and requires the parents to demonstrate changes in their behaviors as well as in the child's (Wells & Forehand, in press).

The program researched by Forehand and associates was originally developed and described by Hanf (1968, 1969). The Hanf-Forehand program has two stages in which different skills are taught to the parents. In the first phase, the parent is taught how to increase his or her reinforcing value to the child, how to give effective commands, and how to use the principles of positive reinforcement and extinction to control the child's behavior. During the second phase, a time-out procedure is taught. The skills are taught to the parents via modeling, feedback, praise, in vivo practice, and homework assignments (see Forehand & Peed, 1979).

Research findings on both the Patterson and Hanf-Forehand programs have generally been favorable, leading one to conclude that parent training is an effective treatment for many conduct-disordered children. Additional research is warranted to investigate the efficacy of these programs with fathers as well as mothers, and with children and families who are more severely disturbed. Nevertheless, the methodology employed in research in this area has included treatment- versus control-group comparisons, naive observers in the home setting, and observational coding systems with demonstrated reliability and validity, lending credibility to the research reports (Wells & Forehand, in press).

The other two behavioral treatments for conduct-disorder problems, home token economy and contingency contracting, have not been as widely researched as the parent-training programs. Home token economies are very similar to the token economies described earlier in this volume. With the therapist's assistance, the parent designs a system in which desirable behaviors of the child are rewarded with tokens and the child's undesirable behaviors are punished through withdrawal of the tokens. The child is then able to purchase rewards with the tokens. Though few studies have demonstrated the efficacy of the home token economy (Wells & Forehand, in press), those that have been done have had encouraging results (for example, Alvord, 1971; Christophersen, Arnold, Hill, & Quilitch, 1972; Christophersen, Barnard, Ford, & Wolf, 1976). More rigorous outcome measures such as home observations and comparisons with parent-training procedures are needed.

Contingency contracting is often used with older children and adolescents. It is similar to a token economy in that certain behaviors are defined as positive and are rewarded, and other behaviors are considered undesirable and are punished. Contracting differs from token economies in that the child or adolescent has much greater input into the behaviors and reinforcers chosen as targets. Thus, contracting is more appropriate for older children or adolescents than is the token economy, since it allows them some input or control over their own welfare. Finally, adolescents and older children are much better able to understand and participate in the negotiations that precede the contract—thus acquiring many therapeutically desirable problem-solving communication skills.

Table 20.1 Sample behavioral contract for a fourteen-year-old girl with truancy, academic, and home behavioral problems.

Janice's Responsibilities/ Parent's Privileges	Janice's Privileges/ Parent's Responsibilities
Attend school each day	Each day at school earns $1.00 to be spent for new clothes
Bring weekly math quizzes home	Each quiz brought home with a "D" or better grade earns Janice a ride in the family car to a point of Janice's choice not more than 10 miles from home.
Be out of bed and dressed by 7:10 A.M. on week days	Breakfast of Janice's choice will be on the table at 7:10. After that it will be thrown out and she will not be allowed to cook anything else.

Bonus Clause: If Janice attends three days or more of school she will earn a shopping trip with her mother for two hours on Saturday afternoon.
Penalty Clause: Janice's use of the phone shall be contingent upon her having been to school that day.

SOURCE: Weathers, L. R., & Liberman, R. P. Modification of family behavior. In D. Marholin (Ed.), Child behavior therapy. New York: Gardner Press, 1977, p. 177. Reproduced with permission of Gardner Press.

In a behavioral contract, the parent's responsibilities are often the child's privileges, and the child's responsibilities are the parent's privileges. Weathers and Liberman (1977) have illustrated this with a contract written for a fourteen-year-old girl referred for truancy, poor academic performance, and home behavior problems (Table 20.1).

Research on contracting has yielded mixed results. Although Stuart, Tripodi, Jayaratne, and Camburn (1976) found that adolescents treated with contingency contracting showed significant (but small) improvements on measures of home and school behaviors relative to a waiting-list control group, others have not had such positive results. For example, Weathers and Liberman (1975) utilized contracting with six predelinquent adolescents and found that neither curfew compliance nor school attendance improved with the introduction of a contract. Only verbal abusiveness, based on the questionable subjective reports of the parents, improved. In a later review of contracting, these same authors concluded that without additional interventions, "most contingency contracts are worth just about as much as the paper they are printed on" (Weathers & Liberman, 1977, p. 181). Although contingency contracting has face validity, future research is needed to establish its effectiveness. A promising line of research would be directed towards the identification of those clients for whom contracts would be effective and those for whom something else is needed.

Social Withdrawal

Children who are socially isolated or withdrawn are receiving increasing attention from behavior therapists. Perhaps because of the very nature of their problems, these children have been relatively ignored in the past. Unlike conduct-disordered children whose behaviors often demand adult attention, socially isolated or withdrawn children cause few problems for the adults in their environment and are thus easily overlooked. However, one dimension of child behavior that consistently emerges from factor-analytic studies of symptom check lists is social withdrawal (Evans & Nelson, 1977; Quay, 1972).

A variety of treatment approaches have been implemented with socially withdrawn children. This section describes the behavioral interventions utilizing operant procedures and modeling. The use of contingent adult attention has been demonstrated to be effective in increasing the amount of isolate children's interactions with peers (for example Allen, Hart, Buell, Harris, & Wolf, 1964; Buell, Stoddard, Harris, & Baer, 1968). There is doubt, however, about whether increasing the amount of social interaction by itself is an appropriate treatment goal (Combs & Slaby, 1977). Consider the example of an isolate child who, during treatment, increased the amount of his or her peer interactions, which resulted in his or her being the recipient of more ridicule and rejection from the peers. Gottman provided evidence that this may occur in some cases. He found no evidence of a relationship between a measure of peer acceptance and the frequency of peer interactions, but did find a significant relationship between a measure of peer rejection and the frequency of peer interaction. From this he concluded that with a greater frequency of peer interactions, there is a greater likelihood that the interactions will be negative, resulting in peer rejection (Gottman, 1977b).

Using the principles of observational learning, O'Connor (1969, 1972) treated isolate preschool children with a narrated film of a withdrawn child who gradually engages in more and more complex social interactions. His findings indicated that children who view such a film increase their social interactions. In his second study (O'Connor, 1972), modeling was shown to produce more stable changes than a shaping procedure. Evers and Schwarz 1973) replicated O'Connor's (1972) findings. However, when Gottman (1977a) controlled for some of the methodological problems of the earlier studies, no differences on any of the behavioral measures or sociometric ratings were found between the group of children viewing the modeling film and the group who saw a control film. Furthermore, Gottman (1977a) questioned the use of low frequency of peer interaction as a method for selecting children in need of treatment and suggested that sociometric measures of peer acceptance are more appropriate.

What appears to be missing from these procedures is the teaching of the specific social, cognitive, and behavioral skills necessary to gain peer acceptance and to minimize the possibility of peer rejection. Once a child is taught these skills, the operant and modeling procedures could be utilized to increase his or her peer interactions. Studies utilizing the combination of these procedures are discussed in the section on cognitive behavioral treatments in this chapter (see also Kendall & Urbain, in press).

Hyperactivity

Although hyperactivity is sometimes considered a school-related problem and is treated within the school setting (see Chapter 21), hyperactive children's problem behaviors often require outpatient treatment as well. It is widely accepted that the term *hyperactivity* applies to a somewhat heterogeneous group of children. However, the core of problem behaviors associated with the term include excessive activity, attentional deficit, distractibility, impulsivity, and poor peer relationships. Medications for hyperactivity have been demonstrated to be effective in the management of the problem. However, when used alone, the lack of improvement in the child's home situation has resulted in a search for additional interventions (Pelham, 1978).

Several investigators (for example, Daniels, 1973; Hall & Broden, 1967) have successfully trained parents to use a number of behavioral techniques to treat their children's hyperactive behaviors. The parent-training procedures described in the conduct-disorder section of this chapter are often used with hyperactive children. It is important to note that these procedures were not designed specifically for the treatment of hyperactivity, and further research is needed to tailor these interventions to the problems of hyperactive children and their families (Mash & Dalby, 1979).

COGNITIVE-BEHAVIORAL TREATMENTS[1]
Impulsivity

The initial impetus for cognitive-behavioral approaches with children was research focusing on the treatment of impulsivity. Impulsivity has been

1. Due to limited research, we have not discussed the cognitive-behavioral treatment of either enuresis and encopresis or fears and phobias. However, in the area of fears and phobias, the work of Kanfer, Karoly, and Newan (1975) is recommended to the interested reader.

considered a cognitive style characterized by rapid responding without adequate deliberation (Kagan, 1966), leading to poor performance on various tasks (Messer, 1976).

Some of the early studies on impulsivity attempted to train impulsive children to slow down before giving an answer to a standardized test (for example, Kagan, Person, & Welch, 1966). Generally, these studies showed that impulsive children could be taught to increase the amount of time between seeing a test item and giving a response, but they continued to make a high number of errors (Craighead et al., 1978; Kendall & Finch, 1979; Messer, 1976). Apparently, just getting the children to slow down is not enough, for the children continue to make a significant amount of errors.

A classic study by Meichenbaum and Goodman (1971) stimulated much of the recent work on the treatment of impulsivity. In this study, a self-instructional treatment program was described. The self-instructions used by Meichenbaum and Goodman included the following elements: (1) questions attempting to identify the task, (2) answers to those questions and plans for completing the task. (3) guidance while performing the task and a means for correcting mistakes, and (4) self-reinforcement for correct responses. Meichenbaum and Goodman (1971) gave the following example of their self-instructions:

Okay, what is it I have to do? You want me to copy the picture with the different lines. I have to go slow and be careful. Okay, draw the line down, down, good; then to the right, that's it; now down some more and to the left. Good, I'm doing fine so far. Remember go slow. Now back up again. No, I was supposed to go down. That's okay. Just erase the line carefully. . . . Good. Even if I make an error I can go on slowly and carefully. Okay, I have to go down now. Finished. I did it. (p. 117)

The children were taught the use of self-instructions individually by an adult through a series of steps:

1. Adult performs task and self-instructs aloud.
2. Child performs task and adult instructs aloud.
3. Child performs task and self-instructs aloud.
4. Child performs task and whispers self-instruction.
5. Child performs task and silently self-instructs.

The children who received the self-instructional training showed significant improvement over children in the control groups on a number of psychometric instruments, but no differences were found on measures of classroom behavior.

Kendall and Finch (1979) developed a treatment program which combines self-instructional training provided via modeling with social praise and a response-cost procedure. The effectiveness of this program was first tested with a single-subject experimental design (Kendall & Finch, 1976). The subject was a nine-year-old boy referred to outpatient treatment for behavior problems. The child performed impulsively on the Matching Familiar Figures (MFF) test (Kagan, 1966), climbed in and out of his chair, and changed the focus of his behavior without apparent reason. These "switches" in behavior were defined as a shift from one behavior to another when the first behavior was not yet complete. Three categories of switches were targeted for treatment: (1) topics of conversation, (2) games played with, and (3) rules of play. The child's therapist provided self-instructional training at the beginning of each therapy session and included a visual prompt stating "stop, listen, look, and think." After self-instructional training, the child was given five dimes and told that he could keep them if he did not switch. Each type of switch was placed under the self-instructions and response-cost contingency in a multiple-baseline design. The number of switches decreased as the treatment was applied to each type of switch and this decrease was maintained at a six-month follow-up. In addition, improvement was obtained on the MFF and teacher reports at both posttreatment and follow-up. This case study was followed by a group comparison-treatment study (Kendall & Finch, 1978) that provided further support for the effectiveness of the cognitive-behavioral training program.

Problem-solving techniques, such as training in Interpersonal Cognitive Problem Solving (ICPS) skills (for example, Spivack & Shure, 1974), have also been investigated with emotionally disturbed children characterized as impulsive. The ICPS program teaches children to think of the consequences of their behavior, to evaluate others' emotions, and to solve interpersonal conflicts through generating and evaluating alternative solutions. A ten-week program described by Spivack and Shure (1974) taught these problem-solving skills using scripts, stories, and role plays. The results suggested that the impulsive children showed improved social adjustment as measured by teacher ratings. However, as Urbain and Kendall (1980) point out, methodological improvements, such as an attention control group, are needed before the effectiveness of the program can be fully determined.

Hyperactivity

Cognitive-behavioral interventions for children's hyperactive behaviors offer much promise as effective treatments. In a sense, they attempt to overcome some of the problems inherent in other treatments of hyperactivity (for example, the lack of generalization with the behavioral interventions and the side effects of the medications). Cognitive-behavioral treatments often focus on the hyperactive child's inability to maintain attention and control impulsivity, the very symptoms that Douglas (1972) suggested may account for most of the deficits found in hyperactive children.

Douglas, Parry, Marton, and Garson (1976) utilized a training procedure with hyperactive boys that was based on Meichenbaum and Goodman's (1971) self-instructional training. Their goal was to teach the hyperactive boys more effective ways to approach cognitive tasks, academic problems, and social situations. They found that the treated subjects showed significantly greater improvement than a control group on several of the psychometric measures, leading them to conclude that cognitive training is an effective treatment for hyperactive children. Unfortunately, like Meichenbaum and Goodman (1971), they did not find improvements on a teacher-rating scale of classroom behavior. Douglas et al. (1976) suggested that the lack of effect on teacher ratings may reflect the training program's concentration on internal thoughts and the development of internal self-control, rather than on the more outwardly observable behavior. A suggested possible solution would be the combination of self-control training with contingency-management techniques.

The cognitive-behavioral treatment package developed by Kendall and Finch (1979)—which is a combination of self-instructional training taught through modeling with contingency-management procedures—was compared to medications (Methylphenidate) in the treatment of hyperactive children (Kendall, Yellin, & Greenberg, 1979). These authors report preliminary findings which indicate that, based on teacher ratings, the cognitive-behavioral procedures produced significant improvements that paralleled those resulting from the medications. That is, though the improvements due to medication were slightly better than those due to the cognitive-behavioral procedures, there were no significant differences between the effectiveness of the two treatment approaches. Additional research should seek to further specify those hyperactive children for whom the cognitive-behavioral procedures are most effective. Research by Bugental, Whalen, and Henker (1977) hints that hyperactive children whose attributional style is one of personal control (rather than external control) are particularly responsive to such self-control treatments.

Perhaps the key cognitive component of the cognitive-behavioral procedures used with both impulsive and hyperactive children is self-instructional training (Meichenbaum, 1975a, 1977). A recent study by Kendall and Wilcox (1979) compared two different types of self-instructional training (each provided via modeling and combined with social praise and a response-cost contingency) with nonself-controlled children. *Concrete* self-instructions were worded so as to refer to the specific training task at hand, whereas *conceptual* self-instructions were worded more globally and abstractly, so as to apply to a broader range of problems. Using the Self-Control Rating Scale (Kendall & Wilcox, 1979) and the hyperactivity items of the Conners Teacher Questionnaire (Conners, 1969), teachers' blind ratings evidenced positive changes for both types of self-instructional training at posttreatment and follow-up, but the *conceptual* self-instructions were superior in facilitating the generalization of improvements in self-control. These results underscore the importance of conceptual self-instructions in attaining generalization from cognitive-behavioral treatments.

Conduct Disorders

As mentioned earlier in this chapter, parent-training programs are among the most effective and common behavioral treatments for conduct disorders. In an attempt to improve a parent-training program, Wells, Forehand, and Griest (1978) added self-control elements to the Hanf-Forehand program. The child's parents were asked to monitor their use of the learned parenting skills (self-monitoring) and to self-reinforce when they used the skills appropriately. The addition of these self-control procedures to the program produced more improvement on the child's behavior at follow-up than the use of parent training alone.

Another cognitive-behavioral treatment for families of conduct-disordered children is conflict-resolution-skills training, primarily designed for older children and adolescents. Therapists utilizing this approach assume that the child's problem behaviors are the result of family conflict caused by poor interaction skills, and they attempt to teach the needed negotiation skills (Wells & Forehand, in press). Basically, these programs train the family members to utilize techniques, such as defining the problem, expressing feelings, and asking for the other's opinion during conflicts. Results of several studies on these techniques are promising (for example, Kifer, Lewis, Green, & Phillips, 1974; Little & Kendall, 1979; Martin & Twentyman, 1976; Robin, Kent, O'Leary, Foster, & Prinz, 1977), although the therapist must be aware of the problems of generalizing the behavior learned in the clinic to the home (Robin et al., 1977; Foster, 1978).

Other investigators utilizing a cognitive behavioral approach with conduct-disordered children have treated the child separate from his or her family. The "think-aloud" program for aggressive boys described by Camp, Blom, Herbert, and van Doorninck (1977) is a good example. This program involved daily thirty-minute training sessions extending over six weeks. Children were taught to use self-instructions on cognitive impersonal tasks as well as in interpersonal situations. Camp et al. (1977) reported an increase in teacher ratings of prosocial behavior and improvement on some of the psychometric tests for the group trained in the program, although no differences on teacher ratings of aggressiveness were found between the treated and nontreated groups. The results of the think-aloud program are encouraging though, and further study is warranted.

Goodwin and Mahoney (1975) treated three aggressive boys with a cognitive modeling film and an interesting procedure. In this "taunting" procedure, the child stood inside a circle while three other children verbally provoked him. The child's behavior was observed during these sessions for any coping responses. The first session was used as a baseline. Treatment consisted of the child being shown a three-minute video tape of a nine-year-old being taunted by five other children. Cognitive coping statements of the taunted child were dubbed onto the video tape. After the first viewing of the video tape, none of the three boys increased their number of coping responses during the taunting game, but after a second viewing when the therapist pointed out the coping statements and discussed them with the child, all three children used more coping responses during the subsequent taunting game. These gains were maintained in a one-week follow-up. Improvements in appropriate classroom behavior were also observed in all three children.

Two studies on the effectiveness of the "turtle" technique (Robin & Schneider, 1976; Schneider, 1974) have shown it to be useful in reducing aggressive behavior in emotionally disturbed children. Children are taught to use imagery relaxation, problem solving, and peer support through a story about a turtle. The turtle is able to exhibit self-control by learning to go into its shell, problem solve, and relax when it is angry.

Social Withdrawal

The behavioral treatments for problems of social withdrawal have been shown to be effective in increasing the amount of social interaction of isolate children. However, they have been criticized for not teaching these children the skills necessary to increase their amount of peer acceptance. For this reason, cognitive and verbal components have been added to the operant and modeling strategies. These components include coaching, role playing, rehearsal, guided practice, information exchange and feedback, and self-control techniques (Combs & Slaby, 1977).

Self-instructional training was included in a treatment program designed by Gottman, Gonso, and Shuler (1976). Two children, low on a sociometric measure of peer acceptance, were treated in this three-stage program.

The first stage consisted of a ten-minute video tape of children who want to join a group of other children. Four vignettes were shown, each narrated by a female voice using coping self-statements. The statements represented an inner debate with the following elements: (1) expressing a desire to initiate interaction, (2) worrying about a negative outcome, (3) a self-debate, (4) deciding to go ahead, (5) approaching the group, (6) greeting the other children, and (7) asking permission to join in or requesting help. The second and third stages involved teaching the subjects how to make friends, dispense positive reinforcement, give appropriate information, and be effective listeners. Role playing, instructions, and practice in the classroom were used. The results of this study were very encouraging, demonstrating that the program, as measured by a sociometric device, resulted in greater peer acceptance for the treated children.

A study by Combs and Lahey (in press) did not provide as positive results for self-instructional training. Three children received two hour-long self-instruction training sessions which included practice in a series of social encounters. Their classroom behavior was observed both before and after treatment, and little change was obtained after self-instructional training. However, when an operant-treatment procedure (the experimenter prompted and reinforced subject and peer interaction) was introduced, an increase was obtained in all the measured social behaviors. The design of this study does not allow a complete evaluation of self-instructional training, since all the subjects received that training first. It is possible that the self-instruction training taught the children the appropriate skills which they chose to use when rewarded during the operant procedure. Furthermore, measures of peer acceptance were not obtained, making it impossible to compare it directly with the Gottman et al. (1976) study.

Oden and Asher (1977) reported using a coaching strategy with third- and fourth-grade isolate children and successfully increasing their sociometric peer acceptance. The coaching consisted of individual sessions describing concepts of how to play with children, practice in using those concepts in social games with peers, and feedback regarding their performance. Although the treatment effects were obtained on the sociometric measure of peer acceptance, behavioral-observation measures did not yield significant differences.

A CLOSING COMMENT

Behavioral approaches to the treatment of outpatient children continue to enjoy a published literature that both describes the procedures to be used in treatment and provides evidence for their effectiveness. Nevertheless, as therapists strive to attain greater generalization of the treatment effects, more attention is being paid to the general process of self-control and the cognitive factors involved. Correspondingly, as interventions shift from treating simple discrete behaviors to more complex behavior patterns, there is an increasing interest in treatment procedures that integrate cognitive behavioral and social-cognitive approaches.

These shifts in emphasis are quite recent, and as yet, we do not have all the answers. Much more needs to be learned about how to best combine and integrate the demonstrated efficiencies of behavior modification with the cognitive activities of the client in the effort to produce marked therapeutic change (Kendall & Hollon, 1979).

SUMMARY

Following a brief description of the historical precursors of outpatient behavior therapy with children, this chapter describes both the behavioral and cognitive-behavioral procedures employed today and the related outcome literature. The major categories of childhood disorders treated on an outpatient basic include fears and phobias, enuresis and encopresis, conduct disorders, social withdrawal, impulsivity, and hyperactivity.

Behavioral interventions, such as desensitization, modeling, and operant procedures, have been the most frequently and successfully employed for fears and phobias. A good deal of research supports the use of the urine-alarm and dry-bed training techniques for problems with childhood enuresis, but the problems of treating encopresis have not been as extensively studied.

Children with conduct disorders, hyperactivity, and social withdrawal have received the attention of therapists from both behavioral and cognitive-behavioral perspectives. Certain behavioral interventions for conduct disorders, such as parent-training programs, have been quite successful, whereas procedures, such as contingency contracting, have produced mixed results. Operant techniques and modeling have been applied for hyperactivity and social withdrawal.

Cognitive-behavioral interventions for conduct disorders, impulsivity/hyperactivity, and social withdrawal employ behavioral strategies and include a special focus on teaching children thinking processes. For example, self-instructions and cognitive problem solving are important components of cognitive-behavioral procedures. Additional research is needed to develop the most efficacious methods for integrating cognitive and behavioral procedures.

CHAPTER 21

BEHAVIOR MODIFICATION IN THE CLASSROOM

Benjamin B. Lahey

University of Georgia

Ronald S. Drabman

University of Mississippi Medical Center

The goal of applications of behavior modification to classroom settings is to create environments in which both learning and classroom behavior are enhanced. Such applications are a natural for a discipline that is heavily based on the principles of learning and have, as a result, been extensively explored. The brief but busy history of these efforts, ranging from about 1965 to the present, can be roughly divided into two stages on the basis of the behavioral strategies advocated. In the first stage, it was assumed that methods that reduced the frequency of behaviors that were incompatible with learning would indirectly increase the rate of academic learning. In the second stage, it was demonstrated that directly modifying academic behavior indirectly reduced the frequency of incompatible behaviors.

In this chapter, we will review and evaluate the major behavioral methods employed in both strategies and attempt to demonstrate the value of each strategy in the classroom. Although an emphasis of any classroom behavior-modification program must be on academic learning, methods that directly reinforce academic behavior cannot be counted on to accomplish indirectly all of the goals of behavior modification. There are many serious aspects of disruptive, aggressive, and social behavior that must be targeted separately. Hence, an effective classroom behavior-modification program should employ a combination of both strategies.

MODIFYING BEHAVIORS INCOMPATIBLE WITH LEARNING

Reinforcement in the Classroom

TEACHER ATTENTION

The first applications of behavior-modification principles were designed to alter behaviors that were either inherently maladaptive and/or were believed to be incompatible with academic learning. Researchers at the University of Washington Laboratory Preschool (Bijou & Baer, 1963) noticed that the probability of adult attention to a child after that child's emission of inappropriate behavior was disproportionately high. They hypothesized that adult attention may have been acting as a reinforcer to maintain the child's inappropriate behavior. To test this hypothesis, it was decided to vary systematically the contingencies under which adult attention would be dispensed.

A typical study used the ABAB design. Ann, for example, was a four-year-old who rarely initiated conversation or cooperative play with adjacent children or responded in any way to overtures directed toward her. Moreover, she was so diffident and passive that she seldom cried or defended herself, even when another child hit her, pushed her, or took her possessions. Behavioral assessment indicated that only 10 percent of her time was spent in social interaction with children. Close scrutiny also revealed that most of the adult attention she received was contingent upon behaviors incompatible with social play.

Within the ABAB design, the 10 percent peer social interaction served as a baseline (A). Next, adult attention was made contingent upon Ann's social interaction with other children (B). During this phase, Ann spent better than 60 percent of her time interacting with children. To determine whether it was the experimental procedure or simply time in preschool that was responsible for the improved behavior, the contingencies were reversed (A) and Ann received adult attention only when she was not interacting with children. Soon after the reversal began, Ann began spending less than 20 percent of her time in interaction with children. Finally, the experimental contingencies were resumed (B) and frequency of interaction with peers again increased. A follow-up check was made several weeks later. At that time, Ann's peer interaction was still higher than baseline although the explicit contingencies had been removed (Allen, Hart, Buell, Harris, & Wolf, 1964).

Procedures in which adult praise and attention are made contingent upon appropriate behavior, while inappropriate behavior is ignored, have proven very successful, especially with young children. Other school behaviors that have been controlled or improved by this method include restricting playmate choice (Bijou & Baer, 1967), motor skills (Johnson, Kelly, Harris, & Wolf, 1966), climbing (Hall & Broden, 1967), cooperative behavior (Hart, Reynolds, Baer, Brawley, & Harris, 1968), regressing crawling (Harris, Johnson, Kelley, & Wolf, 1964), and attending school (Copeland, Brown, & Hall, 1974). Taken together, these studies indicate that teachers are undoubtedly contributing to the maintenance, and perhaps the acquisition, of classroom problem behavior. Children rarely get attention for appropriate behavior. Indeed, the majority of teacher interactions with individual children are of a pejorative nature. Very often, young children engaging in problem behavior are simply performing for the only teacher attention or reinforcement available.

In 1967 Becker and his colleagues at the University of Illinois began to use the methodology and techniques that had proved so successful with individual children with entire classes of elementary school students. They reasoned that if misdirected teacher reinforcement was responsible for maintaining problem behavior in individual children, then training elementary school teachers to contingently praise desirable behavior while ignoring undesirable behavior would be an important contribution to the management of an entire class. In a series of studies, Becker and his colleagues demonstrated that teachers' use or misuse of contingent praise and ignore techniques could predictably create and reduce problem behavior (Becker, Madsen, Arnold, & Thomas, 1967; Madsen, Becker, & Thomas, 1968).

A study by Madsen, Becker, and Thomas (1968) provides a good example of this strategy. Baseline measurement was taken on the following inappropriate behaviors: gross motor, object noise, disturbance and other's property, contact verbalization, turning around, mouthing objects, and isolated play. These behaviors had been selected because they were believed to hinder academic learning.

After baseline-rates of problem behavior had been established, the teacher was asked to write a set of class rules on the board. The children repeated these rules until they knew them. In the third phase, the rules were left visible, and the teacher was instructed to ignore inappropriate behavior. Next, praise for appropriate behavior was added to the already present rules and ignoring. To assess the effect of the treament package, baseline procedures were introduced and rules, praise, and ignoring were removed for a short time. Finally, the study terminated with a return to the treatment package of rules, ignoring inappropriate behavior, and praise for appropriate behavior. Results indicated that the combination of rules, ignoring, and praise was differentially effective in reducing problem behavior. Similar procedures have been used to increase study behavior (Hall, Lund, & Jackson, 1968), decrease off-task behavior (Marlowe, Madsen, Bowen, Reardon, & Logue, 1978), and decrease aggressive behavior (Brown & Elliot, 1965).

Contingent praising and ignoring are powerful techniques and should be part of every teacher's repertoire of instructional procedures. However, they are not without potential problems, and in using them, care should be taken to avoid two pitfalls. First, a teacher must not forget that he or she is but one of several possible reinforcers available in the classroom. Peer reinforcement is a competing reinforcer which grows more powerful as children get older. Sometimes peer reinforcement in the classroom is so powerful that a teacher's ignoring technique leads to greater levels of disruptive behavior (O'Leary, Becker, Evans, & Saudargas, 1969). In such situations, ignoring is not an extinction procedure; it simply makes it easier for alternate reinforcers to create problem behaviors. Second, a teacher may fail to note the importance of descriptive praise. Although saying "Good" to a child is often an effective reinforcer, it is not as effective as describing what the child did that earned the praise (Drabman & Tucker, 1974). The statement, "That was very good the way you raised your hand and waited to be recognized," is preferable to simply saying "Good," because it restates the contingencies and prompts the child to engage in the appropriate behavior again.

Teachers can avoid falling into either of these traps by taking continuous data on any behavior-modification procedure they attempt. Monitoring the data will help teachers discover if they are ignoring too much or not using enough descriptive praise. The data will indicate when changes need to be made. Using behavioral techniques without taking data is not behavior modification; it is simply capricious use of behavioral technology.

BACK-UP REINFORCERS: THE TOKEN ECONOMY

Unfortunately, systematic manipulation of social reinforcement will not always bring behavior to acceptable levels. In some cases, the classroom data, which can be taken by the teacher, teacher's aide, room-mother, or the pupils themselves, will indicate that a more powerful procedure is needed to bring problem behaviors under control. In other cases, the occurrence of appropriate behavior is too infrequent for the effective use of social reinforcement. In such cases, it may be necessary to use a stronger back-up reinforcer.

In a token system, the child is periodically rated on the behaviors in which the teacher is interested and is given some symbol of this rating, called a token. These tokens are exchangeable for back-up reinforcers. At its best, a token-reinforcement program teaches a child to work for symbolic rewards, to delay gratification, and to work on an intermittent schedule. The development of such behaviors is crucial if the child is to be returned to normal classroom procedures.

Although some classroom token programs are costly (Wolf, Giles, & Hall, 1968), most are practical enough for the normal schoolroom (O'Leary & Drabman, 1971), and some cost virtually nothing (Drabman, Spitalnik, & Spitalnik, 1974; Main & Munro, 1977).

What can be used as a token? A token should have several properties: (1) it should be easy to dispense; (2) it should be readily portable; (3) its value should be easily understandable; (4) it should not require extensive outside work by teachers or other personnel; and (5) it should be easily identifiable as the property of the recipient (O'Leary & Drabman, 1971). Most token programs have used check marks or points given by the teacher, although stamps (Wolf, Giles, & Hall, 1968), stars (Barber & Kagey, 1977), and poker chips (Bushell, Wrobel, & Michaelis, 1968) have also been used successfully.

Choosing a token is more a practical than theoretical decision. Checkmark or point systems usually involve fewer administrative problems, but they may not be as interesting or effective as physical tokens. With retarded children, points or check marks probably have very little intrinsic value, and a teacher may have to use physical tokens. The teacher can hand one physical token to the child and then immediately exchange it for a back-up reinforcer. Repeating this procedure while gradually increasing the delay in exchange will teach the child to value the tokens. It is essential that the child learn this value.

Since physical tokens are like money, they can be used to teach practical mathematics to older children. They also allow children a display of wealth, thus increasing their value as reinforcers. The problem with tangible reinforcers is that because they are tangible, they can be thrown, chewed upon, played with, lent, stolen, or used to buy favors (Bushell, Wrobel, & Michaelis, 1968). A teacher who decides to use physical tokens has decided to risk potentially disruptive by-products in favor of the interest and excitement generated by a tangible reinforcement system. As a compromise, a teacher might want to begin the program with points or check marks, and as classroom behavior improves, gradually switch to tangible tokens.

Should children be allowed to accumulate their tokens? If pupils are able to save their tokens, they can "take a holiday" from good work or behavior and use their past earnings. Teachers must decide whether they want to accept this behavior. If they do not want "holidays," yet still want to encourage savings, students can be provided with high-priced reinforcers and allowed to make nonrefundable deposits.

A question often asked by teachers or school psychologists who are initiating a classroom token program is, "What should the tokens buy?" In other words, what should be used as a back-up reinforcer? The answer is simple: "Anything that works." The teacher may judge how well particular reinforcers are working by checking the data. Many studies have used candy, small toys, or trinkets as back-up reinforcers; however, money (Martin, Burkholder, Rosenthal, Tharp, & Thorne, 1968), a class party (Barber & Kagey, 1977), a story (Ulrich, Wolfe, & Bluhm, 1968), and special events (Bushell, Wrobel, & Michaelis, 1968) have also shown excellent results. The opportunity to be tutored in reading by an older schoolmate or a college student can also serve as a reinforcer in a classroom token program (Robertson, DeReus, & Drabman, 1976). For young children, activities like painting, clay, and tumbling mats have proven effective. Young or retarded children also respond well to activities like running errands, cleaning the room, or being a teaching assistant (Drabman & Spitalnik, 1973; Whalen & Henker, 1969).

For older children, activities like playing records, dancing, checkers, games, pool, and Ping-Pong are effective (Rollins, McCandless, Thompson, & Brassell, 1974). Classroom-token problems have also been used effectively with chidlren who have been labeled retarded, autistic, hyperactive, learning disabled, childhood schizophrenic, emotionally disturbed, and delinquent (Lahey, 1979; Lahey & Johnson, 1978).

An example of a working token program will help in understanding this approach (Drabman, 1973). Twenty-four children (ages eleven to fifteen years) in a children's psychiatric hospital were assigned to four classes of six children. Observers monitored the children and recorded instances of aggressive behaviors, noise making, disturbing another's property, inappropriate vocalizations, playing with their own property during lessons, and turning around. During the three-week baseline period, the teachers were asked to handle disruptive behavior in whatever way they felt appropriate. Additionally, the teachers were asked to display the following institutional rules:

1. Come to class on time.
2. Sit in your own seat.
3. Do not leave seat without permission.
4. Keep quiet.
5. Do your own work.
6. Do not distract your neighbor.
7. Do not touch things that do not belong to you.
8. Do not sleep in class.

Teachers were asked to remind the pupils of the rules occasionally and to try to limit their reprimands to individual children.

On the last day of baseline, the workings of the token program were explained, and the children helped choose the reinforcers. They were priced at a ratio of one point for every three cents of object retail value. The reinforcer's "psychological value" (Drabman & Tucker, 1974) was also considered, so that some objects, such as pencils, were priced below their monetary value, and other objects, such as combs, sold for more. Posters containing pictures or facsimiles of the reinforcers, as well as their cost, were displayed in front of the class. The posters served the dual purpose of providing a constant reminder of the token program while allowing the actual prizes to be protected from destruction or theft.

Opaque canisters marked with the name of each child were placed on the teacher's desk along with a dated record sheet and poker chip tokens. Every twenty minutes a timer would ring. When the timer rang, the teacher reset it to prevent a free-time period during token administration. Next, he would decide upon a rating (0 to 10) for each child, based on the child's performance during the preceding twenty minutes. The teacher would then mark the amount of tokens awarded on the record sheet and deposit a corresponding number of chips into each canister. Next, the teacher informed each child of the amount of points he or she had earned. The children were informed only after the teacher had recorded the marks so that they would not attempt to cajole or coerce the teacher.

The poker chip tokens were exchangeable for trinkets or edibles at the end of each class. All tokens not spent could be saved until Fridays. On Fridays, they had to be spent or used as a nonrefundable down payment on a larger prize. After a down payment was received, a child had to complete payment in an agreed upon time limit, or the deposit would be lost. The child who had scored the most points for that day was allowed to select a reinforcer first.

GROUP CONTINGENCIES

The preceding programs stressed individual reinforcement for individual behavior; an alternative is group reinforcement for individual behavior. As an example, a classroom token economy known as the good behavior game will be presented (Barrish, Saunders, & Wolf, 1969).

A regular fourth-grade classroom of twenty-four students was divided into two teams. Classroom rules were re-emphasized, and the game was introduced. The teacher explained that whenever she saw anyone on either team breaking a class rule that team would receive a mark. The winning team (or both teams if neither team had more than five marks) would receive privileges and free time at the end of the day. This procedure was very successful in decreasing out-of-seat and talking-out behavior for the entire class.

Teachers often find group procedures more practical with large classes where individual token administration consumes too much class time. Because of this, several studies have compared the effectiveness of group and individual classroom token economies (Drabman, Spitalnik, & Spitalnik, 1974; Greenwood, Hops, Delquadri, & Guild, 1974; Herman & Tramontana, 1971), and they indicate that both kinds of contingencies are effective in controlling disruptive behavior. However, a group program may not be appropriate when the class is too heterogeneous in behavior. In this case, the class might be divided into homogeneous groups with each group on its own token program.

When choosing between group and individual token-economy programs, teachers often ask, "What will happen to the rest of the class if I initiate a behavioral program for just one child?" Altough the data are not complete (Kazdin, 1979), it seems that the answer may be a positive one. Kazdin (1973d) and Drabman and Lahey (1974) monitored the behavior of untreated classmates while initiating a program involving target children. Both studies reported improved behavior in the untreated classmates. The Drabman and Lahey study also found that the target child received both more positive votes in the sociometric procedure and more positive comments from her peers. It appears, therefore, that teachers who prefer to use behavioral procedures for only some of their pupils will receive dual benefits: both the problem children and their classmates will improve.

Punishment in the Classroom

When disruptive behavior is maintained either wholly or substantially by peer reinforcement, it can be expected to increase if ignored by the teacher. Since peer reinforcement is more immediate, it may be even more powerful than the reinforcers available in a token program. When this is the case, a teacher needs another tool if classroom stability is to be maintained. Some form of punishment is the likely candidate. But what form shall this punishment take?

behavioral psychologists feel that punishment should not be used
~ other more positive alternatives have been unsuccessful. But
since classroom punishment procedures may be necessary, they should be
explored scientifically so that teachers can apply them as effectively as
possible.

Three procedures, which may be subsumed under the rubric of
classroom punishment techniques, have been investigated: response cost,
time out from positive reinforcement, and verbal reprimands.

Response Cost

Response cost may be defined as removal of previously acquired reinforcers contingent upon a response. In the classroom token economy,
response cost is usually accomplished by removal of tokens contingent
upon inappropriate behavior (Iwata & Bailey, 1974; Kaufman & O'Leary,
1972). For example, Iwata and Bailey (1974) took fifteen special-classroom
elementary school children and divided them into two groups. After baseline measurements, one group was given ten free tokens and told that they
would lose them if they did not follow the class rules (response cost). The
other group was not given any tokens but was told that they could earn
ten if they followed rules (positive reinforcement). Both groups had to pay
six tokens for an afternoon-snack reinforcer. After a brief return to baseline for both groups, the systems were switched, so that the group that
had previously been earning tokens was shifted to a response-cost program, and the group that had been losing tokens began a positive-reinforcement program.

Results indicated that the procedures were equally effective in reducing
rule violations and off-task behavior. The pupils did not express a preference for one program over the other. Although the two procedures were
equally effective, we suggest that teachers use the positive-reinforcement
approach whenever possible since this may encourage them to use more
verbal reinforcement (Iwata & Bailey, 1974).

Time Out from Positive Reinforcement

Time out from positive reinforcement has been the classroom punishment
procedure used most often by behavioral teachers and clinicians. Time out
can be defined as contingent removal of the opportunity to earn positive
reinforcement. Because of the way time out has been used in classroom

studies, the procedure might better be labeled contingent social isolation (Drabman & Spitalnik, 1973). A child is placed away from other students (a separate room, a corner of the classroom, and so on) following disruptive behavior. The child remains in isolation for a minimum time period, usually about ten minutes. Return to his or her seat is contingent upon the passage of a fixed period of time or the passage of that time period plus appropriate behavior in the last minutes of the isolation period.

Several classroom studies have used a social-isolation procedure, usually in conjunction with other behavior programs (Drabman & Spitalnik, 1973; Lahey, McNees, & McNees, 1973; Whelan & Haring, 1966). A study that looked at the effects of social isolation as an independent procedure rather than as a segment of a larger classroom program was reported by Drabman and Spitalnik (1973). In this study, three residents of a children's psychiatric hospital were selected because of their high levels of disruptive classroom behavior. A baseline was taken on three types of disruptive behavior—inappropriate vocalizations, aggression, and out-of-seat without permission. Two of these behaviors, out-of-seat and aggression, were selected for the social-isolation punishment procedure. When a student violated previously determined criteria, the teacher told him that because of his misbehavior, he must leave the room. A teaching assistant escorted him to a small room where the child spent the next ten minutes. After this time, the child could return to the classroom.

Results indicated that out-of-seat disruption, which was occurring 34 percent of the time during baseline, decreased to 11 percent of the time with the use of social isolation. Aggression occurred 2.8 percent of the time during baseline, but only .37 percent of the time during the social-isolation phase. On the other hand, vocalization, the unpunished behavior, occurred 32 percent of the time during baseline and continued at about the same rate (28 percent during the isolation phase) Interestingly, when the punishment was removed, the occurrence of the previously punished behavior increased only slightly relative to the unpunished behavior (out-of-seat, 15 percent; vocalization, 40 percent).

This study indicated that social isolation is an effective punisher that can be an important part of a behavioral program. A note of caution is necessary here. Some teachers have viewed behavioral procedures as being used only for punishment. This gives them a faulty perspective. Punishment procedures should never be used unless they are used in conjunction with a reinforcement procedure for an alternative appropriate response. Remember, punishment does not teach children to do anything, only what not to do. It also deprives them of some reinforcers that they have received in the past for performing the undesired acts. A successful behavioral practitioner will therefore always provide reinforcement to children for performing appropriate behavior.

Verbal Reprimands

Teachers often reprimand their students' misbehavior in an attempt to punish it. Several studies have related teachers' verbal reprimands to pupils' behavior. O'Leary and Becker (1968) and O'Leary, Kaufman, Kass, and Drabman (1970) showed that quiet reprimands are more effective than loud reprimands. Thomas, Becker, and Armstrong (1968) have demonstrated that systematically increasing a teacher's disapproving behavior led to parallel increases in disruptive behavior among the pupils.

One of the most interesting studies in this area was conducted by Madsen, Becker, Thomas, Koser, and Plager (1970). A team-taught first-grade classroom of forty-eight children was monitored for inappropriate out-of-seat behavior. Observers also monitored how often the teachers reprimanded children for being out of their seats or told anyone to sit down. They also recorded the number of times that either teacher praised a child for sitting.

After baseline, the experimenters asked the teachers to triple their frequency of sit-down commands. Next, they returned to baseline levels of sit-down commands. Then they returned to the high level of commands of the first treatment phase. Finally, teachers were asked to praise behaviors incompatible with standing.

Results indicated that standing up was functionally related to amount of sit-down commands in that the more sit-down commands the teacher gave, the more the children stood up! In fact, tripling the amount of sit-down commands led to a 33 percent increase in out-of-seat behavior. Praising behavior incompatible with standing up led to a 33 percent decrease in standing-up behavior.

When using punishment, teachers should recall this study and remember that what they believe to be *punishment* might be acting as *reinforcement*. Since the opposite could also be true, the classroom data must be consulted in order to determine what role a particular teacher behavior is playing.

MODIFYING ACADEMIC BEHAVIOR

The behavioral procedures described above when used correctly can be highly effective in reducing inappropriate classroom behavior. As such, they represent important tools for both teachers and consulting psychologists. When such procedures are implemented in the hope of improving academic learning solely by reducing the frequency of behaviors that are incompatible with learning, however, little success can be expected. Decreasing the frequency of disruptions and increasing the frequency of on-task behavior generally does not lead to improved academic performance (Ferritor, Buckholdt, Hamblin, & Smith, 1972; Marholin & Steinman, 1977). These methods can help the children *act* like better students, but not learn more.

Fortunately, however, behavioral principles can also be directly applied to academic instruction with good results. A number of studies indicate that positive reinforcement for correct responding can be used, for example, to improve the acquisition of oral reading (Lahey, 1977), reading comprehension (Lahey, McNees, & Brown, 1973), spelling (Lovitt, Guppy, & Blattner, 1969), handwriting (Trap, Milner-Davis, Joseph, & Cooper, 1978), mathematics (Ayllon, Layman, & Kandel, 1975), English composition (Houten, Morrison, Jarvis, & McDonald, 1974), and science concepts (Brown, Huppler, VanDeventer, York, & Sontag, 1973), among others.

These applications of behavioral methods to academic instruction involve the same basic approach as any other behavioral application. First, the desired response is identified and its frequency is measured. Second, some method is applied to increase the frequency of that response. For example, Lahey, McNees, and Brown (1973) worked with children whose oral reading was on grade level, but whose comprehension of what was read was quite low. A key aspect of what is meant by *reading comprehension* was then identified, in this case, answering questions about the passage just read. When the children were reinforced for correct answers, the frequency of correct answers rose sharply.

The same basic strategy of defining, counting, and modifying academic behavior can be adopted to practically any area of academic instruction. It has even been used to increase creativity in writing (Mahoney & Hopkins, 1973). The most common and least difficult application, however, is to programmed instructional materials. It is a simple matter to increase the efficiency of programmed instruction by reinforcing correct responses to the programmed questions. For example, Holt (1971) used free play as a reinforcer to produce stable 700 percent increases in the rate of correct responding in first- and second-grade reading programs.

Positive reinforcement is by far the most common method used to increase the rate of academic learning, but it is not the only one. Proper pacing of academic instruction and length of student contacts, structuring academic tasks to reduce errors, and signaling children when to respond have all been identified as factors in improved learning (Ayllon & Rosenbaum, 1977; Carnine & Fink, 1978; Scott & Bushell, 1974).

Ironically, methods that improve academic performance also indirectly reduce the frequency of behavior incompatible with learning. One cannot profitably work with disruptive behavior to improve academic learning, but one can improve both academic and general behavior by improving academic performance. For example, Ayllon, Layman, and Kandel (1975) found that when children diagnosed as both hyperactive and learning disabled were given token reinforcement for each correct response in reading and math programs, the rate of correct academic responses rose sharply and the frequency of disruptive behavior dropped dramatically. This same two-part benefit of reinforcing academic behavior was also found by Ayllon and Roberts (1974) with disruptive normal students and has been replicated several times by others (for example, Aaron & Bostow, 1978; Broughton & Lahey, 1978; Marholin & Steinman, 1977), suggesting that it is a highly reliable phenomenon.

Not only is this strategy of directly reinforcing academic behavior a highly effective one, it is also a desirable approach in other ways. First, it is an efficient method; it is much easier for teachers to give tokens based on academic responses than to monitor and evaluate the general behavior of an entire class. Second, the approach appears to have some humanistic benefits as well. Using this approach, teachers do not have to set up extensive rules to control behavior that is *believed* to be incompatible with learning. If children can perform at high academic levels and still walk around a bit or talk softly, teachers might be less inclined to prohibit these activities. Behaviors that are truly incompatible with effective learning *cannot* occur at the same time as effective academic performance. Other behaviors need not necessarily be regulated, at least not for academic purposes.

COMBINED PROGRAMS

We should not be hasty in concluding that programs in which reinforcement is given for academic behavior are a solution to all classroom management problems, however. First of all, although it is clear that it is effective while children are engaged in structured, individual academic work, it would be considerably more difficult to adapt the method to other academic activities, such as science lectures or group discussions. Furthermore, direct reinforcement of academic behavior is not likely to have much impact on the crucial transition periods in the school day when so many serious misbehaviors occur (between classes, going to lunch, and so on).

A complete behavior-modification program for the classroom, then, needs both kinds of programs. Structured academic periods can best be handled by simply providing reinforcement for academic behavior. Behavior during other parts of the day are best handled through reinforcement methods aimed at the behavior problems, and serious misbehaviors during any part of the day that are not handled by the reinforcement programs can perhaps best be dealt with using punishment methods, such as time out.

GENERALIZATION

What will happen when a program, especially a token program, is removed? Behavior modifiers have lost their early optimism and now realize that maintenance is not to be expected but must be programmed (Baer, Wolf, & Risley, 1968; Kazdin & Bootzin, 1972). The goal is to change somehow the reinforcement network for disruptive pupils so that they can function on the same reinforcers as do the majority of their classmates. Unfortunately, this is not easy. In fact, as this review has pointed out, by simply looking at classroom reinforcement contingencies, it is often easier to explain why children misbehave than why they behave.

Little is known regarding the most successful ways to program maintenance. O'Leary and Drabman (1971) suggested a variety of techniques that might achieve generalization, including the following:

1. Providing a good academic program
2. Giving children the expectation that they are doing well
3. Involving the children in the program
4. Teaching the children the ways in which academic achievement will be important later
5. Involving the parents
6. Teaching the teachers behavioral principles

Recently, classroom studies that have used these suggestions as well as other methods to obtain generalization have appeared in the literature (Drabman, 1973; Drabman, Hammer, & Rosenbaum, in press; O'Leary, Drabman, & Kass, 1973). Even these studies give no conclusive information on how to effectively program generalization; they should be seen more as accounts of preliminary success from which further research should stem.

It is known that abrupt withdrawal of a behavioral program does not usually lead to successful generalization. Therefore, some form of gradual withdrawal is probably the key. With token economies, perhaps gradual increases in the length of time necessary to hold the tokens before exchange with concurrent decreases in their purchasing power will lead to generalization. An alternative might be gradually to change the program from contingent and redeemable tokens to contingent but nonredeemable tokens (feedback), and then gradually decrease the occasions of feedback.

PROJECT FOLLOW-THROUGH:
A LARGE-SCALE APPLICATION

When behavioral programs like the ones described above are first presented to teachers and consultants, questions of their practicality are often raised. Can teachers actually use such methods on a daily basis in real classrooms? Is it good for the children in the long run? A good partial answer to those questions can be provided by discussing Project Follow-Through. This federally sponsored program for disadvantaged children experimentally compared a number of different educational models for grades kindergarten through three. The goal of the project was to identify effective methods for educating children disadvantaged by poverty whose average rate of learning was about one-half of the national average.

The two programs in Project Follow-Through that were most successful in improving academic achievement were based on the types of behavioral programs described above, one sponsored by the University of Kansas (Bushell, 1978) and one sponsored by the University of Oregon (Becker & Carnine, 1979). Several thousand children in public schools across the country have been enrolled in the programs for four consecutive school years (kindergarten through third grade). The results of independent evaluations indicate that their average academic achievement has been at or above the national average for each of those years. Clearly, behavior modification can be applied in real classrooms with good results.

CONCLUDING REMARKS

A general framework for the application of principles of behavior modification to classroom settings has been described. We have touched on the most important areas of research and application, but other research programs are exploring other areas of intervention. For example, children have been successfully trained to tutor other children (Robertson, Dereus, & Drabman, 1976) and to aid the teacher in administering general token programs (Craighead & Mercatoris, 1973). Other researchers are looking at the role of the teacher in dealing with social-skills deficits (Combs & Slaby, 1977), are involved in teaching self-control to children (Drabman, Spitalnik, & O'Leary, 1973; Rosenbaum & Drabman, in press), or are testing the benefits of brief daily reports sent to parents describing their child's behavior (Schumaker, Hovell, & Sherman, 1977). Although many of these areas of research are still in their early stages and offer future advances, some applications to public education are already well tested and widely implemented.

SUMMARY

Principles of behavior modification have been successfully applied to classroom settings in a variety of ways to promote academic learning and appropriate behavior. The first techniques developed were designed to directly control inappropriate behavior. These include the use of clear rules, positive reinforcement, soft versus loud reprimands, ignoring minor rule infractions, and time out as a substitute for punishment. When it is necessary to use reinforcers more powerful than praise, tokens may be given out contingent upon appropriate behavior. These tokens can be exchanged later for privileges, activities, prizes, or other back-up reinforcers. This powerful procedure is known as the classroom token economy. Tokens may be given out on an individual basis or based on the behavior of groups of children, and they may be given out contingent on good behavior or deducted from a fixed amount contingent on inappropriate behavior (response cost) with approximately equal effectiveness.

It was originally believed that the modification of inappropriate classroom behavior would indirectly result in improvements in academic learning. When tested, this notion was shown to be incorrect, but fortunately it is easy to adapt behavioral principles to improve directly academic performance. This involves making some form of reinforcement contingent upon small units of correct academic behavior, such as answering a question in group discussion, writing sentences containing many descriptive images, or answering a question correctly in a math workbook. Ironically, it has been found that reinforcing academic behavior indirectly improves general behavior. This is because any behavior that is incompatible with effective learning must be reduced by the child if academic behavior is to improve. Not only is this an efficient method of classroom management (reinforcing academic behavior), but it is also a humane method as well. Teachers need to set up fewer detailed rules when using this approach since most behavior that is truly incompatible with learning will be indirectly managed. It is often necessary, however, to also use direct methods for controlling misbehavior, especially during nonacademic periods of the day.

CHAPTER 22

BEHAVIOR MODIFICATION WITH SEVERELY DISTURBED CHILDREN

Rex Forehand and Beverly M. Atkeson

University of Georgia

. . . Peter didn't look at us, or smile, and wouldn't play the games that seemed as much a part of babyhood as diapers. While he didn't cry, he rarely laughed, and when he did, it was at things that didn't seem funny to us. He didn't cuddle, but sat upright in my lap, even when I rocked him. But children differ and we were content to let Peter be himself. We though it hilarious when my brother, visiting us when Peter was 9 months old, observed that "that kid has no social instincts, whatsoever." Although Peter was a first child, he was not isolated. I frequently put him in his playpen in front of the house, where the school children stopped to play with him as they passed. He ignored them too . . .

Peter's babbling had not turned into speech by the time he was three. His play was solitary and repetitious. He tore paper into long thin strips, bushelbaskets of it every day. He spun the lids from my canning jars and became upset if we tried to divert him. Only rarely could I catch his eye, and then saw his focus change from me to the reflection in my glasses. It was like trying to pick up mercury with chopsticks.

His adventures into our suburban neighborhood had been unhappy. He had disregarded the universal rule that sand is to be kept in sandboxes, and the children themselves had punished him. He walked around a sad and solitary figure, always carrying a toy aeroplane, a toy he never played with. (Eberhardy, 1967, pp. 257–258)

The above description of Peter exemplifies many of the characteristics of severely disturbed children. The behaviors of these children are numerous and varied. They typically lack self-help skills that are commonly acquired as part of the normal developmental process by children. For example, such remedial skills as self-feeding, self-dressing, proper toileting, and self-grooming (for example, showering, bathing, and combing one's hair) are frequently missing. Verbal behavior, particularly as used for communication, and social interactions are also often delayed with these children. In place of prosocial behaviors, severely disturbed children may exhibit a number of antisocial behaviors. For example, stereotyped behaviors, such as head banging and body rocking, are frequently present. In addition, disruptive behaviors, such as screaming, tantruming, fighting, and crying, are also manifested.

Severely disturbed children include those individuals who have been labeled as mentally retarded, autistic, schizophrenic, or psychotic. Compared with many other types of psychological disorders, the prevalence of severely disturbed children is relatively rare. Birnbrauer (1976) reported that the instance of mental retardation ranges from 3 to 5 percent of the population. The instance of infantile autism is even more rare, as only approximately four per ten thousand children are reported to be afflicted with this disorder (Margolies, 1977). Nevertheless, the severity of the behavior of these types of children is extremely dysfunctional. In fact, these types of children have commonly been institutionalized, as parent, teachers, and community resources have been unable to cope with the disorder.

Much effort has been devoted to the differential diagnosis of retarded, autistic, schizophrenic, and psychotic children. For example, Rimland (1964) has proposed that autistic and retarded children differ in a number of ways, including language, musical ability, motor ability, and physical expressions. However, from the behavioral-treatment viewpoint, differential diagnosis has had little utility. As Schreibman and Koegel (1979) have pointed out in their review of autism, differential diagnosis of the various types of severely disturbed children does not suggest differential treatment or differential prognosis. At this time, the strategy of most behavior therapists is to treat behavioral excesses and deficiencies rather than to attempt to differentially diagnose various types of severely disturbed children (Lovaas & Newsom, 1976).

Much speculation regarding the cause of severely disturbed behavior also has appeared in the literature. Ross (1974), among others, has reviewed a number of theories concerning the etiology of autism. These include cognitive, affective, and attachment defects in the individual. For example, the attachment defect proposed by Zaslow and Breger (1969) is based on the proposition that formation of an attachment between the mother and infant fails to occur, and this failure leads to the development of autism. Theories concerning the cause of other types of severe disturbance in children, such as retardation or schizophrenia, also are common. As with the differential diagnosis of various types of severely disturbed behavior, theories of etiology contain little useful information for behavioral treatment. Therefore, further examination of this literature will not be included here.

This chapter will focus primarily on the examination of treatment approaches for behavioral excesses and deficits in the severely disturbed child. Behavioral excesses will be presented first, as most research indicates excessive stereotyped and disruptive behaviors need to be eliminated before prosocial behavior can be taught (for example, Berkson & Mason, 1964; Koegel & Covert, 1972; Lovaas, Litrownick, & Mann, 1971). Once stereotyped and disruptive behavior is decelerated, responsiveness to the environment appears to increase, and prosocial behavior can be taught. Some attention will also be devoted to the literature on teaching parents, teachers, and institutional attendants behavior modification skills, for these individuals are an important and necessary component of any intervention program.

BEHAVIORAL EXCESSES

For the purposes of review, behavioral excesses are grouped into two categories: stereotyped behavior and disruptive behavior. These two types are similar in that both prevent the acquisition of prosocial behavior (for example, Forehand & Baumeister, 1976). However, they differ in that the latter is disruptive, is harmful to others, or otherwise has an adverse effect on the environment. In contrast, stereotyped behavior is not disruptive to the environment or to other individuals in the environment.

Stereotyped Behaviors

Stereotyped acts are highly consistent and repetitive motor-posturing behaviors which are not outer-directed in the sense of being explicitly disruptive and harmful to others. Primary forms of stereotypy are body rocking, head rolling, complex hand movements, head banging, and self-biting. Body rocking consists of the rhythmic forward and backward movement of the torso. Head rolling is the movement of the head from side to side in a rhythmic manner. Complex hand movements consist of either waving the fingers back and forth while holding the hand at arm's length or flicking the fingers immediately in front of the eyes. Head banging is the repetitious hitting of the head against a surface. Self-biting consists of the individual biting some part, usually a hand, of his or her own body. Less pervasive forms of stereotypy include pill rolling, object spinning, digit sucking, body twirling, face slapping, and self-scratching (Forehand & Baumeister, 1976).

These various kinds of stereotypy occur with a particular high frequency among institutionalized individuals. Stereotypy has been observed in approximately two-thirds of the institutionalized retarded populations (Kaufman & Levitt, 1965). When those stereotyped behaviors that are injurious to the individual (for example, head banging) have been examined alone, the incidences range from approximately 8 percent among the retarded (O'Brien, 1974) to 40 percent with schizophrenic children (Greene, 1967).

As noted earlier, the occurrence of stereotyped behavior frequently dominates an individual's behavior and limits positive interaction with the environment. In addition, in the case of self-injurious behavior, harm may occur to the individual as a result. Therefore, it is important to treat these types of behaviors among severely disturbed children.

Much attention recently has been devoted to stereotyped behavior, particularly the self-injurious type. For example, at least ten reviews have appeared in the last three years in which the motivation for the development of such behavior, the detrimental effects of the behavior, and the assessment of the treatment of the behavior have been examined (for example, Carr, 1977; Forehand & Baumeister, 1976; Harris & Ersner-Hershfield, 1978; Johnson & Baumeister, 1978; Picker, Poling, & Parker, 1979; Rincover & Koegel, 1977). These reviews indicate that hundreds of studies addressing stereotyped behavior of severely disturbed children have been conducted.

Behavioral-treatment approaches that have been utilized to decrease stereotyped behaviors can be divided into the following categories: reinforcement of alternate behavior, removal of reinforcement, punishment, and overcorrection. The first procedure involves the use of positive reinforcement contingent upon the occurrence of some behavior other than stereotyped acts. The second procedure involves the removal or absence of positive reinforcement contingent upon the occurrence of the stereotyped behavior. Punishment consists of the presentation of an aversive stimulus contingent upon the stereotyped act. Finally, overcorrection is a package approach that, among other components, involves practicing correct forms of behavior that are incompatible with the stereotyped movements.

Reinforcement of alternate behavior has been shown to be effective in several studies. For example, in an experimental-laboratory study, Mulhern and Baumeister (1969) reduced body rocking in two severely retarded children by programming food reinforcement contingent upon a reduction in rate of rocking for a prescribed period of time. Relative to a base rate of approximately sixty responses per minute, each of the children demonstrated a gradual reduction in rate of body rocking (Forehand & Baumeister, 1976). Other investigators (for example, Repp, Deitz, & Speir, 1974) similarly have demonstrated that reinforcing alternate behavior is effective with a number of different types of stereotyped behavior. In contrast to these positive results, a number of investigators have failed to find that reinforcement of alternate behavior is effective (for example, Measel & Alfieri, 1976; Risley, 1968; Young & Wincze, 1974).

In their review, Harris and Ersner-Hershfield (1978) concluded that the effectiveness of differentially reinforcing alternate behavior is equivocal with stereotyped behavior of severely disturbed children. One difficulty with using this procedure may be finding a period of time in which the stereotyped behavior does not occur. If the behavior occurs at such a high rate that the reinforcer cannot be delivered in the absence of behavior, the ineffectiveness of the procedure is guaranteed. Therefore, it is frequently necessary to use reinforcement of alternate behavior in conjunction with some other intervention procedure that can decrease the initial rate of the stereotyped behavior.

A second procedure that has been utilized to decrease repetitious acts is the removal of positive reinforcement for the occurrence of stereotyped behavior. Removal of reinforcement consists of simply ignoring the behavior, removing some reinforcing object from the child, placing the individual in time out, or removing the sensory-reinforcing consequences of engaging in the stereotyped behavior. Several (for example, Lovaas & Simmons, 1969; Martin & Foxx, 1973) but not all (for example, Myers, 1975) researchers have demonstrated that ignoring stereotyped behavior leads to gradual reductions in the behavior. Unfortunately, particularly in the case of self-injurious behavior, the gradual decrease often is too slow to allow ignoring to be a practical procedure to use.

An alternate type of removal of reinforcement is that in which some type of reinforcing object is removed from the client. For example, Tate and Baroff (1966) reduced head banging and face slapping by removing physical contact from a severely disturbed child for three seconds contingent upon the self-injurious behavior. Other reinforcing events, such as music, tokens, and vibratory stimulation, have also been used effectively as reinforcers with withdrawal contingent upon stereotyped behavior

(Greene, Hoats, & Hornick, 1970; Myers, 1975; Nunes, Murphy, & Ruprecht, 1977).

A third type of removal-of-reinforcement procedure involves time out. With this procedure, the child is put in a place of isolation for a specified period of time contingent upon sterotypy. The assumption in the use of time out is that the individual is removed from an environment that is reinforcing to one that is less reinforcing. Several studies (for example, Hamilton, Stephens, & Allen, 1967; Wolf, Risley, & Mees, 1964) demonstrated that such procedures are effective in reducing stereotyped behavior. However, recent data (Solnick, Rincover, & Peterson, 1977) suggest that time out is not effective unless the environment from which the individual is removed is reinforcing. Unfortunately, with many of our institutions for severely disturbed children, the environment offers little that is reinforcing.

A final type of removal of reinforcement is a procedure recently developed by Rincover (1978). This technique has been labeled extinction and involves removing the sensory consequences that are postulated to maintain the stereotyped behavior. For example, Rincover (1978) found that for a child who spun objects excessively in a stereotyped manner, the noise from the object spinning was maintaining the behavior. Therefore, Rincover eliminated the auditory feedback from the object spinning by carpeting the table upon which the child spun the object. This procedure effectively eliminated object spinning by the child. In another use of sensory extinction, Rincover, Cooke, Peoples, and Packard (1979) eliminated visual feedback from finger and hand movements performed by two children by blindfolding one child and by turning off the overhead lights for a second child. Again, both of these procedures effectively reduced stereotyped behaviors that the children were displaying.

Removal of reinforcement for stereotyped behaviors has been implemented in the forms delineated above. However, it should be noted that there are some limitations to these procedures. One problem is that the stereotyped behavior is free to occur when reinforcement is removed. That is, the removal of reinforcement does not in itself prevent the stereotyped act from occurring. In the case of self-injurious behavior, the continued opportunity for the occurrence of the behavior could be harmful or even fatal. Second, some investigators (for example, Lovaas & Simmons, 1969) recommend against these types of procedures for self-injurious behavior, because of the long period of time required for the behavior to diminish and because of the initial increment in response rate that sometimes occurs with extinction. The third limitation is that the effects of removal of reinforcement frequently appear to be highly situation specific. Generalization to new settings does not occur unless it is deliberately and systematically programmed (for example, Lovaas & Simmons, 1969).

Fourth, there is a legal limitation in that some types of time out procedures are no longer allowed in some institutional settings.

Sensory extinction is the most recently developed technique and the one that has received the least attention. However, it offers several advantages over the other types of removal of reinforcement procedures. As Rincover et al. (1979) have pointed out, the effects appear to be immediate, there are no serious ethical concerns, and it is an easy to implement procedure. At this time, work by other investigators needs to be undertaken to replicate and extend Rincover's work.

It should be noted that it is important when using removal-of-reinforcement procedures that not only should reinforcement be removed for stereotypy, but the absence of stereotypy should be reinforced. A number of investigators (for example, Myers & Deibert, 1971) found that this combination of procedures is effective in decreasing stereotyped behavior.

A third procedure that has been used to decrease stereotyped behavior with the severely disturbed child is punishment. This type of procedure involves the contingent presentation of an aversive stimulus. A considerable variety of stimuli may function as punishers in the sense that they suppress stereotyped behavior. These include electric shock, a slap, facial screening, icing, and ammonia (for extensive reviews, see Forehand & Baumeister, 1976; Harris & Ersner-Hershfield, 1978). Use of electric shock involves the brief application of a mild shock to the individual contingent upon the occurrence of stereotypy. The results of a number of studies (for example, Lovaas, Schaeffer, & Simmons, 1965; Merbaum, 1973; Tate & Baroff, 1966) have demonstrated this procedure to be effective. Suppression of stereotyped behavior typically occurs immediately and has long-lasting effects. However, in most studies, the suppression effects are situation and trainer specific and, consequently, systematic efforts must be taken to build in generalization across trainers and settings (Forehand & Baumeister, 1976). A slap on the hand or some other body part contingent upon stereotyped behavior has also been demonstrated to be effective to decrease repetitious acts (for example, Lovaas, Berberich, Berloff, & Schaeffer, 1966; Romanczyk, 1977). Facial screening involves placing a terry cloth bib over a person's face contingent upon self-injurious behavior. Lutzker (1978) and Zegiob, Jenkins, Becker, and Bristow (1976) have reported data indicating that this procedure is effective in reducing self-injurious behavior of the severely disturbed child.

Drabman, Ross, Lynd, and Cordua (1978) reported that an icing procedure (placing an ice cube in a child's mouth and simultaneously holding his hands down) decreased shirt and/or finger sucking behavior of a retarded child. Ammonia has also been used as a punishment procedure to decrease stereotyped behavior. This procedure involves crushing a capsule of aromatic ammonia under the nose of the child when he or she engages in self-injurious behavior. Tanner and Zeiler (1975) have demonstrated this procedure to be effective in reducing self-injurious behavior; however, as noted by Harris and Ersner-Herschfield (1978), this procedure can result in physical damage to the client. Finally, in their recent review, Harris and Ersner-Hershfield (1978) reported several other procedures that have been effective in reducing stereotyped behavior. These procedures include contingent shaking (Risley, 1968), aversive tickling (Greene & Hoats, 1971), and restraint (Saposnek & Watson, 1974).

Although punishment procedures are effective in reducing stereotyped behavior, it should be noted that these procedures should always be used in combination with reinforcement for appropriate behavior. Furthermore, certain punishment procedures, such as the use of electric shock, now have limited use because of recent court decisions involving the right to treatment of institutionalized individuals (*Wyatt* v. *Stickney,* 1971, Middle District, State of Alabama). Clearly, when instances of abuse are likely, such as with punishment procedures, certain legal/ethical guidelines are needed.

A final procedure that has been employed frequently in the past several years with stereotyped behavior is overcorrection. The overcorrection procedure used for stereotyped behavior is positive practice: the individual practices behaviors that are physically incompatible with the stereotyped behavior (Ollendick & Matson, 1978). For example, for head weaving and hand clapping, Foxx and Azrin (1973) used a positive-practice overcorrection procedure in which the client's head or hands were guided through a series of directed functional movements that were incompatible with head weaving and hand clapping. Similar procedures for self-injurious behavior, such as head banging, has been employed in which the child is guided through a series of body movements that are incompatible with head banging (for example, Harris & Romanczyk, 1976). Included in most overcorrection procedures are a number of steps, such as instruction giving, response prevention, physical restraint, prompting, and reinforcement of responses incompatible with stereotypy. Therefore, overcorrection consists of a number of procedures used in combination. The primary purpose of overcorrection is not only to reduce stereotyped behavior but also to teach the individual appropriate forms of behavior. For example, Wells, Forehand, Hickey, and Green (1977) used an overcorrection procedure involving appropriate toy play with two autistic children; stereotyped behaviors were not only reduced, but with one child, an increase in appropriate toy play also occurred.

The results of numerous articles (for reviews, see Axelrod, Brantner, & Meddock, 1978; Harris & Ersner-Herschfield, 1978; Ollendick & Matson, 1978) demonstrate that overcorrection is effective in reducing stereotyped behavior. However, with few exceptions (Wells et al., 1977), increase in prosocial behavior have not been examined or reported. Research also suggests that overcorrection is more effective than alternate forms of behavior therapy. For example, Harris and Wolchik (1979) found that overcorrection was more effective than time out or differential reinforcement of other behavior. As with other procedures, little evidence has been generated demonstrating the generalization of the effects of overcorrection to novel settings and people without particular training (Harris & Ersner-Herschfield, 1978).

Disruptive Behaviors

Disruptive behaviors refer to acts that are explicitly disruptive, harmful to others, or otherwise have an adverse effect on the environment. Included in this category are behaviors, such as fighting, property damage, physical and verbal assault, stealing, screaming, vomiting, crying, and tantrums. Ross (1972) has reported that this type of behavior occurs frequently in institutionalized children. Furthermore, these behaviors also appear to occur among the noninstitutionalized retarded as well (Forehand & Baumeister, 1976).

As with stereotyped acts, deceleration of disruptive behaviors often is necessary before positive training of other behaviors can be initiated. Disruptive acts often interfere with and preclude the learning of more adaptive social skills. For example, Nordquist and Wahler (1973) have viewed the elimination of disruptive behaviors as an essential component of programs that are designed to generate more socially adaptive behavior, such as language acquisition. Obviously, too, physical harm and damage to property and others can also result from severe disruptive behavior (Forehand & Baumeister, 1976).

As with stereotyped behaviors, reinforcement of alternate behaviors, removal of reinforcement, punishment, and overcorrection have been used to decrease disruptive behaviors. Reinforcement of alternate behavior by the use of food, praise, and other types of reinforcing activities has been shown to decrease stereotyped behaviors (for example, Brawley, Harris, Allen, Fleming, & Peterson, 1969; Nordquist & Wahler, 1973). However, not all investigators have found reinforcing incompatible behaviors to be successful in reducing disruptive acts. For example, Martin, MacDonald, and Omichinski (1971) found that social reinforcement for appropriate eating behavior failed to reduce slopping with three severely retarded girls. Similarly, Risley (1968) reported a case in which food reinforcement of an incompatible behavior failed to decelerate the furniture climbing of a severely disturbed child.

As with stereotyped behavior, the use of reinforcement of alternate behavior would appear to be most effective with disruptive behavior when used in conjunction with another treatment procedure. For example, three studies have demonstrated the combination of reinforcement of alternate behaviors and time out for disruptive behaviors to be effective. Bostow and Bailey (1969) reduced hitting and biting by an institutionalized retardate by delivering food reinforcement contingent upon two-minute periods that were free of aggression. This procedure was coupled with a two-minute time-out period in an isolation booth for each aggressive act. Other researchers (Vukelich & Hake, 1971; Wiesen & Watson, 1967) have obtained similar results.

When considering removal of reinforcement for stereotyped behavior, ignoring, removing a reinforcing object, and placing the individual in time out have been employed. Martin and Foxx (1973) successfully used withdrawal of social reinforcement in an effort to decrease aggression. However, most research has indicated that ignoring alone has been of relatively little use in the suppression of severely disruptive behavior (Harris & Ersner-Herschfield, 1978). For example, Wolf, Risley, Johnston, Harris, and Allen (1967) instructed classroom teachers of an autistic retarded child to ignore him when he pinched others. No effect was observed under this contingency. Similarly, Martin and Iagulli (1974) attempted to use an ignoring procedure to decrease the bedtime tantrums of a severely retarded institutionalized female. Ignoring the tantrum behavior for fifteen days had little effect.

Removal of a reinforcing object, a token in this case, has been shown to be effective in one study. Burchard and Barrera (1972) reported that removal of either thirty or five tokens contingent upon fighting, swearing, and property destruction decreased these behaviors. The loss of thirty tokens was more effective than the loss of five tokens and equally effective as the use of a thirty-minute time out.

The use of time out has been effective in reducing disruption in a number of studies. Wolf, Risley, and Mees (1964) successfully reduced temper tantrums of a severely disturbed child by sending the child to his room upon each occurrence of the behavior. Similarly, stealing, inappropriate eating behavior, screaming, disruptive floor rolling, hitting, kicking, spitting, tantrums, swearing, and property destruction have all been treated effectively by the use of time out (Barton, Guess, Garcia, & Baer, 1970; Burchard & Barrera, 1972; Calhoun & Matherne, 1975; Hamilton & Stephens, 1967; White, Nielsen, & Johnson, 1972). Available data suggest that a short time out (for example, five minutes) can be as effective as a longer time out provided the longer time out does not precede the shorter time out (Pendergrass, 1971; White et al., 1972). Furthermore, for time out to be effective, it can be administered on an intermittent schedule rather than a continuous schedule (Calhoun & Lima, 1977; Clark, Rowbury, Baer, & Baer, 1973).

The time-out procedure would appear to be particularly effective with severely disturbed children. However, as with stereotyped behavior, it should be noted that the use of time out with disruptive behavior should be combined with positive reinforcement for more appropriate behavior. Furthermore, as noted earlier, time out is prohibited in some settings. Finally, as MacDonough and Forehand (1973) and Hobbs and Forehand (1977) have indicated, time out is a complex procedure consisting of a number of parameters (for example, length, method of release, schedule of delivery) which can influence the effectiveness of the procedures. The parameters of time out need to be carefully specified and examined in research with severely disturbed children so that the most effective, efficient, and ethically acceptable procedure can be utilized.

Punishment also has been used as a treatment procedure for disruptive behaviors of severely disturbed children. Electric shock, aversive auditory stimuli, verbal reprimands, spanking, and squirting lemon juice or shaving cream in the mouth of the child have been used as punishment procedures. In the case of shock, Risley (1968) found that shock combined with a verbal command (the word *no*) suppressed an autistic child's climbing behavior after a total of six shocks. This procedure was used only after reinforcement of incompatible behavior and the use of time out had failed to suppress the disruptive behavior. Generalization of suppression of climbing did not occur to the home; therefore, shock for climbing was implemented in the home and immediately reduced the behavior in that setting. Other behaviors that also have been effectively treated with shock include disruptive vocalizations (Hamilton & Standahl, 1969), assaultive behavior (Birnbrauer, 1968; Ludwig, Marx, Hill, & Browning, 1969), property destruction (Bucher & King, 1971), and vomiting (Kohlenberg, 1970; Luckey, Watson, & Musick, 1968; White & Taylor, 1967).

Several conclusions would appear warranted at this time regarding generalization of treatment effects when shock is used with disruptive behavior. First, as in the case of stereotyped movements, suppression of disruptive behavior does not automatically generalize across situations (Bucher & King, 1971; Hamilton & Standahl, 1969; Risley, 1968). However, generalization does occur when systematically programmed (Bucher & King, 1971; Hamilton & Standahl, 1969; Risley, 1968). Second, suppression effects seem to be durable, in some cases lasting at least several months (Kohlenberg, 1970; Luckey et al., 1968; Risley, 1968). Third, suppression of disruptive behavior by shock may be associated with an increase in prosocial behaviors (Luckey et al., 1968; Risley, 1968; White & Taylor, 1967).

Aversive auditory stimuli have also been used to decelerate disruptive behavior. Sajwaj and Hedges (1971) applied a 105-db blast of a bicycle horn to various undesirable dinnertime behaviors, including destructive acts, crying, aggression, and disobedience. The horn blast was contingent upon each occurrence of disruptive behavior. In addition to eliminating the target behaviors, the auditory stimulus had three positive side effects: (1) appropriate dinnertime behaviors doubled; (2) self-injurious acts at dinner, which were never punished, disappeared; and (3) disruptive behaviors during two other periods of the day, living room clean-up and tutorial time, temporarily decreased. However, disruptive behaviors emitted during bedtime clean-up and in the morning generally were not affected by punishing negative dinnertime behavior.

Several studies have used verbal reprimands to punish various disruptive behaviors. Schultz, Wehman, Renzaglia, and Karan (1978) successfully used the contingent application of verbal reprimands as a method for decreasing inappropriate verbalizations of two severely retarded individuals. Henricksen and Doughty (1967) used a verbal reprimand combined with interruption of ongoing negative behavior to decelerate disruptive mealtime activities of profoundly retarded individuals. This procedure effectively reduced the inappropriate mealtime behaviors from a weekly mean of approximately 220 instances per child to about 25 instances per child over a thirteen-week period. Doleys, Wells, Hobbs, Roberts, and Cartelli (1976) used a verbal-reprimand procedure to decrease non-compliance of several retarded children. In each case the reprimand procedure, which consisted of a firm verbal statement expressing disapproval plus a brief period of time in which the experimenter intently glared at the individual, reduced noncompliance and was more effective than either a time out or an overcorrection procedure.

Three additional procedures deserve brief mention. Lovaas, Berberich, Perloff, and Schaeffer (1966) utilized a spanking procedure to decrease disruptive behaviors of severely disturbed children during language training. Conway and Bucher (1974) controlled the tantrums of a severely disturbed child by using a shot of shaving cream in the mouth, while a squirt of lemon juice in the mouth was used by Sajwaj, Libet, and Agras (1974) to control the vomiting of a child.

Clearly, punishment procedures can be effective with disruptive behaviors. However, as with stereotyped behaviors, at least two issues arise. First, ethical/legal restraints have been imposed in many settings to prohibit the use of punishment. Second, the use of punishment should always be used in conjunction with positive reinforcement for prosocial behaviors. As Forehand and Baumeister (1976) have pointed out, the primary goal of decreasing disruptive behaviors is not to produce a passive individual but rather to pave the way for teaching prosocial behaviors.

Another procedure that has been used to decrease disruptive behaviors is overcorrection (Foxx & Azrin, 1972). When treating disruptive behaviors, restitutional overcorrection has been used. With this type of procedure, the individual is required to correct disturbances in the environment that his or her behavior has created. Restitutional overcorrection can take various forms. Foxx and Azrin (1972) required retarded adults who had overturned chairs and tables to restore these items to their correct position, dust them, straighten the rest of the furniture in the room, and apologize to others for the disruption that their behavior caused. With a profoundly retarded individual who vomited frequently, Duker and Seys (1977) successfully used verbal disapproval, having the client wash her face with cold water, clean the vomit from the floor, and clean the surrounding area. She was also required to take off her soiled clothes and replace them with clean ones. Drabman, Cruz, Ross, and Lynd (1979) eliminated drooling by requiring retarded clients to wipe their mouth fifty times with a tissue each time they drooled. As Ollendick and Matson (1976) pointed out, the basic rationale underlying overcorrection is that "the person is required to perform 'restitution' for his inappropriate actions by correcting the situation and restoring the environment to an improved state" (p. 830).

Both Ollendick and Matson (1978) and Axelrod et al. (1978) reviewed a number of studies indicating that restitutional overcorrection is effective in reducing disruptive behaviors of severely disturbed children. However, as Axelrod and his colleagues pointed out, neither the effectiveness of overcorrection relative to alternate procedures nor the side effects of the procedure are clear at this time. Furthermore, they noted the need for a more precise specification of what components in the overcorrection procedure are necessary for it to be effective. As was discussed earlier, when overcorrection for stereotyped behaviors is examined, it can be seen that this procedure does consist of numerous components (for example, instruction giving, prompting, response prevention). The efficient use of restitutional overcorrection could be enhanced by the delineation of which components are the necessary ones.

BEHAVIORAL DEFICITS

Once stereotyped and disruptive behaviors are eliminated, the goal of the behavior therapist becomes one of increasing prosocial behaviors in the severely disturbed child's repertoire. The task becomes one of identifying what skills the child possesses, what skills need refining, and what skills need to be taught. Common behavioral deficits of severely disturbed children occur in self-help, communication, and interactional skills. It should be noted that the task of teaching skills in each of these areas is a monumental one in that frequently only small gains are achieved with the expenditure of immense effort.

Self-Help Skills

Severely disturbed children have been taught a variety of self-help skills. These include dressing, grooming, toileting, and feeding. To teach dressing skills, a backward chaining procedure is frequently used. Initially, this procedure involves breaking the behavior that is being taught into a number of steps. The client is then guided through all the steps with verbal and physical assistance and reinforced for completing the sequence of steps. On subsequent trials, the subject is continually guided through the initial steps in the sequence; however, assistance is faded out on the final steps prior to the completion of the behavior chain. The client is required to complete the final steps on his or her own in order to receive reinforcement. Gradually, the client is required to complete more and more steps without verbal or physical assistance until the entire chain is completed without assistance. An example of a backward chaining procedure involving a dressing skill is putting on a sock. Initially, correctly putting on a sock is divided into the following steps: picking up the sock, placing it near the foot, placing it on the toes, placing it midway on the foot, pulling it up to the heel, and pulling it completely up on the leg. To teach putting on a sock, a client is guided through all of these steps initially and receives reinforcement (for example, praise, edibles) for completing the act with assistance. Subsequently, the client is guided through all the steps except pulling the sock up on the leg. He or she is required to complete this act on his or her own in order to receive reinforcement. On subsequent trials, physical guidance is gradually faded out on each step. In their review, Jacobs and Lewis (1979) report a number of studies which successfully used a backward chaining procedure to teach dressing skills to severely disturbed children (for example, Bensberg, Colwell, & Cassel, 1965; Gorton & Hollis, 1965; Martin, Kehoe, Bird, Jensen, & Dorbeyshire, 1971; Minge & Ball, 1967).

Azrin, Schaeffer, and Wesolowski (1976) have used an alternate approach: a forward chaining procedure. Instead of guiding the client through the initial steps as in backward chaining, the client was required to successfully complete each act of the chain starting with the first behavior rather than the last. Training occurred in intensive four- to six-hour periods in which manual guidance, instruction, and reinforcement were used for completing each step in a chain of behaviors. Positive results were reported in that by the end of the fourth day of training, all twenty retarded clients had reached criterion. Although both backward and forward chaining appear to be successful procedures for teaching dressing, no data are available comparing the relative effectiveness of the two procedures.

Self-grooming has also been a self-help skill that has been taught to severely disturbed children. Jacobs and Lewis (1979) reviewed studies that indicate that tooth brushing, showering, washing, combing hair, trimming and filing nails, and the use of sanitary napkins have all been taught to severely disturbed children. Although it would appear that backward chaining procedures were typically used, many of these studies failed to specify their exact procedures (for example, Bensberg et al., 1965; Hollis & Gorton, 1967). In at least one study (Treffry, Martin, Samuels, & Watson, 1970), a forward chaining procedure was used successfully to teach face washing to severely disturbed children.

The self-help behavior that has received perhaps the most attention is toilet training. Teaching appropriate toileting skills is important not only for sanitary reasons but also to increase the amount of interaction between adults (ward staff, parents, teachers) and severely disturbed children. When children are continually soiled or wet, adults tend to avoid interacting with them. Research data suggest that a substantial proportion of children in state institutions are not toilet trained. Eyman, Tarjan, and Cassidy (1970) reported that 41 percent of the admissions over a two-year period to one state hospital were not toilet trained and another 16 percent were only partially trained. The prevalence of this problem behavior has resulted in it being frequently identified as a behavior deserving treatment.

Birnbrauer (1976) has presented an extensive review of toilet-training studies. One training procedure frequently used consists of placing a severely disturbed child on the toilet at certain times, rewarding the child for using the toilet, and reprimanding, punishing, or ignoring accidents that occur. A number of studies (for example, Baumeister & Klosowski, 1965; Dayan, 1964; Levine & Elliott, 1970) have reported the successful use of this type of program. Azrin and Foxx (1971) have used a similar procedure in their toilet-training studies but have incorporated a restitutional overcorrection component. Whenever accidents occur, clients are required to undress themselves, wash their clothes, shower, obtain clean clothing, and clean the area where the accident occurred. After approximately one week of intensive training, accidents were reported to be at a near zero level. Foxx and Azrin (1973) have presented extensive details for implementing their procedure in their popular book, *Toilet Training the Retarded Child.*

Using a forward chaining procedure, Van Wagenen, Meyerson, Kerr, and Mahoney (1969) utilized a pair of moisture-sensitive pants in which an alarm signaled the beginning of urination by a client. Whenever the alarm sounded, the trainer shouted "No" and moved toward the child. The trainer's actions were designed to stop the child's urination. The child was then placed on the toilet and encouraged to continue urination at that time. On subsequent trials, the trainer's shouting and moving toward the child were faded out and the child began moving toward the toilet independently. Thereafter, the child was taught to anticipate urination, thus eliminating the need for the tone. With forty-five hours of training, Van Wagenen et al. successfully taught eight profoundly retarded children to respond to the tone by going to the toilet and urinating.

Another self-help skill that is frequently absent in severely disturbed children is self-feeding. As with toileting, appropriate mealtime behavior among severely disturbed children is important for sanitary reasons as well as to decrease the aversiveness of the children to the adults working with them. A backward chaining procedure consisting of breaking feeding behaviors down into small steps and using the injestion of food as a reinforcer has been used successfully in a number of studies (for example, Gorton & Hollis, 1965; Zeiler & Jeruly, 1968). Azrin and his colleagues (Azrin & Armstrong, 1973; O'Brien, Bugle, & Azrin, 1972) have developed programs for teaching eating skills that use principles other than those used in backward chaining. These procedures involve teaching feeding during a number of sessions each day in order for the children to receive substantial practice in eating correctly. During each session, an interruption procedure is used to prevent hand feeding and overcorrection is used to have the client clean up the results of eating accidents. Positive practice also occurs as the client practices the correct forms of eating. Azrin and Armstrong (1973) reported developing appropriate eating skills with eleven clients after an average of five days in treatment.

The studies reviewed indicate that dressing, grooming, toileting, and feeding can be taught to severely disturbed children. Both backward chaining and forward chaining procedures have been successfully utilized. The relative effectiveness of these two procedures is unknown. Probably the most effective procedure is one that combines various intervention strategies, such as that used by Azrin and his colleagues to teach feeding.

Several practical problems exist when teaching self-help skills. Most programs involve one-to-one attention or one trainer for a small group of children. When considering most institutions, the staff/client ratio does not make this feasible. Furthermore, ways to promote generalization across time and settings have not been systematically explored. Unless methods to ensure generalization are developed, training will have to occur continually in numerous settings in order for the skills to be used in the various environments in which the clients find themselves.

Communication and Interactional Skills

Teaching communication skills to severely disturbed children has been a goal of many behavior therapists. Compared to the relative ease with which self-help skills can be taught, communication skills involve a far more complex process because more than simple motor movements are required. A number of investigators have delineated programs that can be used to teach verbal skills to children (for example, Lovaas & Newsome, 1976; Marshall & Hegrenes, 1970; Sailor, Guess, & Baer, 1973). These programs each have the following components in common. First, determination of hearing loss and selection of an appropriate reinforcer occur. Subsequently, attention training is undertaken to teach the child to attend to the trainer. Third, the child is taught to imitate. This imitation initially involves motor imitation (for example, simple hand movements) and subsequently vocal imitation (for example, making sounds similar to those made by the trainer). The fourth component is to teach simple and subsequently more complex words by imitation and reinforcement procedures. The individual components of complex words initially are taught, and then these components are combined. Fifth, functional speech is taught in which the client learns the meaning and use of words. This is done by having the client label different objects, request objects that he or she wishes, and describe the action of various objects. As with self-help skills, the basic procedure in teaching language is to break the desired behaviors down into small steps and to reinforce the client for successive approximations at verbalizing the desired response.

Garcia and DeHaven (1974), Margolies (1977), and Lovaas and Newsom (1976) have each reviewed a number of studies indicating that speech can be taught to severely disturbed children. However, Margolies has stressed that although rote words have been taught, the degree to which meaningful language, which is utilized for communication purposes, has been taught successfully is questionable. Furthermore, Garcia and DeHaven (1974) and Lovaas and Newsom (1976) both noted the practical limitations with language training; at the present time in most training programs, one adult typically works with one child for an extended period of time. Use of such methodology is not practical on a large-scale basis.

Carr, Binkoff, Kologinsky, and Eddy (1978) have pointed out that, despite intense training efforts, a number of severely disturbed children do not develop language. Consequently, they demonstrated that sign language could be taught to children in order to give them communication skills. Each of four autistic children was prompted to make a sign for a particular word (for example, apple) and was subsequently reinforced for correctly completing the task. On subsequent trials, the prompting was faded out until the child could make the sign unaided. Thereafter, new signs for additional words were successfully introduced.

Employing yet another procedure, Reid and Hurlbut (1977) taught four spastic retarded individuals to communicate nonverbally by using a pointer and a communication board. The clients were initially taught coordination training by the use of instructions, manual guidance, praise, feedback, and practice. In this phase, each client was taught to point to a particular block on the communication board upon request. Subsequently, identification training was taught in a similar manner. In this phase, the clients were taught to point to a picture on the communication board in response to a verbal request. The pictures on the communication board represented various leisure areas in their environment (e.g., library, TV room, and porch). All clients learned to point to a particular picture on the communication board upon request and subsequently demonstrated that they could use the communication board to inform others about the particular areas of their environment to which they wished to go. Evidently, verbal skills are not necessary for all severely disturbed children to be able to communicate with others.

Some behavior therapists have turned their attention to teaching severely disturbed children conversational skills. In contrast to the remedial-speech and nonverbal training programs in which elementary communication skills are taught, the teaching of conversational skills consists of instructing those children who already have language skills how to use them appropriately in conversations with others. Conversational skills that have been taught include how to ask on-topic questions, make short on-topic statements, indicate interest and enthusiasm in conversations, issue informational facts in a conversation, invite others to engage in activities, and discuss socially appropriate topics. Instructions, modeling, behavioral rehearsal, praise, and fading procedures have been used to teach conversation skills (Humphreys, Forehand, Cheney, & Adams, 1977). Nelson, Gibson, and Cutting (1973) and Kelly, Furman, Phillips, Hathorn, and Wilson (1979) demonstrated that conversational skills can be taught to retarded children. Kelly et al. also found generalized use of the skills as the clients used their conversational skills with retarded and nonretarded peers. Furthermore, improvement was maintained after treatment terminated. Arnold, Sturgis, and Forehand (1977) demonstrated that conversational skills can be taught to parents who can subsequently teach the skills to their severely disturbed children. This is obviously an efficient procedure in terms of the behavior therapist's time.

Strain and his colleagues have been involved in a series of studies designed to teach social interactional skills to severely disturbed children. The skills taught to the children in this program include not only speech and conversational skills but also certain motor skills (for example, touching and cooperating). Using prompting and social reinforcement, Strain, Shores, and Kerr (1976) demonstrated that three preschool behaviorally handicapped children could be taught to increase their positive social behavior with peers. In two subsequent studies, Strain, Shores, and Timm (1977) and Ragland, Kerr, and Strain (1978) taught peers to make social approaches toward identified retarded autistic children who were withdrawn. The peer was trained to initiate interactions through the use of instructions, role playing, and reinforcement for interacting. The results of both studies indicated that the withdrawn children increased their interaction when the peer initiated social responses. Such findings suggest that peers may function effectively as therapists for severely disturbed children.

The results of the studies reviewed in this section indicate that remedial language as well as more advanced conversational skills can be taught to socially interact with peers. However, as was noted earlier, the procedures used to teach verbal, conversational, and social skills to severely disturbed children involve intensive one-to-one training—a luxury not available in many settings designed for the severely disturbed child.

TEACHING WARD STAFF, TEACHERS, AND PARENTS

Behavior therapists are frequently not involved in the actual workings of behavior-modification programming. Instead, they train ward staff in institutional settings, teachers in classrooms, and parents in the home to implement programs with severely disturbed children. The role of the behavior therapist in these instances is to provide the intervention agent (for example, ward staff) with the appropriate skills for actually implementing and completing the behavior-modification program with the child.

Although severely disturbed children have frequently been placed in institutions in the past, the development *and evaluation* of comprehensive programs for training institutional personnel have been absent. This is particularly distressing as institutional staff who work with severely disturbed children report low job satisfaction (Zaharia & Baumeister, 1979a) and demonstrate high staff turnover and absenteeism rates (Zaharia & Baumeister, 1979b). Obviously, training programs for staff are needed to provide these persons with skills to enhance their work effectiveness and job satisfaction.

Jacobs and Lewis (1979) have outlined one staff training program. Although data to support the effectiveness of the program are not available, a brief survey of this program will be offered here in order to provide the reader with a general idea of procedures for training institutional staff personnel. The initial step involves an assessment of the staff and includes determining their attitudes toward clients, their current skill levels in terms of both knowledge and ability to implement programs, and their achievement levels, particularly in the area of reading, as part of the training may involve reading selected materials. Second, determination of what a competent ward staff person should know and be able to do, relative to the initial assessment of what he or she actually can do, leads to a determination of what needs to be taught. Third, individualized instruction, active rather than passive learning, multimedia training packages, and self-paced instruction are viewed as essential ingredients in the training programs for staff. Fourth, a follow-up evaluation following in-service training is necessary, for revisions in programs that have been developed are typically needed. When particular programs are implemented with clients, it is necessary that an accountability system be established in which each staff member has a clear understanding of what is expected of him or her. Furthermore, an adequate incentive system for staff should be established. This had commonly been in the form of feedback or money (for example, Pommer & Streedbeck, 1974).

Clearly, training institutional personnel is a complex process that requires substantial planning, systematic implementation, and continual evaluation. Although comprehensive programs have not been evaluated, several behavior therapists have examined different ways to modify the behavior of institutional personnel. Gardner (1972) found that having behavior-modification skills than having them attend lectures about principles of behavior modification. Praise, written feedback, television feedback, lotteries, and self-recording behavior have been used successfully to teach behavior-modification skills and/or motivate institutional staff to use the skills (for example, Bricker, Morgan, & Grabowski, 1972; Burg, Reid, & Lattimore, 1979; Greene, Willis, Levy, & Bailey, 1978; Iwata, Bailey, Brown, Foshee, & Alpern, 1976). Staff skills that have been identified for modification in these studies include implementing programs, increasing staff interactions with clients, improving the quality of their work, and completing daily tasks on the ward.

Attention is now beginning to focus on the implementation of programs in the classroom setting. With the recent emphasis on deinstitutionalizing severely disturbed children and mainstreaming them into normal environments where possible, the need to develop effective educational programs in public classrooms is evident. Koegel, Russo, and Rincover (1977) have recently reported a training program for teaching teachers to use behavior-modification skills with autistic children. The following skills were taught: use of clear instructions; use of effective prompts; use of shaping procedures; use of immediate, consistent, contingent consequences; and use of discrete training trials. Teachers read a manual, viewed video tapes, and implemented treatment procedures with a child during which time they received feedback from a trainer. The results indicated that all eleven teachers rapidly learned the behavior-modification techniques and generalized their use of the skills to a variety of children.

A number of studies have been completed in which behavior-modification programs have been implemented in classrooms for autistic children (for reviews, see Birnbrauer, 1976; Lovaas & Newsom, Rincover & Koegel, 1977). Disruptive and stereotyped behaviors have been reduced, academic behaviors have been increased, compliance to classroom rules have increased, and prosocial interactional behaviors have increased. A variety of behavior-modification techniques have been used to achieve these ends. These include: programmed instructions; positive reinforcement procedures, including token systems; response cost systems; modeling; and time out for disruptive behaviors.

Although substantial research and a large number of programs have been developed for severely disturbed children in the classroom setting, Rincover and Koegel (1977) pointed out that one problem in the classroom setting is the difficulty of teaching behavior in a group setting (classroom) or maintaining behavior in such a setting after teaching in an individual (one-to-one) setting. Koegel and Rincover (1974) developed a systematic program to address this difficulty. Initially, each of eight children participated in one-to-one training sessions in which they received continuous reinforcement for appropriate responding. Subsequently, the number of children was gradually increased from a one-to-one setting to a two-to-one setting and reinforcement was reduced to an FR 2 schedule. The number of children in the classroom setting continued to increase gradually and reinforcement continued to be faded to a VR 8 schedule. As a result of the gradual increase in number of children and gradual reduction in the reinforcement schedule, the children continued to progress at rates that were achieved during the one-to-one training.

Although it has been demonstrated that severely disturbed children can progress in self-contained rooms in public school systems, more recent emphasis has been on mainstreaming disturbed children. The advantages of placing severely disturbed children in regular classrooms include the availability of appropriate role models and the exposure to the normal curriculum that is taught in regular classrooms. Despite these advantages, placement of severely disturbed children in regular classrooms is often difficult. Russo and Koegel (1977) developed a behavioral program for integrating such children into a normal public school classroom. Working with a five-year-old autistic child, a therapist accompanied the child to a normal kindergarten classroom daily. In addition, the child received three one-hour training sessions after school in which tokens were established as reinforcers. In the normal classroom, the child then received tokens from the therapist for appropriate social behavior, the elimination of self-stimulation, and appropriate verbal response to commands. In the next stage, the teacher was taught to implement the behavior-modification program. The results indicated that all three treated behaviors changed in the desired directions.

Not only is it important for severely disturbed children to acquire skills in an academic setting, it is also important for these children to acquire skills in the home setting. In order for this to occur, parents must acquire the behavior-modification skills necessary to work with their severely disturbed children. Research by Lovaas, Koegel, Simmons, and Long (1973) has demonstrated that training parents can be both an effective and efficient procedure to modify the behavior of severely disturbed children. In their study, training parents to modify the behavior of their autistic children was as effective as intensive inpatient training. The data also suggested that parent training led to better maintenance of gains at follow-up.

Other studies have also demonstrated that parents can modify the behavior of their severely disturbed children (for a review, see Margolies, 1977). Parents have been taught both to decrease the disruptive and stereotyped behaviors of their severely disturbed children and to teach prosocial behaviors. In a recent systematic study of teaching parents to work with their severely disturbed children, Koegel, Glahn, and Neiminen (1978) examined several procedures for obtaining generalization of treatment effects when parents are trained to modify the behavior of their autistic children. The results indicated that a brief demonstration of how to teach a child a new behavior was sufficient for the parents to effectively teach that behavior. However, generalization of the teaching procedure to new child behaviors did not occur until general behavior-modification procedures were taught to the parents. The results of this study suggest that more than specific training on a specific task is necessary for parents to generalize their skills and effectively modify the wide range of behavior difficulties displayed by most severely disturbed children.

Practical problems also exist with training parents to be behavior modifiers. Lovaas et al. (1973) indicated that for parents to be successful behavior modifiers, they must possess the following features: a willingness to use strong consequences, such as food and spankings; a willingness to deny that their children are "ill"; and a willingness to commit a major part of their lives as parents to their children. These three requirements obviously pose a hardship on most parents.

The studies reviewed in this section indicate that institutional staff personnel, teachers, and parents can be taught to work effectively with severely disturbed children. However, the scarcity of data indicating effective teaching approaches suggests that this is a difficult task to accomplish.

Additional research is needed in this area before conclusions can be reached about the effectiveness of training nonprofessionals to work with severely disturbed children.

ETHICAL ISSUES

The conclusion by Lovaas et al. (1973) that effective behavior modifiers of autistic children must be willing to use strong consequences raises one ethical issue that is faced in working with severely disturbed children. When individuals demonstrate pervasive aberrant behavior, aversive consequences are frequently necessary to control such behavior. However, the procedures that are used for such control have often been misused and abused and have resulted in ethical/legal actions being taken to prohibit the use of such techniques. The *Wyatt* v. *Stickney* court ruling (1971) in Alabama mentioned previously serves as an excellent example of the limitation imposed on the use of behavior-therapy techniques by a court ruling. Specific restrictions were placed on the use of time out from positive reinforcement and aversive treatment in the standards issued by the court.

A number of individuals and groups have offered guidelines for the use of aversive treatment with severely disturbed children. For example, Cook, Altman, and Haavik (1978) and Repp and Deitz (1978) have suggested guidelines for the use of aversive treatment with the retarded. In addition, the National Association for Retarded Children has published guidelines for the use of behavioral programs for the institutional retarded (May et al., 1975). These activities suggest that individuals and groups of individuals are concerned about the use of behavior modification with severely disturbed children. This is not surprising, as Forehand and Baumeister (1976) have pointed out that behavior modification has one basic goal: to teach us how to prevail over others. As these authors have stated, behavior modification is especially vulnerable to external control as its emphasis is on "direct control, specificity of force, and manipulation of consequences" (p. 272). It is important to remember that the selection of a particular treatment or strategy with a severely disturbed child must not only take into account the effectiveness of the strategy but also the social acceptability of the approach (Forehand & Baumeister, 1976).

SUMMARY AND CONCLUSIONS

A wide variety of behavior-modification intervention techniques used with severely disturbed children have been discussed in this chapter. In general, all of these have been effective at one point or another. Clearly, however, some (for example, ignoring) are less effective than others (for example, time out). Nevertheless, the available data suggest that there are a wide variety of intervention techniques for not only decreasing excessive behaviors but also increasing deficit behaviors.

The intervention procedures reviewed here are most effective with simple motor-type behaviors and less effective with more complex, cognitive behaviors. For example, the elimination of stereotyped and disruptive behaviors can be achieved with a variety of techniques, such as time out and overcorrection. However, when one moves to more complex, cognitive behaviors, such as functional language, the techniques one has to choose from become more limited and the behavior that one is attempting to teach becomes more difficult. Nevertheless, we do appear to have the beginnings of a technology that may achieve some degree of success, even with complex behaviors.

At least two methodological difficulties have existed in much of the work completed at this time. First, many of the studies have failed to demonstrate the degree of experimental rigor that one would like. The preponderance of uncontrolled case studies has been noted by several investigators (Forehand & Baumeister, 1976; Margolies, 1977). Second, data appear to be particularly lacking when one examines generality of treatment effects. Generalization across time and across settings frequently has not been assessed. The pervasiveness of the behavioral difficulties manifested by most severely disturbed children dictates the importance of assessing generalization and, where needed, developing strategies that will achieve generalized behavior changes.

In view of the two issues just discussed, can we reach any conclusions about the extent to which behavior-modification procedures can produce changes in the behavior of severely disturbed children? Several authors have addressed this issue. After reviewing the literature regarding the behavioral treatment of autism, Margolies (1977) concluded that autistic children following behavioral treatment are clearly not normal. Similarly, Birnbrauer (1976) concluded that retarded individuals treated with behavior-modification techniques are still retarded at the end of treatment. However, both of these investigators reported that behavior modification leads to real change in the behavior of severely disturbed children. Maladaptive behaviors are decreased and prosocial behaviors are increased. As Lovaas et al. (1973) concluded about the improvement achieved with their behavior-modification program for autistic children, the improvement is similar to making from ten to twenty on a one-hundred-step ladder. Clearly, behavior modification is effective with severely disturbed children; however, substantial additional rigorous work is necessary in order to develop behavior-modification techniques that are effective enough to bring the behavior of severely disturbed children into the range of behaviors manifested by normal children.

CHAPTER 23

BEHAVIOR MODIFICATION WITH DELINQUENTS AND CRIMINALS

Jerome S. Stumphauzer

University of Southern California School of Medicine

INTRODUCTION

Perhaps no other area is as controversial as crime and its modification. Crime, whether committed by juveniles or adults, has always been of special interest, not only to students of behavior, but also to politicians, religious leaders, and the public in general. These diverse groups, for example, may all conceptualize crime differently: as behavior, as lawbreaking, as sin, as all of the above, as none of the above. Because of these vastly differing views of crime, and because of media sensationalization of crime—from newspaper headlines to movies and television—crime and corrections are highly emotionally charged topics. In addition, retribution and punishment for law violation are heavily influenced by our cultural and religious heritage ("an eye for an eye, a tooth for a tooth"). These factors should be kept in mind while the reader considers psychological approaches to modifying criminal behavior, because one is dealing with long-standing concepts and traditions.

The behavior modification of crime or, more precisely, the application of psychological learning principles to the behavior of delinquents and criminals has received a good deal of notoriety. In part, this is due to the attention received by the many varied behavioral programs that have been developed for lawbreakers (Nietzel, 1979; Stumphauzer, 1973, 1979), and in part, to the controversy stemming from either misguided or unethical application of these principles to confined prisoners.

A word on concepts and terms. The term *behavioral corrections* will be used in this chapter as a shorthand for behavior modification with delinquents and criminals both in institutions and in community-based programs. Other terms in common use are especially unfortunate. *Delinquency* is the worst and *crime* is not far behind. *Delinquency* has the ring of a human condition too closely akin to a disease. The way it is often used leads one to think that particular youths "have" something called delinquency and (therefore?) they should be treated for "it" or, alternatively, "it" will go away as they "grow out of it." Indeed, it took half a heated symposium debate before a psychoanalyst and I agreed that we were talking about two different things—*delinquency* and *delinquent behavior* (Stumphauzer & Marohn, 1975). For our purposes here, we will be focusing on delinquent behavior. Behavior that is delinquent (that is, that breaks laws) lends itself more meaningfully to observation, measurement, and modification. Likewise, rather than that great social bugaboo *crime,* we will address the more mundane but more accessible *criminal* or *unlawful behavior.* The author has used the title "behavior modification *with* delinquents and criminals" because behaviors other than crimes are often a focus (school achievement, work, and so on). Finally, delinquents and criminals are simply those persons (under or over eighteen) who commit crimes, get caught, and (therefore) get labeled.

Ethical and Legal Issues

Legal challenges to behavior modification and ethical issues have been discussed in general in Chapter 10 and by Martin (1975). Nietzel (1979) addressed these issues specifically as they apply to adult criminals. Stumphauzer (1977) discussed eight general issues, one of which is in particular need of mention here—the utilization of aversion therapy and punishment. Early abuses of aversion-therapy techniques using electric shock or other drastic means (including drugs to induce nausea or to stop breathing), and inaccurately portrayed in Stanley Kubrick's 1976 *A Clockwork Orange,* have resulted in the general curtailment of these procedures with adult criminals. Only one case of such treatment of an adolescent is known to the author (MacCulloh, William, & Birtles, 1971). Although aversion therapy *was* perhaps the hottest issue in behavioral corrections, it has largely been stopped because of legal challenge, questionable effectiveness, and the development of more positive, humane means of improving behavior. This is demonstrated below in the description of the cellblock token economy.

Is punishment synonymous with corrections? To the general public, yes; to psychologists, no. Many people believe, certainly, that criminals should be punished. But as you are probably aware, psychologists have a much more specific usage of the word and its application: *"if the presentation of an aversive stimulus as the consequence of a behavior decreases the strength or frequency of that behavior, then punishment type 1,[1] aversive stimulation has taken place"* (Stumphauzer, 1977, p. 90). Punishment, in *this* sense, is an aversive stimulus that in fact *decreases* behavior. It should be evident that "punishments" like arrest, probation, and imprisonment often *do not* decrease behavior. At first it may seem a legitimate goal for behavior corrections—decreasing criminal behavior by punishment—but the use of physical pain has been repeatedly challenged on both ethical and legal grounds (as cruel and/or unusual punishment). Thus, physical pain is today a rarely acceptable behavior modification intervention. This is not to say that institutional personnel do not continue inflicting pain on inmates by traditional, informal, unscientific means. Two less objectionable forms of punishment are more commonly practiced today in behavioral corrections: *time out* (opportunity for reinforcement briefly withdrawn) and *response cost* (for example, loss of tokens in a token economy). Punishment will be around for a long time, and both its definition and application will remain controversial. This issue and others are discussed in the evaluation of the six programs that follow.

After reviewing these issues, the student may well get the impression that it is impossible to conduct both ethical and effective behavior modification with delinquents and criminals. Indeed, practitioners do not have the freedom to experiment with the behavior of people simply because they are convicted of crimes and labeled criminals. *All* human rights are not given up. Effective *and* ethical behavior modification is possible, but not without careful consideration of these issues and related ones coming on the foreseeable horizon. At this point, there is no indication that an end to either the productivity or the controversy are in sight. The present era can be viewed as a healthy period of growth which is necessarily restrained by concern for basic human rights.

Measurement of Crime

Students of criminal behavior will soon find that their subject matter is exceedingly difficult to measure. For the big picture, the most commonly

1. This was labeled "punishment by application" in Chapter 7.

used index of official, detected crime in the United States is the FBI's annual *Uniform Crime Reports,* which is based on reports submitted voluntarily by individual police departments. The final figures are given as the rate or the frequency of crime per 100,000 population. This frequently cited index suffers not only from lack of uniformity of arrest and record keeping but also from political and fiscal pressures in individual municipalities. This might lead to underestimates of some crimes and the stressing or redefining of other crimes. Cities may want to show, for example, that they do not have a particular problem, or alternatively, that they *do* need funding for a special crime problem. Even with these limitations, these are rates of *official* crime. What about *unofficial* crime? Anonymous surveys of college students, for example, confirm the general belief that large amounts of crime go undetected and that almost everyone has committed acts that, if detected, could result in arrest (Waldo & Chiricon, 1972).

A commonly used measure of correctional or program success is the *recidivism rate,* or the percentage of persons who are convicted *again* after release. This too is a less-than-adequate index because it is often more a measure of court behavior (what police and courts do) rather than of criminal behavior. Also, recidivism is usually an all-or-none measure and does not reflect qualitative or subtle differences in behavior (Braukmann & Fixen, 1975). The problem of measuring criminal behavior is no less complex when one is attempting to assess the criminal activity of even one individual, as will be illustrated in the following case.

Behavioral Analysis of Crime

In a study of mine described in detail elsewhere (Stumphauzer, 1976b), a twelve-year-old girl was referred to a mental health clinic by her school for "uncontrolled stealing for several years." The behavior had not yet been measured. In fact, her behavior fell into the unofficial category: she had not (yet) had any contact with police or the courts, even though several sources (parents, teachers, peers, and herself) all agreed she was a thief. The immediate problem was (1) how to assess the stealing and (2) how to determine its controlling variables. The problem was solved by way of a *behavioral analysis* (Kanfer & Saslow, 1969). Stealing presented particular problems. It was, by its very nature, secret and *not* public behavior-especially if successful! Direct observation was difficult, and like many other crimes, stealing was a fairly *low-frequency* behavior. It was doubtful that stealing would occur at all under direct observation (that is, while being watched). Through the negotiation of a behavioral contract, it was agreed by all parties that stealing incidents would be measured on daily behavior cards (Stumphauzer, 1974a) by parents (at home), by teachers (at school), and simultaneously by the girl in both places. Consensual validation was achieved in that all three sources confirmed a previously estimated base rate of five thefts a week. The behavioral analysis further revealed some of the stimuli, setting events, and reinforcements that led to a high probability of stealing: for example, wanting to buy a snack, not having money, and seeing a purse "unattended" at school. Furthermore, theft and apprehension were socially reinforced by teachers who would give her extra attention at school and by parents when she reached home. Additionally, it seemed important that the girl did *not* receive concomitant attention for any of her numerous good behaviors (school achievement, helping at home, and so on) or for *not* stealing. A self-reinforcement and family-behavioral-contracting program resulted in a rapid cessation of stealing and increases in other, prosocial behaviors. Measurement of the criminal behavior of individuals *is* possible. Measurement of behavior incompatible with crime (for example, school achievement, prosocial activities, and work) in addition may be both easier (more accessible) and desirable (measured so that it can be reinforced in a positive, nonpunitive program).

What follows are descriptions and discussions of three behavioral programs, first for delinquents and then for adult criminals. Each section will (1) begin with an example of a behavioral program in a closed institution or prison, (2) continue with an example "in between" in which there are *some* formal legal or social restrictions (probation, group home, and so on), and (3) end with the description of a totally open, community-based program. Obviously, the six programs described are only illustrative and do not cover the board, as this was not intended as an exhaustive review. More complete coverage of these and many more programs are found elsewhere for delinquents (Stumphauzer, 1970, 1973, 1974b, 1976a, 1979) and for criminals (Nietzel, 1979).

THREE BEHAVIORAL PROGRAMS FOR DELINQUENTS

1. California Youth Authority Project

THE PROBLEM

There is every indication that we will continue to institutionalize young lawbreakers—all the way from temporary "placement" in juvenile halls to the equivalent of prisons for delinquents. Many people believe lawbreaking youths should be locked up just to "be punished" or to "protect society." They are certainly *temporarily* removed from society and thrown together, often in an environment in which they will learn *more* delinquent behavior (Buehler, Patterson, & Furniss, 1966). A vast literature over the past fifty years can be summarized in this one bold statement: locking up delinquents does not improve their behavior. But if we are going to continue locking them up, what effective programs *can* be implemented? This, then, is the problem. Behavioral psychologists were quick to pick up this challenge, perhaps too quick. Often, short-range institutional goals (for example, conformity to institutional rules) have been pursued with this powerful new technology.

THE CYA PROGRAM

The California Youth Authority (CYA) program compared the effectiveness of behavior modification (B Mod) and transactional analysis (TA) in two roughly parallel institutions for delinquents in northern California (Jesness & DeRisi, 1973; Jesness, 1975; Jesness, 1976). It seemed an ideal experimental design: the staff of each was well trained in one or the other modality, delinquent youth aged fifteen to seventeen were randomly assigned to either the B Mod or the TA programs, and multiple-behavior ratings and attitude measures were maintained both while the youths were institutionalized and after release. This seems simple enough, but to my knowledge, so comprehensive a design has never been achieved before or since.

The TA program involved a life-script interview soon after admission to determine each youth's particular script, or broad life pattern, that he appeared to be following. Afterward, three kinds of "mutually agreeable verbal treatment contracts" were negotiated: academic, small group, and social (Jesness, 1975, p. 762). TA treatment focused, both in individual counseling and in small group therapy sessions, on script analysis (analysis of personal and social transactions) and on teaching self-enhancing and socially desirable goals through personal decision and the influence of others ("strokes").

The B Mod program involved contingency management or a token economy in which boys earned "dollars" (reinforcement in the form of paper money) and praise for positive behavior and lost dollars (response cost) for inappropriate behavior. Three classes of behavior were focused on (1) critical behavior deficiencies (those related to parole success, such as fighting), (2) academic behaviors, and (3) convenience behaviors (such as loud talking at bedtime). Dollars were not only used for more desired back-up reinforcers (goods, comforts, and recreation) but also counted toward point-contingent parole from the institution. Detailed behavioral contracts that specified behaviors and consequences were utilized, and charts with measures of these behaviors were posted.

RESULTS AND ISSUES

Jesness (1976) reports parole follow-up and test data on 904 boys. The major findings appear to be that results were amazingly similar, and that both programs were only somewhat superior to regular and comparison institutions. Major breaches of discipline in the institutions apparently were not reduced by either program, but staff responses were different; there was a 60 percent drop in youths sent to detention. Both programs did make substantial gains in academic achievement. Results from a series of attitude surveys suggested that the TA program resulted in more "positive feelings" about the staff, the program, and themselves than the B Mod program. The B Mod program was somewhat superior in ratings of behavior. But what about the bottom line—the recidivism results? Although both the B Mod and the TA programs were superior to the comparison or usual institutions which had a 42 percent recidivism rate, post release arrest records for the two programs still averaged 33 percent at twelve months.

Why are the results of two supposedly different programs so similar? It may be that either the programs were not as different in practice as they might have been or that the measures were not sensitive enough to reflect differences. As noted above, both programs utilized contracting as central to their treatments. Although their conceptual framework may have been different, in actual implementation, both contracting programs specified behaviors and their consequences. It has also been noted to me that points (token reinforcement) were in fact utilized in one of the eight living units in the TA program, thus confounding the experimental design and interpretation of results (Wedge, 1979). The measures of behavior reported are *ratings* of behavior and are usually considered less adequate for reliability and validity than actual measurement of frequency of behaviors. Neither program had an aftercare or follow-through component to continue the program while the youth was on parole, and generalization of results might well have been enhanced if this had been added. Finally, although both programs could certainly be termed successful, they both formally ended in 1972. Why? This final issue has to do with the nature of such research and programming. *Even though a program "works," this does not mean that it will continue.* Program continuation and replication depend on (in addition to such academic proof) funding, political expediency, and the even more nebulous enthusiasm of perhaps one particular program administrator. Differential programming or long-term effectiveness may be of less interest to policy and decision makers than immediate results and cost effectiveness (that is, money spent), and behavioral psychologists will have to address these issues before we will see successful programs both continue and proliferate.

2. Learning House

The Problem

The picture is no less complicated in the gray area between institutionalization and living freely at home. This area can include probation, parole, diversion programs, foster homes, clinic treatment, day care, specialized school placements, and group homes. The problem—effective behavioral programs for youth in a more community-based yet still somewhat legally or socially controlled program—has some very promising solutions. One has been the widely acclaimed Achievement Place model of the group home based on operant-contingency management of delinquents and predelinquents in a family-style setting (Kirigin, Wolf, Braukmann, Fixsen, & Phillips, 1979). A second model of the group home is the Learning House program described below, which extends a social-learning model beyond the group home to parent and self-control with a goal of maintenance and generalization of positive changes.

The Learning House Program

Learning House of Palo Alto, California, is a remarkable behaviorally oriented group home for elementary-age children with multiple problems ranging from incorrigibility to arson, truancy, fighting, and theft (Thoresen, Thoresen, Klein, Wilbur, Becker-Haven, & Haven, 1979). When a child first enters Learning House, a structured, consistent, and comprehensive point system (token economy) helps define and shape appropriate behavior. Later, behavior contracting is utilized to shift the program in the direction of helping children develop and manage their own behavior. In fact, self-control and social-skills training are the heart of the Learning House program. At the same time, the teaching parents and tutors help the children succeed while attending classes in regular schools. A final phase of Learning House residential treatment is a period of self-rating in which each child learns to assess his or her own program and readiness to return home. It is especially noteworthy that the program does *not* end here. Rather, the parent counseling and training that had been taking place on a weekly basis is at last phased into a continuing-care program for the family during the first twelve months *after* the child returns home. The goals of family self-management and the child's self-control are the continuing focus.

Results and Issues

Learning House has been evaluated with a promising new *cost-effectiveness* model (Yates, Haven, & Thoresen, 1979). This model has been useful in pinpointing not only the program's effect on particular behaviors but also its cost. While living at Learning House, the children advanced substantially in measures of academic performance. Of the first thirteen children who completed the Learning House program, nine, or 69 percent, presented no further legal or social problem during the first year of follow-up, a more stringent criterion than simply recidivism. The average cost of treating a child at learning House was $12,847, which is less than an average of $15,000 for more usual *custodial* care for children in California.

Because of the comprehensiveness of the Learning House model and its preliminary results (as well as the continuing success of the Achievement Place model), we should be encouraged to believe that behaviorally oriented family-style residential homes could be a viable large-scale alternative to institutionalization and custodial care. Issues facing the nationwide, commonplace application of these models are many. Shifts in funding from institutions to learning homes must be accomplished, which will meet with political and social resistance. Teaching parents must be trained systematically—a goal already achieved to some degree by the Achievement Place program. Finally, community-based residential-group treatment of delinquents will require education of the general population in order for these learning homes to be accepted into every neighborhood. The model is behaviorally sound and proven; acceptance and widescale application remain other matters.

3. East Side Story

The Problem

There are two ways to look at crime and its modification/prevention. One way is through a traditional official model: police and eventually courts sending youths to institutions, probation, psychological treatment, and even group homes. That way requires that some official agency personnel must catch, label, and somehow determine who may eventually reach a program. I have found the whole system very unsatisfactory, mainly because (1) it reaches a very curious few—it has a low "hit rate," (2) it doesn't work, for the most part, and (3) it cannot and has not met the long-range goals of crime and delinquency prevention. An entirely different approach to the problem of crime is to attempt to study and understand it where it is happening and to intervene directly on a community-wide basis. The problem, then, is how to devise effective behavioral analyses of crime and make interventions based on them directly in the community where criminal behavior is being taught, learned, and maintained. One community under study is the East Side of Los Angeles, which suffers not only from multiple problems of unemployment, poverty, and crime but from a critical gang-violence problem as well—hence the East Side Story.

THE EAST SIDE STORY PROGRAM

The program began with a three-level behavioral analysis of gang violence in one particular community of fifteen thousand residents in which intergang violence (shootings, stabbings, extortion, police confrontation, and fighting) had become common everyday occurrences. First, an on-the-spot behavioral analysis of the community itself was begun with a focus on what part each of the following played in teaching and maintaining gang violence: community design, geography, physical assets and deficits of the city, and principal social influences (parents, teachers, police, business people, clergy). Second, a behavioral study of the one violent gang of four hundred youths that dominates the city was studied directly in terms of how its members were shaping and keeping the violent behavior going (Stumphauzer, Aiken, & Veloz, 1977). Note that none of these individuals were in contact with the program because of any traditional, official lable of "delinquent" or "client." Third, a behavioral analysis of *non*delinquent youth was initiated to develop an understanding of how *naturally occurring* influences in the community were teaching behavior that was *incompatible* with delinquency and violence and to see if these influences could be expanded in terms of prevention (Aiken, Stumphauzer, & Veloz, 1977). The preliminary findings of these analyses were then utilized in the development and implementation of six community anticrime programs with limited federal funding (Veloz & Stumphauzer, 1979). For example, three of the programs engage previously hard-core gang members in behavior that is *incompatible* with gang delinquent behavior: (1) A "dial-an-escort" service to stores, and so on, for senior citizens and women so that they *don't* get robbed; (2) a community revitalization program in which youths canvas their own neighborhood blocks to evaluate high-crime properties (vacant houses, and so on), learning to take *legal* means to correct the situations; and (3) a street-theater group in which youths write, direct, and produce anticrime plays (for example, on gang violence and "angel dust") and present them to peers and other community groups. All six programs are encouraging behavior incompatible with crime and are actively removing or limiting some of the many reinforcers for gang delinquency (attention, praise, freedom from prosecution, material goods) by organizing and educating parents' groups. One group of mothers will blockade a home threatened with violence, and will even walk up to an attacker and take a gun away!

Results and Issues

The initial three-part community analyses generated a great many observations on the chain of events in this community that teach and maintain gang violence. For example: (1) rival gang comes into a territory and commits one of several acts of challenge; (2) a *veterano* (older gang veteran) describes in detail (symbolically models) what *he* did or would do under similar circumstances; (3) gang youth respond with retaliatory behavior; (4) peers and community members reinforce with attention and respect; (5) gang youth respond with pride (self-reinforcing statements); and (6) in some cases, youth are caught by police, usually released, and thus further reinforced. At this stage, these analyses are descriptive and can only be considered suggestive in terms of empirical validation. The study of nondelinquent youth is currently being expanded with the inclusion of more systematic data gathered by nonproblematic youth in the city who are beeped on a random schedule through a vibratactile electronic pager, at which time they record location, companionship, activity, and reinforcement information (Aiken, 1980).

The analyses were useful in developing and evaluating the six anticrime programs. The first year of operation has been completed and each program has had an impact on crime and violent behavior. Those youths engaged in incompatible behaviors have dramatically decreased their criminal behavior (Stumphauzer, 1980).

Issues abound. This is a radical *nontraditional* approach. At times its application comes into conflict with existing traditional thinking and programs. A program that focuses on the development of behavioral assets in delinquent youth is often viewed as "soft" by those persons and agencies who are currently pushing for "getting tough" through stricter enforcement and sending youths to prison. There are ethical issues. Community members can view such programs as intrusive and not want to have any part of, for example, a block watch. This is a Hispanic community very sensitive about "snitching" and reluctant to turn in suspected criminals. Community residents themselves should have the largest input with regard to priorities and community redesign. How can this be achieved?

This community, for example, has a large segment of illegal aliens who are fearful of any stranger, let alone being willing to take part in open community redevelopment. To even a larger degree than the previous two programs, the utilization of community-wide behavioral analyses and intervention would require major changes in policy, funding, and training of those who will focus on modifying or preventing delinquent behavior.

THREE BEHAVIORAL PROGRAMS FOR CRIMINALS

1. The Cellblock Token Economy

THE PROBLEM

Prisons or penal institutions have been around for a long time and, as with delinquents, there is every indication that adult criminals will continue to be locked up—in spite of the fact that there is little evidence of their effectiveness in changing behavior. It might seem reasonable to think that psychologists—especially behavioral psychologists—would have a great deal to offer prisons in the way of corrections programs. Several unfortunate early applications of behavior modification to adult prisoners appear to have set a tone of controversy and legal challenge. For the most part, they utilized either punishment or aversive conditioning in ways that do indeed appear not only cruel but unusual. In the prison hospital at Vacaville, California, an aversion-therapy program was reportedly administering Anectine (a "death drug" derivative of curare which temporarily stops breathing!) to prisoners in order to develop aversions to fighting, stealing and sexually deviant behavior (Mitford, 1973). Subsequent controversy and eventually a lawsuit (*MacKey* v. *Procunier,* 1973) terminated the project. A second program at the state prison mental hospital at Atascadero, California, reportedly administered electric shock to the genitals of inmates while they watched sexually arousing films under the incredibly descriptive program title, "errorless extinction of penile responses" (Weiner, 1972). The title alone would make most men cross their legs. Again, news coverage and lawsuits (for example, *Knecht* v. *Gillman,* 1973) led to the end of not only these programs but, by association, many other behavioral corrections programs. Since these early misguided efforts, the problem has been not only how to develop effective *and humane* behavioral programs in prisons but also how to get public and prison acceptance. A group of behavioral corrections programs conducted over the last several years at the Draper Correctional Center in Elmore, Alabama, have made progress in solving that problem.

The Cellblock Token Economy Programs

The continued success of the Draper programs may well be due to their thorough examination of *existing* punishment and its gradual *replacement* with ultimately more effective *and* humane positive-reinforcement contingencies (Milan & Long, in press). Three related and wide-ranging studies will be reviewed.

The traditional punishment model was evaluated by Milan and McKee (1974). In this study the effect of two types of correctional-officer response—*laissez faire* (remind but not force) and *officer corrects* (traditional control procedures including disciplinary action)—were evaluated as they affected inmates' performance of morning activities (bed making, personal appearance, and so on). The initial laissez-faire condition resulted in 32 percent of morning activities being completed, the officer-corrects condition in 62 percent, and the return to the laissez-faire condition in 35 percent compliance. These results would make a strong case for continuation of punishment, except that under the officer-corrects condition, there was about a *fourfold increase in aggressive incidents* on the cellblock among the inmates—a finding consistent with basic research showing that aversive controls do produce results but also undesirable side effects (Azrin & Holtz, 1966).

In a second study, forty correctional officers at the Draper Correctional Center were trained as behavioral technicians (Smith, Milan, Wood, & McKee, 1976). These officers were able to master the basic skills and to successfully apply principles of behavior modification in the prison. It is especially noteworthy that trained officers were found subsequently to utilize more positive reinforcement than untrained officers.

Finally, the cellblock token economy was evaluated (Milan & McKee, 1976). In a rather complex design, fifty-six inmates received token points (which could be exchanged for a variety of back-up reinforcers) under thirteen experimental conditions—varieties of baseline, usual officer treatment, contingent points, and noncontingent points. The behaviors reinforced with points were chiefly of a custodial nature (being on time, maintenance of living area, and so on). Evaluated over a period of 420 days, results make a strong case for contingent *positive* reinforcement in prisons.

Results and Issues

As reviewed above, the general results of the Draper programs are quite encouraging and *at the same time* are achieved by replacing traditional punitive methods with positive humane programs. However, as in the CYA program, we must ultimately look at the bottom line—the effect of the cellblock token economy on recidivism of inmates, once they are released to the community. Unfortunately, in an eighteen-month follow-up this program was no more effective in reducing further law violation than a no-treatment control group. Perhaps it is unfair to focus on recidivism as the only bottom line. Milan and Long (in press) argue convincingly that the behavior improvement achieved *inside* the institution is, in itself, a desirable goal. The cellblock token economy may be only one necessary component of a comprehensive program to reduce recidivism but is not in itself a *sufficient* condition. In addition, continuity of programs, through parole at least, are suggested.

2. Behavioral Probation

THE PROBLEM

It has been estimated that three-fourths of all court convictions result in probation (Polakow & Doctor, 1974). There are at least five reasons for probation's popularity: (1) the community is more normalizing than institutions; (2) it minimizes psychological and physical degradation; (3) it humanizes rehabilitation; (4) it is thought to be more effective than institutionalization; and (5) it costs less (Carney, 1977). However, probation officers are often overloaded with cases, and the goals of probation are often vague and focus on punishment or aversive controls (Nietzel, 1979). Too often the probation contingency is a loosely stated "stay out of trouble or else" (Stumphauzer, 1974b).

In contrast, the clear-cut contingency contracting of behavior modification seems a natural for application in probation. In a probation-officer training program and six-month follow-up conducted on a consultation basis, it was found that officers certainly could learn the basics of behavioral analysis and behavioral probation planning but rarely continued utilizing these new skills (Burkhart, Behles, & Stumphauzer, 1976; Stumphauzer, Candelora, & Venema, 1976). Reasons given were that (1) caseloads were too high (as many as 150 per officer!); (2) behavioral probation contracting was "more work"; and (3) supervisors had not been trained and the department as a whole was still utilizing traditional probation practices (suggesting that probation officers who utilized behavior contracting would not be reinforced and would perhaps even be punished). The problem, then, is developing effective behavioral probation programs *throughout* probation departments, a goal realized in part in the program outlined below.

THE BEHAVIORAL PROBATION PROGRAMS

Robert Polakow successfully developed the Behavioral Research and Training Program *within* the Los Angeles County Probation Department. As a probation officer himself with a behavioral-psychology background, he and his colleagues have surmounted some of the problems described above. It was not easy. Polakow and Doctor (1974) describe the bureaucratic resistance and their beginnings in doing probation training *from the inside:* documenting behavior, the behavioral point of view, focus on court orders and client needs, the reinforcement of time off probation, and finally, the redefinition of probation activities. Most importantly, the program was effective in getting the court to accept the idea of probationers earning time off probation in this new *systematic* manner (for example, "ten days off probation for each job interview" rather than the vague but all-too-usual "you've been doing pretty good and may get off probation if you keep it up").

In an extended case study, Polakow and Peabody (1975) report a successful behavioral probation program for a twenty-eight-year-old woman convicted of child abuse (including putting her son's hand over an open flame). Behavioral analysis revealed that the woman was inconsistent and relied heavily on punishment. A behavioral probation contract not only specified mother/child interaction (positive reinforcement and time out) but also included one week off probation for every week in which the program was adhered to. By the thirtieth week, effective *positive* reinforcement was being utilized, and the child's acting out was greatly reduced. Follow-up revealed that child abuse had been replaced by effective parenting.

In a more extensive group study, behavioral probation was applied to adult drug offenders (Polakow & Doctor, 1974). Contingency management was compared to regular intensive probation (counseling, persuasion, and coersion). The behavioral probation involved progression through three phases. In the final phase, a written contingency contract specified positive behaviors considered *incompatible* with drug use and crime (employment, and so on) which would result in time off probation. In contrast to usual probation, *no punishing consequences were imposed* other than nonpayment of time off probation.

RESULTS AND ISSUES

Behavioral probation was significantly more effective *both* in decreasing deviant behavior (arrests and violations) and in increasing positive behavior (employment and attendance) than regular intensive probation.

Months on probation were an average of twelve for intensive probation and only seven for behavioral probation.

This last comparison underscores the fact that this program was *cost effective,* that is, it worked better *and* for less money. Polakow and Doctor note that probation costs about one-eighth as much as incarceration—furthering the need for expansion of this kind of program. However, the Behavioral Research and Training Program ended in 1976 because of lack of departmental interest and "costs." According to Polakow (1979), this kind of program has *not* been expanded, replicated, or utilized elsewhere on a large scale. Why not? It seems as though traditional programs continue regardless of their effectiveness. Behavioral probation, which would require changes in probation-officer and court behavior, has not been accepted. Behavioral correction has even more rarely been applied to parole programs after release from prison. Nietzel (1979) reasons that parole is the last phase of the correctional process and there may, therefore, be less enthusiasm and interest in such rehabilitative "embellishments" as behavioral contracting. Wright and James (1974) have proposed a *behavior sentencing* system for courts. The current archaic system somehow relates particular crimes with sentencing to a period of time. After all, what does "doing ten years" have to do with stealing a car? Wright and James suggest replacing this time sentencing with task sentences, such as "ten correct-shopping training sessions" for a shoplifting conviction.

3. Shoplifting Prevention

The Problem

Behavioral programs applied directly in the open community are unusual as was noted earlier in the description of the East Side Story program. Yet this is where crime actually happens, this is where crime is learned, and this is where crime is naturally reinforced. This is also where lawful behavior is learned. If there is ever to be crime prevention, this is where it will have to occur—in the open community and outside the restraints of traditional programs of courts, institutions, probation, and even clinical psychotherapy (Stumphauzer, 1979).

A crime like shoplifting is a good case in point. It is incredibly common. Some believe that if all incidents of shoplifting were reported, it would be *the most frequent crime* in the United States (Weinstein, 1974). Estimates of loss as high as $13 million a day ("To Catch a Thief," 1974) at a cost of $150 a year to each American family ("Christmas Is Coming," 1973) have been suggested.

Although behavioral programs have been developed to control theft in an institutional setting (Azrin & Wesolowski, 1974) and in clinic treatment of children (Reid & Patterson, 1973; Stumphauzer, 1976b), nothing has been done in a systematic way to *prevent* stealing on the spot. This is the problem partly answered in a uniquely creative way by the following program.

THE SHOPLIFTING PREVENTION PROGRAM

Two experiments were devised to measure shoplifting and to prevent it (McNees, Egli, Marshall, Schnelle, & Risley, 1976). They were conducted directly in a department store in Murfreesboro, Tennessee. The manager had noted that they had a shoplifting problem, especially in the young women's clothing department which was not easily watched by management.

In the first study, yellow tags were attached to the price tag of two high-risk items (jeans and tops). Inventory was made each morning to determine shoplifted items (inventory minus items sold). For twenty-six days an initial baseline of shoplifting with no intervention was determined. During the experimental phase, five antishoplifting signs (four messages) were placed in this department for twenty days: (1) shoplifting is stealing, (2) shoplifting is a crime, (3) shoplifting is not uplifting, (4) shoplifting is stealing, and (5) shoplifting helps inflation. Finally, in a return-to-baseline condition, the signs were removed. Measures of both shoplifting and sales were maintained across the three phases of the study.

In the second study, plainly visible red foil stars were attached to the clothing racks containing target merchandise. After an initial baseline measurement period, signs declaring the following were added during the experimental phase: "ATTENTION SHOPPERS AND SHOPLIFTERS. The items you see marked with a red star are items that shoplifters frequently take." Again, measures of both shoplifting and sales were recorded.

RESULTS AND ISSUES

In the first study investigating the effect of adding five antishoplifting signs, the average number of items a day stolen across the three conditions were: baseline, 1.3 items; signs, .88 items; and return-to-baseline, 1.4 items. Although shoplifting was reduced, it was not eliminated. Sales were not affected. In the second study, however, there was a dramatic reduction in shoplifting. For pants, the mean number of jeans taken per day was: baseline, 0.05 jeans; sign condition, 0.03 jeans. For tops, it was: baseline, 0.66

tops; sign condition, 0.06 tops. In summary, McNees et al. were able to both measure and prevent a highly common crime *directly in the natural environment*. Although general antishoplifting signs reduced theft without hurting sales, publicly identifying high-risk merchandise virtually eliminated theft.

This kind of program, elegant in its simplicity and directness of application of behavior technology, is indeed rare. Why? Why aren't its results widely utilized? Why don't others use similar methods to investigate, modify, or *prevent* other criminal behaviors? I believe it is because of our continuing attachment (conditioning?) to traditional programs, traditional training, and traditional jobs. Each has its system of rewards for maintaining itself, and I might add, these rewards come *without reducing crime*. Funding, programs, paychecks, and Ph.D. degrees all continue with their own set of idiosyncratic reinforcers. This kind of approach is *nontraditional*. It doesn't fit our usual job description of policeman, psychologist, or sociologist. Too often, truly creative approaches are only found in psychology experiments. These studies too are not contingent on crime reduction. Instead they are reinforced by attention from colleagues, publication, and perhaps even a degree. They are often time limited. Why continue? Who, then, is to present such a program to policy makers and get it applied on a wide scale over a long period of time? Who is qualified not only to carry out such a large program but also to evaluate and gradually improve it? No person or agency has yet achieved this.

PREVENTION OF CRIMINAL BEHAVIOR

Prevention of crime before it happens may seem the most meaningful goal of all. The National Crime Prevention Institute (1978) suggests the following equation: ability + opportunity + desire = crime. Below I have redefined crime in more behavioral terms:

$$\text{CRIME REPERTOIRE} + \text{STIMULI AND SETTING EVENTS} + \text{PERCEIVED REINFORCEMENT} = \text{CRIMINAL BEHAVIOR}$$

Crime prevention programs must remove some (or a combination) of these elements from the formula. Several such crime-prevention strategies are possible and lend themselves particularly well to a behavioral approach.

One strategy, already touched on in the East Side Story program, is the study of adolescents in high-crime neighborhoods who do *not* become delinquent (Aiken, Stumphauzer, & Veloz, 1977; Aiken, 1980). If we thoroughly understood how these youths (and, by extension, adults) *learn* to stay out of trouble despite the odds in their neighborhood and without intervention of professional agencies, we might be able to teach this naturally occurring self-control (1) directly, to younger children (perhaps in school), or (2) indirectly, to parents in the form of child rearing for nondelinquency. Although these youths may have stimuli and setting events similar to those of gang delinquents, apparently they do not have the same crime behaviors or perceived reinforcements. In the Aiken study cited, two brothers grew up surrounded by violent street-gang members; yet each had some unique ways of either avoiding trouble situations or manipulating or changing the environment to lessen the probability of crime involvement. These brothers in turn could be influential *pro*social models for other *barrio* youth who could learn from them through imitation rather than through the more usual trial-and-too-often-error method.

A second, related strategy is to develop behavior that is *incompatible* with crime (noncrime repertoire). It can include such obvious behaviors as (1) attending school, (2) holding a job, (3) engaging in sports activities, (4) participating in social clubs (boys clubs, adult recreation centers, and so on), and (5) increasing contact with *non*criminal models (peers or family). This may sound as though the best way to keep persons out of trouble—especially in an environment in which crime is highly probable—is to fill their day (and night) with *other* activities. One successful project has done just that (Davidson & Robinson, 1975). Although not a prevention program per se, the principle of incompatible behavior was still utilized. As an alternative to institutionalization, nearly *all* adjudicated hard-core delinquents in Grand Rapids, Michigan, were referred to a special program that included the following: being picked up each morning, attending a token-economy classroom in the morning, working for pay in the afternoon, and participating in an overall behavioral contracting system for the prevention of further crime. Although these youths undoubtedly still had the ability to engage in crime, reinforcement was switched to other behaviors, and setting events (people and places) were changed.

A third approach is to change the environment to prevent crime—to change directly the opportunity or stimuli/setting events. In a provocative book on crime prevention through environmental design, Jeffery (1977) concluded summarily that correctional and treatment methods had clearly not succeeded and that the *only* remaining possibility was to prevent crime through environmental design. This is consistent with a behavioral approach of providing an environment that not only discourages criminal behavior but rather increases the likelihood of incompatible, prosocial behavior. Several levels of environment modification and *re*design are possible from the simple addition of signs in a store to prevent shoplifting (already described), to increasing the lighting on high-crime streets, to taking an active part in the comprehensive design of new inner cities and housing projects.

Is total crime prevention possible? It seems unlikely for several reasons. Asking the question another way sheds some light on the issues. Is crime prevention reinforcing? At present, there is relatively little interest or funding available for crime prevention programs. The bulk of governmental anticrime budgets goes for the continuation of justice, corrections, and treatment programs. Crime prevention would put thousands out of work. Many find their current behaviors of arresting, defending, judging, correcting, and treating highly reinforcing. Finally, the present model of punishment for criminal behavior is also highly reinforcing—for the *punisher*. It is said by some to feel good—there is physical release directed at an object of frustration—and it does work *temporarily* in suppressing behavior (Jeffery, 1977; Stumphauzer, 1973, 1979). This immediate effect is reinforcing, apparently more so than the longer range prevention of criminal behavior. One final point is that crime prevention (the *absence* of criminal behavior) is difficult to demonstrate and prove. With the current tight fiscal policy on spending, governments appear more interested in short-term goals of crime detection and prosecution rather than the longer range prevention of criminal behavior. Although crime prevention may be more cost effective in the long run, politicians appear unwilling to support expensive programs whose results may be several years in coming.

SUMMARY

Modification of criminal behavior is highly controversial because of long-standing traditions, media sensationalization, and early misguided efforts in applying behavior modification to delinquents and adult criminals. Although crime statistics are omnipresent, more exacting measurement of criminal behavior is difficult—although it is possible. Behavioral analysis is a particularly useful approach for measuring and understanding crime and for implementing a program for crime modification.

Three behavioral programs for delinquents (ranging from institution to group home to open community) were described in this chapter. The California Youth Authority project compared the effectiveness of behavior modification and transactional analysis in two institutions for delinquents and found that both with roughly similar results were more effective than usual institutions. Learning House, a behaviorally oriented group home, gave a promising alternative to custodial care and institutionalization. In the East Side Story program, a radically new approach to study and intervention with violent gang members *directly* in their community environment was shown.

Behavior-modification approaches to adult offenders were also illustrated with three programs. The cellblock token economy was a series of related programs that not only examined existing prison discipline but replaced it with more effective and humane methods. A behavioral probation program was described in which probation officers successfully used behavior modification with case loads that included child-abuse and drug-abuse offenses. A shoplifting prevention program was presented as an example of direct environmental manipulation (of signs in a department store) which clearly altered a very common crime—shoplifting.

Finally, behavioral approaches to crime prevention were discussed, including the behavioral analysis of *non*criminals in high-crime communities, the development of behavior incompatible to crime, and the design of environments that discourage crime. The programs reviewed leave considerable room for enthusiasm for the future application of behavior modification to crime. However, this enthusiasm is dampened by (1) continued firm attachment to traditional approaches (in spite of their poor results), (2) short-sighted funding priorities, and (3) an apparent lack of communication with politicians and policy makers, although communication is necessary before these promising new approaches will be applied universally.

CHAPTER 24

BEHAVIORAL
COMMUNITY PSYCHOLOGY

Andrew W. Meyers and Robert Schleser

Memphis State University

THE COMMUNITY MENTAL HEALTH MODEL
History

In the 1950s, evaluations of existing mental health delivery systems revealed the questionable effectiveness of psychotherapy, the inability of traditional mental health practices to meet current service demands, and the limited access, for a large segment of our population, to existing mental health services (Zax & Specter, 1974). The recognition of these problems influenced the U.S. Congress to pass the Mental Health Study Act of 1955 which established the Joint Commission on Mental Health and Illness. This body examined mental health services in the United States; the commission's final report, *Action for Mental Health* (1961), marked the birth of the American community mental health movement (Rappaport, 1977).

The joint commission's report urged that the size of state mental hospital populations be reduced and that this be accomplished, in part, by the construction and staffing of community mental health centers. In the years following the commission's report, legislation to fulfill these goals was enacted.

These legislative guidelines stated that comprehensive community mental health centers must deliver five essential services: twenty-four-hour hospitalization; outpatient services; partial hospitalization, such as day or night hospital care; twenty-four-hour emergency services; and community consultation and education. The services of these mental health centers have been distinguished from traditional clinical activities by (1) an emphasis on treatment in the local community as opposed to the institutional setting; (2) attention to a total community rather than to individual patients; 3) a preventive as opposed to a treatment approach to emotional disorders; (4) the offering of indirect (consultative and educative) services rather than direct services; (5) an emphasis on innovative clinical strategies (for example, crisis intervention); (6) a rational planning process in mental health program decision making; (7) an innovative use of new manpower sources; (8) a recognition of community involvement and control in program development; and (9) an emphasis on identifying sources of stress in the community (Bloom, 1973). These distinctions imply that traditional mental health services have ignored community and environmental influences and have irresponsibly allocated limited resources to direct patient services (Meyers, Craighead, & Meyers, 1974).

Prevention in Community Mental Health

The original joint commission report stressed a treament model for mental health problems, but an underlying assumption of community mental health work involves the value of preventive health interventions. The concept of disability and disease prevention is best illustrated in the field of public health. No disease has ever been treated out of existence, but preventive strategies designed to counteract conditions that cause or contribute to disability have been significantly powerful approaches. The development of vaccines to prevent the spread of infectious diseases, and environmental interventions, such as improved sanitation, have successfully reduced the risk of diseases like smallpox, malaria, and cholera (Rappaport, 1977). Other interventions, such as the fl, of public water supplies and the reduction of highway speed limits, have been associated with reduced rates of dental caries and fewer highway deaths, respectively (Knowles, 1977).

This prevention-based community mental health model represents an attractive set of programs, but community mental health centers have neither delivered the required services nor attained the desired goals. Chu and Trotter (1974) reported few positive effects on existing state mental hospital systems, and they also observed that the development and delivery of services to the poor has received minimal attention. Consultation and education, the prevention-oriented services in the community mental health model, have been severely underemphasized. Cowen (1973), after reviewing the community psychology literature, found that less than 3 percent of the published articles in the area dealt with preventive mental health.

BEHAVIOR MODIFICATION AND COMMUNITY PSYCHOLOGY

Community mental health has come to signify the application of largely traditional clinical activities in community settings (Chu & Trotter, 1974). To build a true community-based preventive mental health model requires an active step beyond the community delivery of these direct treatment services. Just as preventive interventions have partially supplanted direct treatment in the eradication of physical disease, so too must preventive interventions be applied, in addition to existing treatment strategies, to alleviate social, emotional, and behavioral dysfunctions.

The development of preventive mental health interventions requires a broad application of psychological knowledge to community and environmental problems. This examination of the relationship, or fit, between people and their social and physical environments has become known as community psychology. Rappaport (1977) has further defined community psychology as an attempt to find alternatives to treatment for deviance from societal norms. One potential model for community psychology is behavior modification (Atthowe, 1973; Jason, 1977; Meyers et al., 1974; Zifferblatt & Hendricks, 1974).

Behavior modification and community psychology share several conceptual bases. Both disciplines recognize the broad range of influences, from individual cognitive processes to systemwide contingencies, that affect human behavior; both advocate an empirical, interventionist, problem-solving approach to dysfunctional situations (Neitzel, Winett, Mac-Donald, & Davidson, 1977). Additional advantages of a behavioral community psychology include the relative ease with which behavioral programs can be applied and the typically brief training period required for nonprofessional participants (O'Dell, 1974).

The application of an empirically based behavioral approach to community problems requires several elements. First, there must be a behavioral statement of the problem, followed by an analysis of those behaviors and situations that function to maintain the problem. Then, target behaviors must be designated, behavioral objectives must be formulated, and a behavioral intervention designed to achieve these objectives must be developed. Finally, the intervention must be implemented and evaluated, with feedback from the evaluation used to modify and refine future interventions. The behavioral approach to community psychology provides both problem definition leading directly to treatment and evaluation methodology and functional evaluation of the treatment intervention (Meyers, Meyers, & Craighead, in press; Zifferblatt & Hendricks, 1974).

Although a behavioral model offers community psychology a promising prevention paradigm, most community applications of behavioral interventions fall within a more traditional treatment-oriented community mental health delivery system. Winett (1979), in a recent survey of behaviorists active in community research, found that over one-half the respondents were involved in traditional direct-treatment or early-intervention programs delivered in small group settings. Only approximately one-quarter of those surveyed were actively involved in community-level delivery of prevention programming.

Behavior modification delivered in a community mental health treatment model will not be reviewed here, but such interventions have proven relatively successful in school settings, juvenile-justice work, adult corrections, drug-abuse and alcoholism treatment, social-skills development, and work with the elderly (see this text and Nietzel et al., 1977, for reviews of these issues).

This chapter will review nontraditional, prevention-oriented behavioral interventions. Following a public health model *behavioral-preventive interventions* are defined as strategies that either strengthen individuals or modify community systems or environments to reduce the likelihood or prevent the occurrence of dysfunction. Interventions that serve to create more manageable and more pleasant environments, or interventions that develop the ability of community members to cope with social and environmental demands, fall within the domain of this review. Four specific areas will be examined: pollution, energy conservation, health, and skill development.

POLLUTION
Litter

Litter, or misplaced solid waste (Geller, 1979), is unsightly, costly, and dangerous to people, animals, and the environment. Past estimates of the national cost of litter removal have run as high as $1 billion per year ("Keep America Beautiful," 1970; Seed, 1970). Freeman Associates (1977, cited in Geller, 1979) reported that litter is a major factor in five hundred to one thousand highway deaths each year, in at least one house fire every twelve minutes, in one-third of all forest fires, in various health problems (that is, litter aids the breeding of rats, flies, mosquitoes and other disease-carrying pests), and in the death of numerous wild and domestic animals, who ingest or get tangled in garbage. In light of these consequences, litter has been a major target of behavioral community intervention.

Behavioral approaches to litter control have focused on both direct intervention, such as the use of prompts to prevent littering behavior and reinforcers to encourage the removal of existing litter, and indirect interventions, such as the initiation of recycling and waste-reduction programs to produce less litter.

Litter Prevention

Traditional approaches to control the spread of litter, including legal threats and antilitter education programs, have generally been ineffective (Nietzel et al., 1977). A number of studies, which have employed a variety of prompts to reduce littering in a wide range of situations, indicate that behavioral interventions may be an effective alternative.

Marler (1970), in one of the first applications of behavioral principles to litter control, gave campers entering a national forest leaflets containing one of three types of prompts. They found that 90 percent of the campers who received prompts emphasizing the dangers of littering (for example, fire hazard) cleaned their campsites, compared to 72 percent of the campers receiving prompts emphasizing the aesthetic rewards of not littering, 50 percent of those receiving factual prompts, and 75 percent who received no prompt. Although these results seem to indicate the superiority of prompts emphasizing the hazards of litter, evidence indicated that 40 percent of all subjects failed to read their leaflet and that no prompt subjects scored higher on a post-intervention quiz on the effects of littering. These findings suggest the need to design prompts that ensure that essential information will be readily communicated to the littering population.

Dodge (1972) employed an array of antilitter prompts, including personal pleas, bumper stickers, posters, newspaper advertisements, and pamphlets, to saturate an entire town adjacent to a national park. Results indicated a significant decline from baseline both in the number of litterers and the amount of litter left in campsites. These results suggest that salient prompts can be an effective litter-control technique.

Several recent studies compared the effects of various types of prompts containing specific disposal information, general antilittering messages, requests to recycle, and demands to refrain from littering. Generally, prompts containing specific disposal information were the most effective (Geller, 1973; Geller, Witmer, & Orebaugh 1976). Other studies have investigated the effects of littered versus clean environments on later accumulations of litter and found that clean environments tend to reduce subsequent littering behavior (Crump, Nunes, & Crossman, 1977; Finnie, 1973; Tuso, Witmer, & Geller, 1975).

Finally, a number of studies investigated the effects of increasing the number of available trash cans or providing novel or attractive trash cans and found that both interventions produced reductions in littering behavior (Finnie, 1973; Geller & Hayes, 1977; Geller, Mann, & Brasted, 1977; Miller, Albert, Bostick, & Geller, 1976). In summary, behavioral interventions that employed salient prompts containing specific disposal information or that manipulated environmental settings by cleaning the environment and providing attractive trash cans have been moderately effective in litter control.

LITTER REMOVAL

Although prompts alone have been employed successfully to induce people to refrain from littering, they have been ineffective in encouraging inconvenient responses, such as picking up exisitng litter (Geller, 1979). A number of studies have employed a combination of prompts and reinforcers to modify litter-removal behavior.

The first systematic attempt to apply behavioral interventions to litter removal was reported by Burgess, Clark, and Hendee (1971). They investigated the effects of instructions, prompts, and incentives (for example ten cents or a free movie pass) on the amount of trash disposed of properly by children in a movie theater. They found that prompts plus incentives produced substantial increases in the percentage of litter disposed of properly and were significantly more effective than the prompts plus instructions and prompts only conditions.

Clark, Burgess, and Hendee (1972) employed a similar approach in a more extensive demonstration conducted in a national forest campground. These investigators marked and planted litter in the campground and then measured the number of pieces of marked litter removed from campsites. The results of this study clearly indicated that small incentives (for examples, Smokey the Bear shoulder patches, comic books, and Junior Ranger badges) could be employed successfully with a large population in an open setting.

More sophisticated studies assessed the plausibility of implementing unsupervised reinforcement programs (Powers, Osborne, & Anderson, 1973); various schedules of reinforcement (Kohlenberg & Phillips, 1973);

and various contingencies (for example, payment for volume of trash collected versus payment for clean yards) (Chapman & Risley, 1974). Chapman and Risley (1974) compared the effects on children residing in a housing project of verbal appeals, payment for volume, and payment for clean yards in reducing housing-project litter. Results indicated that both incentive conditions were effective in reducing litter, while verbal appeals was not. Payment for clean yards produced the cleanest areas, while payment for volume produced the most trash collected. Evidence suggested that, under the latter condition, children collected litter from inappropriate sources, such as home trash cans or community dumpsters. If the target of litter-reduction programs is a clean environment, then payment for clean areas is the intervention of choice.

Recycling

Both prompting and incentive techniques represent remedial attempts to induce people to engage in proenvironmental behaviors. An alternative approach is to reduce the amount of litter at its source through recycling and other waste-reduction programs.

Geller and his colleagues (Geller, Farris, & Post, 1973; Geller, Wylie, & Farris, 1971) reported the first successful applications of prompting and reinforcement procedures to increase the purchase of returnable bottles. They found that handbills containing prompts to recycle increased convenience-store patrons' purchases of returnable soft drink bottles. In a second study, they demonstrated that prompts alone and prompts plus social recognition were effective in encouraging the purchase of returnable bottles.

Recent studies have investigated the ability of various prompts and incentives to promote recycling behaviors. These efforts included the use of prompts and contests to encourage paper recycling in college dormitories (Geller, Chaffee, & Ingram, 1975; Witmer & Geller, 1976); personal prompts and increased collection sites in an apartment complex (Reid, Luyben, Rawers, & Bailey, 1976); and incentives and increased collection sites in a trailer park (Luyben & Bailey, 1975). The results of this research were encouraging. However, although prompts and incentives have been used successfully to induce recycling behavior, the effects have often been transitory (Nietzel et al., 1977).

Recently, five states (Oregon, Vermont, South Dakota, Maine, and Michigan) have enacted legislation restricting the sale of nonreturnable beverage containers (Geller, 1979), and one state (Minnesota) has passed a law regulating package design to ensure that new containers are environmentally sound (Wahl & Allison, 1975). Legislative interventions such as these, in conjunction with effective behavioral strategies, hold great potential for developing large-scale, durable, cost-effective recycling and waste-management programs.

ENERGY CONSERVATION

Although there is much debate, several estimates indicate that at current consumption levels the world's supply of oil will be so severely depleted by the year 2000 that oil cannot be considered a major resource in future energy programs (Thompson, 1976). However, it is probable that prior to this critical point, the oil-producing nations will begin to restrict oil exports in order to maintain sufficient reserves for their own needs. As a result, the U.S. government has made self-sufficiency, through immediate conservation of fossil fuels and the development of alternative energy supplies (solar, synthetic, and nuclear fuels), our primary energy goal (Carter, 1977).

Transportation

Transportation, particularly private automobile use which accounts for over 30 percent of all petroleum consumed (Hazard, 1975), has been a major target of conservation efforts. These efforts have included reducing the national speed limit to 55 miles per hour and increasing taxes on retail sales of gasoline. Changes like these and soaring gasoline prices have had a moderate impact on gasoline consumption (U.S. Department of Transportation, 1973). A number of behavioral approaches to reducing gasoline consumption have also been explored.

REDUCING VEHICLE MILES TRAVELED

A recent Gallup poll reported that 41 percent of those interviewed would not find it difficult to reduce their driving by 25 percent. Several behavior modification projects have directly explored this possibility.

Hayward and Everett (1976) investigated the effects of four types of feedback (mileage; operating cost; operation and depreciation costs; and operation, depreciation, and social costs) on the number of miles traveled by individual drivers. They found that feedback concerning higher costs produced more negative attitudes toward private automobile use, but no corresponding behavior change in terms of miles traveled. Foxx and Hake (1977) assessed the impact of offering rewards (for example, cash prizes) for reduced mileage and found that a reward group produced a 19.9 percent reduction from baseline in miles traveled compared to a no-treatment control group's 4.5 percent reduction. In a second study, Hake and Foxx (1978) investigated the effects of adding a social-influence factor to the reward condition. They found that the presence of a leader in the reward group significantly enhanced the effects of incentives in reducing miles traveled. These three studies indicate that feedback alone is not an effective mileage-reduction strategy, but that the use of positive-reinforcement contingencies to reduce unnecessary automobile use is promising.

INCREASED DRIVING EFFICIENCY

Although reduced mileage is certainly an appropriate target of intervention, some vehicle miles are essential. As much as 34.1 percent of miles traveled each year are work related (Andrle & Dueker, 1974). An alternative to directly reducing miles traveled is to increase driving efficiency. Runnion, Watson, and McWhorter (1978) demonstrated the utility of using behavioral interventions to increase the mean-miles-per-gallon ratings of short- and long-haul textile company truck drivers. In a two-year period, they studied 195 drivers at fifty-eight mills in a thirty-two-state region driving over 6 million vehicle miles per year. Runnion et al. found that feedback, social recognition, and reinforcement lotteries produced a 5.06 percent and a 2.08 percent increase in miles per gallon during the first year, and 4.18 percent and 8.96 percent increases during the second year, for short- and long-haul truck drivers, respectively. Although these percentages seem small, the net savings were large enough to supply free fuel to the entire truck fleet for a month.

RIDE SHARING

A third approach to gasoline conservation has focused on car- and van-pooling programs. It has been estimated that increasing the mean number of occupants traveling to work from the current 1.4 persons to 3 persons per vehicle would result in a 53 percent fuel savings. Two basic approaches to encourage pooling have been evaluated: (1) organizational efforts to form pools and (2) incentives. Incentives to car pool have included priority lanes for automobiles with two or more occupants (Miller &

Deuser, 1976; Rose & Hinds, 1976); reduced highway and bridge tolls (MacCalden & Davis, 1972); preferred parking (Hirst, 1976; Pratsch, 1975); monetary rewards (Letzkus & Scharfe, 1975); social recognition; and flexible work schedules (Bryant, 1974). Organizational efforts to form car pools have included attempts to facilitate the matching of potential car- and van-pooling members (Andrle & Dueker, 1974; Jones & Derby, 1976; Scheiner & Keiper, 1976) and providing vans and pool coordinators (Owens & Sever, 1977).

In general, behavioral interventions appear to be effective strategies for increasing car and van pooling. However, factors that limit pooling efforts, such as sex and prior acquaintance (Dueker & Levin, 1976), social skills (Barkow, 1974), and demographic factors (Margolin, Misch, & Dobson, 1976), must be considered in future interventions (Reichel & Geller, in press).

MASS TRANSPORTATION

Despite the availability of mass transit (for example, buses and trains), 57 percent of all gasoline consumed for transportation is the result of urban and intercity automobile trips. A fourth approach to reduce private automobile use has been to encourage the use of existing alternative modes of travel. Attempts to increase bus ridership have included the use of priority lanes for buses (Rose & Hinds, 1976), prompts and monetary rewards (Everett, 1973), and various schedules of token reinforcement (Deslauriers & Everett, 1977; Everett, Hayward, & Meyers, 1974). The results of these studies indicate that a substantial increase in bus ridership followed the implementation of contingency programs. However, evidence indicates that increases in bus ridership did not produce a decrease in automobile use. In fact, most new bus riders indicated that walking had been their primary form of transportation (Everett et al., 1974). Deslauriers and Everett (1977) noted that the university setting in which the studies took place may not have allowed an examination of the crucial issues. Although promising, the utility of contingency-management strategies for increasing bus ridership in more competitive transportation settings remains to be evaluated.

Behavioral research in transportation indicates the potential utility of applying behavioral principles to reduce unnecessary automobile use, to encourage efficient driving habits, including car pooling, and to increase the use of more economical modes of travel. However, widespread governmental and private-sector implementation of behavioral programs to reduce transportation energy consumption depends on a demonstration of the cost benefits of these programs.

Home Energy Consumption

Home energy consumption accounts for 20 percent of all energy consumed in the United States (Large, 1973). Behavioral interventions have employed three basic approaches to reduce home energy use—prompts, feedback, and incentives.

Prompts have taken the form of information (for example, pamphlets and flyers) describing the need and various methods to conserve energy. Information alone was effective in changing attitudes about energy conservation but had a minimal effect on active consumption (Bickman, 1972; Hayes & Cone, 1977; Heberlein, 1975; Palmer, Lloyd, & Lloyd, 1978; Winett & Nietzel, 1975). Feedback on energy use has consisted primarily of written information delivered by the experimenter (Winett, Neale, & Grier, 1979). Frequent or daily feedback seems to be most effective, typically resulting in mean energy reductions of 10 to 15 percent (cf. Hayes & Cone, 1977; Seligman & Darley, 1977; Winett et al., 1979). The results of studies investigating weekly or monthly feedback have been equivocal (Winett, Kagel, Battalio, & Winkler, 1978; Seaver & Patterson, 1976). The content of feedback has varied across studies and included kilowatt hours (Kwh) (Winett et al., 1979), percentage of energy-use change (Winett & Nietzel, 1975), and financial cost (Winett et al., 1976). However, only one direct comparison of various types of feedback content has been conducted.

Palmer et al. (1978) directly investigated the effects of daily Kwh feedback with cost feedback. Both strategies were more effective than no feedback. Other studies have evaluated different feedback strategies, such as home meters that signal overuse (Becker & Seligman, in press; Kohlenberg, Phillips, & Proctor, 1976; Zuiches, 1977) and instructing consumers to self-monitor home energy meters (Winett et al., 1979). Winett et al. (1979) compared the effects of self-monitoring with externally delivered feedback on the reduction of electricity consumption. Although both feedback and self-monitoring groups significantly reduced consumption relative to a control group, feedback produced a larger reduction (13 percent from baseline) than self-monitoring (7 percent). This trend continued at both four-week and six-week follow-ups. Although daily feedback delivered externally is moderately effective in reducing energy consumption, the results are often transitory. Once external feedback is withdrawn, energy use increases (cf. Hayes & Cone, 1977). Feedback plus small incentives have been more effective than feedback alone (Hayes & Cone, 1977). Incentives have usually been small monetary rewards (three to fifteen dollars per month) equal to a percentage of the financial value of the energy reduction (cf. Hayes & Cone, 1977; Slavin & Wodarski, 1977; Slavin, Wodarski, & Blackburn, 1978). Larger rewards, such as twenty dollars for a 20 percent reduction in energy consumption (Winett & Nietzel, 1975) or an eighty-dollar prize for winning a conservation contest (McClelland & Cook, 1978a), have occasionally been used. Hayes and Cone (1977) directly compared the effects of various sized payments on the reduction of electricity consumption. They found that decreasing payments for energy saved resulted in corresponding decreases in energy reduction. Returning to the consumer 100 percent of the cost of the energy saved resulted in a mean reduction of 33 percent from baseline; 50 percent payment resulted in a 32 percent reduction; 25 percent payment resulted in a 27 percent reduction; and a 10 percent payment resulted in a 23 percent reduction.

Winett and Nietzel (1975) found that the effects of relatively large incentives (twenty dollars for 20 percent reduction) may be mediated by the climate. They compared feedback and feedback plus incentives on the reduction of gas and electrical consumption. Although both conditions produced reductions (8 percent for feedback and 15 percent for feedback plus incentives) in electricity consumption, gas use for heating was relatively unaffected by the intervention. Winett and Nietzel (1975) reported that gas consumption increased by 5 percent when the temperature dropped to 37° and decreased by 60 percent when the temperature rose to 57°. Similar findings concerning the mediating effects of climate factors and personal comfort were found in interventions designed to reduce electricity consumption in both all-electrical homes during the winter (McClelland & Cook, 1978b) and air-conditioned homes during the summer (Kagal et al., 1976). Interventions in this area must be aware of limitations produced by climate and personal comfort and health.

Small incentives and frequent feedback are effective in reducing home energy consumption (cf. Hayes & Cone, 1977). However, over 4 million Americans live in apartments master-metered for electricity, and 8 to 10 million live in apartments master-metered for natural gas and fuel (Gross, Harper, & Ahlstrom, 1975). A recent study indicated that apartments that were master-metered used approximately 35 percent more energy than similar apartments that were individually metered (Midwest Research Institute, 1975). McClelland and Cook (1978b) suggested that this may be due to the fact that residents in master-metered apartments are unaware of the amount of energy they consume and have no financial incentive to conserve. Although public appeals to conserve and educational programs have been largely ineffective (Slavin & Wodarski, 1977), a number of behavioral interventions have been successful in reducing energy consumption in these settings. Slavin and Wodarski (1977) used a group contingency with master-metered apartment residents. Incentives for conservation were payments of 75 percent of the monetary value of the energy saved for the entire apartment complex. Results indicated an initial

3.3 percent reduction in gas use, which dropped off by the end of two months.

Newsom and Makranczy (1977–1978) initiated a competition between residents in two buildings to reduce electricity use. The prize was fifty dollars for the winning building. They found an overall reduction of 5.25 percent from baseline. Newsom and Makranczy's contest seems to represent a cost-effective way to increase the potential reinforcing value of objectively small incentives.

Behavioral interventions that employed feedback and incentives seem to be moderately effective in producing reductions in home energy consumption, while group contingencies had a slight to moderate effect in master-metered apartment settings. Large rewards and frequent feedback produced larger reductions in consumption than small rewards and infrequent feedback. At present, truly effective interventions that are cost effective have not been developed.

HEALTH

Health care costs have risen at a higher rate than any other sector of the economy (Culliton, 1968) with no measurable impact on overall mortality rates. Total expenditures for health care rose from $12 billion in 1950 to $160 billion in 1977 (Abelson, 1976, 1978). Despite this increase, the mortality rate of cancer remained nearly constant (Monthly Vital Statistics Report, 1975), and although the mortality rate of heart diseases declined slightly, this decrease was largely attributed to lifestyle changes rather than medical interventions (Kristein, Arnold, & Wynder, 1977).

A growing body of research suggests that the major health problems in the United States—cardiovascular disease (heart attacks), carcinomas (cancers), and cerebrovascular disease (strokes)—are related to behavioral and environmental factors. Cigarette smoking has been related to lung cancer (Health Consequences of Smoking, 1975) and other cancers (Lemon & Walden, 1966), emphysema (Diehl, 1969), and heart disease and strokes (Gordon & Thom, 1975; Kahn, 1966). Dietary factors are associated with several cancers (Wynder, 1976) and hypertension (Weinsier, 1976). Type A behavior (that is, an anxious, competitive lifestyle described by Friedman & Roesnman, 1974), obesity (Weinsier, Fuchs, Kay, Triebivasser, & Lancaster, 1976), and physical inactivity (Frank, 1968) have all been associated with the occurrence of heart attacks.

The application of behavioral community interventions is a promising strategy for affecting the occurrence of health-risk factors. Research in this area has focused on three levels of intervention: health screening and entry into treatment; lifestyle change; and environmental-change programs.

Screening and Entry into Treatment

Early diagnosis and treatment is essential in the prevention and treatment of many prevalent health problems. Yet early-screening programs, which relied on screening at central sites and mass mailings to notify targeted populations of the need for and availability of services, did not attract a significant number of community members (Wilber & Barrow, 1972). One reason for this is that the negative consequences of not seeking preventive health care are far removed, whereas the inconvenience of participating in screening or treatment is immediate. Recently, a number of studies compared traditional notification and prompting approaches with various incentive programs to induce people to seek preventive dental services (Iwata & Becksfort, in press) and remedial dental services (Reiss, Piotrowski, & Bailey, 1976) and to participate in a senior citizen nutrition program (Bunck & Iwata, 1978). The results of these studies suggest that simple notification of the need for and availability of services was insufficient to induce people to seek health care services, but the use of incentives (for example, a five-dollar reward, fee reduction, movies, activities) increased the number of people seeking initial screening and entering and completing treatment. Incentive programs were also more cost efficient than prompts involving personal contact (for example, home visits and telephone calls).

Lifestyle-Change Programs

Lifestyle-change programs refer to interventions designed to modify health-risk behaviors, such as smoking, overeating, and poor nutritional habits (see Chapter 15 for a detailed review). Although research has consisted primarily of direct clinical interventions with individuals and small groups of subjects, a few large-scale community programs focusing on multiple-risk-factor reduction have been conducted. Meyer and Henderson (1974) compared the effects of a traditional medical intervention, an educational program, and a behavior modification program on the reduction of certain risk factors. Subjects in the behavioral program, which included modeling techniques, small-group workshops, and behavioral self-control techniques, lost more weight and demonstrated more improvement in dietary habits than subjects in the nonbehavioral groups. Additionally, the behavioral intervention resulted in decreases in smoking rates and serum cholesterol levels and an increase in activity levels.

The Stanford Three-Town study represents the most ambitious attempt to date to affect the health behavior of entire communities (Farquahr, Maccoly, Wood, Alexander, Breitiore, Brown, Haskell, McAllister, Meyer, Nash, & Stern, 1977). Three small northern California cities participated. One town received a public media campaign which included behavioral principles focusing on self-control; the second received the media campaign plus behaviorally based individual and small-group counseling for a selected segment of high-health-risk individuals; the third served as a control community. Results of a two-year follow-up indicated that the risk of heart diseases had increased in the control community, but decreased significantly in the two treatment communities. In addition, there was evidence of beneficial change in knowledge of risk factors, smoking, systolic blood pressure, saturated fat intake, and serum cholesterol. The results of programs such as the Stanford effort suggest that large-scale behaviorally based interventions are a possible and worthwhile approach to the control and prevention of serious health problems.

Environmental-Change Programs

Environmental intervention represents an attempt to structure environments that are conducive to good health. Some approaches have used relatively simple procedures, such as posting nutritional information near vending machines (Wilbur, Zifferblatt, & Zifferblatt, 1978) and cafeteria lines (Zifferblatt, Wilbur, & Pinsky, in press); providing no-smoking instructions in supermarkets (Jason, Clay, & Martin, 1979–1980), elevators (Jason et al., 1979–1980), offices (Jason & Savio, 1978), and shops (Jason & Clay, 1978); and posting prompts to increase physical activity (Brownell, Stunkard, & Albaum, in press).

In general, these attempts have been quite successful in increasing the frequency of positive health behaviors, but they have been limited in scope. In contrast, large-scale government-sponsored educational programs, such as the "buckle up for safety" and antismoking campaigns, have been quite extensive, but generally ineffective (Robertson, Kelley, O"Neill, Wixom, Eiswirth, & Haddon, 1974). These large-scale government interventions must be conducted with the same care and detail that is central to small-scale experimental projects. Although educational programs have produced conflicting results, governmental interventions which manipulate tax and other legal incentives appear to hold great potential for aiding in the development of healthy environments. Evidence is scarce in the health area, but an illustration of this potential can be found in the success of state laws mandating that glass beverage bottles be returnable (Dernback, 1977). The institution of such government programs will require empirical evidence from small-scale demonstration projects.

SKILLS TRAINING

Social competence has been defined as those coordinated sets of behaviors that help people adapt effectively within the context of their social environments (Kirschenbaum, Pedro, & DeVoge, 1980). These behaviors include interpersonal problem solving, decision making, job seeking, child rearing, self-management, and a variety of other skills. The results of several skills-training studies have demonstrated the effectiveness of direct behavioral interventions in helping a variety of populations develop social competence within both remedial and preventive frameworks (Kirschenbaum et al., 1980).

Remedial Approaches

Unemployment has been associated with higher crime rates (Johnson, 1964), alcoholism (Plant, 1967), and poverty (Ferguson, 1971). Although a number of government programs, such as Work Incentive (U.S. Department of Labor, 1977), have been developed, there have been no controlled evaluations of their effectiveness (Azrin, Flores, & Kaplan, 1975). However, a number of recent investigations have indicated the utility of a behavioral approach to developing job-seeking skills. Azrin et al. (1975) reported the successful application of a behavioral intervention to increase the number of jobs obtained by unemployed subjects. The Job Club was a systematic approach to job seeking that included intensive behavioral counseling, interpersonal job-seeking-skills training, a social-information network to alert members to available jobs, and a motivational component. Results indicated that 93 percent of the Job Club participants obtained employment within three months compared to 60 percent of the subjects in a control group. In addition, Job Club participants obtained jobs more quickly and at a higher median salary. The Job Club was later expanded to five national centers and included handicapped people (Azrin & Philip, in press) and welfare recipients (Azrin, Philip, Thienes-Hontos, & Besalel, 1980). Similar success was obtained with these populations.

Other studies have employed behaviorally oriented remedial interventions to teach housekeeping skills to previously institutionalized adults (Bauman & Iwata, 1977), parenting skills to middle-class parents (Clark, Greene, Macrae, McNees, Davis, & Risley, 1977; Risley, Clark, & Cataldo, 1976), and pedestrian skills to mentally retarded individuals (Page, Iwata, & Neef, 1976).

Preventive Approaches

Several studies have investigated childhood predictors of dysfunctional adult behavior (Watt & Lubensky, 1976; Zax, Cowen, Rappaport, Beach, & Laird, 1968). Based on these findings, preventive early-intervention programs have been developed (cf. Cowen, Davidson, & Gesten, in press). One of the most extensive is Cincinnati's Social Skills Development Program (SSDP) (Kirschenbaum et al., in press). SSDP is a behaviorally based program designed to modify through skill development, predictors of dysfunctional adult behavior. Target, or high-risk, children are identified through a mass screening program which includes parent and teacher referral forms, mass screening interviews with teachers, behavioral observation of classroom and free play activities, teachers' competency ratings of children, child-specific teacher interviews, school records, and individual child assessment.

Approximately 15 to 25 percent of the primary-grade children were selected, based on problems found in one or more of the following areas: perceptual/motor skills, affective responses concerning self, peers, family, and school, range of affective responses, sensory preferences, favorite activities, daily activities, interpersonal problem solving, and other aspects of childhood functioning (Kirschenbaum, Bane, Fowler, Klei, Kuykendahl, Marsh, & Pedro, 1976). Based on the initial assessment, specific operationally defined goals were established for each child. The child was then assigned, based on individual need, to either group or individual behavior therapy. Although it is not yet possible to evaluate the effects of such early-intervention programming on the prevention of dysfunctional adult behavior, a number of short-term effects have been found. These effects have included increased cooperative interactions with teachers and increased interpersonal skills (Kirschenbaum et al., in press).

A second area of preventive behavioral intervention has focused on the development of community problem-solving skills. Briscoe, Hoffman, and Bailey (1975) used prompting, shaping, fading, and differential social reinforcement to train problem-identification, problem-solving, and solution-implementation skills to nine low-socioeconomic-class members of a community policy board. Results demonstrated the effectiveness of the behavioral intervention across all three sets of skills.

Training programs that seek to inhibit the development of a variety of dysfunctional or socially inappropriate behaviors through skill training represents the essence of the preventive approach in community intervention. Judging from the findings currently available, behaviorally based early interventions are a particularly promising approach to the remediation or prevention of major life stresses which threaten the quality of life.

A PRACTICAL AND ETHICAL CRITIQUE

Behavioral interventions in community settings offer great promise, but such real-world interventions confront significant practical problems and raise serious ethical questions. Practical problems concern adequate program preparation and community involvement in the intervention process. Ethical problems are related to the imposition of unwanted change efforts on communities and their members.

Practical Issues

PROGRAM PREPARATION

Repucci (1977) and Repucci and Saunders (1974) comprehensively outlined a number of general problems confronting behaviorists involved in large-scale community-change efforts.

1. Institutional or bureaucratic constraints that prevent or retard the application of behavioral programming
2. The political realities produced by external economic, administrative, and other institutional and community forces that often clash with change-agent goals
3. The lack of shared language and shared meaning that complicates communication with community populations
4. The limited ability to modify the behavior of indigenous commu-

nity personnel who actually execute programs but whose behavior is determined by political concerns, philosophies, peer reinforcers, union contracts, and other elements not under change agent control

5. Limited fiscal, manpower, and time resources that interfere with the selection and delivery of reinforcers and the procedure of open-field observation

6. The labeling problem that often results in behaviors being responded to in terms of their label rather than their function (for example, recreation as a mandatory activity rather than a potential reinforcer)

7. The problem of the behavior modifier's perceived inflexibility, which rises from the necessity of consistently applying contingencies

8. The port-of-entry issue that involves overcoming initial resistance from uncooperative bureaucracies and existing staff

9. The necessity of compromise between behavioral principles and the real limits of the natural setting and between the values of the behavior modifier and those of the community (Repucci & Saunders, 1974, pp. 651–658).

Repucci's problem list illustrated the difficulty inherent in transferring interventions from the laboratory to the real world. These practical problems present serious challenges to the community behavior modifier, but Holland (1973) argued that there is nothing inherent in or peculiar to the behavioral approach that limits its ability to confront these issues or to implement environmental-change programs. Behavioral programs—because of their relatively simple language, the ease in training indigenous personnel, and the flexibility produced by continual assessment—may, in fact, be extremely appropriate for such community intervention. Practical problems which occur in environmental interventions can be minimized by recognizing these issues during the initial assessment phase and intervening on them as one would intervene on any other target of behavior change. It is the responsibility of the community behavior-change agent to identify potential program impediments, assess the conditions that maintain these impediments, and incorporate their modification into the overall program structure.

Specific program impediments require specific assessment and treatment procedures, but the general problems raised by Repucci can be tempered by basic program supplements. Necessary program additions include clear and complete communication of program strategies and objectives delivered in the language of the community group; comprehensive perintervention program preparation to maximize effectiveness within political, economic, bureaucratic, and community limitations; contractual relationships and reinforcement procedures to clarify intervention benefits; and small-scale demonstration projects to refine assessment and intervention procedures and clearly illustrate potential program results to all parties (Meyers et al., in press). Meyers, Artz, and Craighead (1976), in their successful attempt to reduce disruptive residential noise, utilized several of these strategies. Extensive preintervention discussion sessions were held with the community residents and administrative officials to clarify program procedures and objectives; contractual reinforcement procedures were employed to make intervention goals more salient; and a small-scale preintervention demonstration project was conducted to hone program procedures and illustrate potential results.

COMMUNITY INVOLVEMENT

Many of the practical problems confronting the community behavior modifier are intimately related to a lack of community involvement in intervention efforts. In most intervention situations, community needs and goals will differ from the change agent's goals and those of individuals, agencies, and institutions that support the agent's intervention activities. Additionally, communities very rarely present unified opinions on local issues. This implies that community problem assessment conducted without local involvement may identify goals and intervention strategies other than those desired by or acceptable to the community. This faulty assessment process should guarantee at least an absence of local cooperation, and possibly, active community resistance to the professional intrusion.

When assessment appropriately identifies goals and procedures acceptable to the community, one must still consider the productivity and meaning of interventions delivered to rather than conducted with and by the community. Desirable results may be obtained, but community members may experience unanticipated outcomes. Although participants may learn to behave in new and perhaps more appropriate ways, they may also learn that their lives and their community are manipulable; that they are relatively powerless; that change and improvement must be initiated and conducted by outside agents. This individual and community conception of powerlessness may have wide-ranging negative effects, from contributing to intrapersonal helplessness (cf. Seligman, 1975) to a further deterioration of community cohesion and autonomy (cf. Warren, 1963).

To confront these issues, the change agent's problem-assessment activities should include community conceptions of problem situations, desirable end-goals, and acceptable and unacceptable intervention strategies. The assessment should also attempt to reach all elements of the community so that minority views will be recognized and represented in the design and conduct of the intervention (Meyers et al., in press).

Ethical Issues

The basic issue of the practicability of externally directed community intervention shades into crucial ethical questions concerning the manipulation and control of communities and their members. The ethical argument raised against behavioral community interventions asserts that behavior-modification procedures allow an individual or group to influence the behavior and personality of other individuals; to impose views and values on others; and to affect individuals' abilities to think for themselves (Subcommittee on Constitutional Rights, 1974). This position emphasizes the threat, produced by the use of behavior-modification procedures, to the individual's constitutional right to self-determination.

Although this position may be philosophically naive, it does represent the common belief that an effective behavior-change technology presents potential dangers of misuse. However, behavioral interventions do not inherently conflict with constitutionally guaranteed rights. At the individual level, behavior-change programs have facilitated the individual's development and use of self-control and environmental-control skills. At community and societal levels, applied behavior analysis has provided the means to analyze and potentially restructure systems of aversive societal control (Holland, 1978).

Even with these recent emphases on paradigm flexibility and individual and community self-control, behavioral community interventions face severe problems. The choice of behavior-change goals and programs, even though they may offer the individual new alternatives and skills, remains a difficult task. Behavior modifiers have no special preparation to select desirable or acceptable behavior-change goals. To prevent a possible autocratic behavioral technology, behavior-change agents must open and share their intervention procedures. A necessary first step is the use of informed consent.

Schwitzgebel and Kolb (1974) stated that the informed consent of a subject is a necessary prerequisite to the conduct of any experiment and that this requirement must be more rigorous when there is risk to the subject. It should be apparent that the prescription of informed consent must also hold for the application of clinical and community interventions. Although informed consent is the keystone of the protection of human subjects and clients, Goldiamond (1974) recognized that any individual's informed consent is responsive to a variety of coercive influences. The malleability of consent indicates that change agents cannot allow the client's choice to absolve them of ethical responsibility.

This ethical dilemma can only be resolved by relying on increased community involvement in the entire intervention process. Interventions that aid in the development of the community's knowledge of principles and skill in the procedures of problem identification and behavior change will allow community members to assume responsibility for the process of community change. Meyers et al. (1974) argued that such skilled populations offer the possibility of self-controlling communities—communities that have the ability to confront and correct local problems, to design and maintain satisfying environments, and to increase community members' social-coping skills. Enlightened community groups increase the probability that power will be more equally distributed through the community and that control will not become unidirectional and coercive. The work of Briscoe et al. (1975), cited earlier, presents an example of an intervention that increases community members' self-determination.

CONCLUSIONS

The development of a behaviorally based community psychology is a relatively recent effort, but the use of behavior-modification procedures to facilitate the growth of individual and community strengths and create more manageable environments is consistent with a preventive health model. Although no definitive evidence exists to support the ability of such interventions to decrease the incidence and intensity of emotional and behavioral dysfunctions, community programs that strengthen community members and produce satisfying environments have obvious benefits.

Beyond the direct benefits received from behavioral interventions, the adoption of a behavioral model brings additional advantages. The first advantage concerns behavior modification's experimental orientation. To examine social problems as experimental questions suggests that, rather than relying on isolated policy decisions, these issues will be dealt with by continuous assessment and repeated intervention. This experimental model produces a continual refinement of program strategies to increase intervention efficiency and retain responsiveness to changes in the problem situation.

The second benefit relates to a common criticism of contemporary Western society, the lack of a sense of community among our people. Sarason (1974) argued that interventions that develop a community's available problem-solving options would improve that community's sense of kinship. Community self-control interventions seem exceptionally appropriate for this task.

The behavior-modification model offers the community both direct and indirect benefits, but community interventions raise new concerns for the social scientist. Any shift in community control or power is essentially a political act, and the behavioral community psychologist, by choice, must forsake the scientist's ideal notion of political neutrality. Rappaport (1977) noted that psychology has rarely been politically neutral, and that the implementation of any social program requires political action. Meyers et al. (in press) suggested that the community change agent serve as an advocate of the community and that, consistent with the model outlined here, this advocacy take the form of an educative, skill-building process.

The interventions presented here are largely small-scale demonstration projects conducted in university settings, and this indicates that behavioral community psychology is still in its infancy. It is an infancy beset with many difficult developmental problems. We can only hope that the model applies the same experimental rigor to its own problems as it does to those of the communities it studies.

SUMMARY

Community psychology is an attempt to understand and to create a better fit between people and their social and physical environments. It is an approach to human behavior problems that adopts a prevention rather than a treatment orientation. One model for community psychology is behavior modification.

Behavioral community psychology includes a wide variety of interventions that serve to either strengthen individuals or modify community systems to reduce the likelihood or prevent the occurrence of behavioral dysfunction. Four areas were reviewed here: pollution control, energy conservation, health interventions, and skills training. Research in these areas is promising, but currently exists at a small-scale demonstration level. Practical and ethical problems in these interventions have been recognized. Recommendations were made for an increased emphasis on community involvement in the entire intervention process.

REFERENCES

Aaron, B. A., & Bostow, D. E. Indirect facilitation of on-task behavior produced by contingent free-time for academic productivity. *Journal of Applied Behavior Analysis*, 1978, *11*, 197.

Abel, G. G., Barlow, D. H., Blanchard, E. B., & Guild, D. The components of rapists' sexual arousal. *Archives of General Psychiatry*, 1977, *34*, 895–908.

Abel, G. G., Blanchard, E. B., Barlow, D. H., & Mavissakalian, M. Identifying specific erotic cues in sexual deviations by audio-taped descriptions. *Archives of Sexual Behavior*, 1975, *8*, 247–260.

Abel, G. G., Blanchard, E. B., & Becker, J. V. An integrated treatment program for rapists. In R. Rada (Ed.), *Clinical aspects of the rapists*. New York: Grune & Stratton, Inc., 1977.

Abel, G. G., Levis, D., & Clancy, J. Aversion therapy applied to taped sequences of deviant behavior in exhibitionism and other sexual deviations: A preliminary report. *Journal of Behavior Therapy and Experimental Psychiatry*, 1970, *1*, 59–66.

Abelson, P. H. Cost-effective health care. *Science*, 1976, *192*, 619.

Abelson, P. H. A view of health research and care. *Science*, 1978, *200*, 845.

Abrahms, J. L., & Allen, G. J. Comparative effectiveness of situational programming, financial payoffs, and group pressure in weight reduction. *Behavior Therapy*, 1974, *5*, 391–400.

Abramson, E. E. Behavioral approaches to weight control: An updated review. *Behavior Research and Therapy*, 1977, *15*, 355–363.

Abramson, E. E., & Stinson, S. G. Boredom and eating in obese and non-obese individuals. *Addictive Behaviors*, 1977, *2*, 181–185.

Abramson, L. Y., Seligman, M. E. P., & Teasdale, J. Learned helplessness in humans: Critique and reformulation. *Journal of Abnormal Psychology*, 1978, *87*, 49–74.

Adesso, V. J., & Glad, W. R. A behavioral test of a smoking typology. *Addictive Behaviors*, 1978, *3*, 35–38.

Agnew, W. M., & Pyke, S. W. *The science game*. Englewood Cliffs, N.J.: Prentice-Hall, 1969.

Agras, W. S. Behavior modification in the general hospital psychiatric unit. In H. Leitenberg (Ed.), *Handbook of behavior modification and behavior therapy*. Englewood Cliffs, N.J.: Prentice-Hall, 1976.

Agras, W. S., Barlow, D. H., Chapin, H. N., Abel, G. G., & Leitenberg, H. Behavior modification of anorexia nervosa. *Archives of General Psychiatry*, 1974, *30*, 279–286.

Aiken, T. W. *Behavioral analysis of nondelinquent invulnerable adolescents from a high juvenile crime community by way of experimental sampling*. Unpublished doctoral dissertation, University of Southern California, 1980.

Aiken, T. W., Stumphauzer, J. S., & Veloz, E. V. Behavioral analysis of nondelinquent brothers in a high juvenile crime community. *Behavioral Disorders*, 1977, *2*, 212–222.

Alberti, R. E., & Emmons, M. L. *Your perfect right* (2nd ed.). San Luis Obispo, Calif.: Impact, 1974.

Alexander, J. K., & Peterson, K. L. Cardiovascular effects of weight reduction. *Circulation*, 1972, *45*, 310–318.

Allen, K. E., Hart, B., Buell, J. S., Harris, F. G., & Wolf, M. M. Effects of social reinforcement on isolate behavior of a nursery school child. *Child Development*, 1964, *35*, 511–518.

Allport, G. W. *Pattern and growth in personality*. New York: Holt, Rinehart & Winston, 1961.

Alvord, J. R. The home token economy: A motivational system for the home. *Corrective Psychiatry and Journal of Social Therapy*, 1971, *17*, 6–13.

American Cancer Society. *Career facts and figures '74*. New York: American Cancer Society, 1974.

American Heart Association. *Heart facts*. 1976.

American Psychiatric Association. Position statement: A call to action for the chronic mental patient. *American Journal of Psychiatry*, 1979, *136*, 748–752.

Andrle, S., & Dueker, K. J. *Attitude toward and evaluation of car-pooling*. Technical Report No. 32. Iowa City, Iowa: Center for Urban Transportation Studies, University of Iowa, 1974.

Annon, J. S. *The behavioral treatment of sexual problems: Volume 2: Intensive therapy*. Honolulu: Enabling Systems, 1975.

Appel, P. W., & Kaestner, E. Interpersonal and emotional problem solving among narcotic drug abusers. *Journal of Consulting and Clinical Psychology*, 1979, *47*, 1125–1127.

Argyle, M., Bryant, B., & Trower, P. Social skills training and psychotherapy: A comparative study. *Psychological Medicine*, 1974, *4*, 435–443.

Arkowitz, H., Lichtenstein, E., McGovern, K., & Hines, P. The behavioral assessment of social competence in males. *Behavior Therapy*, 1975, *6*, 3–13.

Arnold, S., Sturgis, E., & Forehand, R. Training a parent to teach communication skills. *Behavior Modification*, 1977, *1*, 259–276.

Arthur, A. Z. Diagnostic testing and the new alternatives. *Psychological Bulletin*, 1969, *72*, 183–192.

Ashby, W. A., & Wilson, G. T. Behavior therapy for obesity: Booster sessions and long-term maintenance of weight loss. *Behavior Research and Therapy*, 1977, *15*, 451–464.

Ashkenazi, Z. The treatment of encopresis using a discriminative stimulus and positive reinforcement. *Journal of Behavior Therapy and Experimental Psychiatry*, 1975, *6*, 155–157.

Association for Advancement of Behavior Therapy. Ethical issues for human services. *Behavior Therapy*, 1977, *8*, v–vi.

Atthowe, J. Behavior innovation and persistence. *American Psychologist*, 1973, *28*, 34–41.

Atthowe, J. M., Jr., & Krasner, L. A. A preliminary report on the application of contingent reinforcement procedures (token economy) on a "chronic" psychiatric ward. *Journal of Abnormal Psychology*, 1968, *73*, 37–43.

Ausubel, D. P. Causes and types of narcotic addiction: A psychosocial view. *Psychiatric Quarterly*, 1961, *35*, 523–531. (a)

Ausubel, D. P. Personality disorder is disease. *American Psychologist*, 1961, *16*, 69–74. (b)

Axelrod, S., Brantner, J. P., & Meddock, T. D. Overcorrection: A review and critical analysis. *Journal of Special Education*, 1978, *12*, 367–391.

Axline, V. M. *Play therapy*. New York: Ballantine Books, 1947.

Ayllon, T., & Azrin, N. H. The measurement and reinforcement of behavior of psychotics. *Journal of the Experimental Analysis of Behavior*, 1965, *8*, 357–383.

Ayllon, T., & Azrin, N. *The token economy: A motivational system for therapy and rehabilitation.* New York: Appleton-Century-Crofts, 1968.

Ayllon, T., Haughton, E., & Hughes, H. B. Interpretation of symptoms: Fact or fiction. *Behaviour Research and Therapy*, 1965, *3*, 1–8.

Ayllon, T., Layman, D., & Kandel, H. J. A behavioral-educational alternative to drug control of hyperactive children. *Journal of Applied Behavior Analysis*, 1975, *8*, 137–146.

Ayllon, T., & Roberts, M. Eliminating discipline problems by strengthening academic performance. *Journal of Applied Behavior Analysis*, 1974, 7, 71–76.

Ayllon, T., & Rosenbaum, M. S. The behavioral treatment of disruption and hyperactivity in school settings. In B. B. Lahey & A. E. Kazdin (Eds.), *Advances in clinical child psychology*. New York: Plenum, 1977.

Azrin, N. H., & Armstrong, P. M. The "Mini-Meal"—A method for teaching eating skills to profoundly retarded. *Mental Retardation*, 1973, *11*, 9–13.

Azrin, N. H., Flores, T., & Kaplan, S. J. Job-finding club: A group-assisted program for obtaining employment. *Behaviour Research and Therapy*, 1975, *13*, 17–27.

Azrin, N. H., & Foxx, R. M. A rapid method of toilet training the institutionalized retarded. *Journal of Applied Behavior Analysis*, 1971, *4*, 89–99.

Azrin, N. H., & Holz, W. C. Punishment. In W. K. Honig (Ed.), *Operant behavior: Areas of research and application.* New York: Appleton-Century-Crofts, 1966.

Azrin, N. H., Holz, W., & Goldiamond, I. Response bias in questionnaire reports. *Journal of Consulting Psychology,* 1961, *25,* 324–326.

Azrin, N. H., & Philip, R. A. The Job Club method for the job-handicapped: A comparative outcome study. *Rehabilitation Counseling Bulletin,* in press.

Azrin, N. H., Philip, R. A., Thienes-Hontas, P., & Basalel, V. A. Comparative evaluation of the Job Club program with welfare recipients. *Journal of Vocational Behavior,* 1980, *16,* 133–145.

Azrin, N. H., Schaeffer, R. M., & Wesolowski, M. D. A rapid method of teaching profoundly retarded persons to dress by a reinforcement-guidance method. *Mental Retardation,* 1976, *14,* 29–33.

Azrin, N. H., Sneed, T. J., & Foxx, R. M. Dry bed: Rapid elimination of childhood enuresis. *Behavior Research and Therapy,* 1974, *12,* 147–156.

Azrin, N. H., & Wesolowski, M. D. Theft reversal: An overcorrection procedure for eliminating stealing by retarded persons. *Journal of Applied Behavior Analysis,* 1974, 7, 577–581.

Baer, D. M. "Perhaps it would be better not to know everything." *Journal of Applied Behavior Analysis,* 1977, *10,* 167–172.

Baer, D. M., Wolf, M. M., & Risley, T. R. Some current dimensions of applied behavior analysis. *Journal of Applied Behavior Analysis,* 1968, *1,* 91–97.

Baldessarini, R. J. *Chemotherapy in psychotherapy.* Cambridge: Harvard University Press, 1977.

Ball, J. C. Marijuana smoking and the onset of heroin use. In J. O. Cole & J. R. Wittenborn (Eds.), *Drug abuse: Social and psycho-pharmacological aspects.* Springfield, Ill.: Charles C. Thomas, 1966.

Balson, P. M. Case study: Encopresis: A case with symptom substitution? *Behavior Therapy,* 1973, *4,* 134–136.

Bancroft, J., Jones, H., & Pullan, B. A simple transducer for measuring penile erection, with comments on its use in the treatment of sexual disorders. *Behaviour Research and Therapy,* 1966, *4,* 239–241.

Bander, K. W., Steinke, G. V., Allen, G. J., & Mosher, D. L. Evaluation of three dating-specific treatment approaches for heterosexual dating anxiety. *Journal of Consulting and Clinical Psychology,* 1975, *43,* 259–265.

Bandura, A. Influence of models' reinforcement contingencies on the acquisition of imitative responses. *Journal of Personality and Social Psychology,* 1965, *1,* 589–595.

Bandura, A. *Principles of behavior modification.* New York: Holt, Rinehart & Winston, 1969.

Bandura, A. Psychotherapy based upon modeling principles. In A. E. Bergin & S. L.

Garfield (Eds.), *Handbook of psychotheraphy and behavior change: An empirical analysis.* New York: Wiley, 1971. (a)

Bandura, A. Vicarious and self-reinforcement processes. In R. Glaser (Ed.), *The nature of reinforcement.* New York: Academic Press, 1971. (b)

Bandura, A. Self-efficacy: Toward a unifying theory of behavioral change. *Psychological Review,* 1977, *84,* 191–215. (a)

Bandura, A. *Social learning theory.* Englewood Cliffs, N.J.: Prentice-Hall, 1977. (b)

Bandura, A. Reflections on self-efficacy. *Advances in Behaviour Research and Therapy,* 1978, *1,* 237–269.

Bandura, A., Blanchard, E. B., & Ritter, B. The relative efficacy of desensitization and modeling approaches for inducing behavioral, affective, and attitudinal changes. *Journal of Personality and Social Psychology,* 1969, *13,* 173–199.

Bandura, A., Grusec, J. E., & Menlove, F. L. Vicarious extinction of avoidance behavior. *Journal of Personality and Social Psychology,* 1967, *5,* 16–23.

Bandura, A., Jeffery, R. W., & Gajdos, E. Generalizing change through participant modeling with self-directed mastery. *Behaviour Research and Therapy,* 1975, *13,* 141–152.

Bandura, A., Jeffery, R. W., & Wright, C. L. Efficacy of participant modeling as a function of response induction aids. *Journal of Abnormal Psychology,* 1974, *83,* 56–64.

Bandura, A., & Menlove, F. L. Factors determining vicarious extinction of avoidance behavior through symbolic modeling. *Journal of Personality and Social Psychology,* 1968, *8,* 99–108.

Bandura, A., & Walters, R. H. *Social learning and personality development.* New York: Holt, Rinehart & Winston, 1963.

Barbach, L. G. Group treatment of preorgasmic women. *Journal of Sex and Marital Therapy,* 1974, *1,* 139–145.

Barber, R. M., & Kagey, J. R. Modification of school attendance for an elementary population. *Journal of Applied Behavior Analysis,* 1977, *10,* 41–48.

Barber, T. X. *Pitfalls in human research: Ten pivotal points.* New York: Pergamon, 1976.

Barkow, B. *The psychology of car pooling.* Ontario: Ministry of Transportation and Communication, 1974.

Barlow, D. H. Increasing heterosexual responsiveness in the treatment of sexual deviation: A review of the clinical and experimental evidence. *Behavior Therapy,* 1973, *4,* 655–671.

Barlow, D. H. The treatment of sexual deviation: Towards a comprehensive behavioral approach. In K. S. Calhoun, H. E. Adams, & K. M. Mitchell (Eds.), *Innovative treatment methods in psychopathology.* New York: Wiley, 1974.

Barlow, D. H. Aversive procedures. In W. S. Agras (Ed.), *Behavior modification: Principles and clinical applications* (2nd ed.). Boston: Little, Brown, 1978.

Barlow, D. H., Abel, G. G., & Blanchard, E. B. Gender identity change in transsexuals: Follow-up and replications. *Archives of General Psychiatry*, 1979, *36*, 1001–1010.

Barlow, D. H., & Agras, W. S. Fading to increase heterosexual responsiveness in homosexuals. *Journal of Applied Behavior Analysis*, 1973, *6*, 355–366.

Barlow, D. H., Agras, W. S., Leitenberg, H., Callahan, E. J., & Moore, R. C. The contribution of therapeutic instruction to covert sensitization. *Behaviour Research and Therapy*, 1972, *10*, 411–415.

Barlow, D. H., Becker, R., Leitenberg, H., & Agras, W. S. A mechanical strain gauge for recording penile circumference change. *Journal of Applied Behavior Analysis*, 1970, *3*, 73–76.

Barlow, D. H., Hayes, S. C., Nelson, R. O., Steele, D. L., Meeler, M. E., & Mills, J. R. Sex role motor behavior: A behavioral checklist. *Behavioral Assessment*, 1979, *1*, 119–138.

Barlow, D. H., Leitenberg, H., & Agras, W. S. The experimental control of sexual deviation through manipulation of the noxious scene in covert sensitization. *Journal of Abnormal Psychology*, 1969, *74*, 596–601.

Barlow, D. H., Mills, J. R., Agras, W. S., & Steinman, D. L. A comparison of sex-typed minor behavior in male-to-female transsexuals and women. *Archives of Sexual Behavior*, in press.

Barlow, D. H., Reynolds, E. H., & Agras, W. S. Gender identity change in a transsexual. *Archives of General Psychiatry*, 1973, *28*, 569–579.

Barrish, H., Saunders, M., & Wolf, M. Good behavior game: Effects of individual contingencies for group consequences on disruptive behavior in a classroom. *Journal of Applied Behavior Analysis*, 1969, *2*, 119–124.

Barton, E. S., Guess, D., Garcia, E., & Baer, D. M. Improvement of retardates' mealtime behaviors by time-out procedures using multiple baseline techniques. *Journal of Applied Behavior Analysis*, 1970, *3*, 77–84.

Bauer, R. M., & Craighead, W. E. Physiological responses to the imagination of fearful and neutral situations: The effects of imagery instructions. *Behavior Therapy*, 1979, *10*, 389–403.

Bauman, K. E., & Iwata, B. A. Maintenance of independent housekeeping skills using scheduling plus self-recording procedures. *Behavior Therapy*, 1977, *8*, 554–560.

Baumeister, A., & Klosowski, R. An attempt to group toilet train severely retarded patients. *Mental Retardation*, 1965, *3*, 24–26.

Beck, A. T. *Depression: Clinical, experimental and theoretical aspects*. New York: Harper & Row, 1967.

Beck, A. T. General discussion. In R. J. Friedman & M. M. Katz (Eds.), *The psychology of depression: Contemporary theory and research.* New York: J. Wiley, 1974.

Beck, A. T. *Cognitive therapy and the emotional disorders.* New York: International Universities Press, 1976.

Beck, A. T., Ward, C. H., Mendelson, M., Mock, J., & Erbaugh, J. An interview for measuring depression. *Archives of General Psychiatry,* 1961, *4,* 561–571.

Becker, H. S. *Outsiders: Studies in the sociology of deviance.* New York: Free Press, 1963.

Becker, L. S., & Seligman, C. Reducing air conditioning waste by signaling it is cool outside. *Personality and Social Psychology Bulletin,* in press.

Becker, W. C., & Carnine, D. W. Direct instruction: An effective approach to educational intervention with the disadvantaged and low performers. In B. B. Lahey & A. E. Kazdin (Eds.), *Advances in clinical child psychology* (Vol. 3). New York: Plenum, 1979.

Becker, W. C., Madsen, C. H., Arnold, C. R., & Thomas, D. R. The contingent use of teacher attention and praise in reducing classroom behavior problems. *Journal of Special Education,* 1967, *1,* 287–307.

Beckett, H. D. Hypotheses concerning the etiology of heroin addiction. In P. G. Bourne (Ed.), *Addiction.* New York: Academic Press, 1974.

Bellack, A. S. A comparison of self-reinforcement and self-monitoring in a weight reduction program. *Behavior Therapy,* 1976, *7,* 68–75.

Bellack, A. S., Glanz, L., & Simon, R. Positive and negative covert reinforcement in the treatment of obesity. *Journal of Consulting and Clinical Psychology,* 1976, *3,* 490–491.

Bellack, A. S., & Hersen, M. *Behavior modification: An introductory textbook.* New York: Oxford University Press, 1977.

Bellack, A. S., & Hersen, M. Chronic psychiatric patients: Social skills training. In M. Hersen & A. S. Bellack (Eds.), *Behavior therapy in the psychiatric setting.* Baltimore: Williams & Wilkins, 1978.

Bellack, A. S., Hersen, M., & Turner, S. M. Generalization effects of social skills training in chronic schizophrenics: An experimental analysis. *Behaviour Research and Therapy,* 1976, *14,* 391–398.

Bellack, A. S., Rozensky, R., & Schwartz, J. A comparison of two forms of self-monitoring in a behavioral weight reduction program. *Behavior Therapy,* 1974, *5,* 523–530.

Bellack, A. S., & Williamson, D. A. Eating disorders. In D. M. Doleys, R. L. Meredity, & A. R. Ciminero (Eds.), *Behavioral psychology in medicine: Assessment and treatment strategies.* New York: Plenum Press, in press.

Beneke, W. M., & Paulsen, B. K. Long term efficacy of a behavior modification weight loss program: A comparison of two follow-up maintenance strategies. *Behavior Therapy,* 1979, *10,* 8–13.

Beneke, W. M., Paulsen, B., McReynolds, W. T., & Kohrs, M. B. Long-term results of two behavior modification weight loss programs using nutritionists as therapists. *Behavior Therapy*, 1978, *9*, 501–507.

Benjamin, S., Marks, I. M., & Huson, J. Active muscular relaxation in desensitization of phobic patients. In I. M. Marks, A. E. Bergin, P. L. Lang, J. D. Mattarazzo, G. R. Patterson, & H. H. Strupp (Eds.), *Psychotherapy and behavior change*. Chicago, Ill.: Aldine, 1972.

Bennett, P. S., & Maley, R. S. Modification of interactive behaviors in chronic mental patients. *Journal of Applied Behavior Analysis*, 1973, *6*, 609–620.

Bensberg, G. J., Colwell, C. N., & Cassel, R. H. Teaching the profoundly retarded self-help activities by behavior shaping techniques. *American Journal of Mental Deficiency*, 1965, *69*, 674–679.

Bergin, A., & Strupp, H. *Changing frontiers in the science of psychotherapy*. Chicago and New York: Aldine-Atherton, 1972.

Berkson, G., & Mason, W. Stereotyped movements of mental defectives: IV. The effect of toys and the character of the acts. *American Journal of Mental Deficiency*, 1964, *68*, 511–524.

Bernstein, D. A. Behavioral fear assessment: Anxiety or artifact? In H. Adams & P. Unikel (Eds.), *Issues and trends in behavior therapy*. Springfield, Ill.: Thomas, 1973.

Bernstein, D. A., & Borkovec, T. D. *Progressive relaxation: A manual for therapists*. Champaign, Ill.: Research Press, 1973.

Bernstein, D. A., & McAlister, A. The modification of smoking behavior: Progress and problems. *Addictive Behaviors*, 1976, *1*, 89–102.

Bernstein, D. A., & Nietzel, M. T. Procedural variation in behavioral avoidance tests. *Journal of Consulting and Clinical Psychology*, 1973, *41*, 165–174.

Berzins, J. I., Ross, W. F., English, G. E., & Haley, J. V. Subgroups among opiate addicts: Typological investigation. *Journal of Abnormal Psychology*, 1974, *83*, 65–73.

Best, J. A. & Hakstian, A. R. A situation-specific model for smoking behavior. *Addictive Behaviors*, 1978, *3*, 79–92.

Best, J. A., Owen, L. E., & Trentadue, L. Comparison of satiation and rapid smoking in self-managed smoking cessation. *Addictive Behaviors*, 1978, *3*, 71–78.

Bickman, L. Environmental attitudes and actions. *The Journal of Social Psychology*, 1972, *87*, 323–324.

Bieber, B., Bieber, I., Dain, H. J., Dince, P. R., Drellich, M. G., Grand, H. G., Grundlach, R. H., Kremer, M. W., Wilber, C. B., & Bieber, T.D. *Homosexuality*. New York: Basic Books, 1963.

Biglan, A., & Dow, M. G. Toward a "second generation" model of depression treatment: A program specific approach. In L. P. Rehm (Ed.), *Behavior therapy for depression: Present status and future directions*. New York: Academic, in press.

Bijou, S. W., & Baer, D. M. Some methodological contributions from a functional analysis of child development. In L. P. Lipsitt & C. S. Spiker (Eds.), *Advances in child development and behavior* (Vol. 1). New York: Academic Press, 1963.

Bijou, S. W., & Baer, D. M. *Child development: Readings in experimental analysis* (Vol. 3). New York: Appleton-Century-Crofts, 1967.

Bijou, S. W., Peterson, R. F., Harris, F. R., Allen, K. E., & Johnston, M. S. Methodology for experimental studies of young children in natural settings. *Psychological Record,* 1969, *19,* 177–210.

Bindrim, P. Nudity as a quick grab for intimacy in group therapy. *Psychology Today,* 1969, *3,* 24–28.

Birchler, G. R., Weiss, R. L., & Vincent, J. P. A multimethod analysis of social reinforcement exchange between maritally distressed and nondistressed spouse and stranger dyads. *Journal of Personality and Social Psychology,* 1975, *31,* 349–360.

Birk, L., Miller, E., & Cohler, B. Group psychotherapy for homosexual men by male-female co-therapists. *Acta Psychiatrica Scandinavica,* Supplementum 218, 1970, 9–36.

Birnbrauer, J. S. Generalization of punishment effects—A case study. *Journal of Applied Behavior Analysis,* 1968, *1,* 201–211.

Birnbrauer, J. S. Mental retardation. In H. Leitenberg (Ed.), *Handbook of behavior modification.* Englewood Cliffs, N.J.: Prentice-Hall, 1976.

Blalock, N. M. *Causal inferences in nonexperimental research.* Chapel Hill: University of North Carolina Press, 1964.

Blanchard, E. B. The relative contributions of modeling, informational influences, and physical contact in the extinction of phobic behavior. *Journal of Abnormal Psychology,* 1970, *76,* 55–61.

Blaney, P. H. Contemporary theories of depression: Critique and comparison. *Journal of Abnormal Psychology,* 1977, *86*(3), 203–223.

Blaney, P. Cognitive and behavioral therapy of depression: A review of their effectiveness. In L. P. Rehm (Ed.), *Behavior therapy for depression: Present status and future directions.* New York: Academic, in press.

Blinder, B. J., Freeman, D. M. A., & Stunkard, A. J. Behavioral therapy of anorexia nervosa: Effectiveness of activity as a reinforcer of weight gain. *American Journal of Psychiatry,* 1970, *126,* 1093–1098.

Blittner, M., & Goldberg, J. Cognitive self-control factors in the reduction of smoking behavior. *Behavior Therapy,* 1978, *9,* 553–561.

Blom, B. E., & Craighead, W. E. The effects of situational and instructional demand on indices of speech anxiety. *Journal of Abnormal Psychology,* 1974, *83,* 667–674.

Bloom, B. *Community mental health: A historical and critical analysis.* Morristown, N.J.: General Learning Press, 1973.

Bockoven, J. S. *Moral treatment in American psychiatry.* New York: Springer, 1963.

Bollard, R. J., & Woodroffe, B. P. The effect of parent-administered dry bed training and nocturnal enuresis in children. *Behavior Research and Therapy,* 1977, *15,* 159–165.

Boring, E. G. Intelligence as the tests test it. *New Republic,* 1923, *35,* 35–37.

Boring, E. G. When is human behavior predetermined? *Scientific Monthly,* 1957, *84,* 189–196.

Borkovec, T. D. *The comparative effectiveness of systematic desensitization and implosive therapy and the effect of expectancy manipulation on the elimination of fear.* Unpublished doctoral dissertation, University of Illinois, 1970.

Borkovec, T. D. Effects of expectancy on the outcome of systematic desensitization and implosive treatments for analogue anxiety. *Behavior Therapy,* 1972, *3,* 29–40.

Borkovec, T. D. Self-efficacy: Cause or reflection of behavioral change? *Advances in Behaviour Research and Therapy,* 1978, *1,* 163–170.

Borkovec, T. D., Stone, N., O'Brien, G., & Kaloupek, D. Identification and measurement of a clinically relevant target behavior for analogue outcome research. *Behavior Therapy,* 1974, *5,* 503–513.

Borkovec, T. D., Weerts, T. C., & Bernstein, D. A. Assessment of anxiety. In A. R. Ciminero, K. S. Calhoun, & H. E. Adams (Eds.), *Handbook of behavioral assessment.* New York: John Wiley & Sons, 1977.

Borland, B. L., & Rudolph, J. P. Relative effects of low socioeconomic status, parental smoking and poor scholastic performance on smoking among high school students. *Social Science and Medicine,* 1975, *9,* 27–30.

Bostow, D. E., & Bailey, J. B. Modification of severe disruptive and aggressive behavior using brief timeout and reinforcement procedures. *Journal of Applied Behavior Analysis,* 1969, *2,* 31–37.

Bourne, P. G. Issues in addiction. In P. G. Bourne (Ed.), *Addiction.* New York: Academic Press, 1974.

Bowden, C. Determinants of initial use of opioids. *Comprehensive Psychiatry,* 1971, *12,* 136–140.

Brady, J. P. Brevital-relaxation treatment of frigidity. *Behaviour Research and Therapy,* 1966, *4,* 71–77.

Braucht, G. N., Brakarsh, D., Follingstad, D., & Berry, K. L. Deviant drug use in adolescence: A review of psychosocial correlates. *Psychological Bulletin,* 1973, *79,* 92–106.

Braukmann, C. J., & Fixen, D. L. Behavior modification with delinquents. In M. Hersen, R. M. Eisler, & P. M. Miller (Eds.), *Progress in behavior modification.* New York: Academic Press, 1975.

Brawley, E. R., Harris, F. R., Allen, K. E., Fleming, R. S., & Peterson, R. F. Behavior modification of an autistic child. *Behavioral Science,* 1969, *14,* 87–97.

Bray, G. A. *The obese patient.* Philadelphia: Saunders, 1976.

Bray, G. A. (Ed.). *Obesity in America.* U.S. Department of Health, Education, and Welfare. National Institutes of Health, NIH Publication No. 79–359, 1979.

Brecher, E. M. (Ed.). *Licit and illicit drugs.* Boston: Little, Brown, 1972.

Breger, L., & McGaugh, J. Critique and reformulation of "learning theory": Approaches to psychotherapy and neurosis. *Psychological Bulletin,* 1965, *63,* 338–358.

Bricker, W. A., Morgan, D. G., & Grabowski, J. G. Development and maintenance of a behavior modification repertoire of cottage attendants through TV feedback. *American Journal of Mental Deficiency,* 1972, 77, 126–128.

Bridger, W. H., & Mandel, I. J. A comparison of GSR fear responses produced by threat and electrical shock. *Journal of Psychiatric Research,* 1964, *2,* 31–40.

Bridger, W. H., & Mandel, I. J. Abolition of the PRE by instructions in GSR conditioning. *Journal of Experimental Psychology,* 1965, *69,* 476–482.

Brightwell, D. R., & Sloan, C. L. Long-term results of behavior therapy for obesity. *Behavior Therapy,* 1977, *8,* 898–905.

Briscoe, R., Hoffman, D., & Bailey, J. Behavioral community psychology: Training a community board to problem solve. *Journal of Applied Behavior Analysis,* 1975, *8,* 157–168.

Britt, D. B., Kemmerer, W. T., & Robison, J. R. Penile blood flow determination by mercury strain gauge plethysmography. *Investigative Urology,* 1971, *8,* 673–678.

Brockway, B. S. Chemical validation of self-reported smoking rates. *Behavior Therapy,* 1978, *9,* 685–686.

Broughton, S. F., & Lahey, B. B. Direct and collateral effects of positive reinforcement, response-costs, and mixed contingencies for academic behavior. *Journal of School Psychology,* 1978, *16,* 126–136.

Brown, B. S., Gauvey, S. K., Meyers, M. B., & Stark, S. D. In their own words: Addicts' reasons for initiating and withdrawing from heroin. *International Journal of the Addictions,* 1971, *6,* 635–645.

Brown, G. W., & Harris, T. *Social origins of depression.* London: Tavistock Publications, 1978.

Brown, G. W., Harris, T. O., & Peto, J. Life events and psychiatric disorders part 2: Nature and causal link. *Psychological Medicine,* 1973, *3,* 159–176.

Brown, H. A. Role of expectancy manipulation in systematic desensitization. *Journal of Consulting and Clinical Psychology,* 1973, *41,* 405–411.

Brown, L., Huppler, B., Van Deventer, P., York, R., & Sontag, E. Use of reinforcement principles to increase comprehension of instructional filmstrips. *Education and Training of the Mentally Retarded,* 1973, *8,* 50–56.

Brown, P., & Elliott, R. The control of aggression in a nursery school class. *Journal of Experimental Child Psychology,* 1965, *2,* 102–107.

Brownell, K. D. Assessment in the treatment of eating disorders. In D. H. Barlow (Ed.), *Assessment of adult disorders*. New York: Guilford, 1980.

Brownell, K., & Barlow, D. H. The behavioral treatment of sexual deviation. In E. Foa, A. Goldstein, & J. Wolpe (Eds.), *Handbook of behavioral intervention*. New York: John Wiley, 1980.

Brownell, K. D., Hayes, S. C., & Barlow, D. H. Patterns of appropriate and deviant sexual arousal: The behavioral treatment of multiple sexual deviations. *Journal of Consulting and Clinical Psychology*, 1977, *45*, 1144–1155.

Brownell, K. D., Heckerman, C. L., & Westlake, R. J. Therapist and group contact as variables in the behavioral treatment of obesity. *Journal of Consulting and Clinical Psychology*, 1978, *46*, 593–594.

Brownell, K. D., Heckerman, C. L., Westlake, R. J., Hayes, S. C., & Monti, P. M. The effect of couples training and partner cooperativeness in the behavioral treatment of obesity. *Behaviour Research and Therapy*, 1978, *16*, 323–333.

Brownell, K. D., & Stunkard, A. J. Behavioral treatment of obesity in children. *American Journal of Diseases of Children*, 1978, *132*, 403–412.

Brownell, K. D., & Stunkard, A. J. Exercise in the development and control of obesity. In A. J. Stunkard (Ed.), *Obesity*. Philadelphia: Saunders, 1980.

Brownell, K. D., Stunkard, A. J., & Albaum, J. M. Evaluation and modification of exercise patterns in the natural environment. *American Journal of Psychiatry*, in press.

Brownell, K. D., & Venditti, E. M. The etiology and treatment of obesity. In W. E. Fann, I. Karacan, A. D. Pokorny, & R. L. Williams (Eds.), *Phenomenology and the treatment of psychophysiological disorders*. New York: Spectrum, in press.

Bryant, B., Trower, P., Yardley, K., Urbieta, K., & Letemendia, F. J. A survey of social inadequacy among psychiatric patients. *Psychological Medicine*, 1976, *6*, 101–112.

Bryant, D. A. *Study and evaluation of commuter carpool programs in certain metropolitan areas*. Bedford, Mass.: GCA Corporation, Technology Division (GCA-TR-74-8-G), April 1974.

Bucher, B., & Fabricatore, J. Use of patient-administered shock to suppress hallucinations. *Behavior Therapy*, 1970, *1*, 382–385.

Bucher, B., & King, L. W. Generalization of punishment effects in the deviant behavior of a psychotic child. *Behavior Therapy*, 1971, *2*, 68–77.

Budd, K. S., & Baer, D. M. Behavior modification and the law: Implications of recent judicial decisions. *Journal of Psychiatry and Law*, 1976, *4*, 171–244.

Buehler, R. E., Patterson, G. R., & Furniss, J. M. The reinforcement of behavior in institutional settings. *Behavior Research and Therapy*, 1966, *4*, 157–167.

Buell, J., Stoddard, P., Harris, E. R., & Baer, D. M. Collateral social development accompanying reinforcement of outdoor play in a preschool child. *Journal of Applied Behavior Analysis,* 1968, *1,* 167–173.

Bugental, D. B., Whalen, C. K., & Henken, B. Causal attributions of hyperactive children and motivational assumptions of two behavior-change approaches: Evidence for an interactionist position. *Child Development,* 1977, *48,* 874–884.

Bunck, T. J., & Iwata, B. A. Increasing senior citizen participation in a community-based nutritious meal program. *Journal of Applied Behavior Analysis,* 1978, *11,* 75–86.

Burchard, J. D., & Barrera, F. An analysis of timeout and response-cost in a programmed environment. *Journal of Applied Behavior Analysis,* 1972, *5,* 271–282.

Burg, M. M., Reid, D. H., & Lattimore, J. Use of a self-recording and supervision program to change institutional staff behavior. *Journal of Applied Behavior Analysis,* 1979, *12,* 363–375.

Burgess, R. L., Clark, R. N., & Hendee, J. C. An experimental analysis of antilittering procedures. *Journal of Applied Behavior Analysis,* 1971, *4,* 71–75.

Burkhart, B. R., Behles, M. W., & Stumphauzer, J. S. Training juvenile probation officers in behavior modification: Knowledge, attitude change, or behavioral competence? *Behavior Therapy,* 1976, 7, 47–53.

Burt, J. E., & Burt, J. C. *The surgery of love.* New York: Carlton Press, 1975.

Bushell, D. The Behavior Analysis Follow Through Project: An engineering approach to the elementary school classroom. In T. A. Brigham & A. C. Catania (Eds.), *Analysis and modification of social and educational behaviors.* New York: Wiley, 1978.

Bushell, D., Wrobel, P. A., & Michaelis, M. L. Applying "group" contingencies to the classroom study behavior of preschool children. *Journal of Applied Behavior Analysis,* 1968, *1,* 55–61.

Buss, A. H. *Psychopathology.* New York: Wiley, 1966.

Butterfield, F. Love and sex in China. *The New York Times Magazine,* January 13, 1980, 15–17; 43–49.

Cahoon, D. D. Issues and implications of operant conditioning: Balancing procedures against outcomes. *Hospital and Community Psychiatry,* 1968, *19,* 228–229.

Cahoon, D. D., & Crosby, C. C. A learning approach to chronic drug use: Sources of reinforcement. *Behavior Therapy,* 1972, *3,* 64–71.

Calhoon, K. S., & Lima, P. P. Effects of varying schedules of timeout on high- and low-rate behaviors. *Journal of Behavior Therapy and Experimental Psychiatry,* 1977, *8,* 189–194.

Calhoun, K. S., & Matherne, P. The effects of varying schedules of time-out on aggressive behavior of a retarded girl. *Journal of Behavior Therapy and Experimental Psychiatry,* 1975, *6,* 139–144.

Callahan, E. J., & Leitenberg, H. Aversion therapy for sexual deviation: Contingent shock and covert sensitization. *Journal of Abnormal Psychology*, 1973, *81*, 60–73.

Callner, D. A. Behavioral treatment approaches to drug abuse: A critical review of the research. *Psychological Bulletin*, 1975, *82*, 143–164.

Callner, D. A., & Ross, S. M. The reliability and validity of three measures of assertion in a drug addict population. *Behavior Therapy*, 1976, *7*, 659–667.

Callner, D. A., & Ross, S. M. The assessment and training of assertive skills with drug addicts: A preliminary study. *International Journal of the Addictions*, 1978, *13*, 227–239.

Camp, B. W., Blom, G. E., Hebert, F., & van Doorninck, W. J. "Think Aloud": A program for developing self-control in young aggressive boys. *Journal of Abnormal Child Psychology*, 1977, *5*, 157–169.

Campbell, D. T., & Stanley, J. C. Experimental and quasi-experimental designs for research and teaching. In N. L. Gage (Ed.), *Handbook of research on teaching*. Chicago: Rand McNally, 1963.

Cappell, H. An evaluation of tension models of alcohol consumption. In R. J. Gibbons, Y. Israel, H. Kalant, R. E. Popham, W. Schmidt, & R. G. Smart (Eds.), *Research advances in alcohol and drug problems*. New York: Wiley, 1975.

Cappell, H., & Herman, C. P. Alcohol and tension reduction: A review. *Quarterly Journal of Studies on Alcohol*, 1972, *33*, 33–64.

Carlson, C. H., Hersen, M., & Eisler, R. M. Token economy programs in the hospitalized adult psychiatric patients: Current status and recent trends. *Journal of Nervous and Mental Disease*, 1972, *155*, 192–204.

Carney, L. P. *Probation and parole: Legal and social dimensions*. New York: McGraw-Hill, 1977.

Carnine, D. W., & Fink, W. T. Increasing the rate of presentation and use of signals in elementary classroom teachers. *Journal of Applied Behavior Analysis*, 1978, *11*, 35–46.

Carr, E. G. The motivation of self-injurious behavior: A review of some hypotheses. *Psychological Bulletin*, 1977, *84*, 800–816.

Carr, E. G., Binkoff, J. A., Kologinsky, E., & Eddy, M. Acquisition of sign language by autistic children. I: Expressive labeling. *Journal of Applied Behavior Analysis*, 1978, *11*, 489–501.

Carroll, L. J., Yates, B. T., & Gray, J. J. Predicting obesity reduction in behavioral and nonbehavioral therapy from client characteristics: The self-evaluation measure. *Behavior Therapy*, 1980, *11*, 189–197.

Carter, E. N., Rice, A. P., & DeJulio, S. Role of the therapist in the self-control of obesity. *Journal of Consulting and Clinical Psychology*, 1977, *45*, 503.

Carter, J. *The national energy plan*. Nationally televised speech, April 29, 1977.

Castro, L., Rachlin, H. Self-reward, self-monitoring, and self-punishment as feedback in weight control. *Behavior Therapy*, 1980, *11*, 38–48.

Cattell, R. B., & Scheier, I. H. *The meaning and measurement of neuroticism and anxiety.* New York: Ronald, 1961.

Caudill, B. D., & Marlatt, G. A. Modeling influences in social drinking: An experimental analogue. *Journal of Consulting and Clinical Psychology*, 1975, *43*, 405–415.

Cauffman, J. G., Warbuton, E. A., & Shultz, C. S. Health care of school children: Effective referral patterns. *American Journal of Public Health*, 1969, *59*, 86–90.

Cautela, J. R. Treatment of compulsive behavior by covert sensitization. *Psychological Record*, 1966, *16*, 33–41.

Cautela, J. R. Covert sensitization. *Psychological Reports*, 1967, *20*, 459–468.

Cautela, J. R. Behavior therapy and self-control: Techniques and implications. In C. M. Franks (Ed.), *Behavior therapy: Appraisal and status*. New York: McGraw-Hill, 1969.

Cautela, J. R. Rationale and procedures for covert conditioning. In R. D. Rubin, H. Fensterheim, J. D. Henderson, & J. P. Ullmann (Eds.), *Advances in behavior therapy*. New York: Academic Press, 1972.

Cautela, J. R., & Wisocki, P. A. The use of male and female therapists in the treatment of homosexual behavior. In R. Rubin & C. Franks (Eds.), *Advances in behavior therapy, 1968*. New York: Academic Press, 1969.

Cellucci, A. J., & Lawrence, P. S. The efficacy of systematic desensitization in reducing nightmares. *Journal of Behavior Therapy and Experimental Psychiatry*, 1978, *9*, 109–114.

Chaney, E. F., O'Leary, M. R., & Marlatt, G. A. Skill training with alcoholics. *Journal of Consulting and Clinical Psychology*, 1978, *46*, 1092–1104.

Chapman, C., & Risley, T. R. Anti-litter procedures in an urban high-density area. *Journal of Applied Behavior Analysis*, 1974, *7*, 377–384.

Christensen, A., & Arkowitz, H. Preliminary report on practice dating and feedback as treatment for college dating problems. *Journal of Counseling Psychology*, 1974, *21*, 92–95.

Christensen, A., Arkowitz, H., & Anderson, J. Beaus for cupid's errors: Practice dating and feedback for college dating inhibitions. *Behavior Research and Therapy*, 1975, *13*, 321–331.

Christmas is coming. *The Nation*, 1973, *217*, 614.

Christophersen, E. R., Arnold, C. M., Hall, D. W., & Quilitch, H. R. The home point system: Token reinforcement procedures for application by parents of children with behavior problems. *Journal of Applied Behavior Analysis*, 1972, *5*, 485–497.

Christophersen, E. R., Barnard, J. D., Ford, D., & Wolf, M. M. The family training program: Improving parent-child interaction patterns. In E. J. Mash, L. C. Handy, & L. A. Hammerlynck (Eds.), *Behavior modification approaches to parenting*. New York: Brunner/Mazel, 1976.

Chu, F., & Trotter, S. *The madness establishment*. New York: Grossman, 1974.

Ciminero, A. R., Calhoun, K. S., & Adams, H. E. (Eds.). *Handbook of behavioral assessment*. New York: Wiley, 1977.

Clark, H. B., Greene, B. F., Macrae, J. W., McNees, M. P., Davis, J. L., & Risley, T. R. A parent advice package for family shopping trips: Development and evaluation. *Journal of Applied Behavior Analysis*, 1977, *10*, 605–624.

Clark, H. B., Rowbury, T., Baer, A. M., & Baer, D. M. Timeout as a punishing stimulus in continuous and intermittent schedules. *Journal of Applied Behavior Analysis*, 1973, *6*, 443–455.

Clark, J. V., & Arkowitz, H. Social anxiety and self-evaluation of interpersonal performance. *Psychological Reports*, 1975, *36*, 211–221.

Clark, R. N., Burgess, R. L., & Hendee, J. C. The development of antilitter behavior in a forest campground. *Journal of Applied Behavior Analysis*, 1972, *5*, 1–5.

Coan, R. W. Personality variables associated with cigarette smoking. *Journal of Personality and Social Psychology*, 1973, *26*, 86–104.

Cohen, L. K., & Lucye, H. A position on school dental health education. *Journal of School Health*, 1970, *40*, 361–365.

Combs, M. L., & Lahey, B. B. Evaluation of a cognitive social skills training program for young children: Lack of generalized effects. *Behavior Modification*, in press.

Combs, M. L., & Slaby, D. A. Social-skills training with children. In B. B. Lahey & A. E. Kazdin (Eds.), *Advances in clinical child psychology* (Vol. 1). New York: Plenum, 1977.

Conger, A. J., Wallander, J., Mariotto, M. J., & Ward, D. Peer judgments of heterosexual-social anxiety and skill: What do they pay attention to anyhow? *Behavioral Assessment*, in press.

Conger, J. The treatment of encopresis by the management of social consequences. *Behavior Therapy*, 1970, *1*, 386–390.

Conger, J. C., & Farrell, A. D. *Behavioral components of heterosocial skill*. Unpublished manuscript, Purdue University, 1979.

Conger, J. J. Alcoholism: Theory, problem, and challenge. II. Reinforcement theory and the dynamics of alcoholism. *Quarterly Journal of Studies on Alcohol*, 1956, *17*, 291–324.

Conners, C. K. A teacher rating scale for use in drug studies with children. *American Journal of Psychiatry*, 1969, *126*, 884–888.

Conway, J. B., & Bucher, B. D. "Soap in the Mouth" as an aversive consequence. *Behavior Therapy*, 1974, *5*, 154–156.

Cook, J. W., Altman, K., & Haavik, S. Consent for aversive treatment: A model form. *Mental Retardation,* 1978, *16,* 47–51.

Cook, T. D., & Campbell, D. T. (Eds.). *Quasiexperimentation: Design and analysis issues for field settings.* Chicago: Rand McNally, 1979.

Cooke, G. Evaluation of the efficacy of the components of reciprocal inhibition psychotherapy. *Journal of Abnormal Psychology,* 1968, *73,* 464–467.

Cooper, A. J. Disorders of sexual potency in the male: A clinical and statistical study of some factors related to short-term prognosis. *British Journal of Psychiatry,* 1969, *115,* 709–719.

Copeland, R. E., Brown, R. E., & Hall, R. V. The effects of principal-implemented techniques on the behavior of pupils. *Journal of Applied Behavior Analysis,* 1974, *7,* 77–86.

Copemann, C. D. Drug addiction: I. A theoretical framework for behavior therapy. *Psychological Reports,* 1975, *37,* 947–958.

Corah, N. L. The dental practitioners and preventive health behavior. *Health Education Monographs,* 1974, *2,* 226–235.

Cornfield, J., & Mitchell, S. Selected risk factors in coronary disease. *Archives of Environmental Health,* 1969, *19,* 382–391.

Cowen, E. Social and community interventions. *Annual Review of Psychology,* 1973, *24,* 1973.

Cowen, E. L., Davidson, E. R., & Gesten, E. L. Program dissemination and the modification of delivery practices in school mental health. *Professional Psychology,* 1980, *11,* 36–47.

Craighead, L. W. *Evaluation of behavior therapy and a pharmacological approach to the treatment of obesity.* Paper presented at meetings of the Association for the Advancement of Behavior Therapy, San Francisco, December 1979.

Craighead, L. W., & Craighead, W. E. Implications of persuasive communication research for the modification of self-statements. *Cognitive Therapy and Research,* 1980, *4,* 117–134.

Craighead, L. W., Stunkard, A. J., & O'Brien, R. M. *Boosters in the treatment of obesity.* Paper presented at the meetings of the American Psychological Association, Toronto, Canada, August 1978.

Craighead, W. E. The role of muscular relaxation in systematic desensitization. In R. D. Rubin, J. P. Brady, & J. D. Henderson (Eds.), *Advances in behavior therapy* (Vol. 4). New York: Academic, 1973.

Craighead, W. E. Away from a unitary model of depression. *Behavior Therapy,* 1980, *11,* 123–129.

Craighead, W. E., & Mercatoris, M. The use of mentally retarded residents as paraprofessionals: A review. *American Journal of Mental Deficiency,* 1973, *78,* 339–347.

Craighead, W. E., Wilcoxon-Craighead, L., & Meyers, A. W. New directions in behavior modification with children. In M. Hersen, R. Eisler, & P. Miller (Eds.), *Progress in behavior modification* (Vol. 6). New York: Academic Press, 1978.

Creer, T. L., & Davis, M. H. Using a staggered-wakening procedure with enuretic children in an institutional setting. *Journal of Behavior Therapy and Experimental Psychiatry*, 1975, *6*, 23–25.

Crowley, T. J. The reinforcers for drug abuse: Why people take drugs. *Comprehensive Psychiatry*, 1972, *13*, 51–62.

Crump, S. L., Nunes, D. L., & Crossman, E. K. The effects of litter on littering behavior in a forest environment. *Environment and Behavior*, 1977, *9*, 137–146.

Culliton, B. J. Health care economics: The high cost of getting well. *Science*, 1968, *200*, 883–885.

Curran, J. P. An evaluation of a skills training program and a systematic desensitization program in reducing dating anxiety. *Behavior Research and Therapy*, 1975, *13*, 65–68.

Curran, J. P. Skills training as an approach to the treatment of heterosexual-social anxiety: A review. *Psychological Bulletin*, 1977, *84*, 140–157.

Curran, J. P., & Fischetti, M. Heterosexual-social anxiety. In R. Daitzman (Ed.), *Clinical behavior therapy and behavior modification*. New York: Garland, in press.

Curran, J. P., & Gilbert, F. S. A test of the relative effectiveness of a systematic desensitization program and an interpersonal skills training program with date anxious subjects. *Behavior Therapy*, 1975, *6*, 510–521.

Curran, J. P., Gilbert, F. S., & Little, L. M. A comparison between behavioral training and sensitivity training approaches to heterosexual dating anxiety. *Journal of Counseling Psychology*, 1976, *23*, 190–196.

Curran, D., & Parr, D. Homosexuality: An analysis of 100 male cases seen in private practice. *British Medical Journal*, 1957, *1*, 797–801.

Dahlkoetter, J., Callahan, E. J., & Linton, J. Obesity and the unbalanced energy equation: Exercise versus eating habit change. *Journal of Consulting and Clinical Psychology*, 1979, *47*, 898–905.

Danaher, B. G. Research on rapid smoking: Interim summary, and recommendations. *Addictive Behaviors*, 1977, *2*, 151–166.

Danaher, B. G., & Lichtenstein, E. *How to become an ex-smoker*. Englewood Cliffs, N.J.: Prentice-Hall, 1978.

Daniels, L. K. Parental treatment of hyperactivity in a child with ulcerative colitis. *Journal of Behavior Therapy and Experimental Psychiatry*, 1973, *4*, 183–185.

Davidson, W. S., & Robinson, M. J. Community psychology and behavior modification: A community-based program for the prevention of delinquency. *Journal of Corrective Psychiatry and Behavior Therapy*, 1975, *21*, 1–12.

Davis, J. M., Gosenfeld, L., & Tsai, C. C. Maintenance antipsychotic drugs do prevent relapse: A reply to Tobias and MacDonald. *Psychological Bulletin,* 1976, *83,* 431–447.

Davis, J. R., Wallace, C. J., Liberman, R. P., & Finch, B. E. The use of brief isolation to suppress delusional and hallucinatory speech. *Journal of Behavior Therapy and Experimental Psychiatry,* 1976, 7, 269–276.

Davis, W. M., & Smith, S. G. Role of conditioned reinforcers in the initiation, maintenance, and extinction of drug-seeking behavior. *Pavlovian Journal,* 1976, *11,* 222–236.

Davison, G. C. Systematic desensitization as a counterconditioning process. *Journal of Abnormal Psychology,* 1968, *73,* 91–99.

Davison, G. C. Appraisal of behavior modification techniques with adults in institutional settings. In C. M. Franks (Ed.), *Behavior therapy: Appraisal and status.* New York: McGraw-Hill, 1969.

Davison, G. C. Counter-control in behavior modification. In L. A. Hamerlynck, L. C. Handy, & E. J. Mash (Eds.), *Behavior change: Methodology, concepts and practice.* Champaign, Ill.: Research Press, 1973.

Davison, G. C., & Neale, J. M. *Abnormal psychology: An experimental clinical approach* (1st ed.). New York: Wiley, 1974.

Davison, G. C., & Neale, J. M. *Abnormal psychology: An experimental clinical approach* (2nd ed.). New York: Wiley, 1978.

Davison, G. C., & Valins, S. Maintenance of self-attributed and drug-attributed behavior change. *Journal of Personality and Social Psychology,* 1969, *11,* 25–33.

Davison, G. C., & Wilson, G. T. Critique of "Densensitization: Social and cognitive factors underlying the effectiveness of Wolpe's procedure." *Psychology Bulletin,* 1972, *78,* 28–31.

Davison, G. C., & Wilson, G. T. Processes of fear-reduction in systematic desensitization: Cognitive and social reinforcement factors in humans. *Behavior Therapy,* 1973, *4,* 1–21.

Dayan, M. Toilet training retarded children in a state residential institution. *Mental Retardation,* 1964, *2,* 116–117.

Deardorff, C. M., Melges, F. T., Hout, C. N., & Savage, D. J. Situations related to drinking: A factor analysis of questionnaire responses. *Journal of Studies on Alcohol,* 1975, *36,* 1184–1195.

De Carlis, P. "Dr. Dial" program of Oneida-Herkinier County Dental Society. *New York State Dental Journal,* 1973, *39,* 350–353.

De Lahunt, J., & Curran, J. P. Effectiveness of negative practice and self-control techniques in the reduction of smoking behavior. *Journal of Consulting and Clinical Psychology,* 1976, *44,* 1002–1007.

Dengrove, E. Behavior therapy of impotence. *Journal of Sex Research,* 1971, *7,* 177–183.

Dernbach, J. Michigan's bottle bill gives new momentum to national campaign. *Environment Action Bulletin,* April 30, 1977, 3–5.

Deslauriers, B. C., & Everett, P. B. Effects of intermittent and continuous token reinforcement on bus ridership. *Journal of Applied Psychology,* 1977, *62,* 369–375.

Detre, T. P., & Jarecki, H. G. *Modern psychiatric treatment.* Philadelphia: J. B. Lippincott, 1971.

Diehl, H. S. *Tobacco and your health: The smoking controversy.* New York: McGraw-Hill, 1969.

Dische, S. Treatment of enuresis with an enuresis alarm. In I. Kolvin, R. C. MacKeith, & S. R. Meadow (Eds.), *Bladder control and enuresis.* Philadelphia: Lippincott, 1973.

Dodge, M. C. *Modification of littering behavior: An exploratory study.* Masters Thesis, Utah State University, 1972. Reprinted by the Institute for the Study of Outdoor Recreation and Tourism, Logan, Utah.

Doherty, W. J., & Jacobson, N. S. Marriage and the family. In B. B. Wolman (Ed.), *Handbook of developmental psychology.* New York: Prentice-Hall, in press.

Doleys, D. Behavioral treatments for nocturnal enuresis in children: A review of the recent literature. *Psychological Bulletin,* 1977, *84,* 30–54.

Doleys, D. M. Assessment and treatment of childhood encopresis. In A. J. Finch & P. C. Kendall (Eds.), *Clinical treatment and research in child psychopathology.* New York: Spectrum Publications, 1979. (a)

Doleys, D. M. Assessment and treatment of childhood enuresis. In A. J. Finch & P. C. Kendall (Eds.), *Clinical treatment and research in child psychopathology.* New York: Spectrum Publications, 1979. (b)

Doleys, D. M., & Arnold, S. Treatment of childhood encopresis: Full cleanliness training. *Mental Retardation,* 1975, *13,* 14–16.

Doleys, D. M., & Ciminero, A. R. Clinical enuresis: Considerations in treatment. *Journal of Pediatric Psychology,* 1976, *4,* 21–23.

Doleys, D. M., Ciminero, A. R., Tollison, J. W., Williams, C. L., & Wells, K. C. Dry-bed training and retention control training: A comparison. *Behavior Therapy,* 1977, *8,* 541–548.

Doleys, S. M., Wells, K. C., Hobbs, S. A., Roberts, M. W., & Cartelli, L. M. The effects of social punishment on noncompliance: A comparison with timeout and positive practice. *Journal of Applied Behavior Analysis,* 1976, *9,* 471–482.

Dollar, M. L., & Sandell, P. J. Dental programs in schools. *Journal of School Health,* 1961, *31,* 3–15.

Donovan, D. M., Chaney, E. F., & O'Leary, M. R. Alcoholic MMPI subtypes:

Relationship to drinking styles, benefits, and consequences. *Journal of Nervous and Mental Disease,* 1978, *166,* 553–561.

Donovan, D. M., & Marlatt, G. A. Assessment of expectancies and behaviors associated with alcohol consumption: A cognitive-behavioral approach. *Journal of Studies on Alcohol,* in press.

Donovan, D. M., & O'Leary, M. R. Comparison of perceived and experienced control among alcoholics and nonalcoholics. *Journal of Abnormal Psychology,* 1975, *84,* 726–728.

Donovan, D. M., & O'Leary, M. R. The drinking-related locus of control scale: Reliability, factor structure and validity. *Journal of Studies on Alcohol,* 1978, *39,* 759–784.

Donovan, D. M., & O'Leary, M. R. Control orientation among alcoholics: A cognitive social learning perspective. *American Journal of Drug and Alcohol Abuse,* in press.

Douglas, V. I. Stop, look, and listen: The problem of sustained attention and impulse control in hyperactive and normal children. *Canadian Journal of Behavioral Science,* 1972, *4,* 259–282.

Douglas, V. I., Parry, P., Marton, P., & Garson, C. Assessment of a cognitive training program for hyperactive children. *Journal of Abnormal Child Psychology,* 1976, *4,* 389–410.

Drabman, R. S. Child versus teacher administered token programs in a psychiatric hospital school. *Journal of Abnormal Child Psychology,* 1973, *1,* 66–87.

Drabman, R. S., Cruz, G. C. Y., Ross, J., & Lynd, S. Suppression of chronic drooling in mentally retarded children and adolescents: Effectiveness of a behavioral treatment package. *Behavior Therapy,* 1979, *10,* 46–56.

Drabman, R. S., Hammer, D., & Rosenbaum, M. S. Assessing generalization in behavior modification with children: The generalization map. *Behavioral Assessment,* in press.

Drabman, R. S., & Lahey, B. B. Feedback in classroom behavior modification: Effects of the target child and her classmates. *Journal of Applied Behavior Analysis,* 1974, *1,* 591–598.

Drabman, R. S., Ross, J. M., Lynd, R. S., & Cordua, G. D. Retarded children as observers, mediators, and generalization programmers using an icing procedure. *Behavior Modification,* 1978, *2,* 371–385.

Drabman, R. S., & Spitalnik, R. Training a retarded child as a behavioral teaching assistant. *Journal of Behavior Therapy and Experimental Psychiatry,* 1973, *4,* 269–272.

Drabman, R. S., Spitalnik, R., & O'Leary, K. D. Teaching self-control to disruptive children. *Journal of Abnormal Psychology,* 1973, *82,* 10–16.

Drabman, R. S., Spitalnik, R., & Spitalnik, K. Sociometric and disruptive behavior as a function of four types of token economies. *Journal of Applied Behavior Analysis,* 1974, *7,* 93–101.

Drabman, R. S., & Tucker, R. Why classroom token economies fail. *Journal of School Psychology,* 1974, *12,* 178–188.

Droppa, D. C. Behavioral treatment of drug addiction: A review and analysis. *International Journal of the Addictions,* 1973, *8,* 143–161.

Dueker, K. J., & Levin, I. P. *Carpooling: Attitudes and participation.* Technical Report No. 81. Iowa City, Iowa: Center for Urban Transportation Studies, University of Iowa, 1976.

Duker, P. C., & Seys, D. M. Elimination of vomiting in a retarded female using restitutional overcorrection. *Behavior Therapy,* 1977, *8,* 255–257.

Dulany, D. E. Awareness, rules, and propositional control: A confrontation with S-R behavior theory. In T. R. Dixon & D. L. Horton (Eds.), *Verbal behavior and general behavior theory.* Englewood Cliffs, N.J.: Prentice-Hall, 1968.

D'Zurilla, T. J., & Goldfried, M. R. Problem solving and behavior modification. *Journal of Abnormal Psychology,* 1971, *78,* 107–126.

Eberhardy, F. The view from "the couch." *Journal of Child Psychology and Psychiatry,* 1967, *8,* 257–263.

Eddy, N. B., Halbach, H., Isbell, H., & Seevers, M. H. Drug dependence: Its significance and characteristics. In P. H. Blachly (Ed.), *Drug abuse: Data and debate.* Springfield, Ill.: Thomas, 1970.

Edwards, N. B. Case conference: Assertive training in a case of homosexual pedophilia. *Journal of Behavior Therapy and Experimental Psychiatry,* 1972, *3,* 55–63.

Eisler, R. M., Frederiksen, L. W., & Peterson, G. L. The relationship of cognitive variables to the expression of assertiveness. *Behavior Therapy,* 1978, *9,* 419–427.

Eisler, R. M., Hersen, M., Miller, P. M., & Blanchard, E. B. Situational determinants of assertive behaviors. *Journal of Counseling and Clinical Psychology,* 1975, *43,* 330–340.

Ellenberg, M. Impotence in diabetes. *Annals of Internal Medicine,* 1971, *75,* 213–219.

Ellis, A. *Reason and emotion in psychotherapy.* New York: Lyle-Stuart, 1962.

Ellis, A. *The essence of rational psychotherapy: A comprehensive approach to treatment.* New York: Institute for Rational Living, 1970.

Ellis, A. Rational-emotive treatment of impotence, frigidity and other sexual problems. *Professional Psychology,* 1971, *2,* 346–349.

Ellis, A., & Grieger, R. (Eds.). *Handbook of rational-emotive therapy.* New York: Springer, 1977.

Ellis, A., & Harper, R. A. *A guide to rational living.* Hollywood: Wilshire, 1961.

Ellis, A., & Whiteley, J. M. (Eds.). *Theoretical and empirical foundations of rational-emotive therapy.* Monterey, CA: Brooks/Cole, 1979.

Engle, K. B., & Williams, T. K. Effect of an ounce of vodka on alcoholics' desire for alcohol. *Quarterly Journal of Studies on Alcohol,* 1972, *33,* 1099–1105.

Ennis, B. J., & Friedman, P. R. (Eds.). *Legal rights of the mentally handicapped. Volumes 1 & 2.* Practicing Law Institute, The Mental Health Law Project, 1973.

Evans, I. M., & Nelson, R. O. Assessment of child behavior problems. In A. R. Ciminero, K. S. Calhoun, & H. E. Adams (Eds.), *Handbook of behavioral assessment.* New York: Wiley, 1977.

Everett, P. B. The use of the reinforcement procedure to increase bus ridership. *Proceedings of the 81st Annual Convention of the American Psychological Association,* 1973, *8*(2), 891–892.

Everett, P. B., Deslauriers, B. C., Newson, T., & Anderson, V. B. The differential effect of two free ride dissemination procedures on bus ridership. *Transportation Research,* 1978, *12,* 1–6.

Everett, P. B., Hayward, S. C., & Meyer, A. W. Effects of a token reinforcement procedure on bus ridership. *Journal of Applied Behavioral Analysis,* 1974, *7,* 1–9.

Evers, W. L., & Schwarz, J. C. Modifying social withdrawal in preschoolers: The effects of filmed modeling and teacher praise. *Journal of Abnormal Child Psychology,* 1973, *1,* 248–256.

Eyman, R. K., Tarjan, G., & Cassidy, M. Natural history of acquisition of basic skills by hospitalized retarded patients. *American Journal of Mental Deficiency,* 1970, *75,* 120–129.

Eysenck, H. J. (Ed.). *Behavior therapy and the neuroses.* New York: Pergamon, 1960.

Eysenck, H. J. *Experiments in behavior therapy.* New York: Pergamon, 1964.

Eysenck, H. J. *The effects of psychotherapy.* New York: International Science Press, 1966.

Eysenck, H. J. Expectations as causal elements in behavioural change. *Advances in Behaviour Research and Therapy,* 1978, *1,* 171–175.

Farquhar, J. W., Maccoby, N., Wood, P. D. Alexander, J. K., Breitrose, H., Brown, B. W., Jr., Haskell, W. L., McAlister, A. L., Meyer, A. J., Nash, J. D., & Stern, M. P. Community education for cardiovascular health. *Lancet,* 1977, 1192–1195.

Farrell, A. D., Mariotto, M. J., Conger, A. J., Curran, J. P., & Wallander, J. L. Self-ratings and judges' ratings of heterosexual-social anxiety and skill: A generalizability study. *Journal of Consulting and Clinical Psychology,* 1979, *47,* 164–175.

Feighner, J. P., Robins, E., Guze, S. B., Woodruff, R. A., Winokur, R. A., & Munoz, R. Diagnostic criteria for use in psychiatric research. *Archives of General Psychiatry,* 1972, *26,* 57–63.

Feldman, H. W. Ideological supports to becoming and remaining a heroin addict. In R. H. Coombs, L. J. Fry, & P. G. Lewis (Eds.), *Socialization in drug abuse.* Cambridge, Mass.: Schenkman Publishing Co., 1976.

Feldman, M. P., & MacCulloch, M. J. *Homosexual behavior: Therapy and assessment.* Oxford: Pergamon Press, 1971.

Feldman, M. P., MacCulloch, M. J., Mellor, V., & Pinschof, J. The application of anticipatory avoidance learning to the treatment of homosexuality: III. The sexual orientation method. *Behaviour Research and Therapy,* 1966, *4,* 289–299.

Ferguson, J. M. *Learning to eat: Behavior modification for weight control.* Palo Alto, Calif.: Ball, 1975.

Ferguson, R. H. *Unemployment: Its scope, measurement, and effect on poverty* (2nd ed.). Ithaca: New York State School of Industrial and Labor Relations, Cornell University, 1971.

Ferritor, D. E., Buckholdt, D., Hamblin, R. L., & Smith, L. The non-effects of contingent reinforcement for attending behavior on work accomplished. *Journal of Applied Behavior Analysis,* 1972, *5,* 7–18.

Ferster, C. B. Classification of behavioral pathology. In L. Krasner & L. P. Ullmann (Eds.), *Research in behavior modification.* New York: Holt, Rinehart & Winston, 1965.

Ferster, C. B., Nurnberger, J. I., & Levitt, E. B. The control of eating. *Journal of Mathetics,* 1962, *1,* 87–109.

Fichter, M. M., Wallace, C. J., Liberman, R. P., & Davis, J. R. Improving social interaction in a chronic psychotic using discriminated avoidance ("nagging"): Experimental analysis and generalization. *Journal of Applied Behavior Analysis,* 1976, *9,* 377–386.

Fiedler, D., & Beach, L. R. On the decision to be assertive. *Journal of Consulting and Clinical Psychology,* 1978, *46,* 537–546.

Finley, W. W., Besserman, R. L., Bennett, L. F., Clapp, R. K., & Finley, P. M. The effect of continuous, intermittent, and "placebo" reinforcement on the effectiveness of the conditioning treatment for enuresis nocturna. *Behavior Research and Therapy,* 1973, *11,* 289–297.

Finnie, W. C. Field experiments in litter control. *Environment and Behavior,* 1973, *5,* 123–144.

Fischer, J., & Gochros, D. S. W. (Eds.). *Handbook of behavior therapy with sexual problems. Volume 1, General Procedures.* New York: Pergamon Press, 1977.

Fischetti, M., Curran, J. P., & Wessberg, H. W. Sense of timing: A skill deficit in heterosexual-socially anxious males. *Behavior Modification,* 1977, *1,* 179–194.

Flanders, J. A review of research on imitative behavior. *Psychological Bulletin,* 1968, *69,* 316–337.

Flaxman, J. Quitting smoking. In W. E. Craighead, A. E. Kazdin, & M. J. Mahoney (Eds.), *Behavior modification: Principles, issues, and applications*. Boston: Houghton Mifflin, 1976.

Flaxman, J. Quitting smoking now or later: Gradual, abrupt, immediate, and delayed quitting. *Behavior Therapy*, 1978, *9*, 260–270.

Foa, E. B., & Goldstein, A. Continuous exposure and complete response prevention in the treatment of obsessive-compulsive neurosis. *Behavior Therapy*, 1978, *9*, 821–829.

Ford, J. D., & Hogan, D. R. *Assertiveness and social competence in the eye of the beholder*. Paper presented at the meeting of the Association for the Advancement of Behavior Therapy, Chicago, November 1978.

Forehand, R., & Baumeister, A. A. Deceleration of aberrant behavior among retarded individuals. In M. Hersen, R. M. Eisler, & P. M. Miller (Eds.), *Progress in behavior modification* (Vol. 2). New York: Academic Press, 1976.

Forehand, R., & King, H. E. Pre-school children's noncompliance: Effects of short-term therapy. *Journal of Community Psychology*, 1974, *2*, 42–44.

Forehand, R., & King, H. E. Noncompliant children: Effects of parent training on behavior and attitude change. *Behavior Modification*, 1977, *1*, 93–108.

Forehand, R., & Peed, S. Training parents to modify noncompliant behavior of their children. In A. J. Finch, Jr., & P. C. Kendall (Eds.), *Treatment and research in child psychopathology*. New York: Spectrum, 1979.

Foreyt, J. P. (Ed.). *Behavioral treatments of obesity*. New York: Pergamon Press, 1977.

Foreyt, J. P., & Rathjen, D. P. (Eds.). *Cognitive behavior therapy: Research and application*. New York: Plenum, 1978.

Foster, S. L. *Reducing family conflict: The impact of skill-training and generalization programming*. Paper presented at the meetings of the American Psychological Association, Toronto, September 1978.

Fowler, R. S., Fordyce, W. E., Boyd, V. D., & Masock, A. J. The mouthful diet: A behavioral approach to overeating. *Rehabilitation Psychologist*, 1972, *19*, 98–106.

Foxx, R. M., & Azrin, N. H. Restitution: A method of eliminating aggressive-disruptive behavior of retarded and brain damaged patients. *Behaviour Research and Therapy*, 1972, *10*, 15–27.

Foxx, R. M., & Azrin, N. H. The elimination of autistic self-stimulatory behavior by overcorrection. *Journal of Applied Behavior Analysis*, 1973, *6*, 1–14.

Foxx, R. M., & Hake, D. F. Gasoline conservation: A procedure for measuring and reducing the driving of college students. *Journal of Applied Behavioral Analysis*, 1977, *10*, 61–74.

Foxx, R. M., & Rubinoff, A. Behavioral treatment of caffeinism: Reducing excessive coffee drinking. *Journal of Applied Behavior Analysis*, 1979, *12*, 335–344.

Frank, C. W. The course of coronary heart disease: Factors relating to prognosis. *Bulletin of the New York Academy of Medicine,* 1968, *44,* 900–915.

Frank, E., Anderson, C., & Rubinstein, D. Frequency of sexual dysfunction in "normal" couples. *New England Journal of Medicine,* 1978, *299,* 111–115.

Frank, J. D. *Persuasion and healing* (2nd ed.). Baltimore: Johns Hopkins, 1973.

Frankel, A. S. Treatment of multisymptomatic phobia by a self-directed, self-reinforced technique. *Journal of Abnormal Psychology,* 1970, *76,* 496–499.

Frederiksen, L. W., & Williams, J. G. Individualized point systems with a chronic schizophrenic: Component analysis and management in the natural environment. *Journal of Behavior Therapy and Experimental Psychiatry,* 1977, *8,* 205–209.

Freeman Associates. *Public service advertising for the division of litter control.* Presentation to the Virginia Litter Control Board, Richmond, 1977.

Freeman, H. E., & Lambert, J. C. Preventive dental behavior of urban mothers. *Journal of Health and Human Behavior,* 1965, *6,* 141–147.

Freund, K. A laboratory method for diagnosing predominance of homo- or hetero-erotic interest in the male. *Behaviour Research and Therapy,* 1963, *1,* 85–93.

Freund, K. Diagnosing heterosexual pedophilia by means of a test for sexual interest. *Behaviour Research and Therapy,* 1965, *3,* 229–234.

Freund, K. Diagnosing homo- or heterosexuality and erotic age preference by means of a psychophysiological test. *Behaviour Research and Therapy,* 1967, *5,* 209–228.

Freund, K., Knob, K., & Sedlarcek, F. Simple transducer for mechanical plethysmography of the male genital. *Journal of the Experimental Analysis of Behavior,* 1965, *8,* 169–170.

Freund, K., Langevin, R., Cibiri, S., & Zajac, Y. Heterosexual aversion in homosexual males. *British Journal of Psychiatry,* 1973, *122,* 163–169.

Freund, K., McKnight, C. K., Langevin, R., & Cibiri, S. The female child as a surrogate object. *Archives of Sexual Behavior,* 1972, *2,* 119–133.

Freund, K., Nagler, E., Langevin, R., Zajac, A., & Steiner, B. Measuring feminine gender identity in homosexual males. *Archives of Sexual Behavior,* 1974, *3,* 249–261.

Friedman, M., & Rosenman, R. H. *Type A behavior and coronary heart disease.* New York: Random House, 1974.

Fuchs, C. Z., & Rehm, L. P. A self-control behavior therapy program for depression. *Journal of Consulting and Clinical Psychology,* 1977, *45,* 206–213.

Fullerton, D. T., Cayner, J. J., & McLaughlin-Reidel, T. Results of a token economy. *Archives of General Psychiatry,* 1978, *35,* 1451–1453.

Galassi, J. P., De Lo, J. S., Galassi, M. D., & Bastien, S. The college self-expression scale: A measure of assertiveness. *Behavior Therapy,* 1974, *5,* 165–171.

Galassi, J. P., & Galassi, M. D. Validity of a measure of assertiveness. *Journal of Counseling Psychology,* 1974, *21,* 248–250.

Galassi, J. P., & Galassi, M. D. Modification of heterosocial skills deficits. In A. S. Bellack & M. Herson (Eds.), *Research and practice in social skills training*. New York: Plenum Press, 1979.

Galassi, J. P., Galassi, M. D., & Litz, M. C. Assertive training in groups using video feedback. *Journal of Counseling Psychology*, 1974, *21*, 390–394.

Garber, J., & Hollon, S. D. Universal versus personal helplessness in depression: Belief in uncontrollability or incompetence? *Journal of Abnormal Psychology*, 1980, *89*, 56–66.

Garcia, E. E., & DeHaven, E. D. Use of operant techniques in the establishment and generalization of language: A review and analysis. *American Journal of Mental Deficiency*, 1974, *79*, 169–178.

Gardner, J. M. Teaching behavior modification to nonprofessionals. *Journal of Applied Behavior Analysis*, 1972, *5*, 517–521.

Garfield, S. L., & Bergin, A. E. (Eds.). *Handbook of psychotherapy and behavior change* (2nd ed.). New York: Wiley, 1978.

Garfield, S. L., & Kurtz, R. Clinical psychologists in the 1970's. *American Psychologist*, 1976, *31*, 1–9.

Garfield, Z. H., Darwin, P. L., Singer, B. A., & McBrearty, J. F. Effect of "in vivo" training on experimental desensitization of a phobia. *Psychological Reports*, 1967, *20*, 515–519.

Gatchel, R. J., & Price, K. P. (Eds.). *Clinical applications of biofeedback: Appraisal and status*. New York: Pergamon Press, 1979.

Gebhard, P. Factors in marital orgasm. *Journal of Social Issues*, 1966, *22*(2), 88–96.

Geer, J. H., & Turtletaub, A. Fear reduction following observation of a model. *Journal of Personality and Social Psychology*, 1967, *6*, 327–331.

Gelder, M. Behaviour therapy for neurotic disorders. *Behavior Modification*, 1979, *3*, 469–495.

Geller, E. S. Prompting anti-litter behaviors. *Proceedings of the 81st Annual Convention of the American Psychological Association*, 1973, *8*, 901–902. (Summary)

Geller, E. S. Applications of behavioral analysis for litter control. In D. Glenwick & L. Jason (Eds.), *Behavioral community psychology: Progress and prospects*. New York: Praeger Press, 1979.

Geller, E. S., Chaffee, J. L., & Ingram, R. E. Promoting paper-recycling on a university campus. *Journal of Environmental Systems*, 1975, *5*, 39–57.

Geller, E. S., Farris, J. C., & Post, D. S. Prompting a consumer behavior for consumer control. *Journal of Applied Behavior Analysis*, 1973, *6*, 367–376.

Geller, E. S., & Hayes, G. A. *Designing trash receptacles and ash trays for litter control*. Paper presented at the 1977 Congress for Recreation and Parks, Las Vegas, October 1977.

Geller, E. S., Mann, M., & Brasted, W. *Trash can design: A determinant of litter-related behavior.* Paper presented at the meeting of the American Psychological Association, San Francisco, August 1977.

Geller, E. S., Witmer, J. F., & Orebaugh, A. L. Instructions as a determinant of paper-disposal behaviors. *Environment and Behavior,* 1976, *8,* 417–438.

Geller, E. S., Wylie, R. C., & Farris, J. C. An attempt at applying prompting and reinforcement toward pollution control. *Proceedings of the 79th Annual Convention of the American Psychological Association,* 1971, *6,* 701–702. (Summary)

Gershone, J. R., Erickson, E. A., Mitchell, J. E., & Paulson, D. A. Behavioral comparison of a token economy and a standard psychiatric treatment ward. *Journal of Behavior Therapy and Experimental Psychiatry,* 1977, *8,* 381–385.

Gerst, M. D. Symbolic coding processes in observational learning. *Journal of Personality and Social Psychology,* 1971, *19,* 7–17.

Glass, C. R., Gottman, J. M., & Shmurak, S. H. Response acquisition and cognitive self-statement modification approaches in dating skills training. *Journal of Counseling Psychology,* 1976, *23,* 520–526.

Goffman, E. *Asylums.* New York: Doubleday, 1961.

Goldfried, M. R. Systematic desensitization as training in self-control. *Journal of Consulting and Clinical Psychology,* 1971, *37,* 228–234.

Goldfried, M. R., & Davison, G. C. (Eds.). *Clinical behavior therapy.* New York: Holt, Rinehart & Winston, 1976.

Goldfried, M. R., Decenteceo, E. T., & Weinberg, L. Systematic rational restructuring as a self-control technique. *Behavior Therapy,* 1974, *5,* 247–254.

Goldfried, M. R., & D'Zurilla, T. J. A behavioral-analytic model for assessing competence. In C. D. Spielberger (Ed.), *Current topics in clinical comments psychology* (Vol. 1). New York: Academic Press, 1969.

Goldfried, M. R., & Goldfried, A. P. Cognitive change methods. In F. H. Kanfer & A. P. Goldstein (Eds.), *Helping people change.* New York: Pergamon Press, 1975.

Goldfried, M. R., & Pomeranz, D. M. Role of assessment in behavior modification. *Psychological Reports,* 1968, *23,* 75–87.

Goldfried, M. R., & Sprafkin, J. M. *Behavioral personality assessment.* Morristown, N.J.: General Learning Press, 1974.

Goldiamond, I. Toward a constructional approach to social problems: Ethical and constitutional issues raised by applied behavior analysis. *Behaviorism,* 1974, *2,* 1–85.

Goldsmith, J. B., & McFall, R. M. Development and evaluation of an interpersonal skill-training program for psychiatric inpatients. *Journal of Abnormal Psychology,* 1975, *84,* 51–58.

Goldstein, A. J. Separate effects of extinction, counterconditioning and progressive approach in overcoming fear. *Behaviour Research and Therapy,* 1969, *1,* 47–56.

Goldstein, A. P., Heller, K., & Sechrest, L. B. *Psychotherapy and the psychology of behavior change*. New York: Wiley, 1966.

Goldstein, G., & Halperin, K. M. Neuropsychological differences among subtypes of schizophrenia. *Journal of Abnormal Psychology*, 1977, *86*, 34–40.

Gomes-Schwartz, B. The modification of schizophrenic behavior. *Behavior Modification*, 1979, *3*, 439–468.

Goodwin, S. E., & Mahoney, M. J. Modification of aggression through modeling: An experimental probe. *Journal of Behavior Therapy and Experimental Psychiatry*, 1975, *6*, 200–202.

Gordon, T., & Thom, T. The recent decrease in CHD mortality. *Preventive Medicine*, 1975, *4*, 115–125.

Gorton, C. E., & Hollis, J. H. Redesigning a cottage unit for better programming and research for the severely retarded. *Mental Retardation*, 1965, *3*, 16–21.

Gotestam, K. G., & Melin, L. A behavioral approach to drug abuse. *Drug and Alcohol Dependence*, 1980, *5*, 5–25.

Gottman, J. M. The effects of a modeling film on social isolation in preschool children: A methodological investigation. *Journal of Abnormal Child Psychology*, 1977, *5*, 69–78. (a)

Gottman, J. M. Toward a definition of social isolation in children. *Child Development*, 1977, *48*, 513–517. (b)

Gottman, J. M. *Marital interaction: Experimental investigations*. New York: Academic Press, 1979.

Gottman, J. M., Gonso, J., & Schuler, P. Teaching social skills to isolated children. *Journal of Abnormal Child Psychology*, 1976, *4*, 179–197.

Gottman, J. M., & Leiblum, S. R. *How to do psychotherapy and how to evaluate it*. New York: Holt, Rinehart & Winston, 1974.

Gottman, J. M., Markman, H., & Notarius, C. The topography of marital conflict: A sequential analysis of verbal and nonverbal behavior. *Journal of Marriage and the Family*, 1977, *39*, 461–477.

Graber, B., & Kline-Graber, G. Clitoral foreskin adhesions and female sexual function. *The Journal of Sex Research*, 1979, *15*, 205–212.

Graziano, A. M. Parents as behavior therapists. In M. Hersen, R. Eisler, & P. Miller (Eds.), *Progress in behavior modification* (Vol. 4). New York: Academic Press, 1977.

Graziano, A. M., DeGrovanni, I. S., & Garcia, K. A. Behavioral treatment of children's fears: A review. *Psychological Bulletin*, 1979, *86*, 804–830.

Green, A. H. Self-mutilation in schizophrenic children. *Archives of General Psychiatry*, 1967, *17*, 234–244.

Green, L. Temporal and stimulus factors in self-monitoring by obese persons. *Behavior Therapy*, 1978, *9*, 328–341.

Green, R., & Money, J. (Eds.). *Transsexualism and sex reassignment*. Baltimore: Johns Hopkins, 1969.

Greenberg, D. J., Scott, S. B., Pisa, A., & Friesen, D. D. Beyond the token economy: A comparison of two contingency programs. *Journal of Consulting and Clinical Psychology*, 1975, *43*, 498–503.

Greenberg, I., Altman, J. L., & Cole, J. O. Combination of drugs with behavior therapy. In M. Greenblatt (Ed.), *Drugs in combination with other therapies*. New York: Grune & Stratton, 1975.

Greene, B. F., Willis, B. S., Levy, R., & Bailey, J. S. Measuring client gains from staff-implemented programs. *Journal of Applied Behavior Analysis*, 1978, *11*, 395–412.

Greene, R. J., & Hoats, D. L. Aversive tickling: A simple conditioning technique. *Behavior Therapy*, 1971, *2*, 389–393.

Greene, R. J., Hoats, D. L., & Hornick, A. J. Music distortion: A new technique for behavior modification. *Psychological Record*, 1970, *20*, 107–109.

Greenwood, C., Hops, H., Delquardi, J., & Guild, J. Group contingencies for group consequences in classroom management: A further analysis. *Journal of Applied Behavior Analysis*, 1974, *7*, 413–425.

Grings, W., & Lockhart, R. Effects of "anxiety-lessening" instructions and differential set development on the extinction of GSR. *Journal of Experimental Psychology*, 1963, *66*, 292–299.

Grinker, R. A., Miller, J., Sabshin, M., Nunn, R., & Nunally, J. *The phenomenon of depressions*. New York: Hoeber, 1961.

Gruenberg, E. M. The social breakdown syndrome—some origins. *American Journal of Psychiatry*, 1967, *123*, 12–20.

Grunbaum, A. Causality and the science of human behavior. *American Scientist*, 1952, *40*, 665–676.

Gurman, A. S. Treatment of a case of public-speaking anxiety by *in vivo* desensitization and cue-controlled relaxation. *Journal of Behavior Therapy and Experimental Psychiatry*, 1973, *4*, 51–54.

Gurman, A. S., & Kniskern, D. P. Research in marital and family therapy: Progress, perspective, and prospect. In S. L. Garfield & A. E. Bergin (Eds.), *Handbook of psychotherapy and behavior change* (rev. ed.). New York: Wiley, 1979.

Hackett, G., & Horan, J. J. Behavioral control of cigarette smoking: A comprehensive program. *Journal of Drug Education*, 1977, *7*, 71–79.

Hackett, G., & Horan, J. J. Focused smoking: An unequivocably safe alternative to the rapid smoking procedure. *Journal of Drug Education*, 1978, *8*, 261–266.

Hackett, G., & Horan, J. J. Partial component analysis of a comprehensive smoking program. *Addictive Behaviors*, 1979, *4*, 259–262.

Hackett, G., Horan, J. J., Stone, C. I., Linberg, S. E., Nicholas, W. C., & Lukaski, H. C. Further outcomes and tentative predictor variables from an evolving comprehensive program for the behavioral control of smoking. *Journal of Drug Education*, 1977, *7*, 225–229.

Haefner, D. P. School dental health programs. *Health Education Monographs*, 1974, *2*, 212–219.

Hagen, R. L. Group therapy versus bibliotherapy in weight reduction. *Behavior Therapy*, 1974, *5*, 222–234.

Hagen, R. L., Foreyt, J. P., & Durham, T. W. The dropout problem: Reducing attrition in obesity research. *Behavior Therapy*, 1976, *7*, 463–471.

Hake, D. F., & Foxx, R. M. Promoting gasoline conservation: The effects of reinforcement schedules, a leader and self-recording. *Behavior Modification*, 1978, *2*, 339–369.

Hall, C. S., & Lindzey, G. *Theories of personality*. New York: Wiley, 1970.

Hall, R. V., & Broden, M. Behavior changes in brain injured children through social reinforcement. *Journal of Experimental Child Psychology*, 1967, *5*, 463–479.

Hall, R. V., Lund, D., & Jackson, D. Effects of teacher attention on study behavior. *Journal of Applied Behavior Analysis*, 1968, *1*, 1–12.

Hall, S. M., Hall, R. G., Borden, B. L., & Hanson, R. W. Follow up strategies in the behavioral treatment of overweight. *Behavior Research and Therapy*, 1975, *13*, 167–172.

Hall, S. M., Hall, R. G., DeBoer, G., & O'Kulitch, P. Self- and external management compared with psychotherapy in the control of obesity. *Behavior Research and Therapy*, 1977, *15*, 89–95.

Hall, S. M., Hall, R. G., Hanson, R. W., & Borden, B. L. Permanence of two self-managed treatments of overweight in university and community populations. *Journal of Consulting and Clinical Psychology*, 1974, *42*, 781–786.

Hall, R. G., Sachs, D. P. L., & Hall, S. M. Medical risk and therapeutic effectiveness of rapid smoking. *Behavior Therapy*, 1979, *10*, 249–259.

Halmi, K. A. Anorexia nervosa: Demographic and clinical features in 94 cases. *Psychosomatic Medicine*, 1974, *36*, 18–25.

Halmi, K. A., Powers, P., & Cunningham, S. Treatment of anorexia nervosa with behavior modification. *Archives of General Psychiatry*, 1975, *32*, 93–97.

Halzenbuehler, L. C., & Schoeder, H. E. Desensitization procedures in the treatment of childhood disorders. *Psychological Bulletin*, 1978, *85*, 831–844.

Hamburg, S. Behavior therapy in alcoholism: A critical review of broad-spectrum approaches. *Journal of Studies on Alcohol*, 1975, *36*, 69–87.

Hamilton, F., & Maisto, S. A. Assertive behavior and perceived discomfort of alcoholics in assertion-required situations. *Journal of Consulting and Clinical Psychology,* 1979, *47,* 196–197.

Hamilton, J., & Standahl, J. Suppression of stereotyped screaming behavior in a profoundly retarded institutionalized female. *Journal of Experimental Child Psychology,* 1969, *7,* 114–121.

Hamilton, J. W., & Stephens, L. Y. Reinstating speech in an emotionally disturbed, mentally retarded young woman. *Journal of Speech and Hearing Disorders,* 1967, *32,* 383–389.

Hamilton, J. W., Stephens, L., & Allen, P. Controlling aggressive and destructive behavior in severely retarded institutionalized residents. *American Journal of Mental Deficiency,* 1967, *71,* 852–856.

Hamilton, M. A rating scale for depression. *Journal of Neurology, Neurosurgery, and Psychiatry,* 1960, *23,* 56–61.

Hamilton, M., & Schroeder, H. E. A comparison of systematic desensitization and reinforced practice procedures in fear reduction. *Behaviour Research and Therapy,* 1973, *11,* 649–652.

Hammen, C. L., & Glass, D. R., Jr. Depression, activity, and evaluation of reinforcement. *Journal of Abnormal Psychology,* 1975, *84,* 718–721.

Hanf, C. *Modifying problem behaviors in mother-child interaction: Standardized laboratory situations.* Paper presented at the meetings of the Association of Behavior Therapies, Olympia, Washington, April 1968.

Hanf, C. *A two-stage program for modifying maternal controlling during mother-child (m-c) interaction.* Paper presented at the meetings of the Western Psychological Association, Vancouver, April 1969.

Hanson, R. W., Borden, B. L., Hall, S. M., & Hall, R. G. Use of programmed instruction in teaching self-management skills to overweight adults. *Behavior Therapy,* 1976, *7,* 366–373.

Harris, B. Whatever happened to little Albert? *American Psychologist,* 1979, *34,* 151–160.

Harris, F. R., Johnston, M. K., Kelley, C. S., & Wolf, M. M. Effects of positive social reinforcement on regressed crawling of a nursery school child. *Journal of Educational Psychology,* 1964, *55,* 35–41.

Harris, M. G. Self-directed program for weight control: A pilot study. *Journal of Abnormal Psychology,* 1969, *74,* 263–270.

Harris, M. B., & Hallbauer, E. S. Self-directed weight control through eating and exercise. *Behavior Research and Therapy,* 1973, *11,* 523–529.

Harris, S. L., & Ersner-Hershfield, R. Behavioral suppression of seriously disruptive behavior in psychotic and retarded patients: A review of punishment and its alternatives. *Psychological Bulletin,* 1978, *85,* 1352–1375.

Harris, S. L., & Romanczyk, R. G. Treating self-injurious behavior of a retarded child by overcorrection. *Behavior Therapy*, 1976, 7, 235–239.

Harris, S. L., & Wolchik, S. A. Suppression of self-stimulation: Three alternative strategies. *Journal of Applied Behavior Analysis*, 1979, 12, 185–198.

Hart, B. M., Reynolds, N. J., Baer, D. M., Brawley, E. R., & Harris, F. R. Effects of contingent and non-contingent social reinforcement on cooperative play of a preschool child. *Journal of Applied Behavior Analysis*, 1968, 1, 73–76.

Hartman, W. E., & Fithian, M. A. *Treatment of sexual dysfunction*. Long Beach, Calif.: Center for Marital and Sexual Studies, 1972.

Hastings, D. W. *Impotence and frigidity*. Boston: Little, Brown, 1963.

Haughton, E., & Ayllon, T. Production and elimination of symptomatic behavior. In L. P. Ullmann & L. Krasner (Eds.), *Case studies in behavior modification*. New York: Holt, Rinehart & Winston, 1965.

Hayes, S. C., & Cone, J. D. Reducing residential electricity energy use: Payments, information, and feedback. *Journal of Applied Behavior Analysis*, 1977, 10, 425–435.

Hays, W. L. *Statistics for psychologists*. New York: Holt, Rinehart & Winston, 1963.

Hayward, S. C., & Everett, P. B. *A failure of response cost feedback to modify car driving behavior*. Paper presented at the Annual Meeting of the Midwestern Association of Behavioral Analysis, Chicago, Ill., May 1976.

Hazard, J. L. Energy and transportation. *Phi Kappa Phi Journal*, 1975, Winter, 38–41.

Health consequences of smoking. U.S. Public Health Service. (Publication No. 1696). Washington, D.C.: U.S. Government Printing Office, 1975.

Heberlein, T. A. Conservation information: The energy crisis and electricity consumption in an apartment complex. *Energy Systems and Policy*, 1975, 1, 105–117.

Heiman, J., LoPiccolo, L., & LoPiccolo, J. *Becoming orgasmic: A sexual growth program for women*. Englewood Cliffs, N.J.: Prentice-Hall, 1976.

Heiman, J. R., LoPiccolo, L., & LoPiccolo, J. The treatment of sexual dysfunction. In A. S. Gurman & D. P. Kniskern (Eds.), *Handbook of family therapy*. New York: Brunner/Mazel, 1979.

Hekimian, L. J., & Gershon, S. Characteristics of drug abusers admitted to a psychiatric hospital. *Journal of the American Medical Association*, 1968, 205, 125–130.

Henricksen, K., & Doughty, R. Decelerating undesired mealtime behavior in a group of profoundly retarded boys. *American Journal of Mental Deficiency*, 1967, 72, 40–44.

Herman, S. H., Barlow, D. H., & Agras, W. S. An experimental analysis of exposure to "explicit" heterosexual stimuli as an effective variable in changing arousal patterns of homosexuals. *Behavior Research and Therapy*, 1974, 12, 335–345.

Herman, S. H., & Tramontana, J. Instructions and group versus individual reinforcement in modifying disruptive group behavior. *Journal of Applied Behavior Analysis*, 1971, 4, 113–119.

Hersen, M. Token economies in institutional settings: Historical, political, deprivation, ethical and generalization issues. *Journal of Nervous and Mental Disease,* 1976, *162,* 206–211.

Hersen, M. Limitations and problems in the clinical application of behavioral techniques in psychiatric settings. *Behavior Therapy,* 1979, *10,* 65–80.

Hersen, M., & Barlow, D. H. *Single case experimental designs: Strategies for studying behavior change.* New York: Pergamon Press, 1976.

Hersen, M., & Bellack, A. S. A multiple-baseline analysis of social-skills training in chronic schizophrenics. *Journal of Applied Behavior Analysis,* 1976, *9,* 239–245. (a)

Hersen, M., & Bellack, A. S. Social skills training for chronic psychiatric patients: Rationale, research findings, and future directions. *Comprehensive Psychiatry,* 1976, *17,* 559–580. (b)

Hersen, M., & Bellack, A. S. Assessment of social skills. In A. R. Ciminero, K. S. Calhoun, H. E. Adams (Eds.), *Handbook for behavioral assessment.* New York: Wiley, 1977.

Hersen, M., & Bellack, A. S. (Eds.). *Behavior therapy in the psychiatric setting.* Baltimore: Williams & Wilkins, 1978.

Hersen, M., Eisler, R. M., Miller, P. M., Johnson, M. B., & Pinkston, S. G. Effects of practice, instructions, and modeling on components of assertive behavior. *Behaviour Research and Therapy,* 1973, *11,* 443–451.

Hersen, M., Eisler, R. M., Smith, B. S., & Agras, W. S. A token reinforcement ward for young psychiatric patients. *American Journal of Psychiatry,* 1972, *129,* 142–147.

Higgins, G. Aspects of sexual response in spinal cord injured adults. In J. LoPiccolo & L. LoPiccolo (Eds.), *Handbook of sex therapy.* New York: Plenum Press, 1978.

Higgins, R. L., Alonso, R. R., & Pendleton, M. G. The validity of role-play assessments of assertiveness. *Behavior Therapy,* 1979, *10,* 655–662.

Higgins, R. L., & Marlatt, G. A. Fear of interpersonal evaluation as a determinant of alcohol consumption in male social drinkers. *Journal of Abnormal Psychology,* 1975, *84,* 644–651.

Hilgard, E. G., & Bower, G. H. *Theories of learning.* New York: Appleton-Century-Crofts, 1966.

Hirst, E. Transportation energy conservation policies. *Science,* 1976, *192*(4234), 15–20.

Hobbs, S., & Forehand, R. Important parameters in the use of timeout with children: A re-examination. *Journal of Behavior Therapy and Experimental Psychiatry,* 1977, *8,* 365–370.

Hoffman, H. Personality measurement for the evaluation and prediction of alcoholism. In R. E. Tarter & A. A. Sugerman (Eds.), *Alcoholism: Interdisciplinary approaches to an enduring problem.* Reading, Mass.: Addison-Wesley, 1976.

Hogan, D. R. The effectiveness of sex therapy: A review of the literature. In J. LoPiccolo & L. LoPiccolo (Eds.), *Handbook of sex therapy*. New York: Plenum Press, 1978.

Holland, J. Ethical considerations in behavior modification. In M. Shore & S. Golann (Eds.), *Current issues in mental health*. Rockville, Md.: National Institute of Mental Health, DHEW Publication No. (HSM) 73–9029, 1973.

Holland, J. Behaviorism: Part of the problem or part of the solution? *Journal of Applied Behavior Analysis,* 1978, *11,* 163–174.

Holland, J. G., & Skinner, B. F. *The analysis of behavior.* New York: McGraw-Hill, 1961.

Hollingsworth, R., & Foreyt, J. P. Community adjustment of released token economy patients. *Journal of Behavior Therapy and Experimental Psychiatry,* 1975, *6,* 271–274.

Hollis, J. H., & Gorton, C. E. Training severely and profoundly developmentally retarded children. *Mental Retardation,* 1967, *5,* 20–24.

Hollon, S. D., & Beck, A. T. Psychotherapy and drug therapy: Comparisons and combinations. In S. L. Garfield & A. F. Bergin (Eds.), *The handbook of psychotherapy and behavior change* (2nd ed.). New York: Wiley, 1979.

Holroyd, K. A. Cognition and desensitization in the group treatment of test anxiety. *Journal of Consulting and Clinical Psychology,* 1976, *44,* 991–1001.

Holt, G. L. Effect of reinforcement contingencies in increasing programmed reading and mathematics behaviors in first grade children. *Journal of Experimental Child Psychology,* 1971, *12,* 362–369.

Homme, L. E. Perspectives in psychology, XXIV: Control of coverants, the operants of the mind. *Psychological Record,* 1965, *15,* 501–511.

Hoon, E. F., Hoon, P. W., & Wincze, J. The S.A.I.: An inventory for the measurement of female sexual arousal. *Archives of Sexual Behavior,* 1976, *5,* 208–215.

Horan, J. J. Self-help for smokers: Review of O. F. Pomerleau, *Break the smoking habit. Personnel and Guidance Journal,* 1978, *57,* 63.

Horan, J. J., Baker, S. B., Hoffman, A. M., & Shute, R. E. Weight loss through variations in the coverant control paradigm. *Journal of Consulting and Clinical Psychology,* 1975, *43,* 68–72.

Horan, J. J., Hackett, G., & Linberg, S. E. Factors to consider when using expired air carbon monoxide in smoking assessment. *Addictive Behaviors,* 1978, *3,* 25–28.

Horan, J. J., Hackett, G., Nicholas, W. C., Linberg, S. E., Stone, C. I., & Lukaski, H. C. Rapid smoking: A cautionary note. *Journal of Consulting and Clinical Psychology,* 1977, *45,* 341–343.

Horan, J. J., & Johnson, R. G. Coverant conditioning through a self-management application of the Premack principle: Its effect on weight reduction. *Journal of Behavior Therapy and Experimental Psychiatry*, 1971, *2*, 243–249.

Horan, J. J., Linberg, S. E., & Hackett, G. Nicotine poisoning and rapid smoking. *Journal of Consulting and Clinical Psychology*, 1977, *45*, 344–347.

Horan, J. J., Linberg, S. E., & Hackett, G. Reply to Russell and associates on the rapid smoking–nicotine level issue. *Journal of Consulting and Clinical Psychology*, 1980, *48*, 113–114.

Houten, R. V., Morrison, E., Jarvis, R., & McDonald, M. The effects of explicit timing and feedback on compositional response rate in elementary school children. *Journal of Applied Behavior Analysis*, 1974, *7*, 547–555.

Huba, G. J., Wingard, J. A., & Bentler, P. M. Beginning adolescent drug use and peer and adult interaction patterns. *Journal of Consulting and Clinical Psychology*, 1979, *47*, 265–276.

Hull, C. L. *Principles of behavior*. New York: Appleton-Century-Crofts, 1943.

Humphreys, L., Forehand, R., Cheney, T., & Adams, S. V. Training retarded individuals in communication skills: An experimental program. *Journal of Clinical Child Psychology*, 1977, *6*, 33–37.

Hunt, G. A., & Azrin, N. H. A community reinforcement approach to alcoholism. *Behaviour Research and Therapy*, 1973, *11*, 91–104.

Hunt, J. McV. *Intelligence and experience*. New York: Ronald, 1961.

Hunt, M. *Sexual behavior in the 70's*. Chicago: Playboy Press, 1974.

Hunt, W. A., Barnett, L. W., & Branch, L. G. Relapse rates in addiction programs. *Journal of Clinical Psychology*, 1971, *27*, 455–456.

Hunt, W. A., & Matarazzo, J. D. Three years later: Recent developments in the experimental modification of smoking behavior. *Journal of Abnormal Psychology*, 1973, *81*, 107–114.

Husted, J. R. Effect of method of systematic desensitization and presence of sexual communication in the treatment of sexual anxiety by counterconditioning. *Proceedings of the 80th Annual Convention of the American Psychological Association*, 1972, *7*, 325–326.

Ikard, F. F., Green, D. E., & Horn, D. A scale to differentiate between types of smoking as related to the management of affect. *International Journal of Addictions*, 1969, *4*, 649–659.

Intagliata, J. C. Increasing the interpersonal problem-solving skills of an alcoholic population. *Journal of Consulting and Clinical Psychology*, 1978, *46*, 489–498.

Irwin, S. Drugs of abuse: An introduction to their actions and potential hazards. *Journal of Psychedelic Drugs*, 1971, *3*, 5–15.

Isbell, H. Craving for alcohol. *Quarterly Journal of Studies on Alcohol*, 1955, *16*, 38–42.

Israel, A. C., & Saccone, A. J. Follow-up effects of mediator and target of reinforcement on weight loss. *Behavior Therapy*, 1979, *10*, 260–265.

Iwata, B., & Bailey, J. Reward versus cost token systems: An analysis of the effects on students and teacher. *Journal of Applied Behavior Analysis,* 1974, *7,* 567–576.

Iwata, B. A., Bailey, J. S., Brown, K., Foshee, J., & Alpern, M. Modification of institutional staff behavior using a performance-based lottery. *Journal of Applied Behavior Analysis,* 1976, *9,* 417–431.

Iwata, B. A., & Becksfort, C. M. Behavioral research in preventive dentistry: Compliance with personal hygiene regimens via educational and contingency management techniques. *Journal of Applied Behavior Analysis,* in press.

Jackson, J. L., & Calhoun, K. S. Effects of two variable-ratio schedules of timeout: Changes in target and non-target behaviors. *Journal of Behavior Therapy and Experimental Psychiatry,* 1977, *8,* 195–199.

Jacobs, J. W., & Lewis, M. H. Teaching self-help skills to retarded children. In A. J. Finch & P. C. Kendall (Eds.), *Clinical treatment and research in child psychopathology.* New York: Spectrum, 1979.

Jacobson, E. The electrophysiology of mental activities. *American Journal of Psychology,* 1932, *44,* 677–694.

Jacobson, E. *Progressive relaxation.* Chicago: University of Chicago Press, 1938.

Jacobson, N. S. Problem solving and contingency contracting in the treatment of marital discord. *Journal of Consulting and Clinical Psychology,* 1977, *45,* 92–100.

Jacobson, N. S. Specific and nonspecific factors in the effectiveness of a behavioral approach to the treatment of marital discord. *Journal of Consulting and Clinical Psychology,* 1978, *46,* 442–452.

Jacobson, N. S. Behavioral treatments for marital discord: A critical appraisal. In M. Hersen, R. M. Eisler, & P. M. Miller (Eds.), *Progress in behavior modification.* New York: Academic Press, 1979. (a)

Jacobson, N. S. Increasing positive behavior in severely distressed adult relationships. *Behavior Therapy,* 1979, *10,* 311–326. (b)

Jacobson, N. S. Marital problems: Direct strategies for inducing compliance. In J. J. Shelton & R. Levy (Eds.), *Systematic behavior assignments.* Champaign, Ill.: Research Press, in press.

Jacobson, N. S., Elwood, R., & Dallas, M. Assessment of marital dysfunction. In D. H. Barlow (Ed.), *Behavioral assessment of adult disorders.* New York: Guilford Press, in press.

Jacobson, N. S., & Margolin, G. *Marital therapy: Strategies based on social learning and behavior exchange principles.* New York: Brunner/Mazel, 1979.

Jacobson, N. S., Waldron, H., & Moore, D. Toward a behavioral profile of marital distress. *Journal of Consulting and Clinical Psychology,* in press.

Jarvick, M. E. Biological factors underlying the smoking habit. In M. E. Jarvik, J. W. Cullen, E. R. Gritz, T. M. Vogh, & L. J. West (Eds.), *Research on smoking behavior.* NIDA Research Monograph No. 17, December 1977, pp. 122–148. U.S. Dept. of

Health, Education, & Welfare, Public Health Service, Alcohol, Drug Abuse, and Mental Health Administration, National Institute on Drug Abuse, DHEW Publication No. (ADM) 78–581.

Jason, L. Behavioral community psychology: Conceptualizations and applications. *Journal of Community Psychology*, 1977, *5*, 302–312.

Jason, L. A., & Clay, R. Modifying smoking behaviors in a barber shop. *Man-Environment Systems*, 1978, *8*, 38–40.

Jason, L. A., Clay, R., & Martin, M. Reducing cigarette smoke in supermarkets and elevators. *Journal of Environmental Systems*, 1979–1980, *9*, 57–66.

Jason, L. A., & Savio, D. Reducing cigarette smoke in an office setting. *Health Values*, 1978, *2*, 180–185.

Jeffery, C. R. *Crime prevention through experimental design.* Beverly Hills, Calif.: Sage, 1977.

Jeffrey, D. B. A comparison of the effects of external and self-control on the modification and maintenance of weight. *Journal of Abnormal Psychology*, 1974, *83*, 404–410.

Jeffrey, D. B., & Katz, R. C. *Take it off and keep it off.* Englewood Cliffs, N.J.: Prentice-Hall, 1977.

Jeffery, R. W., & Wing, R. R. Frequency of therapist contact in the treatment of obesity. *Behavior Therapy*, 1979, *10*, 186–192.

Jeffery, R. W., Wing, R. R., & Stunkard, A. J. Behavioral treatment of obesity: The state of the art in 1976. *Behavior Therapy*, 1978, *9*, 189–199.

Jellinek, E. M. *The disease concept of alcoholism.* New Brunswick, N.J.: Hillhouse Press, 1960.

Jesness, C. F. Comparative effectiveness of behavior modification and transactional analysis programs with delinquents. *Journal of Consulting and Clinical Psychology*, 1975, *43*, 758–779.

Jesness, C. F. The youth center project: Transactional analysis and behavior modification programs for delinquents. *Behavioral Disorders*, 1976, *1*, 27–36.

Jesness, C. F., & DeRisi, W. Some variations in techniques of contingency management in a school for delinquents. In J. S. Stumphauzer (Ed.), *Behavior therapy with delinquents.* Springfield, Ill.: Charles C. Thomas, 1973.

Johansson, C. R. Tobacco smoke in room air—An experimental investigation of odor perception and irritating effects. *Building Services Engineer*, 1976, *43*, 254–262.

Johnson, E. H. *Crime, correction, and society.* Homewood, Ill.: Dorsey Press, 1964.

Johnson, S. B., & Melamed, B. G. The assessment and treatment of children's fears. In B. Lahey & A. Kazdin (Eds.), *Advances in child clinical psychology* (Vol. 2). New York: Plenum Press, 1979.

Johnson, W. L., & Baumeister, A. A. Self-injurious behavior: A review and analysis of methodological details of published studies. *Behavior Modification*, 1978, *2*, 465–487.

Johnston, M. K., Kelly, C. S., Harris, F. R., & Wolf, M. M. An application of reinforcement principles to development of motor skills of a young child. *Child Development*, 1966, *37*, 379–387.

Joint Commission on Mental Health and Illness. *Action for mental health*. New York: Wiley, 1961.

Jones, B., & Derby, J. Sacramento car-pool project: Interim evaluation report. *Transportation Research Record*, 1976, No. 619, 38–42.

Jones, M. C. A laboratory study of fear: The case of Peter. *Journal of Genetic Psychology*, 1924, *31*, 308–315. (a)

Jones, M. C. The elimination of children's fears. *Journal of Experimental Psychology*, 1924, *7*, 383–390. (b)

Jones, R. R., Vaught, R. S., & Weinrott, M. *Visual versus statistical inference in operant research*. Paper presented at American Psychological Association, Chicago, August 1975.

Kagan, J. Reflection-impulsivity: The generality and dynamics of conceptual tempo. *Journal of Abnormal Psychology*, 1966, *71*, 17–24.

Kagan, J., Pearson, L., & Welch, L. Modifiability of an impulsive tempo. *Journal of Educational Psychology*, 1966, *57*, 359–365.

Kagel, J. H., Battalio, R. C., Winkler, R. C., & Winett, R. A. *Energy conservation strategies: An evaluation of the effectiveness of price changes and information on household-demand for electricity*. Unpublished manuscript, Texas A. & M. University, 1976.

Kahn, H. A. The Dorn study of smoking and mortality among U.S. veterans: Report on eight and one-half years of observation. *National Cancer Institute Monograph*, 1966, *19*, 1–125.

Kanfer, F. H. Vicarious human reinforcements: A glimpse into the black box. In L. Krasner & L. P. Ullmann (Eds.), *Research in behavior modification*. New York: Holt, Rinehart & Winston, 1965.

Kanfer, F. H., & Karoly, P. Self-control: A behavioristic excursion into the lion's den. *Behavior Therapy*, 1972, *3*, 398–416.

Kanfer, F. H., Karoly, P., & Newman, A. *Journal of Consulting and Clinical Psychology*, 1975, *43*, 251–258.

Kanfer, F. H., & Phillips, J. S. *Learning foundations of behavior therapy*. New York: Wiley, 1970.

Kanfer, F. H., & Saslow, G. Behavioral diagnosis. In C. M. Franks (Ed.), *Behavior therapy: Appraisal and status*. New York: McGraw-Hill, 1969.

Kannel, W. B., & Gordon, T. (Eds.). *The Framingham study: An epidemiological investigation of cardiovascular disease*. Section 30. Some characteristics related to the incidence of cardiovascular disease and death: Framingham study, 18 year follow-up. DHEW Publication No. (NIH) 74–599. Superintendent of Documents Stock 1740–00379. Washington, D.C.: U.S. Government Printing Office, 1974.

Kannel, W. B., & Gordon, T. Physiological and medical concomitants of obesity: The Framingham study. In G. A. Bray (Ed.), *Obesity in America*. Washington, D.C.: U.S. Department of Health, Education, and Welfare, NIH Publication No. 79–359, 1979.

Kaplan, H. *The new sex therapy*. New York: Brunner/Mazel, 1974.

Kaplan, H. B., & Meyerowitz, J. H. Social and psychological correlates of drug abuse: A comparison of addict and non-addict populations from the perspective of self-theory. *Social Science and Medicine*, 1970, *40*, 203–225.

Kaplan, H. S., Kohl, R. N., Pomeroy, W. B., Offit, A. K., & Hogan, B. Group treatment of premature ejaculation. *Archives of Sexual Behavior*, 1974, *3*, 443–452.

Katell, A., Callahan, E. J., Fremouw, W. J., & Zilterer, R. E. The effects of behavioral treatment and fasting on eating behaviors and weight loss: A case study. *Behavior Therapy*, 1979, *10*, 579–587.

Kaufman, A., Baron, A., & Kopp, R. E. Some effects of instructions on human operant behavior. *Psychonomic Monograph Supplements*, 1966, *1*, 243–250.

Kaufman, K. F., & O'Leary, K. D. Reward, cost, and self-evaluation procedures for disruptive adolescents in a psychiatric hospital school. *Journal of Applied Behavior Analysis*, 1972, *5*, 293–309.

Kaufman, M. E. The effects of institutionalization on development of stereotyped and social behaviors in mental defectives. *American Journal of Mental Deficiency*, 1967, *71*, 581–585.

Kaufman, M. E., & Levitt, H. A. study of three stereotyped behaviors in institutionalized mental defectives. *American Journal of Mental Deficiency*, 1965, *69*, 467–473.

Kazdin, A. E. Case histories and shorter communications: Nonresponsiveness of patients to token economies. *Behavior Research and Therapy*, 1972, *10*, 417–418.

Kazdin, A. E. The failure of some patients to respond to token programs. *Behavior Therapy and Experimental Psychiatry*, 1973, *4*, 7–14. (a)

Kazdin, A. E. Methodological and assessment considerations in evaluating reinforcement programs in applied settings. *Journal of Applied Behavior Analysis*, 1973, *6*, 517–531. (b)

Kazdin, A. E. Role of instructions and reinforcement in behavior changes in token reinforcement programs. *Journal of Educational Psychology*, 1973, *64*, 63–71. (c)

Kazdin, A. E. The effect of vicarious reinforcement on attentive behavior in the classroom. *Journal of Applied Behavior Analysis*, 1973, *6*, 71–78. (d)

Kazdin, A. E. Statistical analyses for single-case experimental designs. In M. Hersen & D. H. Barlow (Eds.), *Single-case experimental designs: Strategies for studying behavior change*. New York: Pergamon Press, 1976.

Kazdin, A. E. Assessing the clinical or applied significance of behavior change through social validation. *Behavior Modification,* 1977, *1*, 427–452. (a)

Kazdin, A. E. *The token economy: A review and evaluation*. New York: Plenum Press, 1977. (b)

Kazdin, A. E. Chronic psychiatric patients: Ward-wide reinforcement programs. In M. Hersen & A. S. Bellack (Eds.), *Behavior therapy in the psychiatric setting*. Baltimore: Williams & Wilkins, 1978. (a)

Kazdin, A. E. Conceptual and assessment issues raised by self-efficacy theory. *Advances in Behaviour Research and Therapy,* 1978, *1*, 177–185. (b)

Kazdin, A. E. *History of behavior modification: Experimental foundations of contemporary research*. Baltimore: University Park Press, 1978. (c)

Kazdin, A. E. Vicarious reinforcement and punishment in operant programs for children. *Child Behavior Therapy,* 1979, *1*, 13–36.

Kazdin, A. E. *Behavior modification in applied settings* (2nd ed.). Homewood, Ill.: Dorsey Press, 1980. (a)

Kazdin, A. E. *Research design in clinical psychology*. New York: Harper & Row, 1980. (b)

Kazdin, A. E., & Bootzin, R. R. The token economy: An evaluative review. *Journal of Applied Behavior Analysis,* 1972, *5*, 343–372.

Kazdin, A. E., & Wilcoxon, L. A. Systematic desensitization and nonspecific treatment effects: A methodological evaluation. *Psychological Bulletin,* 1976, *83*, 729–758.

Keep America Beautiful, Inc. *Fact sheet: Litter is a national disgrace*. 99 Park Avenue, New York, N.Y. 10016, 1970.

Keesey, R. E. Set-points and body weight regulation. *Psychiatric Clinics of North America,* 1978, *1*, 523–544.

Kegel, A. W. Sexual functions of the pubococcygens muscle. *Western Journal of Obstetrics and Gynecology,* 1952, *60*, 521.

Kelly, J. A., Furman, W., Phillips, J., Hathorn, S., & Wilson, T. Teaching conversational skills to retarded adolescents. *Child Behavior Therapy,* 1979, *1*, 85–97.

Kendall, P. C., & Finch, A. J., Jr. A cognitive behavioral treatment for impulse control: A case study. *Journal of Consulting and Clinical Psychology,* 1976, *44*, 852–857.

Kendall, P. C., & Finch, A. J., Jr. A cognitive-behavioral treatment for impulsivity: A group comparison study. *Journal of Consulting and Clinical Psychology*, 1978, *46*, 110–118.

Kendall, P. C., & Finch, A. J. Developing nonimpulsive behavior in children: Cognitive-behavioral strategies for self-control. In P. C. Kendall & S. D. Hollon (Eds.), *Cognitive-behavioral interventions: Theory, research, and procedures.* New York: Academic Press, 1979.

Kendall, P. C., & Hollon, S. D. (Eds.). *Cognitive-behavioral interventions: Theory, research, and procedures.* New York: Academic Press, 1979.

Kendall, P. C., & Korgeski, G. P. Assessment and cognitive-behavioral interventions. *Cognitive Therapy and Research*, 1979, *3*, 1–21.

Kendall, P. C., & Urbain, E. Social-cognitive approaches to therapy with children. In J. Lackenmeyer & M. Gibbs (Eds.), *Psychology of the abnormal child.* New York: Gardner Press, in press.

Kendall, P. C., & Wilcox, L. E. Self-control in children: Development of a rating scale. *Journal of Consulting and Clinical Psychology*, 1979, *47*, 1020–1029.

Kendall, P. C., Yellin, A., & Greenberg, L. M. *Cognitive-behavioral therapy and methylphenidate with hyperactive children: Preliminary comparisons.* Manuscript submitted for publication, University of Minnesota, 1979.

Kennedy, W. School phobia: Rapid treatment of fifty cases. *Journal of Abnormal Psychology*, 1965, *70*, 285–289.

Kepner, E. Application of learning theory to the etiology and treatment of alcoholism. *Quarterly Journal of Studies on Alcohol*, 1964, *25*, 279–291.

Kifer, R. E., Lewis, M. A., Green, D. R., & Phillips, E. L. Training predelinquent youths and their parents to negotiate conflict situations. *Journal of Applied Behavior Analysis*, 1974, *7*, 357–364.

Kimble, G. A. *Hilgard and Marquis' conditioning and learning.* New York: Appleton-Century-Crofts, 1961.

Kimmel, H. D. Instrumental conditioning of autonomically mediated behavior. *Psychological Bulletin*, 1967, *67*, 337–345.

Kimmel, H. D. Instrumental conditioning of autonomically mediated responses in human beings. *American Psychologist*, 1974, *29*, 325–335.

Kingham, R. J. Alcoholism and the reinforcement theory of learning. *Quarterly Journal of Studies on Alcohol*, 1958, *19*, 320–330.

Kingsley, R. G., & Wilson, G. T. Behavior therapy for obesity: A comparative investigation of long-term efficacy. *Journal of Consulting and Clinical Psychology*, 1977, *45*, 288–298.

Kinsey, A. C., Pomeroy, W. B., & Martin, C. E. *Sexual behavior in the human male.* Philadelphia: W. B. Saunders, 1948.

Kirigin, K. A., Wolf, M. M., Braukmann, C. J., Fixsen, D. L., & Phillips, E. L.

Achievement place: A preliminary outcome evaluation. In J. S. Stumphauzer (Ed.), *Progress in behavior therapy with delinquents*. Springfield, Ill.: Charles C. Thomas, 1979.

Kirschenbaum, D. S., Bane, S., Fowler, R., Klei, B., Kuhkendahl, K., Marsh, M. E., & Pedro, J. L. *Social skills development program: Handbook for helping*. Cincinnati: Cincinnati Health Department, 1976.

Kirschenbaum, D. S., Pedro, J. L., & DeVoge, J. B. A social competency model meets an early intervention program: Description and evaluation of Cincinnati's Social Skills Development Program. In D. F. Ricks & B. S. Dohrenwend (Eds.), *Prevention of mental illness: Research frontiers*. New York: Cambridge University Press, 1980.

Klein, D. C., Fencil-Morse, E., & Seligman, M. E. P. Learned helplessness, depression, and the attribution of failure. *Journal of Personality and Social Psychology*, 1976, *33*, 508–516.

Kleinknecht, R. A., & Bernstein, D. A. Assessment of dental fear. *Behavior Therapy*, 1978, *9*, 626–634.

Knecht v. Gillman, 488 F 2d 1136 (8th Cir. 1973).

Knowles, J. *Doing better and feeling worse*. New York: Norton, 1977.

Kockott, G., Dittmar, F., & Nusselt, L. Systematic desensitization of erectile impotence: A controlled study. *Archives of Sexual Behavior*, 1975, *4*, 493–500.

Koegel, R. L., & Covert, A. The relationship of self-stimulation to learning in autistic children. *Journal of Applied Behavior Analysis*, 1972, *5*, 381–387.

Koegel, R. L., Glahn, T. J., & Nieminen, G. S. Generalization of parent-training results. *Journal of Applied Behavior Analysis*, 1978, *11*, 95–109.

Koegel, R. L., & Rincover, A. Treatment of psychotic children in a classroom environment. I. Learning in a large group. *Journal of Applied Behavior Analysis*, 1974, *7*, 45–59.

Koegel, R. L., Russo, D. C., & Rincover, A. Assessing and training teachers in the generalized use of behavior modification with autistic children. *Journal of Applied Behavior Analysis*, 1977, *10*, 197–205.

Kohlenberg, R. J. The punishment of persistent vomiting: A case study. *Journal of Applied Behavior Analysis*, 1970, *3*, 241–245.

Kohlenberg, R. J. Treatment of a homosexual pedophiliac using *in vivo* desensitization: A case study. *Journal of Abnormal Psychology*, 1974, *83*, 192–195.

Kohlenberg, R. J., & Phillips, T. Reinforcement and rate of litter depositing. *Journal of Applied Behavior Analysis*, 1973, *6*, 391–396.

Kohlenberg, R. J., Phillips, T., & Proctor, W. A behavioral analysis of peaking in residential electricity energy consumption. *Journal of Applied Behavior Analysis*, 1976, *9*, 13–18.

Kraft, T. Behavior therapy and target symptoms. *Journal of Clinical Psychology*, 1969, *25*, 105–109. (a)

Kraft, T. Desensitization and the treatment of sexual disorders. *Journal of Sex Research*, 1969, *5*, 130–134. (b)

Kraft, T. Social anxiety model of alcoholism. *Perceptual and Motor Skills*, 1971, *33*, 797–798.

Krapfl, J., & Vargas, E. (Eds.). *Behaviorism and ethics*. Kalamazoo, Mich.: Behaviordelia, 1977.

Krasner, L., & Ullmann, L. P. *Behavior influence and personality: The social matrix of human action*. New York: Holt, Rinehart & Winston, 1973.

Kratochwill, T. R. (Ed.). *Single-subject research: Strategies for evaluating change*. New York: Academic Press, 1978.

Kristein, M. M., Arnold, C. B., & Wynder, E. L. Health economics and preventive care. *Science*, 1977, *195*, 457–462.

Kuhn, T. S. *The structure of scientific revolutions*. Chicago: University of Chicago Press, 1962.

Lacey, J. I. Psychophysiological approaches to the evaluation of psychotherapeutic process and outcome. In E. Rubinstein & M. B. Parloff (Eds.), *Research in psychotherapy* (Vol. 1). Washington, D.C.: National, 1959.

Lacey, J. I. Somatic response patterning and stress: Some revisions of activation theory. In M. H. Appley & R. Trumbull (Eds.), *Psychological stress: Issues in research*. New York: Appleton-Century-Crofts, 1967.

Lacey, J. I., & Lacey, B. B. Verification and extension of the principle of automatic response stereotypy. *American Journal of Psychology*, 1968, *71*, 50–73.

Lader, M. H., & Mathews, A. M. A physiological model of phobic anxiety and desensitization. *Behaviour Research and Therapy*, 1968, *6*, 411–421.

Lahey, B. B. Research on the role of reinforcement in reading instruction: Some measurement and methodological deficiencies. *Corrective and Social Psychiatry*, 1977, *23*, 27–32.

Lahey, B. B. (Ed.). *Behavior therapy with hyperactive and learning disabled children*. New York: Oxford University Press, 1979.

Lahey, B. B., & Johnson, M. *Psychology and instruction*. Glenview, Ill.: Scott, Foresman, 1978.

Lahey, B. B., McNees, M. P., & Brown, C. C. Modification of deficits in reading for comprehension. *Journal of Applied Behavior Analysis*, 1973, *6*, 475–480.

Lahey, B. B., McNees, M. P., & McNees, M. C. Control of an obscene "verbal tic" through time out in an elementary school classroom. *Journal of Applied Behavior Analysis*, 1973, *6*, 101–104.

Lando, H. A. An objective check upon self-reported smoking levels. *Behavior Therapy*, 1975, *6*, 547–549.

Lando, H. A. Successful treatment of smokers with a broad-spectrum behavioral approach. *Journal of Consulting and Clinical Psychology*, 1977, *45*, 361–366.

Lang, P. J. Fear reduction and fear behavior: Problems in treating a construct. In J. M. Shlien (Ed.), *Research in psychotherapy* (Vol. 3). Washington, D.C.: American Psychological Association, 1968.

Lang, P. J. The mechanics of desensitization and the laboratory study of human fear. In C. M. Franks (Ed.), *Behavior therapy: Appraisal and status*. New York: McGraw-Hill, 1969.

Lang, P. J. Self-efficacy theory: Thoughts on cognition and unification. *Advances in Behaviour Research and Therapy*, 1978, *1*, 187–192.

Lang, P. J., Melamed, B. G., & Hart, J. A psychophysiological analysis of fear modification using an automated desensitization procedure. *Journal of Abnormal Psychology*, 1970, *76*, 220–234.

Lanyon, R. I., & Goodstein, L. D. *Personality assessment*. New York: Wiley, 1971.

Lapouse, R. The epidemiology of behavior disorders in children. *American Journal of Diseases of Children*, 1966, *111*, 594–599.

Large, D. B. (Ed.). *Hidden waste: Potentials for energy conservation*. Washington, D.C.: The Conservation Foundation, 1973.

Lazarus, A. A. Behavior therapy in groups. In G. M. Gazda (Ed.). *Basic approaches to group psychotherapy and group counseling*. Springfield, Ill.: Charles C. Thomas, 1968.

Lazarus, A. A. *Behavior therapy and beyond*. New York: McGraw-Hill, 1971.

Lazarus, A. A. *Clinical behavior therapy*. New York: Brunner/Mazel, 1972.

Lazarus, R., Averill, J., & Opton, E. Towards a cognitive theory of emotion. In M. Arnold (Ed.), *Feelings and emotions*. New York: Academic Press, 1970.

LeBlanc, A. E., Gibbins, R. J., & Kalant, H. Generalization of behaviorally augmented tolerance to ethanol, and its relation to physical dependence. *Psychopharmacology*, 1975, *44*, 241–296.

LeBow, M. D. Can lighter become thinner? *Addictive Behaviors*, 1977, *2*, 87–93.

Leitenberg, H. (Ed.). *Handbook of behavior modification and behavior therapy*. Englewood Cliffs, N.J.: Prentice-Hall, 1976.

Lemon, F. R., & Walden, R. T. Death from respiratory system disease among Seventh-Day Adventist men. *Journal of the American Medical Association*, 1966, *198*, 117–126.

Leon, G. R. Current directions in the treatment of obesity. *Psychological Bulletin*, 1976, *83*, 557–578.

Leon, G. R., & Chamberlain, K. Emotional arousal, eating patterns, and body image as differential factors associated with varying success in maintaining a weight loss. *Journal of Consulting and Clinical Psychology,* 1973, *40,* 474–480.

Letzkus, T., & Scharfe, V. Employer incentive programs. *Proceedings of the 1975 National Conference on Areawide Carpooling.* Houston, Tex., December 8–10, 1975, Washington, D.C.: Federal Highway Administration, Urban Planning Division, 1975.

Levine, M. N., & Elliott, C. B. Toilet training for profoundly retarded with a limited staff. *Mental Retardation,* June 1970, *8,* 48–50.

Levis, D. J. Implosive therapy: A critical analysis of Morganstern's review. *Psychological Bulletin,* 1974, *81,* 155–158.

Levis, D. J., & Hare, N. A review of the theoretical rationale and empirical support for the extinction approach of implosive (flooding) therapy. In M. Hersen, R. M. Eisler, & P. M. Miller (Eds.), *Progress in behavior modification* (Vol. 4). New York: Academic Press, 1977.

Levitt, E. E. *The psychology of anxiety.* New York: Bobbs-Merrill, 1967.

Levitt, E. E., & Edwards, J. A. A multivariate study of correlative factors in youthful cigarette smoking. *Developmental Psychology,* 1970, *2,* 5–11.

Levitz, L. S., & Stunkard, A. J. A therapeutic coalition for obesity: Behavior modification and patient self-help. *American Journal of Psychiatry,* 1974, *131,* 423–427.

Lewinsohn, P. M. Clinical and theoretical aspects of depression. In K. S. Calhoun, H. E. Adams, & K. M. Mitchell (Eds.), *Innovative treatment methods in psychopathology.* New York: Wiley, 1974.

Lewinsohn, P. M., & Amenson, C. S. Some relations between pleasant and unpleasant mood-related events and depression. *Journal of Abnormal Psychology,* 1978, *87*(6), 644–654.

Lewinsohn, P. M., & Graf, M. Pleasant events and depression. *Journal of Consulting and Clinical Psychology,* 1973, *41,* 261–268.

Lewinsohn, P. M., & Libet, J. Pleasant events, activity schedules, and depressions. *Journal of Abnormal Psychology,* 1972, *79,* 291–295.

Lewinsohn, P. M., Lobitz, C., & Wilson, S. "Sensitivity" of depressed individuals to aversive stimuli. *Journal of Abnormal Psychology,* 1973, *81,* 259–263.

Lewinsohn, P. M., & Talkington, J. Studies on the measurement of unpleasant events and relations with depression. *Applied Psychological Measurement,* 1979, *3,* 83–101.

Liberman, R. P., & Davis, J. Drugs and behavior analysis. In M. Hersen, R. M. Eisler, & P. M. Miller (Eds.), *Progress in behavior modification* (Vol. 1). New York: Academic Press, 1975.

Liberman, R. P., Levine, J., Wheeler, E., Sanders, N., & Wallace, C. Experimental evaluation of marital group therapy: Behavioral vs. interaction-insight formats. *Acta Psychiatrica Scandinavia,* 1976, *Supplement.*

Liberman, R. P., Teigen, J., Patterson, R., & Baker, V. Reducing delusional speech in chronic, paranoid schizophrenics. *Journal of Applied Behavior Analysis*, 1973, *6*, 57–64.

Lichtenstein, E., & Danaher, B. G. Modification of smoking behavior: A critical analysis of theory, research, and practice. In M. Hersen, R. M. Eisler, & P. M. Miller (Eds.), *Progress in behavior modification* (Vol. 3). New York: Academic Press, 1976.

Lichtenstein, E., & Glasgow, R. E. Rapid smoking: Side effects and safeguards. *Journal of Consulting and Clinical Psychology*, 1977, *45*, 815–821.

Lichtenstein, E., Harris, D. E., Birchler, G. P., Wahl, J. M., & Schmahl, D. P. Comparison of rapid smoking, warm smoky air, and attention placebo in the modification of smoking behavior. *Journal of Consulting and Clinical Psychology*, 1973, *40*, 92–98.

Lichtenstein, E., & Rodrigues, M. P. Long term effects of rapid smoking treatment for dependent cigarette smokers. *Addictive Behaviors*, 1977, *2*, 109–112.

Lindesmith, A. R. *Addiction and opiates*. Chicago: Aldine, 1968.

Lindner, P. G., & Blackburn, G. L. An interdisciplinary approach to obesity utilizing fasting modified by protein-sparing therapy. *Obesity/Bariatric Medicine*, 1976, *5*, 198–216.

Linehan, M. M. Issues in behavioral interviewing. In J. D. Cone & R. P. Hawkins (Eds.), *Behavioral assessment: New directions in clinical psychology*. New York: Brunner/Mazel, 1977.

Linehan, M. M., & Eagan, K. J. Assertion training for women. In A. S. Bellack & M. Hersen (Eds.), *Research and practice in social skills training*. New York: Plenum Press, 1979.

Linehan, M. M., Goldfried, M. R., & Goldfried, A. P. Assertion therapy: Skill training or cognitive restructuring. *Behavior Therapy*, 1979, *10*, 372–388.

Linehan, M. M., Walker, R. O., Bronheim, S., Haynes, K. F., & Yevzeroff, N. Group vs. individual assertion training. *Journal of Clinical and Consulting Psychology*, in press.

Litman, G. K., Eiser, J. R., Rawson, N. S. B., & Oppenheim, A. N. Differences in relapse precipitants and coping behavior between alcohol relapsers and survivors. *Behaviour Research and Therapy*, 1979, *17*, 89–94.

Little, V. L., & Kendall, P. C. Cognitive-behavioral interventions with delinquents: Problem-solving, role-taking, and self-control. In P. C. Kendall & S. D. Hollon (Eds.), *Cognitive-behavioral interventions: Theory, research, and procedures*. New York: Academic Press, 1979.

Lloyd, R. W., & Salzberg, H. C. Controlled social drinking: An alternative to abstinence as a treatment goal for some alcohol abusers. *Psychological Bulletin*, 1975, *82*, 815–842.

Lobitz, W. C., & LoPiccolo, J. New methods in the behavioral treatment of sexual dysfunction. *Journal of Behavior Therapy and Experimental Psychiatry*, 1972, *3*, 265–271.

Logan, F. A. *Fundamentals of learning and motivation*. Dubuque, Iowa: W. C. Brown, 1969.

Lomont, J. F. Reciprocal inhibition or extinction? *Behaviour Research and Therapy*, 1965, *3*, 209–219.

London, P. *The modes and morals of psychotherapy*. New York: Holt, Rinehart & Winston, 1964.

LoPiccolo, J. Direct treatment of sexual dysfunction in the couple. In J. Money & H. Musaph (Eds.), *Handbook of sexology*. New York: Elsevier/North Holland, 1977. (a)

LoPiccolo, J. From psychotherapy to sex therapy. *Society*, 1977, *14*(5), 60–68. (b)

LoPiccolo, J., & Heiman, J. The role of cultural values in the prevention and treatment of sexual problems. In C. B. Qualls, J. P. Wincze, & D. H. Barlow (Eds.), *The prevention of sexual disorders*. New York: Plenum Press, 1978.

LoPiccolo, J., & Hogan, D. Multidimensional behavioral treatment of sexual dysfunction. In O. Pomerleau & J. P. Brady (Eds.), *Behavioral medicine*. Baltimore: Williams & Wilkins, 1978.

LoPiccolo, J., & Lobitz, W. C. The role of masturbation in the treatment of orgasmic dysfunction. *Archives of Sexual Behavior*, 1972, *2*, 163–172.

LoPiccolo, J., & Steger, J. C. The Sexual Interaction Inventory: A new instrument for assessment of sexual dysfunction. *Archives of Sexual Behavior*, 1974, *3*(6), 585–595.

LoPiccolo, L., & Heiman, J. Sexual assessment and history interview. In L. LoPiccolo & J. LoPiccolo (Eds.), *Handbook of sex therapy*. New York: Plenum Press, 1978.

Lovaas, O. I., Berberich, J. P., Perloff, B. F., & Schaeffer, B. Acquisition of imitative speech by schizophrenic children. *Science*, 1966, *151*, 705–707.

Lovaas, O. I., Koegel, R., Simmons, J. Q., & Long, J. S. Some generalization and follow-up measures on autistic children to behavior therapy. *Journal of Applied Behavior Analysis*, 1973, *6*, 131–166.

Lovaas, O. I., Litrownik, A., & Mann, R. Response latencies to auditory stimuli in autistic children engaged in self-stimulatory behavior. *Behaviour Research and Therapy*, 1971, *9*, 39–49.

Lovaas, O. I., & Newsom, C. D. Behavior modification with psychotic children. In H. Leitenberg (Ed.), *Handbook of behavior modification*. Englewood Cliffs, N.J.: Prentice-Hall, 1976.

Lovaas, O. I., Schaeffer, B., & Simmons, J. Q. Building social behavior in autistic children by the use of electric shock. *Journal of Experimental Research in Personality*, 1965, *1*, 99–109.

Lovaas, O. I., & Simmons, J. Q. Manipulation of self-destruction in three retarded children. *Journal of Applied Behavior Analysis,* 1969, *2,* 143–157.

Lovitt, T. C., Guppy, T. E., & Blattner, J. E. The use of a free-time contingency with fourth graders to improve spelling accuracy. *Behaviour Research and Therapy,* 1969, *1,* 151–156.

Lowe, J. C, & Mikulas, W. L. Use of written material in learning self control of premature ejaculation. *Psychological Reports,* 1975, *37,* 295–298.

Lubin, G. Adjective checklists for the measurement of depression. *Archives of General Psychiatry,* 1965, *12,* 57–62.

Lublin, I. Principles governing the choice of unconditioned stimuli in aversive conditioning. In R. D. Kubin & S. M. Franks (Eds.), *Advances in behavior therapy 1968.* New York: Academic Press, 1969.

Luborsky, L., & Spence, D. P. Quantitative research on psychoanalytic therapy. In S. L. Garfield & A. E. Bergin (Eds.), *Handbook of psychotherapy and behavior change* (2nd ed.). New York: Wiley, 1978.

Luckey, R. E., Watson, C. M., & Musick, J. K. Aversive conditioning as a means of inhibiting vomiting and rumination. *American Journal of Mental Deficiency,* 1968, *73,* 139–142.

Ludwig, A. M., Marx, A. J., Hill, P. A., & Browning, R. M. The control of violent behavior through faradic shock. *Journal of Nervous and Mental Disease,* 1969, *148,* 624–637.

Ludwig, A. M., & Wikler, A. "Craving" and relapse to drink. *Quarterly Journal of Studies on Alcohol,* 1974, *35,* 108–130.

Ludwig, A. M., Wikler, A., & Stark, L. H. The first drink: Psychobiological aspects of craving. *Archives of General Psychiatry,* 1974, *30,* 539–547.

Lutzker, J. R. Reducing self-injurious behavior by facial screening. *American Journal of Mental Deficiency,* 1978, *82,* 510–513.

Luyben, P. D., & Bailey, J. S. *Newspaper recycling behavior: The effects of reinforcement versus proximity of containers.* Unpublished manuscript, Florida State University, 1975.

MacCalden, M., & Davis, C. *Report on priority lane experiment on the San Francisco –Oakland Bay Bridge.* California: Department of Public Works, 1972.

MacCorquodale, K., & Meehl, P. E. On a distinction between hypothetical constructs and intervening variables. *Psychological Review,* 1948, *55,* 95–107.

MacCulloch, M. J., Williams, C., & Birtles, C. J. The successful application of aversion therapy to an adolescent exhibitionist. *Journal of Behavior Therapy and Experimental Psychiatry,* 1971, *2,* 61–66.

MacDonald, M. L. Measuring assertion: A model and method. *Behavior Therapy,* 1978, *9,* 889–899.

MacDonald, M. L., Lindquist, C. U., Kramer, J. A., McGrath, R. A., & Rhyne, L. D. Social skills training: Behavior rehearsal in groups and dating skills. *Journal of Counseling Psychology*, 1975, *22*, 224–230.

MacDonough, T. S., & Forehand, R. Response-contingent time out: Importan. parameters in behavior modification with children. *Journal of Behavior Therapy and Experimental Psychiatry*, 1973, *4*, 231–236.

MacFarlane, J. W., Allen, L., & Honzik, M. P. *A developmental study of the behavior problems of normal children between 21 months and 14 years.* Berkeley: University of California Press, 1954.

MacPhillamy, D. J., & Lewinsohn, P. M. *Pleasant events schedule.* Unpublished paper available from P. M. Lewinsohn, Department of Psychology, University of Oregon, Eugene, Oreg.

Mackey v. Procunier, 477 F. 2d 877 (9th Cir. 1973).

Madsen, C. H., Becker, W. C., & Thomas, D. R. Rules, praise, and ignoring: Elements of elementary classroom control. *Journal of Applied Behavior Analysis*, 1968, *1*, 139–150.

Madsen, C. H., Becker, W. C., Thomas, D. R., Koser, L., & Plager, E. An analysis of the reinforcing function of "sit down" commands. In R. K. Parker (Ed.), *Readings in educational psychology.* Boston: Allyn & Bacon, 1970.

Mahoney, K., Rogers, T., Straw, M., & Mahoney, M. J. *Results and implications of a problem-solving treatment for obesity.* Paper presented at the 11th Annual Convention of the Association for Advancement of Behavior Therapy, Atlanta, December 1977.

Mahoney, M. J. *Cognition and behavior modification.* Cambridge, Mass.: Ballinger, 1974. (a)

Mahoney, M. J. Self-reward and self-monitoring techniques for weight control. *Behavior Therapy*, 1974, *5*, 48–57. (b)

Mahoney, M. J. The sensitive scientist in empirical humanism. *American Psychologist*, 1975, *30*, 864–867.

Mahoney, M. J. *Scientist as subject: The psychological imperative.* Cambridge, Mass.: Ballinger, 1976.

Mahoney, M. J. (Ed.). *Psychotherapy process: Current issues and future directions.* New York: Plenum Press, 1979.

Mahoney, M. J. *Abnormal psychology: Perspectives on human variance.* New York: Harper & Row, 1980.

Mahoney, M. J., & Arnkoff, D. B. Cognitive and self-control therapies. In S. L. Garfield & A. E. Bergin (Eds.), *Handbook of psychotherapy and behavior change* (2nd ed.). New York: Wiley, 1978.

Mahoney, M. J., Kazdin, A. E., & Lesswing, W. J. Behavior modification: Delusion or deliverance? In C. M. Franks & G. T. Wilson (Eds.), *Annual review of behavior therapy: Theory and practice* (Vol. 2). New York: Brunner/Mazel, 1974.

Mahoney, M. J., & Mahoney, K. *Permanent weight control*. New York: Norton, 1976. (a)

Mahoney, M. J., & Mahoney, K. Treatment of obesity: A clinical exploration. In B. J. Williams, S. Martin, & J. P. Foreyt (Eds.), *Obesity: Behavioral approaches to dietary management*. New York: Brunner/Mazel, 1976. (b)

Mahoney, M. J., Moura, N. G. M., & Wade, T. C. Relative efficacy of self-award, self-punishment, self-monitoring techniques for weight loss. *Journal of Consulting and Clinical Psychology*, 1973, *40*, 404–407.

Mahoney, M. J., & Thoresen, C. E. (Eds.). *Self-control: Power to the person*. Monterey, Calif.: Brooks/Cole, 1974.

Main, G. C., & Munro, B. C. A token reinforcement program in a public junior-high school. *Journal of Applied Behavior Analysis*, 1977, *10*, 93–94.

Maisto, S. A., Lauerman, R., & Adesso, V. J. A comparison of two experimental studies investigating the role of cognitive factors in excessive drinking. *Journal of Studies on Alcohol*, 1977, *38*, 145–149.

Maletzky, B. M. "Assisted" covert sensitization in the treatment of exhibitionism. In D. J. Cox & R. J. Daitzman (Eds.), *Exhibitionism: Description, assessment and treatment*. New York: Garland Press, 1980.

Maloney, D. M., Harper, T. M., Braukmann, C. J., Fixsen, D. L., Phillips, E. L., & Wolf, M. M. Teaching conversation-related skills to predelinquent girls. *Journal of Applied Behavior Analysis*, 1976, *9*, 371.

Maloney, K. S., & Hopkins, B. L. The modification of sentence structure and its relationship to subjective judgments of creativity in writing. *Journal of Applied Behavior Analysis*, 1973, *6*, 425–434.

Manganiello, J. A. Opiate addiction: A study identifying three systematically related psychological correlates. *International Journal of the Addictions*, 1978, *13*, 839–847.

Mansdorf, I. J. Reinforcer isolation: An alternative to subject isolation in time-out from positive reinforcement. *Journal of Behavior Therapy and Experimental Psychiatry*, 1977, *8*, 391–393.

Margolies, P. J. Behavioral approaches to the treatment of early infantile autism: A review. *Psychological Bulletin*, 1977, *84*, 249–264.

Margolin, J. B., Misch, M. R., & Dobson, R. D. Incentives and disincentives to ride-sharing behaviors: A program report. *Transportation Research Record*, 1976, No. 592, 41–44.

Marholin, D., & Steinman, W. Stimulus control in the classroom as a function of the behavior reinforced. *Journal of Applied Behavior Analysis*, 1977, *10*, 465–478.

Markman, H. J. Application of a behavioral model of marriage in predicting relationship satisfaction of couples planning marriage. *Journal of Consulting and Clinical Psychology*, 1979, *47*, 743–749.

Marlatt, G. A. Alcohol, stress, and cognitive control. In I. G. Sarason & C. D. Spielberger (Eds.), *Stress and anxiety* (Vol. 3). Washington, D.C.: Hemisphere Publishing, 1976.

Marlatt, G. A. Craving for alcohol, loss of control, and relapse: A cognitive-behavioral analysis. In P. E. Nathan, G. A. Marlatt, & T. Loberg (Eds.), *Alcoholism: New directions in behavioral research and treatment.* New York: Plenum Press, 1978.

Marlatt, G. A. Alcohol use and problem drinking: A cognitive-behavioral analysis. In P. C. Kendall & S. P. Hollon (Eds.), *Cognitive-behavioral interventions: Theory, research, and procedures.* New York: Academic Press, 1979.

Marlatt, G. A., Demming, B., & Reid, J. B. Loss of control drinking in alcoholics: An experimental analogue. *Journal of Abnormal Psychology*, 1973, *81*, 223–241.

Marlatt, G. A., & Donovan, D. M. Psychological perspectives on alcoholism: Behavioral psychology. In E. M. Pattison & E. Kaufman (Eds.), *The American handbook of alcoholism.* New York: Gardner Press, in press.

Marlatt, G. A., & Gordon, J. R. Determinants of relapse: Implications for the maintenance of behavior change. In P. Davidson (Ed.), *Behavioral medicine: Changing health lifestyles.* New York: Brunner/Mazel, 1979.

Marlatt, G. A., Kosturn, C. F., & Lang, A. R. Provocation to anger and opportunity for retaliation as determinants of alcohol consumption in social drinkers. *Journal of Abnormal Psychology*, 1975, *84*, 652–659.

Marlatt, G. A., & Marques, J. K. Meditation, self-control, and alcohol use. In R. B. Stuart (Ed.), *Behavioral self-management: Strategies and outcomes.* New York: Brunner/Mazel, 1977.

Marlatt, G. A., & Rohsenow, D. J. Cognitive processes in alcohol use: Expectancy and the balanced placebo design. In N. K. Mello (Ed.), *Advances in substance abuse: Behavioral and biological research.* Greenwich, Conn.: JAI Press, in press.

Marlatt, G. A., & Rose, F. Addictive disorders. In A. E. Kazdin, A. S. Bellack, & M. Hersen (Eds.), *New perspectives in abnormal psychology.* New York: Oxford University Press, 1980.

Marler, L. A study of anti-litter messages. *Journal of Environmental Education*, 1970, *3*, 52–53.

Marlowe, R. H., Madsen, C. H., Bowen, C. E., Reardon, R. C., & Logue, P. E. Severe classroom behavior problems: Teachers or counsellors. *Journal of Applied Behavior Analysis*, 1978, *11*, 53–66.

Marshall, N. R., & Hegrenes, J. R. Programmed communication therapy for autistic mentally retarded children. *Journal of Speech and Hearing Disorders*, 1970, *35*, 70–83.

Marshall, W. L., Gauthier, J., & Gordon, A. The current status of flooding therapy. In M. Hersen, R. M. Eisler, & P. M. Miller (Eds.), *Progress in behavior modification* (Vol. 7). New York: Academic Press, 1979.

Martin, B., & Twentyman, C. Teaching conflict resolution skills to parents and children. In E. J. Mash, L. C. Handy, & L. A. Hammerlynck (Eds.), *Behavior modification approaches to parenting*. New York: Brunner/Mazel, 1976.

Martin, G. L., Kehoe, B., Bird, E., Jensen, V., & Dorbeyshire, M. Operant conditioning in dressing behavior of severely retarded girls. *Mental Retardation,* 1971, *9,* 27–31.

Martin, G. L., MacDonald, S., & Omichinski, M. An operant analysis of response interactions during meals with severely retarded girls. *American Journal of Mental Deficiency,* 1971, *76,* 68–75.

Martin, J. A., & Iagulli, D. M. Elimination of middle-of-the-night tantrums in a blind, retarded child. *Behavior Therapy,* 1974, *5,* 420–422.

Martin, M., Burkholder, R., Rosenthal, T., Tharp, R., & Thorne, G. Programming behavior change and reintegration into school milieux of extreme adolescent deviates. *Behaviour Research and Therapy,* 1968, *6,* 371–383.

Martin, P. L., & Foxx, R. M. Victim control of the aggression of an institutionalized retardate. *Journal of Behavior Therapy and Experimental Psychiatry,* 1973, *4,* 161–165.

Martin, R. *Legal challenges to behavior modification: Trends in schools, corrections and mental health.* Champaign, Ill.: Research Press, 1975.

Martinson, W. D., & Zerface, J. P. Comparison of individual counseling and a social program with nondaters. *Journal of Counseling Psychology,* 1970, *17,* 36–40.

Mash, E. J., & Dalby, J. T. Behavioral interventions for hyperactivity. In R. Trites (Ed.), *Hyperactivity in children: Etiology, measurement, and treatment implications.* Baltimore: University Park Press, 1979.

Maslow, A. H. *The psychology of science: A reconnaissance.* Chicago: Henry Regnery, 1966.

Masserman, J. H. *Behavior and neurosis.* Chicago: University of Chicago Press, 1943.

Masters, W. H., & Johnson, V. E. *Human sexual response.* Boston: Little, Brown, 1966.

Masters, W. H., & Johnson, V. E. *Human sexual inadequacy.* Boston: Little, Brown, 1970.

Masters, W. H., & Johnson, V. E. *Homosexuality in perspective.* Boston: Little, Brown, 1979.

Mathews, A., Bancroft, J., Whitehead, A., Hackman, A., Julier, D., Bancroft, J., Gath, D., & Shaw, P. The behavioral treatment of sexual inadequacy: A comparative study. *Behavior Research and Therapy,* 1976, *14,* 427–436.

Matson, F. W. Matson replies to Skinner. *Humanist,* 1971, *31,* 2.

Mausner, B. An ecological view of cigarette smoking. *Journal of Abnormal Psychology*, 1973, *81*, 115–126.

Max, L. W. An experimental study of the motor theory of consciousness: II. Action-current responses in deaf mutes during sleep, sensory stimulation and dreams. *Journal of Comparative Psychology*, 1935, *19*, 469–486.

Max, L. W. Experimental study of the motor theory of consciousness: IV. Action-current responses in the deaf during awakening, kinaesthetic imagery, and abstract thinking. *Journal of Comparative Psychology*, 1937, *24*, 301–344.

May, J. G., Risley, T. R., Twardosz, S., Friedman, P., Bijou, S. W., Wexler, D., et al. Guidelines for the use of behavioral procedures in state programs for retarded persons. *Mental Retardation Research*, 1975, *1*.

May, J. G., Risley, T. R., Twardosz, S., Friedman, P., Bijou, S. W., & Wexler, D. *Guidelines for the use of behavioral procedures in state programs for retarded persons.* Arlington, Tex.: National Association for Retarded Citizens, 1976.

Mayer, J. *Overweight: Causes, cost, and control.* Englewood Cliffs, N.J.: Prentice-Hall, 1968.

McAlister, A. L. *Toward the mass communication of behavioral counseling: A preliminary experimental study of a televised program to assist in smoking cessation.* Doctoral dissertation, Stanford University, 1976 (Microfilm 77–7128).

McAuliffe, W. E., & Gordon, R. A. A test of Lindesmith's theory of addiction: The frequency of euphoria among long-term addicts. In R. H. Coombs, L. J. Fry, & P. G. Lewis (Eds.), *Socialization in drug abuse.* Cambridge, Mass.: Schenkman, 1976.

McClelland, D. C., Davis, W. M., Kalin, R., & Wanner, E. *The drinking man.* New York: Free Press, 1972.

McClelland, L., & Cook, S. W. Promoting energy conservation in master-metered apartments through group financial incentives. *Journal of Applied Social Psychology*, September 1978. (a)

McClelland, L., & Cook, S. W. Energy conservation effects of continuous in-home feedback in all-electric homes. *Journal of Applied Social Psychology*, September 1978. (b)

McFall, R. M., & Hammen, C. L. Motivation, structure, and self-monitoring: Role of nonspecific factors in smoking reduction. *Journal of Consulting and Clinical Psychology*, 1971, *37*, 80–86.

McFall, R. M., & Lillesand, D. B. Behavior rehearsal with modeling and coaching in assertion training. *Journal of Abnormal Psychology*, 1971, 77, 313–323.

McFall, R. M., & Twentyman, C. T. Four experiments on the relative contributions of rehearsal, modeling, and coaching to assertion training. *Journal of Abnormal Psychology*, 1973, *81*, 199–218.

McGuire, M. T., Mendelson, J. H., & Stein, S. Comparative psychosocial studies of alcoholic and non-alcoholic subjects undergoing experimentally induced ethanol intoxication. *Psychosomatic Medicine,* 1966, *28,* 13–25.

McKennel, A. C. British research into smoking behavior. In E. F. Borgatta & R. R. Evans (Eds.), *Smoking, health, and behavior.* Chicago: Aldine, 1968.

McLean, P. D. Parental depression: Incompatible with effective parenting. In E. J. Mash, L. C. Handy, & L. A. Hamerlynck (Eds.), *Behavior modification approaches to parenting.* New York: Brunner/Mazel, 1976.

McLean, P. D., & Hakstian, A. R. Clinical depression: Comparative efficacy of outpatient treatments. *Journal of Consulting and Clinical Psychology,* 1979, *47,* 818–836.

McLean, P. D., Ogston, K., & Grauer, L. A behavioral approach to the treatment of depression. *Journal of Behavior Therapy and Experimental Psychiatry,* 1973, *4,* 323–330.

McNamee, H. B., Mello, N. K., & Mendelson, J. H. Experimental analysis of drinking patterns of alcoholics: Concurrent psychiatric observations. *American Journal of Psychiatry,* 1968, *124,* 1063–1069.

McNamee, H. B., Mirin, S. M., Kuehnle, J. C., & Meyer, R. E. Affective changes in chronic opiate use. *British Journal of the Addictions,* 1976, *71,* 275–280.

McNees, P. M., Egli, D. S., Marshall, R. S., Schnelle, J. F., & Risley, T. R. Shoplifting prevention: Providing information through signs. *Journal of Applied Behavior Analysis,* 1976, *9,* 399–405.

McReynolds, W. T., Lutz, R. N., Paulsen, B. K., & Kohrs, M. B. Weight loss resulting from two behavior modification procedures with nutritionists as therapists. *Behavior Therapy,* 1976, *7,* 283–291.

Measel, C. J., & Alfieri, P. A. Treatment of self-injurious behavior by a combination of reinforcement for incompatible behavior and overcorrection. *American Journal of Mental Deficiency,* 1976, *81,* 147–153.

Mechanic, D. The influence of mothers on their children's health attitudes and behavior. *Pediatrics,* 1964, *30,* 444–453.

Mechanic, D. M. Some problems in developing a social psychology of adaptation to stress. In J. E. McGrath (Ed.), *Social and psychological factors in stress.* New York: Holt, Rinehart & Winston, 1970.

Meichenbaum, D. H. Examination of model characteristics in reducing avoidance behavior. *Journal of Personality and Social Psychology,* 1971, *17,* 298–307.

Meichenbaum, D. H. Cognitive modification of test anxious college students. *Journal of Consulting and Clinical Psychology,* 1972, *39,* 370–380.

Meichenbaum, D. H. Cognitive factors in behavior modification: Modifying what clients say to themselves. In C. M. Franks & G. T. Wilson (Eds.), *Annual review of behavior therapy and practice* (Vol. 1). New York: Brunner/Mazel, 1973.

Meichenbaum, D. H. *Cognitive behavior modification*. Morristown, N.J.: General Learning Press, 1974.

Meichenbaum, D. H. Self-instructional methods. In F. Kanfer & A. Goldstein (Eds.), *Helping people change*. New York: Pergamon Press, 1975. (a)

Meichenbaum, D. H. Toward a cognitive theory of self control. In G. Schwartz & D. Shapiro (Eds.), *Consciousness and self regulation: Advances in research*. New York: Plenum Press, 1975. (b)

Meichenbaum, D. H. *Cognitive-behavior modification: An integrative approach*. New York: Plenum Press, 1977.

Meichenbaum, D. H., & Cameron, R. Training schizophrenics to talk to themselves: A means of developing attentional controls. *Behavior Therapy*, 1973, *4*, 515–534.

Meichenbaum, D. H., Gilmore, J. B., & Fedoravicius, A. Group insight versus group desensitization in treating speech anxiety. *Journal of Consulting and Clinical Psychology*, 1971, *36*, 410–421.

Meichenbaum, D. H., & Goodman, J. Training impulsive children to talk to themselves: A means of developing self-control. *Journal of Abnormal Psychology*, 1971, 77, 115–116.

Mello, N. K. Some aspects of the behavioral pharmacology of alcohol. In D. H. Efron (Ed.), *Psychopharmacology: A review of progress*. Washington, D.C.: Government Printing Office (Public Health Service Publication No. 1836), 1968.

Merbaum, M. The modification of self-destructive behavior by a mother-therapist using aversive stimulation. *Behavior Therapy*, 1973, *4*, 442–447.

Merbaum, M., & Lukens, H. C., Jr. Effects of instructions, elicitations, and reinforcements in the manipulation of affective verbal behavior. *Journal of Abnormal Psychology*, 1968, *73*, 376–380.

Messer, S. B. Reflection-impulsivity: A review. *Psychological Bulletin*, 1976, *83*, 1026–1052.

Metz, A. S., & Richards, L. G. Children's preventive visits to the dentist: The relative importance of socio-economic factors and parents' preventive visits. *Journal of American College of Dentistry*, 1967, *34*, 204–212.

Meyer, A. J., & Henderson, J. B. Multiple risk factor reduction in the preventive of cardiovascular disease. *Preventive Medicine*, 1974, *3*, 225–236.

Meyer, R. E., & Mirin, S. M. *The heroin stimulus: Implications for a theory of addiction*. New York: Plenum Press, 1979.

Meyers, A. W., Artz, L., & Craighead, W. E. The effects of instruction, incentive, and feedback on a community problem: Dormitory noise. *Journal of Applied Behavior Analysis*, 1976, *9*, 445–458.

Meyers, A. W., & Craighead, W. E. *Cognitive behavior therapy with children*. New York: Plenum Press, in press.

Meyers, A. W., Craighead, W. E., & Meyers, H. H. A behavioral-preventive approach to community mental health. *American Journal of Community Psychology,* 1974, *2,* 275–285.

Meyers, A. W., Farr, J. H., & Craighead, W. E. Eliminating female orgasmic dysfunction with sexual reeducation. In J. D. Krumboltz & C. E. Thoresen (Eds.), Behavioral counseling methods. New York: Holt, Rinehart, & Winston, 1976.

Meyers, A. W., Meyers, H. H., & Craighead, W. E. Practical and ethical issues in community behavior change. *Behavior Modification,* in press.

Michael, J. Statistical inference for individual organism research: Mixed blessing or curse? *Journal of Applied Behavior Analysis,* 1974, *7,* 647–653.

Midwest Research Institute. *Energy conservation implications of master metering.* MRI Project No. 4008–E. Federal Energy Administration Contract No. C–04–5006.7.00. November 1975.

Mikulus, W. L., & Lowe, J. C. *Self-control of premature ejaculation.* Paper presented at Rocky Mountain Psychological Association, Denver, Colo., 1974.

Milan, M. A., & Long, C. R. Crime and delinquency: The last frontier? In. D. Glenwick & L. Jason (Eds.), *Behavioral community psychology: Progress and prospects.* New York: Praeger Press, in press.

Milan, M. A., & McKee, J. M. Behavior modification: Principles and applications in corrections. In D. Glaser (Ed.), *Handbook of criminology.* Chicago: Rand McNally, 1974.

Milan, M. A., & McKee, J. M. The cellblock token economy: Token reinforcement procedures in a maximum security correctional institution for adult male felons. *Journal of Applied Behavior Analysis,* 1976, *9,* 253–275.

Miller, C., & Deuser, R. Issues in enforcement of busway and bus and car-pool lane restrictions. *Transportation Research Record,* 1976, No. 606, 12–17.

Miller, H. R., & Dermer, S. W. Quasi-experimental follow-up of token-economy and conventional treatment graduates. *Journal of Consulting and Clinical Psychology,* 1979, *47,* 625–627.

Miller, L. C., Schilling, A. F., Logan, D. L., & Johnson, R. L. Potential hazards of rapid smoking as a technique for the modification of smoking behavior. *New England Journal of Medicine,* 1977, *297,* 590–592.

Miller, N., Albert, M., Bostick, D., & Geller, E. S. *Can the design of a trash can influence litter-related behavior?* Paper presented at the meeting of the Southeastern Psychological Association, New Orleans, May 1976.

Miller, P. M. Behavioral treatment of drug addiction: A review. *International Journal of the Addictions,* 1973, *8,* 511–519.

Miller, P. M. *Behavioral treatment of alcoholism.* New York: Pergamon Press, 1976.

Miller, P. M., & Barlow, D. H. Behavioral approaches to the treatment of alcoholism. *Journal of Nervous and Mental Disease*, 1973, *178*, 10–20.

Miller, P. M., & Eisler, R. M. Assertive behavior in alcoholics: A descriptive analysis. *Behavior Therapy*, 1977, *8*, 146–149.

Miller, P. M., Hersen, M., Eisler, R. M., Epstein, L. H., & Wooten, L. S. Relationship of alcohol cues to the drinking of alcoholics and social drinkers: An analogue study. *Psychological Record*, 1974, *24*, 61–66.

Miller, P. M., Hersen, M., Eisler, R. M., & Hilsman, G. Effects of social stress on operant drinking of alcoholics and social drinkers. *Behaviour Research and Therapy*, 1974, *12*, 67–72.

Miller, P. M., & Mastria, M. A. *Alternatives to alcohol abuse: A social learning model.* Champaign, Ill.: Research Press, 1977.

Miller, W. R., & Caddy, G. R. Abstinence and controlled drinking in the treatment of problem drinkers. *Journal of Studies on Alcohol*, 1977, *38*, 986–1003.

Miller, W. R., & Seligman, M. E. P. Depression and learned helplessness in man. *Journal of Abnormal Psychology*, 1975, *84*, 228–238.

Minge, M. R., & Ball, T. S. Teaching of self-help skills to profoundly retarded patients. *American Journal of Mental Deficiency*, 1967, *71*, 864–868.

Minkin, N., Braukmann, C. J., Minkin, B. L., Timbers, G. D., Timbers, B. J., Fixsen, D. L., Phillips, E. L., & Wolf, M. M. The social validation and training of conversational skills. *Journal of Applied Behavior Analysis*, 1976, *9*, 127–139.

Mirin, S. M., Meyer, R. E., & McNamee, H. B. Psychopathology, craving, and mood during heroin acquisition: An experimental study. *International Journal of the Addictions*, 1976, *11*, 525–544.

Mischel, W. *Personality and assessment.* New York: Wiley, 1968.

Mischel, W. Toward a cognitive social learning reconceptualization of personality. *Psychological Review*, 1973, *80*, 252–283.

Mischel, W. *Introduction to personality.* New York: Holt, Rinehart & Winston, 1976.

Mischel, W. On the interface of cognition and personality: Beyond the person-situation debate. *American Psychologist*, 1979, *34*, 740–754.

Mitchell, W. S., & Stoffelmayr, B. E. Application of the Premack Principle to the behavioral control of extremely inactive schizophrenics. *Journal of Applied Behavior Analysis*, 1973, *6*, 419–423.

Mitford, J. *Kind and unusual punishment.* New York: Random House, 1973.

Monthly Vital Statistics Report. Department of Health, Education, and Welfare, 1975.

Morgan, W. G. Nonnecessary conditions or useful procedures in desensitization: A reply to Wilkins. *Psychological Bulletin*, 1973, *79*, 373–375.

Morganstern, K. P. Implosive therapy and flooding procedures: A critical review. *Psychological Bulletin,* 1973, *79,* 318–334.

Morris, R. J. Fear reduction methods. In F. H. Kanfer & A. P. Goldstein (Eds.), *Helping people change.* New York: Pergamon Press, 1975.

Mowrer, O. H. A stimulus–response analysis of anxiety and its role as a reinforcing agent. *Psychological Review,* 1939, *46,* 553–565.

Mowrer, O. H., & Mowrer, W. M. Enuresis: A method for its study and treatment. *American Journal of Orthopsychiatry,* 1938, *8,* 436–459.

Mulhern, T., & Baumeister, A. A. An experimental attempt to reduce stereotypy by reinforcement procedures. *American Journal of Mental Deficiency,* 1969, *74,* 69–74.

Multiple Risk Factor Intervention Trial (MRFIT): A national study of primary prevention of coronary heart disease. *Journal of the American Medical Association,* 1976, *235,* 825–827.

Musante, G. J. The dietary rehabilitation clinic: Evaluative report of a behavioral and dietary treatment of obesity. *Behavior Therapy,* 1976, *7,* 198–204.

Myers, D. V. Extinction, DRO, and response-cost procedures for eliminating self-injurious behavior: A case study. *Behaviour Research and Therapy,* 1975, *13,* 189–192.

Myers, J. J., & Deibert, A. N. Reduction of self-abusive behavior in a blind child by using a feeding response. *Journal of Behavior Therapy and Experimental Psychiatry,* 1971, *2,* 141–144.

Naditch, M. P. Locus of control and drinking behavior in a sample of men in army basic training. *Journal of Consulting and Clinical Psychology,* 1975, *43,* 96.

Nathan, P. E., Titler, N. A., Lowenstein, L. M., Solomon, L., & Rossi, A. M. Behavioral analysis of chronic alcoholism. *Archives of General Psychiatry,* 1970, *22,* 419–430.

National Heart, Lung and Blood Institute Task Force on Arteriosclerosis. DHEW Publication No. (NIH) 72–137. Washington, D.C.: U.S. Government Printing Office, 1971.

National Institute on Alcohol Abuse and Alcoholism. *Alcohol and health.* First, Second, and Third Reports to the U.S. Congress. Washington, D.C.: Department of Health, Education, and Welfare, 1971, 1974, and 1978.

Neher, A. Probability pyramiding, research error, and the need for independent replication. *Psychological Record,* 1967, *17,* 257–262.

Nelson, G. L., & Cone, J. D. Multiple-baseline analysis of a token economy for psychiatric inpatients. *Journal of Applied Behavior Analysis,* 1979, *12,* 255–271.

Nelson, R. O. Methodological issues in assessment via self-monitoring. In J. D. Cone & R. P. Hawkins (Eds.), *Behavior assessment: New directions in clinical psychology.* New York: Brunner/Mazel, 1977.

Nelson, R. O., & Hayes, S. C. Some current dimensions of behavioral assessment. *Behavioral Assessment*, 1979, *1*, 1–16.

Nelson, R., Gibson, F., & Cutting, D. S. Video taped modeling: The development of three appropriate social responses in a mildly retarded child. *Mental Retardation*, 1973, *12*, 24–28.

Newman, I. M. Peer pressure hypotheses for adolescent cigarette smoking. *School Health Review*, 1970, *1*, 15–18. (a)

Newman, I. M. Status configurations and cigarette smoking in a junior high school. *Journal of School Health*, 1970, *40*, 28–31. (b)

Newsom, T. J., & Makranczy, U. J. Reducing electrical consumption of residents living in mass-metered dormitory complexes. *Journal of Environmental Systems*, 1977–78, 7, 215–235.

Nietzel, M. T. *Crime and its modification: A social learning perspective*. New York: Pergamon Press, 1979.

Nietzel, M. T., Winett, R., MacDonald, M., & Davidson, W. *Behavioral approaches to community psychology*. New York: Pergamon Press, 1977.

Nordquist, V. M., & Wahler, R. G. Naturalistic treatment of an autistic child. *Journal of Applied Behavior Analysis*, 1973, *6*, 79–87.

Norton, G. R., & Barske, B. The role of aversion in the rapid smoking treatment procedure. *Addictive Behaviors*, 1977, *2*, 21–25.

Notterman, J. M., Schoenfeld, W. N., & Bersh, P. J. A comparison of three extinction procedures following heart rate conditioning. *Journal of Abnormal and Social Psychology*, 1962, *47*, 674–677.

Nunes, D. L., Murphy, R. J., & Ruprecht, M. L. Reducing self-injurious behavior of severely retarded individuals through withdrawal of reinforcement procedures. *Behavior Modification*, 1977, *1*, 499–516.

O'Banion, K., & Arkowitz, H. *Social anxiety and selective memory for affective information about the self*. Unpublished manuscript, University of Denver, 1975.

O'Brien, C. P. Experimental analysis of conditioning factors in human narcotic addiction. *Pharmacological Reviews*, 1976, *27*, 533–543.

O'Brien, D. *Review of the literature on self-injurious behavior*. Unpublished manuscript, O'Berry Center (Goldsboro, N.C.), 1974.

O'Brien, F., & Azrin, N. H. Developing proper mealtime behaviors of the institutionalized retarded. *Journal of Applied Behavior Analysis*, 1972, *5*, 389–399.

O'Brien, F., Bugle, C., & Azrin, N. H. Training and maintaining a retarded child's proper eating. *Journal of Applied Behavior Analysis*, 1972, *5*, 67–72.

O'Connor, R. D. Modification of social withdrawal through symbolic modeling. *Journal of Applied Behavior Analysis*, 1969, *2*, 15–22.

O'Connor, R. D. Relative efficacy of modeling, shaping, and the combined procedures for modification of social withdrawal. *Journal of Abnormal Psychology,* 1972, *79,* 327–334.

O'Dell, S. Training parents in behavior modification: A review. *Psychological Bulletin,* 1974, *81,* 418–433.

Oden, S., & Asher, S. R. Coaching children in social skills for friendship making. *Child Development,* 1977, *48,* 495–506.

Ogborne, A. C. Two types of heroin reactions. *British Journal of the Addictions,* 1974, *69,* 237–242.

O'Leary, D. E., O'Leary, M. R., & Donovan, D. M. Social skill acquisition and psychosocial development of alcoholics: A review. *Addictive Behaviors,* 1976, *1,* 111–120.

O'Leary, K. D. The effects of self-instruction on immoral behavior. *Journal of Experimental Child Psychology,* 1968, *6,* 297–301.

O'Leary, K. D., & Becker, W. C. The effects of intensity of a teacher's reprimand on children's behavior. *Journal of School Psychology,* 1968, 7, 8–11.

O'Leary, K. D., Becker, W. C., Evans, M. B., & Saudargas, R. A. A token reinforcement program in a public school: A replication and systematic analysis. *Journal of Applied Behavior Analysis,* 1969, *2,* 3–13.

O'Leary, K. D., & Drabman, R. S. Token reinforcement programs in the classroom: A review. *Psychological Bulletin,* 1971, *75,* 379–398.

O'Leary, K. D., Drabman, R. S., & Kass, R. Maintenance of appropriate behavior in a token program. *Journal of Abnormal Child Psychology,* 1973, *1,* 127–138.

O'Leary, K. D., Kaufman, K. F., Kass, R. E., & Drabman, R. S. The effects of loud and soft reprimands on the behaviors of disruptive students. *Exceptional Children,* 1970, *37,* 145–155.

O'Leary, M. R., Donovan, D. M., Freeman, C. W., & Chaney, E. F. Relationship between psychopathology, experienced control, and perceived locus of control: In search of alcoholic subtypes. *Journal of Clinical Psychology,* 1976, *32,* 899–904.

Ollendick, T. H. Behavioral treatment of Anorexia Nervosa: A five year study. *Behavior Modification,* 1979, *3,* 124–135.

Ollendick, T. H., & Matson, J. An initial investigation into the parameters of overcorrection. *Psychological Reports,* 1976, *39,* 1139–1142.

Ollendick, T. H., & Matson, J. L. Overcorrection: An overview. *Behavior Therapy,* 1978, *9,* 830–842.

Orne, M. T. On the social psychology of the psychological experiment: With particular reference to demand characteristics and their implications. *American Psychologist,* 1962, *17,* 776–783.

Orne, M. T., & Scheibe, K. E. The contribution of non-deprivation factors in the production of sensory deprivation effects: The psychology of the "panic button." *Journal of Abnormal and Social Psychology*, 1964, *68*, 3–12.

O'Shea, R. M., & Gray, S. B. Dental patients' attitudes and behavior concerning prevention. *Public Health Reports*, 1968, *83*, 405–410.

Ovesey, L., Gaylin, W., & Hendin, H. Psychotherapy of male homosexuality. *Archives of General Psychiatry*, 1963, *9*, 19–31.

Owens, R. D., & Sever, H. L. *The 3M commute-a-van program: Progress Report II*. St. Paul: 3M Company, 1977.

Packard, R. G. The control of "classroom attention": A group contingency for complex behavior. *Journal of Applied Behavior Analysis*, 1970, *3*, 13–28.

Padfield, M. The comparative effects of two counseling approaches on the intensity of depression among rural women of low socioeconomic status. *Journal of Consulting and Clinical Psychology*, 1976, *23*, 209–214.

Page, T. J., Iwata, B. A., & Neef, N. A. Teaching pedestrian skills to retarded persons: Generalization from the classroom to the natural environment. *Journal of Applied Behavior Analysis*, 1976, *9*, 433–444.

Palmer, A. B. Some variables contributing to the onset of cigarette smoking among junior high school students. *Social Science and Medicine*, 1970, *4*, 359–366.

Palmer, M. H., Lloyd, M. E., & Lloyd, K. E. An experimental analysis of electricity conservation procedures. *Journal of Applied Behavior Analysis*, 1978, *10*, 665–672.

Parker, L. F., & Skorupski, M. S. Conditioned ethanol tolerance. *National Drug Abuse Conference '78 Book of Proceedings*, in press.

Patterson, G. R. *Families: Applications of social learning to family life*. Champaign, Ill.: Research Press, 1971.

Patterson, G. R. Interventions for boys with conduct problems: Multiple settings, treatments, and criteria. *Journal of Consulting and Clinical Psychology*, 1974, *42*, 471–481.

Patterson, G. R., Cobb, J. A., & Ray, R. S. A social engineering technology for retraining aggressive boys. In H. E. Adams & P. Unikel (Eds.), *Issues and trends in behavior therapy*. Springfield, Ill.: Charles C. Thomas, 1973.

Patterson, G. R., & Gullion, M. E. *Living with children*. Champaign, Ill.: Research Press, 1968.

Patterson, G. R., & Reid, J. B. Reciprocity and coercion: Two facets of social systems. In C. Neuringer & J. L. Michael (Eds.), *Behavior modification in clinical psychology*. New York: Appleton-Century-Crofts, 1970.

Patterson, G. R., Reid, J. B., Jones, R. R., & Conger, R. E. *A social learning approach to family intervention: Families with aggressive children*. Eugene, Oreg.: Custalia Press, 1975.

Patterson, G. R., Weiss, R. L., & Hops, H. Training of marital skills: Some problems and concepts. In H. Leitenberg (Ed.), *Handbook of behavior modification*. New York: Prentice-Hall, 1976.

Patterson, R. L., & Teigen, J. R. Conditioning and post-hospital generalization of nondelusional responses in a chronic psychotic patient. *Journal of Applied Behavior Analysis,* 1973, *6,* 65–70.

Pattison, E. M., Sobell, M. B., & Sobell, L. C. (Eds.). *Emerging concepts of alcohol dependence.* New York: Springer, 1977.

Paul, G. L. *Insight vs. desensitization in psychotherapy: An experiment in anxiety reduction.* Stanford: Stanford University Press, 1966.

Paul, G. L. Behavior modification research: Design and tactics. In C. M. Franks (Ed.), *Behavior therapy: Appraisal and status.* New York: McGraw-Hill, 1969. (a)

Paul, G. Chronic mental patient: Current status—future directions. *Psychological Bulletin,* 1969, *71,* 81–94. (b)

Paul, G. L. Outcome of systematic desensitization I: Background, procedures and uncontrolled reports of individual treatment. In C. M. Franks (Ed.), *Behavior therapy: Appraisal and status.* New York: McGraw-Hill, 1969. (c)

Paul, G. L. Outcome of systematic desensitization II: Controlled investigations of individual treatment, technique variations, and current status. In C. M. Franks (Ed.), *Behavior therapy: Appraisal and status.* New York: McGraw-Hill, 1969. (d)

Paul, G. L., & Bernstein, D. A. *Anxiety and behavior: Treatment by systematic desensitization and related techniques.* New York: General Learning Press, 1973.

Paul, G. G., & Lentz, R. J. *Psychosocial treatment of chronic mental patients: Milieu vs. social-learning programs.* Cambridge: Harvard University Press, 1977.

Paul, G. L., Tobias, L. L., & Holly, B. L. Maintenance psychotropic drugs in the presence of active treatment programs. *Archives of General Psychiatry,* 1972, *27,* 106–115.

Paxton, R., & Bernacca, G. Urinary nicotine concentration as a function of time since last cigarette: Implications for detecting faking in smoking clinics. *Behavior Therapy,* 1979, *10,* 523–528.

Paykel, E. S., Prusoff, B. A. Klerman, G. L., Haskell, D., & Dimascio, A. Clinical response to amitriptyline among depressed women. *Journal of Nervous and Mental Disease,* 1973, *156,* 149–165.

Peed, S., Roberts, M., & Forehand, R. Evaluation of the effectiveness of a standardized parent training program in altering the interaction of mothers and their noncompliant children. *Behavior Modification,* 1977, *1,* 323–350.

Pelham, W. E. Hyperactive children. *Psychiatric Clinics of North America,* 1978, *1,* 227–245.

Pendergrass, V. E. Effects of length of time-out from positive reinforcement and schedule of application in suppression of aggressive behavior. *Psychological Record*, 1971, *21*, 75–80.

Penick, S. B., Filion, R., Fox, S., & Stunkard. A. J. Behavior modification in the treatment of obesity. *Psychosomatic Medicine*, 1971, *33*, 49–55.

Percell, L. P., Berwick, P. T., & Beigel, A. The effects of assertive training on self-concept and anxiety. *Archives of General Psychiatry*, 1974, *31*, 502–504.

Perri, M. G., & Richards, C. S. The empirical development of a behavioral role-playing test: Assessment of heterosocial skills in male college students. *Behavior Modification*, 1979, *3*, 337–354.

Perri, M. G., Richards, C. S., & Goodrich, J. D. The heterosocial adequacy test (HAT): A behavioral role-playing test for the assessment of heterosocial skills in male college students. *JSAS Catalog of Selected Documents in Psychology*, 1978, *8*, 16 (Ms. No. 1650).

Peterson, D. R. *The clinical study of social behavior*. New York: Appleton-Century-Crofts, 1968.

Phillips, L., & Draguns, J. G. Classfication of the behavior disorders. *Annual Review of Psychology*, 1971, *22*, 447–482.

Picker, M., Poling, A., & Parker, A. A review of children's self-injurious behavior. *The Psychological Record*, 1979, *29*, 425–452.

Pilkonis, P. A. Shyness public and private and its relationship to other measures of social behavior. *Journal of Personality*, 1977, *45*, 585–595.

Plant, T. F. A. *Alcohol problems: A report to the nation by the Cooperative Commission on the Study of Alcoholism*. New York: Oxford University Press, 1967.

Platt, J., & Labate, C. *Heroin addiction: Theory, research, and treatment*. New York: Wiley, 1976.

Platt, J., Scura, W. C., & Hannon, J. R. Problem-solving thinking of youthful incarcerated heroin addicts. *Journal of Community Psychology*, 1973, *1*, 278–281.

Polakow, R. L. Personal communication to J. S. Stumphauzer, November 19, 1979.

Polakow, R. L., & Doctor, R. M. A behavior modification program for adult drug offenders. *Journal of Research in Crime and Delinquency*, 1974, *3*, 41–45.

Polakow, R. L., & Peabody, D. L. Behavioral treatment of child abuse. *International Journal of Offender Therapy and Comparative Criminology*, 1975, *19*, 100–103.

Pomerleau, O. F. Why people smoke: Current psychobiological models. In P. Davidson (Ed.), *Behavioral medicine: Changing health life styles*. New York: Brunner/Mazel, 1979, in press.

Pomerleau, O. F., & Pomerleau, C. S. *Break the smoking habit: A behavioral program for giving up cigarettes*. Champaign, Ill.: Research Press, 1977.

Pommer, D. A., & Streedbeck, D. Motivating staff performance in an operant learning program for children. *Journal of Applied Behavior Analysis*, 1974, *7*, 217–221.

Poser, E. G. The self-efficacy concept: Some theoretical, procedural and clinical implications. *Advances in Behaviour Research and Therapy*, 1978, *1*, 193–202.

Powell, D. H. A pilot study of occasional heroin users. *Archives of General Psychiatry*, 1973, *28*, 586–594.

Powers, R. B., Osborne, J. B., & Anderson, E. G. Positive reinforcement of litter removal in the natural environment. *Journal of Applied Behavior Analysis*, 1973, *6*, 579–586.

Pratsch, L. *Carpool and buspool matching guide* (4th ed.). Washington, D.C.: U.S. Department of Transportation, Federal Highway Administration, January 1975.

Premack, D. Reversibility of the reinforcement relation. *Science*, 1962, *136*, 255–257.

Premack, D. Reinforcement theory. In D. Levine (Ed.), *Nebraska symposium on motivation*. Lincoln: University of Nebraska Press, 1965.

Presly, A. S., & Walton, H. J. Dimensions of abnormal personality. *British Journal of Psychiatry*, 1973, *122*, 269–276.

Prochaska, J. O., & Marzilli, R. Modifications of the Masters and Johnson approach to sexual problems. *Psychotherapy: Theory Research and Practice*, 1973, *10*, 294–296.

Prytula, R. E., Oster, G. D., & Davis, S. F. The "rat rabbit" problem: What did John B. Watson really do? *Teaching of Psychology*, 1977, *4*, 44–46.

Quay, H. C. Patterns of aggression, withdrawal, and immaturity. In H. C. Quay & J. S. Werry (Eds.), *Psychopathological disorders of childhood*. New York: Wiley, 1972.

Rachlin, H. (Ed.). *Introduction to modern behaviorism*. San Francisco: W. H. Freeman & Co., 1970.

Rachman, S. Systematic desensitization. *Psychological Bulletin*, 1967, *67*, 93–103.

Rachman, S. Clinical applications of observational learning, imitation, and modeling. *Behavior Therapy*, 1972, *3*, 379–397.

Rachman, S. The modification of obsessions: A new formulation. *Behaviour Research and Therapy*, 1976, *14*, 437–443.

Rado, S. An adaptational view of sexual behavior. In P. Hoch & J. Zubin (Eds.), *Psychosexual development in health and disease*. New York: Grune & Stratton, 1949.

Ragland, E. U., Kerr, M. M., & Strain, P. S. Behavior of withdrawn autistic children: Effects of peer social initiations. *Behavior Modification*, 1978, *2*, 565–578.

Ramsey, R. W., & Van Velzen, V. Behavior therapy for sexual perversions. *Behaviour Research and Therapy*, 1968, *6*, 17–19.

Rappaport, J. *Community psychology: Values, research, and action*. New York: Holt, Rinehart & Winston, 1977.

Rathus, S. A. An experimental investigation of assertion training in a group setting. *Journal of Behavior Therapy and Experimental Psychiatry*, 1972, *3*, 81–86.

Rathus, S. A. A 30 item schedule for assessing assertive behavior. *Behavior Therapy*, 1973, *4*, 398–406.

Ray, M. B. The cycle of abstinence and relapse among heroin addicts. In R. H. Coombs, L. J. Fry, & P. G. Lewis (Eds.), *Socialization in drug abuse*. Cambridge, Mass.: Schenkman, 1976.

Ray, O. S. *Drugs, society, and human behavior*. Saint Louis: C. V. Mosby, 1972.

Rayner, J. F., & Cohen, L. K. A position on school dental health education. *Journal of Preventive Dentistry*, 1974, *1*, 11–23.

Reeves, J. L., & Mealiea, W. L. Biofeedback-assisted cue-controlled relaxation for the treatment of flight phobias. *Journal of Behavior Therapy and Experimental Psychiatry*, 1975, *6*, 1–5.

Rehm, L. P. A self-control model of depression. *Behavior Therapy*, 1977, *8*, 787–804.

Rehm, L. P., Fuchs, C. Z., Roth, D. M., Kornblith, S. J., & Romano, J. M. A comparison of self-control and assertion skills treatments of depression. *Behavior Therapy*, 1979, *10*, 429–442.

Rehm, L. P., & Marston, A. R. Reduction of social anxiety through modification of self-reinforcement: An instigation therapy technique. *Journal of Consulting and Clinical Psychology*, 1968, *32*, 565–574.

Reichel, D. A., & Geller, E. S. Applications of behavioral analysis for conserving transportation energy. In A. Baum & J. E. Singer (Eds.), *Advances in environmental psychology* (Vol. 3). Hillsdale, N.J.: Lawrence Erlbaum Associates, Inc., in press.

Reid, D. H., & Hurlbut, B. Teaching nonvocal communication skills to multi-handicapped retarded adults. *Journal of Applied Behavior Analysis*, 1977, *10*, 591–603.

Reid, D. H., Luyben, P. L., Rawers, R. J., & Bailey, J. S. The effects of prompting and proximity of containers on newspaper recycling behavior. *Environment and Behavior*, 1976, *8*, 471–482.

Reid, J. B., & Patterson, G. R. The modification of aggression and stealing behavior of boys in the home setting. In E. Ribes & A. Bandura (Eds.), *Analysis of delinquency and aggression*. Hillsdale, N.J.: Lawrence Erlbaum, 1973.

Reiss, M. L., Piotrowski, W. D., & Bailey, J. S. Behavioral community psychology: Encouraging low-income parents to seek dental care for their children. *Journal of Applied Behavior Analysis*, 1976, *9*, 387–397.

Repp, A. C., & Deitz, D. On the selective use of punishment—Suggested guidelines for administrators. *Mental Retardation*, 1978, *16*, 250–254.

Repp, A. C., Deitz, S. M., & Speir, N. C. Reducing stereotypic responding of retarded persons by the differential reinforcement of other behavior. *American Journal of Mental Deficiency*, 1974, *79*, 279–284.

Repucci, N. Implementation issues for the behavior modifier as institutional change agent. *Behavior Therapy*, 1977, *8*, 594–605.

Repucci, N., & Saunders, J. Social psychology of behavior modification: Problems of implementation in natural settings. *American Psychologist*, 1974, *29*, 649–660.

Reznick, H., & Baleh, P. The effects of anxiety and response cost manipulations on the eating behavior of obese and normal-weight subjects. *Addictive Behaviors*, 1977, *2*, 219–225.

Rhyne, L. D., MacDonald, M. L., McGrath, R. A., Lindquist, C. U., & Cramer, J. A. The role-played dating interactions (RPDI): An instrument for the measurement of male social dating skills. *JSAS Catalog of Selected Documents in Psychology*, 1974, *4*, 42 (Ms. No. 615).

Rimland, B. *Infantile autism: The syndrome and its implications for a neutral theory of behavior*. New York: Appleton-Century-Crofts, 1964.

Rimm, D. C., & Masters, J. C. *Behavior therapy: Techniques and empirical findings* (1st ed.). New York: Academic Press, 1974.

Rimm, D. C., & Masters, J. C. *Behavior therapy: Techniques and empirical findings* (2nd ed.). New York: Academic Press, 1979.

Rincover, A. Sensory extinction: A procedure for eliminating self-stimulatory behavior in developmentally disabled children. *Journal of Abnormal Child Psychology*, 1978, *6*, 299–310.

Rincover, A., Cook, R., Peoples, A., & Packard, D. Sensory extinction and sensory reinforcement principles for programming multiple adaptive behavior change. *Journal of Applied Behavior Analysis*, 1979, *12*, 221–233.

Rincover, A., & Koegel, R. L. Research on the education of autistic children: Recent advances and future directions. In B. B. Lahey & A. E. Kazdin (Eds.), *Advances in clinical child psychology*. New York: Plenum Press, 1977.

Risley, T. R. The effects and side effects of punishing the autistic behaviors of a deviant child. *Journal of Applied Behavior Analysis*, 1968, *1*, 21–34.

Risley, T. R. Behavior modification: An experimental-therapeutic endeavor. In L. A. Hamerlynck, P. O. Davidson, L. E. Acker (Eds.), *Behavior modification and ideal mental health services*. Calgary, Alberta, Canada: University of Calgary Press, 1970.

Risley, T. R., Clark, H. B., & Cataldo, M. F. Behavior technology for the normal, middle-class family. In E. J. Marsh, L. A. Hamerlynck, & L. C. Handy (Eds.), *Behavior modification and families*. New York: Brunner/Mazel, Inc., 1976.

Ritter, B. The use of contact desensitization, demonstration-plus-participation, and demonstration alone in the treatment of acrophobia. *Behavior Research and Therapy*, 1969, *7*, 157–164.

Robertson, L. S., Kelley, A. B., O'Neill, B., Wixom, C. W., Eiswirth, R. S., & Haddon, W. A controlled study of the effect of television messages on safety belt use. *American Journal of Public Health*, 1974, *64*, 1071–1080.

Robertson, S. J., DeReus, D. M., & Drabman, R. S. Peer and college student tutoring as reinforcement in a token economy. *Journal of Applied Behavior Analysis*, 1976, *9*, 169–177.

Robin, A. L., Kent, R., O'Leary, K. D., Foster, S., & Prinz, R. An approach to teaching parents and adolescents problem-solving communication skills: A preliminary report. *Behavior Therapy*, 1977, *8*, 639–643.

Robins, L. *The Viet Nam drug abuser returns*. New York: McGraw-Hill, 1974.

Robinson, E. A., & Price, M. G. Pleasurable behavior in marital interaction: An observational study. *Journal of Consulting and Clinical Psychology*, 1980, *48*, 117–118.

Rogers, C. R. A theory of therapy, personality, and interpersonal relationships, as developed in the client-centered framework. In S. Koch (Ed.), *Psychology: A study of a science* (Vol. 3). New York: McGraw-Hill, 1959.

Rogers, C. R., & Skinner, B. F. Some issues concerning the control of human behavior: A symposium. *Science*, 1956, *124*, 1057–1066.

Rohsenow, D. J., & O'Leary, M. R. Locus of control research on alcoholic populations: A review. I. Development, scales, and treatment. *International Journal of the Addictions*, 1978, *13*, 55–78.

Rollins, H., McCandless, B., Thompson, M., & Brassell, W. Project success environment: An extended application of contingency management to inner city schools. *Journal of Educational Psychology*, 1974, *66*, 167–178.

Romanczyk, R. G. Self-monitoring in the treatment of obesity. *Behavior Therapy*, 1974, *5*, 531–540.

Romanczyk, R. G. Intermittent punishment of self-stimulation: Effectiveness during application and extinction. *Journal of Consulting and Clinical Psychology*, 1977, *45*, 53–60.

Romanczyk, R. G., Tracey, D. A., Wilson, G. T., & Thorpe, G. L. Behavioral techniques in the treatment of obesity: A comparative analysis. *Behavior Research and Therapy*, 1973, *11*, 629–640.

Rose, H. S., & Hinds, D. H. South Dixie Highway contraflow bus and car-pool lane demonstration project. *Transportation Research Record*, 1976, No. 606, 18–22.

Rose, Y. J., & Tryon, W. W. Judgements of assertive behavior as a function of speech, loudness, latency, content, gestures, inflection and sex. *Behavior Modification*, 1979, *3*, 112–123.

Rosen, G. M., Glasgow, R. E., & Barrera, M., Jr. A controlled study to assess the clinical efficacy of totally self-administered systematic desensitization. *Journal of Consulting and Clinical Psychology*, 1976, *44*(2), 208–217.

Rosenbaum, M., & Drabman, R. S. Self-control training in the classroom: A review and critique. *Journal of Applied Behavior Analysis*, in press.

Rosenman, R. H., Friedman, M., Straus, R., Jenkins, C. D., Zyzanski, S. J., &

Wurm, M. Coronary heart disease in the Western Collaborative Group Study: A follow-up experience of 4½ years. *Journal of Chronic Diseases*, 1970, *23*, 173–190.

Rosenthal, T. L. Bandura's self-efficacy theory: Thought *is* father to the deed. *Advances in Behaviour Research and Therapy*, 1978, *1*, 203–209.

Rosenthal, T. L., & Bandura, A. Psychological modeling: Theory and practice. In S. L. Garfield & A. E. Bergin (Eds.), *Handbook of psychotherapy and behavior change*. New York: Wiley, 1978.

Rosenthal, T. L., Hung, J. H., & Kelley, J. E. Therapeutic social influence: Sternly strike while the iron is hot. *Behaviour Research and Therapy*, 1977, *15*, 253–259.

Ross, A. O. *Psychological disorders of children: A behavioral approach to theory, research, and therapy*. New York: McGraw-Hill, 1974.

Ross, R. T. Behavioral correlates of levels of intelligence. *American Journal of Mental Deficiency*, 1972, *76*, 515–519.

Rotter, J. B. *Social learning and clinical psychology*. Englewood Cliffs, N.J.: Prentice-Hall, 1954.

Rozensky, R. H., & Bellack, A. S. Individual differences in self-reinforcement style and performance in self- and therapist-controlled weight reduction programs. *Behavior Therapy*, 1976, *14*, 357–364.

Runnion, A., Watson, J. D., & McWhorter, J. Energy savings in interstate transportation through feedback and reinforcement. *Journal of Organizational Behavior Management*, 1978, *1*, 180–191.

Rush, A. J., Beck, A. T., Kovacs, M., & Hollon, S. D. Comparative efficacy of cognitive therapy in the treatment of depressed outpatients. *Cognitive Therapy and Research*, 1977, *1*, 17–36.

Rush, A. J., Shaw, B., & Khatami, M. Cognitive therapy of depression: Utilizing the couples approach. *Cognitive Therapy and Research*, 1980, *4*, 103–113.

Russell, M. A. H., Raw, M. Taylor, C., Feyerabend, C., & Saloojee, Y. Blood nicotine and carboxy-hemoglobin levels after rapid smoking aversion therapy. *Journal of Consulting and Clinical Psychology*, 1978, *46*, 1423–1431.

Russo, D. C., & Koegel, R. L. A method for integrating an autistic child into a normal public school classroom. *Journal of Applied Behavior Analysis*, 1977, *10*, 579–590.

Ryle, G. *The concept of mind*. New York: Barnes and Noble, 1949.

Sailor, W., Guess, D., & Baer, D. M. Functional language for verbally deficient children: An experimental program. *Mental Retardation*, 1973, *11*, 27–34.

Sajwaj, T., & Hedges, D. *"Side-effects" of a punishment procedure in an oppositional, retarded child*. Paper presented at the meetings of the Western Psychological Association, San Francisco, April 1971.

Sajwaj, T., Libet, J., & Agras, S. Lemon-juice therapy: The control of life-threatening rumination in a six-month-old infant. *Journal of Applied Behavior Analysis*, 1974, *7*, 557–563.

Salmon, R., & Salmon, S. The causes of heroin addiction: A review of the literature. Part II. *International Journal of the Addictions*, 1977, *12*, 937–951.

Salter, A. *Conditioned reflex therapy*. New York: Capricorn, 1949.

Saposnek, D. T., & Watson, L. S. The elimination of the self-destructive behavior of a psychotic child: A case study. *Behavior Therapy*, 1974, *5*, 79–89.

Sarason, I. G. *Abnormal psychology: The problem of maladaptive behavior* (2nd ed.). Englewood Cliffs, N.J.: Prentice-Hall, 1976.

Sarason, S. *The psychological sense of community: Prospects for the community psychology*. San Francisco: Jossey-Bass, 1974.

Sarbin, T. R. Anxiety: Reification of a metaphor. *Archives of General Psychiatry*, 1964, *10*, 630–638.

Sarbin, T. R. On the futility of the proposition that some people be labeled "mentally ill." *Journal of Consulting Psychology*, 1967, *31*, 447–453.

Schachter, S. The interaction of cognitive and physiological determinants of emotional state. In L. Berkowitz (Ed.), *Advances in experimental social psychology* (Vol. 1). New York: Academic Press, 1964.

Schachter, S. Pharmacological and psychological determinants of smoking. *Annals of Internal Medicine*, 1978, *88*, 104–114.

Schachter, S., & Rodin, J. (Eds.), *Obese humans and rats*. Washington, D.C.: Earlbaum, 1974.

Schachter, S., Silverstein, B., Kozlowski, L. T., Perlick, N., Herman, C. P., & Liebling, B. Studies on the interaction of psychological and pharmacological determinants of smoking. *Journal of Experimental Psychology: General*, 1977, *106*, 3–40.

Schachter, S., & Singer, J. E. Cognitive, social, and physiological determinants of emotional state. *Psychological Review*, 1962, *69*, 379–399.

Scheff, T. J. *Being mentally ill: A sociological theory*. Chicago: Aldine, 1966.

Scheiner, J. L., & Keiper, S. A. Car-pool information project: Innovative approaches improve results. *Transportation Research Record*, 1976, No. 619, 16–18.

Schlanger, B. B. Environmental influences on the verbal output of mentally retarded children. *Journal of Speech and Hearing Disorders*, 1954, *19*, 339–343.

Schmahl, D. P., Lichtenstein, E., & Harris, W. E. Successful treatment of habitual smokers with warm, smoky air and rapid smoking. *Journal of Consulting and Clinical Psychology*, 1972, *38*, 105–111.

Schneider, M. Turtle technique in the classroom. *Teaching Exceptional Children*, 1974, *8*, 22–24.

Schneidman, B., & McGuire, L. Group therapy for nonorgasmic women: Two age levels. *Archives of Sexual Behavior*, 1976, *5*, 239–247.

Schover, L. R., Friedman, J., Weiler, S., Heiman, J., & LoPicollo, J. *A multi-axial descriptive system for the sexual dysfunctions.* Unpublished manuscript, 1980. (Available from Dr. L. R. Schover, Department of Psychiatry, SUNY at Stony Brook, Stony Brook, N.Y.)

Schreibman, L. A., & Koegel, R. L. A guideline for planning behavior modification programs for autistic children. In S. M. Turner, K. S. Calhoun, & H. E. Adams (Eds.), *Handbook of behavior therapy.* New York: Wiley, 1979.

Schultz, R., Wehman, P., Renzaglia, A., & Karan, O. Efficacy of contingent social disapproval on inappropriate verbalizations of two severely retarded males. *Behavior Therapy*, 1978, *9*, 657–662.

Schumaker, J. B., Hovell, M. F., & Sherman, J. A. An analysis of daily report cards and parent-managed privileges in the improvement of adolescents' classroom performance. *Journal of Applied Behavior Analysis*, 1977, *10*, 449–464.

Schuster, C. R., & Villareal, J. E. The experimental analysis of opioid dependence. In D. H. Efron (Ed.), *Psychopharmacology: A review of progress.* Washington, D.C.: Government Printing Office (Public Health Service Publication No. 1836), 1968.

Schwartz, J. L. A critical review and evaluation of smoking control methods. *Public Health Reports*, 1969, *84*, 489–506.

Schwitzgebel, R., & Kolb, D. *Changing human behavior: Principles of planned intervention.* New York: McGraw-Hill, 1974.

Scott, J. W., & Bushell, D. The length of teacher contacts and students' off-task behavior. *Journal of Applied Behavior Analysis*, 1974, *7*, 39–44.

Seaver, W. B., & Patterson, A. H. Decreasing fuel oil consumption through feedback and social commendation. *Journal of Applied Behavior Analysis*, 1976, *9*, 147–152.

Sechrest, L. Incremental validity: A recommendation. *Education and Psychological Measurement*, 1963, *23*, 153–158.

Seed, A. H., Jr. Who litters—and why? *Environmental Education*, 1970, *1*, 93–94.

Segraves, R. T. Pharmacological agents causing sexual dysfunction. *Journal of Sex and Marital Therapy*, 1977, *3*, 157–176.

Seligman, C., & Darley, J. M. Feedback as a means of decreasing residential energy consumption. *Journal of Applied Psychology*, 1977, *62*, 363–368.

Seligman, M. E. P. *Helplessness: On depression, development, and death.* San Francisco: W. H. Freeman, 1975.

Selltiz, C., Jahoda, M., Deutsch, M., & Cook, S. W. *Research methods in social relations.* New York: Holt-Dryden, 1959.

Selye, H. *The stress of life.* New York: McGraw-Hill, 1956.

Selye, H. Stress: It's a G.A.S. *Psychology Today*, September 1969, pp. 25–26.

Semans, J. H. Premature ejaculation: A new approach. *Southern Medical Journal,* 1956, *49,* 353–357.

Senter, R. J., Heintzelman, M., Dorfmueller, M., & Hinkle, H. A comparative look at ratings of the subjective effects of beverage alcohol. *Psychological Record,* 1979, *29,* 49–56.

Serber, M. Videotape feedback in the treatment of couples with sexual dysfunction. *Archives of Sexual Behavior,* 1974, *3,* 377–380.

Shapiro, A. K., & Morris, L. A. Placebo effects in medical and psychological therapies. In S. L. Garfield & A. E. Bergin (Eds.), *Handbook of psychotherapy and behavior change* (2nd ed.). New York: Wiley, 1978.

Shaw, B. F. Comparison of cognitive therapy and behavior therapy in the treatment of depression. *Journal of Consulting and Clinical Psychology,* 1977, *45,* 543–551.

Shaw, W. A. The relation of muscular action potentials to imaginal weight lifting. *Archives of Psychology,* 1940, *247,* 50.

Sherman, A. R. Real-life exposure as a primary therapeutic factor in the desensitization treatment of fear. *Journal of Abnormal Psychology,* 1972, *79,* 19–28.

Sidman, M. *Tactics of scientific research.* New York: Basic Books, 1960.

Siegal, S. Evidence from rats that morphine tolerance is a learned response. *Journal of Comparative and Physiological Psychology,* 1975, *89,* 498–506.

Siegal, S. Morphine tolerance acquisition as an associative process. *Journal of Experimental Psychology: Animal Behavior Processes,* 1977, *3,* 1–13.

Sirota, A. D., & Mahoney, M. J. Relaxing on cue: The self-regulation of asthma. *Journal of Behavior Therapy and Experimental Psychiatry,* 1974, *5,* 65–66.

Skinner, B. F. *Walden Two.* New York: Macmillan Co., 1948.

Skinner, B. F. *Science and human behavior.* New York: Free Press, 1953.

Skinner, B. F. Behaviorism at fifty. *Science,* 1963, *140,* 951–958.

Skinner, B. F. *Beyond freedom and dignity.* New York: Knopf, 1971.

Slavin, R. E., Wodarski, J. S., & Blackburn, B. L. *A group contingency for electricity conservation in master metered apartments.* Center for Social Organization of Schools, Johns Hopkins University, 1978. Report No. 242.

Slavin, R. E., & Wodarski, J. S. *Using group contingencies to reduce natural gas consumption in master metered apartments.* Center for Social Organization of Schools, Johns Hopkins University, 1977. Report No. 232.

Smith, G. M. Personality and smoking: A review of the empirical literature. In W. A. Hunt (Ed.), *Learning mechanisms in smoking.* Chicago: Aldine, 1970.

Smith, R. E., Diener, E., & Beaman, A. L. Demand characteristics and the behavioral avoidance measure of fear in behavior therapy analogue research. *Behavior Therapy,* 1974, *5,* 172–182.

Smith, R. E., & Sarason, I. G. Social anxiety and the evaluation of negative interpersonal feedback. *Journal of Consulting and Clinical Psychology*, 1975, *43*, 429.

Smith, R. R., Milan, M. A., Wood, L. F., & McKee, J. M. The correctional officer as a behavioral technician. *Criminal Justice and Behavior*, 1976, *3*, 345–360.

Solnick, J. V., Rincover, A., & Peterson, C. R. Some determinants of the reinforcing and punishing effects of timeout. *Journal of Applied Behavior Analysis*, 1977, *10*, 415–424.

Solomon, E., & Marshall, W. L. A comprehensive model for the acquisition, maintenance, and treatment of drug-taking behaviour. *British Journal of the Addictions*, 1973, *68*, 215–220.

Solomon, R. L. An opponent-process theory of acquired motivation: The affective dynamics of addiction. In J. D. Maser & M. E. P. Seligman (Eds.), *Psychopathology: Experimental models*. San Francisco: W. H. Freeman, 1977.

Solomon, R. L., Kamin, L. J., & Wynne, L. C. Traumatic avoidance learning: The outcomes of several extinction procedures with dogs. *Journal of Abnormal and Social Psychology*, 1953, *48*, 291–302.

Solomon, R. L., & Wynne, L. C. Traumatic avoidance learning: The principles of anxiety conservation and partial irreversibility. *Psychological Review*, 1954, *61*, 353–385.

Spielberger, C. D. *Anxiety: Current trends in theory and research* (Vol. 1). New York: Academic Press, 1972.

Spivack, G., & Shure, M. G. *Social adjustment of young children*. San Francisco: Jossey-Bass, 1974.

Stalonas, P. M., Johnson, W. G., & Christ, M. Behavior modification for obesity: The evaluation of exercise, contingency management, and program adherence. *Journal of Consulting and Clinical Psychology*, 1978, *46*, 463–469.

Stampfl, T. G., & Levis, D. J. Essentials of implosive therapy: A learning-theory-based psychodynamic behavioral therapy. *Journal of Abnormal Psychology*, 1967, *72*, 496–503.

Steffen, J. J., & Myszak, K. A. Influence of pretherapy induction upon the outcome of a self-control weight reduction program. *Behavior Therapy*, 1978, *9*, 404–409.

Steinfield, J. F. The public's responsibility: A bill of rights for the non-smoker. *Rhode Island Medical Journal*, 1972, *55*, 124–126.

Steinglass, P. The conceptualization of marriage from a systems theory perspective. In T. J. Paolino, Jr., & B. S. McCrady (Eds.), *Marriage and marital therapy*. New York: Brunner/Mazel, 1978.

Stevenson, I., & Wolpe, J. Recovery from sexual deviations through overcoming nonsexual neurotic responses. *American Journal of Psychiatry*, 1960, *116*, 737–742.

Strain, P. S., Shores, R. E., & Kerr, M. M. An experimental analysis of "spillover" effects on the social interaction of behaviorally handicapped preschool children. *Journal of Applied Behavior Analysis,* 1976, *9,* 31–40.

Strain, P. S., Shores, R. E., & Timm, M. A. Effects of peer social initiations on the behavior of withdrawn preschool children. *Journal of Applied Behavior Analysis,* 1977, *10,* 289–298.

Strupp, H. H., & Hadley, S. W. A tripartite model of mental health and therapeutic outcomes: With special reference to negative effects in psychotherapy. *American Psychologist,* 1977, *32,* 187–196.

Stuart, R. B. Behavioral control of overeating. *Behaviour Research and Therapy,* 1967, *5,* 357–365.

Stuart, R. B. *Trick or treatment: How and when psychotherapy fails.* Champaign, Ill.: Research Press, 1970.

Stuart, R. B. A three dimensional program for the treatment of obesity. *Behavior Research and Therapy,* 1971, *9,* 177–186.

Stuart, R. B. *Act thin, stay thin.* New York: W. W. Norton Co., 1977.

Stuart, R. B., Tripodi, T., Jayaratne, S., & Camburn, D. An experiment in social engineering in serving the families of predelinquents. *Journal of Abnormal Child Psychology,* 1976, *4,* 243–261.

Stumphauzer, J. S. Behavior modification with juvenile delinquents: A critical review. *Federal Correctional Institution Technical and Treatment Notes,* 1970, *1,* 1–22.

Stumphauzer, J. S. (Ed.). *Behavior therapy with delinquents.* Springfield, Ill.: Charles C. Thomas, 1973.

Stumphauzer, J. S. *Daily behavior card manual.* Venice, Calif.: Behaviormetrics, 1974. (a)

Stumphauzer, J. S. *Six techniques of modifying delinquent behavior.* Leonia, N.J.: Behavioral Sciences Tape Library, 1974. (b)

Stumphauzer, J. S. Modifying delinquent behavior: Beginnings and current practices. *Adolescence,* 1976, *11,* 13–28. (a)

Stumphauzer, J. S. Elimination of stealing by self-reinforcement of alternative behavior and family contracting. *Journal of Behavior Therapy and Experimental Psychiatry,* 1976, *7,* 265–268. (b)

Stumphauzer, J. S. *Behavior modification principles: An introduction and training manual.* Kalamazoo, Mich.: Behaviordelia, 1977.

Stumphauzer, J. S. (Ed.). *Progress in behavior therapy with delinquents.* Springfield, Ill.: Charles C. Thomas, 1979.

Stumphauzer, J. S. *Six community anticrime programs: The first year.* Research report in progress, 1980.

Stumphauzer, J. S., Aiken, T. W., & Veloz, E. V. East side story: Behavioral analysis of a high juvenile crime community. *Behavioral Disorders,* 1977, *2,* 76–84.

Stumphauzer, J. S., Candelora, K., & Venema, H. B. A follow-up of probation officers trained in behavior modification. *Behavior Therapy,* 1976, 7, 713–715.

Stumphauzer, J. S., & Marohn, R. C. *The causes, characteristics and treatment of delinquency: Behavioral vs. psychodynamic perspectives.* Symposium presented to the Institute for Juvenile Research, Chicago, Ill., May 16, 1975.

Stunkard, A. J. (Ed.). *Obesity.* Philadelphia: Saunders, 1980.

Stunkard, A. J., & Brownell, K. D. Work site treatment for obesity. *American Journal of Psychiatry,* in press.

Stunkard, A. J., & Mahoney, M. J. Behavioral treatment of eating disorders. In H. Leitenberg (Ed.), *The handbook of behavior modification.* Englewood Cliffs, N.J.: Prentice-Hall, 1976.

Stunkard, A. J., & Mendelson, M. Obesity and body image: I. Characteristics of disturbances in the body image of some obese persons. *American Journal of Psychiatry,* 1967, *123,* 1296–1300.

Stunkard, A. J., & Penick, S. B. Behavior modification in the treatment of obesity: The problem of maintaining weight loss. *Archives of General Psychiatry,* 1979, *36,* 801–806.

Subcommittee on Constitutional Rights of the Committee on the Judiciary, United States Senate, Ninety-third Congress, second session. *Individual rights and the federal role in behavior modification.* Washington, D.C.: U.S. Government Printing Office, Stock No. 052–070–02620–1, Catalog Y4, 1974.

Sundberg, N. D., Tyler, L. E., & Taplin, J. R. *Clinical psychology: Expanding horizons* (2nd ed.). Englewood Cliffs, N.J.: Prentice-Hall, 1973.

Swan, G. E., & MacDonald, M. L. Behavior therapy in practice: A national survey of behavior therapists. *Behavior Therapy,* 1978, *9,* 799–807.

Swerdhoff, G. Comparison of two methods for referral in a program of school dental health. *Journal of Public Health Dentistry,* 1968, *28,* 241–248.

Szasz, T. S. The psychiatric classification of behavior: A strategy of personal constraint. In L. D. Eron (Ed.), *The classification of behavior disorders.* Chicago: Aldine, 1966.

Talbott, J. A. Care of the chronically mentally ill—Still a national disgrace. *American Journal of Psychiatry,* 1979, *136,* 688–689.

Tamerin, J. S. The importance of psychosocial factors on drinking in alcoholics: Relevance for traffic safety. In S. Israelstam & S. Lambert (Eds.), *Alcohol, drugs, and traffic safety.* Toronto: Addictions Research Foundation, 1975.

Tanner, B. A., & Zeiler, M. Punishment of self-injurious behavior using aromatic ammonia as the aversive stimulus. *Journal of Applied Behavior Analysis,* 1975, *8,* 53–57.

Tate, B. G., & Baroff, G. S. Aversive control of self-injurious behavior in a psychotic boy. *Behaviour Research and Therapy,* 1966, *4,* 281–287.

Taylor, F. G., & Marshall, W. L. Experimental analysis of a cognitive-behavioral therapy for depression. *Cognitive Therapy and Research*, 1977, *1*, 59–72.

Teasdale, J. D., & Bancroft, J. Manipulation of thought content as a determinant of mood and corrugator electromyographic activity in depressed patients. *Journal of Abnormal Psychology*, 1977, *86*(3), 235–241.

Teasdale, J. D. Self-efficacy: Toward a unifying theory of behavioral change? Advances in Behaviour Research and Therapy, 1978, *1*, 211–215.

Terrace, H. S. Stimulus control. In W. K. Honig (Ed.), Operant behavior: Areas of research and application. New York: Appleton-Century-Crofts, 1966.

Tharp, R. G., & Wetzel, R. J. Behavior modification in the natural environment. New York: Academic Press, 1969.

Thomas, D. R., Becker, W. C., & Armstrong, M. Production and elimination of disruptive classroom behavior by systematically varying teacher's behavior. Journal of Applied Behavior Analysis, 1968, *1*, 35–45.

Thompson, R. M. Exploring energy choices. In *Encyclopedia of energy*. New York: McGraw-Hill, 1976.

Thoresen, K. E., Thoresen, C. E., Klein, S. B., Wilbur, C. S., Becker-Haven, J. F., & Haven, W. G. Learning House: Helping troubled children and their parents change themselves. In J. S. Stumphauzer (Ed.), *Progress in behavior therapy with delinquents*. Springfield, Ill.: Charles C. Thomas, 1979.

Thorpe, G. L. Desensitization, behavioral rehearsal, self-instructional training, and placebo effects on assertive-refusal behavior. *European Journal of Behavioural Analysis and Modification*, 1975, *1*, 30–44.

Tobias, L. L., & MacDonald, M. L. Withdrawal of maintenance drugs with long-term hospitalized mental patients: A critical review. *Psychological Bulletin*, 1974, *81*, 107–125.

To catch a thief. *Newsweek*, September 23, 1974, pp. 79–80.

Tomkins, S. A modified model of smoking behavior. In E. F. Borgatta & R. R. Evans (Eds.), *Smoking, health, and behavior*. Chicago: Aldine, 1968.

Townsend, R., House, J., & Addario, D. A comparison of biofeedback-mediated relaxation and group therapy in the treatment of chronic anxiety. *American Journal of Psychiatry*, 1975, *132*, 598–601.

Trap, J. J., Milner-Davis, P., Joseph, S., & Cooper, J. O. The effects of feedback and consequences on transitional cursive letter formation. *Journal of Applied Behavior Analysis*, 1978, *11*, 381–394.

Treffry, D., Martin, G., Samuels, J., & Watson, C. Operant conditioning of grooming behavior of severely retarded girls. *Mental Retardation*, 1970, *8*, 30–34.

Tsoi-Hoshmand, L. Behavioral competence training: A model of rehabilitation. *International Journal of the Addictions*, 1976, *11*, 709–718.

Turner, M. B. *Philosophy and the science of behavior*. New York: Appleton-Century-Crofts, 1967.

Turner, R. W., Ward, M. F., & Turner, D. J. Behavioral treatment for depression: An evaluation of therapeutic components. *Journal of Clinical Psychology*, 1979, *35*, 166–175.

Turner, S. M., Hersen, M., & Bellack, A. S. Effects of social disruption, stimulus interference, and aversive conditioning on auditory hallucinations. *Behavior Modification*, 1977, *1*, 249–258.

Turner, S. M., Hersen, M., Bellack, A. S., & Wells, K. C. Behavioral treatment of obsessive-compulsive neurosis. *Behaviour Research and Therapy*, 1979, *17*, 95–106.

Tuso, M. A., Witmer, J. F., & Geller, E. S. *Littering behavior as a function of response priming and environmental litter*. Paper presented at the meeting of the Midwestern Psychological Association, Chicago, May 1975.

Twentyman, C. T., & McFall, R. M. Behavioral training of social skills in shy males. *Journal of Consulting and Clinical Psychology*, 1975, *43*, 384–395.

Ullman, C. A. Teachers, peers and tests as predictors of adjustment. *Journal of Educational Psychology*, 1957, *48*, 257–267.

Ullmann, L. P. *Abnormal psychology without anxiety*. Paper presented at the meetings of the Western Psychological Association, San Francisco, May 1967.

Ullman, L. P., & Krasner, L. (Eds.), *Case studies in behavior modification*. New York: Holt, Rinehart & Winston, 1965.

Ullmann, L. P., & Krasner, L., *A psychological approach to abnormal behavior* (1st ed.). Englewood Cliffs, N.J.: Prentice-Hall, 1969.

Ullmann, L. P., & Krasner, L. *A psychological approach to abnormal behavior* (2nd ed.). Englewood Cliffs, N.J.: Prentice-Hall, 1975.

Ulrich, R., Wolfe, M., & Bluhm, M. Operant conditioning in the public schools. *Educational Technology Monographs*, 1968, *1*(1).

Underwood, B. J., & Shaughnessy, J. J. *Experimentation in psychology*. New York: Wiley, 1975.

Urbain, E., & Kendall, P. C. A review of social-cognitive problem solving approaches to therapy with children. *Psychological Bulletin*, 1980, *88*, 109–143.

U.S. Department of Labor. *Employment and Training Report of the President*. Washington, D.C.: U.S. Government Printing Office, 1977.

U.S. Department of Transportation, Federal Highway Administration, Office of Highway Planning, Highway Statistics Division. *The effect of speed on automobile gasoline consumption rates*. Washington, D.C., October 1973.

U.S. Public Health Service. *Smoking and health*. Report of the Advisory Committee to the Surgeon General of the Public Health Service. Washington, D.C.: U.S.

Department of Health, Education, and Welfare, 1964. Public Health Service Publication 1103.

U.S. Public Health Service. *The health consequences of smoking*. Washington, D.C.: United States Department of Health, Education, and Welfare, 1975.

U.S. Public Health Service. *Smoking and health: A report of the Surgeon General*. Washington, D.C.: U.S. Department of Health, Education, and Welfare, 1979. DHEW Publication No. (PHS) 79–50066.

Valliant, G. E. A twelve-year follow-up of New York narcotic addicts: III. Some social and psychiatric characteristics. *Archives of General Psychiatry*, 1966, *15*, 599–609.

VanWagenen, R. K., Meyerson, L., Kerr, N. J., & Mahoney, K. Field trails of a new procedure for toilet training. *Journal of Experimental Child Psychology*, 1969, *8*, 147–159.

Veloz, E. V., & Stumphauzer, J. S. *Community anticrime programs*. Manuscript submitted for publication, 1979.

Vincent, J. P., Weiss, R. L., & Birchler, G. R. A behavioral analysis of problem-solving in distressed and nondistressed married and stranger dyads. *Behavior Therapy*, 1975, *6*, 475–487.

Vukelich, R., & Hake, D. F. Reduction of dangerously aggressive behavior in a severely retarded resident through a combination of positive reinforcement procedures. *Journal of Applied Behavior Analysis*, 1971, *4*, 215–225.

Wagner, G., & Ebbehøj, J. *Erective dysfunction caused by abnormal outflow from corpus cavernosum*. Paper presented at the Third International Conference of Medical Sexology, Rome, Italy, October 1978.

Wahl, D., & Allison, G. *Reduce: Targets, means and impacts of source reduction*. League of Women Voters Education Fund, Washington, D.C., 1975.

Waldorf, D. Life without heroin: Some social adjustments during long-term periods of voluntary abstention. In R. H. Coombs, L. J. Fry, & P. G. Lewis (Eds.), *Socialization in drug abuse*. Cambridge, Mass.: Schenkman, 1976.

Wallander, J. L., Conger, A. J., Mariotto, M. J., Curran, J. P., & Farrell, A. D. Comparability of selection instruments in studies of heterosexual-social problem behaviors. *Behavior Therapy*, in press.

Warren, R. *The community in America*. Chicago: Rand McNally, 1963.

Watson, D., & Friend, R. Measurement of social-evaluative anxiety. *Journal of Consulting and Clinical Psychology*, 1969, *33*, 448–457.

Watson, J. B. *Behaviorism*. Chicago: University of Chicago Press, 1924.

Watson, J. B. Can psychology help me rear my child? *McCall's*, September 1927, pp. 44; 72.

Watson, J. B. *Psychological care of infant and child*. New York: Norton, 1928. (a)

Watson, J. B. What about your child? *Cosmopolitan,* October 1928, pp. 76–77; 108; 110; 112. (b)

Watson, J. B., & Rayner, R. Conditioned emotional reactions. *Journal of Experimental Psychology,* 1920, *3,* 1–14.

Watt, N. F., & Lubensky, A. W. Childhood roots of schizophrenia. *Journal of Consulting and Clinical Psychology,* 1976, *44,* 363–375.

Weathers, L. R., & Liberman, R. P. Contingency contracting with families of delinquent adolescents. *Behavior Therapy,* 1975, *6,* 356–366.

Weathers, L. R., & Liberman, R. P. Modification of family behavior. In D. Marholin (Ed.), *Child behavior therapy.* New York: Gardner Press, 1977.

Weber, H. An approach to the problem of fear in children. *Journal of Mental Science,* 1936, *82,* 136–147.

Weber, S. J., & Cook, T. D. Subject effects in laboratory research: An examination of subject roles, demand characteristics, and valid inference. *Psychological Bulletin,* 1972, *77,* 273–295.

Wedge, R. F. Personal communication to J. S. Stumphauzer, November 19, 1979.

Weidner, F. *In vivo* desensitization of a paranoid schizophrenic. *Journal of Behavior Therapy and Experimental Psychiatry,* 1970, *1,* 79–81.

Weil, A. T. Nutmeg as a psychoactive drug. *Journal of Psychedelic Drugs,* 1971, *3,* 72–80.

Weil, A. *The natural mind.* Boston: Houghton Mifflin, 1972.

Weil, G., & Goldfried, M. R. Treatment of insomnia in an eleven-year-old child through self-relaxation. *Behavior Therapy,* 1973, *4,* 282–284.

Weimer, W. B. *Notes on the methodology of scientific research.* Hillsdale, N.J.: Erlbaum, 1979.

Weiner, B. The clockwork cure. *The Nation,* 1972, *215,* 433–436.

Weingaertner, A. H. Self-administered aversive stimulation with hallucinating hospitalized schizophrenics. *Journal of Consulting and Clinical Psychology,* 1971, *36,* 422–429.

Weinsier, R. L. Salt and the development of essential hypertension. *Preventive Medicine,* 1976, *5,* 7–14.

Weinsier, R. L., Fuchs, R. J., Kay, T. D., Triebivasser, J. H., & Lancaster, M. C. Body fat: Its relationship to coronary heart disease, blood pressure, lipids and other risk factors measured in a large male population. *The American Journal of Medicine,* 1976, *61,* 815–824.

Weinstein, G. W. The truth about teenage shoplifting. *Parents Magazine,* April 1974, pp. 42–43; 60–61.

Weisenberg, M. Behavioral motivation. *Journal of Periodontology,* 1973, *44,* 489–499.

Weiss, R. L., Birchler, G. R., & Vincent, J. P. Contractual models for negotiation training in marital dyads. *Journal of Marriage and the Family*, 1974, *36*, 321–331.

Weiss, R. L., & Margolin, G. Assessment of marital conflict and accord. In A. R. Ciminero, K. D. Calhoun, & H. E. Adams (Eds.), *Handbooks of behavioral assessment*. New York: John Wiley, 1977.

Weiss, R. L., & Perry, B. A. *Assessment and treatment of marital dysfunction*. Eugene, Oreg.: Oregon Marital Studies Program, 1979. Available from Robert L. Weiss, Department of Psychology, University of Oregon, Eugene, Oreg. 97403.

Weissberg, M. A comparison of direct and vicarious treatments of speech anxiety: Desensitization, desensitization with coping imagery, and cognitive modification. *Behavior Therapy*, 1977, *8*, 606–620.

Wells, K. C., & Forehand, R. Childhood behavior problems in the home. In S. M. Turner & H. E. Adams (Eds.), *Handbook of behavior therapy*. New York: Wiley, in press.

Wells, K. C., Forehand, R., & Griest, D. *The use of self-control procedures to enhance temporal generality of a parent-training program*. Paper presented at the meetings of the Association for the Advancement of Behavior Therapy, Chicago, November 1978.

Wells, K. C., Forehand, R., Hickey, K., & Green, K. D. Effects of a procedure derived from the overcorrection principle on manipulated and non-manipulated behaviors. *Journal of Applied Behavior Analysis*, 1977, *10*, 679–687.

Wenrich, W. W. *A primer of behavior modification*. Belmont, Calif.: Brooks/Cole, 1970.

Wessberg, H. W., Mariotto, M. J., Cooper, A. J., Conger, J. C., & Farrell, A. D. Ecological validity of roleplays for assessing heterosocial anxiety and skill of male college students. *Journal of Consulting and Clinical Psychology*, 1979, *47*, 525–535.

Wexler, D. B. Reflections on the legal regulation of behavior modification in institutional settings. *Arizona Law Review*, 1975, *17*, 132–143.

Whalen, C. K., & Henker, B. A. Creating therapeutic pyramids using mentally retarded patients. *American Journal of Mental Deficiency*, 1969, *74*, 331–337.

Whelan, R. J., & Haring, N. G. Modification and maintenance of behavior through systematic application of consequences. *Exceptional Children*, 1966, *32*, 281–289.

White, G. D., Nielsen, G., & Johnson, S. M. Timeout duration and the suppression of deviant behavior in children. *Journal of Applied Behavior Analysis*, 1972, *5*, 111–120.

White, J. C., Jr., & Taylor, D. J. Noxious conditioning as a treatment for rumination. *Mental Retardation*, 1967, *5*, 30–33.

Wiesen, A. E., & Watson, E. Elimination of attention seeking behavior in a retarded child. *American Journal of Mental Deficiency*, 1967, *72*, 50–52.

Wiggins, J. S. *Personality and prediction: Principles of personality assessment*. Reading, Mass.: Addison-Wesley, 1973.

Wikler, A. Recent progress in research on the neurophysiological basis of morphine addiction. *American Journal of Psychiatry*, 1948, *105*, 329–338.

Wikler, A. *Opiate addiction*. Springfield, Ill.: Charles C. Thomas, 1953.

Wikler, A. Conditioning factors in opiate addiction and relapse. In D. M. Wilner & G. G. Kassebaum (Eds.), *Narcotics*. New York: McGraw-Hill, 1965.

Wikler, A. Dynamics of drug dependence: Implication of conditioning theory for research and treatment. *Archives of General Psychiatry*, 1973, *28*, 611–616.

Wilber, J. A., & Barrow, J. G. Hypertension—A community problem. *American Journal of Medicine*, 1972, *52*, 653–663.

Wilbur, C. S., Zifferblatt, S. M., & Zifferblatt, M. *Healthy vending: A cooperative pilot program to stimulate good health in the marketplace*. 1978. Unpublished manuscript, National Institute of Health, Bethesda, Maryland.

Wilkins, W. Desensitization: Getting it together with Davison and Wilson. *Psychological Bulletin*, 1972, *78*, 32–36.

Wilkins, W. Desensitization: A rejoinder to Morgan. *Psychological Bulletin*, 1973, *79*, 376–377.

Wilkins, W. Desensitization: Social and cognitive factors underlying the effectiveness of Wolpe's procedure. *Psychological Bulletin*, 1976, *76*, 311–317.

Williams, C. L., Doleys, D. M., & Ciminero, A. R. A two-year follow-up of enuretic children treated with dry bed training. *Journal of Behavior Therapy and Experimental Psychiatry*, 1978, *9*, 285–286.

Williams, J. L. *Operant learning: Procedures for changing behavior*. Monterey, Calif.: Brooks/Cole, 1973.

Williams, K. H., & Goldstein, G. Cognitive and affective responses to lithium in patients with organic brain syndrome. *American Journal of Psychiatry*, 1979, *136*, 800–803.

Williams, M. T., Turner, S. M., Watts, J. G., Bellack, A. S., & Hersen, M. Group social skills training for chronic psychiatric patients. *European Journal of Behavioural Analysis and Modification*, 1977, *1*, 223–239.

Wills, T. A., Weiss, R. L., & Patterson, G. R. A behavioral analysis of the determinants of marital satisfaction. *Journal of Consulting and Clinical Psychology*, 1974, *42*, 802–811.

Wilson, G. T. Alcohol and human sexual behavior. *Behavior Research and Therapy*, 1977, *15*, 239–252.

Wilson, G. T. Booze, beliefs, and behavior: Cognitive processes in alcohol use and abuse. In P. E. Nathan, G. A. Marlatt, & T. Loberg (Eds.), *Alcoholism: New directions in behavioral research and treatment*. New York: Plenum Press, 1978. (a)

Wilson, G. T. Methodological considerations in treatment outcome research on obesity. *Journal of Consulting and Clinical Psychology*, 1978, *46*, 687–702. (b)

Wilson, G. T. The importance of being theoretical: A commentary on Bandura's "Self-efficacy: Towards a unifying theory of behavioral change." *Advances in Behaviour Research and Therapy*, 1978, *1*, 217–230. (c)

Wilson, G. T., & Abrams, D. Effects of alcohol on social anxiety and physiological arousal: Cognitive versus pharmacological processes. *Cognitive Therapy and Research*, 1977, *1*, 195–210.

Wilson, G. T., & Brownell, K. D. Behavior therapy for obesity: Including family members in the treatment process. *Behavior Therapy*, 1978, *9*, 943–945.

Wilson, G. T., & Davison, G. C. Process of fear reduction in systematic desensitization: Animal studies. *Psychological Bulletin*, 1971, *76*, 1–14.

Wilson, G. T., & Lawson, D. M. Expectancies, alcohol and sexual arousal in male social drinkers. *Journal of Abnormal Psychology*, 1976, *85*, 587–594.

Wilson, G. T., & Lawson, D. M. Expectancies, alcohol and sexual arousal in women. *Journal of Abnormal Psychology*, 1978, *87*, 358–367.

Wiltz, N. A., & Patterson, G. R. An evaluation of parent training procedures designed to alter inappropriate aggressive behavior of boys. *Behavior Therapy*, 1974, *5*, 215–221.

Wincze, J. P., Leitenberg, H., & Agras, W. S. The effects of token reinforcement and feedback on the delusional verbal behavior of chronic paranoid schizophrenics. *Journal of Applied Behavior Analysis*, 1972, *5*, 247–262.

Winett, R. A. Behavioral community psychology: Some thoughts on current status and realistic expectations. *The Behavior Therapist*, 1979, *2*, 14–15.

Winett, R. A., Kagel, J., Battalio, R., & Winkler, R. The effects of rebates, feedback and information on electricity consumption. *Journal of Applied Psychology*, 1978, *63*, 73–80.

Winett, R. A., Neale, M. S., & Grier, H. C. The effects of self-monitoring and feedback on residential electricity consumption. *Journal of Applied Behavior Analysis*, 1979, *12*, 173–184.

Winett, R. A., & Nietzel, M. Behavioral ecology: Contingency management of residential energy use. *American Journal of Community Psychology*, 1975, *3*, 123–133.

Winkler, R. C. Management of chronic psychiatric patients by a token reinforcement system. *Journal of Applied Behavior Analysis*, 1970, *3*, 47–55.

Witmer, J. F., & Geller, E. S. Facilitating paper recycling: Effects of prompts, raffles, and contests. *Journal of Applied Behavioral Analysis*, 1976, *9*, 315–322.

Wohlford, P. Initiation of cigarette smoking: Is it related to parental behavior? *Journal of Consulting and Clinical Psychology*, 1970, *34*, 148–151.

Wolf, M. M. Social validity: The case for subjective measurement or how applied behavior analysis is finding its heart. *Journal of Applied Behavior Analysis*, 1978, *11*, 203–214.

Wolf, M. M., Giles, D. K., & Hall, R. V. Experiments with token reinforcement in a remedial classroom. *Behaviour Research and Therapy*, 1968, *6*, 51–64.

Wolf, M. M., Risley, T., Johnston, M., Harris, F., & Allen, E. Application of operant conditioning procedures to the behavior problems of an autistic child: A follow-up and extension. *Behaviour Research and Therapy*, 1967, *5*, 103–111.

Wolf, M., Risley, T., & Mees, H. Application of operant conditioning procedures to the behavior problems of an autistic child. *Behaviour Research and Therapy*, 1964, *1*, 305–312.

Wollersheim, J. P. Effectiveness of group therapy based on learning principles in the treatment of overweight women. *Journal of Abnormal Psychology*, 1970, *76*, 462–474.

Wolpe, J. *Psychotherapy by reciprocal inhibition.* Stanford: Stanford University Press, 1958.

Wolpe, J. *The practice of behavior therapy.* New York: Pergamon Press, 1969.

Wolpe, J. *The practice of behavior therapy* (2nd ed.). New York: Pergamon Press, 1973.

Wolpe, J. Self-efficacy theory and psychotherapeutic change: A square peg for a round hole. *Advances in Behaviour Research and Therapy*, 1978, *1*, 231–236.

Wolpe, J. The experimental model and treatment of neurotic depression. *Behaviour Research and Therapy*, 1979, *17*(6), 555–565.

Wolpe, J. & Lazarus, A. A. *Behavior therapy techniques.* New York: Pergamon Press, 1966.

Wolpin, M. Guided imagining to reduce avoidance behavior. *Psychotherapy: Theory, Research and Practice*, 1969, *6*, 122–124.

Woodward, M. The diagnosis and treatment of homosexual offenders. *British Journal of Delinquency*, 1958, *9*, 44–59.

Wooley, S. C., Wooley, O. W., & Dyrenforth, S. R. Theoretical, practical, and social issues in behavioral treatments of obesity. *Journal of Applied Behavior Analysis*, 1979, *12*, 3–26.

Wright, D. F., Brown, R. A., & Andrews, M. E. Remission of chronic ruminative vomiting through a reversal of social contingencies. *Behaviour Research and Therapy*, 1978, *16*, 134–136.

Wright, J., & James, R. *A behavioral approach to preventing delinquency.* Springfield, Ill.: Charles C. Thomas, 1974.

Wright, L. Handling the encopretic child. *Professional Psychology*, 1973, *4*, 137–144.

Wright, L. Outcome of a standardized program for treating psychogenic encopresis. *Professional Psychology*, 1975, *6*, 453–456.

Wright, L., & Walker, C. E. A simple behavioral treatment program for psychogenic encopresis. *Behavioural Research and Therapy*, 1978, *16*, 209–212.

Wyatt vs. Stickney court case (1971). In B. J. Ennis & P. R. Friedman (Eds.), *Legal rights of the mentally handicapped* (Vol. 1). New York: Practicing Law Institute, 1974.

Wynder, E. L. Nutrition and cancer. *Federation Proceedings,* 1976, *35,* 1309–1315.

Yates, A. J. *Behavior therapy.* New York: Wiley, 1970.

Yates, B. T., Haven, W. G., & Thoresen, C. E. Cost-effectiveness analyses at Learning House: How much change for how much money? In J. S. Stumphauzer (Ed.), *Progress in behavior therapy with delinquents.* Springfield, Ill.: Charles C. Thomas, 1979.

Young, G. C., & Morgan, R. T. T. Overlearning in the conditioning treatment of enuresis. *Behavioral Research and Therapy,* 1972, *10,* 147–151.

Young, J. A., & Wincze, J. P. The effects of the reinforcement of compatible and incompatible alternative behaviors on the self-injurious and related behaviors of a profoundly retarded female adult. *Behavior Therapy,* 1974, *5,* 614–623.

Yukobousky, R., & Fichter, P. Mobility club: A grassroots small town transport concept. *Transportation Research Record,* 1976, No. 559, 89–100.

Zaharia, E. S., & Baumeister, A. A. Cross-organizational job satisfactions of technician-level staff members. *American Journal of Mental Deficiency,* 1979, *84,* 30–35. (a)

Zaharia, E. S., & Baumeister, A. A. Technician losses in public residential facilities. *American Journal of Mental Deficiency,* 1979, *84,* 36–39. (b)

Zaslow, R. W., & Breger, L. A theory and treatment of autism. In L. Breger (Ed.), *Clinical-cognitive psychology: Models and integrations.* Englewood Cliffs, N.J.: Prentice-Hall, 1969.

Zax, M., Cowen, E. L., Rappaport, J., Beach, D. R., & Laird, J. D. Follow-up study of children identified as emotionally disturbed. *Journal of Consulting and Clinical Psychology,* 1968, *32,* 369–374.

Zax, M., & Specter, G. An introduction to community psychology. New York: Wiley, 1974.

Zegiob, L. E., Jenkins, J., Becker, J., & Bristow, A. Facial screening: Effects on appropriate and inappropriate behaviors. *Journal of Behavior Therapy and Experimental Psychiatry,* 1976, *7,* 355–357.

Zeiler, M. D., & Jeruly, S. S. Development of behavior: Self feeding. *Journal of Consulting and Clinical Psychology,* 1968, *32,* 164–168.

Zeiss, A. M., Lewinsohn, P. M., & Munoz, R. F. Nonspecific improvement effects in depression using interpersonal skills training, pleasant activity schedules, or cognitive training. *Journal of Consulting and Clinical Psychology,* 1979, *47,* 427–439.

Zifferblatt, S., & Hendricks, C. Applied behavior analysis of societal problems: Population change, a case in point. *American Psychologist,* 1974, *29,* 750–761.

Zifferblatt, S. M., Wilbur, C. S., & Pinsky, J. L. Changing cafeteria eating habits: A new direction for public health care. *Journal of The American Dietetic Association,* in press.

Zigler, E., & Phillips, L. Social effectiveness and symptomatic behaviors. *Journal of Abnormal and Social Psychology,* 1960, *61,* 231–238.

Zigler, E, & Phillips, L. Psychiatric diagnosis and symptomatology. *Journal of Abnormal and Social Psychology,* 1961, *63,* 69–75. (a)

Zigler, E., & Phillips, L. Social competence and outcome in psychiatric disorder. *Journal of Abnormal and Social Psychology,* 1961, *63,* 264–271. (b)

Zitrin, C. M., Klein, D. F., & Woerner, M. G. Behavior therapy, supportive psychotherapy, imipramine, and phobias. *Archives of General Psychiatry,* 1978, *35,* 307–316.

Zubin, J. The classification of behavior disorders. *Annual Review of Psychology,* 1967, *18,* 373–401.

Zubin, J. The role of vulnerability in the etiology of schizophrenic episodes. In L. J. West & D. E. Flinn (Eds.), *Treatment of schizophrenia: Progress and prospects.* New York: Grune & Stratton, 1976.

Zuckerman, M. Physiological measures of sexual arousal in the human. *Psychological Bulletin,* 1971, *75,* 297–329.

Zuiches, J. J. *Changing family energy behavior through infra-red heat loss evaluation* (Interim Report on Project EA–77–X–01–2118). Institute for Family and Child Study, Michigan State University, 1977.

Zung, W. K. A self-rating depression scale. *Archives of General Psychiatry,* 1965, *12,* 63–70.

AUTHOR INDEX

SUBJECT INDEX

There are many terms used in this book that will be new to a reader unfamiliar with behavior modification. We felt, however, that a glossary would not be of great use, since it would offer definitions completely out of the context of the theories of which they are part. Instead, we have included "definition" subentries for all important terms in the subject index.